CASES AND MATERIALS

LAND LAW

CASES AND MATERIALS

LAND LAW

Gary Watt, MA (Oxon), Solicitor
Senior Lecturer in Law, Nottingham Law School

BLACKSTONE
PRESS LIMITED

First published in Great Britain 1996 by Blackstone Press Limited,
9–15 Aldine Street, London W12 8AW.   Telephone 0181–740 1173

© Nottingham Law School, Nottingham Trent University, 1996

ISBN: 1 85431 532 3

British Library Cataloguing in Publication Data
A CIP catalogue record for this book is available from the British Library.

Typeset by Style Photosetting Limited, Mayfield, East Sussex
Printed by Livesey Limited, Shrewsbury, Shropshire

FOREWORD

All law students are aware that if they are to succeed in their studies they will need commitment and determination. In addition to this they must be provided with good teaching and good materials, and whilst this is normally the case with the teaching it is not always true of the material.

However, help is at hand. Blackstone Press, in association with Nottingham Law School, have developed a unique series of Study Manuals which it is hoped will assist hard-pressed students to achieve their ultimate goal.

The Study Texts replicate, as far as possible, the experience of being guided through a subject by an expert tutor. These Cases and Materials manuals are intended to provide you with the experience, necessary for all law students, of dealing with primary sources (e.g. cases and statutes) and academic commentaries (e.g. journal articles). The idea is for them to serve as a portable library. You should, of course, take full advantage of any opportunity to explore at first hand the vast range of materials available in a well-stocked library.

Of course, in using this volume you have an advantage over the student using a library. The materials have been extracted and are presented in the same order as they are dealt with in the Study Text. This will enable you to analyse the materials and understand the way in which they complement and expand upon the guidance given by the Study Text.

With the above approach in mind, we have presented the cases, statutes and other material without linking commentary. In addition, the extracts from the cases are often longer than can be found in many casebooks. This will encourage you to become familiar with the need to extract from a judgment the important paragraphs, and to realise that statements of general principle and statutory provisions often become more understandable when considered in context.

Not all cases referred to in the Study Text are reproduced, only those necessary for answering the Self Assessment Questions (SAQs) and working through the Activities. Some chapters include an outline answer to End of Chapter Assessment Questions in the Study Text, but these are only provided for guidance and should not be regarded as the only answer that could be given.

We hope that you will find these volumes useful, and that they will help you develop your legal skills as well as your understanding of the law.

CONTENTS

PREFACE

Land law is like chess. The pieces are for the most part simple to identify and the characteristics of each piece are basically straightforward, but when the game is played the pieces combine in complex and difficult forms. The aim of this volume is to identify the pieces and the rules in the clearest possible way using selected statutes and cases, extracts from journal articles, law reform proposals, scholarly texts and illustrative questions and answers. The student will see that land law has thrown up some fascinating games.

Primarily, of course, this volume is intended to accompany the *Distance Learning Text* on *Land Law*. The author of the Learning Text is Dr Roger Sexton, a 'Grandmaster' of land law, to whom I am grateful for providing the structural basis for the present volume. It is an extensive resource which should assist students of any land law degree course to approach the subject with the confidence and authority that comes from using primary source materials.

This volume is to be your portable library, and as such I have extracted for your use that which is relevant from a typical University Law Library. The extracts, wherever possible, are of sufficient length to encourage independent reflection. Distance learning students will do well to make their own connections and discoveries and it is hoped that the present volume will provide scope for this.

You may never be a criminal, you may never commit a tort, but you will invariably have some right or interest in land. I hope that this volume will encourage interest in this area of law.

Gary Watt
Nottingham Law School

ACKNOWLEDGMENTS

Nottingham Law School and the publishers would like to thank the following for permission to reproduce copyright material:

Butterworths & Co. (Publishers) Ltd for extracts from the All England Law Reports, *New Law Journal* and Radcliffe and Cross, *The English Legal System*.

Cambridge University Press for extracts from *Cambridge Law Journal*.

Clarendon Press, Oxford, for extracts from Lawson and Rudden, *The Law of Property* and B. Nicholls, *Introduction to Roman Law*.

The Estates Gazette for extracts from The Estates Gazette Law Reports.

Her Majesty's Stationery Office for extracts from the Law Commission and Scottish Law Commission Reports and Law Commission Working Papers and the Land Registry Certificate.

The Incorporated Council of Law Reporting for England & Wales for extracts from the Law Reports and the Weekly Law Reports.

Law Book Company of Australia for extracts from the Australian Law Journal Reports.

Times Newspapers Ltd for extracts from The Times Law Reports.

Sweet & Maxwell for extracts from *Modern Law Review*, the English Reports, *The Conveyancer and Property Lawyer* and B. Harvey, *Settlements of Land*.

TABLE OF CASES

Cases reported in full are shown in heavy type. The page at which the report is printed is shown in heavy type.

TABLE OF STATUTES

Statutes, and sections thereof, which are set out in full or in part are shown in heavy type. The page at which the statute or section is printed is shown in heavy type.

CHAPTER ONE

INTRODUCTION TO THE TYPES OF PROPERTY RIGHTS IN LAND

1.1   Introduction

**Lawson, F.H. and Rudden, B., The Law of Property 2nd edn,
Oxford: Clarendon Press, 1982, pp. 6–9**

REAL RELATIONS

Having sketched in outline the sort of persons that can have legal relations with things and the kind of things subject to those relations, it is time to consider the relations themselves. The obvious ones are *possession* and *ownership* and they are easy to illustrate. If there is a library book on my desk then I have possession of it but not ownership. If I ask a friend to lend me a jug of milk and he does so then I acquire possession of the jug and he remains owner; but I acquire ownership of the milk and *owe him* its value, and he owns the abstract thing which is my debt to him.

Ownership would seem to the layman to be a simple notion. It is merely a question of *meum* and *tuum*. If the thing is mine, I own it; if it is not, I do not. Often the law conforms to this simple way of looking at ownership. Thus for example, a person may live alone in a house which he has bought and paid for, no one else has any rights over it, and his title is registered in the Land Registry; and he may have in his garage a car which he has bought direct from the manufacturer. In both cases he can correctly say, without qualification, that the thing is his. Or he may reasonably say that he is an absolute owner.

But even in such simple cases it is evident that the words absolute owner are being used to express two quite different ideas: that his ownership is both *indisputable* and that it is *unshared*. The ownership is asserting at the same moment that he and no one else is entitled to the house and car, and that his interest in them is exclusive and complete; or, in negative terms, that no other person can regard the things as his and that no other person can do anything which cuts down their use or reduces their value. The one assertion relates to what lawyers call 'title', the other to the content of ownership. In English law, as we shall see, it is perfectly possible to have one without the other.

Title
Some ways of acquiring title are original in the sense that a person is the first ever owner of a thing: if I write a song I own the copyright. Usually, however, things are acquired from someone else. A person buying a thing wants to be sure that it is the seller's to sell. With movable objects there are few problems—the seller's *possession* of the thing is normally good enough evidence of his *ownership*.

In the case of land, however, the matter is rather more complex. The word 'title' belongs to the vocabulary of a purchaser's solicitor who is trying to ensure that his client will be safe in buying the house and cannot be turned out by anyone else. He is concerned to see that his client gets what is called a good title. In the event of dispute the question of who is *entitled* to it—the issue of title—may have to be tested by a lawsuit in which, although the plaintiff's object would be to obtain possession of the thing, he must try to prove that element of ownership which is the right to immediate possession. . . .

The content of ownership

. . . The main elements are (a) the right to make physical use of a thing; (b) the right to the income from it, in money, in kind, or in services; and (c) the power of management, including that of alienation. Thus the owner of a car may drive it, hire it out, or sell it. And of course within these areas he may do the same things more generously: take the children for a drive, lend it to a friend, give it away. The owner of a house may live there, lease it, or sell it; and so on.

There are certain advantages to be obtained by keeping in the same hands the right or power to do all these things. A buyer normally wants them all and it is inconvenient if the seller cannot give him them. On the other hand, there has always been a need to detach some elements of ownership from others and to vest them in different persons, a need felt most strongly in regard to land. One of the main tasks of the law of property is to reconcile this need with the advantages of simplicity. . . .

Gray, K., Property in Thin Air,
[1991] *Cambridge Law Journal* 252–307 at 292–294

. . . The classic common law criteria of 'property' have tended to rest a twin emphasis on the assignability of the benefits inherent in a resource and on the relative permanence of those benefits if unassigned. Before a right can be admitted within the category of 'property' it must, according to Lord Wilberforce in *National Provincial Bank Ltd v Ainsworth* [1965] AC 1175, be 'definable' identifiable by third parties, capable in its nature of assumption by third parties, and have some degree of permanence or stability. This preoccupation with assignability of benefit and enforceability of burden doubtless owes much to the fact that the formative phases of the common law concept of property coincided with a remarkable culture of bargain and exchange. Non-transferable rights or rights which failed on transfer were simply not 'property'. Within the crucible of transfer lawyers affected to demarcate rights of 'property' from rights founded in contract and tort or, for that matter, from human rights and civil liberties. Only brief reflection is required in order to perceive the horrible circularity of such hallmarks of 'property'. If naively we ask which rights are proprietary, we are told that they are those rights which are assignable to and enforceable against third parties. When we then ask which rights these may be, we are told that they comprise, of course, the rights which are traditionally identified as 'proprietary'. 'Property' is 'property because it is 'property': property status and proprietary consequence confuse each other in a deadening embrace of cause and effect. . . .
. . . In their respective preoccupations with resource allocation and institutional justification, lawyers and philosophers alike have largely failed to identify the characteristic hallmark of the common law notion of 'property'. If our own travels in search of 'property' have indicated one thing, it is that the criterion of 'excludability' gets us much closer to the core of 'property' than does the conventional legal emphasis on the assignability or enforceability of benefits. For 'property' resides not in consumption of benefits but in control over benefits. 'Property' is not about *enjoyment of access* but about *control over access*. 'Property' is the power-relation constituted by the state's endorsement of private claims to regulate the access of strangers to the benefits of particular resources. If, in respect of a given claimant and a given resource, the exercise of such regulatory control is physically impracticable or legally abortive or morally or socially undesirable, we say that such a claimant can assert no 'property' in that resource and for that matter can lose no 'property' in it either. Herein lies an important key to the 'propertiness' of property . . . .

Nicholls, Barry, An Introduction To Roman Law,
Oxford: Clarendon Press, 1962, p. 153

OWNERSHIP

. . . It can indeed be said that ownership is either so simple as to need no explanation or so elusive as to defy definition. At its simplest it is the difference between mine and thine, at its most sophisticated it is the ultimate right, the right behind all other rights. The elusive character of ownership can be appreciated if one attempts to give a precise meaning to the often-repeated statement that Roman ownership is markedly, and to some of its critics excessively, 'absolute'.

The most obvious sense in which ownership may be 'absolute' is that of enjoyment. Though there is no Roman definition of ownership, there is no lack of Romanistic ones, and these are usually in terms of enjoyment. Thus, the commentators adapted the definition of usufruct by adding to the rights of use and enjoyment the right of abuse—*ius utendi fruendi abutendi*. The adaptation is a little forced, since 'abuse' has to include alienation, but it is also, in its emphasis on the plenitude of enjoyment conferred by ownership, misleading. In the first place, no enjoyment can ever be absolute in the sense that it is free from any restrictions whatever. At the very least the use, enjoyment, and abuse of his property by one owner must be reconciled with the equal use, enjoyment, and abuse by all other owners of their property. In a simple sense this is one of the functions of law. Moreover, in all but the crudest system of law there will be other restrictions which, in the general interest, are imposed on the enjoyment of the owner, and the extent of these restrictions will depend very largely on the political and economic ideas of the time. The enjoyment of the modern English owner is far less absolute than that of his Roman predecessor, but this difference in the content of ownership derives from a difference not in the technical legal character of ownership but in the extent to which the public law restricts the rights of the owner in the general interest. For this reason the French Civil Code, thought it declares that ownership is 'the right to enjoy and dispose of things in the most absolute way', adds the proviso that such enjoyment must not contravene the general law. . . .

BERKELEY v POULETT AND OTHERS (1976) EG 911, Court of Appeal

FACTS: A purchaser of a mansion house claimed that certain pictures, a statue and a sundial had passed with the conveyance as fixtures to the land.

SCARMAN LJ: . . . The answer today to the question whether objects which were originally chattels have become fixtures, that is to say part of the freehold, depends upon the application of two tests: (1) the method and degree of annexation; (2) the object and purpose of annexation . . .

. . . Since *Leigh* v *Taylor* the question is really one of fact. The two tests were explained in that case by the Lord Chancellor (see the report at pp. 158 and 159), who commented that not the law but our mode of life has changed over the years; that what has changed is 'the degree in which certain things have seemed susceptible of being put up as mere ornaments whereas at our earlier period the mere construction rendered it impossible sometimes to sever the thing which was put up from the realty'. In other words, a degree of annexation which in earlier times the law would have treated as conclusive may now prove nothing. If the purpose of the annexation be for the better enjoyment of the object itself, it may remain a chattel, notwithstanding a high degree of physical annexation. Clearly, however, it remains significant to discover the extent of physical disturbance of the building of the land involved in the removal of the object. If an object cannot be removed without serious damage to, or destruction of, some part of the realty, the case for its having become a fixture is a strong one. The relationship of the two tests to each other requires consideration. If there is no physical annexation there is no fixture. *Quicquid plantatur solo solo cedit*. Nevertheless an object, resting on the ground by its own weight alone, can be a fixture, if it be so heavy that there is no need to tie it into a foundation, and if it were put in place to improve the realty. *Prima facie*, however, an object resting on the ground by its own weight alone is not a fixture: see *Megarry and Wade*, p. 716. Conversely, an object affixed to realty but capable of being removed without much difficulty may yet be a fixture, if, for example, the purpose of its affixing be that 'of creating a beautiful room as a whole' (Neville J in *In Re Whaley* [1908] 1 Ch 615 at p. 619). And in the famous instance of *Lord Chesterfield's Settled Estates* [1911] 1 Ch 237 Grinling Gibbons carvings, which had been affixed to a suite of rooms 200 years earlier, were held to be fixtures. Today so great are the technical skills of affixing and removing objects to land or buildings that the second test is more likely than the first to be decisive. Perhaps the enduring significance of the first test is a reminder that there must be some degree of physical annexation before a chattel can be treated as part of the realty.

When one seeks to apply the law to the facts of this case, it is necessary to discriminate between what is relevant but not decisive and what is decisive. Investigatory expertise of a high order has been devoted by both sides to discovering how the pictures were affixed to the panelling and the wall in the two rooms. Fascinating though the investigation was, its conclusion (whether it be, as Mr Millett contended, that the pictures were really put up as an integral part, with the panelling, of the wall-covering, or, as Mr Browne-Wilkinson contended, were put into recesses left for them) is not, in my judgment, decisive. It is enough to say that the pictures were firmly fixed and that their removal needed skill and experience if it were to be done without damage to the wall and panelling. Certainly they were firmly enough fixed to become fixtures if that was the object and purpose of their affixing. But, if ordinary skill was used, as it was, in their removal, they could be taken down, and in the event were taken down, without much trouble and without damage to the structure of the rooms. The decisive question is therefore as to the object and purpose of their affixing. Pictures had hung in the two rooms for centuries. 'The Return' had been in the ante-room for a very long time—perhaps ever since it was painted. The 7th Earl decided in the early part of the 20th century to install in the two rooms the panelling and so designed it that there were recesses for pictures. It is this feature which lends plausibility to the suggestion that the pictures, fitted into the recesses left for them, were not to be enjoyed as objects in themselves but as part of the grand architectural design of the two rooms. The Vice-Chancellor rejected this view. So do I. When the panelling was installed in the two rooms the design was either panelled walls with recesses for pictures to be enjoyed as pictures, or rooms having walls which were a composite of panelling and pictures: in other words, the pictures were to be part of a composite mural. I think the former was the truth. The panelling was Victorian, the pictures a heterogeneous collection. According to Sothebys' expert they were of different dates in the 17th and 18th centuries, of different styles, by different hands, the sort of set anyone could put together at any time—very different, I would comment, from that unity of design, the 'Elizabethan Room' in the case of *In re Whaley*. There was a particular Poulett family interest in 'The Return' and in the two coronation portraits, but this interest focused attention not on the design of the room but on the pictures themselves. Notwithstanding the painstaking and attractive arguments of Mr Millett for the plaintiff, I find, applying the second test, that the pictures were not fixtures. They were put in place on the wall to be enjoyed as pictures. The panelling presented a technical problem in putting them up. The way the carpenter, or whoever it was, solved the problem is not decisive in determining their legal character. But the purpose in putting them there is.

The statue and the sundial give rise in my judgment to no difficulty. Neither was at the time of the sale physically attached to the realty. The sundial was a small object and, once the Earl had detached it (as he did many years earlier) from its pedestal, it ceased to be part of the realty. The statue was heavy. It weighed 10 cwt and stood 5 ft 7 in high on its plinth. There is an issue as to whether it was cemented into the plinth or rested on its own weight. The question is not decisive, for, even if it was attached by a cement bond, it was (as events proved) easily removable. However, upon the balance of probability, I agree with the Vice-Chancellor in thinking it was not attached. The best argument for the statue being a fixture was its careful siting in the West Lawn so as to form an integral part of the architectural design of the west elevation of the house. The design point is a good one so far as it goes: it explains the siting of the plinth, which undoubtedly was a fixture. But what was put upon the plinth was very much a matter for the taste of the occupier of the house for the time being. We know that at one time the object on the plinth had been a sundial. At the time of the sale it was this statue of a Greek athlete. The plinth's position was architecturally important: it ensured that whatever stood on it would be correctly positioned. But the object it carried could be whatever appealed to the occupier for the time being. Sundial or statue—it did not matter to the design, so long as it was in the right place—a result ensured by the plinth which was firmly fixed into the ground. Being, as I think, unattached, the statue was, *prima facie*, not a fixture, but, even if it were attached, the application of the second test would lead to the same conclusion. . . .

. . . Accordingly, I agree with the Vice-Chancellor. The action fails *in limine*. The plaintiff cannot show either that the pictures, statue and sundial were fixtures . . .

1.2 Property Rights which Give Immediate Use and Enjoyment of Land

1.2.1 FEE SIMPLE ESTATE

See **4.1**.

1.2.2 LEASES

See **Chapters 17** to **20**.

1.3 Property Rights Against Land Owned by Other People

1.3.1 MORTGAGES

See **Chapter 29** to **33**.

1.3.2 RESTRICTIVE COVENANTS

See **Chapters 26** to **28**.

1.3.3 EASEMENTS

See **Chapters 23** to **25**.

1.3.4 PROFITS À PRENDRE

See **Chapters 23** to **25**.

1.3.5 RENTCHARGES

RENTCHARGES ACT 1977

1. Meaning of 'rentcharge'
For the purposes of this Act 'rentcharge' means any annual or other periodic sum charged on or issuing out of land, except—
    (a)   rent reserved by a lease or tenancy, or
    (b)   any sum payable by way of interest.

2. Creation of rentcharges prohibited
    (1)   Subject to this section, no rentcharge may be created whether at law or in equity after the coming into force of this section.
    (2)   Any instrument made after the coming into force of this section shall, to the extent that it purports to create a rentcharge the creation of which is prohibited by this section, be void.
    (3)   This section does not prohibit the creation of a rentcharge—
    (a)   which has the effect of making the land on which the rent is charged settled land by virtue of section 1(1)(v) of the Settled Land Act 1925;
    (b)   which would have that effect but for the fact that the land on which the rent is charged is already settled land or is held on trust for sale;
    (c)   which is an estate rentcharge;
    (d)   under any Act of Parliament providing for the creation of rentcharges in connection with the execution of works on land (whether by way of improvements, repairs or otherwise) or the commutation of any obligation to do such work; or
    (e)   by, or in accordance with the requirements of, any order of a court.

3. Extinguishment of rentcharges
    (1)   Subject to this section, every rentcharge shall (if it has not then ceased to have effect) be extinguished at the expiry of the period of 60 years beginning—
    (a)   with the passing of this Act, or

(b)   with the date on which the rentcharge first became payable, whichever is the later; and accordingly the land on which it was charged or out of which it issued shall, at the expiration of that period, be discharged and freed from the rentcharge. . . .

1.3.6 RIGHTS OF OCCUPATION UNDER THE MATRIMONIAL HOMES ACT

MATRIMONIAL HOMES ACT 1983

1.   Rights concerning matrimonial home where one spouse has no estate, etc
(1)   Where one spouse is entitled to occupy a dwelling house by virtue of a beneficial estate or interest or contract or by virtue of any enactment giving him or her the right to remain in occupation, and the other spouse is not entitled, then, subject to the provisions of this Act, the spouse not so entitled shall have the following rights (in this Act referred to as 'rights of occupation')—
(a)   if in occupation, a right not to be evicted or excluded from the dwelling house or any part thereof by the other spouse except with the leave of the court given by an order under this section;
(b)   if not in occupation, a right with the leave of the court so given to enter into and occupy the dwelling house.
(2)   So long as one spouse has the rights of occupation, either of the spouses may apply to the court for an order—
(a)   declaring, enforcing, restricting or terminating those rights, or
(b)   prohibiting, suspending or restricting the exercise by either spouse of the right to occupy the dwelling house, or
(c)   requiring either spouse to permit the exercise by the other of that right.
(3)   On an application for an order under this section, the court may make such order as it thinks just and reasonable having regard to the conduct of the spouses in relation to each other and otherwise, to their respective needs and financial resources, to needs of any children and to all the circumstances of the case, and, without prejudice to the generality of the foregoing provision—
(a)   may except part of the dwelling house from a spouse's rights of occupation (and in particular a part used wholly or mainly for or in connection with the trade, business or profession of the other spouse),
(b)   may order a spouse occupying the dwelling house or any part thereof by virtue of this section to make periodical payments to the other in respect of the occupation,
(c)   may impose on either spouse obligations as to the repair and maintenance of the dwelling house or the discharge of any liabilities in respect of the dwelling house.
(4)   Orders under this section may, in so far as they have a continuing effect, be limited so as to have effect for a period specified in the order or until further order.
(5)   Where a spouse is entitled under this section to occupy a dwelling house or any part thereof, any payment or tender made or other thing done by that spouse in or towards satisfaction of any liability of the other spouse in respect of rent, rates, mortgage payments or other outgoings affecting the dwelling house shall, whether or not it is made or done in pursuance of an order under this section, be as good as if made or done by the other spouse.
(6)   A spouse's occupation by virtue of this section shall, for the purposes of the Rent (Agriculture) Act 1976, and of the Rent Act 1977 (other than Part V and sections 103 to 106), be treated as possession by the other spouse and [for the purposes of Part IV of the Housing Act 1985 [and Part I of the Housing Act 1988] (secure tenancies)] be treated as occupation by the other spouse.
(7)   Where a spouse is entitled under this section to occupy a dwelling house or any part thereof and makes any payment in or towards satisfaction of any liability of the other spouse in respect of mortgage payments affecting the dwelling house, the person to whom the payment is made may treat it as having been made by that other spouse, but the fact that that person has treated any such payment as having been so made shall not affect any claim of the first-mentioned spouse against the other to an interest in the dwelling house by virtue of the payment.
(8)   Where a spouse is entitled under this section to occupy a dwelling house or part thereof by reason of an interest of the other spouse under a trust; all the provisions of

subsections (5) to (7) above shall apply in relation to the trustees as they apply in relation to the other spouse.

(9) . . .

(10) This Act shall not apply to a dwelling house which has at no time been a matrimonial home of the spouses in question; and a spouse's rights of occupation shall continue only so long as the marriage subsists and the other spouse is entitled as mentioned in subsection (1) above to occupy the dwelling house, except where provision is made by section 2 of this Act for those rights to be a charge on an estate or interest in the dwelling house.

(11) It is hereby declared that a spouse who has an equitable interest in a dwelling house or in the proceeds of sale thereof, not being a spouse in whom is vested (whether solely or as a joint tenant) a legal estate in fee simple or a legal term of years absolute in the dwelling house, is to be treated for the purpose only of determining whether he or she has rights of occupation under this section as not being entitled to occupy the dwelling house by virtue of that interest.

2. Effect of rights of occupation as charge on dwelling house

(1) Where, at any time during the subsistence of a marriage, one spouse is entitled to occupy a dwelling house by virtue of a beneficial estate or interest, then the other spouse's rights of occupation shall be a charge on that estate or interest, having the like priority as if it were an equitable interest created at whichever is the latest of the following dates, that is to say—

    (a) the date when the spouse so entitled acquires the estate or interest,

    (b) the date of the marriage, and

    (c) the 1st January 1968 (which is the date of commencement of the Act of 1967).

(2) If, at any time when a spouse's rights of occupation are a charge on an interest of the other spouse under a trust, there are, apart from either of the spouses, no persons, living or unborn, who are or could become beneficiaries under the trust, then those rights shall be a charge also on the estate or interest of the trustees for the other spouse, having the like priority as if it were an equitable interest created (under powers overriding the trusts) on the date when it arises.

(3) In determining for the purposes of subsection (2) above whether there are any persons who are not, but could become, beneficiaries under the trust, there shall be disregarded any potential exercise of a general power of appointment exercisable by either or both of the spouses alone (whether or not the exercise of it requires the consent of another person).

(4) Notwithstanding that a spouse's rights of occupation are a charge on an estate or interest in the dwelling house, those rights shall be brought to an end by—

    (a) the death of the other spouse, or

    (b) the termination (otherwise than by death) of the marriage,

unless in the event of a matrimonial dispute or estrangement the court sees fit to direct otherwise by an order made under section 1 above during the subsistence of the marriage.

(5) . . .

(6) . . .

(7) . . .

(8) Where the title to the legal estate by virtue of which a spouse is entitled to occupy a dwelling house (including any legal estate held by trustees for that spouse) is registered under the Land Registration Act 1925 or any enactment replaced by that Act—

    (a) registration of a land charge affecting the dwelling house by virtue of this Act shall be effective by registering a notice under that Act, and

    (b) a spouse's rights of occupation shall not be an overriding interest within the meaning of that Act affecting the dwelling house notwithstanding that the spouse is in actual occupation of the dwelling house.

(9) A spouse's rights of occupation (whether or not constituting a charge) shall not entitle that spouse to lodge a caution under section 54 of the Land Registration Act 1925.

(10) Where—

    (a) a spouse's rights of occupation are a charge on the estate of the other spouse or of trustees for the other spouse, and

    (b) that estate is the subject of a mortgage within the meaning of the Law of Property Act 1925, then, if, after the date of creation of the mortgage, the charge is registered under section 2 of the Land Charges Act 1972, the charge shall, for the purposes of section 94 of that Act of 1925 (which regulates the rights of mortgagees to make further advances ranking in priority to subsequent mortgages), be deemed to be a mortgage subsequent in date to the first-mentioned mortgage.

(11) It is hereby declared that a charge under subsection (1) or (2) above is not registrable under section 2 of the Land Charges Act 1972 or subsection (8) above unless it is a charge on a legal estate.

8.   Dwelling house subject to mortgage

(1)   In determining for the purposes of the foregoing provisions of this Act (including Schedule 1) whether a spouse or former spouse is entitled to occupy a dwelling house by virtue of an estate or interest, there shall be disregarded any right to possession of the dwelling house conferred on a mortgagee of the dwelling house under or by virtue of his mortgage, whether the mortgagee is in possession or not; but the other spouse shall not by virtue of the rights of occupation conferred by this Act have any larger right against the mortgagee to occupy the dwelling house than the one first mentioned has by virtue of his or her estate or interest and of any contract with the mortgagee, unless under section 2 above those rights of occupation are a charge, affecting the mortgagee, on the estate or interest mortgaged.

(2)   Where a mortgagee of land which consists of or includes a dwelling house brings an action in any court for the enforcement of his security, a spouse who is not a party to the action and who is enabled by section 1(5) or (8) above to meet the mortgagor's liabilities under the mortgage, on applying to the court at any time before the action is finally disposed of in that court, shall be entitled to be made a party to the action if the court—

(a)   does not see special reason against it, and

(b)   is satisfied that the applicant may be expected to make such payments or do such things in or towards satisfaction of the mortgagor's liabilities or obligations as might affect the outcome of the proceedings or that the expectation of it should be considered under section 36 of the Administration of Justice Act 1970.

(3)   Where a mortgagee of land which consists or substantially consists of a dwelling house brings an action for the enforcement of his security, and at the relevant time there is—

(a)   in the case of unregistered land, a land charge of Class F registered against the person who is the estate owner at the relevant time or any person who, where the estate owner is a trustee, preceded him as trustee during the subsistence of the mortgage, or

(b)   in the case of registered land, a subsisting registration of a notice under section 2(8) above or a notice or caution under section 2(7) of the Act of 1967,

notice of the action shall be served by the mortgagee on the person on whose behalf the land charge is registered or the notice or caution entered, if that person is not a party to the action.

1.3.7   INTEREST UNDER A CONSTRUCTIVE TRUST

LLOYDS BANK PLC v ROSSET [1991] 1 AC 107, House of Lords

FACTS: Mr. Rosset had received a loan to buy a derelict house on the understanding that the house should be in his name alone. Mrs. Rosset did a limited amount of work helping the renovation of the house, in particular she helped with the interior decorations. However, the vast bulk of the work was carried out by contractors employed and paid for by the husband.

Following matrimonial problems the husband left home, leaving his wife and children in the premises. The loan which the husband had taken out was not, in the event, repaid. Consequently, the bank brought proceedings for possession. The husband raised no defence to that action, but the wife did resist. She claimed to have a beneficial interest in the house under a constructive trust. She also claimed to have been in actual occupation of the property at the time of the completion of the loan (mortgage) from the bank. Accordingly, she claimed to have an interest in the land which would override the bank's

right to enforce its security. (Section 70(1)(g) of the Land Registration Act 1925 provides that the rights of any person in actual occupation of land shall be 'overriding'.) The judge at first instance held in favour of the bank, but the Court of Appeal allowed the wife's appeal. The bank appealed to the House of Lords.
HELD: The appeal was allowed.

LORD BRIDGE OF HARWICH: . . . the judge based his inference of a common intention that Mrs. Rosset should have a beneficial interest in the property under a constructive trust essentially on what Mrs. Rosset did in and about assisting in the renovation of the property between the beginning of November 1982 and the date of completion on 17 December 1982. Yet by itself this activity, it seems to me, could not possibly justify any such inference. It was common ground that Mrs. Rosset was extremely anxious that the new matrimonial home should be ready for occupation before Christmas if possible. In these circumstances it would seem the most natural thing in the world for any wife, in the absence of her husband abroad, to spend all the time she could spare and to employ any skills she might have, such as the ability to decorate a room, in doing all she could to accelerate progress of the work quite irrespective of any expectation she might have of enjoying a beneficial interest in the property. The judge's view that some of this work was work 'upon which she could not reasonably have been expected to embark unless she was to have an interest in the house' seems to me, with respect, quite untenable. The impression that the judge may have thought that the share of the equity to which he held Mrs. Rosset to be entitled had been 'earned' by her work in connection with the renovation is emphasised by his reference in the concluding sentence of his judgment to the extent to which her 'qualifying contribution' reduced the cost of the renovation.

On any view the monetary value of Mrs. Rosset's work expressed as a contribution to a property acquired at a cost exceeding £70,000 must have been so trifling as to be almost *de minimis*. I should myself have had considerable doubt whether Mrs. Rosset's contribution to the work of renovation was sufficient to support a claim to a constructive trust in the absence of writing to satisfy the requirements of section 51 of the Law of Property Act 1925 even if her husband's intention to make a gift to her of half or any other share in the equity of the property had been clearly established or if he had clearly represented to her that that was what he intended. But here the conversations with her husband on which Mrs. Rosset relied, all of which took place before November 1982, were incapable of lending support to the conclusion of a constructive trust in the light of the judge's finding that by that date there had been no decision that she was to have any interest in the property. The finding that the discussion 'did not exclude the possibility' that she should have an interest does not seem to me to add anything of significance.

These considerations lead me to the conclusion that the judge's finding that Mr. Rosset held the property as constructive trustee for himself and his wife cannot be supported and it is on this short ground that I would allow the appeal. . . .

The first and fundamental question which must always be resolved is whether, independently of any inference to be drawn from the conduct of the parties in the course of sharing the house as their home and managing their joint affairs, there has at any time prior to acquisition, or exceptionally at some later date, been any agreement, arrangement or understanding reached between them that the property is to be shared beneficially. The finding of an agreement or arrangement to share in this sense can only, I think, be based on evidence of express discussions between the partners, however imperfectly remembered and however imprecise their terms may have been. Once a finding to this effect is made it will only be necessary for the partner asserting a claim to a beneficial interest against the partner entitled to the legal estate to show that he or she acted to his or her detriment or significantly altered his or her position in reliance on the agreement in order to give rise to a constructive trust or a proprietary estoppel.

In sharp contrast with this situation is the very different one where there is no evidence to support a finding of an agreement or arrangement to share, however reasonable it might have been for the parties to reach such an arrangement if they had applied their minds to the question, and where the court must rely entirely on the conduct of the parties both as the basis from which to infer a common intention to share the property beneficially and as the conduct relied on to give rise to a constructive trust. In this situation direct contributions to the purchase price by the partner who is not the legal owner, whether initially or by payment of mortgage instalments, will readily justify the inference necessary to the creation of a constructive trust. But, as I read the authorities, it is at least extremely doubtful whether anything less will do.

The leading cases in your Lordships' House are *Pettitt* v *Pettitt* [1970] AC 777 and *Gissing* v *Gissing* [1971] AC 866. Both demonstrate situations in the second category to which I have referred and their Lordships discuss at great length the difficulties to which these situations give rise. The effect of these two decisions is very helpfully analysed in the judgment of Lord MacDermott LCJ in *McFarlane* v *McFarlane* [1972] NI 59.

Outstanding examples on the other hand of cases giving rise to situations in the first category are *Eves* v *Eves* [1975] 1 WLR 1338 and *Grant* v *Edwards* [1986] Ch 638. In both these cases, where the parties who had cohabited were unmarried, the female partner had been clearly led by the male partner to believe, when they set up home together, that the property would belong to them jointly. In *Eves* v *Eves* the male partner had told the female partner that the only reason why the property was to be acquired in his name alone was because she was under 21 and that, but for her age, he would have had the house put into their joint names. He admitted in evidence that this was simply an 'excuse.' Similarly in *Grant* v *Edwards* the female partner was told by the male partner that the only reason for not acquiring the property in joint names was because she was involved in divorce proceedings and that, if the property were acquired jointly, this might operate to her prejudice in those proceedings. As Nourse LJ put it, at p. 649:

> Just as in *Eves* v *Eves* [1975] 1 WLR 1338, these facts appear to me to raise a clear inference that there was an understanding between the plaintiff and the defendant, or a common intention, that the plaintiff was to have some sort of proprietary interest in the house; otherwise no excuse for not putting her name on to the title would have been needed.

The subsequent conduct of the female partner in each of these cases, which the court rightly held sufficient to give rise to a constructive trust or proprietary estoppel supporting her claim to an interest in the property, fell far short of such conduct as would by itself have supported the claim in the absence of an express representation by the male partner that she was to have such an interest. It is significant to note that the share to which the female partners in *Eves* v *Eves* and *Grant* v *Edwards* were held entitled were one quarter and one half respectively. In no sense could these shares have been regarded as proportionate to what the judge in the instant case described as a 'qualifying contribution' in terms of the indirect contributions to the acquisition or enhancement of the value of the houses made by the female partners.

I cannot help thinking that the judge in the instant case would not have fallen into error if he had kept clearly in mind the distinction between the effect of evidence on the one hand which was capable of establishing an express agreement or an express representation that Mrs. Rosset was to have an interest in the property and evidence on the other hand of conduct alone as a basis for an inference of the necessary common intention. . . .

For the reasons I have indicated I would allow the appeal. . . .

1.3.8   LICENCES BY ESTOPPEL

INWARDS v *BAKER* [1965] 1 All ER 446, Court of Appeal

FACTS: Baker junior was keen to build himself a bungalow, but he could not afford the price of an empty site. His father had some spare land. Baker senior said to his son, 'Why not put the bungalow on my land and make the bungalow a little bigger?'. Baker junior did exactly that, and made the bungalow his permanent home.

Baker senior retained ownership of the fee simple to the land, and so the house also became **Baker senior's** property. All was well while both senior and junior were still alive, but when Baker senior died his will (made long before the bungalow was built) left the land in question not to Baker junior but to Inwards. Inwards brought proceedings to recover possession of the bungalow. These proceedings failed.

HELD: The Court of Appeal found that where a landowner (L) encourages a third party (T) to expend money and/or effort on L's land, and T reasonably assumes that he will have some degree of permanence on the land, T acquires some sort of right with respect to the land. This right is (in principle) binding on third parties.

1.3.9 ESTATE CONTRACTS

See **5.2.2** and **5.2.2.2**.

1.3.10 OPTIONS

See **5.2.2.2**.

CHAPTER TWO

SOME BASIC CONCEPTS OF PROPERTY LAW

2.1 The Trust

See **Chapters 11 to 13**.

2.2 Real Property and Personal Property

**Megarry, Sir R, and Wade, H.W.R., The Law of Real Property, 5th edn,
London: Stevens & Sons Limited, 1984, p. 10**

Meaning of 'Real Property'

As is the case with so many expressions in English law, the explanation of the term 'real property' is historical.

In early law, property was deemed 'real' if the courts would restore to a dispossessed owner the thing itself, the '*res*,' and not merely give compensation for the loss. Thus If X forcibly evicted Y from his freehold land, Y could bring a 'real' action whereby he could obtain an order from the court that X should return the land to him. But if X took Y's sword or glove from him, he could bring only a personal action which gave X the choice of either returning the article or paying the value thereof. Consequently a distinction was made between real property (or 'realty'), which could be specifically recovered, and personal property (or 'personalty'), which was not thus recoverable. Nature has provided one division of property, namely into immovables (i.e. land) and movables; the English division into real and personal property is similar with one important exception. In general, all interests in land are real property, with the exception of leaseholds (or 'terms of years'), which are classified as personalty.

This peculiar exception was first of all due to the fact that leases were foreign to the feudal system of landholding by tenure, under which, in its earliest form, the social and economic status of every member of society was fixed. Originally leases were rather regarded as personal business arrangements under which one party allowed the other the use of his land in return for a rent. They were, in other words, personal contracts, operating *in personam* between the parties and not creating or transferring any rights *in rem*, i.e. rights in the land itself which could affect feudal status. Leases helped to supply a useful form of investment for a society which knew nothing of stocks and shares. Money might be employed in buying land and letting it out on lease in order to obtain an income from the capital, or in buying a lease for a lump sum which would be recovered with interest out of the produce of the land. These were commercial transactions, more in the sphere of money than of land, as land-owning was then understood. Once leaseholds were classed with personal property it was discovered that the position was not without its advantages. Not only were leases then immune from feudal burdens and the intricate legal procedure required for freeholds: they could be bequeathed by will in times when wills of other land were still not allowed. Thus the illogical position continued until it became too well settled to alter.

Leaseholds are still, therefore, personalty in law. But having now for so long been recognised as interests in land and not merely contractual rights, they have been classed under the paradoxical heading of chattels real. 'The first word indicates their personal nature (cattle were the most important chattels in early days, hence the name), the second shows their connection with land. The three types of property may, therefore, be classified thus:

Land   { (i)   Realty.
              { (ii)   Chattels real.
Personality { (iii) Pure personalty.

... The legislation of 1925 abolished many of the remaining differences between the law governing realty and that governing personalty. For example, before 1926, if a person died intestate (i.e. without a will), all his realty passed to his heir, while his personalty was divided between certain of his relatives; again, realty could be entailed and personalty could not. After 1925, however, realty and personalty both pass on intestacy to certain relatives, and both kinds of property can be entailed. Nevertheless, the distinction still remains of importance.

Real property itself comprises two distinct genera, called corporeal and incorporeal hereditaments. 'Hereditament' indicates property which descended to the heir on intestacy before 1926, i.e. realty as opposed to personalty. Corporeal hereditaments are lands, buildings, minerals, trees and all other things which are part of or affixed to land – in other words, the physical matter over which ownership is exercised. Incorporeal hereditaments, on the other hand, are not things at all, but rights. Certain rights were classified as real property, so that on intestacy before 1926 they also descended to the heir, rather than to the relatives entitled to personalty. The most important incorporeal hereditaments are easements, profits and rentcharges, but there are others also. . . .

CHAPTER THREE

TENURES

3.1 Feudal Tenures

Simpson, A.W.B., An Introduction to the History of the Land Law,
1st edn, Oxford: Oxford University Press, 1961, p. 2

. . . The doctrine of tenure has its origin in the state of social organization known as 'feudalism'. 'Feudalism' is undoubtedly a vague and imprecise term, with a number of connotations. For our immediate purpose it is sufficient to note that the feudal structure of society, which was firmly established in England after the Norman Conquest, involved dependent land holding—the holding of land in return for the rendering of sevices, typically military sevice. Even before the Conquest land tenure of a sort was known; the *loan* of land created a relationship between lender and holder which closely resembles the feudal relationship between lord and tenant of post-Conquest times, and the relationship between the Saxon lord and the village community where he held sway could be described in tenurial terms. How widespread tenure was in Anglo-Saxon England is a moot point, and a somewhat artificial one; until there was a theory of tenure the question can hardly be asked. What is clear is that the Norman administrators did have a theory of tenure, and applied it universally; all land whatsoever was held of some lord, and ultimately of the Crown. This is fully recognized in Domesday Book (1086) and certainly no such rigid doctrine could possibly have existed before 1066; indeed, in England alone was feudalism so universalized. On the Continent feudal land-holding did not engulf all land; some tracts of land—called allodial lands—escaped the net. In Domesday Book the compilers sometimes seem puzzled by a landholder who seems to have no lord, but such puzzlement is assumed to arise rather from ignorance of the facts than from any exception to the universal application of the concept of tenure. The consequence of this was that feudal law did not become the law of the knightly, aristocratic class, nor the law of some parts of the country alone; it became the common law of England.

This triumph of order was made possible by the Conquest, and by the high degree of administrative efficiency attained by King William's staff. The invasion of England by a band of military adventurers made it necessary to quarter this military aristocracy on the conquered land; William had to reward his followers and preserve his military strength for the future. He was able to achieve both these ends by parcelling up the land of the country amongst his followers, who became his tenants for their land, holding by his grant. In return he bargained for services; and most of his tenants were bound to serve in the Royal army and bring with them a specified number of knights. The tenure thus created was knight-service, the typical feudal tenure, and it was wholly Norman. The tenant who owed the service of ten knights was said to hold ten *knight's fees*, and so on; there is some evidence to show that the quota of knights due was fixed in multiples of five or ten knights. The immediate tenants of the Crown were called his tenants in chief, and there were probably about fifteen hundred of these tenants by 1086.

Now when it is said that the country was granted out by the King to his tenants in chief it must not be imagined that any process of wholesale eviction took place. At the bottom of the social scale were those humble peasants who actually wrested the agricultural wealth of the country from the soil; it was their labour which made the whole paraphernalia of knights and castles possible. At the time of the Conquest many were slaves, the property of some Saxon lord; some were free men who had a lord, but who did not hold their lands of their lord, for their personal relationship of dependence was unconnected with their enjoyment of land. Others perhaps could be regarded as tenants, who held of their lords. The greater part of these peasants would be bound by custom to perform various duties of a public nature, such as to repair bridges, and also other duties which were of personal benefit to the Saxon lord of the village community in which they lived—for example they might be bound to provide him with a food rent, or to labour on the land of their lord. The tendency before the Conquest had been for the peasants of a village community to become increasingly dependent upon the local lord, and it has been suggested that it may have often happened that the peasants surrendered their lands into the local lord's hands and received them back again in return for an obligation to labour on their lord's land; in return for a greater degree of subservience the peasants received the protection of a powerful man. In general the effect of the Norman Conquest was only to substitute a new, alien, lord for his Saxon predecessor. What a tenant in chief acquired by the enjoyment of rights over land and services due from peasants who cultivated that land; to the peasant it may not have seemed that anything very momentous had occurred. . . .

The King's immediate grantee—the tenant in chief *ut de corona*—could retain his land and provide knights by paying for them, and keeping them in his household, but more frequently he provided his quota by subinfeudation. This took the form of a grant by the tenant in chief of one parcel of land to some lesser man, X, the land to be held of the grantor in return for the service of one or more knights in the Royal army. The grantee, X, in his turn could again subinfeudate to another, Y, a part or the whole of his parcel of land, and in this way any number of rungs in the ladder could be created. Upon such a subinfeudation the grantor and grantee could reach any bargain they wished as to the services, but this in no way concerned the lord of whom the grantor held, for the service due to him remained burdened on the land, unaffected by subinfeudation. . . .

The provision of an army was but one of the requirements of medieval society. By the creation of tenures involving other forms of service the land, which was the major source of wealth, could be made to yield to lords whatever goods or labour they required. It is important to realise that no fixed rules governed the type or nature of the services which could be stipulated for upon a grant of land. The result was the creation of tenures which range from the ludicrous to the obscene and from the onerous to the nominal. A few examples will illustrate this diversity. In the reign of John we find that William, Earl Warren granted lands in Stamford to be held for the service of finding annually a mad bull to divert his lordship, whilst there are several grants of land for the service of holding the seasick King's head on his trips across the channel. Straw for the royal privy had to be found by one unfortunate landholder, and the tenant of lands in Suffolk, one Rolland, was obliged upon Christmas Day to make a leap, a whistle and a fart *coram domino rege*, a service subseqently commuted for a less embarrassing money payment. At the other end of the scale come really heavy burdens—tenants in chief who owe the service of forty or more knights, those who hold at substantial rents in kind, and those who hold in return for onerous services, such as the duty of caring for falcons and hounds. Upon this diversity of social relationships the medieval lawyers imposed a deceptively simple classification of tenures. The basis for this classification—which was only achieved by degrees—was the nature of the service due. . . .

MABO v *QUEENSLAND* (1992) 66 ALJR 408, High Court of Australia

FACTS: In this case the High Court of Australia had to consider whether certain islands were subject to the native title of the indigenous inhabitants, or whether they were lands held by the Crown.
HELD: Native title should be preserved.

BRENNAN J:
The feudal basis of the proposition of absolute Crown ownership
The land law of England is based on the doctrine of tenure. In English legal theory, every parcel of land in England is held either mediately or immediately of the King who is the Lord Paramount; the term 'tenure' is used to signify the relationship between tenant and

lord (*Attorney-General of Ontario* v *Mercer* (1883) LR 8 App Cas 767 at 771–772), not the relationship between tenant and land. The characteristic of feudalism 'is not tenere terram, but tenere terram de X' (Pollock and Maitland, *The History of English Law* (2nd edn, 1898, reprinted 1952), vol. 1, p. 234n). It is implicit in the relationship of tenure that both lord and tenant have an interest in the land; 'The King had *"dominium directum"*, the subject *"dominium utile"'* (at p. 773; Co Litt 16). Absent a *'dominium directum'* in the Crown, there would be no foundation for a tenure arising on the making of a grant of land. When the Crown acquired territory outside England which was to be subject to the common law, there was a natural assumption that the doctrine of tenure should be the basis of the land law. Perhaps the assumption did not have to be made. After all, as Holdsworth observed . . . the universal application of the doctrine of tenure is a purely English phenomenon.

(QUIA EMPTORES) (1289–90)

A Statute of Our Lord The King, Concerning the Selling and Buying of Land

Chapter 1   Freeholders may sell their lands; so that the feoffee do hold of the chieflord
. . . Our lord the King, in his Parliament at Westminster after Easter, the eighteenth year of his reign, that is to wit, in the quinzime of Saint John Baptist, at the instance of the great men of the realm, granted, provided, and ordained, that from henceforth it shall be lawful to every freeman to sell at his own pleasure his lands and tenements, or part of them; so that the feoffee shall hold the same lands or tenements of the chief lord of the same fee, by such service and customs as his feoffor held before.

TENURES ABOLITION ACT 1660

An Act takeing away the Court of Wards and Liveries and Tenures in Capite and by Knights Service and Purveyance, and for setling a Revenue upon his Majesty in Lieu thereof

4.   All tenures to be created by the King hereafter to be in free and common socage
And . . . that all tenures hereafter to be created by the King Majestic his heires or successors upon any gifts or grants of any mannours landes tenements or hereditaments of any estate of inheritance at the common law shall be in free and common soccage, and shall be adjudged to be in free and common soccage onely, and not by knight service or in capite, and shall be discharged of all wardship value and forfeiture of marriage livery primer-seizin ouster le main aide pur faier fitz chivalier & pur file marrier, any law statute or reservation to the contrary thereof any wise notwithstanding.

3.2   Leasehold Tenures

See **2.2** and **Chapters 17** to **22**.

CHAPTER FOUR

ESTATES

4.1   Fee Simple

4.1.1   MODIFIED FEES SIMPLE

4.1.1.1   Public policy

BLATHWAYT v CAWLEY (BARON) AND OTHERS **[1976] AC 397, House of Lords**

FACTS: A clause of a testator's will provided that, in the event that one of the beneficiaries under his will should 'be or become a Roman Catholic . . . the estate hereby limited to him shall cease and determine and be utterly void'. It later transpired that a life tenant did indeed become a Roman Catholic. The judge at first instance held that his estate should be forfeit.
HELD: The House of Lords unanimously upheld the condition subsequent.

LORD WILBERFORCE: . . . as to public policy. The argument under this heading was put in two alternative ways. First, it was said that the law of England was now set against discrimination on a number of grounds including religious grounds, and appeal was made to the Race Relations Act 1968 which does not refer to religion and to the European Convention of Human Rights of 1950 which refers to freedom of religion and to enjoyment of that freedom and other freedoms without discrimination on ground of religion. My Lords, I do not doubt that conceptions of public policy should move with the times and that widely accepted treaties and statutes may point the direction in which such conceptions, as applied by the courts, ought to move. It may well be that conditions such as this are, or at least are becoming, inconsistent with standards now widely accepted. But acceptance of this does not persuade me that we are justified, particularly in relation to a will which came into effect as long ago as 1936 and which has twice been the subject of judicial consideration, in introducing for the first time a rule of law which would go far beyond the mere avoidance of discrimination on religious grounds. To do so would bring about a substantial reduction of another freedom, firmly rooted in our law, namely that of testamentary disposition. Discrimination is not the same thing as choice: it operates over a larger and less personal area, and neither by express provision nor by implication has private selection yet become a matter of public policy.

4.2   Fee Tail

FINES AND RECOVERIES ACT 1833

15.   Power of actual tenants in tail, after 31st December, 1833, to dispose of entailed lands in fee simple or for less estate, saving the rights of certain persons.
. . . After the thirty-first day of December one thousand eight hundred and thirty-three every actual tenant in tail, whether in possession, remainder, contingency or otherwise,

shall have full power to dispose of for an estate in fee simple absolute or for any less estate the lands entailed, as against all persons claiming the lands entailed by force of any estate tail which shall be vested in or might be claimed by, or which but for some previous act would have been vested in or might have been claimed by, the person making the disposition at the time of his making the same, and also as against all persons, including the King's most excellent Majesty, whose estates are to take effect after the determination or in defeasance of any such estate tail; saving always the rights of all persons in respect of estates prior to the estate tail in respect of which such disposition shall be made, and the rights of all other persons, except those against whom such disposition is by this Act authorised to be made.

4.3 Life Estates

See **Chapter 11**.

4.4 Reform

The Law Commission (Law Com. No. 181) Transfer of Land: Trusts of Land

Entailed Interests

16.1 In the working paper we proposed that the creation of new entailed interests should be prevented. This proposal met with strong approval from several consultees. At present, entailed interests can only be constituted behind a strict settlement. Given that our recommendations are designed to minimise use of the Settled Land Act 1925, it seems logical to suggest that there should be no new entails, particularly as the latter would have little purpose outwith the framework of a strict settlement. We recommend that an attempt to create an entailed interest in land should operate as a grant of a fee simple absolute, unless the grantor has an equitable interest only. In this latter case, the attempt to create an entail will take effect as a declaration of trust on the part of the settlor or the personal representative that the land is held on trust (under the new system) for the grantee absolutely. It is at present possible to create entailed interests in personalty. Given that we are concerned to approximate the positions of trusts of real and personal property, we further recommend that it should no longer be possible to create entailed interests in personal property. . . .

Conditional and Determinable Fees

17.1   By virtue of section 7 of the Law of Property Act 1925, a fee simple which is subject to a legal or equitable right of entry or re-entry is a fee simple absolute and hence a legal estate. Our recommendations are not designed to affect this provision, and these estates would continue to be legal estates. However, where a person is granted a conditional or determinable fee in land which does not come within section 7 the land would be held on trust under the new system, the trustees being the grantor or personal representatives (as appropriate).

Sexton, R., 'The Law Commission's report on trusts of land, at last a law for contemporary society?' *Trust Law and Practice*, January 1989, p. 66

The continued existence of outmoded rights in land

As every law student knows, land law is still cluttered up with strange devices such as fees fail, determinable fees and fees upon condition subsequent. The Commission does propose (cl. 16 of the Bill) that no new entails should be created; any attempt to create an entail would in future result in a fee simple being transferred. This proposal does not, however, go far enough.

In its working paper, the Commission proposed to convert all existing fees tail into fees simple, but this is another proposal which has disappeared (without any explanation) from the final report. The Commission should have stuck by its original proposal. Indeed it should have gone further. Modified fees should also be banned, and any existing ones converted into absolute fees simple (many modified fees where the 'modification' relates to marriage or religion must surely infringe the European Convention on Human Rights). . . .

4.5 End of Chapter Assessment Question

'As every law student knows, land law is cluttered up with strange devices such as fees tail, determinable fees and fees upon condition subsequent. The Law Commission [merely] proposes that no new entails should be created. This proposal does not, however, go far enough.' (Article in *Trust Law and Practice*.)

Critically examine this statement.

4.6 End of Chapter Assessment Outline Answer

On 8 June 1989 the Law Commission published a Report titled 'Transfer of Land: Trusts of Land' (Law Com. No. 181). The Report considered entailed interests and modified fees simple. It recommended that no new entailed interests should be created, but it did not recommend the prohibition of new modified fees. Although fees tail are now very few in number, and modified fees are virtually non-existent, it can still be argued that the Law Commission did not go far enough in its proposals for reform of these estates.

The fee tail is a strange legal relic which has somehow survived into the late twentieth century. Fees tail were first recognised as estates in land in 1285. Until the nineteenth century land (particularly the large country estate) was often subject to a fee tail. Very few exist today. A fee tail is an estate of inheritance, i.e. it can pass from generation to generation within the same family and lasts as long as the original grantee or any of his lineal descendants are alive. However, there are strict rules governing which of the descendants may inherit the fee tail. When an owner of the fee tail dies the rules ensure that the land must pass to the 'heir' of the deceased owner. Thus the land will pass first to the eldest male descendant and only if there is no male descendant will the land pass to the eldest female descendant. A fee simple is different. As the word 'simple' informs us, it may be left to anybody, whether or not they are the 'heir'.

Before 1833 the fee tail was a useful device for keeping land within the family, but since the Fines and Recoveries Act 1833 the person who owns the fee tail estate in possession (known as the 'tenant in tail') may, if they are of full age, 'bar' the entail by a relatively cheap and simple process. Barring the entail converts the fee tail into a fee simple. The result is that the fee tail, once it has been transformed into a fee simple, may be sold or given away to persons outside the family. Consequently, there can be no good reason for creating a fee tail today.

In its 1989 Report the Law Commission acknowledged the irrelevance of fees tail to modern land ownership by recommending legislation to prevent the creation of any new fees tail (para. 16.1). However, in making this recommendation, the Law Commission did not go far enough. The Working Paper which preceded the Report had recommended that existing fees tail should be converted into fees simple. It is regrettable that this recommendation did not appear in the final report, it could have saved future tenants in tail the expense of having to bar the entail. Further, the very concept of inheritance by the 'heir' might be thought of as unsuitable to a modern statute, providing as it does for inheritance by males in preference to females. It sits uneasily in the statute books with the Sex Discrimination Act 1975. There are not many tenants in tail nowadays, but any that do exist will necessarily incur the expense of executing a disentailing assurance (barring the entail) before being able to leave the land to, say, a daughter in preference to a son.

The vast majority of fees in existence today are 'absolute', which means that, in principle, they will last for ever. An almost negligible minority of fees are said to be 'modified'.

The determinable fee simple is a fee simple which is modified in such a way that it will terminate automatically upon the occurrence of a specified event. The specified event must be such that it may never occur. Examples include: 'to John Smith in fee simple until he marries Fanny Bloggs' and 'to Ann Green in fee simple during the time that she remains a faithful protestant'. The essence of the modification is that it is of a temporal nature, using words such as 'until', 'while' and 'during'.

The fee simple upon condition subsequent can be defined as a fee simple where the grantee is given an apparently absolute fee simple to which a clause is added to the effect that if a stated condition is broken, the estate shall be forfeit. For example: 'To John Smith in fee simple provided that he never marries Fanny Bloggs' and 'to Ann Green in fee simple unless she forsakes the Protestant religion'. The essence of the modification is that it is of a conditional nature, using words such as 'provided that', 'on condition', 'unless' and 'but not if'.

In its 1989 Report the Law Commission considered modified fees (para. 17.1) and had the opportunity to recommend their abolition. The Commission did not take this opportunity and today it is still possible to create modified fees simple.

One argument in favour of their abolition is that they are out of line with modern ideas of freedom, particularly religious freedom. As things presently stand modified fees limiting freedom to marry and freedom of religion are valid. Indeed, as recently as 1975, the House of Lords unanimously upheld a condition subsequent which provided for forfeiture on the grantee becoming a Roman Catholic (*Blathwayt* v *Lord Cawley* [1975] 3 All ER 625). Lord Wilberforce, delivering the leading speech, acknowledged that 'conditions such as this are, or at least are becoming, inconsistent with standards now widely accepted' but upheld the condition because in 1936, when the fee had been granted, the condition had been added through the exercise, not of discrimination, but of choice. His Lordship did tacitly acknowledge, however, that the condition might have infringed the European Convention on Human Rights of 1950 which protects the enjoyment of freedoms without discrimination on ground of religion. In coming to the conclusion it did, the House of Lords side-stepped a dilemma. It is not actually the dilemma between the grantor's freedom of disposition and the grantee's freedom of religion. Nothing ever prevented the grantee from becoming a Roman Catholic! It is the dilemma between the grantor's freedom of disposition and the grantee's freedom as a property owner to hold a valuable estate without the threat that it might be lost through the exercise of freedom of religion. The Law Commission also side-stepped this dilemma in failing to recommend the abolition of modified fees. This is also regrettable, for it is a dilemma that only Parliament can resolve.

Fees tail, determinable fees and fees upon condition subsequent are 'strange devices' indeed. The creation of new ones should be prohibited, and those that already exist should be converted to fees simple.

CHAPTER FIVE

LEGAL AND EQUITABLE RIGHTS IN LAND

5.1 Creation and Transfer of Legal Property Rights

SMITH v *BUSH* [1990] 1 AC 849, House of Lords

This case is included because of a useful summary of conveyancing procedure provided by Lord Templeman. The decision in the case itself is of more direct relevance to the tort of negligence.

LORD TEMPLEMAN: Each year one million houses may be bought and sold. Apart from exceptional cases the procedure is always the same. The vendor and the purchaser agree a price but the purchaser cannot enter into a contract unless and until a mortgagee, typically a building society, offers to advance the whole or part of the purchase price. A mortgage of 80 per cent or more of the purchase price is not unusal. Thus, if the vendor and the purchaser agree a price of £50,000 and the purchaser can find £10,000, the purchaser then applies to a building society for a loan of £40,000. The purchaser pays the building society a valuation fee and the building society instructs a valuer who is paid by the building society. If the valuer reports to the building society that the house is good security for £40,000, the building society offers to advance £40,000 and the purchaser contracts to purchase the house for £50,000. The purchaser, who is offered £40,000 on the security of the house, rightly assumes that a qualified valuer had valued the house at not less than £40,000.

At the date when the purchaser pays the valuation fee, the date when the valuation is made and at the date when the purchaser is offered an advance, the sale may never take place. The amount offered by way of advance may not be enough, the purchaser may change his mind, or the vendor may increase his price and sell elsewhere. For many reasons a sale may go off, and in that case, the purchaser has paid his valuation fee without result and must pay a second valuation fee when he finds another house and goes through the same procedure. The building society which is anxious to attract borrowers and the purchaser who has no money to waste on valuation fees, do not encourage or pay for detailed surveys. Moreover, the vendor may not be willing to suffer the inconvenience of a detailed survey on behalf of a purchaser who has not contracted to purchase and may exploit minor items of disrepair disclosed by a detailed survey in order to obtain a reduction in the price.

The Law Commission Working Paper No. 92, Transfer of Land: Formalities for Contracts for Sale etc. of Land, London: HMSO, 1985, p. 9

General principles

5.2   We consider that there are three general principles which must be taken into account so far as possible in any reform in this area.

(i)   No reform should increase the likelihood of contracts for the sale (or other disposition) of land becoming binding before the parties have been able to obtain legal advice. This is not to say, however, that any reform should itself result in formalities which can only be undertaken by lawyers and not, for example, by the parties themselves if they so decide.

(ii)   Any reform if unable to reduce the risk of injustice should at least not increase it. In particular, the imposition of any formal requirements should not be so inflexible that hardship or unfairness is perceived in cases of minor non-compliance.

(iii)   Any reform should simplify or at least not complicate conveyancing. Although this is an argument for reducing formalities, so containing professionals' fees and assisting 'do-it-yourself' conveyancers, certainty and reliability are often essential in dealings with land and may call for extra formalities.

Is land different?

5.3   The question of whether land should be treated differently from other property is important, and one which deserves serious consideration. There are many other forms of property which may be worth far more than a piece of land, yet no formalities are required for contracts relating to them. If one can contract to buy or sell £1 million pounds' worth of shares without formality, why should even the smallest interest in land require any contractual formality? One reason conventionally given is that land has the particular characteristic that many people may acquire interests in or over one piece of land. For this reason, it is said, some formality must be required in dealings with land if confusion is not to arise as to whom owns what. From this point of view section 40(1) is obviously linked with the other sections of the Law of Property Act 1925 which require formalities for dealings with land. While we find this argument persuasive in relation to the completion of contracts, i.e., the actual creation of interests in land, even then it may not be totally compelling, because some third party interests can be created in other forms of property. More persuasive is the point that in principle each particular piece of land is unique, so that for contracts relating to land the important remedy of specific performance is much more likely to be available.

5.4   Another convincing argument, in our view, is that while there are other forms of property as valuable as land, for example, a Rolls Royce motorcar, most people do not deal in such property. For most people, the most significant transaction they will ever enter into is one relating to land, in particular the sale or purchase of a dwelling house. From this point of view, insisting on some formalities for the sale or purchase of land can be seen as a form of consumer protection for ordinary people who are engaged in a transaction which they will enter into only a few times in their lifetime, and which will often involve them in major financial commitments. However, the consumer protection approach is obviously not so appropriate for business transactions, for example, contracts for the grant of leases of commercial premises.

5.5   On balance, it is our provisional view that contracts for the sale of land should still be treated differently. . . .

5.1.1   FORMALITIES FOR A DEED: THE MODERN RULE

LAW OF PROPERTY (MISCELLANEOUS PROVISIONS) ACT 1989

1.   Deeds and their execution

(1)   Any rule of law which —

(a)   restricts the substances on which a deed may be written;

(b)   requires a seal for the valid execution of an instrument as a deed by an individual; or

(c)   requires authority by one person to another to deliver an instrument as a deed on his behalf to be given by deed,

is abolished.

(2)   An instrument shall not be a deed unless —

(a)   it makes it clear on its face that it is intended to be a deed by the person making it or, as the case may be, by the parties to it (whether by describing itself as a deed or expressing itself to be executed or signed as a deed or otherwise); and

(b)   it is validly executed as a deed by that person or, as the case may be, one or more of those parties.

(3)   An intrument is validly executed as a deed by an individual if, and only if—

   (a) it is signed —

      (i) by him in the presence of a witness who attests the signature; or

      (ii) at his direction and in his presence and the presence of two witnesses who each attest the signature; and

   (b) it is delivered as a deed by him or a person authorised to do so on his behalf. . . .

LAW OF PROPERTY ACT 1925

52. Conveyances to be by deed

(1)   All conveyances of land or of any interest therein are void for the purpose of conveying or creating a legal estate unless made by deed.

(2)   This section does not apply to —

   (a) assents by a personal representative;

   (b) disclaimers made in accordance with [sections 178 to 180 or sections 315 to 319 of the Insolvency Act 1986], or not required to be evidenced in writing;

   (c) surrenders by operation of law, including surrenders which may, by law, be effected without writing;

   (d) leases or tenancies or other assurances not required by law to be made in writing;

   (e) receipts not required by law to be under seal;

   (f) vesting orders of the court or other competent authority;

   (g) conveyances taking effect by operation of law.

5.2   Creation of Equitable Interests in Land

5.2.1   CREATION OF EQUITABLE INTERESTS IN LAND BY EXPRESS TRUST

LAW OF PROPERTY ACT 1925

53. Instruments required to be in writing

(1)   Subject to the provisions hereinafter contained with respect to the creation of interests in land by parol—

   (a) no interest in land can be created or disposed of except by writing signed by the person creating or conveying the same, or by his agent thereunto lawfully authorised in writing, or by will, or by operation of law;

   (b) a declaration of trust respecting any land or any interest therein must be manifested and proved by some writing signed by some person who is able to declare such trust or by his will;

   (c) a disposition of an equitable interest or trust subsisting at the time of the disposition, must be in writing signed by the person disposing of the same, or by his agent thereunto lawfully authorised in writing or by will.

(2)   This section does not affect the creation or operation of resulting, implied or constructive trusts.

5.2.2   CREATION OF EQUITABLE INTERESTS BY A CONTRACT TO CONVEY OR CREATE A LEGAL ESTATE OR INTEREST

5.2.2.1   Formalities for contracts to sell estates or interests in land

See also **5.1**.

(Note that s. 40 (below) has been repealed by s. 2 of the Law of Property (Miscellaneous Provisions) Act 1989. *Steadman* v *Steadman* has also been superseded by s. 2 of the 1989 Act.)

LAW OF PROPERTY ACT 1925

40.   Contracts for sale, etc, of land to be in writing

(1)   No action may be brought upon any contract for the sale or other disposition of land or any interest in land, unless the agreement upon which such action is brought, or some memorandum or note thereof, is in writing, and signed by the party to be charged or by some other person thereunto by him lawfully authorised.

(2)   This section applies to contracts whether made before or after the commencement of this Act and does not affect the law relating to part performance, or sales by the court.

STEADMAN v *STEADMAN* [1976] AC 536, House of Lords

FACTS: Mr. and Mrs. Steadman were divorced, but the property side of the break-up had not been concluded. During the course of negotiating a settlement of the wife's disputed claim to joint ownership of the matrimonial home, the husband made an oral offer to pay to Mrs. Steadman lump sums of £1,500 (in return for which she would surrender her interest in the matrimonial home) and £100 (by way of child maintenance). They reached an oral agreement on these terms. Accordingly, he paid the £100 as agreed, but she refused to sign the land transfer when it was presented to her. The registrar who first heard the case held that preparing the transfer document was an act of part performance by the husband. On appeal to a county court judge, the judge held that there had been no act of part performance. In the Court of Appeal the judgment was again reversed. That court held that the payment of the £100 was an act of part performance, even though it had been made by way of child maintenance and was therefore not directly referable to the matrimonial home. The wife appealed to the House of Lords.

HELD: The appeal was dismissed. On the balance of probabilities, and taking into account all the facts of the case, there had been acts of part performance of the oral agreement to transfer the wife's interest in the matrimonial home.

LORD REID: . . . . The sole question for your Lordships' decision is whether the admitted facts amount to part performance within the meaning of section 40(2). In my view it is clear that the oral agreement of March 2, 1972, is indivisible and not severable. The whole must stand or fall. Indeed the contrary was not seriously argued. And it is clear that the payment of £100 to the wife as ordered by the magistrates' court was, taking the words in their ordinary sense, in part performance of the agreement. The husband also relies on the following other acts by him or his solicitor as being further part performance; (1) the intimation of the agreement to the magistrates and his abandonment of his attempts to have all arrears of maintenance remitted, and (2) sending to the wife the transfer which she refused to sign and incurring the cost of its preparation. I am very doubtful about the first of these but I am inclined to think that the second could be regarded as part performance. It is the universal custom that a deed of transfer of an interest in land is prepared by the solicitor of the transferee so the wife or her solicitor as her agent must have known that the husband would incur the cost of preparation of the deed in carrying out the agreement.

But the wife's case is that we must not take 'part performance' in its ordinary meaning because the phrase has acquired a highly technical meaning over the centuries.

This matter has a very long history. Section 40 replaced a part of section 4 of the Statute of Frauds 1677 (29 Car. 2, c. 3), and very soon after the passing of that Act authorities on this matter began to accumulate. It is now very difficult to find from them any clear guidance of general application. But it is not difficult to see at least one principle behind them. If one party to an agreement stands by and lets the other party incur expense or prejudice his position on the faith of the agreement being valid he will not then be allowed to turn round and assert that the agreement is unenforceable. Using fraud in its older and less precise sense, that would be fraudulent on his part and it has become proverbial that courts of equity will not permit the statute to be made an instrument of fraud.

If must be remembered that this legislation did not and does not make oral contracts relating to land void: it only makes them unenforceable. And the statutory provision must be pleaded; otherwise the court does not apply it. So it is in keeping with equitable principles that in proper circumstances a person will not be allowed 'fraudulently' to take advantage of a defence of this kind. There is nothing about part performance in the Statute of Frauds. It is an invention of the Court of Chancery and in deciding any case not clearly covered by authority I think that the equitable nature of the remedy must be kept in mind. . . .

The argument for the wife, for which there is a good deal of authority, is that no act can be relied on as an act of part performance unless it relates to the land to be acquired and can only be explained by the existence of a contract relating to the land. But let me suppose a case of an oral contract where the consideration for the transfer of the land was not money but the transfer of some personal property or the performance of some obligation. The personal property is then transferred or the obligation is performed to the knowledge of the owner of the land in circumstances where there can be no restitutio in integrum. On what rational principle could it be said that the doctrine of part performance is not to apply? And we were not referred to any case of that kind where the court had refused to apply it. The transfer of the personal property or the performance of the obligation would indicate the existence of a contract but it would not indicate that that contract related to that or any other land.

I think that there has been some confusion between this supposed rule and another perfectly good rule. You must not first look at the oral contract and then see whether the alleged acts of part performance are consistent with it. You must first look at the alleged acts of part performance to see whether they prove that there must have been a contract and it is only if they do so prove that you can bring in the oral contract. . . .

I am aware that it has often been said that the acts relied on must necessarily or unequivocally indicate the existence of a contract. It may well be that we should consider whether any prudent reasonable man would have done those acts if there had not been a contract but many people are neither prudent nor reasonable and they might often spend money or prejudice their position not in reliance on a contract but in the optimistic expectation that a contract would follow. So if there were a rule that acts relied on as part performance must of their own nature unequivocally show that there was a contract, it would be only in the rarest case that all other possible explanations could be excluded.

In my view, unless the law is to be divorced from reason and principle: the rule must be that you take the whole circumstances, leaving aside evidence about the oral contract, to see whether it is proved that the acts relied on were done in reliance on a contract: that will be proved if it is shown to be more probable than not.

Authorities which seem to require more than that appear to be based on an idea, never clearly defined, to the effect that the law of part performance is a rule of evidence rather than an application of an equitable principle. I do not know on what ground any court could say that, although you cannot produce the evidence required by the Statute of Frauds, some other kind of evidence will do instead. But I can see that if part performance is simply regarded as evidence, then it would be reasonable to hold not only that the acts of part performance must relate to the land but that they must indicate the nature of the oral contract with regard to the land. But it appears to me to be a fundamental departure from the true doctrine of part performance, and it is not supported by recent authorities...

LAW OF PROPERTY (MISCELLANEOUS PROVISIONS) ACT 1989

2. Contracts for sale etc of land to be made by signed writing

(1)   A contract for the sale or other disposition of an interest in land can only be made in writing and only by incorporating all the terms which the parties have expressly agreed in one document or, where contracts are exchanged, in each.

(2)   The terms may be incorporated in a document either by being set out in it or by reference to some other document.

(3)   The document incorporating the terms or, where contracts are exchanged, one of the documents incorporating them (but not necessarily the same one) must be signed by or on behalf of each party to the contract.

(4)   Where a contract for the sale or other disposition of an interest in land satisfies the conditions of this section by reason only of the rectification of one or more documents in pursuance of an order of a court, the contract shall come into being, or be deemed to have come into being, at such time as may be specified in the order.

(5)   This section does not apply in relation to—

(a)   a contract to grant such a lease as is mentioned in section 54(2) of the Law of Property Act 1926 (short leases);

(b)   a contract made in the course of a public auction; or

(c)   a contract regulated under the Financial Services Act 1986;

and nothing in this section affects the creation or operation of resulting, implied or constructive trusts.

(6)   In this section—

'disposition' has the same meaning as in the Law of Property Act 1925;

'interest in land' means any estate, interest or charge in or over land or in or over the proceeds of sale of land.

(7)   Nothing in this section shall apply in relation to contracts made before this section comes into force.

(8)   Section 40 of the Law of Property Act 1925 (which is superseded by this section) shall cease to have effect.

5.2.2.2   Estate contracts

SPIRO v GLENCROWN PROPERTIES LTD AND ANOTHER
[1991] 1 All ER 600, Chancery Division

FACTS: The vendor granted the purchaser an option to buy certain property. The central question was whether the option itself was a 'contract for sale' in accordance with section 2 of the Law of Property Miscellaneous Provisions Act 1989, or whether the option was merely an irrevocable offer of sale which did not become a contract until a notice exercising the option had been served.

HELD: The reason for the formality requirements laid down in section 2 of the LP(MP)A 1989 was to ensure an adequate evidential record of the consent of the contracting parties to the terms of their contract. Accordingly, the formality requirements of section 2 would only apply to the original grant of the option, as this was the document which enshrined the bi-lateral agreement of the parties. The notice exercising the option was exercised unilaterally and would therefore not have to comply with section 2.

HOFFMANN J: Apart from authority, it seems to me plain enough that s. 2 was intended to apply to the agreement which created the option and not to the notice by which it was exercised. Section 2, which replaced s. 40 of the Law of Property Act 1925, was intended to prevent disputes over whether the parties had entered into a binding agreement or over what terms they had agreed. It prescribes the formalities for recording their mutual consent. But only the grant of the option depends upon consent. The exercise of the option is a unilateral act. It would destroy the very purpose of the option if the purchaser had to obtain the vendor's counter-signature to the notice by which it was exercised. The only way in which the concept of an option to buy land could survive s. 2 would be if the purchaser ensured that the vendor not only signed the agreement by which the option was granted but also at the same time provided him with a counter-signed form to use if he decided to exercise it. There seems to be no conceivable reason why the legislature should have required this additional formality.

. . . the underlyiing principles are clear enough. The granting of the option imposes no obligation upon the purchaser and an obligation upon the vendor which is contingent upon the exercise of the option. When the option is exercised, vendor and purchaser come under obligations to perform as if they had concluded an ordinary contract of sale. And the analogy of an irrevocable offer is, as I have said, a useful way of describing the position of the purchaser between the grant and exercise of the option. Thus in the recent case of *J Sainsbury plc v O'Connor (Inspector of Taxes)* [1990] STC 516 at 532 Millett J used it to explain why the grantee of an option to buy shares did not become the beneficial owner until he had exercised the option.

But the irrevocable offer metaphor has much less explanatory power in relation to the position of the vendor. The effect of the 'offer' which the vendor has made is, from his point of view, so different from that of an offer in its primary sense that the metaphor is of little assistance. Thus in the famous passage in *London and South Western Rly Co v Gomm* (1882) 20 ChD 562 at 581, [1881–5] All ER Rep 1190 at 1193 Jessel MR had no use for it in explaining why the grant of an option to buy land confers an interest in the land upon the grantee:

The right to call for a conveyance of the land is an equitable interest or equitable estate. In the ordinary case of a contract for purchase there is no doubt about this, and an option for repurchase is not different in its nature. A person exercising the option has to do two things, he has to give notice of his intention to purchase, and to pay the purchase-money; but as far as the man who is liable to convey is concerned, his estate or interest is taken away from him without his consent, and the right to take it away being vested in another, the covenant giving the option must give that other an interest in the land. . . .

The purchaser's argument requires me to say that 'irrevocable offer' and 'conditional contract' are mutually inconsistent concepts and that I must range myself under one or other banner and declare the other to be heretical. I hope that I have demonstrated this to be a misconception about the nature of legal reasoning. An option is not strictly speaking either an offer of a conditional contract. It does not have *all* the incidents of the standard form of either of these concepts. To that extent it is a relationship *sui generis*. But there are ways in which it resembles each of them. Each analogy is in the proper context a valid way of characterising the situation created by an option. The question in this case is not whether one analogy is true and the other false, but which is appropriate to be used in the construction of s. 2 of the Law of Property (Miscellaneous Provisions) Act 1989. . . .

Perhaps the most helpful case for present purposes is *Re Mulholland's Will Trusts, Bryan* v *Westminster Bank Ltd* [1949] 1 All ER 460. A testator had let premises to the Westminster Bank on a lease which included an option to purchase. He appointed the bank his executor and trustee and after his death the bank exercised the option. It was argued for his widow and children that the bank was precluded from exercising the option by the rule that a trustee cannot contract with himself. Wynn-Parry J was pressed with the irrevocable offer metaphor, which, it was said, led inexorably to the conclusion that when the bank exercised the option, it was indeed entering into a contract with itself. But the judge held that if one considered the purpose of the self-dealing rule, which was to prevent a trustee from being subjected to a conflict of interest and duty, the only relevant contract was the grant of the option. The rule could only sensibly be applied to a consensual transaction. While for some purposes it might be true to say that the exercise of the option brought the contract into existence, there could be no rational ground for applying the self-dealing rule to the unilateral exercise of a right granted before the trusteeship came into existence. The judge quoted the passage I have cited from Jessel MR in *Gomm's* case and said ([1949] 1 All ER 460 at 464):

As I understand that passage, it amounts to this, that, as regards this option, there was between the parties only one contract, namely the contract constituted by the provisions in the lease which I have read creating the option. The notice exercising the option did not lead, in my opinion, to the creation of any fresh contractual relationship between the parties, making them for the first time vendors and purchasers, nor did it bring into existence any right in addition to the right conferred by the option. . . .

In my judgment there is nothing in the authorities which prevents me from giving s. 2 the meaning which I consider to have been the clear intention of the legislature. On the contrary, the purposive approach taken in cases like *Mulholland* encourages me to adopt a similar approach to s. 2. And the plain purpose of s. 2 was, as I have said, to prescribe the formalities for recording the consent of the parties. It follows that in my view the grant of the option was the only 'contract for the sale or other disposition of an interest in land' within the meaning of the section and the contract duty complied with the statutory requirements. There must be judgment for the plaintiff against both defendants with costs.

(a)   The vendor must take good care of the property and consult the purchaser before taking managerial decisons regarding the property.

MOHAMED HAJI ABDULLAH AND ANOTHER v *GHELA MANEK SHAH* [1959] AC 124,
Privy Council

FACTS: The vendor owned a row of three shops. At the time the contract of sale for the shops was signed all three of them were leased to tenants. Between contract and completion one of the tenants (unexpectedly) terminated his tenancy. The vendor, without asking the purchaser, immediately relet the shop. The premises would have been more valuable to the purchaser had they remained unlet. The purchaser claimed specific performance of the contract of sale and also claimed compensation for the financial loss arising out of the sub-letting.

HELD: Both under the Indian Transfer of Property Act 1882 and under English law the vendor should have consulted the purchaser about the proposed reletting. Consequently, the purchaser was entitled to a reduction in the agreed completion price, by way of compensation.

LORD SOMERVELL OF HARROW: The obligations imposed by section 55(1)(e) are substantially those imposed on a vendor under English law.

The Court of Appeal cited with approval the opinion of Mulla and Gour in their textbooks on the Indian Act that the vendor's duties to a purchaser under paragraph (e), although he is not a trustee, are the same as they would be if section 15 of the Indian Trusts Act, 1882, were applicable. That section reads as follows:

15. A trustee is bound to deal with the trust property as carefully as a man of ordinary prudence would deal with such property if it were his own; and in the absence of a contract to the contrary a trustee so dealing is not responsible for the loss, destruction, or deterioration of the trust property.

This is substantially the position of a trustee in relation to property under English law. Their Lordships therefore agree with the courts below that English principles and authorities are relevant and of assistance.

On this basis it seems plain that the vendors had no right without consultation with the purchasers to diminish the value of the property as it was after the surrender by reletting. . . .

The purchasers sought alternatively to support the decision of the Court of Appeal on the terms of the contract, and on a general proposition that a purchaser ought always to be consulted with regard to a new letting. It is unnecessary to consider circumstances other than the present, which are in their Lordships' opinion covered by section 55(1)(e).

Their Lordships will therefore humbly advise Her Majesty that the appeal be dismissed and the order of the Court of Appeal confirmed. The appellants must pay the costs of the appeal.

(b) The risk of anything untoward happening to the property passes to the purchaser when the contract is signed.

HILLINGDON ESTATES CO. v STONEFIELD ESTATES LTD
[1952] 1 Ch 62, Chancery Division

FACTS: In this case the parties having already contracted to sell and purchase certain freehold land, and the purchaser having already paid a deposit in accordance with the contract, the local authority made a compulsory purchase order affecting some of the freehold land. As a result the purchase of that land was never completed. The purchasers brought the present action, alleging that they should be entitled to be discharged from the contract, and should be able to claim a refund of their deposit together with interest thereon. The defendants counterclaimed for specific performance of the contract upon the original terms, including the original price, despite the fact that the purchasers could no longer build on the land as they had intended.

HELD: The vendor was entitled to insist upon the completion of the sale, even though the purchaser would subsequently have to convey the land to the local authority.

VAISEY J: . . . I should have thought that the situation must have arisen in a great many cases, and, in the large majority of them, must have been a most important point for consideration in the position of the parties (that is to say, vendors and purchasers) as between themselves; and the complete absence of authority rather suggests to my mind that, although this doctrine of frustration may operate in some circumstances, it does not operate normally in the case of contracts for the sale of land.

What is the effect of the compulsory purchase order on the rights and position of, first, the purchasers, and, secondly, the vendors? Undoubtedly the position of the vendors in an unperformed contract for the sale of land is radically different, in quality and in nature, from that of the purchasers. I have always understood (and indeed it is a common-place) that when there is a contract by A to sell land to B at a certain price, B becomes the owner in equity of the land, subject, of course, to his obligation to perform his part of the contract by paying the purchase-money; but subject to that, the land is the land of B, the purchaser. What is the position of A, the vendor? He has, it is true, the legal estate in the land, but, for many purposes, from the moment the contract is entered into he holds it as trustee for B, the purchaser. True, he has certain rights in the land remaining, but all those rights are conditioned and limited by the circumstance that they are all referable to his right to recover and receive the purchase-money. His interest in the land when he has entered into a contract for sale is not an interest in land; it is an interest in personal estate, in a sum of money; and it seems to me that in a case such as this, when the date for completion is long past, the purchasers, subject to the payment of that purchase-money, are to be regarded as the owners of the land. So I think they are; and the effect of this notice to treat and this compulsory purchase process is merely to place an obligation on those who are already the owners of the land in question. The compulsory purchase order does not affect the vendors; they have no interest in the matter save in respect of the purchase-money which they are entitled to be paid. The persons who are affected by the compulsory purchase order are the owners of the land, namely, the plaintiffs, i.e., the purchasers.

AMALGAMATED INVESTMENT & PROPERTY CO. LTD v JOHN WALKER & SONS LTD [1976] 3 All ER 509, Court of Appeal

FACTS: The defendants (the well-known whisky firm) contracted to buy an old building which they planned to demolish and replace with modern offices. The local authority then 'listed' the building as one of 'special architectural or historic interest', thus effectively preventing the development. The purchasers claimed rescission of the contract on the ground of 'mutual mistake', which is to say that both parties had thought, at the time of the contract, that the land would be suitable for development and would not be subject to a listing. On the other side, the vendors sought specific performance of the contract.

LAWTON LJ: . . . Anybody who buys property knows, and certainly those who buy property as property developers know, that there are all kinds of hazards which have to be taken into consideration. There is the obvious hazard of planning permission. There is the hazard of fiscal and legislative changes. There is the hazard of existing legislation being applied to the property under consideration—compulsory purchase, for example. Amongst the hazards are the provisions of section 54 of the Town and Country Planning Act 1971. That seems now to be a well-known hazard, as is shown by the form of inquiry before contract which was made by the purchasers in this case. They used a printed form. The printed form asked whether the property had been listed. Similarly, when they came to make a search in the local registry of land charges, once again they made specific inquiries as to whether there had been any listing of the premises. All that adds up, in my judgment, to indicating that those who deal in property nowadays appreciate the existence of these kind of risks. At common law anyone entering into a contract for the purchase of real property had to accept the risk of damage to the property after the contract had been made. Damage to the property nowadays can arise from causes other than fire and tempest. Financial loss can arise from government intervention. This is a risk which people have to suffer. . . .

SIR JOHN PENNYCUICK: In the present case, the contract was one of which, upon the date of its signature, specific performance would have been ordered. Consequently, the purchasers became in equity the owners of the property, subject , of course, to vendor's lien: see *Williams on Vendor and Purchasers*, 4th edn. (1936), p. 547. The listing struck down the value of the property as might a fire or a compulsory purchase order or a number of other events. It seems to me, however, that the listing did not in any respect prevent the contract from being carried to completion according to its terms; that is to say, by payment of the balance of the purchase price and by conveyance of the property. The property is none the less the same property by reason that listing imposed a fetter upon its use. . . . One cannot say that the circumstances in which performance, i.e., completion, will be called for would render that performance a thing radically different from that which was undertaken by the contract. On the contrary, completion, according to the terms of the contract, would be exactly what the purchasers promised to do, and of course the vendors.

For those reasons, I would dismiss the appeal.

Thompson M. P., Must a Purchaser buy a Charred Ruin? (1984) 48 Conv 43

In 1876, Sir George Jessel MR said that 'if anything happens to the estate between the time of the sale and the time of completion of purchase it is at the risk of the purchaser. If it is a house that is sold, and the house is burnt down, the purchaser loses the house.' [*Lysaght* v *Edwards* (1876) 2 ChD 499 at p. 507]. The purpose of this article is to examine this statement with a view to showing that, although it has long been taken as representing the conventional wisdom in this area, it is possible that if directly challenged today, it may not remain as an accurate statement of the law, so that if the house is burnt down between contract and conveyance, the loss falls on the vendor, irrespective of whether or not it was his fault that the damage occurred.

THE EFFECT OF A CONTRACT OF SALE

To explain why it is the purchaser who is said to have to bear the risk of disasters befalling the property between contract and conveyance, it is necessary to examine the effect on the parties' position of an enforceable contract coming into existence. From very early days, it has been said that the effect of a contract for the sale of land is that the vendor becomes a trustee of the property; a doctrine which is now well-settled. Because it is a trust which arises irrespective of the intentions of the parties, it has been classified as being a constructive trust. While it is too late to argue against the view that some sort of trust arises, it is contended that it is misleading to describe it as a constructive trust and that it is better to regard it as *sui generis*.

Why does a trust of any sort arise due to the existence of a valid contract for the sale of land? The answer was provided by Lord Parker, delivering the opinion of the Privy Council, who said:

> It is sometimes said that under a contract for the sale of an interest in land the vendor becomes a constructive trustee for the purchaser of the interest contracted to be sold subject to a lien for the purchase money; but however useful such a statement may be as illustrating a general principle of equity, it is only true *if and so far as* a Court of Equity would under all the circumstances grant specific performance of the contract.

This is an important statement of principle, in that it emphasises that the creation of the trust is dependent on the availability of specific performance. The trust that arises does so because of the operation of the maxim: equity looks on that which ought to be done as done; a principle best illustrated by the doctrine of *Walsh* v *Lonsdale* (1882) 21 ChD 9, CA. . . .

Normally constructive trusts require no written evidence. In the case of a contract for the sale of land, however, this is not so. In the absence of part performance, an oral contract is now enforceable by action, with the consequence that specific performance is unavailable and the doctrine of conversion does not operate. A trust is not, therefore, created. So, although if there is an enforceable contract, the vendor is recognised as the owner at law and the purchaser as the owner in equity—the paradigm trust—it is more helpful to view the situation as very much an individual type of trust. One should not forget that its existence depends on the availability of specific performance. . . . The trust that arises on the formation of an enforceable contract for sale is what lies behind the notion that from that date the risk of damage to the property rests with the purchaser. Subject to the duty on the vendor to take reasonable care of the property, the purchaser is the owner in equity and is, therefore, the one to bear the risk of damage not caused by the vendor's default. This result could have been achieved by the use of implied contractual terms and, indeed, the law would probably have been easier to explain if this had been the case. Nevertheless, the explanation of the risk passing to the purchaser lies in the utilisation of the law of trusts, although . . . the type of trust involved is an inappropriate method by which to achieve this.

5.2.2.3   A contract to create rights in land itself create an equitable interest in the land

WALSH v LONSDALE (1882) 21 ChD 9, Court of Appeal

FACTS: A landlord and tenant had entered into a contract for a seven year lease and the tenant had gone into possession, but the parties had forgotten to execute the formal deed needed for a valid legal lease. The rent clause in the contract provided that under the lease the rent should be per year payable in advance at the beginning of each year (the precise figure would depend upon the number of looms run by the tenant for his business). Despite the absence of a deed granting a legal lease, the landlord demanded the rent in advance in accordance with the contractual term. Indeed, he attempted to recover the rent due by exercising his right of distress. The tenant claimed that as there was no deed and therefore no proper lease, any rent should be payable in arrear. He therefore claimed an injunction against the action for distress.
HELD: The landlord could claim rent in advance. The contract had created an equitable lease enforceable between the parties. The terms of this lease would correspond to the terms of the contract.

JESSEL MR: . . . The question is one of some nicety. There is an agreement for a lease under which possession has been given. Now since the *Judicature Act* the possession is held under the agreement. There are not two estates as there were formerly, one estate at common law by reason of the payment of the rent from year to year, and an estate in equity under the agreement. There is only one Court, and the equity rules prevail in it. The tenant holds under an agreement for a lease. He holds, therefore, under the same terms in equity as if a lease had been granted, it being a case in which both parties admit that relief is capable of being given by specific performance. That being so, he cannot complain of the exercise by the landlord of the same rights as the landlord would have had if a lease had been granted. On the other hand, he is protected in the same way as if a lease had been granted; he cannot be turned out by six months' notice as a tenant from year to year. He has a right to say, 'I have a lease in equity, and you can only re-enter if I have committed such a breach of covenant as would if a lease had been granted have entitled you to re-enter according to the terms of a proper proviso for re-entry.' That being so, it appears to me that being a lessee in equity he cannot complain of the exercise of the right of distress merely because the actual parchment has not been signed and sealed.

5.2.3   AN INFORMAL GRANT OF RIGHTS IN LAND IS TREATED AS A CONTRACT AND SO CREATES AN EQUITABLE INTEREST IN LAND

(Note that the cases in this section must now be read subject to s. 2 of the Law of Property (Miscellaneous Provisions) Act 1989.)

PARKER v TASWELL (1858) 2 De G & J 559, Lord Chancellor's Court

FACTS: A landlord and tenant signed a document which purported to grant a lease to the tenant. The document did not bear a seal, and therefore could not constitute the grant of a legal lease by deed.
HELD: A purported grant of land which lacked the necessary formality should be deemed to be a contract which could be enforced by a decree of specific performance. The discretionary remedy of specific performance was awarded in this case.

THE LORD CHANCELLOR: . . . the instrument now in question could not amount to a lease, because it was not signed by an agent lawfully authorized by writing, nor was it signed in the name of the principal, so as to render it a lease binding upon the lessor. Assuming, however, that it had been signed in the name of the lessor, and would therefore have amounted to a lease, as containing words of present demise, yet there is nothing, in the Act to prevent its being used as an agreement, though void as a lease because not under seal.

The Legislature appears to have been very cautious and guarded in language, for it uses the expression 'shall be void at law' — that is as a lease. If the Legislature had intended to deprive such a document of all efficacy, it would have said that the instrument should be 'void to all intents and purposes.' There are no such words in the Act. I think it would be too strong to say that because it is void at law as a lease, it cannot be used as an agreement enforceable in equity, the intention of the parties having been that there should be a lease, and the aid of equity being only invoked to carry that intention into effect. . . .

5.2.3.1   Limits on the principle that a contract or informal grant creates an equitable interest

COATSWORTH v JOHNSON [1886–90] All ER Rep 547, Court of Appeal

FACTS: Johnson entered into an agreement to lease a farm to Coatsworth for twenty-one years. The agreement contained a clause to farm 'in good and husband-like manner'. Coatsworth took possession of the farm without a formal deed being executed in his favour. Within a few months of his taking possession he had allowed the condition of the land to deteriorate very badly. Johnson took the rather drastic step of evicting Coatsworth from the farm. Coatsworth sued for wrongful eviction, contending that the agreement created an equitable lease lasting 21 years.

HELD: Coatsworth's failure to take good care of the farm was a substantial breach of the contract which meant that he had 'unclean hands' in the sight of equity. He would therefore be denied the discretionary remedy of specific performance of the contract. He was evicted.

LORD ESHER MR: . . . If there is a tenancy at will, how is the landlord to put an end to it? By giving notice to quit, and that is all. He has not to assign any reasons for giving that notice. Supposing there had been no breach of any covenant, he could have given that notice to quit so far as it is a tenancy at will. If it is a tenancy at will, the question of whether there is a breach of covenant or not is immaterial. But it is argued that it was not a tenancy at will, because, under the circumstances, the court of equity would have decreed specific performance of the lease; and it is said that now both sides of the court would consider that as done which the court of equity would have decreed to be done. That proposition is not to be denied.

That raises this question: Would the court of equity in this case have decreed specific performance? If it would, then that is to be considered as done, and then there is a lease. But if it would not, then, there being no lease at common law, it being in the position that the court of equity would not decree specific performance for a lease, then it is no lease at common law. But the proposition is this: It is admitted that, before the Conveyancing Act 1881, if there had been a breach of the contract as to cultivation, the court of equity would not have decreed specific performance. But it is said that, although the tenant has declined or neglected to cultivate in the way mentioned in the agreement, nevertheless the court of equity would decree specific performance, because it is said that the Conveyancing Act 1881, by s. 14, has altered the contract; and that now there is no breach of the contract to cultivate in a particular way, unless, besides the non-cultivation, there has been a demand by the landlord, or a notice by the landlord, not properly observed by the tenant. In other words, that s. 14 of the Conveyancing Act 1881, has altered the contract, and that it is not confined merely to relief in the case of breach of the contract.

It is clear to my mind that s. 14 of the Conveyancing Act 1881, has not altered the contract at all. It has merely dealt with relief, or non-relief, on the assumption that that particular stipulation of the contract has been broken. If the contract is not altered, then by the non-cultivation there is a breach of the contract. Would the court of equity then decree specific performance, there being in existence at the time this state of facts? The moment the plaintiff went into equity, and asked for specific performance, and it was proved that he himself was guilty of the breach of contract, which the defendant says he is by not cultivating, the court of equity would refuse to grant specific performance, and would leave the parties to their other rights. Then, if the court of equity would not grant specific performance, we are not to consider specific performance as granted. Then the case is at an end. It is a lease at will. . . .

5.3   End of Chapter Assessment Question

(a)   Norma owns the legal fee simple estate (unregistered title) in 'Ramsey House'. Two months ago she entered into a written agreement (not in the form of a deed) to let Ramsey House to Matthew for five years. The agreement specifically stated that the house should be used for residential purposes only.

Matthew has just been made redundant, and is now considering using Ramsey House for a business repairing bicycles. He has heard rumours that Norma is about to sell the house.

Advise Matthew, who is concerned that, as his lease is not in the form of a deed, he might be evicted by Norma.

And

(b)   Last week, by a written contract, Teresa agreed to sell 'Taylor Cottage' to Henry, the sale to be completed in six weeks time.

Unfortunately yesterday, a bus racing one of its competitors to the next stop, crashed into Taylor Cottage causing considerable damage.

This morning Teresa demolished a small outhouse which stood at the bottom of the garden of Taylor Cottage.

Advise Henry, who wants either to rescind the contract or at least obtain a reduction in the previously agreed price.

5.4   End of Chapter Assessment Outline Answer

PART A

Section 52 of the LPA 1925 requires, subject to certain exceptions not applicable here, that grants (and transfers) of legal rights be made by deed. The agreement of two months ago is not in the form of a deed, and therefore cannot be a legal lease.

Matthew has however, almost certainly got an equitable lease. A line of nineteenth century cases, culminating in *Walsh* v *Lonsdale* (1882) 21 ChD 9 (decided just after the Judicature Acts) held that any contract for a lease (or informal grant of a lease) is regarded by Equity as creating an equitable lease. In Equity the parties to the contract or informal transaction have the same rights and duties they would have had, had a deed been executed.

Subject to certain points raised below, Matthew will be able to invoke the principle in *Walsh* v *Lonsdale* and claim that the written agreement confers on him an equitable lease.

One possible initial stumbling block for Matthew is that for an agreement to create an equitable lease, it must be a legally valid contract. Contracts for the sale or transfer of rights in land (unlike most contracts) are subject to special requirements as to form. Section two of the 1989 Law of Property Miscellaneous Provisions Act requires land contracts to be in a written document signed by both parties, including all the agreed terms. Thus if (say) Matthew did not sign the agreement, or some of the agreed terms did not appear in the document, the agreement would be VOID. Consequently Matthew would not have an equitable lease.

Assuming that the agreement did comply with section two, then Matthew has an equitable lease, but the continued existence of that lease is under threat from another direction.

Matthew's right to an equitable lease depends upon his right to claim the equitable remedy of specific performance of the agreement. If Matthew is in substantial breach of his agreement he will lose the right to specific performance ('He who comes to Equity must have clean hands') and thus destroy his equitable lease. Matthew does not want to suffer the fate of the tenant farmer in *Coatsworth* v *Johnson* [1886–90] All ER Rep 547, who lost his equitable lease because he failed to comply with the obligation to farm 'in a husbandlike manner'. Matthew must abandon his plan to run a bike-repair business from the house.

PART B

The first point to make is that if the 'contract' between Henry and Teresa does not comply with Section 2 of the 1989 Act, then the contract is void, and Henry can repudiate the 'arrangement' without fear of being sued by Teresa.

Assuming the contract complies with section two, then in principle an ancient rule of Equity will operate on that contract. Applying the maxim 'Equity looks on as done that which ought to be done', somebody who has contracted to buy a piece of land is regarded in Equity as owner of that land even though the legal estate has not yet been conveyed to him. That in particular means that the 'risk' of anything untoward happening to a property passes to a purchaser when the contract is signed, not (at the later stage) when the legal estate is conveyed to the purchaser.

Thus if a building is destroyed by fire or other calamity between contract and completion, the (unfortunate) purchaser must complete the deal. Applied to Taylor Cottage, this principle would mean that Henry would have to accept a conveyance of the badly damaged building and pay the full price.

The principle that 'the risk passees on contract not completion' has been heavily criticised in recent years, and in 1990 the Law Society drew up a new set of standard conditions for the sale of land, clause five of which is crucial. Clause five provides that the seller of land must 'transfer the property in the same state as it was at the date of the contract', and also that if between contract and completion 'the physical state of the property makes it unusable for its purpose' the buyer can rescind the contract.

Thus, provided the contract signed last week incorporated clause five, Henry can certainly claim compensation from Teresa, and (alternatively) if the property is uninhabitable, rescind the contract.

If the contract did not include clause five, then Henry must complete the deal. He will have to hope that his solicitor arranged insurance for the cottage from the date of the contract.

The point regarding the outhouse is only relevant if Henry cannot rescind the contract because of the bus damage. Another consequence (more beneficial to purchasers) of the theory that a purchaser becomes owner in Equity on contract not completion is the rule that the vendor must take managerial decisions with respect to the land only in consultation with the purchaser. In *Abdullah* v *Shah* [1959] AC 124 the vendor immediately relet part of the property which had fallen vacant between contract and completion. The purchaser, who would have preferred the property empty, was awarded a reduction in price by the Judicial Committee of the Privy Council.

In the same way Henry (if forced to complete the deal despite the bus damage), can claim a reduction in price to compensate for the demolition of the outhouse.

CHAPTER SIX

DIFFERENCE IN VALIDITY BETWEEN LEGAL PROPERTY RIGHTS AND EQUITABLE PROPERTY RIGHTS

6.1 The Elements of the Doctrine of Notice

A bona fide purchaser for value of a legal estate or legal interest without notice of equitable interests burdening the legal estate or interest will take free of those equitable interests provided that those equitable interests are subject to 'the doctrine of notice'. We will now consider each element of the doctrine in turn.

6.1.1 BONA FIDE

PILCHER v *RAWLINS* (1872) 7 Ch App 259

The following dictum should be noted, knowledge of the facts of the case is not essential.

SIR W. M. JAMES LJ: I propose simply to apply myself to the case of a purchaser for valuable consideration, without notice, obtaining, upon the occasion of his purchase, and by means of his purchase deed, some legal estate, some legal right, some legal advantage; and, according to my view of the established law of this Court, such a purchaser's plea of a purchase for valuable consideration without notice is an absolute, unqualified, unanswerable defence, and an unanswerable plea to the jurisdiction of this Court. Such a purchaser, when he has once put in that plea, may be interrogated and tested to any extent as to the valuable consideration which he has given in order to show the *bona fides* or *mala fides* of his purchase, and also the presence or the absence of notice; but when once he has gone through that ordeal, and has satisfied the terms of the plea of purchase for valuable consideration without notice, then, according to my judgment, this Court has no jurisdiction whatever to do anything more than to let him depart in possession of that legal estate, that legal right, that legal advantage which he has obtained, whatever it may be. In such a case a purchaser is entitled to hold that which, without breach of duty, he has had conveyed to him.

6.1.2 PURCHASER FOR VALUE

6.1.2.1 The meaning of value

See *Midland Bank Trust Co. Ltd* v *Green* [1981] AC 513 (**8.1.3**).

6.1.2.2   Marriage as 'value'

Until the passing of the Law Reform (Miscellaneous Provisions) Act 1970 an engagement to marry was a legally enforceable contract and the promise to marry was, accordingly, 'value' for the purposes of the doctrine of notice.

6.1.3   OF A LEGAL ESTATE OR LEGAL INTEREST

See *Pilcher* v *Rawlins* (above at **6.1.1**).

6.1.4   WITHOUT NOTICE

6.1.4.1   Actual notice

A purchaser has actual notice of documents in his possession, even if he has not read them. 'Notice' is not the same as 'knowledge'.

6.1.4.2   Constuctive notice

HUNT v *LUCK* [1902] 1 Ch 428 (Court of Appeal)

The following dictum should be noted, the facts of the case are not essential. Vaughan Williams LJ affirmed the judgment of Farwell J in the court below.

VAUGHAN WILLIAMS LJ: In my opinion, the judgment of Farwell J was quite right. . . .

In his judgment he, after quoting the older authorities, said: 'The rule established by these two cases may be stated thus: (1) A tenant's occupation is notice of all that tenant's rights, but not of his lessor's title or rights; (2) actual knowledge that the rents are paid by the tenants to some person whose receipt is inconsistent with the title of the vendor is notice of that person's rights.' In the present case I do not understand that any one suggests, and, if it is suggested, in my opinion the suggestion is ill-founded, that there was actual knowledge that the rents were paid by the tenants to some person whose receipt would be inconsistent with the title of the mortgagor, Gilbert. We have, therefore, to apply the first of the rules stated by the learned judge. Now, what does that mean? It means that, if a purchaser or a mortgagee has notice that the vendor or mortgagor is not in possession of the property, he must make inquiries of the person in possession—of the tenant who is in possession—and find out from him what his rights are, and, if he does not choose to do that, then whatever title he acquires as purchaser or mortgagee will be subject to the title or right of the tenant in possession.

That, I believe, is a true statement of the law . . .

BARCLAYS BANK PLC v *O'BRIEN* [1993] 4 All ER 417 (House of Lords)

FACTS: Mrs O'Brien, the claimant, was surety for a loan made by the bank to her husband. Mr O'Brien's business had been struggling and the loan was taken out to resolve some of its financial problems. The loan was secured by a mortgage on the matrimonial home, in which Mrs O'Brien had an equitable interest. Mrs O'Brien signed the mortgage documents at the bank without reading them and without taking independent legal advice. In due course Mr O'Brien defaulted in repayment of the loan and the bank sought to enforce its security by taking possession of the matrimonial home. Mrs O'Brien claimed that the mortgage should be set aside, alleging that Mr O'Brien had assured her that the loan was of £60,000 only. It was, in fact, a loan of £135,000.

HELD: A wife who has been induced to stand as a surety for her husband's debts by his undue influence, misrepresentation or other legal wrong has an equity as against him to set aside the transaction. The bank took with constructive notice of Mrs O'Brien's equity and therefore would be unable to enforce its later equity by taking possession of the matrimonial home.

LORD BROWNE-WILKINSON: . . . The large number of cases of this type coming before the courts in recent years reflects the rapid changes in social attitudes and the distribution of wealth which have recently occurred. Wealth is now more widely spread. Moreover a high proportion of privately owned wealth is invested in the matrimonial home. Because of the recognition by society of the equality of the sexes, the majority of matrimonial homes are now in the joint names of both spouses. Therefore in order to raise finance for the business enterprises of one or other of the spouses, the jointly owned home has become a main source of security. The provision of such security requires the consent of both spouses.

In parallel with these financial developments, society's recognition of the equality of the sexes has led to a rejection of the concept that the wife is subservient to the husband in the management of the family's finances. A number of the authorities reflect an unwillingness in the court to perpetuate law based on this outmoded concept. Yet, as Scott LJ in the Court of Appeal rightly points out, although the concept of the ignorant wife leaving all financial decisions to the husband is outmoded, the practice does not yet coincide with the ideal. . . . In a substantial proportion of marriages it is still the husband who has the business experience and the wife is willing to follow his advice without bringing a truly independent mind and will to bear on financial decisions. The number of recent cases in this field shows that in practice many wives are still subjected to, and yield to, undue influence by their husbands. Such wives can reasonably look to the law for some protection when their husbands have abused the trust and confidence reposed in them.

On the other hand, it is important to keep a sense of balance in approaching these cases. It is easy to allow sympathy for the wife who is threatened with the loss of her home at the suit of a rich bank to obscure an important public interest, viz the need to ensure that the wealth currently tied up in the matrimonial home does not become economically sterile. If the rights secured to wives by the law renders vulnerable loans granted on the security of matrimonial homes, institutions will be unwilling to accept such security, thereby reducing the flow of loan capital to business enterprises. It is therefore essential that a law designed to protect the vulnerable does not render the matrimonial home unacceptable as security to financial institutions.

With these policy considerations in mind I turn to consider the existing state of the law. . . .

In my judgment, if the doctrine of notice is properly applied, there is no need for the introduction of a special equity in these types of cases. A wife who has been induced to stand as a surety for her husband's debts by his undue influence, misrepresentation or some other legal wrong has an equity as against him to set aside that transaction. Under the ordinary principles of equity, her right to set aside that transaction will be enforceable against third parties (eg against a creditor) if either the husband was acting as the third party's agent or the third party had actual or constructive notice of the facts giving rise to her equity. Although there may be cases where, without artificiality, it can properly be held that the husband was acting as the agent of the creditor in procuring the wife to stand as surety, such cases will be of very rare occurrence. The key to the problem is to identify the circumstances in which the creditor will be taken to have had notice of the wife's equity to set aside the transaction.

The doctrine of notice lies at the heart of equity. Given that there are two innocent parties, each enjoying rights, the earlier right prevails against the later right if the acquirer of the later right knows of the earlier right (actual notice) or would have discovered it had he taken proper steps (constructive notice). In particular, if the party asserting that he takes free of the earlier rights of another knows of certain facts which put him on inquiry as to the possible existence of the rights of that other and he fails to make such inquiry or take such other steps as are reasonable to verify whether such earlier right does or does not exist, he will have constructive notice of the earlier right and take subject to it. Therefore where a wife has agreed to stand surety for her husband's debts as a result of undue influence or misrepresentation, the creditor will take subject to the wife's equity to set aside the transaction if the circumstances are such as to put the creditor on inquiry as to the circumstances in which she agreed to stand surety.

It is at this stage that, in my view, the 'invalidating tendency' or the law's 'tender treatment' of married women, becomes relevant. As I have said above in dealing with undue influence, this tenderness of the law towards married women is due to the fact that, even today, many wives repose confidence and trust in their husbands in relation to their financial affairs. This tenderness of the law is reflected by the fact that voluntary dispositions by the wife in favour of her husband are more likely to be set aside than other dispositions by her: a wife is more likely to establish presumed undue influence of class 2B by her husband than by others because, in practice, many wives do repose in their husbands trust and confidence in relation to their financial affairs. Moreover the informality of business dealings between spouses raises a substantial risk that the husband has not accurately stated to the wife the nature of the liability she is undertaking, ie he has misrepresented the position, albeit negligently.

Therefore, in my judgment a creditor is put on inquiry when a wife offers to stand surety for her husband's debts by the combination of two factors: (a) the transaction is on its face not to the financial advantage of the wife; and (b) there is a substantial risk in transactions of that kind that, in procuring the wife to act as surety, the husband has committed a legal or equitable wrong that entitles the wife to set aside the transaction.

It follows that, unless the creditor who is put on inquiry takes reasonable steps to satisfy himself that the wife's agreement to stand surety has been properly obtained, the creditor will have constructive notice of the wife's rights. . . .

LAW OF PROPERTY ACT 1925

199. Restrictions on constructive notice

(1) A purchaser shall not be prejudicially affected by notice of—

(i) any instrument or matter capable of registration under the provisions of the Land Charges Act 1925, or any enactment which it replaces, which is void or not enforecable as against him under that Act or enactment, by reason of the non-registration thereof;

(ii) any other instrument or matter or any fact or thing unless—

(a) it is within his own knowledge, or would have come to his knowledge if such inquiries and inspection had been made as ought reasonably to have been made by him; or

(b) in the same transaction with respect to which a question of notice to the purchaser arises, it has come to the knowledge of his counsel, as such, or of his solicitor or other agent, as such or would have come to the knowledge of his solicitor or other agent, as such, if such inquiries and inspections had been made as ought reasonably to have been made by the solicitor or other agent.

(2) Paragraph (ii) of the last subsection shall not exempt a purchaser from any liability under, or any obligation to perform or observe, any covenant, condition, provision, or restriction contained in any instrument under which his title is derived, mediately or immediately; and such liability or obligation may be enforced in the same manner and to the same extent as if that paragraph had not been enacted.

(3) A purchaser shall not by reason of anything in this section be affected by notice in any case where he would not have been so affected if this section had not been enacted.

(4) This section applies to purchases made either before or after the commencement of this Act.

6.1.4.3 Imputed notice

KINGSNORTH FINANCE CO. LTD v TIZARD AND ANOTHER [1986] 1 WLR 783, High Court

FACTS: Mr. and Mrs. Tizard lived in the matrimonial home, Willowden, which had been built using funds to which they had made roughly equal contributions. Only Mr. Tizard's name appeared on the title deeds. The marriage later broke down and Mrs. Tizard moved out. However, she occasionally slept at Willowden in her husband's absence, and often spent time there looking after the children of the marriage. Mr. Tizard wished to mortgage the property to Kingsnorth. They instructed brokers to investigate the property, who in turn appointed a surveyor. Kingsnorth believed that Mr. Tizard was unmarried, on account of his application form, but the surveyor's searches revealed that he was 'recently separated'. In the event the mortgage was completed on the basis of the survey and application form, with Kingsnorth never having had actual notice of the fact that Mr. Tizard was married.

HELD: The surveyor should have communicated to his principals the fact that Mr. Tizard had recently separated from his wife. This should have prompted further searches which should then have led to Mrs. Tizard. Mrs. Tizard had not truly ceased to be in actual occupation, as her occupation had only temporarily been disturbed. Following *Hunt* v *Luck*, the surveyor had constructive notice of Mrs. Tizard's interest. This notice would be imputed to Kingsnorth.

JUDGE JOHN FINLAY QC: The house Willowdown was the matrimonial home of Mr. Tizard and his wife, the second defendant. The property was vested in Mr. Tizard alone. Mrs. Tizard claims an equitable interest in it. The plaintiffs are seeking to enforce their legal charge. The question in this action is whether that legal charge is subject to or overrides the equitable interest, if any, which Mrs. Tizard has. That is the question between the plaintiffs and Mrs. Tizard. Between Mr. and Mrs. Tizard there is also the question whether Mrs. Tizard has an equitable interest and if so what it is. . . .

In 1982 the marriage broke down. Mr. and Mrs. Tizard agreed that Willowdown and the adjoining land should be sold and the net proceeds divided between them in equal shares. This was not done before Mr. Tizard emigrated and it has not been done since.

Mrs. Tizard moved into the spare bedroom when the marriage broke down. Willowdown had four bedrooms: the master bedroom, which until then the spouses had used and which continued to be used by Mr. Tizard; two bedrooms occupied by the two children respectively, and the spare bedroom which was a room with a double bed. In November 1982 Mrs. Tizard began to sleep not always but sometimes at her sister's house, about four miles away. She would sleep at Willowdown when Mr. Tizard was not spending the night there. He was away quite often, and kept her informed when he would not be there. If she slept at her sister's, Mrs. Tizard would drive over early in the morning, give the children breakfast and get them ready for school, and then make herself ready to go to work at 9 am. She returned to give the children and herself an evening meal. She would leave if Mr. Tizard returned in the evening, but stay the night, sleeping in the spare bedroom, if he was not to be there. Sometimes he was away for several nights, occasionally even weeks. Mrs. Tizard formed a relationship with a Mr. Mead; and instead of going to her sister's when she was not sleeping at Willowdown, Mrs. Tizard began to go to Mr. Mead's cottage, which also was not far away. Most of her wardrobe she kept at Willowdown: her clothes were in three of the four wardrobe compartments in the master bedroom. Her toiletries, her dressing gown, her nightwear and so forth were also at Willowdown. These arrangements I find continued until the time in mid-1983 when Mrs. Tizard found a note from Mr. Tizard saying that he was going on holiday abroad with the boy twin. Neither he nor the boy has returned.

I find that Mrs. Tizard contributed substantially to the successive property ventures by putting up money for the first deposit, by contributing through the earnings of hers which went into the common pool out of which mortgage instalments and building costs were paid, and by her labour. No accounts were kept of the spouses' respective contributions whether in money or in labour either before or after they were married. I find that they contributed substantially equally. Mrs. Tizard is entitled to half of the equity. Furthermore, I find that Mrs. Tizard remained at all material times in occupation of Willowdown House. Mr. Tizard, the owner of the legal estate, was in occupation, until he departed for the Americas in about June 1983. That circumstance does not however prevent Mrs. Tizard also being in occupation. . . .

The brokers whose fee was to be £1,240 were Bradshaws. They instructed a chartered surveyor, Mr. Marshall, to carry out an inspection. He did so on 13 March 1983, and made a report dated 15 March. Mr. Wigmore, for the plaintiffs, accepts that Mr. Marshall must be treated as the agent of the plaintiffs. . . .

In his evidence Mr. Marshall made it clear that he was suspicious; he was on the lookout for signs of female occupation; not the occupation of a wife, but that of a girl friend. He found no such signs, but his evidence made it clear that he regarded it as his duty to look for them. He drew the line however at opening cupboards and drawers. Mr. Marshall's understanding of his duty to look for signs of occupation by anyone else accords with mine. That being the scope of his duty, I consider that he should have enlarged on his answer to the question, 'Who occupies the property?' The answer that he gave was. 'Applicant, son and daughter.' That was founded in part on his own observation; in part on what Mr. Tizard told him. He should, in my view, have added, either in the 'Occupation' or in the 'General observations' section, 'Applicant states that he is separated from wife who lives nearby,' or something to that effect.

My reason for that view is this. It is common ground that Mr. Marshall was acting as agent of the plaintiffs. He was not instructed by the plaintiffs. He was instructed by Bradshaws. Before Mr. Marshall inspected the property, Bradshaws had the document dated 12 March 1983 which Mr. Tizard signed. What Mr. Tizard told Bradshaws about his material status at that stage can be inferred from what he told them later when he signed the plaintiffs' form, namely, that he was 'single.' In a document which gives only one alternative to 'single,' namely, 'married,' 'single' must signify either bachelor or spinster as the case may be, or a widow or widower, or a person whose marriage has been dissolved. It cannot mean 'married but separated.' As Bradshaws were instructing Mr. Marshall to make an inspection on behalf of the plaintiffs, they were acting as the plaintiffs' agents for that purpose. The fact that Mr. Marshall was looking for evidence of the occupation of a female cohabitee coupled with what I infer from the two documents signed by Mr. Tizard was Bradshaw's understanding of Mr. Tizard's marital status, implies that Mr. Marshall approached his inspection on the footing that Mr. Tizard was not married; when it appeared that he was, I consider that he had a duty to communicate this new information to his principals. It follows in my judgment that the knowledge of the agent, Mr. Marshall, that Mr. Tizard had a wife is to be taken to be the knowledge of the principal, the plaintiffs.

The plaintiffs received Mr. Tizard's application in which he described himself as single; and received Mr. Marshall's report in which there was mention of a son and daughter. The application mentioned two 'children or other dependants' who were stated to be both aged 15. The application had a space in which there fell to be inserted 'Age of spouse next birthday.' It was left blank. It also contained spaces for insertion of the spouse's name, and the name and address of the spouse's employers: and in these spaces there appeared 'N/A', not applicable. The application left it in doubt whether the two 15-year old dependants were children or others, but Mr. Marshall's report made it clear that they were son and daugter of the applicant. Had Mr. Marshall's report indicated that Mr. Tizard was married, it seems to me to be clear that bearing in mind that the application stated over Mr. Tizard's signature that he was single, the plaintiffs would have been put on notice that further investigation was required. Indeed, even if I am wrong in my view that Mr. Marshall should have reported what Mr. Tizard said about his wife, the reference to 'son and daughter' in the report should have alerted the plaintiffs to the need to make further inquiries. Primarily, the plaintiffs are to be taken to have been aware that Mr. Tizard was married and had described himself as single; and in these circumstances their further inquiries should have led them to Mrs. Tizard.

Section 199(1) of the Law of Property Act 1925 provides:

A purchaser shall not be prejudicially affected by notice of—(i) any instrument or matter capable of registration under the provisions of the Land Charges Act 1925, or any enactment which it replaces, which is void or not enforceable as against him under that Act or enactment, by reason of the non-registration thereof; (ii) any other instrument or matter or any fact or thing unless—(a) it is within his own knowledge, or would have come to his knowledge if such inquiries and inspections had been made as ought reasonably to have been made by him; or (b) in the same transaction with respect to which a question of notice to the purchaser arises, it has come to the knowledge of his counsel, as such, or of his solicitor or other agent, as such, or would have come to the knowledge of his solicitor or other agent, as such, if such inquiries and inspections had been made as ought reasonably to have been made by the solicitor or other agent.

'Purchaser' in that provision, includes a mortgagee: see section 205(1) of the Act.

Although a spouse's statutory rights of occupation under section 1 of the Matrimonial Homes Act 1983, and the statutory provisions replaced by that Act are capable of protection by registration as a Class F land charge, by virtue of the Land Charges Act 1972, the equitable interest of such a spouse in the matrimonial home is not capable of being so protected. The plaintiffs were prejudicially affected by the knowledge of their agent, Mr. Marshall, that Mr. Tizard, contrary to what he had said in his application, was married: see section 199(1)(ii)(b). That put them on notice that further inquiries were necessary; the inquiries which in these circumstances ought reasonably to have been made by the plaintiffs would, in my judgment, have been such as to have apprised them of the fact that Mrs. Tizard claimed a beneficial interest in the property; and accordingly, they would have had notice of such equitable rights as she had and the mortgage in these circumstances takes effect subject to these rights: see Section 199(1)(ii)(a).

I arrive at that conclusion without having considered the question: does the occupation of Mrs. Tizard affect the mortgagees with notice of her rights, or are they only so affected if, as Mr. Wigmore submits, they are aware of her occupation, that is, if they find her in occupation?

On the balance of probabilities, I find that the reason Mr. Marshall did not find Mrs. Tizard in the house was that Mr. Tizard had arranged matters to achieve that result. He told Mrs. Tizard that on a particular Sunday, and I find in fact that it was the Sunday that Mr. Marshall did inspect, he was going to entertain friends to lunch and would she take the children out for the day. She did; and having regard to the manner in which I find that the signs of he occupation were temporarily eliminated by Mr. Tizard, the reasonable inference is that he made this request so that Mr. Marshall could inspect and find no evidence of Mrs. Tizard's occupation.

In *Caunce* v *Caunce* [1969] 1 WLR 286 Stamp J held that where a wife who had an equitable interest in a property being mortgaged to the bank by he husband was resident with him in the property, that circumstance did not result in the bank taking the property fixed with notice of her rights because, finding her in occupation, the bank made no inquiry of her. Stamp J said, at p. 293:

Here it is said that the plaintiff was in possession or occupation. No inquiry was made of her and therefore the bank is fixed with notice of her equitable interest. In my judgment, it is here that the fallacy arises, for the plaintiff, unlike the deserted wife, was not in apparent occupation or possession. She was there, ostensibly, because she was the wife, and her presence was wholly consistent with the title offered by the husband to the bank.

In *Williams & Glyn's Bank Ltd* v *Boland* [1981] AC 487, 505, Lord Wilberforce said in the passage I have already read: 'But the presence of the vendor, with occupation, does not exclude the possibility of occupation of others.' He went on to say there were observations suggesting the contrary in *Caunce* v *Caunce* [1969] 1 WLR 286 but he agreed with the disapproval of those and with the assertion expressed by Russell LJ in *Hodgson* v *Marks* [1971] Ch 892, 934. Russell LJ there stated:

I would only add that I do not consider it necessary to this decision to pronounce on the decision in *Caunce* v *Caunce* [1969] 1 WLR 286. In that case the occupation of the wife may have been rightly taken to be not her occupation but that of her husband. In so far, however, as some phrases in the judgment might appear to lay down a general proposition that inquiry need not be made of any person on the premises if the proposed vendor himself appears to be in occupation, I would not accept them.

I have already stated my finding that the wife was in occupation. In the circumstances in which she was, I find that her occupation was not that of her husband. Guided by the high authority of the two passages I have just cited, Lord Wilberforce in *Williams & Glyn's Bank Ltd* v *Boland* [1981] AC 487, 505, and Russell LJ in *Hodgson* v *Marks* [1971] Ch 892, 934, I conclude that had Mrs. Tizard been found to be in occupation by the plaintiffs or their agent and so found in the context of what had been said by Mr. Tizard to Mr. Marshall and stated or implied in the forms he had signed, they, the plaintiffs, would clearly either have learned of her rights by inquiry of her or been fixed with notice of those rights had not inquiry of her been made.

In the light of my finding that Mr. Marshall's information about Mr. Tizard's wife is to be imputed to the plaintiffs and my conclusion that further inquiries should have been made by the plaintiffs because of that imputed knowledge, do I ask myself whether such an inspection as would have disclosed that Mrs. Tizard was in the premises is one which ought reasonably to have been made by them, or is the proper question: can the plaintiffs show that no such inspection was reasonably necessary? The latter appears to me to be the proper way to put it. The plaintiffs did not make any further inquiries or inspections; had they done so it would have been open to them to contend that they had done all that was reasonably required and if they still had no knowledge of Mrs. Tizard's rights or claims, that they were not fixed with notice of them. But in the absence of further inquiries or inspections, I do not think that it is open to the plaintiffs to say that if they had made a further inspection they would still not have found Mrs. Tizard in occupation.

I would put it briefly thus. Mr. Tizard appears to have been minded to conceal the true facts; he did not do so completely; the plaintiffs had, or are to be taken to have had, information which should have alerted them to the fact that the full facts were not in their possession and that they should make further inspections or inquiries; they did not do so; and in these circumstances I find that they are fixed with notice of the equitable interest of Mrs. Tizard. . . .

Thompson, M. P., The Purchaser as Private Detective
Kingsnorth Trust Ltd v *Tizard* (1986) 50 Conv 283

. . . A company which seems to be quite heavily involved in the second mortgage market is Kingsnorth Trust Ltd. Its efforts to ensure that the mortgage has priority over beneficial interests provide a cautionary tale of the difficulties caused by *Boland*. . . .

In *Kingsnorth Trust Ltd* v *Tizard* [1986] 1 WLR 783 the issue was whether [Kingsnorth Trust Ltd] were bound by Mrs. Tizard's interest on the basis of constructive notice. Judge Finlay QC, sitting as a High Court judge, held in favour of the wife.

In deciding as he did, the judge laid much stress on the wife being in occupation of the property and whether this was discoverable by making reasonable inquiries. It will be argued below that this issue was approached in an unsatisfactory manner by the judge. . . .

In reaching this conclusion, Judge Finlay used various strands of reasoning. He accepted that, in the light of *Boland*, the approach of Stamp J in *Caunce* v *Caunce* [1969] 1 WLR 286, that if a vendor or mortgagor was in occupation of the house, no inquiries need be addressed to other occupants, could no longer be sustained. Hence he accepted that if a purchaser failed to make such inspections as ought reasonably to have been made, thereby failing to discover that another person was in occupation, then he would be fixed with constructive notice of that occupier's interest. This is surely right. What is more questionable is the judge's finding that the inquiries made in the present case were unreasonably deficient.

The judge considered that Mr. Marshall had been put on inquiry that there was another occupier of the house. This was because when the inspection was being performed, Mr. Tizard apologised for the state of the house ascribing it to the fact that his wife had left him some time ago to move in with someone else nearby. In addition to this, the view was expressed that the existence of the two children was sufficient in itself to put Mr. Marshall on guard that further inquiries were necessary to establish whether anyone else lived there. The onus of inquiry was not discharged, it was held, by an inspection of the house at a time pre-arranged with the mortgagor.

Various themes are run together in this reasoning caused, it is suggested, by a failure to appreciate the different significance of occupation in registered and unregistered land. In registered land, the importance of occupation is not to put a purchase on notice that the occupier has rights. Provided that the occupier has a recognised proprietary interest, the significance of occupation is that section 70(1)(g) of the Land Registration Act 1925 without further ado converts that right into an overriding interest. Conversely, the effect of occupation in unregistered land is less mechanical. The fact of occupation serves to put a purchaser on notice that the occupier might have rights over the property and that inquiry should be made as to whether that is so. Whereas if in registered conveyancing occupation exists as a fact, it is immaterial whether or not it was discoverable, this is not true in unregistered conveyancing, where the issue is what reasonable inquiries and inspections would reveal.

The real issue on this case was not whether Mr. Marshall had notice of whether Mrs. Tizard was in occupation; it was whether he had notice of her rights. Given that he had been told that she had only recently left the house, it seems reasonable that he should ask where she lived so that questions could be addressed to her to ascertain whether she had any interest in the property. It should be pointed out here that, even if what Mr. Tizard had said was tue, Mrs. Tizard could still have had an interest adversely affecting the mortgage. While unless she actually was in occupation, a sale could take place with vacant possession, she would nevertheless have had a prior claim to her share in the proceeds of sale. Indeed, this was the result of the case as Mrs. Tizard was quite happy for the house to be sold. It would seem, therefore, to be imperative for inquiries to be addressed to her to ensure that the house was good security for the money advanced. . . .

It is necessary that the vendor should be asked whether he shares the house with anyone else. Additionally he should be asked if he either is or was married. If the answers reveal the existence of anybody, then inquiries where possible should be made of that person. Further, an inspection of the property should be carried out. If such an inspection gives no cause to suspect adverse rights then, *pace* Judge Finlay, even if this inspection was performed at a time arranged with the vendor, the purchaser should be held to have done all that is required of him by section 199 of the Law of Property Act 1925. For the purchaser to insist on doing more carries the inevitable implication that he suspects the vendor of deceit. Such demands should not be considered to be within the scope of reasonable inquiries. . . .

While the position of a first mortgagee, who acquires his interest at the time the property is bought, has been substantially eased, the position of purchasers and other mortgagees has become extremely parlous. They are faced with invidious choices. They can further alter their conduct to resemble that of an enthusiastic private investigator and accept the need to behave in a potentially offensive manner towards a householder. Unfortunately they could not even then be sure of safeguarding their position. So far as mortgagees are concened, they can simply accept that the security for a number of mortgages will inevitably be lost, regarding that as an ordinary business hazard or finally insurance could be taken out against the risk of each mortgage being rendered substantially worthless. Any of these options will, of course, inevitably increase the transaction cost of conveyancing.

Many would applaud the actual decision in *Boland* but be less happy with the implications of the reasoning. . . . unless some modification of *Boland* is effected in the courts, one can only view with sympathy the continuing, yet unavailing, attempts by companies such as Kingsnorth Trust Ltd to come to terms with it.

CHAPTER SEVEN

THE IMPACT OF THE 1925 LEGISLATION

7.1 Legal Estates and Interests and the 1925 Legislation

LAW OF PROPERTY ACT 1925

1. Legal estates and equitable interests

(1) The only estates in land which are capable of subsisting or of being conveyed or created at law are—

    (a) An estate in fee simple absolute in possession;

    (b) A term of years absolute.

(2) The only interests or charges in or over land which are capable of subsisting or of being conveyed or created at law are—

    (a) An easement, right, or privilege in or over land for an interest equivalent to an estate in fee simple absolute in possession or a term of years absolute;

    (b) A rentcharge in possession issuing out of or charged on land being either perpetual or for a term of years absolute;

    (c) A charge by way of legal mortgage;

    (d) ... and any other similar charge on land which is not created by an instrument;

    (e) Rights of entry exercisable over or in respect of a legal term of years absolute, or annexed, for any purpose, to a legal rentcharge.

(3) All other estates, interests, and charges in or over land take effect as equitable interests.

(4) The estates, interests, and charges which under this section are authorised to subsist or to be conveyed or created at law are (when subsisting or conveyed or created at law) in this Act referred to as 'legal estates,' and have the same incidents as legal estates subsisting at the commencement of this Act; and the owner of a legal estate is referred to as 'an estate owner' and his legal estate is referred to as his estate.

(5) A legal estate may subsist concurrently with or subject to any other legal estate in the same land in like manner as it could have done before the commencement of this Act.

(6) A legal estate is not capable of subsisting or of being created in an undivided share in land or of being held by an infant.

(7) Every power of appointment over, or power to convey or charge land or any interest therein, whether created by a statute or other instrument or implied by law, and whether created before or after the commencement of this Act (not being a power vested in a legal mortgagee or an estate owner in right of his estate and exercisable by him or by another person in his name and on his behalf), operates only in equity.

(8) Estates, interests, and charges in or over land which are not legal estates are in this Act referred to as 'equitable interests', and powers which by this Act are to operate in equity only are in this Act referred to as 'equitable powers'.

7.2   Legal Estates Existing After 1925

7.2.1   TERM OF YEARS ABSOLUTE

See **Chapter 17**.

LAW OF PROPERTY ACT 1925

205.   General definitions

(1) (xxvii)   'Term of years absolute' means a term of years (taking effect either in possession or in reversion whether or not at a rent) with or without impeachment for waste, subject or not to another legal estate, and either certain or liable to determination by notice, re-entry, operation of law, or by a provision for cesser on redemption, or in any other event (other than the dropping of a life, or the determination of a determinable life interest); but does not include any term of years determinable with life or lives or with the cesser of a determinable life interest, nor, if created after the commencement of this Act, a term of years which is not expressed to take effect in possession within twenty-one years after the creation thereof where required by this Act to take effect within that period; and in this definition the expression 'term of years' includes a term for less than a year, or for a year or years and a fraction of a year or from year to year.

7.2.2   FEE SIMPLE ABSOLUTE IN POSSESSION

7.2.2.1   'Absolute'

LAW OF PROPERTY (AMENDMENT) ACT 1926

1.   Conveyances of legal estates subject to certain interests

(1)   Nothing in the Settled Land Act 1925 shall prevent a person on whom the powers of a tenant for life are conferred by paragraph (ix) of subsection (1) of section twenty of that Act from conveying or creating a legal estate subject to a prior interest as if the land had not been settled land.

(2)   In any of the following cases, namely—

(a)   where a legal estate has been conveyed or created under subsection one of this section, or under section sixteen of the Settled Land Act 1925, subject to any prior interest, or

(b)   where before the first day of January, nineteen hundred and twenty-six, land has been conveyed to a purchaser for money or money's worth subject to any prior interest whether or not on the purchase the land was expressed to be exonerated from, or the grantor agreed to indemnify the purchaser against, such prior interest,

the estate owner for the time being of the land subject to such prior interest may, notwithstanding any provision contained in the Settled Land Act 1925, but without prejudice to any power whereby such prior interest is capable of being overreached, convey or create a legal estate subject to such prior interest as if the instrument creating the prior interest was not an instrument or one of the instruments constituting a settlement of the land.

(3)   In this section 'interest' means an estate, interest, charge or power of charging subsisting, or capable of arising or of being exercised, under a settlement, and, where a prior interest arises under the exercise of a power, 'instrument' includes both the instrument conferring the power and the instrument exercising it.

LAW OF PROPERTY ACT 1925

7.   Saving of certain legal estates and statutory powers

(1)   A fee simple which, by virtue of the Lands Clauses Acts . . . or any similar statute, is liable to be divested, is for the purposes of this Act a fee simple absolute, and remains liable to be divested as if this Act had not been passed [and a fee simple subject to a legal or equitable right of entry or re-entry is for the purposes of this Act a fee simple absolute].

(2) A fee simple vested in a corporation which is liable to determine by reason of the dissolution of the corporation is, for the purposes of this Act, a fee simple absolute.

(3) The provisions of—

(a) ...;

(b) the Friendly Societies Act 1896, in regard to land to which that Act applies;

(c) any other statutes conferring special facilities or prescribing special modes (whether by way of registered memorial or otherwise) for disposing of or acquiring land, or providing for the vesting (by conveyance or otherwise) of the land in trustees or any person, or the holder for the time being of an office or any corporation sole or aggregate (including the Crown);

shall remain in full force.

This subsection does not authorise an entailed interest to take effect otherwise than as in equitable interest.

CHAPTER EIGHT

STATUS OF EQUITABLE INTERESTS AFTER 1925

8.1 Registration of Land Charges

LAW OF PROPERTY ACT 1925

198. Registration under the Land Charges Act 1925 to be notice

(1) The registration of any instrument or matter [in any register kept under the Land Charges Act 1972 or any local land charges register] shall be deemed to constitute actual notice of such instrument or matter, and of the fact of such registration, to all persons and for all purposes connected with the land affected, as from the date of registration or other prescribed date and so long as the registration continues in force.

LAND CHARGES ACT 1972

1. The registers and the index

(1) The registrar shall continue to keep at the registry in the prescribed manner the following registers, namely—

    (a) a register of land charges;

    (b) a register of pending actions;

    (c) a register of writs and orders affecting land;

    (d) a register of deeds of arrangement affecting land;

    (e) a register of annuities,

and shall also continue to keep there an index whereby all entries made in any of those registers can readily be traced.

(2) Every application to register shall be in the prescribed form and shall contain the prescribed particulars.

(3) Where any charge or other matter is registrable in more than one of the registers kept under this Act, it shall be sufficient if it is registered in one such register, and if it is so registered the person entitled to the benefit of it shall not be prejudicially affected by any provision of this Act as to the effect of non-registration in any such register. . . .

2. The register of land charges

(1) If a charge on or obligation affecting land falls into one of the classes described in this section, it may be registered in the register of land charges as a land charge of that class.

(2) A class A land charge is—

    (a) a rent or annuity or principal money payable by instalments or otherwise, with or without interest, which is not a charge created by deed but is a charge upon land (other than a rate) created pursuant to the application of some person under the provisions of any Act of Parliament, for securing to any person either the money spent by him or the costs, charges and expenses incurred by him under such Act, or the money advanced by him for repaying the money spent or the costs, charges and expenses incurred by another person under the authority of an Act of Parliament; or

(b) a rent or annuity or principal money payable as mentioned in paragraph (a) above which is not a charge created by deed but is a charge upon land (other than a rate) created pursuant to the application of some person under any of the enactments mentioned in Schedule 2 to this Act.

(3) A Class B land charge is a charge on land (not being a local land charge . . .) of any kind described in paragraph (a) of subsection (2) above, created otherwise than pursuant to the application of any person.

(4) A Class C land charge is any of the following (not being a local land charge), namely—

    (i) a puisne mortgage;

    (ii) a limited owner's charge;

    (iii) a general equitable charge;

    (iv) an estate contract;

and for this purpose—

    (i) a puisne mortgage is a legal mortgage which is not protected by a deposit of documents relating to the legal estate affected;

    (ii) a limited owner's charge is an equitable charge aquired by a tenant for life or statutory owner under the Capital Transfer Tax Act 1984 or under any other statute by reason of the discharge by him of any capital transfer tax or other liabilities and to which special priority is given by the statute;

    (iii) a general equitable charge is any equitable charge which—

        (a) is not secured by a deposit of documents relating to the legal estate affected; and

        (b) does not arise of affect an interest arising under a trust for sale or a settlement; and

        (c) is not a charge given by way of idemnity against rents equitable apportioned or charged exclusively on land in exoneration of other land and against the breach or non-observance of covenants or conditions; and

        (d) is not included in any other class of land charge;

    (iv) an estate contract is a contract by an estate owner or by a person entitled at the date of the contract to have a legal estate conveyed to him to convey or create a legal estate, including a contract conferring either expressly or by statutory implication a valid option to purchase, a right of pre-emption or any other like right.

(5) A Class D land charge is any of the following (not being a local land charge), namely—

    (i) an Inland Revenue Charge;

    (ii) a restrictive covenant;

    (iii) an equitable easement;

and for this purpose—

    (i) an Inland Revenue charge is a charge on land, being a charge acquired by the Board under the Capital Transfer Tax Act 1984;

    (ii) a restrictive covenant is a covenant or agreement (other than a covenant or agreement between a lessor and a lessee) restrictive of the user of land and entered into on or after 1st January 1926;

    (iii) an equitable easement is an easement, right or privilege over or affecting land created or arising on or after 1st January 1926, and being merely an equitable interest.

(6) A Class E land charge is an annuity created before 1st January 1926 and not registered in the register of annuities.

(7) A Class F land charge is a charge affecting any land by virtue of the Matrimonial Homes Act 1983.

(8) A charge or obligation created before 1st January 1926 can only be registered as a Class B land charge or a Class C land charge if it is acquired under a conveyance made on or after that date.

(9) . . .

3. Registration of land charges

(1) A land charge shall be registered in the name of the estate owner whose estate is intended to be affected. . . .

4.   Effect of land charges and protection of purchasers

(1)   A land charge of Class A (other than a land improvement charge registered after 31st December 1969) or of Class B shall, when registered, take effect as if it had been created by a deed of charge by way of legal mortgage, but without prejudice to the priority of the charge.

(2)   A land charge of Class A created after 31st December 1888 shall be void as against a purchaser of the land charged with it or of any interest in such land, unless the land charge is registered in the register of land charges before the completion of the purchase.

(3)   After the expiration of one year from the first conveyance occurring on or after 1st January 1889 of a land charge of Class A created before that date the person entitled to the land charge shall not be able to recover the land charge or any part of it as against a purchaser of the land charged with it or of any interest in the land, unless the land charge is registered in the register of land charges before the completion of the purchase.

(4)   If a land improvement charge was registered as a land charge of Class A before 1st January 1970, any body corporate which, but for the charge, would have power to advance money on the security of the estate or interest affected by it shall have that power notwithstanding the charge.

(5)   A land charge of Class B and a land charge of Class C (other than an estate contract) created or arising on or after 1st January 1926 shall be void as against a purchaser of the land charged with it, or of any interest in such land, unless the land charge is registered in the appropriate register before the completion of the purchase.

(6)   An estate contract and a land charge of Class D created or entered into on or after 1st January 1926 shall be void as against a purchaser for money or money's worth (or, in the case of an Inland Revenue charge, a purchaser within the meaning of the Capital Transfer Tax Act 1984) of a legal estate in the land charged with it, unless the land charge is registered in the appropriate register before the completion of the purchase.

(7)   After the expiration of one year from the first conveyance occurring on or after 1st January 1926 of a land charge of Class B or Class C created before that date the person entitled to the land charge shall not be able to enforce or recover the land charge or any part of it as against a purchaser of the land charged with it, or of any interest in the land, unless the land charge is registered in the appropriate register before the completion of the purchase.

(8)   A land charge of Class F shall be void as against a purchaser of the land charged with it, or of any interest in such land, unless the land charge is registered in the appropriate register before the completion of the purchase.

11.   Date of effective registration and priority notices

(1)   Any person intending to make an application for the registration of any contemplated charge, instrument or other matter in pursuance of this Act or any rule made under this Act may give a priority notice in the prescribed form at least the relevant number of days before the registration is to take effect.

(2)   Where a notice is given under subsection (1) above, it shall be entered in the register to which the intended application when made will relate.

(3)   If the application is presented within the relevant number of days thereafter and refers in the prescribed manner to the notice, the registration shall take effect as if the registration had been made at the time when the charge, instrument or matter was created, entered into, made or arose, and the date at which the registration so takes effect shall be deemed to be the date of registration.

(4)   Where—

   (a)   any two charges, instruments or matters are contemporaneous; and

   (b)   one of them (whether or not protected by a priority notice) is subject to or dependent on the other; and

   (c)   the latter is protected by a priority notice,

the subsequent or dependent charge, instrument or matter shall be deemed to have been created, entered into or made, or to have arisen, after the registration of the other.

(5)   Where a purchaser has obtained a certificate under section 10 above, any entry which is made in the register after the date of the certificate and before the completion of the purchase, and is not made pursuant to a priority notice entered on the register on or before the date of the certificate, shall not affect the purchaser if the purchase is completed before the expiration of the relevant number of days after the date of the certificate.

(6)   The relevant number of days is—
    (a)   for the purposes of subsections (1) and (5) above, fifteen;
    (b)   for the purposes of subsection (3) above, thirty;
or such other numbers as may be prescribed; but in reckoning the relevant number of days for any of the purposes of this section any days when the registry is not open to the public shall be excluded.

13.   Saving for overreaching powers

(1)   The registration of any charge, annuity or other interest under this Act shall not prevent the charge, annuity or interest being overreached under any other Act, except where otherwise provided by that other Act.

(2)   The registration as a land charge of a puisne mortgage or charge shall not operate to prevent that mortgage or charge being overreached in favour of a prior mortgagee or a person deriving title under him where, by reason of a sale or foreclosure, or otherwise, the right of the puisne mortgagee or subsequent chargee to redeem is barred.

HOLLINGTON BROTHERS LTD v RHODES AND ANOTHER [1951] 2 All ER 578,
Chancery Division

FACTS: H 'leased' some offices to R for seven years by a document which was not a deed. R therefore acquired only an equitable lease. R took possession of the premises but failed to register his lease as a land charge (equitable leases are registrable as Class C(iv) Land Charges under the Land Charges Act 1972—the successor statute to the Land Charges Act 1925 which was then in force). H later sold his reversion to D, the sale being expressly 'subject to and with the benefit of such tenancies as may affect the premises'.
HELD: The equitable lease was valid against H, but not against D, despite the fact that D undoubtedly had notice of the existence of the tenancy.

HARMAN J: . . . held that there was no contract between the plaintiffs and the defendants as alleged by the plaintiffs and continued: If I am right, the action fails and I need go no further, but it may be useful that I should express a view on two further points which were fully argued before me:—(i) assuming that there was a contract such as the plaintiffs alleged, was there a breach by the defendants; and (ii) if so, what is the proper measure of damages? After 1925 by virtue of the Land Charges Act 1925, s. 10(1), this contract came within class C(iv) as a 'charge or obligation affecting land,' and, therefore, might be registered as a land charge in the register of land charges. Accordingly, by virtue of s. 13 (2), this being a land charge of class C, it is void '. . . against a purchaser of the land charged therewith, or of any interest in such land, unless the land charge is registered in the appropriate register before the completion of the purchase . . .'. Moreover, by the Law of Property Act 1925, s. 199(1)(i), a purchaser is not to be prejudicially affected by notice of any instrument or matter capable of registration under the Land Charges Act 1925, which is void against him by reason of non-registration. This land charge was not registered, and, accordingly, it is said that it was void against Daymar Estates Ltd., notwithstanding their notice or knowledge, and, moreover, that there was no duty lying on the plaintiffs to register the contract to prevent this result.
    . . . The defendants' answer to this point was that Daymar Estates Ltd, did not contract to obtain, and did not by the assignment get, any estate in the land expressed to override the plaintiffs' rights, and that, consequently, they took subject to those rights, which are expressly mentioned, and that the land which they purchased was, in fact, only an interest in the land subject to the rights of the plaintiffs in it. This argument seemed to me attractive because it appears at first glance wrong that a purchaser, who knows perfectly well of rights and is expressed to take subject to them, should be able to ignore them.
    . . . It seems to me, however, that this argument cannot prevail having regard to the words in s. 13(2) of the Land Charges Act 1925, coupled with the definition of 'land' in s. 20(6) of the Act. The fact is that it was the policy of the framers of the legislation of 1925 to get rid of equitable rights of this kind unless registered. . . .
    . . . Finally, as under the Land Charges Act 1925, s. 13(2), an unregistered estate contract is void as against a purchaser of the land, and under the Law of Property Act 1925, s. 199(1), the purchaser is not to be prejudicially affected by it, I do not see how that which

is void and which is not to prejudice the purchaser can be validated by some equitable doctrine. There is, after all, no great hardship in this. The plaintiffs could, at any time until the completion of the assignment to Daymar Estates Ltd, have preserved their rights by registration, just as the defendants could have protected their obligations by completing the underlease, of which Daymar Estates Ltd, could not have complained as they knew all about it. . . .

8.1.1   SEARCHES OF THE LAND CHARGES REGISTER

OAK CO-OPERATIVE BUILDING SOCIETY v BLACKBURN AND OTHERS
[1968] 1 Ch 730, Court of Appeal

FACTS: The defendant, Francis David Blackburn, had granted a mortgage of his land. This mortgage was registered in the Land Charges register against the name 'Francis David Blackburn'. Later Mr. Blackburn agreed to sell his land to a Ms. Caines. She registered this agreement (an estate contract) as a class C(iv) Land Charge against the name 'Frank David Blackburn'. She entered into possession of the land on the strength of the agreement. Still later Mr. Blackburn granted the second mortgage on his land to a building society. Before making the loan the building society searched the Land Charges register against the name 'Francis Davis Blackburn'. This search revealed the first mortgage, but not the estate contract. On the strength of the results of the search, the building society made a loan to Mr. Blackburn secured by a second mortgage on his land. In due course Mr. Blackburn fell behind on his mortgage repayments and was declared bankrupt. The building society brought the present action for, *inter alia*, a possession order against Ms. Caines. The judge at first instance granted the building society possession of the property on grounds that although the building society's search was not carried out accurately, the more important fact was that Ms. Caines had failed to register her interest correctly. Ms. Caines appealed to the Court of Appeal.

HELD: The appeal was allowed. Ms. Caines had registered her interest against a legitimate variation of the estate owner's name. Such a registration would have been ineffective against the building society had it searched the estate owner's correct names, but it would be effective against a building society (or other 'purchaser'), as here, which had failed to make a proper search.

RUSSELL LJ: An estate agent lived in Southport. His full names were Francis David Blackburn. In the conveyance and mortgage later mentioned he was so described. He carried on business in Southport as Frank D. Blackburn or Frank David Blackburn, and he was generally known as 'Frank' and not as 'Francis.' He owned a freehold house, No. 34 Union Street, Southport, Lancashire, which was conveyed to him on sale in December, 1957, by a Mrs. Allinson, and which he simultaneously mortgaged to a building society. On January 10, 1958, he agreed in writing to sell the house to the third defendant for £2,000 payable by instalments consisting of capital and interest payable over a period of 15 years with a deposit of £100. No solicitor acted; and the third defendant received no copy of the agreement. The third defendant moved into occupation and has lived there ever since, paying the instalments up to April, 1965. She has paid in all £700 and has saved the instalments due since then. No copy of the contract is available. It is not known in what version of his name Blackburn figured in the contract. It was not then registered as a land charge.

In August, 1959, Blackburn executed a puisne second mortgage of the property.

In December, 1959, the third defendant for some reason visited a solicitor. He applied to register the contract as a Class C(iv) land charge—an estate contract—against the property, 34 Union Street. In this application the name of the estate owner was given as 'Surname—Blackburn: Christian names—Frank David.' In that name the land charge was registered: nothing was said to Blackburn, who was not asked for a copy of the contract.

In December, 1962, Blackburn mortgaged the property to the plaintiffs, Oak Co-operative Building Society, paying off the existing first and second mortgages. He only paid two instalments in February and May, 1963, and in June, 1965, the plaintiffs roused themselves from torpor and started proceedings claiming payment, possession, foreclosure and sale, including a claim for possession against the third defendant. Possession was ordered against her and she appeals.

The question is whether her estate contract is valid against the subsequent legal charge to the plaintiffs as being effectively registered as an estate contract, or whether the use of the name 'Frank' rather than 'Francis' invalidates it.

. . . The application for an official search certificate was against the name 'Francis Davis Blackburn'.

. . . Section 17 [Land Charges Act 1925] provides for an official search. A proposing purchaser (for example) may lodge a requisition for such a search and thereupon the registrar shall 'make the search required, and shall issue a certificate setting forth the result thereof'. Subsection (3) provides that in favour of the intending purchaser as against the person interested under the instrument (here the estate contract) 'the certificate, according to the tenor thereof, shall be conclusive, affirmatively or negatively, as the case may be.' Subsection (4) provides that every such requisition shall be in writing 'specifying the name against which he desires search to be made, or in relation to which he requires a certificate of result of search, and other sufficient particulars.'

. . . The real problem is, what is meant by the name or the names of the estate owner in this legislation?

As a matter of theoretical approach it is obvious that it is intended or hoped by the legislation that every registered land charge will be safeguarded by registration because due diligence in search will reveal it: and correspondingly that every duly diligent search will reveal every registered land charge affecting the land to be purchased. It is realised that if an official search certificate is issued there may be a blunder for which some innocent person must suffer, and section 17(3) provides, for example, that if a nil certificate is given the owner of the land charge suffers, however valid his registration. But it would be supposed that it would be intended to reduce error to a minimum. What then is meant by the requirement that the name—surname and Christian names—of the estate owner be given when requisitioning a search? People use different names at different times and for different purposes. But the matter now under consideration relates to two things: first, the investigation into the soundness of the paper title of a proposed vendor by a proposed purchaser: second, the attempt to prevent by registration the disposal by the owner of that paper title of the legal estate in a manner which will override the interest of the owner of the land charge.

In the case of a request for an official search, which of course takes place before completion after the title examined, we can only think that the name or names referred to in the request should be that or those appearing on the title. A nil certificate here as to Francis Davis *Blackburn* would not have served to override the third defendants land charge had it been registered in the name of Francis David *Blackburn*, though it *could* have been issued. . . .

. . . If a proposing purchaser here had requested a search in the correct full names he would have got a clean certificate and a clear title under section 17(3) of the Land Charges Act 1925, and would have suffered no harm from the fact that the registration was not in such names: and a person registering who is not in a position to satisfy himself what are the correct full names runs that risk. But if there be registration in what may be fairly described as a version of the full names of the vendor, albeit not a version which is bound to be discovered on a search in the correct names, we would not hold it a nullity against someone who does not search at all, or who (as here) searches in the wrong name.

There is one objection to this approach, and that is that provision is made for personal as distinct from official search: . . .

. . . But we think that anyone who nowadays is foolish enough to search personally deserves what he gets: and if the aim of the statute is to arrive at a sensible working system that aim is better furthered by upholding a registration such as this than protecting a personal searcher from his folly. . . .

DILIGENT FINANCE CO. LTD v *ALLEYNE AND ANOTHER* (1972) 23 P&CR 346, Chancery Division

FACTS: Diligent Finance Co. Ltd brought this action for possession of a matrimonial home currently occupied by the second defendant, Cynthia Alleyne. She had been deserted by

her husband, Erskine Owen Alleyne, the first defendant to the action. The plaintiff was the holder of a mortgage against the matrimonial home which had been executed in the name of the first defendant only. The second defendant had registered her matrimonial rights of occupation as a 'Class F' land charge against the name Erskine Alleyne. She should have registered her charge against her husband's full name, Erskine Owen Alleyne, for that was the name appearing on the conveyance to him and on the mortgage to the plaintiff.
HELD: The Class F land charge did not rank ahead of the legal charge of the plaintiff. The plaintiff was awarded possession.

FOSTER J: . . . Valiant efforts have been made by the second defendant to discover what the true names are of her husband—who in fact went back to Barbados the day after he had obtained the new charge, i.e. on February 19 1970—but a certificate of registration of birth which is forthcoming and which is dated March 2 1972, shows a certificate of registration of birth but under the column 'Baptismal name if added after registration of birth' there is given no name at all, and counsel for the second defendant told me that he had tried to get a baptismal certificate but that it had not been forthcoming.

The question therefore is whether the court is entitled to assume from the conveyancing documents which I have mentioned that the first defendant's name Erskine Owen Alleyne is in fact his real and full name. It was pointed out on behalf of the plaintiff that no one was in a better position to know what the full name of her husband was than his wife, and further it was pointed out that the second defendant must have known that the freehold property was mortgaged to the Greater London Council where one could find the name Erskine Owen Alleyne.

In my judgment, in the absence of any other evidence— and there is none— it is right for the court, following Ungoed-Thomas J's statement in the court below and Russell L J, in the Court of Appeal, to assume in the absence of evidence to the contrary that the proper name of a person is that in which the conveyancing documents have been taken. It is unfortunate, to say the least, that the Class F registration was not made against the proper name Erskine Owen Alleyne but only against Erskine Alleyne, but that is a mistake which I for my part cannot unfortunately rectify. If follows that the official certificate granted to the plaintiff on February 13 1970, under section 17(3) of the Land Charges Act 1925 is conclusive and that the Class F charge does not rank ahead of the legal charge of the plaintiff.

8.1.2   EQUITABLE INTERESTS REGISTRABLE AS LAND CHARGES

SHILOH SPINNERS LTD v HARDING [1973] AC 691, House of Lords

FACTS: The plaintiffs had assigned their leasehold interest to a company, T Ltd., which promised to meet certain leasehold obligations. Upon a failure by T Ltd. to meet any of those obligations, the plaintiffs were to be entitled to exercise a right of re-entry. This right of re-entry was not registered as a Land Charge. The question therefore arose whether it was binding on a purchaser from T Ltd.
HELD: The equitable right of re-entry did not fall within any of the categories of Land Charges. Accordingly, it did not need to be protected by registration as a Land Charge, and would be binding on the purchaser.

LORD WILBERFORCE: The right of entry, it is said, is unenforceable against the respondent, although he took with actual notice of it, because it was not registered as a charge under the Land Charges Act 1925. There is no doubt that if it was capable of registration under that Act, it is unenforceable if not registered: the appellants deny that it was so capable either (i) because it was a legal right, not an equitable right, or (ii) because if equitable, it does not fall within any of the classes or descriptions of charges registration of which is required.

I consider first whether the right of entry is legal in character or equitable, using these adjectives in the technical sense in which they are used in the 1925 property legislation. The question is purely one of statutory definition, the ingredients of which are found in sections 1 and 205(1)(x) of the Law of Property Act 1925. The contention that the right is legal was not accepted by Burgess V-C or advanced in the Court of Appeal below, nor was it contained in the printed case signed by eminent counsel, though if it were upheld it would be decisive of the case. The appellants were, however, permitted to lodge an amended case raising the point. I set out for convenience section 1(1), (2) and (3) of the Act. The definition section 205(1)(x) uses the same verbiage and adds nothing to the argument.

(1) The only estates in land which are capable of subsisting or of being conveyed or created at law are—(a) An estate in fee simple absolute in possession; (b) A term of years absolute. (2) The only interests or charges in or over land which are capable of subsisting or of being conveyed or created at law are—(a) An easement, right, or privilege in or over land for an interest equivalent to an estate in fee simple absolute in possession or a term of years absolute; (b) A rentcharge in possession issuing out of or charged on land being either perpetual or for a term of years absolute; (c) A charge by way of legal mortgage; (d) Land tax, tithe rentcharge, and any other similar charge on land which is not created by an instrument; (e) Rights of entry exercisable over or in respect of a legal term of years absolute, or annexed, for any purpose, to a legal rentcharge. (3) All other estates, interests, and charges on or over land take effect as equitable interests.

The right of entry in this case is not contained in a lease, so as to be annexed to a reversion, nor is it exercisable for a term of years, or (comparably with a fee simple) indefinitely. Its duration is limited by a perpetuity period. Whether it can be said to be 'exercisable over or in respect of a legal term of years absolute' appears obscure. It is not exercisable for a legal term of years (whether that granted by the lease or any other term): it is not so exercisable as to determine a legal term of years. To say that a right of entry is exercisable in respect of a legal term of years appears to me, with respect, to be without discernible meaning. The effect of this right of entry is to cause a legal term of years to be divested from one person to another upon an event which may occur over a perpetuity period. It would, I think, be contrary to the whole scheme of the Act, which requires the limiting and vesting of legal estates and interests to be by reference to a fee simple or a term of years absolute, to allow this to rank as a legal interest. In my opinion it is clearly equitable.

. . . There is certainly nothing exhaustive about the expression 'equitable interests'—just as certainly it has no clear boundaries. The debate whether such rights as equity, over the centuries, has conferred against the holder of the legal estate are truly proprietary in character, or merely *in personam*, or a hybrid between the two, may have lost some of its vitality in the statutory context but the question inevitably rises to mind whether the 'curtain' or 'overreaching' provisions of the 1925 legislation extend to what are still conveniently called 'equities' or 'mere equities' such as rights to rectification, or to set aside a conveyance. There is good authority, which I do not presume to doubt, for a sharp distinction between the two—I instance Lord Upjohn in *National Provincial Bank Ltd* v *Hastings Car Mart Ltd* [1965] AC 1175, 1238 and *Snell's Principles of Equity*, 25th edn. (1960) p. 38. I am impressed by the decision in *E. R. Ives Investment Ltd* v *High* [1967] 2 QB 379 in which the Court of Appeal held that a right by estoppel—producing an effect similar to an easement—was not registrable under Class D(iii). Lord Denning MR referred to the right as subsisting only in equity. Danckwerts LJ thought it was an equity created by estoppel or a proprietary estoppel: plainly this was not an equitable interest capable of being overreached, yet no member of the court considered that the right—so like an easement—could be brought within Class D(iii). The conclusion followed, and the court accepted it, that whether it was binding on a purchaser depended on notice. All this seems to show that there may well be rights, of an equitable character, outside the provisions as to registration and which are incapable of being overreached.

That equitable rights of entry should be among them is not in principle unacceptable. First, rights of entry, before 1925, were not considered to confer an interest in the land. They were described as bare possibilities (*Challis's Real Property*, 3rd edn. (1911), p. 76) so that it is not anomalous that equitable rights of entry should not be treated as equitable interests. Secondly, it is important that section 10 of the Land Charges Act 1925 should be given a plain and ordinary interpretation. It is a section which involves day to day operation by solicitors doing conveyancing work: they should be able to take decisions and advise their clients upon a straightforward interpretation of the registration classes, not upon one depending upon a sophisticated, not to say dsiputable, analysis of other statutes. Thirdly, the consequence of equitable rights of entry not being registrable is that they are subject to the doctrine of notice, preserved by section 199 of the Law of Property Act. This may not give complete protection, but neither is it demonstrable that it is likely to be less effective than the present system of registration against names. I am therefore of opinion that Class D(iii) should be given its plain prima facie meaning and that so read it does not comprise equitable rights of entry. It follows that non-registration does not make the appellants' rights unenforceable in this case.

8.1.3 CONSEQUENCES OF FAILURE TO REGISTER A LAND CHARGE

MIDLAND BANK TRUST CO. LTD v *GREEN* [1981] AC 513, House of Lords

FACTS: In this case a father owned a farm. He granted his son an option to purchase the farm at any time in the next ten years. The son should have registered this option (technically a form of 'estate contract') as a Class C(iv) Land Charge, but he omitted to do so. Father and son later fell out. In order to deprive the son, the father sold the farm (worth about £40,000) to his wife for just £500. The wife, of course knew all about the option. After the wife's death, her son brought an action against her estate to establish that his option was binding on the land. The Court of Appeal held that the wife's estate was bound by the option. That court held that 'money or money's worth' meant a fair price, which clearly £500 was not. The executors of the wife's estate appealed to the House of Lords.
HELD: The wife's estate was not bound by her son's option.

LORD WILBERFORCE: My Lords, this appeal relates to a 300-acre farm in Lincolnshire called 'Gravel Hill Farm.' It was owned by Walter Stanley Green ('Walter') and since 1954, let to his son Thomas Geoffrey Green ('Geoffrey') who farmed it as tenant. Walter owned another larger farm which he farmed jointly with another son Robert Derek Green ('Robert'), the appellant. In 1960 Walter sold this other farm to Robert at £75 per acre.

On March 24, 1961, Walter granted to Geoffrey an option to purchase Gravel Hill Farm, also at £75 per acre. The option was granted for the consideration of £1, and so was contractually binding upon Walter. It was to remain open for ten years. It seems that the reason why this transaction was entered into, rather than one of sale to Geoffrey, was to save estate duty on Walter's death.

This option was, in legal terms, an estate contract and so a legal charge, Class C, within the meaning of the Land Charges Act 1925. The correct and statutory method for protection of such an option is by means of entering it in the Register of Land Charges maintained under the Act. If so registered, the option would have been enforceable, not only (contractually) against Walter, but against any purchaser of the farm.

The option was not registered, a failure which inevitably called in question the responsibility of Geoffrey's solicitor. . . .

. . . the case appears to be a plain one. The 'estate contract,' which by definition (section 11) includes an option of purchase, was entered into after January 1 1926: Evelyne took an interest (in fee simple) in the land 'for valuable consideration'—so was a 'purchaser': she was a purchaser for money—namely £500: the option was not registered before the completion of the purchase. It is therefore void as against her.

In my opinion this appearance is also the reality. The case is plain: the Act is clear and definite. Intended as it was to provide a simple and understandable system for the protection of title to land, it should not be read down or glossed: to do so would destroy the usefulness of the Act. Any temptation to remould the Act to meet the facts of the present case, on the supposition that it is a hard one and that justice requires it, is, for me at least, removed by the consideration that the Act itself provides a simple and effective protection for persons in Geoffrey's position—*viz*—by registration.

The respondents submitted two arguments as to the interpretation of section 13(2): the one sought to introduce into it a requirement that the purchaser should be 'in good faith': the other related to the words 'in money or money's worth.'. . .

As to the requirement of 'good faith' we are faced with a situation of some perplexity. The expression 'good faith' appears in the Law of Property Act 1925 definition of 'purchaser' ('a purchaser in good faith for valuable consideration'), section 205(1)(xxi); in the Settled Land Act 1925, section 117(1)(xxi) (ditto); in the Administration of Estates Act

1925, section 55(1)(xviii) ('"Purchaser" means a lessee, mortagee or other person who in good faith acquires an interest in property for valuable consideration') and in the Land Registration Act 1925, section 3(xxi) which does not however, as the other Acts do, include a reference to nominal consideration. So there is certainly some indication of an intention to carry the concept of 'good faith' into much of the 1925 code. What then do we find in the Land Charges Act 1925? We were taken along a scholarly peregrination through the numerous Acts antecedent to the final codification and consolidation in 1925....

My Lords, I recognise that the inquiring mind may put the question: why should there be an omission of the requirement of good faith in this particular context? I do not think there should be much doubt about the answer. Addition of a requirement that the purchaser should be in good faith would bring with it the necessity of inquiring into the purchaser's motives and state of mind. The present case is a good example of the difficulties which would exist. If the position was simply that the purchaser had notice of the option, and decided nevertheless to buy the land, relying on the absence of notification, nobody could contend that she would be lacking in good faith. She would merely be taking advantage of a situation, which the law has provided, and the addition of a profit motive could not create an absence of good faith. But suppose, and this is the respondents' argument, the purchaser's motive is to defeat the option, does this make any difference? Any advantage to oneself seems necessarily to involve a disadvantage for another: to make the validity of the purchase depend upon which aspect of the transaction was prevalent in the purchaser's mind seems to create distinctions equally difficult to analyse in law as to establish in fact: avarice and malice may be distinct sins, but in human conduct they are liable to be intertwined. The problem becomes even more acute if one supposes a mixture of motives. Suppose—and this may not be far from the truth—that the purchaser's motives were in part to take the farm from Geoffrey, and in part to distribute it between Geoffrey and his brothers and sisters, but not at all to obtain any benefit for herself, is this acting in 'good faith' or not? Should family feeling be denied a protection afforded to simple greed? To eliminate the necessity for inquiries of this kind may well have been part of the legislative intention. Certainly there is here no argument for departing—violently—from the wording of the Act....

My Lords, I can deal more shortly with the respondents' second argument. It relates to the consideration for the purchase. The argument is that the protection of section 13(2) of the Land Charges Act 1925 does not extend to a purchaser who has provided only a nominal consideration and that £500 is nominal. A variation of this was the argument accepted by the Court of Appeal that the consideration must be 'adequate'—an expression of transparent difficulty. The answer to both contentions lies in the language of the subsection. The word 'purchaser,' by definition (section 20(8)), means one who provides valuable consideration—a term of art which precludes any inquiry as to adequacy. This definition is, of course, subject to the context. Section 13(2), proviso, requires money or money's worth to be provided: the purpose of this being to exclude the consideration of marriage. There is nothing here which suggests, or admits of, the introduction of a further requirement that the money must not be nominal.

The argument for this requirement is based upon the Law of Property Act 1925 which, in section 205(1)(xxi) defining 'purchaser' provides that 'valuable consideration' includes marriage but does not include a 'nominal consideration in money.' The Land Charges Act 1925 contains no definition of 'valuable consideration,' so it is said to be necessary to have resort to the Law of Property Act definition: thus 'nominal consideration in money,' is excluded. An indication that this is intended is said to be provided by section 199(1)(i). I cannot accept this. The fallacy lies in supposing that the Acts—either of them—set out to define 'valuable consideration'; they do not: they define 'purchaser,' and they define the word differently (see the first part of the argument). 'Valuable consideration' requires no definition: it is an expression denoting an advantage conferred or detriment suffered. What each Act does is, for its own purposes, to exclude some things from this general expression: the Law of Property Act includes marriage but not a nominal sum in money; the Land Charges Act excludes marriage but allows 'money or money's worth.' There is no coincidence between these two; no link by reference or necessary logic between them. Section 199(1)(i) by referring to the Land Charges Act 1925, necessarily incorporates—for the purposes of this provision—the definition of 'purchaser' in the latter Act, for it is only against such a 'purchaser' that an instrument is void under this Act. It cannot be read as incorporating the Law of Property Act definition into the Land Charges Act. As I have pointed out the land charges legislation has contained its own definition since 1888, carried through, with the addition of the reference to 'money or money's worth' into 1925. To exclude a nominal sum of money from section 13(2) of the Land Charges Act would be to rewrite the section.

This conclusion makes it unnecessary to determine whether £500 is a nominal sum of money or not. But I must say that for my part I should have great difficulty in so holding. 'Nominal consideration' and a 'nominal sum' in the law appear to me, as terms of art, to refer to a sum or consideration which can be mentioned as consideration but is not necessarily paid. To equate 'nominal' with 'inadequate' or even 'grossly inadequate' would embark the law upon inquiries which I cannot think were contemplated by Parliament.

I would allow the appeal.

8.1.4   OTHER REGISTERS ASSOCIATED WITH THE LAND CHARGES REGISTER

8.1.4.1   The register of pending actions

PEREZ-ADAMSON v PEREZ-RIVAS [1987] 2 WLR 500, Court of Appeal

FACTS: A wife included in her divorce petition a plea for ancillary relief by way of, *inter alia*, a property adjustment order. She registered this claim against the former matrimonial home as a pending land action. Later, the husband took out a loan with a bank and granted the bank a mortgage over the matrimonial home as security. The bank had failed to make a search of the Land Charges registery and so was unaware of the wife's claim. The husband realised all his assets and left the country without paying off the loan with the bank. The judge at first instance set aside the bank's charge on the matrimonial home. The bank appealed.
HELD: The appeal was dismissed. The wife's pending land action took priority over all subsequent charges on the property.

DILLON LJ: . . . It is common ground in these proceedings, in so far as it is material, that the legal charge in favour of the bank was made for valuable consideration and that the bank acted in relation to it in good faith. It is also clear that the bank had no express notice of any intention on the part of the husband to defeat the wife's claim for financial relief. The case turns on the effect of the registration under section 5 of the Act of 1972. . . .

The position therefore is that the long-established procedure for the registration of a lis pendens has to be married with the code under the Matrimonial Causes Act 1973 for property adjustment as between spouses. The Land Charges Act 1972 also includes provisions for the registration of various other property rights or interests which have in some cases been previously the subject of registration under quite different statutes.

Taking the whole together, I would accept the view of Stamp LJ that the code, as we now have it, has the effect that the registration of the lis pendens in respect of the wife's claim for property adjustment gives her priority over any subsequent conveyance or mortgage of the property executed by the husband. Mr. Lightman urges that that is only so if the other party to the transaction, being supposed to know of the claim for ancillary relief and the property adjustment order, is to be held to have had notice of intention on the part of the husband to defeat the wife's claim for financial relief. If the bank or other third party, not having actual knowledge of the registration and of the existence of the claim for ancillary relief, did not ask any questions, it might be difficult to establish that it had notice of an intention on the part of the husband to defeat the claim for ancillary relief. If the bank or third party did ask but was given a specious but untruthful answer, it would be well nigh impossible for a court to hold that the bank or other third party had the requisite notice of the husband's intention. There would be a very serious lacuna in the protection for the wife which Stamp LJ thought so desirable.

In my judgment there is no such lacuna, and so, for these reasons which are substantially the same as those which the judge in the court below gave, I would dismiss the appeal because the wife's claim for a property adjustment order has priority to the bank's charge and the wife has obtained, from the order of the judge now under appeal an order for the transfer of the proceeds of the property to her. The property was sold pending the hearing, it being common ground that neither spouse was then occupying it.

I would dismiss the appeal.

NICHOLLS LJ: I agree. . . .

The effect of registration of a pending land action in the register of pending actions is, as provided in section 198(1) of the Law of Property Act 1925, that the registration is 'deemed to constitute actual notice of [the] . . . matter . . . to all persons and for all purposes connected with the land affected . . .' In this case the 'matter' consists of the proceedings in which the property transfer order is being claimed. . . .

MATRIMONIAL CAUSES ACT 1973

24.   Property adjustment orders in connection with divorce proceedings, etc

(1)   On granting a decree of divorce, a decree of nullity of marriage or a decree of judicial separation or at any time thereafter (whether, in the case of a decree of divorce or of nullity of marriage, before or after the decree is made absolute), the court may make any one or more of the following orders, that is to say—

(a)   an order that a party to the marriage shall transfer to the other party, to any child of the family or to such person as may be specified in the order for the benefit of such a child such property as may be so specified, being property to which the first-mentioned party is entitled, either in possession or reversion;

(b)   an order that a settlement of such property as may be so specified, being property to which a party to the marriage is so entitled, be made to the satisfaction of the court for the benefit of the other party to the marriage and of the children of the family or either or any of them;

(c)   an order varying for the benefit of the parties to the marriage and of the children of the family or either or any of them any ante-nuptial or post-nuptial settlement (including such a settlement made by will or codicil) made on the parties to the marriage;

(d)   an order extinguishing or reducing the interests of either of the parties to the marriage under any such settlement;

subject, however, in the case of an order under paragraph (a) above, to the restrictions imposed by section 29(1) and (3) below on the making of orders for a transfer of property in favour of children who have attained the age of eighteen.

(2)   The court may make an order under subsection (1)(c) above notwithstanding that there are no children of the family.

(3)   Without prejudice to the power to give a direction under section 30 below for the settlement of an instrument by conveyancing counsel, where an order is made under this section on or after granting a decree of divorce or nullity of marriage, neither the order nor any settlement made in pursuance of the order shall take effect unless the decree has been made absolute.

8.1.4.2   The register of writs and orders affecting land

INSOLVENCY ACT 1986

336.   Rights of occupation etc of bankrupt's spouse

. . .

(2)   Where a spouse's rights of occupation under the Act of 1983 are a charge on the estate or interest of the other spouse, or of trustees for the other spouse, and the other spouse is adjudged bankrupt—

(a)   the charge continues to subsist notwithstanding the bankruptcy and, subject to the provisions of that Act, binds the trustee of the bankrupt's estate and persons deriving title under that trustee, and

(b)   any application for an order under section 1 of that Act shall be made to the court having jurisdiction in relation to the bankruptcy.

(3)   Where a person and his spouse or former spouse are trustees for sale of a dwelling house and that person is adjudged bankrupt, any application by the trustee of the bankrupt's estate for an order under section 30 of the Law of Property Act 1925 (powers of

court where trustees for sale refuse to act) shall be made to the court having jurisdiction in relation to the bankruptcy.

(4)   On such an application as is mentioned in subsection (2) or (3) the court shall make such order under section 1 of the Act of 1983 or section 30 of the Act of 1925 as it thinks just and reasonable having regard to—

(a)   the interests of the bankrupt's creditors,

(b)   the conduct of the spouse or former spouse, so far as contributing to the bankruptcy,

(c)   the needs and financial resources of the spouse or former spouse,

(d)   the needs of any children, and

(e)   all the circumstances of the case other than the needs of the bankrupt.

8.2 End of Chapter Assessment Question

In 1960 Ruth purchased the fee simple in Grand Villa, a large country house with two acres of grounds. The title was unregistered in an area which did not become an area of compulsory registration until 1988. Grand Villa was conveyed to Ruth in her sole name.

Four weeks ago William purchased Grand Villa from Ruth. Since the execution of the conveyance, the following matters have come to light.

(a) Martin, Ruth's husband, has returned from an extended business trip to Malaysia, and is alarmed to discover that Ruth has sold Grand Villa to William. Martin claims that, since in 1980 he paid £200,000 for a total reconstruction of Grand Villa, he has 'rights' which bind William.

(b) David has arrived at Grand Villa and has produced a document (not in the form of a deed) which Ruth and David signed six months ago. The document is a lease for fifteen years of part of the grounds of Grand Villa.

(c) Harry, owner of neighbouring Blackview, has arrived at Grand Villa and produced a deed executed some time in the 1920s. (The exact date is difficult to read.) This deed was executed by the then owner of Grand Villa, and contains a restrictive covenant in favour of the owners of Blackview to the effect that Grand Villa is to be used for residential purposes only. William plans to convert Grand Villa into a conference centre.

Advise William as to whether any of these matters will affect him.

8.3 End of Chapter Assessment Outline Answer

(a) There are TWO types of right which Martin can claim against Grand Villa. The first is his 'Rights of Occupation' granted by the Matrimonial Homes Acts. These rights automatically arise from the fact that he is Ruth's spouse and she had sole title to the matrimonial home.

The 'Rights of Occupation' are classed as an equitable interest, but are not subject to the doctrine of notice; they are registrable as a Land Charge 'Class F'. Almost certainly Martin did not know that he needed to register his Class F charge, and thus it is almost certain that his rights of occupation will not bind William.

Martin's second right is the constructive trust interest which he obtained in Grand Villa through paying £200,000 for a total reconstruction. Cases such as *Lloyds Bank* v *Rosset* (see **1.3.7**) hold that substantial contributions to the cost of purchasing or reconstructing a property will give rise to a constructive trust interest in the contributor's favour.

A constructive trust interest is subject to the equitable Doctrine of Notice. Thus Martin's interest will bind William unless William can prove that he is a bona fide purchaser for value of a legal estate (or interest) without notice of Martin's interest. It is reasonably clear that William is a bona fide purchaser for value of a legal estate. Thus William will take Grand Villa free from Martin's interest if he can prove that at the time of the conveyance he was without notice of Martin's claim.

'Notice' comes in three forms, actual, constructive and imputed. It would appear that at the time of the purchase William had no actual knowledge (i.e. actual notice) of Martin's constructive trust interest. However Martin will probably contend that William had constructive notice of Martin's interest.

Under the constructive notice rule a purchaser of land must make all those enquiries which a reasonable purchaser makes. In particular he must inspect the land for signs of occupiers other than the vendor and investigate the title deeds. If a purchaser fails to make a reasonable enquiry which would have revealed an equitable interest, he will be stuck with constructive notice of that interest.

Martin's interest is not the sort which is revealed in title deeds. But it is the sort which may gain protection from the rule in *Hunt* v *Luck* [1902] 1 Ch 45. If on inspecting the land the (potential) purchaser sees signs of a person other than the vendor occupying the land, then the purchaser must seek out that other person and enquire of him what claim he has to the land.

We must hope that William made a proper inspection of Grand Villa, and that when he made that inspection there were no signs that Martin lived there. . . . Only if that is the case will William be without notice of Martin's interest.

If William employed a surveyor to inspect the land, we must hope that there were no signs of Martin when the surveyor called to inspect. This is because of the imputed notice rule. If a purchaser employs an agent then any (actual or constructive) notice which comes to that agent is automatically attributed to the purchaser with the result that he is bound by the relevant equitable interest.

(b)   As the document granting the lease is not a deed, David has only got an equitable lease. Post-1925 such a lease is not subject to the doctrine of notice. It is registrable as an 'Estate Contract' land charge. It is unlikely that David (who probably did not take legal advice) will have registered. If he has not registered then his equitable lease will be void against William, as William is (apparently) a purchaser for money or money's worth of a legal estate. Moreover it will be void against William even if he actually knew of the equitable lease. (See *Hollington Brothers* v *Rhodes* [1951] 2 All ER 578.)

(c)   Whether the restrictive covenant benefiting Blackview binds William may well depend upon the date it was entered into. The deed produced by Harry must be carefully examined to see whether or not it was executed after 1925.

If it transpires that the 'residential purposes' only covenant was entered into after 1925, then it will be registrable as a land charge. It will only bind William if it was correctly registered as a land charge against the name of the owner of Grand Villa who (back in the 'twenties') entered into the restrictive covenant. If the covenant was not correctly registered it will be void against William, even if he knew about the covenant through looking at the title deeds.

If the covenant was entered into before 1926 then it will not be registrable as a land charge; it will be subject to the old doctrine of notice.

As mentioned earlier, the purchaser of land is expected to investigate the title deeds. If William inspected the deeds and saw the restrictive covenant mentioned, he would have actual notice. If his solicitor inspected the deeds and saw the covenant, William would have imputed notice.

If William (or his solicitor) failed to investigate title properly, with the result that the covenant ought to have been discovered from the deeds but wasn't, then William will have constructive (or constructive imputed) notice.

The duty to investigate deeds is not however a duty to investigate documents back to the time immemorial. It is a duty to go back to the 'root of title'; the root is the most recent conveyance which is at least fifteen years old. When William purchased Grand Villa the root would have been the conveyance to Ruth in 1960. If (as is possible) the 'residential only' covenant is not mentioned in that conveyance (nor in any later document such as a mortgage of Grand Villa produced by Ruth to William or his solicitor), then William will not have notice of the covenant and will not be bound by it.

CHAPTER NINE

REGISTRATION OF TITLE — THE BASIC PRINCIPLES

9.1 Introduction

Lawson, F. H. and Rudden, B., *The Law of Property*, 2nd edn, Oxford: Clarendon Press, 1982, Chapter XVI

REGISTRATION

. . . Registration has been accepted wholeheartedly for ships, for bills of sale, and for various kinds of companies; and there has been no difficulty in insisting on companies keeping registers of shares and shareholders. Moreover, the practice of proving wills has always carried with it registration.

With land the story has been very different. The obvious advantages attaching to registration have had to fight against many adverse forces, of which the most important have been the desire of landowners and their lawyers to keep transactions secret and the difficulty of placing all the immensely complicated mass of interests that may coexist in land on a single register. During the latter half of the nineteenth century there were among reformers of real property law two opposing schools of thought, the one insisting that registration should be pushed forward as rapidly as possible, the other insisting on its difficulty without a preliminary simplification of the law and on the probability that it would be found unnecessary once the law was simplified. The dispute between the two schools helped to prevent anything being done on either side, but eventually the simplifiers won. Registration has been extended greatly in many ways, but perhaps not so much as if the movement in favour of it had alone held the field. . . .

9.2 Register of Estates not Register of Plots

LAND REGISTRATION ACT 1925

1. Registers to be continued

(1) The Chief Land Registrar shall continue to keep a register of title to freehold land and leasehold land.

(2) The register need not be kept in documentary form.

2. What estates may be registered

(1) After the commencement of this Act, estates capable of subsisting as legal estates shall be the only interests in land in repect of which a proprietor can be registered and all other interests in registered land (except overriding interests and interests entered on the register at or before such commencement) shall take effect in equity, as minor interests, but all interests (except undivided shares in land) entered on the register at such commencement which are not legal estates shall be capable of being dealt with under this Act:

Provided that, on the occasion of the first dealing with any such interest, the register shall be rectified in such manner as may be provided by rules made to secure that the entries therein shall be similar to those which would have been made if the title to the land had been registered after the commencement of this Act.

9.3 Grades of Title

LAND REGISTRATION ACT 1925

5. Effect of first registration with absolute title

Where the registered land is a freehold estate, the registration of any person as first proprietor thereof with an absolute title shall vest in the person so registered an estate in fee simple in possession in the land, together with all rights, privileges, and appurtenances belonging or appurtenant thereto, subject to the following rights and interests, that is to say,—

(a) Subject to the incumbrances, and other entries, if any, appearing on the register; and

(b) Unless the contrary is expressed on the register, subject to such overriding interest, if any, as affect the registered land; and

(c) Where the first proprietor is not entitled for his own benefit to the registered land subject, as between himself and the persons entitled to minor interests, to any minor interests of such persons of which he has notice,

but free from all other estates and interests whatsoever, including estates and interests of His Majesty.

6. Effect of first registration with possessory title

Where the registered land is a freehold estate, the registration of any person as first proprietor thereof with a possessory title only shall not affect or prejudice the enforcement of any estate, right or interest adverse to or in derogation of the title of the first proprietor, and subsisting or capable of arising at the time of registration of that proprietor; but save as aforesaid, shall have the same effect as registration of a person with an absolute title.

7. Qualified title

(1) Where an absolute title is required, and on the examination of the title it appears to the registrar that the title can be established only for a limited period, or only subject to certain reservations, the registrar may, on the application of the party applying to be registered, by an entry made in the register, except from the effect of registration any estate, right, or interest—

(a) arising before a specified date; or

(b) arising under a specified instrument or otherwise particularly described in the register,

and a title registered subject to such excepted estate, right, or interest shall be called a qualified title.

8. Application for registration of leasehold land

(1) Where the title to be registered is a title to a leasehold interest in land—

(a) any estate owner (including a tenant for life, statutory owner, personal representative, or trustee for sale, but not including a mortgagee where there is a subsisting right of redemption), holding under a lease for a term of years absolute of which more than twenty-one are unexpired, whether subject or not to incumbrances; or

(b) any other person (not being a mortgagee as aforesaid and not being a person who has merely contracted to buy the leasehold interest) who is entitled to require a legal leasehold estate held under such a lease as aforesaid (whether subject or not to incumbrances) to be vested in him,

may apply to the registrar to be registered in respect of such estate, or in the case of a person not being in a fiduciary position to have registered in his stead any nominee, as proprietor with an absolute title, with a good leasehold title or with a possessory title:

Provided that—

(i)   Where an absolute title is required, the applicant or his nominee shall not be registered as proprietor until and unless the title both to the leasehold and to the freehold, and to any intermediate leasehold that may exist, is approved by the registrar;

(ii)   Where a good leasehold title is required, the applicant or his nominee shall not be registered as proprietor until and unless the title to the leasehold interest is approved by the registrar;

(iii)   Where a possessory title is required, the applicant or his nominee may be registered as proprietor on giving such evidence of title and serving such notices, if any, as may for the time being be precsribed;

(iv)   If on an application for registration with a possessory title the registrar is satisfied as to the title to the leasehold interest, he may register it as good leasehold, whether the applicant consents to such registration or not, but in that case no higher fee shall be charged than would have been charged for registration with possessory title. . . .

9.   Effect of first registration with absolute title

Where the registered land is a leasehold interest, the registration under this Act of any person as first proprietor thereof with an absolute title shall be deemed to vest in such person the possession of the leasehold interest described, with all implied or expressed rights, privileges, and appurtenances attached to such interest, subject to the following obligations, rights, and interests, that is to say—

(a)   Subject to all implied and express covenants, obligations, and liabilities incident to the registered land; and

(b)   Subject to the incumbrances and other entries (if any) appearing on the register; and

(c)   Unless the contrary is expressed on the register, subject to such overriding interests, if any, as affect the registered land; and

(d)   Where such first proprietor is not entitled for his own benefit to the registered land subject, as between himself and the persons entitled to minor interest, to any minor interests of such persons of which he has notice;

but free from all other estates and interests whatsoever, including estates and interests of His Majesty.

10.   Effect of first registration with good leasehold title

Where the registered land is a leasehold interest, the registration of a person as first proprietor thereof with a good leasehold title shall not affect or prejudice the enforcement of any estate, right or interest affecting or in derogation of the title of the lessor to grant the lease, but, save as aforesaid, shall have the same effect as registration with an absolute title.

11.   Effect of first registration with possessory title

Where the registered land is a leasehold interest, the registration of a person as first proprietor thereof with a possessory title shall not affect or prejudice the enforcement of any estate, right, or interest (whether in respect of the lessor's title or otherewise) adverse to or in derogation of the title of such first registered proprietor, and subsisting or capable of arising at the time of the registration of such proprietor; but, save as aforesaid, shall have the same effect as registration with an absolute title.

12.   Qualified title

(1)   Where on examination it appears to the registrar that the title, either of the lessor to the reversion or of the lessee to the leasehold interest, can be established only for a limited period, or subject to certain reservations, the registrar may, upon the request in writing of the person applying to be registered, by an entry made in the register, except from the effect of registration any estate, right or interest—

(a)   arising before a specified date, or

(b)   arising under a specified instrument, or otherwise particularly described in the register,

and a title registered subject to any such exception shall be called a qualified title.

(2)   Where the registered land is a leasehold interest, the registration of a person as first proprietor thereof with a qualified title shall not affect or prejudice the enforcement of any

estate, right, or interest appearing by the register to be excepted, but save as aforesaid, shall have the same effect as registration with a good leasehold title or an absolute title, as the case may be.

20.   Effect of registration and dispositions of freeholds

(1)   In the case of a freehold estate registered with an absolute title, a diposition of the registered land or of a legal estate therein, including a lease thereof, for valuable consideration shall, when registered, confer on the transferee or grantee an estate in fee simple or the term of years absolute or other legal estate expressed to be created in the land dealt with, together with all rights, privileges, and appurtenances belonging or appurtenant thereto including (subject to any entry to the contrary in the register) the appropriate rights and interests which would, under the Law of Property Act 1925, have been transferred if the land had not been registered, subject—

(a)   to the incumbrances and other entries, if any, appearing on the register [and any charge for capital transfer tax subject to which the disposition takes effect under section 73 of this Act]; and

(b)   unless the contrary is expressed on the register, to the overrriding interests, if any, affecting the estate transferred or created,

but free from all other estates and interests whatsoever, including estates and interests of His Majesty, and the disposition shall operate in like manner as if the registered transferor or grantor were (subject to any entry to the contrary in the register) entitled to registered land in fee simple in possession for his own benefit.

(2)   . . .

(3)   . . .

(4)   Where any such disposition is made without valuable consideration, it shall, so far as the transferee or grantee is concerned, be subject to any minor interests subject to which the transferor or grantor held the same, but, save as aforesaid, shall, when registered, in all respects, and in particular as respects any registered dealings on the part of the transferee or grantee, have the same effect as if the disposition had been made for valuable consideration.

69.   Effect of registration on the legal estate

(1)   The proprietor of land (whether he was registered before or after the commencement of this Act) shall be deemed to have vested in him without any conveyance, where the registered land is freehold, the legal estate in fee simple in possession, and where the registered land is leasehold the legal term created by the registered lease, but subject ot the overriding interests, if any, including any mortgage term or charge by way of legal mortgage created by or under the Law of Property Act 1925, or this Act or otherwise which has priority to the registered estate.

(2)   Where any legal estate or term left outstanding at the date of first registration (whether before or after the commencement of this Act), or disposed of or created under section forty-nine of the Land Transfer Act 1875, before the commencement of this Act, becomes satisfied, or the proprietor of the land becomes entitled to require the same to be vested in or surrendered to him, and the entry, if any, for protecting the same on the register has been cancelled, the same shall thereupon, without any conveyance, vest in the proprietor of the land, as if the same had been conveyed or surrendered to him as the case may be.

(3)   If and when any person is registered as first proprietor of land in a compulsory area after the commencement of this Act, the provisions of the Law of Property Act 1925 for getting in legal estates shall apply to any legal estate in the land which was expressed to be conveyed or created in favour of a purchaser or lessee before the commencement of this Act but which failed to pass or to be created by reason of the omission of such purchaser or lessee to be registered as proprietor of the land under the Land Transfer Acts 1875 and 1897, and shall operate to vest that legal estate in the person so registered as proprietor on his registration, but subject to any mortgage term or charge by way of legal mortgage having priority thereto.

(4)   The estate for the time being vested in the proprietor shall only be capable of being disposed of or dealt with by him in manner authorised by this Act.

(5)   Nothing in this section operates to render valid a lease registered with possessory or good leasehold title.

77. Conversion of title

(1)   Where land is registered with a good leasehold title, or satisfies the conditions for such registration under this section, the registrar may, and on application by the proprietor shall, if he is satisfied as to the title to the freehold and the title to any intermediate leasehold, enter the title as absolute.

(2)   Where land is registered with a possessory title, the registrar may, and on application by the proprietor shall—

(a)   if he is satisfied as to the title, or

(b)   if the land has been so registered for at least twelve years and he is satisfied that the proprietor is in possession,

enter the title in the case of freehold land as absolute and in the case of leasehold land as good leasehold.

(3)   Where land is registered with a qualified title, the registrar may, and on application by the proprietor shall, if he is satisfied as to title, enter it in the case of freehold land as absolute and in the case of leasehold land as good leasehold.

(4)   If any claim adverse to the title of the proprietor has been made, an entry shall not be made in the register under this section unless and until the claim has been disposed of.

(5)   No fee shall be charged for the making of an entry in the register under this section at the instance of the registrar or on an application by the proprietor made in connection with a transfer for valuable consideration of the land to which the application relates.

(6)   Any person, other than the proprietor, who suffers loss by reason of any entry on the register made by virtue of this section shall be entitled to be indemnified under this Act as if a mistake had been made in the register.

9.3.1   UPGRADING OF TITLE

LAND REGISTRATION ACT 1986

1.   Conversion of title

(1)   . . .

(2)   In the case of land registered with a possessory title before the commencement of this Act—

(a)   subsection (2)(b) of section 77 of the 1925 Act as substituted by this section applies only where the land has been so registered for a period of at least 12 years after that commencement, but

(b)   nothing in this section affects the operation of subsection (3)(b) of section 77 of the 1925 Act as originally enacted (which provides for conversion of a possessory title after 15 years' registration in the case of freehold land and 10 years' registration in the case of leasehold land) in relation to a period of registration beginning before that commencement.

9.4   The Form of the Register

LAND REGISTRATION ACT 1925

110.   Provisions as between vendor and purchaser

On a sale or other disposition of registered land to a purchaser other than a lessee or chargee—

(1)   The vendor shall, notwithstanding any stipulation to the contrary, at his own expense furnish the purchaser with an authority to inspect the register, and, if required, with a copy of the subsisting entries in the register and of any filed plans and copies or abstracts of any documents or any part thereof noted on the register so far as they respectively affect the land to be dealt with (except charges or incumbrances registered or protected on the register which are to be discharged or overrridden at or prior to completion):

Provided that—

(a)   unless the purchase money exceeds one thousand pounds the costs of the copies and abstracts of the said entries plans and documents shall, in the absence of any stipulation to the contrary, be borne by the purchaser requiring the same; . . .

HM Land Registry

TITLE NUMBER : CS65432

C. CHARGES REGISTER (continued)

Entry No.	
2.	(19 November 1989) The land is subject to the rights of way on foot only over the passageway tinted blue on the filed plan.
3.	(31 July 1990) A Transfer of the land in this title dated 29 June 1990 made between (1) HERBERT DUDLEY RANSOM and (2) SAM DAVID JUNIOR and ANN JUNIOR contains restrictive covenants. *NOTE:- Copy in Certificate.*

***** END OF REGISTER *****

NOTE A : A date at the beginning of an entry is the date on which the entry was made in the Register.

NOTE B : This certificate was officially examined with the register on 31 July 1990. This date should be stated on any application for an official search based on this certificate.

Page 2.

HM Land Registry

TITLE NUMBER : CS65432

Edition date : 31 July 1990

A. PROPERTY REGISTER
containing the description of the registered land and the estate comprised in the Title

COUNTY   DISTRICT

SUMMERSHIRE   REXTON

Entry No.	
1.	(19 November 1989) The Freehold land edged with red on the plan of the above Title filed at the registry and being 12 Ink Way, Rossby.
2.	(19 November 1989) The land has the benefit of a right of way on foot only over the passageway tinted brown on the filed plan.
3.	(31 July 1990) The land in this title has the benefit of the rights granted by but is subject to the rights reserved by the Transfer dated 29 June 1990 referred to in the Charges Register.

B. PROPRIETORSHIP REGISTER
stating nature of the Title, name, address and description of the proprietor of the land and any entries affecting the right of disposing thereof

TITLE ABSOLUTE

Entry No.	
1.	(31 July 1990) Proprietor(s): SAM DAVID JUNIOR and ANN JUNIOR both of 12 Ink Way, Rossby, Rexton, Summershire.

C. CHARGES REGISTER
containing charges, incumbrances etc. adversely affecting the land and registered dealings therewith

Entry No.	
1.	(19 November 1989) A Conveyance of the land in this title and other land dated 19 April 1923 made between (1) Frederick Obb (Vendor) and (2) Gertrude Mary East (Purchaser) contains the following covenants:- "And the purchaser for herself her heirs executors administrators and assigns hereby covenants with the Vendor his heirs and assigns that she will perform and observe the stipulations set out in the First Schedule hereto so far as they relate to the hereditaments hereby assured THE FIRST SCHEDULE above referred to (a) No caravan shall be allowed upon the premises and the Vendor or owner or owners of adjoining premises may remove and dispose of any such caravan and for that purpose may forcibly enter upon any land upon which a breach of this stipulation shall occur and shall not be responsible for the safe keeping of any such caravan or for the loss thereof or any damage thereto or to any fence or wall (b) No earth gravel or sand shall at any time be excavated or dug out of the land except for the purpose of excavations in connection with the buildings erected on the land and no bricks or tiles shall at any time be burnt or made nor any clay or lime be burnt on the land."

Continued on the next page

9.4.1 THE PROPERTY PART

The Law Commission (Law Com. No. 125) Property Law: Land Registration, London: HMSO, 26 October 1983

Boundaries

2.17 It has long been an accepted principle that the boundaries indicated by the register are *general boundaries* only. This is known as the 'general boundaries rule' and is now expressed in rule 278, which is in the following terms:—

278.—(1) Except in cases in which it is noted in the Property Register that the boundaries have been fixed, the filed plan or General Map shall be deemed to indicate the general boundaries only.

(2) In such cases the exact line of the boundary will be left undetermined—as, for instance, whether it includes a hedge or wall and ditch, or runs within or beyond it; or whether or not the land registered includes the whole or any portion of an adjoining road or stream.

(3) When a general boundary only is desired to be entered in the register, notice to the owners of the adjoining lands need not be given.

(4) This rule shall apply notwithstanding that a part or the whole of a ditch, wall, fence, road, stream or other boundary is expressly included in or excluded from the title or that it forms the whole of the land comprised in the title.

The effect of this rule is that no guarantee is given by the Land Registry that the legal boundary is the centre of a fence, hedge or ditch or on one side of it or the other; and if the boundary is a road or stream, there will usually be no guidance as to whether the title includes the whole or any part of that road or stream.

2.18 A procedure does however remain whereby applications may be made for the boundaries of registered land to be fixed; if they are so fixed the filed plan is then 'deemed to define accurately the fixed boundaries'. This procedure is rarely used: of some 8.3 million titles now registered only about 20 are registered with fixed boundaries, and since 1970 only four applications to fix boundaries have been made, of which only one was pursued to completion.

Criticisms of the present law and practice . . .

2.20 . . . Boundary disputes are both a source and a product of ill-feeling between neighbours; and we have no doubt that the vagueness with which boundaries have traditionally been defined is an important contributory factor to these disputes. . . .

Merits of the General Boundaries Rule . . .

2.25 If boundaries are to be fixed, notice clearly has to be served on all neighbouring owners and their titles have to be investigated. The fixing of boundaries, not only on all first registrations but also on many dealings with registered land, would involve an enormous amount of work for the Registry, but without commensurate return because the existence of the general boundaries rule means that land can be brought onto the Register without costly surveys or any elaborate investigative procedure. The rule also facilitates the work of mapping in the Registry; a return to a system of registration with precise and accurate boundaries would seriously hamper the work of bringing new land onto the Register. We regard that as being far too high a price to pay for the somewhat nebulous benefits to be derived from a reversion to the system of fixed boundaries. There are clear advantages in getting land onto the Register as soon as possible, not only to facilitate and simplify conveyancing, but also to secure the real advantages of superior identification which the registered system provides. . . .

Conclusion

2.28 We recommend that the general boundaries rule should be retained. We consider that the likelihood of boundary disputes can best be reduced by improvements in conveyancing practice.

CHAPTER TEN

OVERRIDING INTERESTS AND MINOR INTERESTS

10.1 Overriding Interests

LAND REGISTRATION ACT 1925

70. Liability of registered land to overriding interests

(1)   All registered land shall, unless under the provisions of this Act the contrary is expressed on the register, be deemed to be subject to such of the following overriding interests as may be for the time being subsisting in reference thereto, and such interests shall not be treated as incumbrances within the meaning of this Act, (that is to say):—

(a)   Rights of common, drainage rights, customary rights (until extinguished), public rights, profits à prendre, rights of sheepwalk, rights of way, watercourses, rights of water, and other easements not being equitable easements required to be protected by notice on the register;

(b)   Liability to repair highways by reason of tenure, quit-rents, crown rents, heriots, nd other rents and charges (until extinguished) having their origin in tenure;

(c)   Liability to repair the chancel of any church;

(d)   Liability in respect of embankments, and sea and river walls;

(e)   ..., payments in lieu of tithe, and charges of annuities payable for the redemption of tithe rentcharges;

(f)   Subject to the provisions of this Act, rights acquired or in course of being acquired under the Limitation Acts;

(g)   The rights of every person in actual occupation of the land or in receipt of the rents and profits thereof, save where enquiry is made of such person and the rights are not disclosed;

(h)   In the case of a possessory, qualified, or good leasehold title, all estates, rights, interests, and powers excepted from the effect of registration;

(i)   Rights under local land charges unless and until registered or protected on the register in the prescribed manner;

(j)   Rights of fishing and sporting, seignorial and manorial rights of all descriptions (until extinguished), and franchises;

(k)   Leases granted for a term not exceeding twenty-one years;

(l)   In respect of land registered before the commencement of this Act, rights to mines and minerals, and rights of entry, search, and user, and other rights and reservations incidental to or required for the purpose of giving full effect to the enjoyment of rights to mines and minerals or of property in mines or minerals, being rights which, where the title was first registered before the first day of January, eighteen hundred and ninety-eight, were created before that date, and where the title was first registered after the thirty-first day of December, eighteen hundred and ninety-seven, were created before the date of first registration:

Provided that, where it is proved to the satisfaction of the registrar that any land registered or about to be registered is exempt from land tax, or tithe rentcharge or payments in lieu of tithe, or from charges or annuities payable for the redemption of tithe rentcharge, the registrar may notify the fact on the register in the prescribed manner.

(2)   Where at the time of first registration any easement, right, privilege, or benefit created by an instrument and appearing on the title adversely affects the land, the registrar shall enter a note thereof on the register.

(3)   Where the existence of any overriding interest mentioned in this section is proved to the satisfaction of the registrar or admitted, he may (subject to any prescribed exceptions) enter notice of the same or of a claim thereto on the register, but no claim to an easement, right, or privilege not created by an instrument shall be noted against the title to the servient land if the proprietor of such land (after the prescribed notice is given to him) shows sufficient cause to the contrary.

10.1.1   S. 70(1)(a) . . . PROFITS À PRENDRE, . . . AND EASEMENTS NOT BEING EQUITABLE EASEMENTS REQUIRED TO BE PROTECTED BY NOTICE ON THE REGISTER

CELSTEEL LTD AND OTHERS v ALTON HOUSE HOLDINGS LTD AND ANOTHER
[1985] 1 WLR 204, Chancery Division

FACTS: The case involved registered land. A right of way had been granted to the plaintiffs by a written agreement. The easement thus created was an equitable easement. The plaintiff exercised its right of way openly, but had never protected the equitable easement by a notice of entry on the register. The question before the court was whether the unprotected equitable easement was binding upon a purchaser of the servient land ('servient land' is land over which an easement is exercised).

HELD: The equitable easement would bind the purchaser of the servient land, despite the plaintiff's failure to protect it by notice of entry on the register. This was because an equitable easement qualifies as an 'overriding interest' within s. (70)(1)(a) of the Land Registration Act 1925.

SCOTT J: . . . Paragraph (a) of section 70(1) protects as overriding interests the following rights:

> Rights of common, drainage rights, customary rights (until extinguished), public rights, profit à prendre, rights of sheepwalk, rights of way, watercourses, rights of water, and other easements not being equitable easements required to be protected by notice on the register.

The rights over the rear driveway which the third plaintiff acquired by virtue of the facts pleaded in the paragraphs of the statement of claim which I have mentioned were certainly rights of way. If they were legal rights of way then the second defendants are bound by them. If they were only equitable rights of way then I must decide whether or not they are excepted from paragraph (a) by the phrase 'not being equitable easements required to be protected by notice on the register.'

The third plaintiff's entitlement to the easements comprised in the intended lease of garage 52 for the intended 120 year term is an *equitable* entitlement. It could only become a *legal* entitlement by the grant to him of the lease contracted to be granted and the registration of that lease at Her Majesty's Land Registry. But the meaning and scope of the provision 'equitable easements required to be protected by notice on the register' is somewhat obscure. In *E R Ives Investment Ltd* v *High* [1967] 2 QB 379 it was held by the Court of Appeal that easements acquired in equity by proprietory estoppel were not equitable easements for the purposes of section 10(1) Class D(iii) of the Land Charges Act 1925. Lord Denning MR expressed the view that 'equitable easements' referred simply to that limited class of rights which before the 1925 property legislation were capable of being conveyed or created at law but thereafter were capable of existing only in equity: see p. 395. In *Poster* v *Slough Estates Ltd* [1969] 1 Ch 495 Cross J declined, at pp. 506–507, to disagree with Lord Denning MR's view of the meaning of the expression and held that a right to re-enter premises after termination of a lease and to remove fixtures therefrom was not an 'equitable easement' for the purposes of the Land Charges Act 1925. These authorities might be thought to suggest by analogy that equitable easements in section 70(1)(a) should be given a similarly limited meaning. I am, however, reluctant to do that because in general the clear intention of the Land Registration Act 1925 is that equitable interests should be protected either by entry on the register or as overriding interests and, if equitable easements in general are not within the exception in paragraph (a), it would follow that they would rank as overriding interests and be binding upon registered proprietors of servient land even though such proprietors did not have and could not by any reasonable means have obtained any knowledge of them. That result could not possibly be supported. In my view, therefore, the dicta in the two cases are not applicable to the construction of 'equitable easements' in paragraph (a) of section 70(1). . . .

In my opinion, the words 'required to be protected' in paragraph (a) should be read in the sense 'need to be protected.' The exception in the paragraph was, in my view, intended to cover all equitable easements other than such as by reason of some other statutory provision or applicable principle of law, could obtain protection otherwise than by notice on the register. The most obvious example would be equitable easements which qualified for protection under paragraph (g) as part of the rights of a person in actual occupation. In my view I must examine the easement claimed by the third plaintiff and consider whether there is any statutory provision or principle of law which entitles it to protection otherwise than by entry of notice on the register.

The matter stands in my opinion thus. At the time when Mobil acquired its registered leasehold title the third plaintiff's right to an easement of way for the benefit of garage 52 over a part of the property enjoyed under that leasehold title was an equitable and not a legal right. It was, in ordinary conveyancing language, an equitable easement. It was not protected by any entry on the register. On the other hand it was at the relevant time openly exercised and enjoyed by the third plaintiff as appurtenant to garage 52. Section 144 of the Land Registration Act 1925 contains power for rules to be made for a number of specified purposes. The Land Registration Rules 1925 (SR & O 1925 No. 1093) were accordingly made and rule 258 provides:

> Rights, privileges, and appurtenances appertaining or reputed to appertain to land or demised, occupied, or enjoyed therewith or reputed or known as part or parcel of or appurtenant thereto, which adversely affect registered land, are overriding interests within section 70 of the Act, and shall not be deemed incumbrances for the purposes of the Act.

The third plaintiff's equitable right of way over the rear driveway was, in my view, at the time when Mobil acquired its registered leasehold title, a right enjoyed with land for the purposes of this rule. It was plainly a right which adversely affected registered land including the part of the rear driveway comprised in Mobil's lease. Rule 258 categorises such a right as an overriding interest. Section 144(2) of the Act provides that 'Any rules made in pursuance of this section shall be of the same force as if enacted in this Act.' Accordingly, in my judgment, the third plaintiff's right ranks as an overriding interest, does not need to be protected by entry of notice on the register and is binding on Mobil.

Mr. Davidson submitted that there was no power under section 144(1) for rules to add to the overriding interests specified in the various paragraphs of section 70(1). He submitted that rule 258 was ultra vires and of no effect. I do not agree. Sub-paragraph (xxxi) of section 144(1) enables rules to be made,

> for regulating any matter to be prescribed or in respect of which rules are to or may be made under this Act and any other matter or thing, whether similar or not to those above mentioned, in respect of which it may be expedient to make rules for the purpose of carrying this Act into execution.

This is a power in very wide terms. In my view, it is in terms wide enough to justify rule 258 and I see no reason why it should be given a limited effect.

Accordingly, for these reasons, the third plaintiff's equitable right of way over the rear driveway enjoyed with garage 52 was and is, in my judgment, binding on Mobil.

Thompson, M.P., Equitable Easements in Registered Land (1986) 50 Conv 31

. . . commentators have tended to emphasise the undersirability of equitable easements being regarded as overriding interests, whilst recognising the possibility that they might be. In support of this argument are the considerations that the opposite view would make the last 13 words of the paragraph [LRA 1925, s. 70(1)(a)] redundant and that if equitable easements were intended to be overriding interests, a less tortuous method of drafting could easily have been employed to this effect. Together with these points is the policy consideration that it is desirable that section 70 is construed narrowly to enhance the reliability of the register. As against this, however, it does not seem to be conspicuously rational to include equitable *profits* as overriding interests but to exclude equitable easements as the Act appears to do, if this argument is correct. In addition, equitable easements were overriding interests under the predecessor to the Land Registration Act 1925 and it is not entirely clear that this position was meant to be changed.

On balance, the better view seemed clearly to be that equitable easements were not within the ambit of section 70(1)(a). This view was not fully accepted, however, in *Celsteel Ltd* v *Alton House Holdings Ltd* [1985] 1 WLR 204. The facts, somewhat simplified, were that the plaintiff held an equitable lease of a garage together with a right of vehicular access over a driveway which also provided access to and egress from a petrol station. The defendant, an oil company, was registered as proprietor with a leasehold title of the petrol station. There was no mention of the plaintiff's right of way on the register. The defendant planned to erect a car wash which, when built, would substantially interfere with the plaintiff's right. The issue therefore, in an action for injunctive relief, was whether or not the equitable easement was an overriding interest. In a reserved judgment, delivered in June 1984 but, regrettably, not fully reported until June 1985, Scott J held that it was.

In reaching this conclusion, it may be observed that the judge's reasoning is somewhat obscure. He declined to construe the term, equitable easements, in the narrow sense suggested in earlier decisions involving unregistered land. This was because he felt that if equitable easements were construed narrowly and, as a category were excluded from paragraph (a), then a wide category of rights would rank as overriding interests despite their being undiscoverable by a purchaser of the servient tenement: a result he regarded as objectionable. The writer would agree with this statement of policy but would confess to finding the reasoning somewhat baffling, as the simplest method of achieving the desired policy objective would be to hold first that equitable easements were to be defined widely, and secondly that the concluding thirteen words of paragraph (a) meant that equitable easements were not overriding interests.

Scott J rejected the plaintiff's argument that as nothing in the Act requires equitable easements to be protected by a notice, it therefore followed that all equitable easements were overriding interests. Instead, he held that within the ambit of paragraph (a) were only those easements which did not need to be protected on the register. Such easements were those that qualified for protection under paragraph (g) as part of the rights of a person in actual occupation of the land. In addition, he held that equitable easements enjoyed openly were also overriding interests. This was the consequence of Rule 258, which provides that:

> Rights, privileges, and appurtenances appertaining or reputed to appertain to land or demised, occupied or enjoyed therewith or reputed or known as part or parcel of or appurtenant thereto, which adversely affect registered land, are overriding interests within section 70 of the Act, and shall not be deemed incumbrances for the purpose of the Act.

Because at the time when the defendant acquired its registered leasehold interest, the plaintiff exercised his right of way, Rule 258 transformed it into an overriding interest. Thus, an equitable easement is an overriding interest if either the owner of it is in actual occupation of the servient land or actually exercises it at the time that the servient land is transferred. If it falls into neither category, it is overridden by a transfer for value, unless it is registered.

It appears that an alternative line of reasoning to reliance on Rule 258 to reach the same conclusion in *Celsteel* was available, although not canvassed. Section 70(1)(a), it will be recalled, lists as overriding interests *profits à prendre* . . . rights of way, watercourses, rights of water, and other easements not being equitable easements required to be protected by notice on the register. As is the case with *profits*, it will be observed that no distinction is made between legal and equitable rights of way. The implication seems to be, therefore, that all rights of way are overriding interests, be they legal or equitable. Why rights of way should be treated differently from other easements is, of course, not obvious, but to look for rhyme and reason in this ill-drafted paragraph is not a conspicuously rewarding task.

10.1.2 SECTION 70(1)(G) A VERY DIFFERENT AND IMPORTANT OVERRIDING INTEREST

WILLIAMS & GLYN'S BANK LIMITED v BOLAND AND ANOTHER
[1981] AC 487, House of Lords

FACTS: The title to the land was registered. Mr Boland ('H') bought a house, registered title, in his sole name. His wife ('W') made substantial contributions to the cost of acquisition, and therefore acquired a constructive trust interest in the house. While H and W were living happily together in the house, H decided to borrow some more money. Without telling his wife, he borrowed it from the bank. He granted the bank a mortgage by registered charge. The bank did not go to the trouble of sending an employee to the house, and certaiinly did not ask W any questions. H defaulted in repaying the loan, and the bank now wished to enforce their mortgage by taking possession of the house and selling. The issue was as follows: Was W's interest binding on the bank? If it was, the bank would effectively be prevented from enforcing its security.
HELD: the wife's equitable interest was binding on the bank as an 'overriding interest' due to the fact that the wife was in 'actual occupation' of the land (Land Registration Act 1925, s. 70(1)(g)).

LORD WILBERFORCE: . . . The system of land registration, as it exists in England, which long antedates the Land Registration Act 1925, is designed to simplify and to cheapen conveyancing. It is intended to replace the often complicated and voluminous title deeds of property by a single land certificate, on the strength of which land can be dealt with. In place of the lengthy and often technical investigation of title to which a purchaser was committed, all he has to do is to consult the register; from any burden not entered on the register, with one exception, he takes free. Above all, the system is designed to free the purchaser from the hazards of notice—real or constructive—which, in the case of unregistered land, involved him in enquiries, often quite elaborate, failing which he might be bound by equities. The Law of Property Act 1925 contains provisions limiting the effect of the doctrine of notice, but it still remains a potential source of danger to purchasers. By contrast, the only provisions in the Land Registration Act 1925 with regard to notice are provisions which enable a purchaser to take the estate free from equitable interests or equities whether he has notice or not. (See, for example, section 3(xv) s.v. 'minor interests'). The only kind of notice recognised is by entry on the register.

The exception just mentioned consists of 'overriding interests' listed in section 70. As to these, all registered land is stated to be deemed to be subject to such of them as may be subsisting in reference to the land, unless the contrary is expressed on the register. The land is so subject regardless of notice actual or constructive. In my opinion therefore, the law as to notice as it may affect purchasers of unregistered land, whether contained in decided cases, or in a statute (the Conveyancing Act 1882, section 3, Law of Property Act, section 199) has no application even by analogy to registered land. Whether a particular right is an overriding interest, and whether it affects a purchaser, is to be decided upon the terms of section 70, and other relevant provisions of the Land Registration Act 1925, and upon nothing else.

In relation to rights connected with occupation, it has been said that the purpose and effect of section 70(1)(g) of the Land Registration Act 1925 was to make applicable to registered land the same rule as previously had been held to apply to unregistered land: see *per* Lord Denning MR in *National Provincial Bank Ltd* v *Hastings Car Mart Ltd* [1964] Ch 665, 689, and in this House [1965] AC 1175, 1259.

I adhere to this, but I do not accept the argument which learned counsel for the appellant sought to draw from it. His submission was that, in applying section 70(1)(g), we should have regard to and limit the application of the paragraph in the light of the doctrine of notice. But this would run counter to the whole purpose of the Act. The purpose, in each system, is the same, namely, to safeguard the rights of persons in occupation, but the method used differs. In the case of unregistered land, the purchaser's obligation depends upon what he has notice of—notice actual or constructive. In the case of registered land, it is the fact of occupation that matters. If there is actual occupation, and the occupier has rights, the purchaser takes subject to them. If not, he does not. No further element is material.

I now deal with the first question. Were the wives here in 'actual occupation'? These words are ordinary words of plain English, and should, in my opinion, be interpreted as such. Historically they appear to have emerged in the judgment of Lord Loughborough LC in *Taylor* v *Stibbert* (1794) 2 Ves Jun 437, 439–440, in a passage which repays quotation:

> . . . whoever purchases an estate from the owner, knowing it to be in possession of tenants, is bound to inquire into the estates, those tenants have. It has been determined, that a purchaser being told, particular parts of the estate were in possession of a tenant, without any information as to his interest, and taking it for granted it was only from year to year, was bound by a lease, that tenant had, which was a surprise upon him. That was rightly determined; for it was sufficient to put the purchaser upon inquiry, that he was informed, the estate was not in the *actual possession* of the person, with whom he contracted; that he could not transfer the ownership and possession at the same time; that there were interests, as to the extent and terms of which it was his duty to inquire.

They were taken up in the judgment of the Privy Council in *Barnhart* v *Greenshields* (1853) 9 Moo PCC 18. The purpose for which they were used, in that case, was evidently to distinguish the case of a person who was in some kind of legal possession, as by receipt of the rents and profits, from that of a person actually in occupation as tenant. Given occupation, i.e., presence on the land, I do not think that the word 'actual' was intended to introduce any additional qualification, certainly not to suggest that possession must be 'adverse': it merely emphasises that what is required is physical presence, not some entitlement in law. So even if it were necessary to look behind these plain words into history, I would find no reason for denying them their plain meaning.

Then, were the wives in actual occupation? I ask: why not? There was physicial presence, with all the rights that occupiers have, including the right to exclude all others except those having similar rights. The house was a matrimonial home, intended to be occupied, and in fact occupied by both spouses, both of whom have an interest in it: it would require some special doctrine of law to avoid the result that each is in occupation. . . . There are observations which suggest the contrary in the unregistered land case of *Caunce* v *Caunce* [1969] 1 WLR 286, but I agree with the disapproval of these, and with the assertion of the propostion I have just stated by Russell LJ in *Hodgson* v *Marks* [1971] Ch 892, 934. Then it was suggested that the wife's occupation was nothing but the shadow of the husband's—a version I suppose of the doctrine of unity of husband and wife. This expression and the argument flowing from it was used by Templeman J in *Bird* v *Syme-Thomson* [1979] 1 WLR 440, 444, a decision preceding and which he followed in the present case. The argument was also inherent in the judgment in *Caunce* v *Caunce* [1969] 1 WLR 286 which influenced the decisions of Templeman J. It somewhat faded from the arguments in the present case and appears to me to be heavily obsolete. . . .

This brings me to the second question which is whether such rights as a spouse has under a trust for sale are capable of recognition as overriding interests—a question to my mind of some difficulty. The argument against this is based upon the structure of the Land Registration Act 1925 and upon specific provisions in it.

As to structure, it is said that the Act recognises three things: (a) legal estates, (b) minor interests, which take effect in equity, (c) overriding interests. These are mutually exclusive: an equitable interest, which is a minor interest, is incapable of being at the same time an overriding interest. The wife's interest, existing under or behind a trust for sale, is an equitable interest and nothing more. To give it the protection of an overriding interest would, moreover, contradict the principle according to which such an equitable interest can be overreached by an exercise of the trust for sale. As to the provisions of the Act, particular emphasis is placed on section 3(xv) which, in defining 'minor interests' specifically includes in the case of land held on trust for sale 'all interests and powers which are under the Law of Property Act 1925 capable of being overriden by the trustees for sale 'and excludes, expressly, overriding interests. Reliance is also placed on section 86, which, dealing analogously, so it is said, with settled land, prescribes that successive or other interests created by or arising under a settlement take effect as minor interests and not otherwise, and on section 101 which, it is argued, recognises the exclusive character of minor interests, which in all cases can be overridden.

My Lords, I find this argument formidable. To reach a conclusion upon it involves some further consideration of the nature of trusts for sale, in relation to undivided shares. The trust upon which, in this case, the land is to be held are defined—as 'statutory trusts'—in section 35 of the Law of Property Act 1925, i.e.:

> ... upon trust to sell the same and to stand possessed of the net proceeds of sale, after payment of costs, and of the net rents and profits until sale after payment of rates, taxes, cost of insurance, repairs, and other outgoings, upon such trusts, and subject to such powers and provisions, as may be requisite for giving effect to the rights of the persons ... interested in the land.

In addition to this specific disposition, the general provisions as to trusts for sale in sections 23 to 31, where not inconsistent, appear to apply. The right of occupation of the land pending sale is not explicitly dealt with in these sections and the position as to it is obscure. Before the Act the position was that owners of undivided shares (which could exist at law) had concurrent rights of occupation. In *Bull v Bull* [1955] 1 QB 234, it was held by the Court of Appeal, applying *In Re Warren* [1932] 1 Ch 42, that the conversion of these legal estates into equitable interests by the Law of Property Act 1925 should not affect the mutual rights of the owners. Denning LJ, in a judgment which I find most illuminating, there held, at p. 238 in a factual situation similar to that of the instant cases, that 'when there are two equitable tenants in common, then, until the place is sold, each of them is entitled concurrently with the other to the possession of the land and to the use and enjoyment of it in a proper manner.' And he referred to section 14 of the Law of Property Act 1925 which provides that the Act 'shall not prejudicially affect the interest of any person in possession or in actual occupation of land to which he may be entitled in right of such possession or occupation'.

How then are these various rights to be fitted into the scheme of the Land Registration Act 1925? It is clear, at least, that the interests of the co-owners under the 'statutory trusts' are minor interests—this fits with the definition in section 3(xv), But I can see no reason why, if these interests, or that of any one of them, are or is protected by 'actual occupation' they should remain merely as 'minor interests.' On the contrary, I see every reason why, in that event, they should acquire the status of overriding interests. And, moreover, I find it easy to accept that they satisfy the opening, and governing, words of section 70, namely, interests subsisting in reference to the land. As Lord Denning MR points out, to describe the interests of spouses in a house jointly bought to be lived in as a matrimonial home as merely an interest in proceeds of sale, or rents and profits until sale, is just a little unreal: see also *Elias* v *Mitchell* [1972] Ch 652, *per* Pennycuick V-C with whose analysis I agree, and contrast, *Cedar Holdings Ltd* v *Green* [1981] Ch 129 (which I consider to have been wrongly decided). . . .

. . . I would only add, in conclusion, on the appeal as it concerns the wives a brief observation on the conveyancing consequences of dismissing the appeal. These were alarming to Templeman J, and I can agree with him to the extent that whereas the object of a land registration system is to reduce the risks to purchasers from anything not on the register, to extend (if it be an extension) the area of risk so as to include possible interests of spouses, and indeed, in theory, of other members of the family or even outside it, may add to the burdens of purchasers, and involve them in enquiries which in some cases may be troublesome.

But conceded, as it must be, that the Act, following established practice, gives protection to occupation, the extension of the risk area follows necessarily from the extension, beyond the paterfamilias, of rights of ownership, itself following from the diffusion of property and earning capacity. What is involved is a departure from an easy-going practice of dispensing with enquiries as to occupation beyond that of the vendor and accepting the risks of doing so. To substitute for this a practice of more careful enquiry as to the fact of occupation, and if necessary, as to the rights of occupiers can not, in my view of the matter, be considered as unacceptable except at the price of overlooking the widespread development of shared interests of ownership. In the light of section 70 of the Act, I cannot believe that Parliament intended this, though it may be true that in 1925 it did not foresee the full extent of this development. . . .

The Law Commission (Law Com. No. 115) Property Law: the Implications of *Williams & Glyn's Bank Ltd* v *Boland*, London: HMSO, August 1982, Cmnd. 8636

70.   We are now in a position to point to those aspects of the law affected by *Boland* which we consider to be in need of reform, and to suggest what the aims of that reform should be. The consistency of *Boland* with current social policy which favours the protection of the wife in the matrimonial home is in contrast to its inconsistency with the policy of property law which upholds the security of titles, the marketability of land and the simplification of conveyancing. Whilst the law as developed in *Boland* confers a measure of protection on the wife's interest in the matrimonial home, areas of uncerainty as to the existence of that protection remain. First, there is the uncertainty about the *fact of occupation*, the purchaser not knowing whether he has discovered all the occupiers and the co-owner not knowing whether he or she will be in actual occupation at the relevant time. Secondly, there is the uncertainty as to the *right of occupation*, which may be lost through the co-owner's interest being converted into money. Thirdly, there is the uncertainty as to *co-ownership* itself, that is to say whether or not on particular facts it exists at all, and if so what is its extent. In our view the aims of law reform in this field should be to uphold social policy in the protection of the matrimonial home, to remove unnecessary complications in property law and conveyancing, and, in accordance with these general aims, to remove or reduce these areas of uncertainty. . . .

The conveyancing problem: how may a co-owner ensure that his interest is protected against a purchaser and the purchaser ensure that he takes free of co-ownersip interests of which he is unaware?

73.   The simplest and most effective way to deal with this problem would be for co-ownership interests not to be enforceable as overriding interests, or through the operation of the doctrine of constructive notice, but to be recorded on the appropriate register under the Land Registration Act 1925 (registered land) or the Land Charges Act 1972 (unregistered land). These Acts provide for the registration of certain interests and contain machinery by which purchasers take subject to these interests if they appear on the register and free of them if they do not.

HODGSON v MARKS AND ANOTHER [1971] 1 Ch 892, Court of Appeal

FACTS: The plaintiff transferred her legal title in certain land to her lodger on the understanding, orally agreed, that the plaintiff would remain equitable owner of the property. In course of time the lodger sold the house to the first defendant. The first defendant then raised a mortgage on the security of the house, the mortgagee being the second defendant to this action. The plaintiff commenced the present proceedings for a declaration that the house should be transferred to her and that the second defendant's mortgage should not be binding on her. The judge at first instance found against the plaintiff and she appealed.

HELD: The plaintiff's rights, being the rights of a person 'in actual occupation' of the land, had the status of overriding interests and were therefore binding upon the defendants.

RUSSELL LJ: . . . It is a principle of law (and of the Land Registration Act 1925) that a person in occupation is protected in his rights by that occupation, unless, of course, the rights are such that they require registration if they are to be protected. A purchaser must pay heed to anyone in occupation if he is to be sure of getting a good title. It was argued, on the basis of a quotation from the judgment of Vaughan Williams LJ in *Hunt* v *Luck* [1902] 1 Ch 428, 432 that this does not apply when the vendor is in occupation, and that (as is the fact) there is no reported case of unregistered land where a purchaser was fixed with constructive notice of the rights of any other occupier when the vendor was in occupation, and that any other view would lead to an impossible burden of inquiry on a purchaser and more particularly on a lender of money on mortgage such as the building society. (As to the defendant building society it is plain that it made no inquiries on the spot save as to repairs; it relied on Mr. Marks, who lied to it: and I waste no tears on it.) I do not think this is a real problem. Conveyancing is conducted generally upon a basis of good faith, with something of a long stop in the shape of covenants for title. Moreover, I do not consider that it is correct in law to say that any rights of a person who is in occupation will be overridden whenever the vendor is, or appears to be, also in occupation.

I do not think it desirable to attempt to lay down a code or catalogue of situations in which a person other than the vendor should be held to be in occupation of unregistered land for the purpose of constructive notice of his rights, or in actual occupation of registered land for the purposes of section 70(1)(g). It must depend on the circumstances, and a wise purchaser or lender will take no risks. Indeed, however wise he may be he may have no ready opportunity of finding out; but, nevertheless, the law will protect the occupier. Reliance upon the untrue ipse dixit of the vendor will not suffice. Take the present case—though the test of occupation must be objective. Mr Evans was only a lodger, and whether in law he was in occupation at all is at least doubtful. But the plaintiff was there for Mr. Marks to see and he saw her on two occasions. He did not introduce himself to her as an intending purchaser. He made no inquiry of her. He assumed her to be Mr. Evans' wife who knew all about the proposed purchase. This assumption may well have stemmed from a lie told by Mr. Evans, though neither Mr. Marks nor Mrs. Marks actually said so. Nonetheless, there was the plaintiff *de facto* living in the house as her house, and, if the judge's gloss were to be accepted, I should say just as much in apparent actual occupation of it as before the transfer to Mr. Evans; and, indeed, if Mr. Evans had stopped lodging there before the registration in Mr. Marks' name she would unquestionably have been in actual occupation. In short, unless it can be established in law that a person is not to be regarded as in actual occupation for the purposes of section 70(1)(g) merely because the vendor appears also to be occupying the property, it seems to me that the judge's decision on this point cannot be supported. (I observe that it was necessary for the defendants' argument on actual occupation to contend that if the plaintiff had said in conversation to Mr. Marks that it was her house and Mr. Evans her lodger, and Mr. Marks had believed Mr. Evans when he said, 'The old lady has a bee in her bonnet and is talking rubbish,' her interest would not have been enforceable against Mr. Marks because she was not in actual occupation and, accordingly, without an overriding interest.) I do not accept that proposition of law. Accordingly, I would hold that the plaintiff was at all material times a person in actual occupation of the property. . . .

To the whole of this, I venture to think, somewhat amorphous approach to the problem, the answer seems to me to be that an overriding interest is just that. A registered proprietor cannot transfer free from an overriding interest. Registration itself is subject to overriding interests. Moreover, a person who remains in actual occupation does not do anything to abandon the rights which her actual occupation protects, unless on inquiry she does not reveal them: that is what section 70(1)(g) enacts. The plaintiff did not arm Mr. Evans with the apparent ability or power to deal with the property free from any overriding interest.

I would only add that I do not consider it necessary to this decision to pronounce on the decision in *Caunce* v *Caunce* [1969] 1 WLR 286. In that case the occupation of the wife may have been rightly taken to be not her occupation but that of her husband. In so far, however, as some phrases in the judgment might appear to lay down a general proposition that enquiry need not be made of any person on the premises if the proposed vendor himself appears to be in occupation, I would not accept them.

Accordingly, I would allow the appeal with such order as may be consequential on the establishment by the plaintiff of her overriding beneficial entitlement to the premises.

ABBEY NATIONAL BUILDING SOCIETY v CANN AND ANOTHER
[1991] AC 56, House of Lords

FACTS: George Cann purchased a maisonette in his sole name. His mother (who lived with him) made a substantial contribution to the cost of the acquisition and thus was entitled to a constructive trust interest. At about 11.45 on the 13 August ('the date of completion') furniture removers acting on behalf of Mrs. Cann started laying carpets and bringing in her furniture. (She herself was on holiday in the Netherlands.) At 12.20 the same day, a land transfer was executed in favour of George. As is normal in these situations, he immediately executed a mortgage in favour of the building society. The society were, of course, lending a substantial proportion of the purchase price, and were taking the mortgage as security for the loan. Both the land transfer and the mortgage were registered on the 13 September ('the date of registration') by which time Mrs. Cann was living in the maisonette with her son. After some time, George defaulted in repaying the loan. Mrs. Cann then claimed that her constructive trust interest was an overriding interest under s. 70(1)(g), binding on the building society.

HELD: Her claim failed.

LORD OLIVER OF AYLMERTON: In the Court of Appeal Mrs Cann's claim failed because, in the view of all members of the court, she was aware that the balance of the purchase price of 7, Hillview, over and above the net amount to be produced by the sale of 30, Island Road, was going to be raised by George Cann by mortgage of the premises. Having thus impliedly authorised him to raise this amount on mortgage she must necessarily have authorised him to that extent to create a charge to the society having priority to her interest and could not, as against the society, complain that George had exceeded a limitation on his authority of which the society was unaware. Dillon LJ, however, took the view that the events which took place between 11.45 a.m. and 12.20 p.m on 13 August did constitute actual occupation of the property by Mrs. Cann sufficient to enable her to claim an overriding interest, a proposition which was doubted by Ralph Gibson and Woolf LJJ. . . .

. . . the relevant date for determining the existence of overriding interests which will 'affect the estate transferred or created' is the date of registration. This does, of course, give rise to the theoretical difficulty that since a transferor remains the registered proprietor until registration of the transfer, it would be possible for him, in breach of trust, to create overriding interests, for instance, by grant of an easement or of a lease, which would be binding on the transferee and against which the transferee would not be protected by an official search. That would, of course, equally be the case in a purchase of unregistered land where the purchaser pays the price in advance of receiving a conveyance. I cannot, however, find in the theoretical possibility of so improbable an event a context for preferring the judge's construction.

The question remains, however, whether the date of registration is also the relevant date for determining whether a claimant to a right is in actual occupation. It is to be noted that it is not the actual occupation which gives rise to the right or determines its existence. Actual occupation merely operates as the trigger, as it were, for the treatment of the right, whatever it may be, as an overriding interest. Nor does the additional quality of the right as an overriding interest alter the nature or quality of the right itself. If it is an equitable right it remains an equitable right. As was observed in *Williams & Glyn's Bank Ltd v Boland* [1981] AC 487, 504, the purpose of section 70(1)(g) was to make applicable to registered land the same rule for the protection of persons in actual occupation as had been applied in the case of unregistered land in, for instance, *Hunt v Luck* [1902] 1 Ch 428. In relation to legal rights it does nothing, for it is not easy to conceive of a legal right in the land which would not already be an overriding interest under some other head, as, for instance, paragraphs (a) or (k). Again, as regards equitable rights in an occupier which arise before completion and are supported by occupation at that date there is no difficulty. A chargee who advances money and so acquires an equitable charge prior to the creation of the occupier's right does not lose his priority because the occupier's right becomes an overriding interest. That interest remains what it always was, an interest subject to the prior equity of the chargee which, on registration, is fortified by the legal estate. Equally, a chargee advancing his money after the creation of the occupier's equitable right is, as one would expect, subject to such right.

The case which does give rise to difficulty if the date of registration is the relevant date for determining whether there is a claimant in actual occupation is one in which the sequence of events is that the right, unaccompanied by occupation, is created before completion and before the chargee has advanced his money and then subsequently the claimant enters into actual occupation after completion and remains in occupation up to the date when the registration of the charge is effected. The chargee in that event would have no possibility of discovering the existence of the claimant's interest before advancing his money and taking his charge, but would nevertheless, be subject, on registration, to the claimant's prior equitable interest which, *ex hypothesi*, would not have been subject to the charge at its creation.

   This does indeed produce a conveyancing absurdity and there is, as Nicholls LJ observed [1989] Ch 350, 374B–C, an internal context for supposing that the legislature, in enacting paragraph (g), must have been contemplating an occupation which preceded and existed at completion of a transfer or disposition. Not only was the paragraph clearly intended to reflect the rule discussed in *Hunt* v *Luck* with regard to unregistered conveyancing, but the reference to inquiry and failure to disclose cannot make any sense unless it is related to a period in which such inquiry could be other than otiose. That absurdity can, I think, be avoided only by the route which the Court of Appeal adopted and by referring the 'actual occupation' in paragraph (g) to the date of completion of the transaction by transfer and payment of the purchase money. Section 70(1) refers to such interests 'as may be for the time being subsisting' and in order to affect 'the estate transferred or created' on registration such interests would no doubt require to be subsisting on that date. But I see no insuperable difficulty in holding that the actual occupation required to support such an interest as a subsisting interest must exist at the date of completion of the transaction giving rise to the right to be registered, for that is the only date at which the inquiry referred to in paragraph (g) could, in practice, be made and be relevant. I agree, therefore, with the conclusion of the Court of Appeal in *Rosset* [1989] Ch 350 that it is at that moment that it falls to be determined whether there is an actual occupation for the purposes of paragraph (g). I do not think that I can improve upon Nicholls LJ's analysis when he said, in the course of his judgment in Rosset, at p. 374:

> If this is right, the pieces of the jigsaw fit together reasonably well. A purchaser or mortgagee inspects and inquires before completion, in the established fashion. Or he fails to do so, at this own risk. He then completes the transaction, taking an executed transfer or mortgage. Whether or not an overriding interest under paragraph (g) subsists so far as his freehold or mortgage is concerned falls to be determined at that moment. If an overriding interest does subsist, then his estate when registered takes subject to that interest. If it does not, then subsequently entry of a person into occupation before the transfer or mortgage has been registered, and 'completed' for the purposes of section 19, does not have the consequence of creating an overriding interest under paragraph (g) in relation to that freehold or mortgage. . . .

I have, up to this point, been content to assume that the facts of the instant case justify the proposition which found favour with Dillon LJ, that she was in actual occupation of the property at the material time. This is, of course, essentially a question of fact, but there is the serious question of what, in law, can amount to 'actual occupation' for the purposes of section 70(1)(g). In *Williams & Glyn's Bank Ltd* v *Boland* [1981] AC 487, 504. Lord Wilberforce observed that these words should be interpreted for what they are, that is to say, ordinary words of plain English. But even plain English may contain a variety of shades of meaning. At the date of completion Mrs. Cann was not personally even in England, leave alone in personal occupation of the property, and the trial judge held that the acts done by Mr. Abraham Cann and Mr. George Cann amounted to

> no more than the taking of preparatory steps leading to the assumption of actual residential occupation on or after completion, whatever the moment of the day when completion took place . . .

For my part, I am content to accept this as a finding of fact which was amply justified by the evidence before him, and I share the reservations expressed by Ralph Gibson and Woolf LJJ in the Court of Appeal. It is, perhaps, dangerous to suggest any test for what is essentially a question of fact, for 'occupation' is a concept which may have different connotations according to the nature and purpose of the property which is claimed to be occupied. It does not necessarily, I think, involve the personal presence of the person claiming to occupy. A caretaker or the representative of a company can occupy, I should have thought, on behalf of his employer. On the other hand, it does, in my judgment, involve some degree of permanence and continuity which would rule out mere fleeting presence. A prospective tenant or purchaser who is allowed, as a matter of indulgence, to go into property in order to plan decorations or measure for furnishing would not, in ordinary parlance, be said to be occupying it, even though he might be there for hours at a time. Of course, in the instant case, there was, no doubt, on the part of the persons involved in moving Mrs. Cann's belongings, an intention that they would remain there and would render the premises suitable for her ultimate use as a residential occupier. Like the trial judge, however, I am unable to accept that acts of this preparatory character carried out by courtesy of the vendor prior to completion can constitute 'actual occupation' for the purposes of section 70(1)(g). Accordingly, all other considerations apart, Mrs Cann fails, in my judgment, to establish the necessary condition for the assertion of an overriding interest.

Baughen, S., Some Lessons of *Cann* (1991) 55 Conv 116

At first glance *Cann* seems so uniformly in favour of the mortgagee that it would be tempting to believe that it had removed nearly all the uncertainties that have surrounded section 70(1)(g). Persons such as Mrs. Cann can no longer establish an equitable interest prior to completion. All they can obtain at this stage is a potential equitable interest. They will find it extremely difficult to establish 'actual occupation' at the date of completion. Assuming they can clear these hurdles, they will always lose out to a mortgagee, even if their potential equitable interest came first in time, if the property could not have been purchased 'but for' the mortgage. Finally, even if they succeed on all these points, they will be taken to have postponed their interest to that of the mortgagee if they knew a mortgage *might* have to be taken out. However, several uncertainties still remain.

First, there is the application of the 'but for' test. *Cann* illustrates the difficulty in applying such a test in cases of dishonesty. What *actually* happened was that £25,000 was taken out on mortgage. What *should have* happened was that only £4,000 was taken out. In the latter situation 'but for' Mrs. Cann vacating Island Road it could not have been sold and the greater part of the purchase price could not have been released. Their Lordships did not need to consider the problem of conflicting 'but for' interests because they resolved the dilemma posed by the dishonesty by focusing on what actually happened. But what if there had been a mortgage for only £4,000? The financial scales would not be substantially tilted towards Mrs. Cann, but could the mortgagee still prevail by arguing that 'but for' its lending the final £4,000 Hillview could not have been purchased? The matter could be resolved by applying the 'consent' principles of *Henning*, but suppose George had fraudulently told his mother he would make up the shortfall by his savings, and she had no reasonable grounds to disbelieve him?

Secondly, there is the issue of re-mortgages. A distinction must be drawn between further advances which have no relevance to the initial purchase, as in *Boland*, and re-mortgages which discharge the initial mortgage. The former will not take priority over the rights of those in 'actual occupation' unless they can be taken to have consented to this. The 'but for' argument is inapplicable. However, it will apply to straight re-mortgages. 'But for' the first mortgage there would be no purchase. Therefore, 'but for' the second mortgage there would be no discharge from the first mortgage. There will never be a time when the legal estate is held free from encumbrances. However, if the re-mortgage is for an amount greater than that required to discharge the first mortgage, the surplus will be treated on the same principles as *Boland*. It, therefore, follows that mortgagees must still continue to exercise the greatest care in surveying the property on which they propose to lend money.

Thirdly, a question mark still hangs over what acts can constitute 'actual occupation.' *Cann* leaves open the question of whether acts taking place prior ro the acquisition of the equitable interest which gives the *right* to occupation, are still relevant to this issue. Until this point is clarified, mortgagees need to remember that those in 'actual occupation' may not only be those claiming title through the vendor but may extend to those whose title will, on completion derive from the intending purchaser. The former's rights will usually be revealed by a thorough survey before exchange. However, the latter's can only be revealed between exchange and completion. If there is a significant delay in completion, mortgagees would be advised to make a second survey during this period and to make such a survey a condition of the advance.

Fourthly, there is the possibility that overriding interests under section 70(1)(a) and section 70(1)(k) may be created by a fraudulent vendor in the gap between transfer and registration. This is an extension of a problem that was already latent in that such interests would have been created by the vendor prior to completion without anyone being able to discover them. They will only lose priority if those claiming under them knew of the vendor's fraud. The purchaser can protect itself against such interests being created *after* completion by immediately going into 'actual occupation' then, so as to become protected by section 70(1)(g). However, there is nothing a mortgagee can do to protect itself against such a situation.

STRAND SECURITIES v CASWELL AND ANOTHER [1965] 1 Ch 958, Court of Appeal

FACTS: Caswell took a 39 year lease of a London flat. As the lease was for over 21 years, it should have been registered. Caswell did not register the lease. The practical effect of this failure to register the lease was that it only took effect as an equitable lease. The reversion was sold to Strand. They would only be bound by Caswell's lease if it was an overriding interest within the Land Registration Act 1925, s. 70(1)(g). Caswell did not personally live in the flat, but was an occasional visitor. The permanent occupant of the flat was his step-daughter. He let her live there rent-free, as her marriage had broken down.
HELD: Caswell was not in actual occupation of the premises and therefore could not claim to have an overriding interest under s. 70(1)(g).

LORD DENNING MR: . . . Even if the first defendant did not apply in time to register his sublease, he is not necessarily defeated. He may have an 'overriding interest' within section 70(1)(g). This subsection expressly preserves 'the rights of every person in actual occupation of the land or in receipt of 'the rents and profits thereof.' [His Lordship stated the facts and continued]: Section 70(1)(g) as an important provision. Fundamentally its object is to protect a person in actual occupation of land from having his rights lost in the welter of registration. He can stay there and do nothing. Yet he will be protected. No one can buy the land over his head and thereby take away or diminish his rights. It is up to every purchaser before he buys to make inquiry on the premises. If he fails to do so, it is at his own risk. He must take subject to whatever rights the occupier may have. Such is the doctrine of *Hunt v Luck* [1902] 1 Ch 428 for unregistered land. Section 70(1)(g) carries the same doctrine forward into registered land but with this difference. Not only is the actual occupier protected, but also the person from whom he holds. It is up to the purchaser to inquire of the occupier, not only about the occupier's own rights, but also about the rights of his immediate superior. The purchaser must ask the occupier: 'To whom do you pay your rent?' And the purchaser must inquire what the rights of that person are. If he fails to do so, it is at his own risk for he takes subject to 'the rights of every person in actual occupation of the land or in receipt of the rents and profits thereof.'

In this case it is clear that the second defendant was in actual occupation of the flat. The plaintiffs, therefore, took subject to her rights, whatever they were; see *National Provincial Bank Ltd v Hastings Car Mart Ltd* [1964] Ch 665. She was not a tenant but only a licensee; see *Foster v Robinson* [1951] 1 KB 149; *Cobb v Lane* [1952] 1 All ER 1199. She had no contractual right to stay there. Her licence could be determined at any time and she would have to go in a reasonable time thereafter; see *Minister of Health v Bellotti* [1944] KB 298. So the plaintiffs could get her out, provided always that they could get rid of the first defendant's sublease.

But although the second defendant was in actual occupation, it is said that the first defendant was also in actual occupation. We have had several cases lately in which we have held that 'possession in law is, of course, single and exclusive but occupation may be shared with others or had on behalf of others'; see *Hills (Patents) Ltd v University College Hospital Board of Governors* [1956] 1 QB 90, and *Willis v Association of Universities of the British Commonwealth* [1965] 1 QB 140. In this case it is said that the first defendant did share the actual occupation of the flat with the second defendant.

I would like to hold that the first defendant was sharing the occupation of the flat with the second defendant. But I cannot bring myself to this conclusion. The truth is that he allowed her to be in actual occupation, and that is all there is to it. She was a licensee rent free and I fear that it does not give him protection. It seems to be a very rare case—a case which the legislature did not think of. For it is quite clear that if the second defendant had paid a token sum as rent, or for use and occupation, to the first defendant, he would be 'in receipt of the rents and profits' and his rights would be protected under section 70(1)(g). Again if the first defendant put his servant or caretaker into the flat, rent free, he would be protected because his agent would have actual occupation on his behalf. It is odd that the first defendant is not protected simply because he let his stepdaughter in rent free. Odd as it is, however, I fear the words of the statute do not cover this case and the first defendant does not succeed on this point. . . .

WEBB v *POLLMOUNT* [1966] 1 Ch 584, Chancery Division

FACTS: L granted to Webb a legal lease to last for seven years, the lease was overriding under s. 70(1)(k). The lease also granted to Webb an option to purchase the fee simple reversion. No notice or caution was entered on the register to protect Webb's option. The fee simple was sold to Pollmount Ltd, who claimed that the option was not binding on it. HELD: Section 70(1)(g) would assist Webb. He was actually occupying the leased property at the time of the sale. Therefore his option was an overriding interest within s. 70(1)(g).

UNGOED-THOMAS . . . As a matter of first impression, 'land' in section 70(1)(g) does not appear to me to refer to an estate in land, but to the physical land. The references which are contained in the subparagraph to 'actual occupation' and 'receipt of the rents and profits thereof' indicate this conclusion: and (g) is not limited to the rights of every tenant or estate owner, but extends to the rights of every person in actual occupation. 'Registered land' and 'land' are by definition not limited to estates in land, but include physical land. In this case, the only registered land is land comprised in the title mentioned in the pleadings, namely, 'the freehold property, No. 139, High Street, Plumstead.' In the Property Register under the heading 'The Freehold Land Shown and Numbered as below on H.M. Land Registry General Map' and sub-heading 'Short Description' the entry is '139, High Street, Plumstead.' It is the Proprietorship Register which shows the title and the proprietor. The registered land as appearing from the register is the physical land, 139, High Street, Plumstead. . . .

In section 70(1)(g) itself, notice is covered by the concluding words 'save where inquiry is made of such person and the rights are not disclosed.' Thus, in this very subsection, 'the rights' are contrasted with and therefore are not defined or ascertained by reference to what constitutes notice of these rights. Notice, before the Act, is replaced by the express provision relating to notice in sub-paragraph (g) itself. So, it seems to me, that the question whether an option to purchase is a right within section 70(1)(g) has to be decided independently of what constitutes notice of those rights. But, were it necessary, for the purposes of this case, to decide what has not hitherto been decided, whether before 1926 occupation by the lessee gave constructive notice of an option to purchase contained in his lease, I would decide that it did so (in accordance with the statement in Williams on Vendor and Purchaser, 4th edn. (1936). vol. 1, p. 636, and the judgments in *Hunt* v *Luck* [1902] 1 Ch 428 and *Barnhart* v *Greenshields* (1853) 9 Moo PCC 18).

It was suggested for the defendant that 'the right of every person in actual occupation of the land' should be construed as the rights by virtue of which a person is in actual occupation of the land. The short answer to this, it seems to me, is that it does not say so; and the wording is in marked contrast with the wording in section 14 of the Law of Property Act 1925, where reference is made to the interest of a person in possession or occupation of land 'to which he may be entitled in right of such possession or occupation.' It is neither, in my view, consistent with the wording of section 70(1)(g) of the Land Registration Act 1925, nor with the authorities from which I have quoted.

Although an option to purchase does not, like an option to renew, 'touch,' 'concern' or 'affect' 'the land demised and regarded as the subject-matter of the lease ' (so as, e.g., to bind the reversion under the Grantees of Reversions Act 1540), what we are concerned with here is not whether it so 'affects' 'the land demised' and is within the relationship of landlord and tenant as considered in the judgment of the Court of Appeal in *Woodall* v *Clifton* [1905] 2 Ch 257, but whether within section 20(1)(b) it is an interest 'affecting the estate transferred' to the defendant. That it is capable of affecting the estate transferred to the defendant is not disputed; e.g., if the defendant had notice of it before transfer to him.

So, it seems to me to fall within Russell LJ's test in *National Provincial Bank Ltd* v *Hastings Car Mart Ltd* [1964] Ch 665 of 'being capable of enduring through different ownerships of the land according to normal conceptions of title to real property.' And if it, thus, in the circumstances of this case, is a right 'affecting the estate transferred,' within the requirement of section 20(1)(b), it seems to me that it is 'for the time being subsisting in reference to 'registered land within the requirement of section 70(1). My conclusion, therefore, is that subject to deciding the question as to the effect of section 59, the option to purchase appears to be an overriding interest. . . .

10.2 Minor Interests

10.2.1 PROTECTION OF MINOR INTERESTS

LAND REGISTRATION ACT 1925

20. Effect of registration of dispositions of freeholds

   (1)   In the case of a freehold estate registered with an absolute title, a disposition of the registered land or of a legal estate therein, including a lease thereof, for valuable consideration shall, when registered, confer on the transferee or grantee an estate in fee simple or the terms of years absolute or other legal estate expressed to be created in the land dealt with, together with all rights, privileges, and appurtenances belonging or appurtenant thereto, including (subject to any entry to the contrary in the register) the appropriate rights and interests which would, under the Law of Property Act 1925, have been transferred if the land had not been registered, subject—

   (a)   to the incumbrances and other entries, if any, appearing on the register [and any charge for [inheritance tax] subject to which the disposition takes effect under section 73 of this Act]; and

   (b)   unless the contrary is expressed on the register, to the overriding interests, if any, affecting the estate transferred or created,

but free from all other estates and interests whatsoever, including estates and interests of His Majesty, and the disposition shall operate in like manner as if the registered transferor or grantor were (subject to any entry to the contrary in the register) entitled to the registered land in fee simple in possession for his own benefit.

LYUS v *PROWSA DEVELOPMENTS* [1982] 1 WLR 1044, Chancery Division

FACTS: The land was registered. A land transfer was executed, expressly subject to a minor interest which had not been protected by entry on the register.
HELD: The purchaser was bound by the minor interest.

DILLON J: . . . It has been pointed out by Lord Wilberforce in *Midland Bank Trust Co. Ltd* v *Green* [1981] AC 513, 531, that it is not fraud to rely on legal rights conferred by Act of Parliament. Under section 20, the effect of the registration of the transferee of a freehold title is to confer an absolute title subject to entries on the register and overriding interests, but, 'free from all other estates and interests whatsoever, including estates and interests of His Majesty . . .' In *Miles* v *Bull* (*No. 2*) [1969] 3 All ER 1585, Bridge J expressed the view that the words which I have quoted embraced, *prima facie*, not only all kinds of legal interests, but all kinds of equitable interests: see p. 1589. He therefore held, at p. 1590, as I read his judgment, that actual or constructive notice on the part of a purchaser of an unregistered interest would not have the effect of imposing a constructive trust on him. The interest in *Miles* v *Bull* (*No. 2*) was the interest in the matrimonial home of a deserted wife who had failed to protect her interest by registration under the Matrimonial Homes Act 1967. The contract for sale between the husband, who was the registered proprietor, and the purchaser provided that the house concerned was sold, subject to such rights of occupation as might subsist in favour of the wife, with a proviso that this was not to imply that the wife had, or would after completion have any such rights as against the purchaser. Plainly, therefore, the clause was only included in the contract for the protection of the husband who was the vendor. The wife was to get no fresh rights, and it was not in *Miles* v *Bull* (*No. 2*) a stipulation of the bargain between the vendor and the purchaser that the purchaser should give effect to the rights as against the vendor of the deserted wife. *Miles* v *Bull* (*No. 2*) is thus distinguishable from the facts of the present case as I interpret those facts.

It seems to me that the fraud on the part of the defendants in the present case lies not just in relying on the legal rights conferred by an Act of Parliament, but in the first defendant reneging on a positive stipulation in favour of the plaintiffs in the bargain under which the first defendant acquired the land. That makes, as it seems to me, all the difference. It has long since been held, for instance, in *Rochefoucauld* v *Boustead* [1897] 1 Ch 196, that the provisions of the Statute of Frauds 1677 (29 Car, 2 c. 3), now incorporated in certain sections of the Law of Property Act 1925, cannot be used as an instrument of fraud, and that it is fraud for a person to whom land is agreed to be conveyed as trustee for another to deny the trust and relying on the terms of the statute to claim the land for himself. *Rochefoucauld* v *Boustead* was one of the authorities on which the judgment in *Bannister* v *Bannister* [1948] 2 All ER 133 was founded.

It seems to me that the same considerations are applicable in relation to the Land Registration Act 1925. If, for instance, the agreement of October 18, 1979, between the bank and the first defendant had expressly stated that the first defendant would hold Plot 29 upon trust to give effect for the benefit of the plaintiffs to the plaintiffs' agreement with the vendor company, it would be difficult to say that that express trust was overreached and rendered nugatory by the Land Registration Act 1925. The Land Registration Act 1925 does not, therefore affect the conclusion which I would otherwise have reached in reliance on *Bannister* v *Bannister* and the judgment of Lord Denning MR in *Binions* v *Evans* [1972] Ch 359 had Plot 29 been unregistered land.

The plaintiffs are, therefore, entitled to succeed in this action. The appropriate relief in that event is that specific performance should be ordered as against the second defendants of the sale to the plaintiffs of Plot 29, with the completed house thereon, on the terms of the agreement of January 30, 1978, made between the plaintiffs and the vendor company.

Kenny, P.H., Constructive Trust of Registered Land (1983) 46 MLR 96

Lyus v *Prowsa* [1982] 1 WLR 1044 concerned the enforceability of an unregistered third-party interest which was not an overriding interest against a transferee of registered land. The question was whether a purchaser was bound by a previous contract to sell part of the land to the plaintiff. The court held that the principle that a statute cannot be used as an instrument of fraud applied to the Land Registration Act 1925 and that in this case the purchaser was bound by a constructive trust ot the unregistered estate contract. . . .

The case is as important for what was omitted as for what was decided. Key sections of the Land Registration Act were not referred to: section 74 which states that no 'person dealing with a registered estate or charge shall be affected with notice of a trust express implied or constructive' was ignored. Similarly, section 59(1) providing that matters registerable in the case of unregistered land under the Land Charges Act 1972 are to be 'protected only by lodging a creditor's notice, a bankruptcy inhibition or a caution against dealings with the land or charge' was ignored. Presumably, the same sweeping principles of equity would have sidestepped these provisions.

The court here showed the usual judicial reluctance to grapple firmly with the mechanics of land registration. This arm's-length approach to the registration system led it not to give effect to the prescriptive system of registration in the Land Registration Act 1925. In the same way that the effect of non-registration of an estate contract is prescribed by section 4 of the Land Charges Act 1972 and had to be given effect to in *Midland Bank Trust Co. Ltd* v *Green* [1981] AC 513 so the need to register an equivalent interest in registered land is prescribed by section 59(1) of the Land Registration Act 1925 which, with section 20 and section 34(4), should have been given effect to by the court. The legislation for both registered and unregistered land makes mandatory provision for registration and is specific on the effect of non-registration. The estate contract could, under the Land Registration Act, have been protected against the charge only by registration giving priority over the charge with the bank's consent. If there is a principle of equity which allows such transparently clear provisions to be sidestepped it should at least be described with greater precision and result from a less cavalier treatment of the relevant legislation.

Harpum, C., Constructive Trusts and Registered Land
[1983] *Cambridge Law Journal* 54

The decision of Dillon J in *Lyus* v *Prowsa Developments Ltd* [1982] 1 WLR 1044 is another example of judicial unwillingness to come to terms with the Land Registration Act 1925. . . .

The consequences of the decision are far-reaching. A novel method has been found of assigning the burden of a contract that relates to property. The property is simply sold subject to those contractual rights and by the medium of a constructive trust the purchaser becomes bound by them even though he could not otherwise have been. The equitable obligation arises from the undertaking in the contract to sell the property and no mention of the liability need appear on the title. In this way, the burden of positive covenants may be transferred to a purchaser, the vendor thereby escaping liability. It also means that unregistered equitable encumbrances may be made to bind purchasers. For example, A contracts to grant a lease of unregistered land to B. B neglects to register the agreement as a Class C(iv) land charge. A then sells the land to C 'subject to' B's contract. Although by reason of section 4(6) of the Land Charges Act 1972, C should take free of B's unregistered charge: *Hollington Brothers Ltd* v *Rhodes* [1951] 2 All ER 578 *Lyus* suggests that he will not, because a constructive trust will be imposed upon him. What then if C sells the land to D without any reservation in favour of B's rights, but where D is fully aware of them and perhaps pays less for the land as a result? If the basis of the imposition of the constructive trust in *Lyus* was to prevent unconscionable conduct, then D too should be a constructive trustee. If that is correct, what has become of *Midland Bank Trust Co Ltd* v *Green* [1981] AC 513? The *Lyus* constructive trust looks to be 'remedial' rather than 'substantive' and as such without much precedent in English law, which has tended to treat constructive trusts as part of the law of property, preferring to develop the remedial possibilities of estoppel instead. It remains to be seen whether the *Lyus* constructive trust is a one-case mutant or the progenitor of a new species. . . .

PEFFER v RIGG AND ANOTHER [1977] 1 WLR 285, Chancery Division

FACTS: Title to the land was registered. Mr. Peffer and Mr. Rigg purchased a house as an investment and in order to accommodate a relative. The house was registered in Mr. Rigg's sole name, but it was agreed that he would hold the legal title on trust for himself and Mr. Peffer as tenants in common in equal shares. This arrangement was confirmed by an express deed of trust at a later date. On their divorce Mr. Rigg transferred the house to Mrs. Rigg for £1, as part of the divorce settlement. Mrs. Rigg was, accordingly, registered as sole legal proprietor. She was fully aware, throughout of the trust in favour of Mr. Peffer. Unfortunately Mr. Peffer had failed to protect his interest on the register and so the question arose whether Mrs. Rigg was bound by his interest.

HELD: Even if the £1 consideration could be treated as valuable consideration, it was still necessary for the purchaser to show that she had purchased in good faith. This she had failed to do. Consequently, she could not take advantage of the Land Registration Act, s. 59(6) which provides that 'a purchaser aquiring title under a registered disposition' shall not be concerned with unprotected minor interests, apart from overriding interests. Her lack of 'good faith' meant that she wasn't to be regarded as a 'purchaser', at all, for the purposes of this section.

In any event, the purchaser had known that the property she had received was trust property. She would therefore be liable as a constructive trustee, under normal trust principles, to account to the plaintiff for his share of the property.

GRAHAM J: . . . was the letting to Mr. and Mrs. Lewis by the defendants a breach of trust *qua* the plaintiff? I do not think so. . . .

The purported transfer, however, of the whole of the beneficial interest in the property by the first defendant to the second defendant on the occasion of the divorce agreement in the light of their knowledge of the true facts as I have found them, seems to me to be in a very different position. It was argued by Mr. Banks, for the second defendant, that the property was transferred to her for valuable consideration as part of the divorce agreement and that, therefore, the combined effect of sections 20 and 59 of the Land Registration Act 1925 protected the second defendant against any claim or interest of the plaintiff because there is no entry on the register in his favour prior to the transfer to the second defendant.

This argument would be convincing if it were not for my finding that the second defendant at the time knew perfectly well that the first defendant could not transfer to her more than a half share of the property. It is this knowledge which seems to me to cause great difficulty to her and prevents her argument succeeding for a number of different reasons put forward by Mr. Poulton for the plaintiff at the second hearing. He argues first that the purported transfer from the first defendant to the second defendant of the beneficial interest of the whole of the property of 103, Leighton Road was expressed to be for the consideration of £1. This is a nominal consideration and not valuable consideration and it follows that the second defendant is not protected by section 20 of the Land Registration Act 1925. In accordance with the provisions of section 20(4) she can only take subject to any minor interests subject to which the first defendant held the same. He was party to the trust deed of May 30, 1968, and clearly had notice of the plaintiff's half interest in the property. The second defendant can therefore only take subject to the minor interest of the plaintiff in the property subject to which the first defendant held it.

The argument to the contrary is that the transfer was only part of the whole agreement entered into by the first and second defendants on the occasion of the divorce and it is not therefore right to limit the consideration for the transfer to the £1 expressed to be therefor. The consideration, there, was a great deal more and included all the obligations undertaken by the second defendant. Such consideration was therefore not nominal but valuable within section 20 and the second defendant received the protection of the section. I do not see why, when the parties have chosen to express a transfer as being for a nominal consideration, the court should seek to hold that the consideration was in fact otherwise than as agreed and stated. If, however, the proper view is that there was valuable consideration for the transfer here, then it is argued as follows. There is a contrast between sections 20 and 59 of the Act. Section 20(1) protects any 'transferee' for valuable consideration. By section 18(5) 'transfer' and 'transferee' in relation to freehold land have very wide meanings but are not specifically defined in section 3. It is to be noted, however, that section 20, though it mentions valuable consideration, does not mention 'good faith' as being necessary on the part of the transferee, nor does it mention notice. It can be argued therefore that the section seems to be saying that a transferee whether he has good faith or not, and whether he has notice or not, takes free of all interests (other than overriding interests) provided he has given valuable consideration.

This at first sight seems a remarkable proposition and though undoubtedly the property legislation of 1925 was intended to simplify such matters of title as far as possible, I find it difficult to think that section 20 of this Act can have been intended to be as broad in scope as this. Similar doubt is expressed in *Brickdale & Stewart-Wallace's Land Registration Act 1925*, 4th edn. (1939), p. 107, note (1). The provisions for rectification in section 82 as against a proprietor in possession who has been a party to a fraud, mistake or an omission in consequence of which rectification of the register is sought also seems to me to show that section 20 must be read with some limitations: see also *Ruoff & Roper*.

Registered Conveyancing, 3rd edn. (1972), p. 417. Section 59(6) on the other hand speaks of a 'purchaser' not being affected by matters which are not protected by a caution or other entry on the register. By definition, however (see section 3(xxi)), 'purchaser' means a purchaser in good faith for valuable consideration. It seems clear therefore that as a matter of construction a purchaser who is not in fact one 'in good faith' will be concerned with matters not protected by a caution or other entry on the register, at any rate, as I hold, if he has notice thereof. If these sections 20 and 59 are read together in the context of the Act they can be reconciled by holding that if the 'transferee' spoken of in section 20 is in fact a 'purchaser' he will only be protected if he has given valuable consideration and is in good faith. He cannot in my judgment be in good faith if he has in fact notice of something which affects his title as in the present case. Of course if he and, *a fortiori*, if a purchaser from him has given valuable consideration and in fact has no notice he is under no obligation to go behind the register, and will in such a case be fully protected. This view of the matter seems to me to enable the two sections to be construed consistently together without producing the unreasonable result of permitting a transferee purchaser to take advantage of the Act, and divest himself of knowledge of defects in his own title, and secure to himself a flawless title which he ought not in justice to be allowed to obtain. This view of the Act produces a result which is also produced by applying the principles applicable in the case of a constructive trust, which I will now consider.

On the evidence in this case I have found that the second defendant knew quite well that the first defendant held the property on trust for himself and the plaintiff in equal shares. The second defendant knew this was so and that the property was trust property when the transfer was made to her, and therefore she took the property on a constructive trust in accordance with general equitable principles: see *Snell's Principles of Equity*, 27th edn. (1973), pp. 98–99. This is a new trust imposed by equity and is distinct from the trust which bound the first defendant. Even if, therefore, I am wrong as to the proper construction of sections 20 and 59, when read together, and even if section 20 strikes off the shackles of the express trust which bound the first defendant, this cannot invalidate the new trust imposed on the second defendant. . . .

CLARK v *CHIEF LAND REGISTRAR* [1993] 2 WLR 141, Chancery Division, Ferris J; [1994] 3 WLR 593, Court of Appeal, Nourse LJ

FACTS: The Jarvises, the owners of 'Spinner's Corner', owed the Clarks money under a judgment debt. The Clarks, in an effort to enforce their judgment, obtained a 'charging order' against Spinners Corner. This gave them an interest in Spinners Corner similar to that of an equitable mortgagee. They perfectly correctly 'protected' their interest by lodging a Caution.

The Jarvises then executed a legal mortgage of Spinners Corner to Jones. When Jones presented his mortgage for registration as a mortgage by registered charge, the Land Registry made a mistake. They omitted to send a warning of the proposed transaction to the Clarks. Thus the Clarks did not object to Jones registering his mortgage by registered charge.

HELD: Jones was not bound by the Clarks charging order, (even though Jones presumably knew of the Caution). However, the Clarks were entitled to claim compensation from the Land registry, whose negligence had effectively destroyed their rights.

FERRIS J: . . . On the footing that, as I have now held, the charging order obtained by the plaintiffs charges the land, the registrar contends that the plaintiffs have nevertheless suffered no loss as the result of the failure to give notice pursuant to their caution. (By 'their caution' I mean the caution lodged on 29 November 1990 in respect of their charging order absolute. Although the caution in respect of the charging order nisi remained on the register for some time it had no substantive effect after 29 November 1990). The caution remains on the register and it is said that it has the effect that, if the second defendant were to obtain the surplus proceeds of sale not required to satisfy the charge in favour of Barclays Bank Plc, he would have to satisfy the interests of the plaintiffs as cautioners before he could take anything in satisfaction of his own charge. This contention, if it were right, would be advantageous to the plaintiffs, who would not then need to seek an indemnity from the registrar. The plaintiffs do not, however, support it. On their behalf Mr. Nugee submits that it is manifestly wrong. . . .

. . . The effect of a caution was considered by the Court of Appeal in *Barclays Bank Ltd* v *Taylor* [1974] Ch 137. In this case the land certificate of registered land had been deposited with the bank by way of security and the bank had registered at the Land Registry a notice of deposit which, under the rules, had effect as a caution under section 54 of the Land Registration Act 1925. Subsequently the bank was granted a legal mortgage but before this had been registered the registered proprietors entered into a contract to sell the land to purchasers who lodged a caution to protect their interest as purchasers under the contract. The bank subsequently took steps to register its legal charge and notice of this application was given to the purchasers as cautioners. The purchasers claimed that the bank's charge should be registered only subject to their contract. The Court of Appeal held that the bank's unregistered mortgage and the purchasers' contract were both minor interests which took effect in equity only and that the priority beween them was governed by the normal rules, the interest which was first in time having priority. In giving the judgment of the court, Russell LJ made a number of observations which bear upon the effect of a caution, at p. 147:

The caution lodged on behalf of the purchasers had no effect whatever by itself on priorities: it simply conferred on the cautioners the right to be given notice of any dealing proposed to be registered . . . so that they might have the opportunity of contending that it would be a dealing which would infringe their rights and to which the applicants for the registration were not as against them entitled: . . . [The purchasers'] caution did not and could not confer on their equitable entitlement or interest any priority over the bank's equitable charge . . .

Later he observed:

counsel for [the purchasers] was quite unable to point to any provision in the statute which stated that their caution as such gave them priority in respect of their equitable interest over the earlier equitable interest of the bank under its mortgage. If such had been the intention of the legislature, it would not have been difficult for the statute to have so provided: see the express provision in section 29 on priorities between registered charges . . .

The argument on behalf of the plaintiffs was that the registrar's contention concerning the plaintiffs' caution seeks to give to that caution precisely the effect on priorities which the Court of Appeal said that a caution does not and cannot have. Moreover the suggestion that the plaintiffs have priority over the second defendant is contrary to section 29 of the Act of 1925 under which

Subject to any entry on the contrary on the register, registered charges on the same land shall as between themselves rank according to the order in which they are entered on the register, and not according to the order in which they are created.

Looking at the register immediately after the second defendant's charge was registered, that charge ranked, it is said, subject only to the prior charge of Barclays Bank Plc. It cannot rank subject to the plaintiffs' charging order, because that charging order has not been entered on the register.

The registrar's answer to this argument is based upon section 59 of the Act of 1925 and *Parkash* v *Irani Finance Ltd* [1970] Ch 101 Section 59(1) provides:

A writ, order, deed of arrangement, pending action, or other interest which in the case of unregistered land may be protected by registration under the Land Charges Act 1925 shall, where the land affected or the charge securing the debt affected is registered, be protected only by lodging a creditor's notice, a bankruptcy inhibition or a caution against dealings with the land or the charge.

As I have mentioned, section 3(3) of the Charging Orders Act 1979 now expressly permits a charging order to be protected by a notice and even before that Act was passed the registrar allowed this as a matter of discretion. However these facts do not affect the submission of the registrar, which was based on section 59(6) which provides that, subject to certain immaterial exceptions,

a purchaser acquiring title under a registered disposition, shall not be concerned with any . . . order . . . or other document, matter, or claim (not being an overriding interest) which is not protected by a caution or other entry on the register, whether he has or has not notice thereof, express, implied, or constructive.

The argument is that where a charging order *is* protected by a caution or other entry on the register a purchaser *is* 'affected by it' and that, in the context, 'affected by it' means that he takes subject to it. It was submitted that this had been held to be so in *Parkash* v *Irani Finance Ltd* and that this view was endorsed in *Megarry and Wade, The Law of Real Property*, 5th edn. (1984), p. 213, footnote 88.

In *Parkash* v *Irani Finance Ltd* [1970] Ch 101 the defendant obtained a charging order on registered land which it protected by lodging a caution. The plaintiff entered into a contract to purchase the land and his solicitors obtained an official search which, by an error, did not disclose the caution. The plaintiff then completed his purchase and executed a legal charge over the property. When the transfer in favour of the plaintiff and the charge executed by him were presented for registration, notice was given to the defendant as cautioner. The defendant objected to these instruments being registered until its charge had been redeemed. The registrar, in accordance with the rules, ordered that the following questions be referred to the court: (a) whether the caution should continue to have effect or be cancelled; and (b) if the caution was to continue to have effect the order of priority in which the charging order to Irani, the transfer to the plaintiff and the charge to the plaintiff's mortgagee should be entered on the register. The report of the argument shows that it was accepted on behalf of the plaintiff that, unless there was something to give priority to the transfer in his favour (which at that stage took effect in equity only by virtue of section 106 of the Land Registration Act 1925) the prior equity of Irani must prevail. It was contended that the plaintiff's transfer should have priority because the plaintiff had no notice of the interest protected by the caution and, if it were not for the caution, would have become a purchaser for value without notice. The main argument for Irani was that the ordinary doctrine of notice had no application to registered land. If it were applicable it would be in conflict with section 59. The plaintiff's mortgagee supported the plaintiff's argument and raised other arguments which do not matter for present purposes.

Plowman J rejected the plaintiff's argument based on the absence of notice. In doing so he referred to section 59(6) and said [1970] Ch 101, 110:

> It is true, as was stressed in the argument before me, that what the subsection says is that a purchaser is *not* affected by notice, express, implied or constructive, of matters capable of protection by a caution and not so protected and that (unlike the case of a notice of lease under section 48(1) of the Act) it does not say in terms that a purchaser *is* affected by a notice of matters capable of protection by caution, which *are* so protected, but that, in my judgment, is implicit in the scheme of the Act and in the subsection.

He went on to hold first that the appropriate form of protection for a charging order is a caution (this may, it seems, have been before the registrar began to allow protection by notice); secondly that once the caution is registered the cautioner could only lose his protection in various specific ways which were not applicable to that case; and thirdly, at p. 111:

> that therefore he does not lose it merely because a purchaser of the property does not know of its existence, even if the purchaser's ignorance is the result of a mistake of the Land Registry, short of a failure to act on an application to register the caution in the first place.

His ultimate conclusion, at p. 112, was that 'Irani's caution should continue to have effect and that it takes priority over the transfer of 10 August 1967 and the charge of the same date.'

I have thought it necessary to summarise *Parkash v Irani Finance Ltd* [1970] Ch 101 in some detail because Mr. Nugee contended, on behalf of the plaintiffs, that although the reasoning of Plowman J might appear to support the registrar's argument, this was not in fact the case. Mr. Nugee supported that part of the reasoning which rejected the argument that the principles of notice applicable to unregistered land were also applicable to registered land, in so far as this reasoning did not depend on section 59(6). That was all that was necessary to decide the case. The plaintiff could not establish that he was a purchaser of a legal estate because, at the time when the matter came before the court, he did not have the legal estate. Accordingly the contest was between two equitable interests and, in accordance with the principles subsequently applied in *Barclays Bank Ltd v Taylor* [1974] Ch 137, the interest of Irani prevailed because it was first in time. When, at the end of his judgment, Plowman J said that Irani's caution took priority over the transfer in favour of the plaintiff and the charge executed by him, he should be taken as meaning that the charging order protected by the caution took priority. That was, in substance the answer to the second question which had been referred to the court by the registrar. I note that Mrs. Crampin sought instructions as to what entries had been made in the register pursuant to the order of Plowman J, but the answer was unhelpful as it appears that the registrar indemnified Irani and cancelled the caution, so leaving the field open for registration of the plaintiff and his mortgagee.

Mr. Nugee contended that the observations of Plowman J on section 59(6) were unnecessary to his decision and, in so far as they suggest that a caution has, in some respects at least, an effect similar to that of a notice, they were inconsistent with section 56(2) and with the emphatic statements of the Court of Appeal in *Barclays Bank Ltd* v *Taylor* and ought not to be followed. *Parkash* v *Irani Finance Ltd* [1970] Ch 101 was cited in argument in *Barclays Bank Ltd* v *Taylor* [1974] Ch 137 but was not commented upon in the judgment. In my judgment Mr. Nugee's submissions concerning *Parkash* v *Irani Finance Ltd* [1970] Ch 101 are correct. I doubt whether Plowman J intended to suggest that a caution had much the same effect as a notice. In so far as his language, may suggest otherwise I must, I think, decline to apply it. If I were to do so I would, it appears to me, ignore the binding reasoning of *Barclays Bank Ltd* v *Taylor* [1974] Ch 137.

NOURSE LJ: . . . The views expressed by . . . this court in *Barclays Bank Limited* v *Taylor* are decisive of the caution point. They have the very great merit of having been based essentially on those provisions—sections 54 to 56 of the Act of 1925—which were clearly intended to describe and declare the nature and effect of cautions against dealings. They show that it is for that purpose unnecessary to look beyond those provisions. The deletion of Sir George Curtis's and Mr. Ruoff's original firm opinion that cautions do not confer any kind of priority, an opinion which is as correct now as it was then, is of no significance. The lack of priority remains implicit in the revised version. Moreover, the attempts made in argument to depreciate the manifest value of the views expressed in *Barclays Bank Ltd* v *Taylor* were unsuccessful.

The principal consequence of the arguments advanced on behalf of the Chief Land Registrar and Mr. Ketteringham was to demonstrate the unwisdom of straying from sections 54 to 56 to other provisions of the Act of 1925. It is hardly surprising that counsel were able to extract from legislation 'of exceptionally low quality' provisions which, on a myopic view, give some semblance of support for those arguments. None of those provisions can prevail over the clear effect of sections 54 to 56.

In this court, as in the courts below, the Chief Land Registrar relied principally on section 59(1) and (6) of the Act of 1925 and *Parkash* v *Irani Finance Ltd* [1970] Ch 101. For the reasons given by Ferris J [1993] Ch 294, 311F to 313H, I agree with him that those provisions and that decision do not assist them. For myself, I am certain that Plowman J a judge of great experience in conveyancing matters, did not intend to suggest that a caution had much the same effect as a notice.

The other provision of the Act of 1925 on which the Chief Land Registrar mainly relied was section 20(1)(a). While I would certainly accept that cautions, once recorded in the Registry, are 'entries . . . appearing on the register' within that provision and that, what it means is 'subject to rights and interests created by any document or transaction recorded as an entry'—see *Kitney* v *MEPC Ltd* [1977] 1 WLR 981, 989G—like Ferris J, I am unable to see how it can elevate cautions to a status and effect not given to them by sections 54 to 56. The same answer can be given to an argument based on that part of rule 220(3) which empowers the registrar to order that the caution shall continue to have effect.

In my view Ferris J's decision of the caution point was, like his decision of the charging order point, correct. As I have said, the Chief Land Registrar's contention as to the rectification point was abandoned during the argument in this court. There can be no doubt that the judge's decision of that point was also correct.

10.3   End of Chapter Assessment Question

George is currently setting himself up as a farmer. In the last month he has acquired the following property rights.

(a)   A freehold title to Broad Field acquired from Harry. The title is unregistered, and Harry was only able to produce one title deed, the conveyance to him when he bought the land ten years ago.

(b)   The grant of a new lease for 30 years over Wide Field.

(c)   The grant of a new lease over Low Field for 8 years.

(d)   The grant of a profit to graze 100 sheep on East Moor. The profit is to last for George's lifetime.

(e)   An agreement for a right of way across West Meadow to get to Broad Field.

Advise George as to:

(i)   which of these property rights will acquire substantive registration;

(ii)   the effects of such registration;

(iii)   the consequences of failure to register a title which should have been registered;

(iv)   whether any of the rights which are not capable of substantive registration should be protected by an entry on the Register of Title or on the Land Charges Register.

10.4   End of Chapter Assessment Outline Answer

(a)(i)   When George buys Harry's freehold title to Broad Field there will be clearly a 'conveyance on sale' which will oblige George to register that title. (Since 1990 the whole country has been a compulsory area of registration of title.)

(b)(i)   When George applies for the first registration of his freehold title to Blue Field, there will be the problem that he will only be able to produce a 'root of title' which is ten years old, rather than the requisite fifteen. As things stand at the moment somebody (call him X) might still come along and (1) produce documents proving that X was originally owner of Broad Field and (2) prove that X's rights have not yet been 'time-barred' by adverse possession.

The Land Registry are thus unlikely to grant George an 'absolute title' guaranteeing that he is outright owner of the land. They might conceivably grant George a 'Qualified Title' guaranteeing that, except for claims arising more than ten years ago which are not time-barred, he is owner of the land. However, it is not the general practice for the registry to grant qualified titles.

Almost certainly the Registry will grant George a possessory title. This will not guarantee George against any competing claims to Broad Field which arise before the date of registration. The value of this possessory title to George will initially be limited. But if he remains in undisputed control of Broad Field for twelve years his title will be upgraded to absolute. (Assuming George registers in early 1996, he will get an absolute title in 2008.)

(c)(i)   If George fails to register within two months of the conveyance, the legal title to Broad Field will revest in Harry in trust for George. George will thus only have an equitable fee simple.

This 'sanction' is not a severe one. George can always apply for late registration, which will revest the legal title in himself. The registry could charge him a 'late fee', but in practice the registry only rarely require the payment of such a fee.

(a)(ii) As the lease of Wide Field is over twenty-one years, it will also require registration.

(b)(ii) If the freehold reversion to Wide Field is registered with absolute title, then George will be granted an absolute leasehold title to the field, giving him a firm guarantee that he has a thirty year lease.

If the reversion is unregistered then George will only get a good leasehold title (unless he can persuade his landlord to produce his deeds to the registry). Good leasehold guarantees George's lease only on the assumption that the landlord's title is sound. (I.e., if somebody came along and proved that he had a better title to Wide Field than George's 'landlord', George will lose his lease and will have no claim against the registry.)

(c)(ii) If George fails to register within two months he will cease to have a legal lease and will (in effect) only have an equitable lease. George can always apply for late registration, which will revest a legal lease in himself. Again, the registry might possibly charge him a 'late fee'.

(a)(iii) A lease for not more than twenty-one years is not capable of substantive registration.

(d)(iii) Provided the lease of Low Field is by deed, there is no further action which George need take to protect his right to Low Field. If the reversion to Low Field is unregistered, then George has a legal lease which is automatically binding on the whole world. If the reversion to the lease is registered then George will have an overriding interest within the Land Registration Act 1925, s. 70(1)(k) which will be binding on the purchaser of the reversion. (George need not worry about whether he is an 'actual occupation'.)

(d)(iv) A profit is not capable of substantive registration. As this profit only lasts for George's lifetime, it is outside the scope of the Law of Property Act 1925, s. 1(2) and is purely equitable. Thus if the title to East Moor is unregistered, George should register his profit as a class D(iii) landcharge. If he fails to do so, his profit would be void against a purchaser for money or money's worth of East Moor.

If the title to East Moor is registered, George need do nothing to protect his profit. He has an overriding interest within the Land Registration Act 1925, s. 70(1)(a), a provision which extends to both legal and equitable profits.

(d)(v) This right is clearly an equitable easement (there is no deed) and it is not capable of substantive registration. If the title to West Meadow is unregistered, George should register his easement as a class D(iii) landcharge. If he fails to do so, his easement will be void against a purchaser for money or money's worth of West Meadow.

If the title to West Meadow is registered, then it is debatable whether George's easement is an overriding or minor interest. The wording of section 70(1)(a) suggests that an equitable easement can only be a minor interest. However in *Alton House* Scott J held that an equitable easement was an overriding interest which bound a purchaser of the servient land even though it had not been protected by an entry on the register.

This is a very questionable decision, and George should act on the assumption that it is wrong. He should protect his interest by entry of a Notice or Caution. A 'Notice' is preferable, but to enter one against West Meadow he will need to produce the Land Certificate to the registry.

If the owner of West Meadow will not agree to the production of the Land Certificate, then George should lodge a 'Caution'. In theory this only entitles him to fourteen days warning of proposed transactions with West Meadow, though in practice all but foolhardy purchasers will be put off by the presence of the Caution.

CHAPTER ELEVEN

SETTLEMENTS OF LAND

11.1 Introduction

Harvey, B.W., *Settlements of Land*, London: Sweet & Maxwell, 1973, p. 3

. . . It is now comparatively rare to find large tracts of land in England still the subject of the traditional family settlement. There are in essence two reasons, one economic and one fiscal.

The economic reason is that from about the middle of the nineteenth century onwards it became plain that there was no inherent superiority in land as an investment for wealth. Investment in land which had been in the family for many years had, it is true, a strong sentimental attraction, but at this time the growth of the joint stock company combined with readily available facilities for lending money at interest, whether privately or to the government, provided alternative uses for wealth. England was becoming more of a trading than of an agricultural nation and the demand for coal and other minerals made it more desirable for mineral leases to be granted for exploitation of the underground wealth of the land. The growth of the population also put pressure on land for housing development. Land subject to the traditional family settlements was ill-suited for these purposes. Large tracts were vested in limited owners with inadequate powers of disposition, the land itself being burdened with charges in favour of other members of the family. Agricultural depression, too, became an issue in 1879 when the government appointed a Royal Commission to investigate the condition of farmers. The depression was caused basically by the repeal of the Corn Laws which after a time resulted in the cheap importation of foreign grain. Farming tended to be inefficient and unscientific and tenant farmers suffered particularly badly. Landlords were forced to lower rents, but the fixed charges payable out of their land, if settled, remained. The result in their case too was a decline in standards of living . . . so that it became much less easy for any settlor to ordain whether the family wealth should be held in the form of land or personalty.

The fiscal reason stems from the drastic steepening of the rates of income tax, surtax and estate duty since the early 1900s. . . . The impact of taxation, which bears on the nominal value of money, has been increased by a steady decline in the real value (or purchasing power) of the currency. Apart from a period between the wars, the average loss in value of the pound since 1900 has been about 4 per cent per annum. This reduces the value of £1 to 1/4d. (7p.) over seventy years. These taxes are adverse to large landholdings in that as far as taxes on income are concerned, in order to retain spending power it is necessary to keep raising rents (where not controlled by statute) or otherwise make the land yield money, and owners were often either unable or unwilling to do this. . . .

11.2   The Traditional Strict Settlement

SETTLED LAND ACT 1925

THIRD SCHEDULE

PART I   IMPROVEMENTS, THE COSTS OF WHICH ARE NOT LIABLE TO BE
REPLACED BY INSTALMENTS

(i)   Drainage, including the straightening, widening, or deepening of drains, streams, and watercourses:

(ii)   Bridges:

(iii)   Irrigation; warping:

(iv)   Drains, pipes, and machinery for supply and distribution of sewage as manure:

(v)   Embanking or weiring from a river or lake, or from the sea, or a tidal water:

(vi)   Groynes; sea walls; defences against water:

(vii)   Inclosing; straightening of fences; re-division of fields:

(viii)   Reclamation; dry warping:

(ix)   Farm roads; private roads; roads or streets in villages or towns:

(x)   Clearing; trenching; planting:

(xi)   Cottages for labourers, farm-servants, and artisans, employed on the settled land or not:

(xii)   Farmhouses, offices, and outbuildings, and other buildings for farm purposes:

(xiii)   Saw-mills, scutch-mills, and other mills, water-wheels, engine-houses, and kilns, which will increase the value of the settled land for agricultural purposes or as woodland or otherwise:

(xiv)   Reservoirs, tanks, conduits, watercourses, pipes, wells, ponds, shafts, dams, weirs, sluices, and other works and machinery for supply and distribution of water for agricultural, manufacturing, or other purposes or other consumption:

(xv)   Tramways; railways; canals; docks:

(xvi)   Jetties, piers, and landing places on rivers, lakes, the sea, or tidal waters, for facilitating transport of persons and of agricultural stock and produce, and of manure and other things required for agricultural purposes, and of minerals, and of things required for mining purposes:

(xvii)   Markets and market-places:

(xviii) Streets, roads, paths, squares, gardens, or other open spaces for the use, gratuitously or on payment, of the public or of individuals, or for dedication to the public, the same being necessary or proper in connexion with the conversion of land into building land:

(xix)   Sewers, drains, watercourses, pipe-making, fencing, paving, brick-making, tile-making, and other works necessary or proper in connexion with any of the objects aforesaid:

(xx)   Trial pits for mines, and other preliminary works necessary or proper in connexion with development of mines:

(xxi)   Reconstruction, enlargement, or improvement of any of those works:

(xxii)   The provision of small dwellings, either by means of building new buildings or by means of the reconstruction, enlargement, or improvement of existing buildings, if that provision of small dwellings is, in the opinion of the court, not injurious to the settled land or is agreed to by the tenant for life and the trustees of the settlement:

(xxiii) Additions to or alterations in buildings reasonably necessary or proper to enable the same to be let:

(xxiv) Erection of buildings in substitution for buildings within an urban sanitary district taken by a local or other public authority, or for buildings taken under compulsory powers, but so that no more money be expended than the amount received for the buildings taken and the site thereof:

(xxv)   The rebuilding of the principal mansion house on the settled land:

Provided that the sum to be applied under this head shall not exceed one-half of the annual rental of the settled land.

PART II   IMPROVEMENTS, THE COSTS OF WHICH THE TRUSTEES OF THE SETTLEMENT OR THE COURT MAY REQUIRE TO BE REPLACED BY INSTALMENTS

(i)   Residential houses for land or mineral agents, managers, clerks, bailiffs, woodmen, gamekeepers and other persons employed on the settled land, or in connexion with the management or development thereof:

(ii)   Any offices, workshops and other buildings of a permanent nature required in connexion with the management or development of the settled land or any part thereof:

(iii)   The erection and building of dwelling houses, shops, buildings for religious, eduational, literary, scientific, or public purposes, market places, market houses, places of amusement and entertainment, gasworks, electric light or power works, or any other works necessary or proper in connexion with the development of the settled land, or any part thereof as a building estate:

(iv)   Restoration or reconstruction of buildings damaged or destroyed by dry rot:

(v)   Structural additions to or alterations in buildings reasonably required, whether the buildings are intended to be let or not, or are already let:

(vi)   Boring for water and other preliminary works in connexion therewith.

PART III   IMPROVEMENTS, THE COSTS OF WHICH THE TRUSTEES OF THE SETTLEMENT AND THE COURT MUST REQUIRE TO BE REPLACED BY INSTALMENTS

(i)   Heating, hydraulic or electric power apparatus for buildings, and engines, pumps, lifts, rams, boilers, flues, and other works required or used in connexion therewith:

(ii)   Engine houses, engines, gasometers, dynamos, accumulators, cables, pipes, wiring, switchboards, plant and other works required for the installation of electric, gas, or other artificial light, in connexion with any principal mansion house, or other house or buildings; but not electric lamps, gas fittings, or decorative fittings required in any such house or building:

(iii)   Steam rollers, traction engines, motor lorries and moveable machinery for farming or other purposes.

11.3   Introduction to the Settled Land Acts

11.3.1   SETTLED LAND DEFINED

SETTLED LAND ACT 1925

1.   What constitutes a settlement

(1)   Any deed, will, agreement for a settlement or other agreement, Act of Parliament, or other instrument, or any number of instruments, whether made or passed before or after, or partly before and partly after, the commencement of this Act, under or by virtue of which instrument or instruments any land, after the commencement of this Act, stands for the time being—

(i)   limited in trust for any persons by way of succession; or

(ii)   limited in trust for any person in possession—

(a)   for an entailed interest whether or not capable of being barred or defeated;

(b)   for an estate in fee simple or for a term of years absolute subject to an executory limitation, gift, or disposition over on failure of his issue or in any other event;

(c)   for a base or determinable fee or any corresponding interest in leasehold land;

(d)   being an infant, for an estate in fee simple or for a term of years absolute; or

(iii)   limited in trust for any person for an estate in fee simple or for a term of years absolute contingently on the happening of any event; or

(iv)   . . .

(v)   charged, whether voluntary or in consideration of marriage or by way of family arrangement, and whether immediately or after an interval, with the payment of any rentcharge for the life of any person, or any less period, or of any capital, annual, or periodical sums for the portions, advancement, maintenance, or otherwise for the benefit of any persons, with or without any term of years for securing or raising the same;
creates or is for the purposes of this Act a settlement and is in this Act referred to as a settlement, or as the settlement, as the case requires:
Provided that, where land is the subject of a compound settlement, references in this Act to the settlement shall be construed as meaning such compound settlement, unless the context otherwise requires.

(2)   Where an infant is beneficially entitled to land for an estate in fee simple or for a term of years absolute and by reason of an intestacy or otherwise there is no instrument under which the interest of the infant arises or is acquired, a settlement shall be deemed to have been made by the intestate, or by the person whose interest the infant has acquired.

(3)   . . .

(4)   An estate or interest not disposed of by a settlement and remaining in or reverting to the settlor, or any person deriving title under him, is for the purposes of this Act an estate or interest comprised in the subject of the settlement and coming to the settlor or such person under or by virtue of the settlement.

(5)   Where—
    (a)   a settlement creates an entailed interest which is incapable of being barred or defeated, or a base or determinable fee, whether or not the reversion or right of reverter is in the Crown, or any corresponding interest in leasehold land; or
    (b)   the subject of a settlement is an entailed interest, or a base or determinable fee, whether or not the reversion or right of reverter is in the Crown, or any corresponding interest in leasehold land;
the reversion or right of reverter upon the cesser of the interests so created or settled shall be deemed to be an interest comprised in the subject of the settlement, and limited by the settlement.

(6)   Subsections (4) and (5) of this section bind the Crown.

(7)   This section does not apply to land held upon trust for sale.

2.   What is settled land

Land which is or is deemed to be the subject of a settlement is for the purposes of this Act settled land, and is in relation to the settlement referred to in this Act as the settled land.

4.   Authorised method of settling land inter vivos

(1)   Every settlement of a legal estate in land inter vivos shall, save as in this Act otherwise provided, be effected by two deeds, namely, a vesting deed and a trust instrument and if effected in any other way shall not operate to transfer or create a legal estate.

(2)   By vesting deed the land shall be conveyed to the tenant for life or statutory owner (and if more than one as joint tenants) for the legal estate the subject of the intended settlement:
Provided that, where such legal estate is already vested in the tenant for life or statutory owner, if shall be sufficient, without any other conveyance, if the vesting deed declares that the land is vested in him for that estate.

(3)   The trust instrument shall—
    (a)   declare the trusts affecting the settled land;
    (b)   appoint or constitute trustees of the settlement;
    (c)   contain the power, if any, to appoint new trustees of the settlement;
    (d)   set out, either expressly or by reference, any powers intended to be conferred by the settlement in extension of those conferred by this Act;
    (e)   bear any ad valorem stamp duty which may be payable (whether by virtue of the vesting deed or otherwise) in respect of the settlement.

5.   Contents of vesting deeds

(1)   Every vesting deed for giving effect to a settlement or for conveying settled land to a tenant for life or statutory owner during the subsistence of the settlement (in this Act

referred to as a 'principal vesting deed') shall contain the following statements and particulars, namely:—

(a)   A description, either specific or general, of the settled land;

(b)   A statement that the settled land is vested in the person or persons to whom it is conveyed or in whom it is declared to be vested upon the trusts from time to time affecting the settled land;

(c)   The names of the persons who are the trustees of the settlement;

(d)   Any additional or larger powers conferred by the trust instrument relating to the settled land which by virtue of this Act operate and are exercisable as if conferred by this Act on a tenant for life;

(e)   The name of any person for the time being entitled under the trust instrument to appoint new trustees of the settlement. . . .

6.   Procedure in the case of settlements by will

Where a settlement is created by the will of an estate owner who dies after the commencement of this Act—

(a)   the will is for the purposes of this Act a trust instrument; and

(b)   the personal representatives of the testator shall hold the settled land on trust, if and when required so to do, to convey it to the person who, under the will, or by virtue of this Act, is the tenant for life or statutory owner, and, if more than one, as joint tenants.

7.   Procedure on change of ownership

(1)   If, on the death of a tenant for life or statutory owner, or of the survivor of two or more tenants for life or statutory owners, in whom the settled land was vested, the land remains settled land, his personal representatives shall hold the settled land on trust, if and when required so to do, to convey it to the person who under the trust instrument or by virtue of this Act becomes the tenant for life or statutory owner and, if more than one, as joint tenants.

13.   Dispositions not to take effect until vesting instrument is made

Where a tenant for life or statutory owner has become entitled to have a principal vesting deed or a vesting assent executed in his favour, then until a vesting instrument is executed or made pursuant to this Act in respect of the settled land, any purported disposition thereof inter vivos by any person, other than a personal representative (not being a disposition which he has power to make in right of his equitable interests or powers under a trust instrument), shall not take effect except in favour of a purchaser of a legal estate without notice of such tenant for life or statutory owner having become so entitled as aforesaid but, save as aforesaid, shall operate only as a contract for valuable consideration to carry out the transaction after the requisite vesting instrument has been executed or made, and a purchaser of a legal estate shall not be concerned with such disposition unless the contract is registered as a land charge.

Nothing in this section affects the creation or transfer of a legal estate by virtue of an order of the court or the Minister or other competent authority.

11.3.2   ACCIDENTAL SETTLEMENTS CONVEYING LAND SUBJECT TO A RIGHT TO RESIDE

BINIONS v EVANS [1972] 1 Ch 359, Court of Appeal

FACTS: The trustees of the Tredegar Estate owned a cottage in which there resided rent-free Mrs. Evans, the widow of an employee of the Estate. The trustees sold the cottage to Binions, expressly on the condition that Mrs. Evans should be allowed to live there for the rest of her life. Binions paid a reduced price because of this condition. Binions nevertheless tried to evict Mrs. Evans; he claimed that she had no propietary interest in the land.

HELD: Not surprisingly, Binions found no sympathy in the Court of Appeal. The majority of the Court of Appeal (Megaw and John Stephenson LJJ) held that the conveyance to Binions created a life interest in favour of Mrs. Evans. Therefore the land was 'settled land' within the meaning of the 1925 Act, with Mrs. Evans as life tenant.

LORD DENNING MR: . . . Seeing that the defendant has no legal estate or interest in the land, the question is what right has she? At any rate, she has a contractual right to reside in the house for the remainder of her life or as long as she pleases to stay. I know that in the agreement it is described as a tenancy: but that does not matter. The question is: What is it in reality? To my mind it is a licence, and no tenancy. It is a privilege which is personal to her. On all the modern cases, which are legion, it ranks as a contractual licence, and not a tenancy: see *Shell-Mex and BP Ltd v Manchester Garages Ltd* [1971] 1 WLR 612.

What is the status of such a licence as this? There are a number of cases in the books in which a similar right has been given. They show that a right to occupy for life, arising by contract, gives to the occupier an equitable interest in the land: just as it does when it arises under a settlement: see *In re Carne's Settled Estates* [1899] 1 Ch 324 and *In re Boyer's Settled Estates* [1916] 2 Ch 404. The courts of equity will not allow the landlord to turn the occupier out in breach of the contract: see *Foster v Robinson* [1951] 1 KB 149, 156; nor will they allow a purchaser to turn her out if he bought with knowledge of her right—*Errington v Errington and Woods* [1952] 1 KB 290, 299.

It is instructive to go back to the cases before the Supreme Court Judicature Act 1873. They show that, if a landlord, by a memorandum in writing, let a house to someone, let us say to a widow, at a rent, for her life or as long as she pleased to stay, the courts of equity would not allow the landlord to turn her out in breach of his contract. If the landlord were to go to the courts of law and obtain an order in ejectment against her, as in *Doe d Warner v Browne*, 8 East 165, the courts of equity would grant an injunction to restrain the landlord from enforcing his rights at law, as in *Browne v Warner* (1808) 14 Ves 409. The courts of equity would give the agreement a construction, which Lord Eldon LC called an 'equitable construction,' and construe it as if it were an agreement to execute a deed granting her a lease of the house for her life—*Browne v Warner*, 14 Ves 156, 158. They would order the landlord specifically to perform the contract, so construed, by executing such a deed. This court did so in *Zimbler v Abraham* [1903] 1 KB 577. This means that she had an equitable interest in the land. So much so that if a purchaser wished to buy her interest from her, he had to pay her its full value as such. Malins V-C so held in *In re King's Leasehold Estates* (1873) LR 16 Eq 521, 527, where he described it as an 'equitable interest.' It follows that, if the owner sold his reversion to another, who took with notice of the widow's interest, his successor could not turn her out any more than he could. She would have, I should have thought, at least as strong a case as the occupier in *Webb v Paternoster* (1619) Poph 151, which received the blessing of Lord Upjohn in *National Provincial Bank Ltd v Hastings Car Mart Ltd* [1965] AC 1175, 1239.

Suppose, however, that the defendant did not have an equitabe interest at the outset, nevertheless it is quite plain that she obtained one afterwards when the Tredegar Estate sold the cottage. They stipulated with the plaintiffs that they were to take the house 'subject to' the defendant's rights under the agreement. They supplied the plaintiffs with a copy of the contract: and the plaintiffs paid less because of her right to stay there. In these circumstances, this court will impose on the plaintiffs a constructive trust for her benefit: for the simple reason that it would be utterly inequitable for the plaintiffs to turn the defendant out contrary to the stipulation subject to which they took the premises. That seems to me clear from the important decision *Bannister v Bannister* [1948] 2 All ER 133, which was applied by the judge, and which I gladly follow.

This imposing of a constructive trust is entirely in accord with the precepts of equity. As Cardozo J once put it: 'A constructive trust is the formula through which the conscience of equity finds expression,' see *Beatty v Guggenheim Exploration Co.* (1919) 225 NY 380, 386: or, as Lord Diplock put it quite recently in *Gissing v Gissing* [1971] AC 886, 905, a constructive trust is created 'whenever the trustee has so conducted himself that it would be inequitable to allow him to deny to the cestui que trust a beneficial interest in the land acquired.'

. . . At any rate when the licensee is in actual occupation of the land, so that the purchaser must know he is there, and of the rights which he has: see *Hodgson v Marks* [1971] Ch 892. Whenever the purchaser takes the land impliedly subject to the rights of the contractual licensee, a court of equity will impose a constructive trust for the beneficiary. So I still adhere to the proposition I stated in *Errington v Errington and Woods* [1952] 1 KB 290, 299; and elaborated in *National Provincial Bank Ltd v Hastings Car Mart Ltd* [1964] Ch 665, 686–689, namely, that when the licensee is in actual occupation, neither the licensor nor anyone who claims through him can disregard the contract except a purchaser for value without notice.

5. *Conclusion*

In my opinion the defendant, by virtue of the agreement, had an equitable interest in the cottage which the court would protect by granting an injunction against the landlords restraining them from turning her out. When the landlords sold the cottage to a purchaser 'subject to' her rights under the agreement, the purchaser took the cottage on a constructive trust to permit the defendant to reside there during her life, or as long as she might desire. The courts will not allow the purchaser to go back on that trust. I entirely agree with the judgment of Judge Bulger. I would dismiss this appeal.

STEPHENSON LJ: . . . The words 'tenant for life' are not used, but that in one sense is what the landlords are agreeing that this widow should become. If, however, these words were in the agreement they would be used like 'tenant at will' in the context of the whole agreement as conferring a life interest, whatever called or however described, which was determinable by the so-called tenant for life on four weeks' notice or by ceasing permanently to live in the cottage.

Apart from authority, I would not have thought that such an interest could be understood to amount to a tenancy for life within the meaning of the Settled Land Act 1925, and I would have thought that the other terms of her tenancy (as I think it ought properly to be called) are inconsistent with a power to ask for the legal estate to be settled on her or to sell the cottage. But *Bannister* v *Bannister* [1948] 2 All ER 133 is a clear decision of this court that such words as have been used in this agreement (excepting, I must concede, the words 'as tenant at will of them') create a life interest determinable (apart from the special considerations introduced by the Settled Land Act 1925) on the beneficiary ceasing to occupy the premises and the landlords hold the cottage on trust to permit her to occupy it 'during her life or as long as she lives' as Judge Bulger held and subject thereto in trust for them.

I therefore find it unnecessary to consider or decide the vexed questions (1) whether this agreement is or creates an irrevocable contractual licence to occupy; and (2) whether such a licence has been elevated to a status equivalent to an estate or interest in land. . . .

UNGURIAN v *LESNOFF AND OTHERS* [1989] 3 WLR 840, Chancery Division

FACTS: Ms. Lesnoff gave up her Polish nationality, secure home and academic career, in order to take up residence with Mr. Ungurian in Muswell Hill, London. They lived at No. 136, Muswell Hill Road as *de facto* husband and wife. Ms. Lesnoff made substantial improvements to the premises throughout the four years of their relationship and she remained in the premises after their separation. The home was registered in Mr. Ungurian's sole name. He brought this present action to recover possession of the premises.

HELD: Ms. Lesnoff would be entitled to a life interest in the property, with the result that she became the tenant for life under a strict settlement.

VINELOTT J: . . . In summary . . ., I am not satisfied that the house was bought by Mr. Ungurian with the intention that it would belong to Mrs. Lesnoff, either immediately or when she gave up her flat in Poland and obtained permission to live permanently abroad; but I am satisfied that it was bought with the common intention that Mrs. Lesnoff would be entitled to live there with her children, sharing it with Mr. Ungurian when he was in England, and with any of his children who were here for the purpose of being educated. I am satisfied that Mrs. Lesnoff went through with this plan, initiated in Beirut and later elaborated, in the expectation that Mr. Ungurian would provide her with a secure home and that she burnt her boats by giving up her flat in Wraclow in the belief that he had done so. The question is whether these facts, and the work subsequently done by Mrs. Lesnoff, give rise, either to a constructive trust under which Mrs. Lesnoff became entitled to a beneficial interest in the house, or to a licence to reside, or to an estoppel preventing Mr. Ungurian from denying her right to reside in the house.

Mr. Pascoe submitted that these facts found the inference that there was a bargain or common intention that Mrs. Lesnoff was to have a beneficial interest, and that the interest should be commensurate with the extent to which the value of the house was improved by her labours. I accept that Mrs. Lesnoff and her sons did do a great deal of work to the house, though I think that in retrospect Mrs. Lesnoff has probably come to exaggerate both the extent of the work she did, and in particular the skilled work. Mrs. Lesnoff gave a graphic account of wielding a pickaxe. No doubt her solicitors had retailed to her the facts in *Eves v Eves* [1975] 1 WLR 1338 which they drew to the attention of Mr. Ungurian's solicitors. In the course of her evidence this was reduced to a claim that she used a pickaxe to lever doorframes away from the brickwork where they needed to be replaced. I doubt whether Mrs. Lesnoff used a tool as clumsy as a pickaxe at all, unless possibly she picked up one that had been left lying around by workmen and put it to some temporary, and possibly inappropriate, use. I am not persuaded that, as she claimed, she mastered the art of plastering walls. As I have said, I am satisfied that she and her sons did a substantial amount of work, but I think she did the work on the understanding that she had the right to reside in the house and because she wanted to make it more comfortable for her and Mr. Ungurian, and for her growing sons. Mr. Ungurian in particular wanted some privacy and the alterations to the ground floor were designed to that end.

In my judgment, the inference to be drawn from the circumstances in which the property was purchased and the subsquent conduct of the parties—the intention to be attributed to them—is that Mrs. Lesnoff was to have the right to reside in the house during her life. It would be to that extent her house, and although the expectation was that Mr. Ungurian would live there with her when he was in England, and that Paul, and possibly in due course his younger son also, would be accommodated there while they were being educated, that result would flow from the continued relationship between Mrs. Lesnoff and Mr. Ungarian and would be dependent on it. It must be borne in mind that Mr. Ungurian was a man of considerable means with flats in Beirut, Amman and Switzerland. He was providing a house as a home for a woman much younger than himself who would be likely to survive him. I do not think that full effect would be given to this common intention by inferring no more than an irrevocable licence to occupy the house. I think the legal consequences which flow from the intention to be imputed to the parties was that Mr. Ungurian held the house on trust to permit Mrs. Lesnoff to reside in it during her life unless and until Mr. Ungurian, with her consent, sold the property and bought another residence for her in substitution for it.

If that is the right conclusion, then the house became settled land within the Settled Land Act 1925 and Mrs. Lesnoff is tenant for life and entitled to call for the execution of a vesting deed and for the appointment of trustees. Any understanding that Mr. Ungurian was not to be entitled with her consent to sell the house and apply the proceeds, in whole or in part, towards the purchase of another house would be avoided by section 106 of the Settled Land Act 1925. . . .

11.4   Who is the Life Tenant under the Settled Land Act?

SETTLED LAND ACT 1925

19.   Who is tenant for life

(1)   The person of full age who is for the time being beneficially entitled under a settlement to possession of settled land for his life is for the purposes of the Act the tenant for life of that land and the tenant for life under that settlement.

(2)   If in any case there are two or more persons of full age so entitled as joint tenants, they together constitute the tenant for life for the purposes of this Act.

(3)   If in any case there are two or more persons so entitled as joint tenants and they are not all of full age, such one or more of them as is or are for the time being of full age is or (if more than one) together constitute the tenant for life for the purposes of this Act, but this subsection does not affect the beneficial interests of such of them as are not for the time being of full age.

(4)   A person being tenant for life within the foregoing definitions shall be deemed to be such notwithstading that, under the settlement or otherwise, the settled land, or his estate or interest therein, is incumbered or charged in any manner or to any extent, and notwithstanding any assignment by operation of law or otherwise of his estates or interest under the settlement, whether before or after it came into possession, other than an assurance which extinguishes that estate or interest.

20.   Other limited owners having powers of tenant for life

(1)   Each of the following persons being of full age shall, when his estate or interest is in possession, have the powers of a tenant for life under this Act, (namely):—

(i)   A tenant in tail, including a tenant in tail after possibility of issue extinct, and a tenant in tail who is by Act of Parliament restrained from barring or defeating his estate tail, and although the reversion is in the Crown, but not including such a tenant in tail where the land in respect whereof he is so restrained was purchased with money provided by Parliament in consideration of public services;

(ii)   A person entitled to land for an estate in fee simple or for a term of years absolute with or subject to, in any of such cases, an executory limitation, gift, or disposition over on failure of his issue or in any other event;

(iii)   A person entitled to a base or determinable fee, although the reversion or right of reverter is in the Crown, or to any corresponding interest in leasehold land;

(iv)   A tenant for years determinable on life, not holding merely under a lease at a rent;

(v)   A tenant for the life of another, not holding merely under a lease at a rent;

(vi)   A tenant for his own or any other life, or for years determinable on life, whose estate is liable to cease in any event during that life, whether by expiration of the estate, or by conditional limitation, or otherwise, or to be defeated by an executory limitation, gift, or disposition over, or is subjet to a trust for accumulation of income for any purpose;

(vii)   A tenant by the curtesy;

(viii)   A person entitled to the income of land under a trust or direction for payment thereof to him during his own or any other life, whether or not subject to expenses of management or to a trust for accumulation of income for any purpose, or until sale of the land, or until forfeiture, cesser or determination by any means of his interest therin, unless the land is subject to an immediate binding trust for sale;

(ix)   A person beneficially entitled to land for an estate in fee simple or for a term of years absolute subject to any estates, interests, charges, or powers of charging, subsisting or capable of being exercised under a settlement;

(x)   . . .

(2)   In every such case as is mentioned in subsection (1) of this section, the provisions of this Act referring to a tenant for life, either as conferring powers on him or otherwise, shall extend to each of the persons aforesaid, and any reference in this Act to death as regards a tenant for life shall, where necessary, be deemed to refer to the determination by death or otherwise of the estate or interest of the person on whom the powers of a tenant for life are conferred by this section.

(3)   For the purposes of this Act the estate or interest of a tenant by the curtesy shall be deemed to be an estate or interest arising under a settlement made by his wife.

(4)   Where the reversion or right of reverter or other reversionary right is in the Crown, the exercise by a person on whom the powers of tenant for life are conferred by this section of his powers under this Act, binds the Crown.

23.   Powers of trustees, etc, when there is no tenant for life

(1)   Where under a settlement there is no tenant for life nor, independently of this section, a person having by virtue of this Act the powers of a tenant for life then—

(a)   any person of full age on whom such powers are by the settlement expressed to be conferred; and

(b)   in any other case the trustees of the settlement;

shall have the powers of a tenant for life under this Act.

(2)   This section applies to trustees of settlements of land purchased with money provided by Parliament in consideration of public services where the tenant in tail is restrained from barring or defeating his estate tail, except that, if the tenant in tail is of full age and capacity, the powers shall not be exercised without his consent, but a purchaser shall not be concerned to see or inquire whether such consent has been given.

34.   Appointment of trustees by court

(1)   If at any time there are no trustees of a settlement, or where in any other case it is expedient, for the purposes of this Act, that new trustees of a settlement be appointed, the court may, if it thinks fit, on the application of the tenant for life, statutory owner, or of any

other person having, under the settlement, an estate or interest in the settled land, in possession, remainder or otherwise, or, in the case of an infant, of his testamentary or other guardian or next friend, appoint fit persons to be trustees of the settlement.

(2) The persons so appointed, and the survivors and survivor of them, while continuing to be trustees or trustee, and, until the appointment of new trustees, the personal representatives or representative for the time being of the last surviving or continuing trustee, shall become and be the trustees or trustee of the settlement.

11.5   Who are the Trustees of the Settlement for the Purposes of the Settled Land Act?

SETTLED LAND ACT 1925

30.   Who are trustees for purposes of Act

(1)   Subject to the provisions of this Act, the following persons are trustees of a settlement for the purposes of this Act, and are in this Act referred to as the 'trustees of the settlement' or 'trustees of a settlement', namely—

(i)   the persons, if any, who are for the time being under the settlement, trustees with power of sale of the settled land (subject or not to the consent of any person), or with power of consent to or approval of the exercise of such a power of sale, or if there are no such persons; then

(ii)   the persons, if any, for the time being, who are by the settlement declared to be trustees thereof for the purposes of the Settled Land Acts 1882 to 1890, or any of them, or this Act, or if there are no such persons; then

(iii)   the persons, if any, who are for the time being under the settlement trustees with power of or upon trust for sale of any other land comprised in the settlement and subject to the same limitations as the land to be sold or otherwise dealt with, or with power of consent to or approval of the exercise of such a power of sale, or, if there are no such persons; then

(iv)   the persons, if any, who are for the time being under the settlement trustees with future power of sale, or under a future trust for sale of the settled land, or with power of consent to or approval of the exercise of such a future power of sale, and whether the power or trust takes effect in all events or not, or, if there are no such persons; then

(v)   the persons, if any, appointed by deed to be trustees of the settlement by all the persons who at the date of the deed were together able, by virtue of their beneficial interests or by the exercise of an equitable power, to dispose of the settled land in equity for the whole estate the subject of the settlement.

(2)   . . .

(3)   Where a settlement is created by will, or a settlement has arisen by the effect of an intestacy, and part from this subsection there would be no trustees for the purposes of this Act of such settlement, then the personal representatives of the deceased shall, until other trustees are appointed, be by virtue of this Act the trustees of the settlement, but where there is a sole personal representative, not being a trust corporation, it shall be obligatory on him to appoint an additional trustee to act with him for the purposes of this Act, and the provisions of the Trustee Act 1925 relating to the appointment of new trustees and the vesting of trust property shall apply accordingly.

CHAPTER TWELVE

THE STATUTORY POWERS OF THE LIFE TENANT

12.1   Life Tenant's Statutory Powers of Disposition: General

The thinking in 1925 was *not* to give the life tenant totally unrestricted powers over the settled land. Rather it was to give him only those powers which a 'reasonable landowner' would want. Unfortunately, in the light of changed economic conditions, some of these powers are today inadequate.

12.2   The Statutory Powers

SETTLED LAND ACT 1925

38.   Powers of sale and exchange
A tenant for life—
    (i)   May sell the settled land, or any part thereof, or any easement, right or privilege of any kind over or in relation to the land; and
    (ii)   . . .
    (iii)   May make an exchange of the settled land, or any part thereof, or of any easement, right, or privilege of any kind, whether or not newly created, over or in relation to the settled land, or any part thereof, for other land, or for any easement, right or privilege of any kind, whether or not newly created, over or in relation to other land, including an exchange in consideration of money paid for equality of exchange.

39.   Power of Minister to acquire and dispose of land
   (1)   Subject to the provisions of this Act, the Minister may acquire (by purchase, lease or exchange) land which in his opinion is suitable for afforestation or for purposes connected with forestry, together with any other land which must necessarily be acquired therewith, and may place any land acquired by him under this section at the disposal of the Commissioners. . . .

41.   Power to lease for ordinary or building or mining or forestry purposes
A tenant for life may lease the settled land, or any part thereof, or any easement, right, or privilege of any kind over or in relation to the land, for any purpose whatever, whether involving waste or not, for any term not exceeding—
    (i)   In case of a building lease, nine hundred and ninety-nine years;
    (ii)   In case of a mining lease, one hundred years;
    (iii)   In case of a forestry lease, nine hundred and ninety-nine years;
    (iv)   In case of any other lease, fifty years;

44.   Regulations respecting building leases

(1)   Every building lease shall be made partly in consideration of the lessee, or some person by whose direction the lease is granted, or some other person, having erected or agreeing to erect buildings, new or additional, or having improved or repaired or agreeing to improve or repair buildings, or having executed or agreeing to execute on the land leased, an improvement authorised by this Act for or in connexion with building purposes.

(2)   A peppercorn rent or a nominal or other rent less than the rent ultimately payable, may be made payable for the first five years or any less part of the term.

(3)   Where the land is contracted to be leased in lots, the entire amount of rent to be ultimately payable may be apportioned among the lots in any manner:

Provided that—

(i)   the annual rent reserved by any lease shall not be less than [50p]; and

(ii)   the total amount of the rent reserved on all leases for the time being granted shall not be less than the total amount of the rents which, in order that the leases may be in conformity with this Act, ought to be reserved in respect of the whole land for the time being leased; and

(iii)   the rent reserved by any lease shall not exceed one-fifth part of the full annual value of the land comprised in that lease with the buildings thereon when completed.

47.   Capitalisation of part of mining rent

Under a mining lease, whether the mines or minerals leased are already opened or in work or not, unless a contrary intention is expressed in the settlement there shall be from time to time set aside, as capital money arising under this Act, part of the rent as follows, namely—where the tenant for life or statutory owner is impeachable for waste in respect of minerals, three fourth parts of the rent, and otherwise one fourth part thereof, and in every such case the residue of the rent shall go as rents and profits.

51.   Power to grant options

(1)   A tenant for life may at any time, either with or without consideration, grant by writing an option to purchase or take a lease of the settled land, or any part thereof, or any easement, right, or privilege over or in relation to the same at a price or rent fixed at the time of the granting of the option.

(2)   Every such option shall be made exercisable within an agreed number of years not exceeding ten.

(3)   The price or rent shall be the best which, having regard to all the circumstances, can reasonably be obtained and either—

(a)   may be a specified sum of money or rent, or at a specified rate according to the superficial area of the land with respect to which the option is exercised, or the frontage thereof or otherwise; or

(b)   in the case of an option to purchase contained in a lease or agreement for a lease, may be a stated number of years' purchase of the highest rent reserved by the lease or agreement; or

(c)   if the option is exercisable as regards part of the land comprised in the lease or agreement, may be a proportionate part of such highest rent;

and any aggregate price or rent may be made to be apportionable in any manner, or according to any system, or by reference to arbitration.

(4)   An option to take a mining lease may be coupled with the grant of a licence to search for and prove any mines or minerals under the settled land, or any part thereof, pending the exercise of the option.

(5)   The consideration for the grant of the option shall be capital money arising under this Act.

63.   Power to complete predecessor's contracts

A tenant for life may make any disposition which is necessary or proper for giving effect to a contract entered into by a predecessor in title, and which if made by that predecessor would have been valid as against his successors in title.

64. General power for the tenant for life to effect any transaction under an order of the court

(1)   Any transaction affecting or concerning the settled land, or any part thereof, or any other land (not being a transaction otherwise authorised by this Act, or by the settlement) which in the opinion of the court would be for the benefit of the settled land, or any part thereof, or the persons interested under the settlement, may, under an order of the court, be effected by a tenant for life, if it is one which could have been validly effected by an absolute owner.

(2)   In this section 'transaction' includes any sale, . . . exchange, assurance, grant, lease, surrender, reconveyance, release, reservation, or other disposition, and any purchase or other acquisition, and any covenant, contract, or option, and any application of capital money . . . and any compromise or other dealing, or arrangement; . . . , and 'effected' has the meaning appropriate to the particular transaction; and the references to land include references to restrictions and burdens affecting land.

65. Power to dispose of mansion

(1)   The powers of disposing of settled land conferred by this Act on a tenant for life may be exercised as respects the principle mansion house, if any, on any settled land, and the pleasure grounds and park and lands, if any, usually occupied therewith:

Provided that those powers shall not be exercised without the consent of the trustees of the settlement or an order of the court—

(a) if the settlement is a settlement made or coming into operation before the commencement of this Act and the settlement does not expressly provide to the contrary; or

(b) if the settlement made or coming into operation after the commencement of this Act and the settlement expressly provides that these powers or any of them shall not be exercised without such consent or order.

(2)   Where a house is usually occupied as a farmhouse, or where the site of any house and the pleasure grounds and park and lands, if any, usually occupied therewith do not together exceed twenty-five acres in extent, the house is not to be deemed a principal mansion house within the meaning of this section, and may accordingly be disposed of in like manner as any other part of the settled land.

67. Sale and purchase of heirlooms under order of court

(1)   Where personal chattels are settled so as to devolve with settled land, or to devolve therewith as nearly as may be in accordance with the law or practice in force at the date of the settlement, or are settled together with land, or upon trusts declared by reference to the trusts affecting land, a tenant for life of the land may sell the chattels or any of them.

(2)   The money arising by the sale shall be a capital money arising under this Act, . . .

71. Power to raise money by mortgage

(1)   Where money is required for any of the following purposes namely:—

(i)   Discharging an incumbrance on the settled land or part thereof;

(ii)   Paying for any improvement authorised by this Act or by the settlement;

(iii)   Equality of exchange;

(iv)   (v) . . .;

(vi)   *Redeeming a compensation rentcharge in respect of the extinguishment of manorial incidents and affecting the settled land*;

(vii)   Commuting any additional rent made payable on the conversion of a perpetually renewable leasehold interest into a long term;

(viii) Satisfying any claims for compensation on the conversion of a perpetually renewable leasehold interest into a long term by any officer, solicitor, or other agent of the lessor in repect of fees or remuneration which would have been payable by the lessee or under-lessee on any renewal;

(ix)   Payment of the costs of any transaction authorised by this section or either of the two last preceding sections;

the tenant for life may raise the money so required, on the security of the settled land, or of any part thereof, by a legal mortgage, and the money so raised shall be capital money for that purpose, and may be paid or applied accordingly. . . .

12.3 Invalidation of All Restrictions on a Life Tenant's Powers

SETTLED LAND ACT 1925

106. Prohibition or limitation against exercise of powers void, and provision against forfeiture

(1) If in a settlement, will, assurance, or other instrument executed or made before or after, or partly before and partly after, the commencement of this Act a provision is inserted—

(a) purporting or attempting, by way of direction, declaration, or otherwise, to forbid a tenant for life or statutory owner to exercise any power under this Act, or his right to require the settled land to be vested in him; or

(b) attempting, or tending, or intended, by a limitation, gift, or dispositon over of settled land, or by a limitation, gift, or disposition of other real or any personal property, or by the imposition of any condition, or by forfeiture, or in any other manner whatever, to prohibit or prevent him from exercising, or to induce him to abstain from exercising, or to put him into a position inconsistent with his exercising any power under this Act, or his right to require the settled land to be vested in him;

that provision, as far as it purports, or attempt, or tends, or is intended to have, or would or might have, the operation aforesaid, shall be deemed to be void. . . .

109. Saving for additional or larger powers under settlement

(1) Nothing in this Act precludes a settlor from conferring on the tenant for life, or (save as provided by the last preceding section) on the trustees of the settlement, any powers additional to or larger than those conferred by this Act.

(2) Any additional or larger powers so conferred shall, as far as may be, notwithstanding anything in this Act, operate and be exercisable in the like manner, and with all the like incidents, effects, and consequences, as if they were conferred by this Act, and, if relating to the settled land, as if they were conferred by this Act on a tenant for life.

12.4 Safeguards Against the Life Tenant Abusing His Position

SETTLED LAND ACT 1925

101. Notice to trustees

(1) Save as otherwise expressly provided by this Act, a tenant for life or statutory owner, when intending to make a sale, exchange, lease, mortage, or charge or to grant an option—

(a) shall give notice of his intention in that behalf to each of the trustees of the settlement, by posting registered letters, containing the notice, addressed to the trustees severally, each at his usual or last known place of abode in the United Kingdom; and

(b) shall give a like notice to the solicitor for the trustees, if any such solicitor is known to the tenant for life or statutory owner, by posting a registered letter, containing the notice, addressed to the solicitor at his place of business in the United Kingdom;

every letter under this section being posted not less than one month before the making or granting by the tenant for life or statutory owner of the sale, exchange, lease, mortgage, charge, or option, or of a contract for the same:

Provided that a notice under this section shall not be valid unless at the date thereof the trustee is a trust corporation, or the number of trustees is not less than two.

(2) . . .

(3) . . .

(4) Any trustee, by writing under his hand, may waive notice either in any particular case, or generally, and may accept less than one month's notice.

(5) A person dealing in good faith with the tenant for life is not concerned to inquire respecting the giving of any such notice as is required by this section.

107. Tenant for life trustee for all parties interested

(1)   A tenant for life or statutory owner shall, in exercising any power under this Act, have regard to the interests of all parties entitled under the settlement, and shall, in relation to the exercise thereof by him, be deemed to be in the position and to have the duties and liabilities of a trustee for those parties.

(2)   The provision by a tenant for life or statutory owner, at his own expense, of dwellings available for the working classes on any settled land shall not be deemed to be an injury to any interest in reversion or remainder in that land, but such provision shall not be made by a tenant for life or statutory owner without the previous approval in writing of the trustees of the settlement.

110. Protection of purchasers, etc

(1)   On a sale, exchange, lease, mortgage, charge, or other disposition, a purchaser dealing in good faith with a tenant for life or statutory owner shall, as against all parties entitled under the settlement, be conclusively taken to have given the best price, consideration, or rent, as the case may require, that could reasonably be obtained by the tenant for life or statutory owner, and to have complied with all the requisitions of this Act.

(2)   A purchaser of a legal estate in settled land shall not, except as hereby expressly provided, be bound or entitled to call for the production of the trust instrument or any information concerning that instrument or any ad valorem stamp duty thereon, and whether or not he has notice of its contents he shall, save as hereinafter provided, be bound and entitled if the last or only principal vesting instrument contains the statements and particulars required by this Act to assume that—

(a)   the person in whom the land is by the said instrument vested or declared to be vested is the tenant for life or statutory owner and has all the power of a tenant for life under this Act, including such additional or larger powers, if any, as are therein mentioned;

(b)   the persons by the said instrument stated to be the trustees of the settlement, or their successors appearing to be duly appointed, are the properly constituted trustees of the settlement;

(c)   the statements and particulars required by this Act and contained (expressly or by reference) in the said instrument were correct at the date thereof.

(d)   the statements contained in any deed executed in accordance with this Act declaring who are the trustees of the settlement for the purposes of this Act are correct;

(e)   the statements contained in any deed of discharge, executed in accordance with this Act, are correct:

Provided that, as regards the first vesting instrument executed for the purpose of giving effect to—

(a)   a settlement subsisting at the commencement of this Act; or

(b)   an instrument which by virtue of this Act is deemed to be a settlement; or

(c)   a settlement which by virtue of this Act is deemed to have been made by any person after the commencement of this Act; or

(d)   an instrument *inter vivos* intended to create settlement of a legal estate in land which is executed after the commencement of this Act and does not comply with the requirements of this Act with respect to the method of effecting such a settlement;

a purchaser shall be concerned to see—

(i)   that the land disposed of to him is comprised in such settlement or instrument;

(ii)   that the person in whom the settled land is by such vesting instrument vested, or declared to be vested, is the person in who it ought to be vested as tenant for life or statutory owner;

(iii)   that the persons thereby stated to be the trustees of the settlement are the properly constituted trustees of the settlement. . . .

CHAPTER THIRTEEN

TRUSTS FOR SALE OF LAND

13.1 Trusts for Sale Defined

LAW OF PROPERTY ACT 1925

205. General definitions

(1)(xxix) 'Trust for sale', in relation to land, means an immediate binding trust for sale, whether or not exercisable at the request or with the consent of any person, and with or without a power at discretion to postpone the sale; 'trustees for sale' mean the persons (including a personal representative) holding land on trust for sale; and 'power to postpone a sale' means power to postpone in the exercise of a discretion;

LAW OF PROPERTY ACT 1925

25. Power to postpone sale

(1) A power to postpone sale shall, in the case of every trust for sale of land, be implied unless a contrary intention appears.

(2) Where there is a power to postpone the sale, then (subject to any express direction to the contrary in the instrument, if any, creating the trust for sale) the trustees for sale shall not be liable in any way for postponing the sale, in the exercise of their discretion, for any indefinite period; nor shall a purchaser of a legal estate be concerned in any case with any direction respecting the postponement of a sale.

(3) The foregoing provisions of this section apply whether the trust for sale is created before or after the commencement or by virtue of this Act.

(4) Where a disposition or settlement coming into operation after the commencement of this Act contains a trust either to retain or sell land the same shall be construed as a trust to sell the land with power to postpone the sale.

RE HERKLOT'S WILL TRUSTS [1964] 1 WLR 583, Chancery Division

FACTS: A testatrix left the residue of her estate on trust for sale, and provided that 'Miss Gordon' should be entitled to the income on the residue for her life. Miss Gordon was also entitled 'to reside in my said house during her life for so long as she wishes'. A codicil to the will granted the plaintiff a share in the residue, providing also that he could take a conveyance of the testatrix's home, if he wished, in part settlement of his claim to the residue. Miss Gordon proposed to sell the house and the plaintiff brought the present action to restrain her by injunction from doing so.
HELD: The testatrix could not have intended the land to have been settled land, with the necessary consequence that Miss Gordon would have been able to sell the house at will, for this would have been inconsistent with the terms of the codicil. The house was held on trust for sale, subject to the consents of Miss Gordon and the plaintiff.

UNGOED-THOMAS J: The definition of trust for sale in the Settled Land Act 1925, refers to the definition in section 205(1)(xxix) of the Law of Property Act, 1925, which, in so far as material, reads; '"Trust for sale", in relation to land, means an immediate binding trust for sale, whether or not exercisable at the request or with the consent of any person, and with or without a power at discretion to postpone the sale.' For the plaintiff it is said that, on the true construction of the will and codicil, there is an immediate binding trust for sale within the meaning of this definition because the definition itself provides for it being binding despite the need for the consent of any person, and that on the true construction of this will and codicil, the consent of the plaintiff to a sale is required.

Looking at the terms of this will and codicil, by clause 4 of the will the property was given upon trust to sell, with a power to postpone the sale indefinitely. Clause 5 provided that out of the proceeds of such sale the funeral and testamentary expenses shall be paid. Quite clearly, down to that stage, there is an immediate binding trust for sale, with emphasis placed upon the power to postpone sale. So there is so far, within the contemplation of the testatrix, an operative trust for sale which was expected to provide cash for stated purposes.

Clause 6 provided that the trustees should invest the residue in authorised investments. Then in clause 7, the testatrix provided for the payment of the income to Miss Gordon during her life 'without prejudice to the trust for sale herein contained and shall permit her to reside in my said house during her life for so long as she wishes.' The words 'without prejudice to the trust for sale herein contained' emphasise that at that stage the testatrix did not wish the trust for sale to be prejudiced in any way.

The defendants say that the testatrix dealt with the house in the second part of clause 7, by the express provision that it was to be without prejudice to the trust for sale, which she had emphatically stated in the first part of the clause, with the result, they claim, that there was a modification of the trust for sale so that the trustees were not to sell the house without the consent of Miss Gordon. I think it would be placing much too much weight on the words 'without prejudice to the trust for sale herein contained' to conclude from them that the testatrix intended with regard to the house that the house should be taken out of the trusts for sale in which she had previously included it. Clause 7, however, went on to provide that Miss Gordon had permission to reside in the house 'during her lifetime for as long as she wishes.' If effect is to be given to this provision the result is that the house cannot be sold without her consent. . . .

. . . Looking again at clause 7 of the will, it does not appear to me that the provision that Miss Gordon should be permitted to reside in this house so long as she wished is inconsistent with the trust for sale for which the testatrix had expressly provided. I have to construe the will and, so far as possible, to reconcile the provisions of the will in accordance with what, so far as I can gather from the terms of the will and codicil, are the testatrix's intentions. Reading this provision for residence in clause 7 of the will, coming as it does in the clause which deals with the income of the investments of the trust, it does not appear to me that the testatrix there contemplated that the provision for residence should take this property out of the trust for sale. It is certainly reconcilable with the trust for sale because the effect would simply be that if Miss Gordon wished to reside in this house, it was not to be sold. I find nothing in the fact that her consent to the sale was required in that way inconsistent with the definition of trust for sale contained in section 205(1)(xxix) of the Law of Property Act, 1925.

13.2   Trusts for Sale Subject to Consents

LAW OF PROPERTY ACT 1925

26.   Consents to the execution of a trust for sale

(1)   If the consent of more than two persons is by the disposition made requisite to the execution of a trust for sale of land, then, in favour of a purchaser, the consent of any two such persons to the execution of the trust or to the exercise of any statutory or other powers vested in the trustees for sale shall be deemed sufficient.

(2)   Where the person whose consent to the execution of any such trust or power is expressed to be required in a disposition is not *sui juris* or becomes subject to disability, his consent shall not, in favour of a purchaser, be deemed to be requisite to the execution of the trust or the exercise of the power; but the trustees shall, in any such case, obtain the

separate consent of the parent or testamentary or other guardian of an infant or of the . . . receiver (if any) of a person suffering from mental disorder. . . .

13.3 Powers of Trustees for Sale

13.3.1 DISPOSITIONS OTHER THAN SALE

LAW OF PROPERTY ACT 1925

28. Powers of management, etc, conferred on trustees for sale

(1) Trustees for sale shall, in relation to land or to manorial incidents and to the proceeds of sale, have all the powers of a tenant for life and the trustees of a settlement under the Settled Land Act 1925 including in relation to the land the powers of management conferred by that Act during a minority: and where by statute settled land is or becomes vested in the trustees of the settlement upon the statutory trusts, such trustees and their successors in office shall also have all the additional or larger powers (if any) conferred by the settlement on the tenant for life, statutory owner, or trustees of the settlement, and (subject to any express to the contrary) all capital money arising under the said powers shall, unless paid or applied for any purpose authorised by the Settled Land Act 1925 be applicable in the same manner as if the money represented proceeds of sale arising under the trust for sale.

13.3.2 DELEGATION OF MANAGEMENT AND LEASING POWERS

LAW OF PROPERTY ACT 1925

29. Delegation of powers of management by trustees for sale

(1) The powers of an incidental to leasing, accepting surrenders of leases and management, conferred on trustees for sale whether by this Act or otherwise, may, until sale of the land, be revocably delegated from time to time, by writing, signed by them, to any person of full age (not being merely an annuitant) for the time being beneficially entitled in possession to the net rents and profits of the land during his life or for any less period: and in favour of a lessee such writing shall, unless the contrary appears, be sufficient evidence that the person named therein is a person to whom the powers may be delegated, and the production of such writing shall, unless the contrary appears, be sufficient evidence that the delegation has not been revoked.

(2) Any power so delegated shall be exercised only in the names and on behalf of the trustees delegating the power.

(3) The persons delegating any power under this section shall not, in relation to the exercise or purported exercise of the power, be liable for the acts or defaults of the person to whom the power is delegated, but that person shall, in relation to the exercise of the power by him, be deemed to be in the position and to have the duties and liabilities of a trustee.

13.4 Involvement of Beneficiaries in the Trust for Sale

13.4.1 DUTY TO CONSULT BENEFICIARIES

LAW OF PROPERTY ACT 1925

26. Consents to the execution of a trust for sale

. . .

(3) Trustees for sale shall so far as practicable consult the persons of full age for the time being beneficially interested in possession in the rents and profits of the land until sale, and shall, so far as consistent with the general interest of the trust, give effect to the wishes of

such persons, or, in the case of dispute, of the majority (according to the value of their combined interests) of such persons, but a purchaser shall not be concerned to see that the provisions of this subsection have been complied with.

In the case of a trust for sale, not being a trust for sale created by or in pursuance of the powers conferred by this or any other Act, this subsection shall not apply unless the contrary intention appears in the disposition creating the trust.

13.4.2 SECTION 30 OF THE LAW OF PROPERTY ACT 1925

LAW OF PROPERTY ACT 1925

30. Powers of court where trustees for sale refuse to exercise powers
(1) If the trustees for sale refuse to sell or to exercise any of the powers conferred by either of the last two sections, or any requisite consent cannot be obtained, any person interested may apply to the court for a vesting or other order for giving effect to the proposed transaction or for an order directing the trustees for sale to give effect thereto, and the court may make such order as it thinks fit.

(2) The county court has jurisdiction under this section where the land which is to be dealt with in the court does not exceed the county court limit in capital value or net annual value for rating.

13.5 Appointment, Retirement and Removal of Trustees

13.5.1 METHOD OF APPOINTMENT OF TRUSTEES

TRUSTEE ACT 1925

40. Vesting of trust property in new or continuing trustees
(1) Where by a deed a new trustee is appointed to perform any trust, then—
(a) if the deed contains a declaration by the appointor to the effect that any estate or interest in any land subject to the trust, or in any chattel so subject, or the right to recover or receive any debt or other thing in action so subject, shall vest in the persons who by virtue of the deed become or are the trustees for performing the trust, the deed shall operate, without any conveyance or assignment, to vest in those persons as joint tenants and for the purposes of the trust the estate interest or right to which the declaration relates; and
(b) if the deed is made after the commencement of this Act and does not contain such a declaration, the deed shall, subject to any express provision to the contrary therein contained, operate as if it had contained such a declaration by the appointor extending to all the estates interests and rights with respect to which a declaration could have been made.

(2) Where by a deed a retiring trustee is discharged under the statutory power without a new trustee being appointed, then—
(a) if the deed contains such a declaration as aforesaid by the retiring and continuing trustees, and by the other person, if any, empowered to appoint trustees, the deed shall, without any conveyance or assignment, operate to vest in the continuing trustees alone, as joint tenants, and for the purposes of the trust, the estate, interest, or right to which the declaration relates; and
(b) if the deed is made after the commencement of this Act and does not contain such a declaration, the deed shall, subject to any express provision to the contrary therein contained, operate as if it had contained such a declaration by such persons as aforesaid extending to all the estates, interests and rights with respect to which a declaration could have been made.

(3) An express vesting declaration, whether made before or after the commencement of this Act, shall, notwithstanding that the estate, interest or right to be vested is not expressly referred to, and provided that the other statutory requirements were or are

complied with, operate and be deemed always to have operated (but without prejudice to any express provision to the contrary contained in the deed of appointment or discharge) to vest in the persons respectively referred to in subsections (1) and (2) of this section, as the case may require, such estates, interests and rights as are capable and ought to be vested in those persons. . . .

13.6   End of Chapter Assessment Question

You are consulted by Sarah in connection with the making of her will. Sarah owns two properties: a large family house, 'The Gables', which she has recently inherited from her husband Thomas; and a country cottage.

Sarah lives at The Gables with her elder sister Jane. Soon after Thomas's death Sarah asked Jane to live with her because of Sarah's ill health. Jane has little money of her own and is rather inexperienced about financial matters.

Sarah tells you that she wishes Jane to be able to live at The Gables for as long as she wishes, and that on Jane's death or on Jane's ceasing to reside at The Gables, for the property to pass to Thomas's godson, James, who has always shown a great interest in the property. However Sarah is particularly anxious that Jane should not be able to use The Gables in order to raise any finance for herself.

With regard to the cottage, Sarah wants a close friend, Amy, to live there if she wishes and that after Amy's death the proceeds of sale are to be divided equally between Sarah's cousin's children. Sarah adds that the cottage is situated rather remotely and so if Amy wishes she should be allowed to sell the cottage and buy another property which is more suitable for her.

Advise Sarah.

13.7   End of Chapter Assessment Outline Answer

It is clear that by her will Sarah should create a two separate trusts, one over The Gables and the other over the remote cottage. In theory Sarah has two forms of trust of land to choose from, namely the strict settlement and the trust for sale.

A strict settlement for The Gables can be ruled out immediately. Where there is a strict settlement the life beneficiary (life tenant) of the trust *must* be given control over the land, *must* hold the legal title to the land, and *must* have the power to sell the land and/or grant leases for up to fifty years. The now antiquated Settled Land Act 1925 makes this very clear, see especially section 106. A strict settlement of The Gables would have the disastrous result of putting Jane in total charge.

A strict settlement with respect to the cottage seems *at first sight* a very attractive proposition. The disposition would read something like to 'Amy for life, remainder to [trustees] on trust for sale to hold the proceeds in trust for Sarah's cousin's children in equal shares.' Amy, as Sarah desires, would have the power to sell the cottage. The proceeds of sale would have to be paid not to Amy but to the 'Trustees for the purposes of the Settled Land Act'; however Amy would have the power to direct that the SLA trustees invest those proceeds in the purchase of an alternative residence.

On more careful thought, it is suggested that a strict settlement of the cottage is not a good idea. It will cause problems either during Amy's lifetime or on her death.

If Amy is made a life tenant and decides to sell during her lifetime she may have problems with purchasers' solicitors unfamiliar with the concept of settled land. 'What is this settled land? What is this vesting assent you are waving at me as part of the title deeds? And are you serious when you say that I pay the purchase price not to you but to the SLA trustees? I was never taught any of this at Trendyville Law School!'

If Amy is made a Life Tenant but decides to keep the cottage, there is a very complex transition which will occur on her death. This transition could well go wrong if the solicitors involved are unfamiliar with settled land.

When Amy dies the strict settlement ends *immediately*. The SLA trustees will have no more functions to perform, though they may think otherwise and try and interfere. What should happen is that the executors appointed by Amy's will should get an ordinary grant of probate in the usual way. This grant will extend to the *ex*-settled land. Amy's executors should then execute an *ordinary* assent in favour of the trustees who must then sell the property and split the proceeds amongst the cousins' children.

It is therefore much better for Sarah to create an immediate trust for sale, on trust for Amy for life, remainder to the cousins' children in equal shares. This has the theoretical disadvantage that control of the cottage does not belong to Amy. But this problem can be met firstly, by appointing young intelligent trustees who can be relied upon to respect Amy's wishes; secondly, by carefully drafting the trust. The trust for sale should contain the following clauses.

(1)   A provision that any sale should only be with Amy's consent.

(2)   A provision that if sale is postponed, Amy shall be allowed to live in the cottage.

(3)   A provision that if Amy requests the cottage be sold, the power to postpone sale should no longer apply and the trustees must sell as soon as reasonably practicable. (In view of the recession it would be unwise to insert a clause providing that Amy can insist on immediate sale.)

(4)   A provision that if the cottage is sold the trustees shall have the power to invest the proceeds in the purchase of alternative accommodation or other land.

(5)   A provision that Amy can insist that the trustees invest proceeds of sale in alternative accommodation for herself.

(6)   A provision that the trustees shall have the same powers of disposition as an outright owner, but any disposition must be with Amy's consent.

(Clause (4) is necessary because courts have held that when trustees for sale sell all the land they hold they cease to have the power to invest in land. Clause (6) is necessary as a precaution. Without it the trustees have the same outdatedly restricted powers as life tenants. E.g. suppose somebody offered to take a 99-year lease of the cottage on terms which the trustees think are very favourable. Clause (6) enables the trustees, provided Amy agrees, to accept the offer.)

To return to The Gables, the position is (ironically) more straightforward. Sarah should create a trust for sale, being careful to appoint reliable trustees. The equitable interests under the trust will simply read, 'to Jane for life or until her ceasing to reside in The Gables, remainder to James'. The trust should include:—

(1)   A provision that any sale should only be with James and Jane's consent.

(2)   A provision that if sale is postponed, Sarah shall be allowed to live in the cottage.

(3)   A provision similar to (4) above.

(4)   A provision similar to (6) above.

CHAPTER FOURTEEN

CO-OWNERSHIP OF LAND — THE BASIC CONCEPTS

14.1   Introduction

Lawson, F. H. and Rudden, B., The Law of Property, 2nd edn,
Oxford: Clarendon Press, 1982, p. 82

CO-OWNERSHIP

Ownership of the same thing at the same time and in the same way by a number of persons has been general from early times. Indeed, some students of primitive law think that ownership by communities such as families, tribes, and clans everywhere preceded ownership by individuals. Roman law admitted common ownership and it has survived everywhere in one form or another.

Even in the modern world there are many occasions on which this may happen. A man may, for instance, die intestate leaving two unmarried sons who go on living together in his house; they do not choose to divide it into two self-contained flats but use most of the rooms in common. In many countries marriage usually makes some at least of what was hitherto the separate property of each of the spouses their common property; and in England it is common for husband and wife to operate a joint banking account. Or two men may run a business in partnership, which involves using the same factory or office in common.

English law has always known two kinds of co-ownership, in accordance with which several persons enjoy what are called concurrent interests. They are called respectively joint ownership and ownership in common. In speaking of land the terms joint tenancy and tenancy in common are used, but this is used of freehold owners and has nothing to do with the law of leases. The difference between them is that whereas if one owner or tenant in common dies, his share passes to his successors, whether by will or on an intestacy, one joint tenant's share accrues on his death to the other joint tenants, so that when all the joint tenants but one are dead the last survivor becomes sole owner tenant.

Lawyers have tried to explain this right of survivorship in a thoroughly artificial way by saying that whereas tenants in common are regarded as holding undivided shares in the land, each share being capable of being alienated, joint tenants do not own shares, but each joint tenant owns the whole, subject to the concurrent ownership of the other joint tenants. When one dies the others do not in theory acquire anything that they had not already, but are merely relieved of the presence of a competing tenant.

The phrase 'undivided shares' has a long history and is much used in modern statutes, so it is a burden we must accept. But it would be meaningless to call a share 'undivided' if by that were meant not separate from the other shares. The simplest way to grasp the position of tenants in common is to think of shares in a company. The shareholders each have a separate thing which they can alienate or leave to pass on their death. It is the property in which the share subsists—the company—which is undivided. So two tenants in common of a house each have a separate, though intagible, asset; it is the house which is not divided into distinct 'shares'. . . .

14.2 Joint Tenancy

14.2.1 RIGHT OF SURVIVORSHIP

The Law Commission, Working Paper No. 105, Transfer of Land: Title on Death, London: HMSO, 1987, p. 47

Co-ownership
2.43   Modern English co-ownership of land is built on the concept of the trust for sale. On the death of a legal co-owner (who has to be a joint tenant since 1925) his surviving co-owner or co-owners take by the *jus accrescendi* (right of survivorship). If co-ownership remains in existence, then there must be at least two trustees (unless the sole one is a trust corporation) before any disposition involving capital money can be effected. If co-ownership has ceased and the sole survivor is beneficially entitled, the position will differ according as the title is registered or unregistered. It will also differ according as the beneficial entitlement in the sole survivor has come about by the operation of the *jus accrescendi* on the end of a beneficial joint tenancy or by the inheritance of the undivided beneficial joint tenancy or by the inheritance or the undivided beneficial share of the deceased by his surviving co-tenant in common. If the title is registered and there was a beneficial joint tenancy before the death, there should be no restriction relating to the co-ownership on the register and the Registrar will merely delete the deceased's name from the proprietorship register, leaving the survivor as unrestricted sole proprietor, unless the Registrar has reason to believe that a severance of the joint tenancy had occurred by or at the date of death. If the title is registered and there was restriction on the register at death because the co-owners were not then joint owners, the Registrar will need to have evidence of the vesting in the survivor of the whole beneficial interest before he removes the restricton from the register. If the title is unregistered and the co-owners appeared as beneficial joint tenants on the title deeds at the death, then the Law of Property (Joint Tenants) Act 1964 seems to provide purchasers from the survivor with full protection so long as the provisions of that Act are fulfilled. If, however, the title is unregistered and the 1964 Act does not apply, the survivor will either have to appoint a new trustee to act with him or (uniquely if the transaction is one such as a sale at an under value which trustes do not have authority to make) show the passage to him of the deceased's equitable share by assent or assignment. . . .

14.3   The Reform of Co-ownership in 1925 — the Main Objective

LAW OF PROPERTY ACT 1925

34. Effect of future dispositions to tenants in common
    (1)   An undivided share in land shall not be capable of being created except as provided by the Settled Land Act 1925 or as hereinafter mentioned.
    (2)   Where, after the commencement of this Act, land is expressed to be conveyed to any persons in undivided shares and those persons are of full age, the conveyance shall (notwithstanding anything to the contrary in this Act) operate as if the land had been expressed to be conveyed to the grantees, or, if there are more than four grantees, to the four first named in the conveyance, as joint tenants upon the statutory trusts hereinafter mentioned and so as to give effect to the rights of the persons who would have been entitled to the shares had the conveyance operated to create those shares:
    Provided that, where the conveyance is made by way of mortgage the land shall vest in the grantees or such four of them as aforesaid for a term of years absolute (as provided by this Act) as joint tenants subject to cesser on redemption in like manner as if the mortgage money had belonged to them on a joint account, but without prejudice to the beneficial interests in the mortage money and interest. . . .

35.   Meaning of the statutory trusts

For the purposes of this Act land held upon the 'statutory trust' shall be held upon the trusts and subject to the provisions following, namely, upon trust to sell the same and to stand possessed of the net proceeds of sale, after payment of costs and of the net rents and profits until sale after payment of rates, taxes, costs of insurance, repairs, and other outgoings, upon such trusts, and subject to such powers and provisions, as may be requisite for giving effect to the rights of the persons (including an incumbrancer of a former undivided share or whose incumbrance is not secured by a legal mortgage) interested in the land and the right of a person who, if the land had not been made subject to a trust for sale by virtue of this Act, would have been entitled to an entailed interest in an undivided share in the land, shall be deemed to be a right to a corresponding entailed interest in the net proceed of sale attributable to that share.

Where—

(a)   an undivided share was subject to a settlement, and

(b)   the settlement remains subsisting in respect of other property and

(c)   the trustees thereof are not the same persons as the trustees for sale,

then the statutory trusts include a trust for the trustees for sale to pay the proper proportion of the net proceeds of sale or other capital money attributable to the share to the trustees of the settlement to be held by them as capital money arising under the Settled Land Act 1925.

14.4   The Modern Conveyancing Practice to create an Express Trust for Sale

WALKER v *HALL* (1984) 5 FLR 126, Court of Appeal

FACTS: An unmarried couple had been living together as *de facto* man and wife and had purchased a house in joint names as a family home. During the relationship they pooled their earnings to pay various expenses, and to repay the mortgage by instalments. A short while later the couple separated, Mrs. Walker leaving Mr. Hall in the family home. He continued to pay off the mortgage instalments from his own funds, with the result that his contributions to the price of the property far outweighed hers. Mrs. Walker claimed a beneficial share in the property.

HELD: In the absence of an express declaration as to the extent of her beneficial interest, Mrs. Walker's share would be determined, according to normal trust principles, with reference only to the extent of her financial contribution to the value of the property. *Per curiam*: solicitors acting for joint purchasers of land should ascertain, and declare by express deed of trust, the parties' intentions as to the extent of their respective beneficial shares in the land.

DILLON LJ: . . . The transfer of 33 Foxberry Road to Mr Hall and Mrs Walker is in the common form of a Land Registry Transfer. It transfers the property to Mr Hall and Mrs Walker as joint tenants but contains no statement of what their respective beneficial interests are to be. Ten years ago Bagnall J in *Cowcher* v *Cowcher* [1972] 1 WLR 425 at p. 442 drew attention to the desirability that solicitors should take steps to find out and declare what the beneficial interests are to be, when the legal estate in a house is acquired by two persons in their joint names. The difficulties which otherwise arise, and which can so easily be avoided by a little care on the part of the solicitors, were emphasized recently by Griffiths LJ in *Bernard* v *Josephs* (1983) 4 FLR 178. I would wish to underline the point as strongly as I can and to suggest that the courts may soon have to consider whether a solicitor acting for joint purchasers is not guilty of negligence if he fails to find out and record what the joint purhasers' beneficial interests in the relevant property are to be. . . .

If there is evidence that both parties were to have beneficial interests in the house, and there is no further evidence at all to indicate the extent of those interests, the conclusion would be that equity follows the law, and the parties holding the legal estate as joint tenants, are entitled beneficially as joint tenants also. As Lord Upjohn pointed out in *Pettitt* v *Pettitt* [1970] AC 777 at pp. 813–14:

... in the absence of all other evidence, if the property is conveyed ... to the spouses jointly that operates to convey the beneficial interest to the spouses jointly, i.e. with benefit of survivorship, but it is seldom that this will be determinative.

In particular, the law of trusts has concentrated on how the purchase money has been provided and it has been consistently held that where the purchase money for property acquired by two or more persons in their joint names has been provided by those persons in unequal amounts, they will be beneficially entitled as between themselves in the proportions in which they provided the purchase money. This is the basic doctrine of the resulting trust.

GOODMAN v *GALLANT* [1986] 2 WLR 236, Court of Appeal

FACTS: A married couple purchased a house in their joint names and held it as beneficial joint tenants in equity. The husband left his wife (the plaintiff) and the defendant moved in with her. They purchased the husband's interest from him, the conveyance providing that the plaintiff and defendant were to hold the property on trust for sale as joint tenants in equity. The defendant left and the plaintiff served a notice severing the tenancy. She then issued a summons for a declaration as to their respective shares in the property. She claimed to be entitled to a three-quarters share. The registrar held that the express declaration of the joint tenancy in equity had established their respective beneficial shares, upon severance, as half and half. The judge at first instance upheld the registrar's conclusion and the plaintiff appealed to the Cout of Appeal.
HELD: The appeal was dismissed.

SLADE LJ: ... sections 34 to 36, while importing a trust for sale in certain cases where it would not otherwise have arisen, are designed merely to simplify the mechanics of conveyancing. They have no effect whatever on the nature and extent of the respective beneficial interest in the proceeds of sale of the several persons interested. Accordingly, in our judgment, the provisions of clause 2(a) of the conveyance, by which *express trusts* are declared concerning the beneficial interests in the property or its proceeds of sale, cannot be regarded as otiose. The position is quite the contrary.

In a case where the legal estate in property is conveyed to two or more persons as joint tenants, but neither the conveyance nor any other written document contains any express declaration of trust concerning the beneficial interests in the property (as would be required for an express declaration of this nature by virtue of section 53(1)(b) of the Law of Property Act 1925), the way is open for persons claiming a beneficial interest in it or its proceeds of sale to rely on the doctrine of 'resulting, implied or constructive trusts': see section 53(2) of the Law of Property Act 1925. In particular, in a case such as that, a person who claims to have contributed to the purchase price of property which stands in the name of himself and another can rely on the well known presumption of equity that a person who has contributed a share of the purchase price of property is entitled to a corresponding proportionate beneficial interest in the property by way of implied or resulting trust: see, for example, *Pettitt* v *Pettitt* [1970] AC 777, 813–814, *per* Lord Upjohn. If, however, the relevant conveyance contains an express declaration of trust which comprehensively declares the beneficial interests in the property or its proceed of sale, there is no room for the application of the doctrine of resulting implied or constructive trusts unless and until the conveyance is set aside or rectified; until that event the declaration contained in the document speaks for itself.

... in the absence of any claim for rectification or rescission, the provision in the conveyance declaring that the plaintiff and the defendant were to hold the proceeds of sale of the property 'upon trust for themselves as joint tenants' concludes the question of the respective beneficial interests of the two parties in so far as that declaration of trust, on its true construction, exhaustively declares the beneficial interests.

CHAPTER FIFTEEN

SEVERANCE OF JOINT TENANCIES

15.1 Methods of Severance

Since 1925, a legal tenancy cannot be severed. Any severance affects only the equitable interests under the trust for sale. In this section we shall consider the various methods of severance of the equitable joint tenancy.

15.1.1 TOTAL ALIENATION

If a joint tenant sells (or gives away inter vivos) his equitable interest, that effects a severance.

15.1.2 BANKRUPTCY

RE DENNIS (A BANKRUPT) [1992] 3 WLR 204, Chancery Division

FACTS: A husband and wife were beneficial joint tenants of certain freehold properties. On 21 September 1982 the husband failed to comply with a bankruptcy notice and as a consequence of this failure a bankruptcy petition was served on him. Before he was actually declared bankrupt his wife died, having devised her estate on her children. The trustee in bankruptcy applied for a declaration that the two freeholds were vested in him. HELD: The joint tenancy had been severed by the final adjudication of bankruptcy, and not by the failure to comply with the notice, nor by service of the petition. Accordingly, the joint tenancy had not been severed before the wife's death and the two properties could not devolve as part of her estate. They had vested in her husband by right of survivorship and were now vested in the trustee in bankruptcy.

SIR DONALD NICHOLLS V-C: A joint tenancy is severed if a joint tenant disposes of his interest *inter vivos*. Such a disposition may be voluntary, for example a gift or a sale; it may be involuntary, as occurs upon bankruptcy when the bankrupt's property vests in his trustee. In the present case the position when Mrs. Dennis died was that her husband had not yet been adjudicated bankrupt. He had committed an act of bankruptcy and a petition had been presented. The petition had been followed by a receiving order. This was after Mrs. Dennis' death, but in any event a receiving order does not operate to divest a debtor of his property. If authority is needed for that proposition, it can be found in the decision of the Court of Appeal in *Rhodes* v *Dawson* (1886) 16 QBD 548. Thus, by the moment of Mrs. Dennis' death on 24 February 1983, there had been no alienation by her husband of his interest in the joint tenancy.

Subsequently he became bankrupt. At that moment he was divested of his property. At that moment there was therefore an involuntary alienation by him of his property. The concluding words of section 18(1) of the Bankruptcy Act 1914 provide for the consequence of an adjudication in these terms: 'and thereupon the property of the bankrupt shall become divisible among his creditors and shall vest in a trustee.' To the like effect is section 53 which provides:

(1) Until a trustee is appointed, the official receiver shall be the trustee for the purposes of this Act, and, immediately on a debtor being adjusted bankrupt, the property of the bankrupt shall vest in the trustee. (2) On the appointment of a trustee, the property shall forthwith pass to and vest in the trustee appointed.

Both these statutory provisions provide that there vests in the trustee 'the property of the bankrupt.' Section 38 specifies what the expression means. By way of introduction to section 38 I should refer to the familiar provisions in section 37 concerning relation back of a trustee's title. The material part of section 37(1) provides:

The bankruptcy of a debtor . . . shall be deemed to have relation back to, and to commence at, the time of the act of bankruptcy being committed on which a receiving order is made against him. . . .

Section 38 provides:

The property of the bankrupt divisible amongst his creditors, and in this Act referred to as the property of the bankrupt, shall not comprise the following particulars. . . . —Two types of property are then specified which I need not refer to. The section then continues—'But it shall comprise the following particulars:—(a) All such property as may belong to or be vested in the bankrupt at the commencement of the bankruptcy, or may be acquired by or devolve on him before his discharge; . . .

It is clear, therefore, that the property which vests in the trustee when an adjudication order is made includes property which was vested in the bankrupt at an earlier date. Here, when the relevant act of bankruptcy occurred, Mr. Dennis was a beneficial joint tenant of the two properties. In my view, however, the effect of section 38(a) is not to vest title in the trustee retrospectively in the sense that under the Act he is deemed to have had title at the commencement of the bankruptcy; the effect of section 38(a) is to vest in the trustee, when adjudication occurs, title to property which is identified by reference to the property which belonged to the bankrupt at the commencement of the bankruptcy. The consequence of this may be, and in some cases will be, to divest a third party of title to property which since the commencement of the bankruptcy he has acquired from the bankrupt. That divesting occurs when the adjudication order is made, not before. Hence in the present case Mr. Dennis had not been divested of his interest under the joint tenancy when his wife died. When she died the joint tenancy still subsisted. . . .

In the result, therefore, the adjudication of Mr. Dennis as bankrupt after the death of his wife did not have the effect of severing retrospectively the joint tenancy before her death. On the contrary, upon adjudication there vested in Mr. Dennis' trustee the entire beneficial interest in the two properties which, on Mrs. Dennis' death, had passed to Mr. Dennis as the surviving joint tenant. I shall therefore make the declarations sought. . . .

15.1.3 PARTIAL ALIENATION

A partial alienation would occur where a joint tenant mortgaged or leased his or her interest.

15.1.4 CONTRACT TO ALIENATE

If a joint tenant contracts to sell, lease, or mortgage his interest that will effect a severance.

15.1.5 WRITTEN NOTICE AND INFORMAL SEVERANCE UNDER THE LAW OF PROPERTY ACT 1925

LAW OF PROPERTY ACT 1925

36. Joint tenancies

(1) Where a legal estate (not being settled land) is beneficially limited to or held in trust for any persons as joint tenants, the same shall be held on trust for sale, in like manner as if the persons beneficially entitled were tenants in common, but not so as to sever their joint tenancy in equity.

(2) No severance of a joint tenancy of a legal estate, so as to create a tenancy in common land, shall be permissible, whether by operation of law or otherwise, but this subsection does not affect the right of a joint tenant to release his interest to the other joint tenants, or the right to sever a joint tenancy in an equitable interest whether or not the legal estate is vested in the joint tenants:

Provided that, where a legal estate (not being settled land) is vested in joint tenants beneficially, and any tenant desires to sever the joint tenancy in equity, he shall give to the other joint tenants a notice in writing of such desire or do such other acts or things as would, in the case of personal estate, have been effectual to sever the tenancy in equity, and thereupon under the trust for sale affecting the land the net proceeds of sale, and the net rents and profits until sale, shall be held upon the trusts which would have been requisite for giving effect to the beneficial interests if there had been an actual severance.

Nothing in this Act affects the right of a survivor of joint tenants, who is solely and beneficially interested, to deal with his legal estate as if it were not held on trust for sale.

(3) Without prejudice to the right of a joint tenant to release his interest to the other joint tenants no severance of a mortgage term or trust estate, so as to create a tenancy in common, shall be permissible.

15.1.5.1 Severance by written notice

LAW OF PROPERTY ACT 1925

196. Regulations respecting notices

(1) Any notice required or authorised to be served or given by this Act shall be in writing.

(2) Any notice required or authorised by this Act to be served on a lessee or mortgagor shall be sufficient, although only addressed to the lessee or mortgagor by that designation, without his name, or generally to the persons interested, without any name, and notwithstanding that any person to be affected by the notice is absent, under disability, unborn, or unascertained.

(3) Any notice required or authorised by this Act to be served shall be sufficiently served if it is left at the last-known place of abode or business in the United Kingdom of the lessee, lessor, mortgagee, mortgagor, or other person to be served, or, in case of a notice required or authorised to be served on a lessee or mortgagor, is affixed or left for him on the land or any house or building comprised in the lease or mortgage, or, in case of a mining lease, is left for the lessee at the office or counting-house of the mine.

(4) Any notice required or authorised by this Act to be served shall also be sufficiently served, if it is sent by post in a registered letter addressed to the lessee, lessor, mortgagee, mortgagor, or other person to be served, by name, at the aforesaid place of abode or business, office, or counting-house, and if that letter is not returned through the post office undelivered; and that service shall be deemed to be made at the time at which the registered letter would in the ordinary course be delivered. . . .

RE 88 BERKELEY ROAD, N.W.9. [1971] 1 All ER 254, Chancery Division

FACTS: Two unmarried ladies, Miss Eldridge and Miss Goodwin, were joint tenants of their home, 88 Berkeley Road. Eldridge announced that she was getting married. Goodwin consulted solicitors, who advised her to sever the joint tenancy. The solicitors drafted a notice of severance and this was sent by recorded delivery to Eldridge at her 'residence', 88 Berkeley Road. When the postman called, Eldridge had already gone to work. Goodwin signed for the letter. Goodwin died soon afterwards. In the ensuing proceedings, Eldridge swore that she had never seen the letter. The question was whether there had been an effective severance of the joint tenancy.

HELD: There had been a severance, because the letter had not been 'returned undelivered' and was therefore notice of severance was deemed to have been properly served.

PLOWMAN J: Mr. Bramall's second submission was, if he will allow me to say so, an ingenious one. He pointed to the words in section 196(4)—and I quote: '. . . if that letter is not returned through the post office undelivered'—and he submitted that the facts of the present case showed that the letter was delivered into the hand of Miss Goodwin: in other words, it was really delivered to the sender, because the solicitors who sent it were Miss Goodwin's solicitors and her agents for this purpose, and that, since the letter was delivered into the hands of the sender, it was in effect returned through the Post Office undelivered.

Again, I do not feel able to accept that submission. In my view, the words '. . . if that letter is not returned through the post office undelivered' refer to the ordinary case of the Post Office being unable to effect delivery at the address on the letter for some reason or other, such as that the addressee has gone away or the house is shut or empty. It does not, in my judgment, apply to a case like the present where the letter has in fact been delivered by the postman at the address to which it was sent.

The third submission which Mr. Bramall made was to this effect, that where a section in an Act of Parliament is potentially creating an unjust situation, as would be the case here if the notice is to be taken as having been received by the plaintiff although she never received it, then the Act ought to be construed strictly, and that that involves strict proof that the relevant document—the letter containing the notice of severance, in this case—was in fact served. And Mr. Bramall pointed out that Mr. Bender, who was an assistant solicitor in the firm of solicitors who were Miss Goodwin's solicitors at this time and who was responsible for dealing with this matter, could not actually prove putting the notice of severance in the envelope with the covering letter before it was sent. In my judgment, the onus of proof on the defendants here is no higher than proof that, on the balance of probabilities, that was done; and I feel no difficulty in reaching the conclusion that, on the balance of probabilities, it was in fact done.

For those reasons, I cannot accept Mr. Bramall's submissions on section 196(4). . . .

In those circumstances, and with some regret having regard to my findings of fact, I feel bound to conclude that the notice of severance, even though never received by the plaintiff, was in fact sufficiently served for the purposes of section 36(2) of the Law of Property Act 1925 with the consequence that the joint tenancy was severed during the lifetime of Miss Goodwin.

HARRIS v GODDARD [1983] 1 WLR 1203, Court of Appeal

FACTS: A husband and wife were beneficial joint tenants of the matrimonial home, from which the husband ran his retail business. After some time, the wife left and served a divorce petition. Paragraph 3 of the petition prayed that 'such order may be made by way of transfer or property and/or settlement of property and/or variation of settlement in respect of the former matrimonial home . . . and otherwise as may be just'. Three days before the hearing of the petition the husband was involved in a car crash, resulting in a coma from which he never recovered. The husband's executors sought a declaration that the joint tenancy of the former matrimonial home had been effectively severed before the husband's death. They pointed to paragraph 3 of the divorce petition as constituting a valid notice of severance within the proviso to s. 36(2) of the Law of Property Act 1925.

HELD: Severance had not been effected before the husband's death. A notice of severance within s. 36(2) had to evince an intention to sever immediately. The paragraph in the petition had merely expressed the wife's desire to invite the court to exercise its jurisdiction to apportion property entitlements according to justice. She could not have known the precise course that the court might take.

LAWTON LJ: I start with section 36. It dealt with beneficial tenancies, which must mean all joint tenancies, including those held by husbands and wives. The section makes no special provisions by way of giving extra rights or raising presumptions in favour of spouses. When severance is said to arise under section 36(2), not from the giving of a notice in writing, but from '[doing] . . . other acts or things' which would, in the case of personal estate, have been effectual to sever a joint tenancy in equity, the fact that the parties were married may make the drawing of inferences easier. It is, in my judgment, only in this limited evidential context that the existence of the married state has any relevance. In reaching this conclusion I have followed what Russell LJ said in *Bedson* v *Bedson* [1965] 2 QB 666, 689–690 rather than the obiter statement of Lord Denning MR in the same case at p. 678. Lord Denning MR said that spouses holding as beneficial joint tenants cannot sever their interests so as to convert them into tenancies in common. The trial judge seems to have been influenced to some extent by what Lord Denning MR said. Since in this case severance is said to have come about by a notice in writing the sole question is whether that which is said to be the notice did show that Mrs. Harris desired to sever the joint tenancy.

In *Williams* v *Hensman* (1861) 1 Johns & Hem 546, 557, Page-Wood V-C said that a joint tenancy could be severed in three ways, that is, by disposal of one of the interests, by mutual agreement and 'by any course of dealing sufficient to intimate that the interests of all were mutually treated as constituting a tenancy in common.' The words in section 36(2) 'do such other acts or things as would . . . have been effectual to sever the tenancy' put into statutory language the other ways of effecting severance to which Page Wood V-C referred in *Williams* v *Hensman*. The words 'and any tenant desires to sever the joint tenancy in equity, he shall give to the other joint tenants a notice in writing of such desire' operate to extend the mutual agreement concept of severance referred to in *Williams* v *Hensman*. Unilateral action to sever a joint tenancy is now possible. Before 1925 severance by unilateral action was only possible when one joint tenant disposed of his interest to a third party. When a notice in writing of a desire to sever is served pursuant to section 36(2) it takes effect forthwith. It follows that a desire to sever must evince an intention to bring about the wanted result immediately. A notice in writing which expresses a desire to bring about the wanted result at some time in the future is not, in my judgment, a notice in writing within section 36(2). Further the notice must be one which allows an intent to bring about the consequences set out in section 36(2), namely, that the net proceeds of the statutory trust for sale 'shall be held upon the trusts which would have been requisite for giving effect to the beneficial interests if there had been an actual severance.' I am unable to accept Mr. Berry's submission that a notice in writing which shows no more than a desire to bring the existing interest to an end is a good notice. It must be a desire to sever which is intended to have the statutory consequences. . . .

Perhaps this case should be a cautionary tale for those who draft divorce petitions when the spouses hold property as joint tenants in equity. The decision of Plowman J in *In re Draper's Conveyance* [1969] 1 Ch 486 is an example of how starting legal proceedings can sever a joint tenancy. In that case a wife, after a decree nisi but before a decree absolute, issued a summons under section 17 of the Married Women's Property Act 1882 asking for an order that a house in the joint names of herself and her husband be sold and the proceeds of sale distributed in accordance with the parties' respective interests therein. An affidavit sworn by the wife in support of the summons contained this paragraph:

> In the premises I humbly ask that the said property may be sold and that the proceeds of sale thereof may be distributed equally; alternatively that the respondent pay me one half of the value of the said property with vacant possession. . . .

Plowman J adjudged that the summons and the affidavit together effected a severance during the lifetime of the husband. I agree that it did; but it is not clear from the judgment whether the judge regarded the summons or the affidavit or both as notices in writing or whether the service of the summons and the filing of the affidavit were acts which were effectual to sever the joint tenancy. I do not share the doubts about the correctness of this judgment on this point which Walton J expressed in *Nielson-Jones* v *Fedden* [1975] Ch 222, 236 relying on *In re Wilks* [1981] 3 Ch 59. The fact that the wife in *In re Draper's Conveyance* [1969] 1 Ch 486 could have withdrawn the summons is a factor which could have been taken into account in deciding whether what was done was effectual to sever the joint tenancy in equity. The weight of that factor would have depended upon all the other circumstances and was in that case clearly negligible.

I would dismiss the appeal.

RE DRAPER'S CONVEYANCE [1969] 1 Ch 486, Chancery Division

FACTS: A husband and wife held the matrimonial home in joint tenants in equity. Some time later the wife served a divorce petition. Between decree nisi and decree absolute of the divorce, the wife sought an order under the Married Women's Property Act 1882 in terms that the house be sold and the proceeds apportioned according to the parties respective interests therein.

The registrar granted the wife an order for possession but the husband died shortly afterwards and the house was not sold. The wife issued a summons to determine the basis on which she currently held title to the matrimonial home.

HELD: The wife's summons and supporting affidavit under the Married Women's Property Act 1882 evinced an intention to sever the joint tenancy.

PLOWMAN J: . . . Mr. Cooke, . . . puts it in two ways; first, he submits that the wife's conduct was such as to effect a severance of the joint tenancy, and in relation to that matter he relies on the summons of February 11 1966, in the Probate, Divorce and Admiralty Division, coupled with the orders which were made by that court, coupled with the plaintiff's solicitor's letter of June 7 1966. And he says, either as a result of those three matters or as a result of any of them, the joint tenancy became severed by conduct, and he referred me to the decision of Havers J in *Hawkesley* v *May* [1956] 1 QB 304. The part of that case which is relevant for present purposes depends upon these facts, which I read from the headnote: 'A settled fund was held by trustees upon trusts under which on attaining the age 21 the plaintiff and his younger sister became absolutely entitled as joint tenants.' The question was whether that joint tenancy had become severed, and Havers J. said:

> The joint tenancy was capable of being severed by the plaintiff on attaining the age of 21. There are a number of ways by which a joint tenancy may be servered. In *Williams* v *Hensman* (1861) 1 Johns & Hem 546 Page-Wood V-C in the course of his judgment, said: 'A joint-tenancy may be severed in three ways: in the first place, an act of any one of the persons interested operating upon his own share may create a severance as to that share. The right of each joint-tenant is a right by survivorship only in the event of no severance having taken place of the share which is claimed under the jus accrescendi. Each one is at liberty to dispose of his own interest in such manner as to sever it from the joint fund—losing, of course, at the same time, his own right of survivorship. Secondly, a joint-tenancy may be severed by mutual agreement. And, in the third place, there may be a severance by any course of dealing sufficient to intimate that the interests of all were mutually treated as constituting a tenancy in common. When the severance depends on an inference of this kind without any express act of severance, it will not suffice to rely on an intention, with respect to the particular share, declared only behind the backs of the other persons interested.'

Havers J continued:

> The first method indicated, namely, an act of any one of the persons interested operating upon his own share, obviously includes a declaration of intention to sever by one party.' . . .

So from that case I derive this; a declaration by one of a number of joint tenants of his intention to sever operates as a severance. Mr. Cooke also, as I have said, relied upon the notice in writing which under section 36(2) of the Law of Property Act, 1925, is allowed in the case of a joint tenancy in land, although not in personalty, and he submits that the summons to which I have already referred, although not signed, amounted to a notice in writing on the part of the wife that she desired to sever the joint tenancy in equity. I say 'although not signed by the wife or by anybody on her behalf' because there is no requirement in the subsection of a signature.

. . . I feel little doubt that in one way or the other this joint tenancy was severed in equity before the end of February 1966, as a result of the summons which was served on the husband and as a result of what the wife stated in her affidavit in support of the summons. . . .

15.1.6   INFORMAL SEVERANCE

BURGESS v RAWNSLEY [1975] 1 Ch 429, Court of Appeal

FACTS: Mr. Honick (a widower) and Mrs. Rawnsley (a widow) met at a scripture rally in Trafalgar Square. They became close friends and bought as joint tenants the fee simple to the house of which Mr. Honick had hitherto been a tenant. However, they later fell out. It was orally agreed that Honick should buy out Mrs. Rawnsley's interest for £750. Before matters could finally be resolved, Honick died. The issue before the court was whether there had or had not been a severance.

HELD: The oral agreement (though not an enforceable contract) had been sufficient to sever the joint tenancy.

LORD DENNING MR: . . . Nowadays everyone starts with the judgment of Sir William Page Wood V-C in *Williams* v *Hensman* (1861) 1 John & Hem 546, 557, where he said:

> A joint tenancy may be severed in three ways: in the first place, an act of any one of the persons interested operating upon his own share may create a severance as to that share. . . . Secondly, a joint tenancy may be severed by mutual agreement. And, in the third place, there may a severance by any course of dealing sufficient to intimate that the interests of all were mutually treated as constituting a tenancy in common. When the severance depends on an inference of this kind without any express act of severance, it will not suffice to rely on an intention, with respect to the particular share, declared only behind the backs of the other persons interested. You must find in this class of cases a course of dealing by which the shares of all the parties to the contest have been effected, as happened in the cases of *Wilson* v *Bell* (1843) 5 IrEqR 501 and *Jackson* v *Jackson* (1804) 9 Ves Jun 591.

In that passage Page Wood V-C distinguished between severance 'by mutual agreement' and severance by a 'course of dealing.' That shows that a 'course of dealing' need not amount to an agreement, expressed or implied, for severance. It is sufficient if there is a course of dealing in which one party makes clear to the other that he desires that their shares should no longer he held jointly but be held in common. I emphasise that it must be made clear to the other party. That is implicit in the sentence in which Page Wood V-C says:

> it will not suffice to rely on an intention, with respect to the particular share, declared only behind the backs of the other persons interested.

Similarly it is sufficient if both parties enter on a course of dealing which evinces an intention by both of them that their shares shall henceforth be held in common and not jointly. As appears from the two cases to which Page Wood V-C referred of *Wilson* v *Bell* 5 IrEqR 501 and *Jackson* v *Jackson* 9 Ves Jun 591.

I come now to the question of notice. Suppose that one party gives a notice in writing to the other saying that he desires to sever the joint tenancy. Is that sufficient to effect a severance? I think it is. It was certainly the view of Sir Benjamin Cherry when he drafted section 36(2) of the Law of Property Act 1925. It says in relation to real estates:

> . . . where a legal estate (not being settled land) is vested in joint tenants beneficially, and any tenant desires to sever the joint tenancy in equity, he shall give to the other joint tenants a notice in writing of such desire or do such other acts or things as would, in the case of personal estate, have been effectual to sever the tenancy in equity, and thereupon under the trust for sale affecting the land the net proceeds of sale, and the net rents and profits until sale, shall be held upon the trusts which would have been requisite for giving effect to the beneficial interests if there had been an actual severance.

I have underlined the important words. The word 'other' is most illuminating. It shows quite plainly that, in the case of personal estate one of the things which is effective in equity to sever a joint tenancy is 'a notice in writing' of a desire to sever. So also in regard to real estate.

Taking this view, I find myself in agreement with Havers J in *Hawkesley* v *May* [1956] 1 QB 304, 313–314, and of Plowman J in *In re Draper's Conveyance* [1969] 1 Ch 486. I cannot agree with Walton J [1975] Ch 222, 234–235, that those cases were wrongly decided. It would be absurd that there should be a difference between real estate and personal estate in this respect. Suppose real estate is held on a joint tenancy on a trust for sale and is sold and converted into personal property. Before sale, it is severable by notice in writing. It would be ridiculous if it could not be severed afterwards in like manner. I look upon section 36(2) as declaratory of the law as to severance by notice and not a a new provision confined to real estate. A joint tenancy in personal estate can be severed by notice just as a joint tenancy in real estate. . . .

It remains to apply these principles to the present case. I think there was evidence that Mr. Honick and Mrs. Rawnsley did come to an agreement that he would buy her share for £750. That agreement was not in writing and it was not specifically enforceable. Yet it was sufficient to effect a severance. Even if there was not any firm agreement but only a course of dealing, it clearly evinced an intention by both parties that the property should henceforth be held in common and not jointly.

On these grounds I would dismiss the appeal.

SIR JOHN PENNYCUICK: . . . I think it may be helpful to state very shortly certain views which I have formed in the light of the authorities.

(1) I do not think rule 3 in Page Wood V-C's statement, 1 John & Hem 546, 557, is a mere sub-heading of rule 2. It covers only acts of the parties, including, it seems to me, negotiations which, although not otherwise resulting in any agreement, indicate a common intention that the joint tenancy should be regarded as severed.

I do not overlook the words which I have read from Page Wood V-C's statement, namely, that you must find a course of dealing by which the shares of all the parties to the contract have been affected. But I do not think those words are sufficient to import a binding agreement.

(2) Section 36(2) of the Law of Property Act 1925 has radically altered the law in respect of severance by introducing an entirely new method of severance as regards land, namely, notice in writing given by one joint tenant to the other.

(3) Pre-1925 judicial statements, in particular that of Stirling J in *In re Wilks, Child* v *Bulmer* [1891] 3 Ch 59, must be read in the light of this alteration in the law; and, in particular, I do not see why the commencement of legal proceedings by writ or originating summons or the swearing of an affidavit in those proceedings, should not in appropriate circumstances constitute notice in writing within the meaning of section 36(2). The fact that the plaintiff is not obliged to prosecute the proceedings is I think irrelevant in regard to notice.

(4) Perhaps in parenthesis because the point does not arise, the language of section 36(2) appears to contemplate that even under the existing law notice in writing would be effective to sever a joint tenancy in personalty; see the words 'such other act or thing.' The authorities to the contrary are rather meagre and I am not sure how far this point was ever really considered in relation to personalty before 1925. If this anomaly does exist, and I am afraid I am not prepared to say positively that it does not exist, the anomaly is quite indefensible and should be put right as soon as possible.

(6) An uncommunicated declaration by one party to the other or indeed a mere verbal notice by one party to another clearly cannot operate as a severance.

(7) The policy of the law as it stands today, having regard particularly to section 36(2), is to facilitate severance at the instance of either party, and I do not think the court should be over zealous in drawing a fine distinction from the pre-1925 authorities.

(8) The foregoing statement of principles involves criticism of certain passages in the judgments of Plowman J and Walton J in the two cases cited. Those cases, like all other cases, depend on their own particular facts, and I do not myself wish to go on to apply these *obiter* statements of principle to the actual decisions in these cases.

Finally, I would say that if, contrary to my view, there was a resulting trust in this case, I should have no doubt that, on the particular facts in the case, the resulting trust would be for Mr. Honick and for Mrs. Rawnsley in equal shares. I was referred to *Robinson v Preston* (1858) 4 Kay & J 505. The circumstances of the present case are I think plainly such as to take this case out of the general principle laid down in that case as applicable apart from particular circumstances.

I would dismiss the appeal.

15.2   Matters which are Not a Severance

15.2.1   UNILATERAL ORAL STATEMENTS

Lord Denning in *Burgess v Rawnsley* (**15.1.6** above) took the view that even a unilateral oral statement by one joint tenant to the other(s) could amount to severance. This view is not shared by any other judge (ancient or modern) and is clearly wrong.

15.2.2   SUBSEQUENT USE OF PROPERTY FOR BUSINESS PURPOSES

BARTON v *MORRIS* [1985] 2 All ER 1032, Chancery Division

FACTS: A farm was conveyed to two cohabitees on express trust for themselves as joint tenants in equity. 'The property was run as a guest house and small farm on a partnership basis and Miss Barton kept partnership accounts which showed the farm as a partnership asset'.

HELD: The use of the property for the purpose of a partnership did not, on the facts of the present case, sever the joint tenancy.

NICHOLLS J: In this action it is common ground that Miss Barton and Mr Morris carried on their business as a partnership at will, with profits and losses being shared equally. There was no written partnership agreement. . . .

Counsel for the plaintiff advanced the case in favour of severance in two ways. He accepted that the onus of establishing severance lay on the plaintiff, but he pointed out that equity leans in favour of tenancies in common. He observed, and I accept, that in a case such as this, the evidence of Mr Morris as the survivor must be viewed with caution. He drew my attention, amongst other authorities, to the judgment of Lord Denning MR in *Burgess v Rawnsley* [1975] 3 All ER 142 at 146–147, [1975] Ch 429 at 438–439. Lord Denning MR referred to Page Wood V-C's well-known classification in *Williams v Hensman* (1861) 1 John & H 546 at 557–558, 70 ER 862 at 867, of the three ways in which a joint tenancy may be severed. In short the third of these three modes of severance is by any course of dealing sufficient to intimate that the interests of the joint tenants were mutually treated as constituting a tenancy in common. . . .

. . . Here, submitted counsel for the plaintiff, there was such a course of dealing. The property was made subject to a joint tenancy declared in August 1979, but at that stage Miss Barton and Mr Morris did not want a formal partnership agreement. They wanted to see how the business went. By the autumn of 1980 Miss Barton had paid off the whole of the bank loan from her own money and the way ahead had become clearer. It was submitted that in this manner there had been a change in the situation. Further funds had been injected by Miss Barton as a matter of necessity, and thereafter the property and the partnership became inextricably interwoven. What happened, and this is the course of dealing relied on, was that Miss Barton prepared draft accounts to the knowledge of Mr Morris, showing the property as a partnership asset. The two of them then visited Mr Howells, and without dissent from Mr Morris Miss Barton indicated that the property was to be included for the sake of completeness. Matters then proceeded on that footing.

. . . To my mind the evidence establishes clearly that when the express declaration of joint tenancy in the conveyance was executed by the parties in about mid-August 1979, they both knew what the effect of that joint tenancy would be, and they both intended that the property should automatically accrue to the survivor on the death of the first to die. I accept the evidence of Miss Malthouse, the solicitor who acted for the parties on their purchase, concerning what passed between her and Miss Barton and Mr Morris on this topic prior to completion. In particular, beneficial joint tenancy was Miss Barton's intention, even though she was providing the lion's share of the purchase price. Again, it is plain from the evidence that from the outset the parties hoped and intended that the farmhouse would be used by them as a guest-house, and indeed, they took over one booking from their vendor. They planned to carry on such a business there together, with the house also being their home. Improvements and decorations would be necessary and Mr Morris was to carry out the heavy physical work. . . .

In those circumstances I am wholly unable to accept that the events relied on by counsel for the plaintiff as constituting the course of dealing he submits do in fact do so. . . .

15.2.3 'SEVERANCE BY WILL'

A joint tenancy cannot be severed by will.

CHAPTER SIXTEEN

THE PROBLEMS WHEN CO-OWNERS FALL OUT

16.1 Tenancy in Common Arising Because There is a Constructive Trust

16.1.1 DISPOSITIONS BY A SINGLE TRUSTEE

16.1.1.1 Registered title

ELIAS v MITCHELL AND ANOTHER [1972] 1 Ch 652, Chancery Division

FACTS: Two business partners had fallen out. One was the sole registered proprietor of their business premises, but both had 'shares' (as tenants in common) in the premises. The partner who was not the registered proprietor had left those premises.
HELD: The interest of the 'departed' partner was a minor interest which could be protected by lodging a caution.

PENNYCUICK V-C: . . . When one reads the definition of 'minor interests' in section 3(xv) it seems to me perfectly clear that although what is defined is simply 'minor interests.' that is intended as a definition of minor interests in land. The opening words 'interests not capable of being disposed of or created by registered dispositions and capable of being overridden . . . by the proprietors unless protected as provided by this Act . . .' relate straight back to section 2(1): '. . . all other interests in registered land . . . shall take effect in equity as minor interests . . .' Reading those two subsections together it seems to me clear that the entire subject matter of the definition of 'minor interests' consists of interests in land. Then one finds in section 3(xv)(a) that interests under a trust for sale are expressly included among minor interests; and it follows that those particular interests under a trust for sale are treated, for the purpose of this Act, as being minor interests in land.

Then one comes to section 54(1): 'Any person interested . . . howsoever, in any land . . . may lodge a caution . . .' If it is right to say that an interest in the proceeds of sale being by definition a minor interest is, within the intendment of this Act, an interest in land, then there is no doubt that a person interested in the proceeds of sale is a person interested in land for the purpose of section 54(1) and can accordingly lodge a caution. If there were any doubt on this point, it would, I think, be set at rest by section 101(3) which provides that minor interests may be protected by entry on the register of cautions. So that subsection in terms provides that minor interests, which by definition include interests under a trust for sale, may be protected by entry on the register, and that means that such interests are interests in land within the scope of section 54.

I should at this stage refer to the statutory provision which preceded section 54 of the Act of 1925, namely, section 96 of the Land Registry Act 1862:

Any person interested under an agreement, or otherwise howsoever, in any land or charge registered in the name of any other person, may lodge a caveat with the registrar to the effect that no disposition of such land or charge be made until notice has been served upon the cautioner.

It will be seen that under that section a person who was an equitable tenant in common of land could have lodged a caveat, he being at that date indisputably a person interested in land. So in that respect section 54 of the Act of 1925, as I have construed it, reproduces the pre-existing law, but if section 54 had a narrower scope it would be altering the pre-existing law by excluding from the persons having the right to lodge a caution equitable tenants in common who have now become persons interested only in the proceeds of the sale of the land. I mention that point because it is, I think, of intrinsic importance and it is one on which reliance has been placed in more than one of the authorities on other sections raising a comparable point. I should make it clear that my conclusion would be the same apart from that point. I say that because the point was raised at a very late stage in the hearing and was perhaps not fully argued.

Mr. Hames contended that the expression 'minor interests' does not indicate exclusively interests in land and that an interest in the proceeds of the sale of land is not in itself an interest in land. He stressed that under the legislation of 1925 an interest in an undivided share in land can no longer exist and that an interest in the proceeds of sale of land does not itself constitute land. That is undoubtedly so, but the question is whether in the context of this particular Act such an interest is a minor interest within the definition in section 3(xv). For the reasons which I have given I have reached the conclusion that it is. . . .

Apart from authority then, I conclude that the plaintiff, having an interest in the proceeds of sale under this trust for sale, is a person interested in the land within the meaning of section 54 and as such is in a position to lodge a caution. That seems to me an entirely sensible provision in accordance with the general scheme of the Act. Indeed, it would be strange if a person having an interest in the proceeds of sale of land were not in a position to obtain a protection against some threatened misapplication of the land by the registered proprietor. . . .

16.1.2   DISPOSITIONS BY MORE THAN ONE TRUSTEE

LAW OF PROPERTY ACT 1925

2. Conveyances overreaching certain equitable interests and powers

(1)   A conveyance to a purchaser of a legal estate in land shall overreach any equitable interest or power affecting that estate, whether or not he has notice thereof, if—

(i)   the conveyance is made under the powers conferred by the Settled Land Act 1925 or any additional powers conferred by a settlement, and the equitable interest or power is capable of being overreached thereby, and the statutory requirements respecting the payment of capital money arising under the settlement are complied with;

(ii)   the conveyance is made by trustees for sale and the equitable interest or power is at the date of the conveyance capable of being overreached by such trustees under the provisions of sub-section (2) of this section or independently of that sub-section, and the statutory requirements respecting the payment of capital money arising under a disposition upon trust for sale are complied with;

(iii) the conveyance is made by a mortgagee or personal representative in the exercise of his paramount powers, and the equitable interest or power is capable of being overreached by such conveyance, and any capital money arising from the transaction is paid to the mortgagee or personal representative;

(iv)   the conveyance is made under an order of the court and the equitable interest or power is bound by such order, and any capital money arising from the transaction is paid into, or in accordance with the order of, the court.

(2)   Where the legal estate affected is subject to a trust for sale, then if at the date of a conveyance made after the commencement of this Act under the trust for sale or the powers conferred on the trustees for sale, the trustees (whether original or substituted) are either—

(a)   two or more individuals approved or appointed by the court or the successors in office of the individuals so approved or appointed; or

(b)   a trust corporation,

any equitable interest or power having priority to the trust for sale shall, notwithstanding any stipulation to the contrary, be overreached by the conveyance, and shall, according to its priority, take effect as if created or arising by means of a primary trust affecting the proceeds of sale and the income of the land until sale.

(3)   The following equitable interests and powers are excepted from the operation of subsection (2) of this section, namely—

(i)   Any equitable interest protected by a deposit of documents relating to the legal estate affected;

(ii)   The benefit of any covenant or agreement restrictive of the user of land;

(iii)   Any easement, liberty, or privilege over or affecting land and being merely an equitable interest (in this Act referred to as an 'equitable easement');

(iv)   The benefit of any contract (in this Act referred to as an 'estate contract') to convey or create a legal estate, including a contract conferring either expressly or by statutory implication a valid option to purchase, a right of pre-emption, or any other like right;

(v)   Any equitable interest protected by registration under the Land Charges Act 1925 other than—

(a)   an annuity within the meaning of Part II of that Act;

(b)   a limited owner's charge or a general equitable charge within the meaning of that Act.

(4)   Subject to the protection afforded by this section to the purchaser of a legal estate, nothing contained in this section shall deprive a person entitled to an equitable charge of any of his rights or remedies for enforcing the same.

27.   Purchaser not to be concerned with the trusts of the proceeds of sale which are to be paid to two trustees or to a trust corporation

(1)   A purchaser of a legal estate from trustees for sale shall not be concerned with the trusts affecting the proceeds of sale of land subject to a trust for sale (whether made to attach to such proceeds by virtue of this Act or otherwise), or affecting the rents and profits of the land until sale, whether or not those trusts are declared by the same instrument by which the trust for sale is created.

(2)   Notwithstanding anything to the contrary in the instrument (if any) creating a trust for sale of land or in the settlement of the net proceeds, the proceeds for sale or other capital money shall not be paid to or applied by the direction of fewer than two persons as trustees for sale, except where the trustee is a trust corporation, but this subsection does not affect the right of a sole personal representative as such to give valid receipts for, or direct the application of, proceeds of sale or other capital money, nor, except where capital money arises on the transaction, render it necessary to have more than one trustee.

CITY OF LONDON BUILDING SOCIETY v FLEGG [1988] 1 AC 54, House of Lords

FACTS: Mr. and Mrs. Flegg had both contributed to the purchase of a house; the title to the house was registered in the names of their daughter and son-in-law (the Maxwell-Browns). The Fleggs, as a consequence of their contributions, each had an interest as a tenant in common under a resulting trust. All four lived in the house, and were therefore in 'actual occupation'. The house was subsequently mortgaged to the building society by the Maxwell-Browns. The building society argued that the mortgage, being executed by two trustees, overreached the rights of Mr. and Mrs. Flegg and that, as a result, they could sell the house 'over the heads' of the Fleggs.
HELD: The argument of the building society succeeded.

LORD TEMPLEMAN: . . . The respondents claim to be entitled to overriding interests because they were in actual occupation of Bleak House on the date of the legal charge. But the interests of the respondents cannot at one and the same time be overreached and overridden and at the same time be overriding interests. The appellants cannot at one and the same time take free from all the interests of the respondents yet at the same time be subject to some of those interests. The right of the respondents to be and remain in actual occupation of Bleak House ceased when the respondents' interests were overreached by the legal charge save in so far as their rights were transferred to the equity of redemption. As persons interested under the trust for sale the respondents had no right to possession as against the appellants and the fact that the respondents were in actual occupation at the date of the legal charge did not create a new right or transfer an old right so as to make the right enforceable against the appellants.

One of the main objects of the legislation of 1925 was to effect a compromise between on the one hand the interests of the public in securing that land held in trust is freely marketable and, on the other hand, the interests of the beneficiaries in preserving their rights under the trusts. By the Settled Land Act 1925 a tenant for life may convey the settled land discharged from all the trusts powers and provisions of the settlement. By the Law of Property Act 1925 trustees for sale may convey land held on trust for sale discharged from the trusts affecting the proceeds of sale and rents and profits until sale. Under both forms of trust the protection and the only protection of the beneficiaries is that capital money must be paid to at least two trustees or a trust corporation. . . .

For these reasons and for the reasons to be given by my noble and learned friend, Lord Oliver of Aylmerton, I would allow this appeal and restore the order of Judge Thomas who ordered the respondents to deliver up Bleak House to the appellants.

LORD OLIVER OF AYLMERTON: . . . I turn to consider whether, in fact, the decision of this House in *Boland* [1981] AC 487 does lead to the conclusion that the occupying co-owner's interest unde the statutory trusts is, by reason of his occupation, one which is incapable of being overreached. It has, I think, to be borne in mind when reading both the judgments in the Court of Appeal in that case and the speeches in the House that they were prepared and delivered against a background of fact which precluded any argument that the interests of Mrs. Boland and Mrs. Brown had been overreached under the provisions of the Law of Property Act 1925. . . .

Considered in the context of a transaction complying with the statutory requirements of the Law of Property Act 1925 the question of the effect of section 70(1)(g) of the Land Registration Act 1925 must, in my judgment, be approached by asking first what are the 'rights' of the person in occupation and whether they are, at the material time, subsisting in reference to the land. In the instant case the exercise by the registered proprietors of the powers conferred on trustees for sale by section 28(1) of the Law of Property Act 1925 had the effect of overreaching the interests of the respondents under the statutory trusts upon which depended their right to continue in occupation of the land. The appellants took free from those trusts (section 27) and were not, in any event, concerned to see that the respondents' consent to the transaction was obtained (section 26). If, then, one asks what were the subsisting rights of the respondents referable to their occupation, the answer must, in my judgment, be that they were rights which, vis-à-vis the appellants, were, *eo instante* with the creation of the charge, overreached and therefore subsisted only in relation to the equity of redemption. I do not, for my part, find in *Boland's* case [1981] AC 487 anything which compels a contrary conclusion. Granted that the interest of a co-owner pending the execution of the statutory trust for sale is, despite the equitable doctrine of conversion, an interest subsisting in reference to the land the subject matter of the trust and granted also that *Boland's* case establishes that such an interest, although falling within the definition of minor interest and so liable to be overriden by a registered disposition, will, so long as it subsists, be elevated to the status of an overriding interest if there exists also the additional element of occupation by the co-owner, I cannot for my part accept that, once what I may call the parent interest, by which alone the occupation can be justified, has been overreached and thus subordinated to a legal estate properly created by the trustees under their statutory powers, it can, in relation to the proprietor of the legal estate so created, be any longer said to be a right 'for the time being subsisting.' Section 70(1)(g) protects only the rights in reference to the land of the occupier whatever they are at the material time—in the instant case the right to enjoy in specie the rents and profits of the land held in trust for him. Once the beneficiary's rights have been shifted from the land to capital moneys in the hands of the trustees, there is no longer an interest in the land to which the occupation can be referred or which it can protect. If the trustees sell in accordance with the statutory provisions and so overreach the beneficial interests in reference to the land, nothing remains to which a right of occupation can attach and the same result must, in my judgment, follow vis-à-vis a chargee by way of legal mortgage so long as the transaction is carried out in the manner prescribed by the Law of Property Act 1925, overreaching the beneficial interests by subordinating them to the estate of the chargee which is no longer 'affected' by them so as to become subject to them on registration pursuant to section 20(1) of the Land Registration Act 1925. In the instant case, therefore, I would, for my part, hold that the charge created in favour of the appellants overreached the beneficial interests of the respondents and that there is nothing in section 70(1)(g) of the Land Registration Act 1925 or in *Boland's* case which has the effect of preserving against the appellants any rights of the respondents to occupy the land by virtue of their beneficial interests in the equity of redemption which remains vested in the trustees. . . .

Swadling, W.J., 'The Conveyancer's Revenge, *City of London Building Society* v *Flegg* [1987] 2 WLR 1266' (1987) 51 Conv 451 at 454

. . . In *Flegg* it was assumed that overreaching was effected by the Law of Property Act 1925 itself. Lord Templeman thought that the relevant statutory provisions were contained in sections 27 and 28 whilst Lord Oliver preferred to think that it was an amalgam of sections 2, 26, 27 and 28 of the Law of Property Act and section 17 of the Trustee Act 1925 which triggered the process. It is submitted, however, that this approach is incorrect. Overreaching . . . occurs through the exercise of a trustee's powers and is dependent on the purchaser taking without notice of a breach of trust. All the statutory provisions do is to relieve the purchaser from making inquiries where certain procedures are followed. They do not facilitate the overreaching of the beneficial interests themselves which is dependent on the powers conferred by the trust instrument or statutory trust for sale.

On either view, however, it is important that the beneficial interests exist behind a trust for sale since only a purchaser from trustees for sale can claim the protection given by the legislation. Here the House of Lords held that such a trust was imposed by statute. Lord Oliver, however, did find some difficulty with the point. This was because he acknowledged that the way in which the equitable interest of the parents arose, i.e. under a resulting trust, is not specifically dealt with by that part of the 1925 legislation which imposes trusts for sale in certain situations.

> Nevertheless, section 34(1) [Law of Property Act 1925] provides that an undivided share shall not be capable of being created except as provided by the Settled Land Act 1925 or as thereinafter mentioned and section 36(4) of the Settled Land Act 1925 provides in terms that an undivided share in land shall not be capable of being created except under a trust instrument or under the Law of Property Act 1925, and shall then only take effect behind a trust for sale.

This, his Lordship reasoned, established the trust for sale as the conveyancing machinery for ownership of undivided shares. With respect, the result is nothing of the sort. What it means is that if an interest behind a resulting trust is to arise at all then it must do so *despite* the statute using the maxim that equity will not allow a statute to be used as an engine of fraud. If the legislation on the one hand prevents the interest from coming into being it is difficult to see how on the other it turns what would otherwise be a bare trust into a trust for sale. How can it apply to something it forbids? Lord Templeman did not feel that the point even merited discussion. With the drastic consequences such a finding can have on equitable co-owners it is a pity that the whole question was not more fully ventilated. . . .

The Law Commission, Working Paper No. 106, Trusts of Land: Overreaching, London: HMSO, 1988

7. Provisional conclusion

7.1   It is our present view that there is a case for reforming the law on 'overreaching' for private trusts (i.e. when interests in land become instead interests in money). We are also at the moment of the opinion that, in principle, the law would better balance the practical concerns of purchasers and mortgagees against the special needs of beneficiaries for the land itself if it prevented their interests being 'overreached' without their consent where they are in actual occupation and of full age. In other words, we tentatively favour Proposal II [see below]. In addition, we would repeat the suggestion that the 'overreaching' machinery should be available for the protection of purchasers and mortgagees in respect of interests under bare trusts too.

Proposal II: no overreaching without consent of occupying beneficiaries
6.5 . . . it could be suggested that no overreaching should be possible without every beneficiary's consent. It may be argued that the duty to consult is far too limited and that the only way to protect beneficiaries adequately is to involve them directly in every sale or mortgage. However, this wide proposal would be impracticable. The purchaser/mortgagee could have no acceptable means of ascertaining who all the beneficiaries are, and they might not be of full age.
6.6 However, requiring consent of those beneficiaries in occupation may well strike the right balance between beneficiaries and purchasers. Accordingly this Proposal actually is that the interest of an occupying beneficiary should only be capable of being overreached with his or her consent, irrespective of whether the beneficiary has sought to protect himself by an entry on the register. The proposal is consistent with the approach to the rights of occupiers seen in *Boland* and achieves the effect of the Court of Appeal decision in *Flegg*. In cases of a sole registered proprietor or sole estate owner it appears inconsistent to protect benficiaries in actual occupation only until a second trustee is appointed. Further if interests in actual occupation are worth protecting, they ought to be protected whether or not the property was originally conveyed to or subsequently vested in joint owners at law. . . .

Harpum, C., Overreaching, Trustees' Powers and the Reform of the 1925 Legislation, [1990] *Cambridge Law Journal* 277–333

THE BASIS OF OVERREACHING
A number of misconceptions exist about overreaching. The first is that overreaching is something that occurs only in relation to land. It is undoubtedly true that the expression 'overreaching' gained currency during the 19th century and appears always to have been used in connection with dispositions of land. That association has been firmly cemented by the provisions of the Law of Property Act 1925, s. 2, which set out the circumstances in which a conveyance of a legal estate in land will overreach any equitable interest or power affecting that land. But overreaching must take place in relation to other forms of property. A trustee who sells trust investments must necessarily hold the proceeds of sale on the same trusts as the original investment. It must also follow from this that the basis of overreaching does not lie in the statutory provisions of section 2 of the Law of Property Act 1925. It must have a common law basis if it applies to personalty, and there are clear accounts of the effects of overreaching that pre-date the 1925 property legislation.

The second misconception is that overreaching is connected with the doctrine of conversion, at least in relation to trusts for sale. Because of that doctrine, it is said that the interests of the beneficiaries are from the inception of the trust in the proceeds of sale. Such a view is untenable as an explanation of overreaching. First, a disposition under a mere *power* of sale will overreach just as much as a disposition under a trust for sale, and this is so even though the doctrine of conversion is usually relevant to determine whether beneficial interests are in land or in personalty. Overreaching applies as much to trusts for sale of personalty as to trusts of realty. Thirdly, overreaching is concerned to transfer trusts from the original subject-matter of the trust to the *actual* proceeds *after* sale. The beneficial interests of those entitled under a trust for sale, by reason of the doctrine of conversion, are regarded for certain purposes as interests in the *notional* proceeds of sale *from the date of the creation of the trust*. There is no inevitability about the application of the doctrine of conversion to trusts for sale, and indeed the doctrine suffers from inherent logical flaws. The correct approach in every case is, it is suggested, to ask whether, as a matter of policy and for the particular purpose in issue, the interests of the beneficiaries should be regarded as interests in the subject matter of the trust or in the proceeds. It is not easy to predict whether the doctrine of conversion will ever again be used to explain overreaching. Lord Oliver, who in analysing the interests of tenants in common in *City of London Building*

Society v *Flegg* [[1988] 1 AC 54], favoured a strict application of the doctrine of conversion, certainly assumed that overreaching occurred on sale, but at the same time cited with approval the statement that '[t]he whole purpose of the trust for sale is to make sure, by shifting the equitable interests away from the land and into the proceeds of sale, that a purchaser of the land takes free from the equitable interests'.

The third misconception—apparently confined to trusts for sale of land—has it that overreaching will take place whenever the trustees for sale make *any* disposition, whether it is within their powers or not, provided the proceeds of the disposition are made to two trustees or to a trust corporation in accordance with the Law of Property Act 1925, s. 27(2). This view forms the foundation of the Law Commission's Working Paper No. 106, *Trusts of Land: Overreaching*, and seems to rest on the assumption that the provisions of the Law of Property Act 1925 a self-contained code for the operation of overreaching. It is said to derive support from the decision of the House of Lords in *City of London Building Society* v *Flegg*.

Leaving aside the statutory provisions of the Law of Property Act for the present, it would be very odd indeed if *ultra vires* dispositions could overreach. Dispositive powers are not inherently different from powers of appointment, and it would be reasonable to expect some parallel to the equitable doctrine of fraud on a power to be applicable to powers of disposition. If an *intra vires* appointment made in fraud of an equitable power is void, the same might be expected *a fortiori* of a transfer of property made in the absence or in excess of a power of disposition. An analysis of the authorities suggests that this is indeed the case.

16.2   Section 30 and the Co-ownership Trust for Sale

RE MAYO [1943] 1 Ch 302, Chancery Division

FACTS: Trustees were divided two against one on the decision whether or not to sell certain freehold properties held by them under a trust for sale. The single trustee took out a summons under s. 30 of the Law of Property Act 1925 for an order directing his co-trustees to concur in a sale.

HELD: The two trustees were directed to concur in the sale of the property.

SIMONDS J: [after stating the facts:] The result of the residuary devise, having regard to the provisions of s. 36 of the Settled Land Act, 1925, was that the property was held on trust for sale, but, superadded to that trust, there is a statutory power of postponement. It appears to me that the judicial discretion conferred by s. 30 of the Law of Property Act, 1925, must be exercised in the same way as the discretion which is exercisable by the court in the case of an instrument containing an express trust for sale. The trust for sale will prevail, unless all three trustees agree in exercising the power to postpone. The principle is established by *In re Roth* (1896) 74 LT 50, and *In re Hilton* [1909] 2 Ch 548. Here there is no suggestion of *mala fides* on the part of the testator's son, who claims that the sale should not be postponed. If that were established, the position would be different, but in the present case I think that the son is reasonable in asking for the property to be sold. It has been urged that the same considerations should influence the court as those by which it would have been influenced before 1925 on applications under the Partition Acts. I do not think that the analogy is in any way of assistance. Here there is an express trust for sale imposed by the statute with a power to postpone the sale. I cannot exercise the discretion in any other way than I should have exercised it if there had been an express trust for sale, with a power of postponement, in the will. I must direct the trustees to concur with the testator's son in taking all necessary steps for the sale of the property.

The Law Commission (Law Com. No. 181) Transfer of Land: Trusts of Land,
London: HMSO, 8 June 1989

Powers of the Court

12.1   The courts have interpreted section 30 of the Law of Property Act so broadly as to enable them, in settling a dispute relating to a trust for sale, to give effect to what they perceive to be the purpose of the trust or the intention of the parties in acquiring the trust land. It is our view that the courts should have a similarly broad power to settle disputes concerning trust of land under the new system.

12.2   There are, however, two main problems with this interpretation. The first, which might be described as a problem of 'form', is that this approach sits uneasily upon the statutory formulation of the trust for sale. Although the 'primary purpose' doctrine may mitigate the artificiality of this formulation, nevertheless it begs many questions about the nature of the trust for sale. The second, or 'substantive', problem is that the doctrine cannot satisfactorily deal with the implications of the duty to sell. The imposition of this duty continues to restrict adversely the courts' discretion.

12.3   The source of the first problem is that any interpretation of the section 30 discretion should, logically, be rationalised in terms of the trust for sale scheme as a whole. The formal terms of the trust for sale are, as we have seen, quite unsuited to modern conditions of home ownership. Whether or not one remains within the traditional approach, these terms impose some degree of artificiality upon any exercise of the discretion. If, on the one hand, primacy is given to the duty to sell (following the interpretation adopted by Simonds J, in *Re Mayo* [1943] 1 Ch 302 the trust for sale is defined in such a way as to remain within the constraints imposed by a 'traditional' approach. If, on the other hand, the doctrine of the 'primary purpose' is applied, this artificiality can only be neutralised by formulating reasons for the displacement of the primacy of the duty to sell. There is something odd about a doctrine whose essential purpose is so obviously the circumvention of an inconvenient provision. It is not that there is anything illogical or unrealistic about the substance of the approach, rather it is that this 'creative' interpretation hangs upon the practical unsuitability of the statutory definition. It is somewhat unsatisfactory that court practice should be thus adapted to the inadequacies of the trust for sale.

12.4   As regards the second problem, the imposition of a duty to sell means that, although the court may make 'such order as it thinks fit', this discretion may be restricted to a power to either order or refuse a sale. This makes the court's discretion rather 'one-dimensional'. On this view, it is not (for example) possible for the court to refuse to order a sale and yet impose an occupation rent. This obviously limits the effectiveness of the discretion as a means of doing justice to all parties.

12.5   Our recommendations in relation to section 30 should be viewed in the context of the proposed new system as a whole. It is our view that a restructuring of the trust powers, and in particular the elimination of the duty to sell, should clear the way for a genuinely broad and flexible approach. The courts will not be required to give preference to sale, and, in making orders, will not be restricted to making ones which are simply ancillary to sale.

16.2.1   SOLUTIONS THE COURT MAY ADOPT

16.2.1.1   Refuse a sale

RE BUCHANAN-WOLLASTON'S CONVEYANCE [1939] 1 Ch 738, Court of Appeal

FACTS: A piece of open ground at Lowestoft in Suffolk separated four houses from the sea. That piece of land was up for sale, the owners of the four houses pooled their money together in order to buy the land as tenants in common law. They were anxious to preserve their view of the sea. One of the four subsequently sold his house and moved away. He then applied to the court for an order that the piece of land should be sold and the proceeds divided. He argued that as the land was held on trust for sale it followed that if any of the four asked for a sale, a sale must take pace.
HELD: This argument was firmly rejected. Where land was bought for a specific purpose and that purpose could still be fulfilled, the courts would normally refuse to order a sale.

SIR WILFRID GREEN MR: . . . The statutory trust for sale is one which must be exercised and was intended by the Legislature to be exercised subject to the power of the Court to enforce it. That appears in s. 30. But the Legislature must be taken to have known the principles upon which the court of equity proceeds when asked by one of a body of trustees, or other persons who are not in agreement, to lend its assistance for the purpose of carrying out a trust; the Legislature must be taken to have known the principles upon which those powers are exercised, and the power of the Court to enforce the trust for sale must be exercised in regard to the statutory trust for sale according to well-known and ordinary principles. I am not going to enter into a discussion of the question whether or not the provisions of the Act in creating this trust for sale have the effect of overriding or nullifying any provisions in the instrument which in some way clog or fetter the trust for sale. That is a question which came into the discussion in the case of *In re Flint* [1927] 1 Ch 570, before Astbury J. If and when that particular question comes to be considered again, it will require perhaps some full examination, but what I am saying now is not affected by the decision in that case, because it seems to me that the court of equity, when asked to enforce the trust for sale, whether one created by a settlement or a will or one created by the statute, must look into all the circumstances of the case and consider whether or not, at the particular moment and in the particular circumstances when the application is made to it, it is right and proper that such an order shall be made. In considering a question of that kind, in circumstances such as these, the Court is bound to look at the contract into which the parties have entered and to ask itself the question whether or not the person applying for execution of the trust for sale is a person whose voice should be allowed to prevail. In the present case, Farwell J approached the matter from that angle and gave a perfectly definite and unhesitating answer to it, with which I entirely agree. He said in effect 'Here is a person who has contracted with others for a particular purpose, and the effect of the contract is to impose upon the power of the trustees to sell this land, certain restrictions.' Without going into the question which I mentioned a moment ago as to overriding or not overriding those things, he said: 'It is not right that the court of equity should in those circumstances, on the invitation of a person who has not acted in accordance with the contract, and is opposed by other persons interested, exercise the power of the Court and make an order for sale.' That, of course, does not mean that in other circumstances, at some future time, the Court will not lend its aid. Circumstances may change. If all the parties died and all their houses were sold, I apprehend, for example, that the Court, if asked to enforce a statutory trust for sale, would not be disposed to listen to arguments against such a sale adduced by people who had no real interest in keeping this land unsold. Questions of that kind can be decided if and when they arise. . . .

RE EVER'S TRUST [1980] 3 All ER 399, Court of Appeal

FACTS: A cohabiting couple bought a house as joint tenants, in order to house themselves and the three children for who they had responsibility. The relationship broke down, and the man left. The other four members of the family continued to live in the house. The man applied to court under s. 30 of the Law of Property Act 1925 for an order of sale.
HELD: The application for sale was refused. The greater part of the purpose of acquiring the house (housing the family of five) could still be fulfilled.

ORMROD LJ: . . . The usual practice in these cases has been to order a sale and a division of the proceeds of sale, thus giving effect to the express purpose of the trust. But the trust for sale has become a very convenient and much used conveyancing technique. Combined with the statutory power in the trustees to postpone the sale, it can be used to meet a variety of situations, in some of which an actual sale is far from the intentions of the parties at the time when the trust for sale comes into existence. So, when asked to exercise its discretionary powers under s. 30 to execute the trust, the court must have regard to its underlying purpose. In *Re Buchanan-Wollaston's Conveyance* [1939] 2 All ER 302, [1939] Ch 738 four adjoining landowners purchased a plot of land to prevent it being built on and held it on trust for sale. They also convenanted with one another that the land would not be dealt with except with the unanimous agreement of the trustees. Subsequently one of them wished to sell, but some of the other trustees objected so the plaintiff applied to the court under s. 30 for an order for sale. At first instance Farwell J refused the order, saying ([1939] Ch 217 at 223):

The question is this: Will the court assist the plaintiff to do an act which would be directly contrary to his contract with the other parties, since it was plainly the intention of the parties to the said contract that the land should not be sold save with the consent of them all?

His decision was upheld in this court, but on a broader basis. Greene MR said ([1939] 2 All ER 302 at 308, [1939] Ch 738 at 747):

> . . . it seems to me that the court of equity, when asked to enforce the trust for sale, whether one created by a settlement or a will or one created by the statute, must look into all the circumstances of the case and consider whether or not, at the particular moment and in the particular circumstances when the application is made to it, it is right and proper that such an order shall be made. In considering a question of that kind, in circumstances such as these, the court is bound to look at the contract into which the parties have entered and to ask itself the question whether or not the person applying for execution of the trust for sale is a person whose voice should be allowed to prevail. . . .

This approach to the exercise of the discretion given by s. 30 has considerable advantages in these 'family' cases. It enables the court to deal with substance (that is, reality) rather than form (that is, convenience of conveyancing); it brings the exercise of the discretion under this section, so far as possible, into line with the exercise of the discretion given by s. 24 of the Matrimonial Causes Act 1973; and it goes some way to eliminating differences between legitimate and illegitimate children in accordance with present legislative policy (see for example the Family Law Reform Act 1969, Part II).

. . . Under s. 30 the primary question is whether the court should come to the aid of the applicant at the particular moment, and in the particular circumstances when the application is made to it *Re Buchanan-Wollaston's Conveyance* [1939] 2 All ER 302 at 308, [1939] Ch 738 at 747). In the present case, at the present moment and in the existing circumstances, it would be wrong to order a sale. But circumstances may change unpredictably. It may not be appropriate to order a sale when the child reaches 16 years, a purely arbitrary date, or it may become appropriate to do so much sooner, for example on the mother's remarriage or on it becoming financially possible for her to buy the father out. In such circumstances it will probably be wiser simply to dismiss the application while indicating the sort of circumstances which would, *prima facie*, justify a further application. The ensuing uncertainty is unfortunate, but, under this section, the court has no power to adjust property rights or to redraft the terms of the trust. Ideally, the parties should now negotiate a settlement on the basis that neither of them is in a position to dictate terms. We would, therefore, dismiss the father's appeal, but would vary the order to dismiss the application on the mother's undertaking to discharge the liability under the mortgage, to pay the outgoings and maintain the property, and to indemnify the father so long as she is occupying the property.

16.2.1.2 Refuse a sale but charge a co-owner in possession rent

DENNIS v McDONALD [1981] 1 WLR 810, Family Division, Purchas J; [1982] 1 All ER 590, Court of Appeal, Arnold P

FACTS: A co-habiting couple bought a house as tenants in common in equal shares. They eventually had five children. The relationship broke up because of the man's violence. The woman left home, but only had care of the two youngest children. The three older children continued to live with their father in the house. He continued to make the mortgage repayments. The woman made an application under s. 30 of the Law of Property Act 1925 for an order for sale of the property.

HELD: The order for sale was refused. One of the primary purposes of the trust as originally envisaged was to provide a home for the family, and this purpose was still subsisting. However, the man would have to pay an 'occupation rent' to the woman throughout the duration of his residence in the property. This rent was fixed at half a 'fair rent' for the premises.

PURCHAS J: In support of his first contention Mr. Coningsby relied, *inter alia*, on *In re Evers' Trust* [1980] 1 WLR 1327. This case is a clear authority for the proposition that where the circumstances in which the trust for sale originated envisaged as one of the primary objects the provision of a home for the family rather than an immediate sale, then the proper approach to the exercise of the discretion granted by section 30 of the Law of Property Act 1925 is not to make an order for sale: see also the dictum of Lord Denning MR in *Williams (JW)* v *Williams (MA)* [1976] Ch 278, 285. There is no doubt that this is such a case. Subject to what follows hereafter in this judgment it would not be proper to make an immediate order for the sale of the property; nor would it be either convenient or appropriate to make such an order suspended during any specific period, e.g., the minority of the youngest of the children enjoying the property as his home. Mr. Walker, whilst keeping his options open, has not seriously argued against this proposition.

The main argument has revolved around the right or otherwise of the plaintiff to receive an occupation rent as a co-tenant who is excluded from the property. Mr. Coningsby has referred me to a judgment of Lord Denning MR in *Jones (AE)* v *Jones (FW)* [1977] 1 WLR 438, 441:

> First the claim for rent. It is quite plain that these two people were in equity tenants in common having a three-quarter and one-quarter share respectively. One was in occupation of the house. The other not. Now the common law said clearly that one tenant in common is not entitled to rent from another tenant in common, even though that other occupies the whole . . . As between tenants in common, they are both equally entitled to occupation and one cannot claim rent from the other. Of course, if there was an ouster, that would be another matter: or if there was a letting to a stranger for rent that would be different, but there can be no claim for rent by one tenant in common against the other whether at law or in equity.

In *Jones (AE)* v *Jones (FW)* the plaintiff failed not only on the ground that no occupation rent could be claimed by one tenant in common from another but also upon, the ground of equitable estoppel. . . .

In the instant case the plaintiff is clearly not a free agent. She was caused to leave the family home as a result of the violence or threatened violence of the defendant. In any event, whatever might have been the cause of the breakdown of the association, it would be quite unreasonable to expect the plaintiff to exercise her rights as a tenant in common to occupy the property as she had done before the breakdown of her association with the defendant. In my judgment she falls into exactly the kind of category of person excluded from the property in the way envisaged by Lord Cottenham LC in *M'Mahon* v *Burchell* 2 Ph 127. Therefore, the basic principle that a tenant in common is not liable to pay an occupation rent by virtue merely of his being in sole occupation of the property does not apply in the case where an association similar to a matrimonial association has broken down and one party is, for practical purposes, excluded from the family home.

I should add that I have thought it proper to consider the wider implications of what I believe to be the wide ambit of the meaning of the word 'exclusion' in the context of joint tenants because I am reluctant to see any extension of the concept of 'constructive desertion' after it has to a large extent been successfully eliminated by the provisions of section 1(2)(b) of the Matrimonial Causes Act 1973. On the particular facts of this case, however, I am satisfied that by his acts of violence and threats of continuing violence the defendant forced the plaintiff to leave the home and thereafter prevented her returning to it in circumstances amounting to constructive desertion. Whatever may be the true test of 'expulsion' or 'ouster' I have no doubt that the plaintiff in this case was expelled by the conduct of the defendant from the property and prevented by him from enjoying her rights as a tenant in common.

. . . The approach which I adopt is that as each party has a right to occupy the property but the occupation rent arises as a result of the exclusion of the plaintiff in the manner already described in this judgment, then the plaintiff's rights as against the defendant must envisage that the respondent himself has a right to occupy the property akin to the sort of protection given to a protected tenant. For these reasons I think that the proper way to assess the amount of the occupation rent for which the defendant is liable is that this should be half the fair rent which would be assessed by the rent officer for a letting unfurnished of the whole of the property to a protected tenant. An inquiry should be ordered, therefore, to assess this figure for the years 1977 to 1980 inclusive. In such an inquiry the defendant should be entitled to credit for any sums paid in respect of the property which enhances its capital value but not for any sums paid in the ordinary maintenance and repair of the property.

ARNOLD P: . . . [it is said] there is that one should look, not at the detriment to the plaintiff, but at the advantage to the defendant and that he should be regarded as illicitly enjoying, and therefore accountable for, one-half of what he would have to pay for the property if he entered the property market as a willing tenant and found a willing landlord ready to let it to him.

I am bound to say in the circumstances of this case that that is somewhat unrealistic. He occupies this property not because he has been able to negotiate in the market and obtain it but because he is a tenant in common. He occupies it in respect of, and by right of, his beneficial interest. He is not, therefore, subject to the vagaries of the market and starts off with a right of occupation. Something would have to be allowed in some way for that. Moreover, it is difficult to see what justification there is for charging a person in his position with such extra payment as a tenant would have to make by reason of the scarcity of relevant accommodation in the market. If one is setting out to achieve a fair solution in a situation in which plainly the defendant has to pay something, I can think of no better way of regulating that than by doing one's best to assess a fair rent for the property, with all its advantages and defects, and eliminating the scarcity element. If one does that, one finds oneself in the position of operating sub-ss. (1) and (2) of s. 70 of the 1977 Act, and with the exception of sub-s. (3) of s. 70 which, in my judgment, should be eliminated, I would adopt what the judge has said about the method, subject only to this. . . .

16.2.1.3   Order a sale

JONES v CHALLENGER [1961] 1 QB 176, Court of Appeal

FACTS: Husband and wife bought their matrimonial home as joint tenants. The marriage broke down and the wife went to live with another man. The husband was left alone in the house. The wife applied for an order of sale under the Law of Property Act 1925 s. 30.
HELD: With the end of the marriage the underlying purpose of the trust had come to an end. Consequently, the Court of Appeal ordered a sale.

DEVLIN LJ: . . . In the case we have to consider, the house was acquired as the matrimonial home. That was the purpose of the joint tenancy and, for so long as that purpose was still alive, I think that the right test to be applied would be that in *In re Buchanan-Wollaston's Conveyance* [[1939] 1 Ch 738]. But with the end of the marriage, that purpose was dissolved and the primacy of the duty to sell was restored. No doubt there is still a discretion. If the husband wanted time to obtain alternative accommodation, the sale could be postponed for that purpose, but he has not asked for that. If he was prepared to buy out the wife's interest, it might be proper to allow it, but he has not accepted a suggestion that terms of that sort should be made. In these circumstances, there is no way in which the discretion can properly be exercised except by an order to sell, because, since they cannot now both enjoy occupation of the property, that is the only way whereby the beneficiaries can derive equal benefit from their investment, which is the primary object of the trust. . . .

16.2.1.4.   Order a sale but suspend the order for a short period.
The possibility of making an order in this form was expressly recognised by the Court of Appeal in *Jones v Challenger*.

16.3   The Modern Position of Husband and Wife Co-owners on a Marriage Break-up

WILLIAMS v WILLIAMS [1977] 1 All ER 28, Court of Appeal

FACTS: A married couple purchased a house in joint names, the husband providing the majority of the purchase price. The marriage was later dissolved and the wife remained in

the house with the four sons of the family. She paid the mortgage instalments thereafter. The youngest son having reached the age of 12, the husband applied under the Law of Property Act 1925, s. 30 for an order of sale. The judge at first instance granted the order of sale as requested. The wife appealed.
HELD: The appeal was allowed.

LORD DENNING MR: . . . It seems to me that in this case the judge was in error in applying the old approach. He did not give proper effect to the modern view, which is to have regard to the needs of the family as a whole before a sale is ordered. We have here the wife and the four sons still in the house. The youngest son is only 13 years of age and still at school. It would not be proper at this stage to order the sale of the house, unless it were shown that alternative accommodation could be provided at a cheaper rate, and some capital released. That has not been shown here.

The truth is that the approach to these cases has been transformed since the Matrimonial Proceedings and Property Act 1970 and the Matrimonial Causes Act 1973 which have given the power to the court after a divorce to order the transfer of property. In exercising any discretion under section 30 of the Law of Property Act 1925, those Acts must be taken into account. The discretion should be exercised on the principles stated by this court in *Jackson* v *Jackson* [1971] 1 WLR 1539, 1543.

I would add this: An application about a matrimonial home should not be restricted to section 30 of the Law of Property Act 1925. In view of the wide powers of transfer and adjustment which are available under the new matrimonial property legislation it seems to me that the applications should be made to the Family Division under the relevant provisions. If taken out in another division, they should be transferred to a judge of the Family Division. In this very case it seems to me that the right course (which the wife's advisers ought to have taken before) is that they should now, and at once, take out the appropriate application under section 24 of the Matrimonial Causes Act 1973 for any necessary orders and so on to be made with regard to the house and the property. That application should be brought on together with an application under section 30.

I would therefore be in favour of allowing the appeal, setting aside the order for sale made by Foster J and remitting the matter for further consideration by a judge of the Family Division when an application has been taken out under the matrimonial property legislation. I would allow the appeal accordingly. . . .

MESHER v *MESHER AND HALL* [1980] 1 All ER 126, Court of Appeal

FACTS: This case properly belongs in a book on family law. The matrimonial home was in the joint names of husband and wife. On an application for a property adjustment order under ss. 23–25 of the Matrimonial Causes Act 1973 the judge at first instance ordered that the property should be transferred into the wife's sole name. The husband appealed.
HELD: The judge's order was set aside and a new order made, in the terms set out at the end of the following extract.

DAVIES LJ: . . . matters are very evenly balanced; and in these circumstances counsel for the husband submits that it would be quite wrong to deprive the husband of the substantial asset which his half-interest in the house represents. Indeed he referred us to the very recent decision of this court in *Wachtel* v *Wachtel* [1973] 1 All ER 829 and suggested that as a result of the observations of Lord Denning MR in that case there would be something to be said for cutting down the wife's share to one-third. But he did not ask for such an order. He was content that this valuable asset should be divided equally.

Counsel for the wife, however, strongly supported the order. She pointed out that, after 14 years of marriage, it was the husband who broke it up, as the judge rightly said, and that, despite what this court said in *Wachtel* v *Wachtel*, under the express words of s. 5(1) of the Matrimonial Proceedings and Property Act 1970, conduct is a matter to put into the scales. She points out that owing to the forthcoming marriage between the wife and Mr Jones, the husband will be absolved from the liability to maintain the wife and that the order of £4 per week in respect of the daughter is on the low side.

So far as that last point is concerned, it is obviously open to the wife to apply for an increase if the circumstances justify it. But as far as the main problem is concerned, one has to take a broad approach to the whole case. What is wanted here is to see that the wife and daughter, together no doubt in the near future with Mr Jones, should have a home in which to live rather than that she should have a large sum of available capital. With that end in view, I have come to the conclusion that counsel's submission for the husband is right. It would, in my judgment, be wrong to strip the husband entirely of any interest in the house. I would set aside the judge's order so far as concerns the house and substitute instead an order that the house is held by the parties in equal shares on trust for sale but that it is not to be sold until the child of the marriage reaches a specified age or with the leave of the court. . . .

THOMPSON v THOMPSON [1985] 3 WLR 17, Court of Appeal

FACTS: The order of a court of the family division in divorce proceedings, made in 1981, directed that the ex-husband and ex-wife, who remained the trustees for sale, should postpone sale of the home 'until the youngest child of the family . . . reaches the age of 17 years or finishes further education, whichever is later, or further order'. The ex-wife continued to live in the home with the two children, the youngest of whom was (in 1985) aged 11. The ex-wife wanted to move from the home; ironically the ex-husband would not agree. She sought and obtained an order for sale under section 24A of the Matrimonial Causes Act 1973.
HELD: The order was granted.

OLIVER LJ: . . . The questions which arise on this appeal, therefore, appear to me to be (1) it is permissible for a property adjustment order made under section 24 of the Act of 1973 to contain a provision for the court to make some further order in the future as to the circumstances in which the property may be sold? (2) If so, and if the order made contains, either expressly or by necessary implication, such a provision, can an order declaring that the trust for sale may be executed in circumstances other than those expressed in the original order be made in exercise of the court's matrimonial jurisdiction under section 24, or is the further order referred to restricted to an order made under the court's general equitable jurisdiction over the administration and execution of trusts? (3) Does the court, once the order has been made, have any jurisdiction to order that the trust be executed by selling the property otherwise than under section 17 or the Act of 1882 or section 30 of the Act of 1925?

Now as regards the first question, it should be said that Mr Laurie has not argued that it is inappropriate for an order of this sort to contain some provision for the court to make further orders in future unascertained events as to the administration or execution of the trusts established by the order. And that, indeed, is scarcely surprising, for such provision is virtually common form. The order in the instant case is in the familiar *Mesher* form, and it has for years been customary to include some such provision, however worded. Indeed, such inclusion in fact stems from *Mesher v Mesher and Hall (Note)* [1980] 1 All ER 126 itself, which though decided in 1973 was not reported until 1980, where this court ordered the matrimonial home to be held by the parties in equal shares on trust for sale but not to be sold until the child of the marriage reached a specified age or 'with the leave of the court.' That was effected in the order in fact drawn up by attaching a proviso that the house was not to be sold so long as the child of the marriage was under the age of 17, 'or until further order.'. . .

Thus, it is demonstrable that the use of the formula, 'until further order' in these orders, is amply supported by the authority of this court, and it must be assumed that it was inserted by this court in the orders mentioned for a specific purpose.

That brings me to the second question, namely, the effect of the inclusion of these words in the order. Mr. Laurie's submissions, and, as I read it, the judgment of the judge, effectively deprive them of any substantial practical effect. What is said is that there is no power under the Matrimonial Causes Act 1973 to order a sale. The most that the court can do under section 24 in the exercise of its power to vary a settlement under subsection (1)(c) is to order that the execution of the trust for sale shall be suspended until a particular event. It cannot reserve to itself a power to reconsider the suspensive events by a formula of this sort, for that would be reserving a power to vary the order made under section 24, and that is prohibited by section 31. Accordingly, the 'further order' referred to is not an order made in exercise of the matrimonial jurisdiction, for there can be no such order. It must therefore be an order under the general equitable jurisdiction of the court over the administration of trusts, and the only appropriate order is either one under section 30 of the Law of Property Act 1925, which can be made only where the trustees or one of them refuses to sell, or an order under section 57 of the Trustee Act 1925, conferring a new or varied power of sale on the trustees. Such an order, if sought in the county court can, in the absence of consent, be made only in relation to trust property of a value within the limits of the court's equitable jurisdiction. . . .

Whatever, therefore, may be the position as regards an order made in exercise of the power conferred by section 30 of the Law of Property Act 1925, there is no doubt about the county court's jurisdiction to make an order for sale under section 24A of the Matrimonial Causes Act 1973. In any case, therefore, where such an order can be made, the question of limits on the court's equity jurisdiction becomes academic. . . .

ALLEN v ALLEN [1974] 3 All ER 389, Court of Appeal

This case is included here as it provides an example of a form of property adjustment order that can be made under the Matrimonial Causes Act 1973, s. 24.

BUCKLEY LJ: . . . Taking all the circumstances into consideration I have come to the conclusion that the solution favoured by the learned judge was in fact a solution which would be the most satisfactory for these boys in particular and for the family as a whole. I think the learned judge, therefore, arrived at the right conclusion. But I think it would be better that his order should be varied in its terms (the precise drafting can be considered later) to provide that the former matrimonial home should be transferred to the husband and the wife, to be held on trust for sale, with a direction that the sale should not take place until the younger child had attained the age of 17 years, or had finished his full-time education, whichever date should be the earlier, without either the consent of both the parents or under an order of the court, and that during that limited period the property should be held in trust for the wife to the exclusion of the husband for the purpose of her providing a home there for the children of the family, and, in particular, the two boys, and that at the expiration of that limited period it should then be held on trust for the two spouses in equal shares.

Now it would follow from that that the husband would no longer have any right to reside in the home during the limited period which I have referred to, and I think it right that the order should be so framed as to give him a reasonable time to get out. The learned judge ordered him to leave within two months from the date of his order, and I think it would be right if the order is altered on the lines I suggest that he should still be given a reasonable time, whatever might now be a reasonable time, to find other accommodation and to make his move.

In substance, therefore, I for my part would dismiss this appeal, but I would vary the learned judge's order in the way I have indicated.

HARVEY v HARVEY [1982] 2 WLR 283, Court of Appeal

FACTS: The parties' marriage had broken down and the judge at first instance had made a 'Mesher' order (see above) in terms that the husband should leave the matrimonial home and that the property should be transferred into the joint names of the parties, to be held by them on trust for sale in equal shares; sale to be postponed until the youngest child attained the age of 16 or completed her full-time education, whichever was later. At the time of sale the wife would, under the 'Mesher' order be at liberty to purchase the husband's share at a fair valuation to be made at the time. The husband had left the home and obtained council accommodation. The wife appealed.
HELD: A new order was substituted for that of the judge, in terms appearing in the following extract from the judgment of Purchas J.

PURCHAS J: . . . The judge made an order in relation to the matrimonial home which provided that the husband, who at that time was in occupation, should vacate it with the purpose of the wife returning with the children. The order also provided that the property should be held in the joint names of the two parties to the marriage, on trust for sale in equal shares, that sale to be postponed until the youngest child of the family should attain the age of 16 years or complete her full time education, whichever was the later date and then further provided that the wife should be at liberty to purchase the husband's share at a valuation then to be made. Unless the circumstances of the family alter dramatically during the next few years, the latter part of that order would appear to be mainly academic in all the circumstances.

The difficulty which arises in all cases of this kind is that if an order for the sale of an asset of limited value such as this is made, even if it is postponed until after the house is required for the purpose of bringing up the children, then the share available to each of the equity, in practice is said not to be sufficient to provide either party with a roof over his or her head. That depends on numerous circumstances. In this case we are relieved of one problem as the result of the turn of events. That is that we are concerned now that the wife should have a roof over her head, but at the same time, although the husband has such a shelter, it would be wrong to deprive him of some benefit of his interest in the asset, provided that can be done without doing violence to the terms of section 25 of the Matrimonial Causes Act 1973.

The problem is one of what is practical and what is reasonable. So far as their earning capacity is concerned at the moment, the figures were agreed. The husband earns about twice as much as the wife. His figure, before deductions for national insurance contributions and the like, is £107 odd per week, and the wife earns £52.50 a week.

It is unlikely that, if this property were shared equally, the wife would be able to buy out the husband's interest. In the meanwhile she is under the obligation to provide a home for three children. In the circumstances prevailing today, it would be rash to assume that, at the age of 16, each of these children will no longer be a responsibility of the wife. Experience shows that very often young people stay in their homes longer than that during the early stages of what one hopes will be their early careers, so that in any event I would have considered that 16 was far too early a point in time at which to allow a sale of the roof over the wife's head, without any kind of relief.

Taking all these circumstances into account, and bearing in mind the charge in section 25 of the Act of 1973 that so far as one can possibly do it the parties ought to be placed in the position in which they would have been if the marriage had not broken down, one must remember that, in fact, this asset would never have been available to either of the parties as a capital or income producing asset as such, whilst they both survived and whilst their marriage subsisted; so that although it is attractive to say that one party or the other is being kept out of their money, that is not in accordance with the approach of section 25. They would not have had the asset to realise during the currency of their marriage unless they had both agreed to obtain less expensive accommodation after their family had grown up and left them. . . .

It is going to be a few years before the mortgage is paid off. I would accede partly to the submissions that were made before the judge and which were repeated before us by Miss Solomon, that the court ought to take the course which would enable the wife to go on living in the matrimonial home for as long as it is reasonable for her to do so.

I also take the opportunity of considering the proportion of interest in that house which it would be fair to order. We have a certain amount of information from the judgment and from the papers in the case. The wife has had the major burden of bringing up the family. She has not received very much financial help from the husband. I think that an equal division of this asset, as envisaged by the judge, was too favourable in all the circumstances, to the husband, bearing in mind that the wife will continue in occupation of the house, will be responsible for its upkeep, for paying the rates and the mortgage. She should have more than half an interest in this asset and I would divide the interest in the asset as to two-thirds in favour of the wife and one-third in favour of the husband. If and when a sale takes place, the proceeds ought to be divided in those proportions between the parties. At the same time, after the mortgage has been paid off, or after the wife has been relieved of all her responsibilities towards the family (if a date has to be fixed I would suggest 18 years of age for the youngest of the children) whichever is the later of the two incidents, the wife should pay to the husband by way of an occupational rent—and I do not think it is technically such a payment but I use that expression to describe it—to recognise that she is having the enjoyment of a property which she owns jointly, albeit not in equal proportions, with the husband. What that figure should be, it is impossible to determine at this stage. It is a matter that ought to be determined as being a reasonable, market figure, but it should be fixed by reference to the registrar at the appropriate time.

That having been said, I am of the opinion that the wife is entitled to live in this home as long as she chooses so to do, subject to certain obvious conditions. I do that on the basis that was adopted in the case of *Martin (BH)* v *Martin (D)* [1978] Fam 12 that, had the marriage not broken down, that is precisely what she would have been entitled to do.

I would vary the judge's order, first of all to say that the asset, the matrimonial home at 143, Wakeman Road, London, N.W.10, be transferred into the joint names of the wife and the husband on trust for sale in shares of two-thirds to the wife and one-third to the husband, and further that such sale shall be postponed during the lifetime of the wife her re-marriage, or voluntary removal from the premises, or her becoming dependent upon another man. I have in mind that if she begins to cohabit with another man in the premises, then obviously that man ought to take over the responsibility of providing accommodation for her. Until one or other of those events occur, she should be entitled to continue to reside at these premises, but after the mortgage has been paid off, or the youngest child has reached the age of 18, whichever is the latter, she should pay an occupation rent to be assessed by the registrar. To that extent I would allow this appeal and vary the order made by the judge.

16.4   The Rights of Co-owners in Equity — are they Interests in Land?

RE KEMPTHORNE [1930] 1 Ch 268, Chancery Division

FACTS: The testator owned a half-share in land as tenant in common. He died in 1927. His will was in terms which might be baldly summarised thus: 'I leave my real estate to X and my personal estate to Y'. The main question for resolution was whether the his 'undivided share' under the tenancy in common went to X or Y.
HELD: The testator's share as a tenant in common went to Y.

LAWRENCE LJ: . . . Maugham J in deciding this case, followed the decision of Clauson J, in *In re Price* [1928] Ch 579. In that case Clauson J, after carefully and exhaustively reviewing the provisions of the new Acts, came to the conclusion that the statutory imposition of a trust for sale operated to convert an undivided share of real estate into a corresponding share of the proceeds of sale of the entirety, and accordingly that as from the passing of the Act of 1925 the interest of the owner of the undivided share became personal estate and passed as such. I agree with Clauson J that this is the true effect of the recent legislation in the case of an unsettled undivided share of real estate. It follows, therefore, that on January 1, 1926, before the will in the present case became operative, the testator's undivided shares in question ceased to be 'freehold property,' and on his death they passed under the bequest of his personal estate.

Mr Grant contended that the decision in *In re Price* was wrong, and that the undivided shares in question remained 'freehold property,' In support of this contention he relied on the provisions of s. 28(1) of the Act of 1925. That section, however, so far from supporting his contention tends in the opposite direction. It recognizes the distinction between settled land and land held upon trust for sale, and, in the concluding words of the first paragraph, negatives the idea that the proceeds of sale under a trust for sale should devolve in the same manner as capital money arising from a sale of settled land. It enacts in terms that all capital money arising under the powers which the trustees might exercise under s. 28 should (unless paid or applied for any of the purposes authorized by the Settled Land Act, 1925) 'be applicable in the same manner as if the money represented proceeds of sale arising under the trust for sale'; and the sub-section goes on to provide that all land acquired under this sub-section (that is to say, by the exercise of any of the powers thereby conferred) should be conveyed to the trustees on trust for sale; thus drawing a sharp distinction between capital money arising from a sale of land under a trust for sale and capital money arising from a sale of settled land (whether consisting of an undivided share or of the entirety) under the provisions of the Settled Land Act, 1925. In the latter case, s. 75(5) of the Settled Land Act, 1925, provides that the proceeds of sale shall devolve in the same manner as the land from which such proceeds arise would have devolved, whereas in the case of a sale under the statutory trust for sale there is no provision to be found in either of the Acts which operates to re-convert the proceeds into land. . . .

16.4.1 THE MODERN POSITION — THE RIGHTS OF CO-OWNERS ARE INTERESTS IN LAND

BULL v BULL [1955] 1 QB 234, Queen's Bench Division

FACTS: Bull, 'the son', bought a house. His mother paid a substantial part of the purchase price. The mother thus acquired an equitable interest in the house. It followed that the son held the house on trust for sale for himself and his mother as tenants in common. The son later got married, and the mother fell out with her new daughter-in-law. The son sided with his wife, and told his mother to leave. When she refused he sued to evict her, contending that she was a trespasser. He argued that she had no interest in the land itself, but only an interest 'in money'.

HELD: Notwithstanding the imposition of a trust for sale by the 1925 legislation, the mother had a right to live in the home.

DENNING LJ: . . . My conclusion, therefore, is that, when there are two equitable tenants in common, then, until the place is sold, each of them is entitled concurrently with the other to the possession of the land and to the use and enjoyment of it in a proper manner; and that neither of them is entitled to turn out the other.

The question may be asked: What is to happen when the two fall out, as they have done here? The answer is that the house must then be sold and the proceeds divided between mother and son in the proper proportions. The son is the legal owner and he holds it on the statutory trusts for sale. He cannot at the present moment sell the house because he cannot give a valid receipt for the proceeds. It needs two trustees to give a receipt; see section 14 of the Trustee Act, 1925. The son could get over this difficulty by appointing another trustee (under section 36(6) of the Trustee Act, 1925) who would agree with him to sell the house. The two trustees would no doubt have to consider the mother's wishes, but as the son appears to have made the greater contribution he could in theory override her wishes about a sale: see section 26(3) of the Law of Property Act, 1925. The difficulty of the two trustees would be a practical difficulty because, so long as the mother is there, they could not sell with vacant possession.

The mother is entitled to rely on her equitable interest as tenant in common, which is preserved by two sections of the Law of Property Act, 1925. The first section 14 which provides that the Act 'shall not prejudicially affect the interest of any person in possession or in actual occupation of land to which he may be entitled in right of such possession or occupation.' The second is section 35 which says that the trust for sale is subject to such provisions as may be requisite for giving effect to the rights of the persons interested in the land. The mother here is in possession and in actual occupation as equitable co-owner and by virtue of that interest she could not be turned out by the trustees except with her consent. In this situation if the trustees wished to sell with vacant possession the only thing they could do would be to apply to the court under section 30 of the Law of Property Act, 1925, on the ground that the mother's consent could not be obtained. The court could then make such order as it thought fit and this would include, I think, an order to turn the mother out if it was right and proper for such an order to be made: compare *In re Buchanan-Wollaston's Conveyance* [1939] 1 Ch 738 and *In re Hyde's Conveyance* (1952) LJN 58.

My conclusion is, therefore, that the son, although he is the legal owner of the house, has no right to turn his mother out. She has an equitable interest which entitles her to remain in the house as tenant in common with him until the house is sold. If they fall out the house should be sold and the proceeds divided between them in the proper proportions; but he cannot at his will turn her out into the street. The house cannot be sold with vacant possession unless she consents to it. If she unreasonably refuses her consent, the son, by taking proper steps, can obtain an order for sale from the court and in aid of it the court can order the mother to go; but the court would only make such an order if it was satisfied that it was right and proper to do so and on such terms as to alternative accommodation as it thought right to impose. I find myself, therefore, in agreement with the county court judge and I would dismiss this appeal. . . .

16.4.2   CASES WHERE THE DOCTRINE OF CONVERSION HAS BEEN APPLIED TO CO-OWNERS

BARCLAY v *BARCLAY* [1970] 2 QB 677, Court of Appeal

FACTS: A testator left a bungalow on trust for sale for five beneficiaries in equal shares. As it happened, one of the beneficiaries was living in the bungalow at the time of the testator's death. One of the non-occupying beneficiaries claimed possession of the bungalow with a view to carrying out a sale in accordance with the trust for sale. The judge at first instance felt himself bound by *Bull* v *Bull* to postpone the sale of the house until such time as the occupying beneficiary might consent to the sale. The plaintiff appealed.
HELD: Appeal allowed. The occupying beneficiary was evicted and a sale ordered to proceed. The underlying purpose of the trust for sale was that the land should be sold and the proceeds divided between the beneficiaries.

LORD DENNING MR: In this present case there was an express trust for sale: and an implied power to postpone the sale: see section 25(1). That makes this case look, at first sight, like *Bull* v *Bull* [1955] 1 QB 234. But I think it is quite distinguishable. In *Bull* v *Bull* the prime object of the trust was that the parties should occupy the house together. They were entitled to the possession of it in undivided shares. That made them, in equity, tenants in common. An equitable tenancy in common arises whenever two or more persons become entitled to the possession of property (or the rents and profits thereof) in undivided shares. They may become so entitled by agreement, or under a will, or by inference, as often happens when husband and wife acquire their matrimonial home. The legal owner holds the legal estate on trust for them as tenants in common.

The present case is very different. The prime object of the trust was that the bungalow should be sold. None of the five beneficiaries was given any right or interest in the bungalow itself. None of them was entitled to the possession of it. The testator, by his will, expressly directed that it was to be sold and the proceeds divided between them. In such a situation there was no tenancy in common of the bungalow itself, but at most in the proceeds of sale. The case falls within the words of Devlin LJ in *Jones* v *Challenger* [1961] 1 QB 176, 184:

> The conversion of the property into a form in which both parties can enjoy their rights equally is the prime object of the trust; the preservation of the house as a home for one of them singly is not an object at all. If the true object of the trust is made paramount . . . there is only one order that can be made.

So we have the clear distinction. In *Bull* v *Bull* [1955] 1 QB 234 the prime object was that the house should be occupied by them both. So they were tenants in common of the house itself. In the present case, the prime object of the testator was that the bungalow should be sold and the proceeds divided. So the beneficiaries were not tenants in common of the bungalow, but only of the proceeds after it was sold.

The main argument of Mr. Cheyne before us was that there should be no order for possession. He said that Mrs. Winifred Barclay was a trustee who should apply under section 30 of the Law of Property Act, 1925, for directions. We have read through section 30 many times. It has no application to this case at all. Mrs. Barclay, as trustee, has not refused to sell or to exercise any of her powers. It is not a case where a requisite consent cannot be obtained. This case does not come within that section at all. This is a plain case where Mr. Allan Barclay has no interest in the bungalow. He has tried to assert an equitable tenancy by virtue of *Bull* v *Bull* [1955] 1 QB 234, but that has no application to the present case. I think that the appeal should be allowed and judgment given for possession.

CEDAR HOLDINGS LTD v *GREEN AND ANOTHER* [1981] 1 Ch 129, Court of Appeal

FACTS: Husband and wife owned the matrimonial home as joint tenants. The marriage broke down. H and X went to Cedar asking for a loan. The husband's new partner falsely represented that she was his wife. The husband and his partner executed a deed mortgaging the home to Cedar Holdings. This mortgage was, of course, fraudulent and void against the legal estate. Cedar Holdings argued, however, that s. 63 of the Law of Property Act 1925 should apply. The gist of that section is that where a person executes a 'conveyance' of Blackacre, that conveyance is deemed to pass on whatever title to land that the conveyor had in Blackacre. Accordingly, Cedar claimed that even if they could not claim a charge over the whole of the property, they could at least claim the husband's beneficial share as security. The wife counter-claimed that the land was not subject to a charge at all. The judge at first instance found in favour of the wife. The plaintiff's appealed.

HELD: The appeal was dismissed. The rights of the husband under the trust for sale were not an 'interest in land' for the purposes of section 63. Cedar Holdings Ltd thus had no security at all for their loan.

BUCKLEY LJ: . . . The device of the statutory trust for sale in respect of property vested in co-owners must have been very prominent in the minds of those who framed the 1925 property legislation. Had they intended the Law of Property Act 1925, section 63, to have a different kind of operation from that which the Conveyancing Act 1881, section 63, had been designed to achieve, I would certainly have expected some indication of this fact in section 63. Instead, section 63 of the Act of 1881 was left intact by the amending Act (Law of Property Act 1922) and was consolidated without any change in its language into the Act of 1925. In my judgment, upon the true construction of section 63 a beneficial interest in the proceeds of sale of land held upon the statutory trusts is not an interest in that land within the meaning of the section and a conveyance of that land is not effectual to pass a beneficial interest in the proceeds of sale. It follows that, in my judgment, in the present case the legal charge executed by the first defendant was not effectual to charge his beneficial interest in the proceeds of sale of 12, Preston Road. . . .

16.5   Law of Property (Joint Tenants) Act 1964

LAW OF PROPERTY (JOINT TENANTS) ACT 1964

1.   Assumptions on sale of land by survivor of joint tenants

(1)   For the purposes of section 36(2) of the Law of Property Act 1925, as amended by section 7 of and the Schedule to the Law of Property (Amendment) Act 1926, the survivor of two or more joint tenants shall in favour of a purchaser of the legal estate, be deemed to be solely and beneficially interested if he conveys as beneficial owner or the conveyance includes a statement that he is so interested.

Provided that the foregoing provisions of this subsection shall not apply if, at any time before the date of the conveyance by the survivor—

(a)   a memorandum of severance (that is to say a note or memorandum signed by the joint tenants or one of them and recording that the joint tenancy was severed in equity on a date therein specified) had been endorsed on or annexed to the conveyance by virtue of which the legal estate was vested in the joint tenants; or

(b)   [a bankruptcy order] made against any of the joint tenants, or a petition for such an order, had been registered under the Land Charges Act 1925, being an order or petition of which the purchaser has notice, by virtue of the registration, on the date of the conveyance by the survivor.

(2)   The foregoing provisions of this section shall apply with the necessary modifications in relation to a conveyance by the personal representatives of the survivor of joint tenants as they apply in relation to a conveyance by such a survivor.

. . .

3. Exclusion of registered land

This Act shall not apply to any land the title of which has been registered under the provisions of the Land Registration Acts 1925 and 1936.

16.6 Co-ownership of Registered Land

RE GORMAN (A BANKRUPT) [1990] 1 WLR 616, Chancery Division

FACTS: The land registry transfer to husband and wife co-proprietors did not specify whether they held as joint tenants in equity, or as tenants in common. However, the transfer did declare that the survivor of them could give a valid receipt for capital monies. Further, the registration did not include any restriction on transfer by the survivor of them. The couple divorced and the husband was later declared bankrupt. The present action was brought by the husband's trustee in bankruptcy for an order for the sale of the property. The judge held that the property belonged solely to the wife, on the basis, *inter alia*, that she had paid off all the mortgage instalments. The trustee appealed.

HELD: The appeal was allowed. The declaration that the survivor of the husband and wife could give a valid receipt of capital monies was consistent only with the existence of a joint tenancy in equity. Accordingly the land was now held by them as tenants in common in equal shares, the husband's bankruptcy having severed the joint tenancy, and so the trustee in bankruptcy would be entitled to recover the husband's share by sale.

VINELOTT J: . . . The position is shortly this. Section 58(3) of the Land Registration Act 1925 provides, so far as material, that in the case of joint proprietors, where the number of proprietors is reduced to below a certain level:

> no disposition shall be registered except under an order of the court, or of the registrar after inquiry into title [the subsection then continues]— and, subject to general rules, such as entry under this subsection as may be prescribed shall be obligatory unless it is shown for their own benefit, or can give valid receipts for capital money, or that one of them is a trust corporation.

I observe in passing that the language of that subsection is in fact reflected in the declaration in this case. Rules have been made and, under section 144(2) of the Act of 1925, the rules are to 'be of the same force as if enacted in this Act.' Rule 213(1) and (2) of the Land Registration Rules 1925 provides:

> (1) An entry under section 58(3) shall be in form 62, and need only be made where, by law, the survivor of the joint proprietors will not have power to give a valid receipt for capital on a disposition of the land or charge, or where the registrar, for any special reason, considers that such an entry would be desirable. (2) Such an entry may at any time be made with the consent of joint proprietors entitled in their own right.

Form 62 reads:

> When the number of joint proprietors has been reduced to one, unless such proprietor is a trust corporation, no registered disposition of the land . . . shall be made except under an order of the registrar, after an inquiry into title, or an order of the court.

The effect of subrules (1) and (2), together with section 58(3), is that in the case of joint proprietors an entry in the terms of form 62 must be included, unless the registrar is satisfied that the survivor of joint proprietors will have power to give a valid receipt for the purchase price. The law is so stated in *Ruoff and Roper, Registered Conveyancing*, 5th edn. (1986), p. 398, where it is said:

> Where two or more persons (not being charitable or Settled Land Act trustees) are jointly registered as proprietors, the Chief Land Registrar is under an obligation to enter a restriction to prevent a sole survivor of them from executing a disposition which

involves capital money. The situation is precisely that with which the practitioner is familiar in unregistered conveyancing.

It is plain in the circumstances of this case, that the registrar must have been satisfied that the declaration represented an agreement between Mr. and Mrs. Gorman, and that he could only have been so satisfied if either the original transfer had been signed by both, or if he had been informed by the solicitors who acted for Mr. and Mrs. Gorman that it reflected an agreement between them. Both were represented by the same firm of solicitors. They were in fact Mrs. Gorman's family solicitors.

Mr. Hunter then submitted that the claim that the declaration on the transfer, even if unsigned, was evidence of an agreement, is a new point not raised before the judge and which this court, sitting as an appellate court, ought not to entertain. He submitted that Mrs. Gorman might have been able to rebut this claim, if properly raised at the proper time. Then, he submitted, he might have been able to adduce evidence that the declaration was added without her knowledge or consent and was added by her solicitors as what he called 'a conveyancing device,' that is to facilitate a sale by the survivor without the need to appoint an additional trustee.

I do not think there is any substance in that argument. First, it cannot be said that it was a conveyancing device. If not in truth joint tenants, the effect of putting the transfer before the registrar as recording an agreement between them, was that the parties were deprived of the protection of an entry which would prevent a survivor from dealing with the property for his or her own benefit. In taking that course, the solicitors would have been guilty of grave dereliction of their duty to their clients.

As to the claim that the point is a new point, the position is this. Mr. Parker, in opening his case, relied on the declaration as concluding the question as to the beneficial title of the property. During or shortly after the short adjournment it was drawn to his attention, either by Mr. Hunter or the judge (I am not certain which) that the transfer had not been signed by the transferees; he nonetheless relied on the transfer as evidence of an agreement between the parties. No claim was made that the declaration had been added to the transfer without Mrs. Gorman's knowledge and consent, and Mr. Hunter did not apply for an adjournment to adduce evidence to this effect. The reason is not far to seek. Mrs. Gorman was well aware that the trustee relied on the declaration in the transfer. At no time did she suggest, either before the application was made by the trustee, or in her evidence in opposition to it, that the declaration had been made without her authority. In her first affidavit in opposition she said:

My late father did not trust my husband and at the time of giving me £2,000 he expressed the wish that the property be held by me alone. My former husband would not agree and persuaded me to arrange for the property to be transferred into our joint names. I was not aware at that time that it was possible to hold a property in joint names and for the beneficial interest to be expressed unequally.

That, as I see it, is a clear statement that she understood at the time of the transfer that the property would be conveyed into the joint names of herself and her husband and would not be held in trust for themselves as tenants in common in unequal shares.

16.7   End of Chapter Assessment Question

In 1987 four friends, Steven, Julia, Mark and Tracey, purchased a cottage called 'The Retreat' for the purpose of a holiday home. The conveyance to them contained no express declaration of a trust for sale. Title to The Retreat was unregistered. The purchase money was provided equally and at the time of the purchase Tracey was only 17 years of age.

In January 1994 Julia became short of cash and therefore obtained a bank loan which was secured on her interest in The Retreat.

Some months later Steven also found himself in financial difficulties. However his solution to the problem was to create frequent arguments with the others in which he would demand that they 'buy him out'. These outbursts were ignored by the others and Steven eventually stopped using The Retreat.

In October 1994 Steven and Julia were killed in a car accident. By their wills Steven left all his property to his mother Violet, and Julia left all her property to her sister, Karen. Mark is keen to sell The Retreat and has just found a purchaser who wants an early completion. Tracey vehemently opposes the proposed sale as since the deaths of Steven and Julia she has been living at The Retreat permanently. Violet is in agreement with Mark, but Karen is uncertain.

Advise Mark as to:

(a)   exactly who owns The Retreat and in what proportions;

(b)   his prospects of forcing a sale.

16.8   End of Chapter Assessment Outline Answer

The Legal Ownership of the Retreat
As the friends were co-owners, a trust for sale was imposed on them in 1987. However, only Steven, Julia and Mark became trustees, as Tracey was under 18 and only adults can be appointed trustees. Tracey would NOT become a trustee on her attaining the age of 18.
   The only event after 1987 to affect the trusteeship of the legal title is the death of Steven and Julia. This event (as a result of the survivorship rule) leaves Mark as the only trustee, though not (as we shall see) the sole beneficiary.

Can Mark Sell Without a Court Order?
In theory, yes, in practical reality, no. Mark appears to be a sole surviving joint tenant, so he might try and take advantage of the Law of Property (Joint Tenants) Act 1964. Alternatively, to give added reassurance to the purchaser, he could appoint a friend as co-trustee, and the two of them convey The Retreat to the purchaser. Either way a sale would overreach the equitable interests of Tracey and any other beneficiary.
   The practical reality is, however, that no purchaser, even a very keen one, is going to buy with Tracey in permanent occupation. Undoubtedly Tracey has the right to occupy the property until it is sold (see *Bull* and *Boland*). On the sale taking place her rights will be overreached (*Flegg*) and she will become a trespasser vis-à-vis the purchaser. But the purchaser will 'acquire' the problem of taking proceedings to evict Tracey. No sane purchaser (particularly one keen to move in quickly) is going to buy in these circumstances.
   Thus Mark will be forced to take section 30 proceedings. (See below.)

The Equitable Owneship of The Retreat
The initial position
There appears to be nothing to rebut the initial presumption of joint tenancy. Note in particular that the four contributed equally to the cost. However, there might be a tenancy

in common (in equal shares) if the court found there was a business element to the arrangements, e.g. if they envisaged holiday lettings of The Retreat when none of them wanted to use it themselves.

Current Position if Parties Initially Tenants in Common
An equitable interest as tenants in common can be left by will. Therefore after the car crash Violet and Karen would become tenants in common in equity alongside Mark and Tracey.

Current Position if Parties Initially Equitable Joint Tenants

The Effect of Julia's Mortgage
This clearly severs her equitable interest, converting it into a one quarter share as tenant in common. On her death this equitable interest will pass by her will (subject to the mortgage) to Karen.

The Effect of Steven's Frequent Arguments
It is possible to sever by informal argreement, or by conduct which indicates that the parties are treating the joint tenancy as at an end (*Burgess* v *Rawnsley*). As the outbursts were ignored by the other three it seems that there has been no informal severance by conduct/agreement.

However, Lord Denning was of the view in *Burgess* that an oral unilateral statement would effect a severance. This rather impractical view is unsupported by authority, but if it were correct then presumably the outbursts would affect a severance. As a result Violet would inherit a quarter share.

If (as is probably the case) Steven has not severed, then Violet does not inherit any interest in The Retreat. The 'survivorship' rule operates between joint tenants; the law of succession has no application to a joint tenancy interest. The current equitable ownership would be Julia one quarter with the other three-quarters belonging to Mark and Tracey as joint tenants.

Mark's prospects of getting an order of sale
Violet's support is probably irrelevant, as she only has an interest if either the parties were initially tenants in common or if Steven has severed. If Violet has no interest and Karen comes out against a sale then a majority by value would be against sale.

But it is submitted that Mark has the trump card. The purpose for which the property was acquired has clearly failed, and that normally means that the court in its discretion will order a sale under the Law of Property Act 1925, s. 30. (See *Jones* v *Challenger*, contrast *Re Buchanan-Wollaston*.)

A refusal of sale would be very unfair on Mark, as he would be left with his money locked up in an asset he no longer has any use for. In *Dennis* v *McDonald* the Court of Appeal adopted a compromise whereby a sale was refused but the co-owner in occupation had to pay a rent. However, that was a case of a broken-down cohabitation, very different from this one!

A much more sensible compromise, *and one which can be reached without the expense of litigation*, is for Tracey to buy out the interests of the other parties involved. Mark should propose this in '*Calderbank*' letters sent to Tracey and Karen. (A '*Calderbank*' letter is a letter sent 'without prejudice' to legal action that might be taken by the person sending the letter.)

CHAPTER SEVENTEEN

LEASES — THE BASIC REQUIREMENTS

17.1 Duration of Leases

17.1.1 FIXED-TERM LEASES

LACE v *CHANTLER* [1944] 1 KB 368, Court of Appeal

FACTS: The question in the Court of Appeal, was whether a lease 'for the duration of the war' was valid as a legal lease.

HELD: It was not possible to construe the lease as a long lease determinable on the cessation of the war. It was therefore a lease of indeterminate maximum duration and thus was not capable of being a legal lease.

LORD GREENE MR: Normally there could be no question that this was an ordinary weekly tenancy, duly determinable by a week's notice, but the parties in the rent-book agreed to a term which appears there expressed by the words 'furnished for duration,' which must mean the duration of the war. The question immediately arises whether a tenancy for the duration of the war creates a good leasehold interest. In my opinion, it does not. A term created by a leasehold tenancy agreement must be expressed either with certainty and specifically or by reference to something which can, at the time when the lease takes effect, be looked to as a certain ascertainment of what the term is meant to be. In the present case, when this tenancy agreement took effect, the term was completely uncertain. It was impossible to say how long the tenancy would last. Mr Sturge in his argument has maintained that such a lease would be valid, and that, even if the term is uncertain at its beginning when the lease takes effect, the fact that at some future time it will be rendered certain is sufficient to make it a good lease. In my opinion, that argument is not to be sustained. . . .

The question then arises whether it can take effect in any other way. It was suggested that the difficulty would be got over by construing the tenancy as a lease for a long period, e.g., ninety-nine years, determinable on the cessation of the war. In my opinion, it is impossible to construe this tenancy in that way. It is true that, in *Great Northern Railway Co.* v *Arnold* (1916) 33 TLR 114, Rowlatt J found it possible to treat a tenancy for the duration of the last war, the rent being payable weekly, as though a lease for nine hundred and ninety-nine years terminable on the cessation of the war had been created. He had some assistance in arriving at that conclusion in the fact that there was a definite undertaking by the landlords not to serve a notice to quit during the period. The actual words, as stated in the head-note, were: 'The landlords said that they did not intend that he should be subject to a week's notice.' That case can, in my opinion, only be supported because of the presence of that term of the agreement.

Is there any other possible construction? It is not contended that this tenancy agreement can be construed as though it were a grant of a freehold interest. The only way in which one could convert this into a freehold interest would be by construing it as an agreement for a life tenancy terminable at the end of the war. It is impossible to construe this agreement as anything of the kind.

Lastly, Mr Sturge argued that the agreement could be construed as an agreement to grant a licence. In my opinion, it is impossible to construe it in that sense. The intention was to create a tenancy and nothing else. The law says that it is bad as a tenancy. The court is not then justified in treating the contract as something different from what the parties intended, and regarding it merely as a contract for the granting of a licence. That would be setting up a new bargain which neither of the parties ever intended to enter into. The relationship between the parties must be ascertained on the footing that the tenant was in occupation and was paying a weekly rent. Accordingly, it must be the relationship of weekly tenant and landlord and nothing else.

PRUDENTIAL ASSURANCE CO. LTD v LONDON RESIDUARY BODY AND OTHERS
[1992] 2 AC 386, House of Lords

FACTS: This case involved a 'lease' granted by a council, and intended to 'continue until . . . the land is required by the council for the purposes of the widening of' a highway. The issue was whether the tenancy might be determined earlier.
HELD: As all leases need by definition to be of a certain duration, it followed that the lease granted by the council was void. However, the tenant's possession, and payment of a yearly rent, meant that the tenant had established an informal legal yearly tenancy. Such a tenancy could be determined on the giving of six months' notice.

LORD TEMPLEMAN: Now it is said that when in the present case the tenant entered pursuant to the agreement and paid a yearly rent he became a tenant from year to year on the terms of the agreement including clause 6 which prevents the landlord from giving notice to quit until the land is required for road widening. This submission would make a nonsense of the rule that a grant for an uncertain term does not create a lease and would make nonsense of the concept of a tenancy from year to year because it is of the essence of a tenancy from year to year that both the landlord and the tenant shall be entitled to give notice determining the tenancy. . . .

My Lords, I consider that the principle in *Lace* v *Chantler* [1944] KB 368 reaffirming 500 years of judicial acceptance of the requirement that a term must be certain applies to all leases and tenancy agreements. A tenancy from year to year is saved from being uncertain because each party has power by notice to determine at the end of any year. The term continues until determined as if both parties made a new agreement at the end of each year for a new term for the ensuing year. A power for nobody to determine or for one party only to be able to determine is inconsistent with the concept of a term from year to year: see *Doe d Warner* v *Browne*, 8 East 165 and *Cheshire Lines Committee* v *Lewis & Co.*, 50 LJQB 121. In *In re Midland Railway Co's Agreement* [1971] Ch 725 there was no 'clearly expressed bargain' that the term should continue until the crack of doom if the demised land was not required for the landlord's undertaking or if the undertaking ceased to exist. In the present case there was no 'clearly expressed bargain' that the tenant shall be entitled to enjoy his 'temporary structures' in perpetuity if Walworth Road is never widened. In any event principle and precedent dictate that it is beyond the power of the landlord and the tenant to create a term which is uncertain.

A lease can be made for five years subject to the tenant's right to determine if the war ends before the expiry of five years. A lease can be made from year to year subject to a fetter on the right of the landlord to determine the lease before the expiry of five years unless the war ends. Both leases are valid because they create a determinable certain term of five years. A lease might purport to be made for the duration of the war subject to the tenant's right to determine before the end of the war. A lease might be made from year to year subject to a fetter on the right of the landlord to determine the lease before the war ends. Both leases would be invalid because each purported to create an uncertain term. A term must either be certain or uncertain. It cannot be partly certain because the tenant can determine it at any time and partly uncertain because the landlord cannot determine it for an uncertain period. If the landlord does not grant and the tenant does not take a certain term the grant does not create a lease.

The decision of the Court of Appeal in *In re Midland Railway Co.'s Agreement* [1971] Ch 725 was taken a little further in *Ashburn Anstalt* v *Arnold* [1989] Ch 1. That case, if it was correct, would make it unnecessary for a lease to be of a certain duration. In an agreement for the sale of land the vendor reserved the right to remain at the property after completion as licensee and to trade therefrom without payment of rent.

> save that it can be required by Matlodge [the purchaser] to give possession on not less than one quarter's notice in writing upon Matlodge certifying that it is ready at the expiration of such notice forthwith to proceed with the development of the property and the neighbouring property involving, *inter alia*, the demolition of the property.

The Court of Appeal held that this reservation created a tenancy. The tenancy was not from year to year but for a term which would continue until Matlodge certified that it was ready to proceed with the development of the property. The Court of Appeal held that the term was not uncertain because the vendor could either give a quarter's notice or vacate the property without giving notice. But of course the same could be said of the situation in *Lace v Chantler* [1944] KB 368. The cumulative result of the two Court of Appeal authorities *In re Midland Railway Co.'s Agreement* [1971] Ch 725 and *Ashburn's* case [1989] Ch 1 would therefore destroy the need for any term to be certain.

In the present case the Court of Appeal were bound by the decisions in *In re Midland Railway Co.'s Agreement* and *Ashburn's* case. In my opinion both these cases were wrongly decided. A grant for an uncertain term does not create a lease. A grant for an uncertain term which takes the form of a yearly tenancy which cannot be determined by the landlord does not create a lease. I would allow the appeal. The trial judge, Millett J, reached the conclusion that the six months' notice served by the London Residuary Body was a good notice. He was of course bound by the Court of Appeal decisions but managed to construe the memorandum of agreement so as to render clause 6 ineffective in fettering the right of the landlord to serve a notice to quit after the landlord had ceased to be a road widening authority. In the circumstances this question of construction need not be considered. For the reasons which I have given the order made by Millett J must be restored. The plaintiffs must pay the costs of the second to fourth defendants before the House and in the courts below.

17.1.2   PERIODIC TENANCIES

LADIES' HOSIERY AND UNDERWEAR, LTD v PARKER
[1930] 1 Ch 304, Court of Appeal

FACTS: A fixed-term lease had come to an end and the tenant had remained in occupation. In other words, the tenant had 'held over' informally. In due course the landlord sold his reversion to the plaintiff company, but the plaintiff company received no rent from the tenant. The plaintiff brought the present action for an order of possession, asserting that the defendant was, at most, merely a weekly tenant.

HELD: Although it might, on other facts, be possible to infer that the defendant had continued in possession as a yearly tenant, such an inference was not possible here. The defendant was a weekly tenant. The 'period' of the tenancy should be determined by reference to the period according to which the rent had been calculated, not by reference to the time of rental payments. Thus a rent of £1,000 per annum, paid weekly, would give rise to a yearly tenancy. In the present case rent was set at £2.00 per week. Accordingly, this was a weekly periodic tenancy.

MAUGHAM J: . . . In the present case, the lease or agreement is one for three years at a rent of £2 a week. It is not a lease for three years at a rent of £104 per annum payable weekly: and it is observable that £2 a week is a rent which, as we all know, is not exactly divisible into the number of days either of an ordinary year or of a leap year. I cannot find, and counsel have been unable to find, any case exactly in point; but I have come to the conclusion that there is no reason for extending the views, which are binding on me, as to the terms which justify the inference that a tenancy is from year to year, and that in this case, narrow as the distinction is, the holding over of the premises after the expiration of the agreement of October 10 1914, would have resulted only, and did result only, in the tenant's being a tenant from week to week.

In coming to that conclusion I derive support from the judgment of Parke B in *Braythwayte* v *Hitchcock* (1842) 10 M & W 494. He says: 'Although the law is clearly settled, that where there has been an agreement for a lease and an occupation without payment of rent, the occupier is a mere tenant at will; yet it has been held that if he subsequently pays rent under that agreement, he thereby becomes tenant from year to year. Payment of rent, indeed, must be understood to mean a payment with reference to a yearly holding; for in *Richardson* v *Langridge* (1811) 4 Taunt 128, a party who had paid rent under an agreement of this description, but had not paid it with reference to a year, or any aliquot part of a year, was held nevertheless to be a tenant at will only'. My conclusion, therefore, is that when the defendant Henry Alfred Parker, after the expiration of that agreement, paid the sum of £2 a week to his landlord Jenkins, he was *prima facie* not paying it with reference to a year or an aliquot part of a year, but was paying it with reference to the week in respect of which he made the payment.

In the result the plaintiff company will have a judgment for possession of the premises at the back of No. 18, and the defendants must pay the costs of the action.

The Court of Appeal (Lord Hanworth MR, Lawrence and Romer LJJ) dismissed the appeal.

17.1.3 SPECIAL PROBLEMS CONNECTED WITH THE DURATION OF LEASES

17.1.3.1 Leases for lives

LAW OF PROPERTY ACT 1925

149. Abolition of interesse termini, and as to reversionary leases and leases for lives

(1) The doctrine of interesse termini is hereby abolished.

(2) As from the commencement of this Act all terms of years absolute shall, whether the interest is created before or after such commencement, be capable of taking effect at law or in equity, according to the state interest or powers of the grantor, from the date fixed for commencement of the term, without actual entry.

(3) A term, at a rent or granted in consideration of a fine, limited after the commencement of this Act to take effect more than twenty-one years from the date of the instrument purporting to create it, shall be void, and any contract made after such commencement to create such a term shall likewise be void; but this subsection does not apply to any term taking effect in equity under a settlement, or created out of an equitable interest under a settlement, or under an equitable power for mortgage, indemnity or other like purposes.

(4) Nothing in subsections (1) and (2) of this section prejudicially affects the right of any person to recover any rent or to enforce or take advantage of any covenants or conditions or, as respects terms or interests created before the commencement of this Act, operates to vary any statutory or other obligations imposed in respect of such terms or interests.

(5) Nothing in this Act affects the rule of law that a legal term, whether or not being a mortgage term, may be created to take effect in reversion expectant on a longer term, which rule is hereby confirmed.

(6) Any lease or underlease, at a rent, or in consideration of a fine, for life or lives or for any term of years determinable with life or lives, or on the marriage of the lessee, or any contract therefor, made before or after the commencement of this Act, or created by virtue of Part V of the Law of Property Act 1922, shall take effect as a lease, underlease or contract therefor, for a term of ninety years determinable after the death or marriage (as the case may be) of the original lessee, or of the survivor of the original lessees, by at least one month's notice in writing given to determine the same on one of the quarter days applicable to the tenancy, either by the lessor or the persons deriving title under him, to the person entitled to the leasehold interest, or if no such person is in existence by affixing the same to the premises, or by the lessee or other persons in whom the leasehold interest is vested to the lessor or the persons deriving title under him:

Provided that—

(a) this subsection shall not apply to any term taking effect in equity under a settlement or created out of an equitable interest under a settlement for mortgage, indemnity, or other like purposes;

(b)   the person in whom the leasehold interest is vested by virtue of Part V of the Law of Property Act 1922, shall, for the purposes of this subsection, be deemed an original lessee;

(c)   if the lease, underlease, or contract therefor is made determinable on the dropping of the lives of persons other than or besides the lessees, then the notice shall be capable of being served after the death of any person or of the survivor of any persons (whether or not including the lessees) on the cesser of whose life or lives the lease, underlease, or contract is made determinable, instead of after the death of the original lessee or of the survivor of the original lessees;

(d)   if there are no quarter days specially applicable to the tenancy, notice may be given to determine the tenancy on one of the usual quarter days.

17.1.3.2   Perpetually renewable leases

CAERPHILLY CONCRETE PRODUCTS LTD v OWEN
[1972] 1 WLR 372, Court of Appeal

FACTS: A lease granted a tenant the right to request, by writing, a renewal of the lease for a further five years 'at the same rent and containing the like covenants and provisos as are herein contained (including the option to renew such lease for a further term of five years at the expiration thereof)'. The question was whether this created a perpetually renewable lease convertible, under s. 145 and Schedule 15, para. 5 of the Law of Property Act 1922, into a lease for a term of 2,000 years.
HELD: The lease was perpetually renewable.

SACHS LJ: The question for determination in this appeal is whether the lease of May 6, 1963, is upon a proper construction of clause 4(3) a perpetually renewable lease. That clause, so far as relevant, reads:

> That the landlord will on the written request of the tenant made six months before the expiration of the term hereby created . . . at the expense of the tenant grant to him a lease of the said demised land for the further term of five years from the expiration of the said term hereby granted at the same rent and containing the like covenants and provisos as are herein contained (including an option to renew such lease for the further term of five years at the expiration thereof). . .

I, too, have underlined the words in brackets. It is trite to say that when construing a document such as a lease it is the prime purpose of the courts to seek to adopt a meaning that conforms to the intentions of the parties. Not even the most impeccable conveyancing logic, however neatly expressed, can convince me that in the instant case it was the mutual intention of the parties that the lease should be perpetually renewable. So far as the landlord is concerned it seems to me highly unlikely that he really intended that this particular lease could or should be 'for ever.' My doubts on this question of intention extend also to the tenant—for I would acquit him of any intent to lay a trap through the operation of the words enclosed in the brackets, which we know to have been added to the draft at the very last moment by his solicitors. It is difficult indeed, at any rate so far as I am concerned, to think that two business men would be talking in terms of five years if both—or indeed either— of them truly meant that a lease should be granted which went on *ad infinitum.*

Were I in a position to give effect to the views just expressed that would result in the landlord succeeding in this appeal: but it is necessary to consider whether the authorities which were so fully and so helpfully cited to us permit such a result. An examination of the relevant decisions discloses an area of law in which the courts have manoeuvred themselves into an unhappy position. On the one hand in judgment after judgment (for instance, *Baynham's* case (1796) 3 Ves 295, 298; *Moore* v *Foley* (1801) 6 Ves 232, 235–236 and *Swinburne* v *Milburn* (1884) 9 App Cas 844, 850) it has been proclaimed that the courts lean against holding that a lease is to that extent renewable. On the other hand, by strict adherence to precedent relating to the phrase 'including the present covenant' when following a covenant conferring a right to a renewal on the like covenants and provisos as are contained in the first lease, they appear to have bound themselves to hold that the use of a certain set of words (to which I will refer as 'the formula') causes the lease to be perpetually renewable, even when no layman—at least if he has some elementary knowledge of business—would dream of granting such a lease and, if aware of the technical meaning of the particular phraseology, would almost certainly be aghast at its devastating effect and refuse to sign. One reason for the courts so binding themselves is said to be that the formula is one the effect of which is well known to trained conveyancers, and that this is advantageous, however much of a trap it may constitute for others.

Wilkinson, H. W., Renewable Leases (1981) 131 NLJ 683

. . . Parties who do not want to make a perpetually renewable lease should say so. The *Encylopaedia of Forms and Precedents* 4th edn, vol 11, form 2: 55, pp 340, 341 has a precedent which uses the vital words,

> subject in all other respects to the same stipulations as are herein contained except this clause for renewal.

If that type of phrase is not used, there can be danger. The judges in the *Caerphilly* case saw no remedy apart from statutory intervention. Indeed, Stamp LJ pointed out that statute so far has had the opposite effect from that intended,

> One of the purposes of the Law of Property Act 1922 in converting a purported perpetually renewable lease into a long term of years, was, according to the learned editors of *Wolstenholme and Cherry's Conveyancing Statutes*, to discourage the creation of such leases; and to the extent that it has not done so this is a matter for the legislature.

Need such a reform await legislation? It is suggested that if an appropriate case got to the House of Lords their lordships could say that a perpetually renewable lease is only to be construed out of words which in clear terms provide for it.

17.1.3.3 Tenancy at will

MANFIELD v *BOTCHIN* [1970] 2 QB 612, Queen's Bench Division

FACTS: A written tenancy agreement prescribed that the tenancy should be a tenancy at will, and that an annual rent should be paid. The tenant claimed the protection of the Landlord and Tenant Act 1954, Part II, on the basis that the tenancy was a yearly tenancy according to the rental period.
HELD: The tenancy agreement had created a tenancy at will, not a yearly tenancy. The protection of the Act would not be available to the tenant.

COOKE J: Clause 1 of the agreement read as follows:

> The company shall let and [the tenant] shall take the said premises on a tenancy at will commencing from December 5 1964, at a rental to be calculated at the rate of £1,560 per annum and paid on demand at such time or times as the company may think fit Provided always that if the company should demand the aforesaid rent at fixed periods such demand or acceptance of rent shall not be deemed to create any periodic tenancy. . . .

In my view, the fact that rent was reserved at an annual rate is not in the present case sufficient to override the expressed intention of the parties to create a tenancy at will. The agreement does not provide for the payment of rent at fixed times, but only on demand. It is questionable whether the terms of this provision would strictly empower the landlords to demand rent in advance. If, however, the provision does empower the landlords to demand rent in advance, it seems to me that any advance payment made on such a demand would of necessity be a provisional payment only; and if during the period for which an advance payment had been made either the landlords or the tenant were to exercise his right to determine the tenancy forthwith an appropriate adjustment would have to be made. . . .
  Has, then, anything occurred since the date of the agreement which has altered the relationship of the parties? The tenant relies on the fact that the tenancy subsisted for

nearly five years before the landlords purported to determine it. I cannot think that that is a circumstance which indicates that the parties have altered their relationship since the agreement was made. There is nothing in the actual duration of the tenancy which is inconsistent with the agreement which the parties made, for under the agreement the duration of the tenancy is wholly indeterminate.

Then the tenant relies on the fact that in the main rent was regularly demanded and paid on a monthly basis. I find nothing in this fact which indicates an alteration in the relationship between the parties. Regular demands for and payment of rent are not in themselves inconsistent with a tenancy at will, and indeed in this case they are actually contemplated by the agreement itself, just as they were contemplated in *Doe* d *Bastow* v *Cox* (1874) 11 QB 122. . . .

HESLOP v *BURNS AND ANOTHER* [1974] 3 All ER 406, Court of Appeal

FACTS: A fairly wealthy person allowed two friends to occupy a house he owned rent-free. After his death, the friends remained in possession. They claimed that they had a tenancy at will, which, by s. 9 of the Limitation Act 1939, was deemed to have determined a year after its commencement. Thereafter, they claimed they had occupied the freehold a 'squatters' (see the chapter on adverse possession) and now owned the freehold as of right. HELD: Such a friendly arrangement (made without intent to create legal relations) regarding the occupation the house was to be treated as a licence, not as a tenancy at will. Accordingly, the 'friends' had no right to exclude the deceased (by his executors) from taking possession of the freehold.

STAMP LJ: . . . On the facts of this case it is, in my judgment, abundantly clear that the parties did not enter into any arrangement, far less any arrangement intended to create a legal relationship, as to the terms on which the defendants should occupy the property. There was no contract, no arrangement, no statement by the deceased. The defendants, as I see it, were allowed to move into the property and occupy it simply as a result of the bounty of the deceased and without any arrangements as to the terms on which they should do so. There was no evidence of any discussion whatsoever taking place as to the terms of the occupation. It was by the effect of the bounty of the deceased or, if you will, because of his feelings of affection for Mrs Burns, that the home was provided, and it was, I think, for those reasons that the defendants remained there.

The fact, which was relied on by counsel for the defendants, that the deceased had already said, in relation to each of the properties in Fowler Street and Love Walk, that he would leave it to the defendants, is no evidence that it was the intention of the deceased that the defendants should in the meantime be tenants at will rather than licensees. Counsel for the defendants submitted that, since the deceased intended to provide the defendants with a home, he must have intended to give them an interest in the property. But a tenancy at will was no more apt to achieve that purpose than a revocable personal licence to occupy the property; and if one asks the question what interest he intended them to have, it could only, consistently with counsel's submission, be an interest during the rest of the life of the deceased of such a nature as would exclude him from any right to turn them out. No such interest was created and I find it impossible to infer an intention on the part of the deceased to create such a situation. In my judgment the proper inference is that the defendants at the outset entered into occupation of the premises as licensees and not as tenants at will; not with a right to exclude the deceased from possession. . . .

17.2   The Distinction Between Leases and Licences

17.2.1   EXCLUSIVE POSSESSION AS THE FOUNDATION OF THE LEASE/LICENCE DISTINCTION

STREET v *MOUNTFORD* [1985] 1 AC 809, House of Lords

FACTS: Street granted to Mountford the right to occupy two rooms by a form of agreement described as being a 'licence'. The agreement was subject to a number of conditions.

Mountford signed a declaration by which she acknowledged that the agreement did not give her a protected tenancy. Street sought an order of the county court declaring that the agreement was a licence, and did not constitute a tenancy.

HELD: The agreement was a tenancy, despite the use of the word 'licence'. The test to distinguish a lease from a licence was one of substance, not of form. The crucial question to ask was whether the agreement conferred 'exclusive possession'.

LORD TEMPLEMAN: . . . My Lords, there is no doubt that the traditional distinction between a tenancy and a licence of land lay in the grant of land for a term at a rent with exclusive possession. In some cases it was not clear at first sight whether exclusive possession was in fact granted. . . .

In the case of residential accommodation there is no difficulty in deciding whether the grant confers exclusive possession. An occupier of residential accommodation at a rent for a term is either a lodger or a tenant. The occupier is a lodger if the landlord provides attendance or services which require the landlord or his servants to exercise unrestricted access to and use of the premises. A lodger is entitled to live in the premises but cannot call the place his own. In *Allan* v *Liverpool Overseers* (1874) LR 9 QB 180, 191–192 Blackburn J said:

> A lodger in a house, although he has the exclusive use of rooms in the house, in the sense that nobody else is to be there, and though his goods are stowed there, yet he is not in exclusive occupation in that sense, because the landlord is there for the purpose of being able, as landlords commonly do in the case of lodgings, to have his own servants to look after the house and the furniture, and has retained to himself the occupation, though he has agreed to give the exclusive enjoyment of the occupation to the lodger.

If on the other hand residential accommodation is granted for a term at a rent with exclusive possession, the landlord providing neither attendance nor services, the grant is a tenancy; any express reservation to the landlord of limited rights to enter and view the state of the premises and to repair and maintain the premises only serves to emphasise the fact that the grantee is entitled to exclusive possession and is a tenant. In the present case it is conceded that Mrs. Mountford is entitled to exclusive possession and is not a lodger. Mr. Street provided neither attendance nor services and only reserved the limited rights of inspection and maintenance and the like set forth in clause 3 of the agreement. On the traditional view of the matter, Mrs. Mountford not being a lodger must be a tenant.

There can be no tenancy unless the occupier enjoys exclusive possession; but an occupier who enjoys exclusive possession is not necessarily a tenant. He may be owner in fee simple, a trespasser, a mortgagee in possession, an object of charity or a service occupier. To constitute a tenancy the occupier must be granted exclusive possession for a fixed or periodic term certain in consideration of a premium or periodical payments. The grant may be express, or may be inferred where the owner accepts weekly or other periodical payments from the occupier.

Occupation by service occupier may be eliminated. A service occupier is a servant who occupies his master's premises in order to perform his duties as a servant. In those circumstances the possession and occupation of the servant is treated as the possession and occupation of the master and the relationship of landlord and tenant is not created; . . .

In the present case, the agreement dated 7 March 1983 professed an intention by both parties to create a licence and their belief that they had in fact created a licence. It was submitted on behalf of Mr. Street that the court cannot in these circumstances decide that the agreement created a tenancy without interfering with the freedom of contract enjoyed by both parties. My Lords, Mr. Street enjoyed freedom to offer Mrs. Mountford the right to occupy the rooms comprised in the agreement on such lawful terms as Mr. Street pleased. Mrs. Mountford enjoyed freedom to negotiate with Mr. Street to obtain different terms. Both parties enjoyed freedom to contract or not to contract and both parties exercised that freedom by contracting on the terms set forth in the written agreement and on no other terms. But the consequences in law of the agreement, once concluded, can only be determined by consideration of the effect of the agreement. If the agreement satisfied all the requirements of a tenancy, then the agreement produced a tenancy and the parties cannot alter the effect of the agreement by insisting that they only created a licence. The manufacture of a five-pronged implement for manual digging results in a fork even if the manufacturer, unfamiliar with the English language, insists that he intended to make and has made a spade.

It was also submitted that in deciding whether the agreement created a tenancy or a licence, the court should ignore the Rent Acts. If Mr. Street has succeeded, where owners have failed these past 70 years, in driving a coach and horses through the Rent Acts, he must be left to enjoy the benefit of his ingenuity unless and until Parliament intervenes. I accept that the Rent Acts are irrelevant to the problem of determining the legal effect of the rights granted by the agreement. Like the professed intention of the parties, the Rent Acts cannot alter the effect of the agreement. . . .

. . . in my opinion in order to ascertain the nature and quality of the occupancy and to see whether the occupier has or has not a stake in the room or only permission for himself personally to occupy, the court must decide whether upon its true construction the agreement confers on the occupier exclusive possession. If exclusive possession at a rent for a term does not constitute a tenancy then the distinction between a contractual tenancy and a contractual licence of land becomes wholly unidentifiable.

In *Somma* v *Hazelhurst* [1978] 1 WLR 1014, a young unmarried couple H and S occupied a double bedsitting room for which they paid a weekly rent. The landlord did not provide services or attendance and the couple were not lodgers but tenants enjoying exclusive possession. But the Court of Appeal did not ask themselves whether H and S were lodgers or tenants and did not draw the correct conclusion from the fact that H and S enjoyed exclusive possession. The Court of Appeal were diverted from the correct inquiries by the fact that the landlord obliged H and S to enter into separate agreements and reserved power to determine each agreement separately. The landlord also insisted that the room should not in form be let to either H or S or to both H and S but that each should sign an agreement to share the room in common with such other persons as the landlord might from time to time nominate. The sham nature of this obligation would have been only slightly more obvious if H and S had been married or if the room had been furnished with a double bed instead of two single beds. If the landlord had served notice on H to leave and had required S to share the room with a strange man, the notice would only have been a disguised notice to quit on both H and S. The room was let and taken as residential accommodation with exclusive possession in order that H and S might live together in undisturbed quasi-connubial bliss making weekly payments. The agreements signed by H and S constituted the grant to H and S jointly of exclusive possession at a rent for a term for the purposes for which the room was taken and the agreement therefore created a tenancy. Although the Rent Acts must not be allowed to alter or influence the construction of an agreement, the court should, in my opinion, be astute to detect and frustrate sham devices and artificial transactions whose only object is to disguise the grant of a tenancy and to evade the Rent Acts. I would disapprove of the decision in this case that H and S were only licensees and for the same reason would disapprove of the decision in *Aldrington Garages Ltd*, v *Fielder* (1978) 37 P & CR 461 and *Sturolson & Co* v *Weniz* (1984) 272, EG 326.

In the present case the Court of Appeal, 49 P & CR 324 held that the agreement dated 7 March 1983 only created a licence. Slade LJ, at p. 329 accepted that the agreement and in particular clause 3 of the agreement 'shows that the right to occupy the premises conferred on the defendant was intended as an exclusive right of occupation, in that it was thought necessary to give a special and express power to the plaintiff to enter. . .' Before your Lordships it was conceded that the agreement conferred the right of exclusive possession on Mrs. Mountford. Even without clause 3 the result would have been the same. By the agreement Mrs. Mountford was granted the right to occupy residential accommodation. The landlord did not provide any services or attendance. It was plain that Mrs. Mountford was not a lodger. Slade LJ proceeded to analyse all the provisions of the agreement, not for the purpose of deciding whether his finding of exclusive possession was correct, but for the purpose of assigning some of the provisions of the agreement to the category of terms which he thought are usually to be found in a tenancy agreement and of assigning other provisions to the category of terms which he thought are usually to be found in a licence. Slade LJ may or may not have been right that in a letting of a furnished room it was 'most unusual to find a provision in a tenancy agreement obliging the tenant to keep his rooms in a 'tidy condition' (p. 329). If Slade LJ was right about this and other provisions there is still no logical method of evaluating the results of his survey. Slade LJ reached the conclusion that 'the agreement bears all the hallmarks of a licence rather than a tenancy save for the one important feature of exclusive occupation': p. 329. But in addition to the hallmark of exclusive occupation of residential accommodation there were the hallmarks of weekly payments for a periodical term. Unless these three hallmarks are decisive, it really becomes impossible to distinguish a contractual tenancy from a contractual licence save by reference to the professed intention of the parties or by the judge awarding marks for drafting. Slade LJ was finally impressed by the statement at the foot of the agreement by Mrs. Mountford 'I understand and accept that a licence in the above form does not and is not intended to give me a tenancy protected under the Rent Acts.' Slade LJ said, at p. 330:

> it seems to me that, if the defendant is to displace the express statement of intention embodied in the declaration, she must show that the declaration was either a deliberate sham or at least an inaccurate statement of what was the true substance of the real transaction agreed between the parties; . . .

My Lords, the only intention which is relevant is the intention demonstrated by the agreement to grant exclusive possession for a term at a rent. Sometimes it may be difficult to discover whether, on the true construction of an agreement, exclusive possession is conferred. Sometimes it may appear from the surrounding circumstances that there was no intention to create legal relationships. Sometimes it may appear from the surrounding circumstances that the right to exclusive possession is referable to a legal relationship other than a tenancy. Legal relationships to which the grant of exclusive possession might be referable and which would or might negative the grant of an estate or interest in the land include occupancy under a contract for the sale of the land, occupancy pursuant to a contract of employment or occupancy referable to the holding of an office. But where as in the present case the only circumstances are that residential accommodation is offered and accepted with exclusive possession for a term at a rent, the result is a tenancy.

The position was well summarised by Windeyer J sitting in the High Court of Australia in *Radaich v Smith* (1959) 101 CLR 209, 222, where he said:

> What then is the fundamental right which a tenant has that distinguishes his position from that of a licensee? It is an interest in land as distinct from a personal permission to enter the land and use it for some stipulated purpose or purposes. And how is it to be ascertained whether such an interest in land has been given? By seeing whether the grantee was given a legal right of exclusive possession of the land for a term or from year to year or for a life or lives. If he was, he is a tenant. And he cannot be other than a tenant, because a legal right of exclusive possession is a tenancy and the creation of such a right is a demise. To say that a man who has, by agreement with a landlord, a right of exclusive possession of land for a term is not a tenant is simply to contradict the first proposition by the second. A right of exclusive possession is secured by the right of a lessee to maintain ejectment and, after his entry, trespass. A reservation to the landlord, either by contract or statute, of a limited right of entry, as for example to view or repair, is, of course, not inconsistent with the grant of exclusive possession. Subject to such reservations, a tenant for a term or from year to year or for a life or lives can exclude his landlord as well as strangers from the demised premises. All this is long established law: see *Cole on Ejectment* (1857) pp. 72, 73, 287, 458.

My Lords, I gratefully adopt the logic and the language of Windeyer J. Henceforth the courts which deal with these problems will, save in exceptional circumstances, only be concerned to inquire whether as a result of an agreement relating to residential accommodation the occupier is a lodger or a tenant. In the present case I am satisfied that Mrs. Mountford is a tenant, that the appeal should be allowed, that the order of the Court of Appeal should be set aside and that the respondent should be ordered to pay the costs of the appellant here and below.

Waite, A. J., Leases and Licences: The True Distinguishing Test (1987) 50 MLR 226

. . . In *Crancour Ltd v Da Silvaesa* (1986) 52 P & CR 204 Ralph Gibson LJ said:

> It is not necessary in my opinion for this court to decide . . . whether the principles laid down in *Street v Mountford* [1985] 1 AC 809 mean that, as a matter of law, premises made

available for a term at a rent for residential accommodation must imply a grant of exclusive possession, whatever the terms and circumstances of the agreement, unless the landlord provides attendance or services which require the landlord or his servants to exercise unrestricted access to and use of the premises. I incline to the view that *Street* v *Mountford* does lay down such a rule where the accommodation is intended for use as ordinary separate and private residential accommodation and in the absence of any exceptional circumstances. I understand the basis of the rule to be that possession of rooms for occupation as ordinary residential accommodation must, from its nature, be intended by both parties to be exclusive except where, as stated, the landlord requires unrestricted access for the provision of services or attendance.

It is suggested that this approach is open to criticism. It involves reading too much into a single passage in *Street* v *Mountford*. It is submitted that the touchstone of a tenancy remains exclusive possession. Lord Templeman's 'lodger' test is simply one of several ways in which a claim to exclusive possession can be negatived. . . . A fundamental question underlying the whole of the present discussion relates to the nature of the requisite exclusive possession. Must there be a right to exclusive possession or does the fact of it suffice? . . . The text of Lord Templeman's speech in *Street* v *Mountford* is somewhat ambiguous. However, if the above analysis of the sham is accepted then it is the right to (*i.e.* the grant of) exclusive possession which is decisive. This is clearly the view of the judges in *Crancour*. Ralph Gibson LJ in dealing with Lord Templeman's analysis of *Somma* v *Hazlehurst* [1978] 1 WLR 1014 said; 'the House of Lords is there saying, first, that the agreement in that case constituted the grant of exclusive possession; second, that the written obligation to share the room was not effective to alter the true nature of the grant . . .' In any case the 'right' as opposed to 'fact' analysis must be correct in principle since a lease is a derivative as opposed to original interest. It must therefore be based on a grant.

A final word is necessary about Lord Templeman's restricted 'lodger' test. It is clear that it is only where the landlord requires unrestricted access to the premises in order to provide attendance or services that the requisite exclusive possession is negated. Some useful guidance on the meaning of ' unrestricted ' has been provided by Ralph Gibson LJ in *Crancour*. The term means that the landlord can come and go at his own convenience irrespective of the presence of the occupier. The amount and frequency of the attendance and services are relevant but not overriding factors. Inevitably there is a grey area which is likely to provide the opportunity for litigation. No doubt equally inevitably the draughts-men will attempt to plug the gap. However, the shadow of the sham will always hover over this type of agreement, and will ensure that 'off the peg' agreements cannot be used to avoid Rent Act protection.

ADDISCOMBE GARDENS v *CRABBE* [1958] 1 QB 513, Court of Appeal

FACTS: The question was whether an agreement for the 'rental' of tennis courts in consideration of monthly payments of 'court fees' was a lease or a licence. The agreement required the grantee to keep the courts 'in good and tenantable repair and condition' and to surrender them at the end of the 'licence' in such condition. It also permitted the owner to enter 'at all reasonable times' to inspect the condition of the premises. In return, the owner, agreed to allow the grantees to 'quietly enjoy' the premises.
HELD: On the question of whether this agreement constituted a lease or a licence, it was held to constitute a lease. The answer was determined by law, and not by the label the parties put on the agreement.

JENKINS L: stated the facts and continued: It is vital to the plaintiffs' claim for possession of the premises that they should be able to establish that this document described as a licence is in truth a licence, as opposed to a tenancy agreement. If it is a mere licence, then the plaintiffs' claim to possession must follow, for the rights granted by it have some time since expired. If, on the other hand, although described as a licence, it has the effect of a tenancy agreement, then *prima facie* the plaintiffs must be faced, before they can get possession, with the task of compliance with the provisions of the Landlord and Tenant Act, 1954. . . .

. . . Taking all those considerations together, I am of opinion that the judge was perfectly right in holding, as he did, that this was a tenancy. He was particularly impressed by the express provision entitling the grantors to enter the premises 'to inspect the condition thereof and for all other reasonable purposes'; and he held that to be an indication that the right to occupy the premises granted to the grantees was intended to be an exclusive right of occupation, that circumstance, as I have said, being at lowest a strong circumstance in favour of the view that there is a tenancy as opposed to a licence.

FAMILY HOUSING ASSOCIATION v JONES [1990] 1 WLR 779, Court of Appeal

FACTS: The plaintiff housing association granted a homeless family the right to live in temporary accommodation. Under the agreement, described as a 'licence' and expressed to deny exclusive possession to the occupier, the occupiers were to pay a weekly 'accommodation charge'. The association retained a key, in order to execute emergency repairs and to provide certain counselling services to tenants. When offered alternative accommodation, the occupiers refused to vacate the premises. The judge at first instance held that the occupier was a licensee, and granted possession to the association. The occupiers appealed.

HELD: The appeal was allowed. According to the substantive test for 'a lease' the present arrangement could not properly be described as a licence. It was a weekly tenancy.

BALCOMBE LJ : *Licence or tenancy*

The decision of the House of Lords in *Street* v *Mountford* [1985] AC 809 represented a sea-change in the law on this subject. Although the difference between a licence and a tenancy had been long established, it was believed by many that a right of exclusive occupation could be granted to an occupier, and that right did not amount to exclusive possession, and hence create a tenancy, if that were the genuine intention of the parties. Lord Templeman, with whose speech all the other Law Lords agreed, disposed of that belief. . . .

Mr. Neuberger, for the housing association before us, did not seek to support the judge's findings that there was no defined term or that occupation could be given up without notice. Clearly the payment of an 'accommodation charge' on a weekly basis is no different from the payment of a weekly rent, which without more creates a weekly tenancy, while payment of that charge in advance would appear to prevent the housing association from determining Mrs. Jones's right to occupy at least before the end of the week in respect of which that charge had been paid; in any event even a licence cannot be determined except on reasonable notice: see *Minister of Health* v *Bellotti* [1944] KB 298. Furthermore, the 'genuine and express agreement that exclusive possession was not granted'—clause 5 of the agreement of 5 February 1985—is as much a label as is the reference to a 'licence' in the same clause and, to use Lord Templeman's spade/fork analogy (even though most garden forks have four tines or prongs), cannot prevent the agreement creating a tenancy if that is its true effect.

This was a self-contained flat, and it is clear that Mrs. Jones and Nicolas were to be its only occupants. Mrs. Jones paid a weekly charge for her right to occupy the flat. Thus the agreement fulfils all the requirements which Lords Templeman, Oliver of Aylmerton and Donaldson of Lymington MR in the several passages quoted above indicate as being appropriate for the creation of a tenancy; the only possible contra-indications are the retention of a key by the housing association and the purposes for which that key was retained. (I leave out of account the judge's reliance on the temporary nature of the accommodation granted: a weekly tenancy, provided it is not a secure tenancy and can be determined on a week's notice, is just as consistent with the provision of temporary accommodation as is a licence.) So I return to the question of the retention of the key and the purposes for which it was retained.

The retention of a key by itself cannot be decisive; a landlord under an undoubted tenancy may retain a key to enable him to exercise a right reserved to him by the tenancy to enter the demised premises to inspect the state of repair. As Lord Donaldson of Lymington MR said in *Aslan* v *Murphy* [1990] 1 WLR 776 there is a spectrum ranging from tenant at the one end to lodger at the other. Whilst the rights retained by the housing association in the present case may be slightly greater than those usually retained by a landlord under a lease, I entertain no doubt that they fall at the 'tenant' end of the spectrum, not the 'lodger' end.

In my judgment, the judge was incorrect in holding that the agreement of 5 February 1985 created a licence: it created a weekly tenancy.

17.2.2 THE MEANING OF EXCLUSIVE POSSESSION

MARCHANT v *CHARTERS* [1977] 1 WLR 1181, Court of Appeal

FACTS: The 'grantee' occupied an apartment in the grantor's premises. The grantor provided daily cleaning and regular changes of bed linen. The question was whether the grantee was a typical 'lodger', that is, a licensee, or whether they were a tenant.
HELD: The grantee was only a licensee.

LORD DENNING MR: . . . Gathering the cases together, what does it come to? What is the test to see whether the occupier of one room in a house is a tenant or a licensee? It does not depend on whether he or she has exclusive possession or not. It does not depend on whether the room is furnished or not. It does not depend on whether the occupation is permanent or temporary. It does not depend on the label which the parties put upon it. All these are factors which may influence the decision but none of them is conclusive. All the circumstances have to be worked out. Eventually the answer depends on the nature and quality of the occupancy. Was it intended that the occupier should have a stake in the room or did he have only permission for himself personally to occupy the room, whether under a contract or not? In which case he is a licensee.

Looking at the position in this case, in my opinion Mr. Charters was not a tenant of this one room. He was only a licensee. A contractual licensee, no doubt, but still only a licensee. So he does not have security of tenure under the Rent Acts. He is not protected against eviction. On this point I differ from the judge. It is sufficient for the deciding of this case. Mr Charters has no right to stay. . . .

17.2.3 RETENTION OF KEYS BY THE GRANTOR

ASLAN v *MURPHY* [1990] 1 WLR 766, Court of Appeal

FACTS: The plaintiff owned a basement room occupied exclusively by the defendant. The agreement under which the occupant held the premises provided that he had a mere 'licence' to occupy the room in common with other licensees, the owner retained the keys to the room. The occupant was also required to vacate the room for 90 minutes each day. The judge at first instance held that the agreement created a 'licence'. The occupier appealed.
HELD: The occupier had been granted exclusive possession and was, accordingly, a tenant of the room. This fact could not be altered unilaterally by the threat of introducing another licensee into the premises.

LORD DONALDSON OF LYMINGTON MR: . . . *General principles*
The status of a tenant is essentially different from that of a lodger and owners of property are free to make accommodation available on either basis. Which basis applies in any particular case depends upon what was the true bargain between the parties. It is the ascertainment of that true bargain which lies at the heart of the problem.

Labelling
The labels which parties agree to attach to themselves or to their agreements are never conclusive and in this particular field, in which there is enormous pressure on the homeless to agree to any label which will facilitate the obtaining of accommodation, they give no guidance at all. As Lord Templeman said in *Street* v *Mountford* [1985] AC 809, 819:

> The manufacture of a five-pronged implement for manual digging results in a fork even if the manufacturer, unfamiliar with the English language, insists that he intended to make and has made a spade.

Exclusive or non-exclusive occupation

This is the touchstone by which the 'spade' of tenancy falls to be distinguished from the 'fork' of lodging. In this context it is necessary to consider the rights and duties of the person making the accommodation available ('the owner') and the rights of other occupiers. The occupier has in the end to be a tenant or a lodger. He cannot be both. But there is a spectrum of exclusivity ranging from the occupier of a detached property under a full repairing lease, who is without doubt a tenant, to the overnight occupier of a hotel bedroom who, however up-market the hotel, is without doubt a lodger. The dividing line—the sorting of the forks from the spades—will not necessarily or even usually depend upon a single factor, but upon a combination of factors.

Pretences

Quite apart from labelling, parties may succumb to the temptation to agree to pretend to have particular rights and duties which are not in fact any part of the true bargain. *Prima facie*, the parties must be taken to mean what they say, but given the pressures on both parties to pretend, albeit for different reasons, the courts would be acting unrealistically if they did not keep a weather eye open for pretences, taking due account of how the parties have acted in performance of their apparent bargain. This identification and exposure of such pretences does not necessarily lead to the conclusion that their agreement is a sham, but only to the conclusion that the terms of the true bargain are not wholly the same as those of the bargain appearing on the face of the agreement. It is the true rather than the apparent bargain which determines the question 'tenant or lodger?'

The effect of the Rent Acts

If an occupier would otherwise be protected by the Rent Acts, he does not lose that protection by agreeing that he will surrender it either immediately or in the future and whether directly and in terms or indirectly, e.g. by agreeing to substitute a shared for an exclusive right of occupation should the owner so require; *Antoniades* v *Villiers* [1990] AC 417, 461. . . .

The judge was, of course, quite right to approach the matter on this basis that it is not a crime, nor is it contrary to public policy, for a property owner to license occupiers to occupy a property on terms which do not give rise to a tenancy. Where he went wrong was in considering whether the whole agreement was a sham and, having concluded that it was not, giving effect to its terms, i.e. taking it throughout at face value. What he should have done, and I am sure would have done if he had known of the House of Lords approach to the problem, was to consider whether the whole agreement was a sham and, if it was not, whether in the light of the factual situation the provisions for sharing the room and those depriving the defendant of the right to occupy it for 90 minutes out of each 24 hours were part of the true bargain between the parties or were pretences. Both provisions were wholly unrealistic and were clearly pretences.

In this court an attempt to uphold the judge's decision was made upon a different basis, namely, the landlord's right to retain the keys. The provisions relevant to this aspect of the agreement are:

1. . . . The licensor will retain the keys to the room and has absolute right of entry at all times for the purpose of exercising such control and (without prejudice to the generality of the foregoing) for the purpose of effecting any repairs or cleaning to the room or building or for the purpose of providing the attendance mentioned in clause 4 hereof or for the purpose of removing or substituting such articles of furniture from the room as the licensor might see fit. The said right of entry is exercisable by the licensor or his servants or agents with or without any other persons (including prospective future licensee of the room). . . . 4. The licensor will provide the following attendance for the licensee: (1) housekeeping (2) lighting of common parts (3) cleaning of common parts (4) window cleaning (5) intercom (6) telephone coin box (7) cleaning of room (8) collection of rubbish (9) provision and laundering of bed linen (10) hot water (11) provision of household supplies.

Provisions as to keys are often relied upon in support of the contention that an occupier is a lodger rather than a tenant. Thus in *Duke* v *Wynne* [1990] 1 WLR 766 . . . the agreement required the occupier 'not to interfere with or change the locks on any part of the premises, [or] give the key to any other than an authorised occupier of the premises.' Provisions as to keys, if not a pretence which they often are, do not have any magic in themselves. It is not a requirement of a tenancy that the occupier shall have exclusive possession of the keys to the property. What matters is what underlies the provisions as to keys. Why does the owner want a key, want to prevent keys being issued to the friends of the occupier or want to prevent the lock being changed?

A landlord may well need a key in order that he may be able to enter quickly in the event of emergency: fire, burst pipes or whatever. He may need a key to enable him or those authorised by him to read meters or to do repairs which are his responsibility. None of these underlying reasons would of themselves indicate that the true bargain between the parties was such that the occupier was in law a lodger. On the other hand, if the true bargain is that the owner will provide genuine services which can only be provided by having keys, such as frequent cleaning, daily bed-making, the provision of clean linen at regular intervals and the like, there are materials from which it is possible to infer that the occupier is a lodger rather than a tenant. But the inference arises not from the provisions as to keys, but from the reason why those provisions formed part of the bargain. On the facts of this case, the argument based upon the provisions as to keys must and does fail for the judge found that 'during the currency of the present agreement virtually 'no services' had been provided.' These provisions may or may not have been pretences, but they are without significance in the context of the question which we had to decide.

17.2.4   POSSESSORY LICENCES AFTER *STREET* v *MOUNTFORD*

17.2.4.1   Acts of generosity or friendship where there is no intent to create legal relations

RHODES v *DALBY* [1971] 2 All ER 1144, Chancery Division

FACTS: Two men were long-standing friends. One owned a bungalow, but was going abroad for two years. The two men signed a document described as 'a gentleman's agreement' not intended to create legal relations. Under that agreement the friend staying in this country took possession of the bungalow during the two year absence. He agreed to pay a quite high 'rent' for being able to live in the bungalow.
HELD: The arrangement was a licence.

GOFF J: . . . The plaintiff fastens on the word 'let', and on the payment of rent. But he cannot use it out of its context. What was admitted was that it was let on a gentleman's agreement. Counsel for the plaintiff very properly conceded that a gentleman's agreement normally means something which is not legally enforceable. I do not see how a letting on a gentleman's agreement, without further explanation, can be held sufficient evidence of a tenancy. . . .

Harris, J. W., Licences and Tenancies—The Generosity Factor (1969) 32 MLR 92

The commonest single factor which appears to have influenced the courts in finding a licence rather than a tenancy, is the element of charitable disposition on the part of the landowner. This may be called 'the generosity factor.' It appears typically in 'family,' 'friendly' or 'personal' arrangements.

A recent example of the generosity factor appeared in *Abbeyfield (Harpenden) Society Ltd* v *Woods* [1968] 1 WLR 374. A charitable society rented an unfurnished bed-sittingroom to Mr. Woods at £9 per week, in a home for old people, on terms that the society would provide food, heating and light and the services of a resident house-keeper. The crucial letter from the Society's officer to Mr. Woods contained these words:

I hope you will understand that in order to make the Abbeyfield House run properly, the Society must reserve the right to take possession of your room should it at its discretion think fit. You will, however, be given at least one month's notice of the Society's desire to take possession, and I do assure you that this right will only be exercised in the event of the Society considering it absolutely essential in the interests of yourself and of the other residents of this house.

It was held by the Court of Appeal that Mr. Woods was not entitled to the protection of the Rent Acts, because the relationship was that of licensor and licensee. Lord Denning MR, said:

> The modern cases show that a man may be a licensee even though he has exclusive possession, even though the word 'rent' is used, and even though the word 'tenancy' is used. The court must look at this agreement as a whole and see whether a tenancy really was intended. In this case there is, besides the one room, the provision of services, meals, a resident housekeeper, and such like. The whole arrangement was so personal in nature that the proper inference is, as the judge found, that he was a licensee on the terms stated in the letter, namely, that the Society would give him one month's notice and would only exercise that right in the event of the Society considering it absolutely essential in the interests of himself and the other residents of the house.

Lord Denning has often used the adjective 'personal' to describe the particular quality of the relationship between licensor and licensee. In *Cobb* v *Lane* [1952] 1 All ER 1199 and *Errington* v *Errington* [1952] 1 KB 290 he contrasted the 'personal privilege' created by a licence with the 'interest in land' created by any tenancy. The ordinary meaning of 'personal' in the context of Mr. Woods' relationship with his landlords would seem to be 'intimate'; and yet there can certainly be tenancies in which the tenant has just as much an every-day relationship with his landlord as did Mr. Woods with the plaintiff Society. Express tenancy agreements in respect of single rooms, where the landlord agrees to provide services, would, if the above words of Lord Denning were taken as a literal guide, all be in danger of being cut down to mere licences. 'Personal' is evidently equivalent to 'non-commercial' or 'charitable'—the generosity factor. Where one party is let into possession of another's land there is, below the level of the various relationships of estate created by grant, the relationship of licensor and licensee created by concession. This is a concept not susceptible of exact definition, and therefore it confers on the judge a discretion to preserve the deserving landlord from the effects of legislation designed to protect tenants.

17.2.4.2 Service occupancies

CRANE v *MORRIS* [1965] 3 All ER 77, Court of Appeal

FACTS: The defendant was employed as a farm worker and granted exclusive possession of a cottage on the farm upon condition that he remained in the employ of the plaintiff. The defendant did not pay rent. When the defendant left the plaintiff's employ and took up work in a factory, the plaintiff brought an action to regain possession of the premises. HELD: The defendant was a mere licensee, not a service tenant.

LORD DENNING MR: . . . At one time it was said (as the judge said here) that, for there to be a service occupation and not a tenancy, the servant must be *required* to occupy the house in order to perform his duties, as distinct from being *permitted* to occupy it. It was also said that the difference between a licence and a tenancy was that, on a tenancy, the occupier had exclusive possession, but on a licence, he had not exclusive possession. We have got long past those days. It is now perfectly well settled that a man may be a licensee (and no tenant) even though he has exclusive possession; see *Errington* v *Errington* [1952] 1 KB 290. And a servant may be a licensee (and no tenant) even though he is not required to live in the house but only permitted to do so for the convenience of his work; see *Torbett* v *Faulkner* [1952] 2 TLR 659. In this particular case I have no doubt whatever that the defendant was not a tenant. He was a licensee in the house, with permission to stay there rent free, so long as he remained in the employment of the farmer. Once he ceased to be in that employment, he could be turned out, being given, of course, a reasonable time to go. It is not necessary to give a licensee notice to quit, any more than it is a tenant at will. A demand is sufficient: and a writ claiming possession is itself a sufficient demand. . . .

NORRIS v *CHECKSFIELD* [1991] 1 WLR 1241, Court of Appeal

FACTS: A coach mechanic had been granted a 'licence' to use a bungalow close to the depot where he worked. A condition of the grant was that he would apply for a passenger service vehicle licence and would drive coaches for his employer. Upon discovering that the mechanic was a disqualified driver, the employer terminated his employment and brought an action for possession of the premises. The judge granted the order and the employee appealed. HELD: The appeal was dismissed. There was a sufficient connection between the employment and the licence to describe it as a 'service licence'. Such a licence came to an end summarily upon the termination of the employment to which it related.

WOOLF LJ: . . . In relation to the thorny issue as to when an employee is a licensee and not a tenant of premises belonging to his employer which he is allowed to occupy, Mr. Seaward, who appeared on behalf of the employee, was prepared to accept Mr. Zeidman's submission on behalf of the employer. Mr. Zeidman submitted that an employee can be a licensee, although his occupation of the premises is not *necessary* for the purposes of the employment, if he is genuinely *required* to occupy the premises for the *better performance* of his duties. In my judgment this submission accurately reflects the law. We have been referred to a number of authorities which set out different tests. The most helpful decision is that of the House of Lords in *Glasgow Corporation* v *Johnstone* [1965] AC 609. In that case Lord Reid, with whose speech Lord Wilberforce agreed, said, at p. 618:

> So, if necessity were the criterion, the appeal would succeed. But if it is sufficient for the respondents to show that their servant is bound to reside there, and that his residing there is of material assistance to them in the carrying out of their activities, then the appellants must fail on this point.

Lord Reid then went on to examine a number of English authorities and concluded this part of his speech by saying, at p. 619:

> In requiring that the occupation should be necessary I think that Mellor J's judgment [in *Smith* v *Seghill Overseers* (1875) LR 10 QB 422] is out of line with the other authorities, and the authorities on this topic appear to me to support the respondent's contention in the present case.

Lord Reid was therefore of the opinion that it would be sufficient if the employee's occupation was of 'material assistance' to his employment. It need not be *'necessary'* for his employment. The same view was taken by Lord Evershed and Lord Hodson. Lord Guest stated the position which must exist for there to be a licence in the following terms, at p. 629:

> The residence must be ancillary to the duties which the servant has to perform (*Smith* v *Seghill Overseers*) or, put in another way, the requirement must be with a view to the more efficient performance of the servant's duties (*Fox* v *Dalby* (1874) LR 10 CP 285).

As Mr. Seaward correctly submitted, it would not suffice if the occupation was a 'fringe benefit' or merely an inducement to encourage the employee to work better. Unless the occupation fulfilled this test, the fact that the employee had exclusive possession and paid rent would almost inevitably establish a service tenancy: see generally *Street* v *Mountford* [1985] AC 809 and *AG Securities* v *Vaughan* [1990] 1 AC 417, 459 *per* Lord Templeman.

If in this case, as was contemplated, when the employee went into occupation he had obtained a PSV licence and had changed the nature of his job so that he became a coach driver, the judge would undoubtedly have been entitled to regard the employee as a licensee. He would then have entered into occupation under a document which described the relationship in terms of a licence and the occupation would be beneficial to the employee's employment on the judge's findings. His occupation would enable him to assist his employer in cases of emergency or on short notice. . . .

Although the employee was unable to obtain the necessary PSV licence to drive coaches, he was on the judge's finding only allowed into occupation on the basis that he would obtain the necessary qualifications and work as a coach driver. In my judgment it would not be sensible, unless compelled to do so, to restrict an employer's ability to grant a licence to situations where the employment which would be benefited by the employee taking up occupation commenced simultaneously with or prior to the occupation of the premises. There may be many circumstances where it would be desirable for the employee to take up occupation before the relevant work commenced. What is required is that there should be a sufficient factual nexus between the commencement of the occupation of the premises and the employment which would benefit from that occupation. If for some reason it becomes apparent that the employee is not going to be able to fulfil the requirements of that employment within a reasonable time, then the position may be different. However, if the situation is one where it is contemplated, as was the position here, that the employee would, within a reasonable time, be able to take up the relevant employment, that will suffice. The fact that the employee during the interval may be performing some other duties which are not affected by the occupation of the premises does not prevent a licence coming into existence. . . .

17.2.5   FLAT-SHARING AGREEMENTS

ANTONIADES v *VILLIERS* [1990] 1 AC 417, House of Lords;
AG SECURITIES v *VAUGHAN* [1990] 1 AC 417, House of Lords

Antoniades v *Villiers*

FACTS: V1 and V2 (a co-habiting couple) each signed on the same day an agreement giving them the right to use a small flat. Clause 16 of each agreement provided: 'The licensor shall be entitled at any time to use the rooms together with the licensee and permit other persons to use all of the rooms together with the licensee'. The question was whether the agreements together constituted a lease of the premises, or whether they were individual licenses.
HELD: The practical reality was that the two documents, read together, granted exclusive possession to the appellants and therefore created a lease. Clause 16 should be ignored. It had been inserted by the grantor as a 'pretence', in an effort to show that V1 and V2 did not together have exclusive possession. The purported 'licences' were 'shams'.

AG Securities v *Vaughan*

FACTS: AGS owned a four-bedroomed flat. Each of the four occupiers had signed a non-exclusive licence. Each licence was signed on a different date, was for a different period, and was at a different rent. The question was whether this arrangement had created one lease or four licences.
HELD: There were four separate licences.

LORD TEMPLEMAN: . . . Parties to an agreement cannot contract out of the Rent Acts; if they were able to do so the Acts would be a dead letter because in a state of housing shortage a person seeking residential accommodation may agree to anything to obtain shelter. The Rent Acts protect a tenant but they do not protect a licensee. Since parties to an agreement cannot contract out of the Rent Acts, a document which expresses the intention, genuine or bogus, of both parties or of one party to create a licence will nevertheless create a tenancy if the rights and obligations enjoyed and imposed satisfy the legal requirements of a tenancy. A person seeking residential accommodation may concur in any expression of intention in order to obtain shelter. Since parties to an agreement cannot contract out of the Rent Acts, a document expressed in the language of a licence must nevertheless be examined and construed by the court in order to decide whether the rights and obligations enjoyed and imposed create a licence or a tenancy. A person seeking residential accommodation may sign a document couched in any language in order to obtain shelter. Since parties to an agreement cannot contract out of the Rent Acts, the grant of a tenancy to two persons jointly cannot be concealed, accidentally or by design, by the creation of two documents in the form of licences. Two persons seeking residential accommodation may sign any number of documents in order to obtain joint shelter. In considering one or more documents for the purpose of deciding whether a tenancy has been created, the court must consider the surrounding circumstances including any relationship between the prospective occupiers, the course of negotiations and the nature and extent of the accommodation and the intended and actual mode of occupation of the accommodation. If the owner of a one-bedroomed flat granted a licence to a husband to occupy the flat provided he shared the flat with his wife and nobody else and granted a similar licence to the wife provided she shared the flat with the husband and nobody else, the court would be bound to consider the effect of both documents together. If the licence to the husband required him to pay a licence fee of £50 per month and the licence to the wife required her to pay a further licence fee of £50 per month, the two documents read together in the light of the property to be occupied and the obvious intended mode of occupation would confer exclusive occupation on the husband and wife jointly and a tenancy at the rent of £100.

Landlords dislike the Rent Acts and wish to enjoy the benefits of letting property without the burden of the restrictions imposed by the Acts. Landlords believe that the Rent Acts unfairly interfere with freedom of contract and exacerbate the housing shortage. Tenants on the other hand believe that the Acts are a necessary protection against the exploitation of people who do not own the freehold or long leases of their homes. The court lacks the knowledge and the power to form any judgment on these arguments which fall to be considered and determined by Parliament. The duty of the court is to enforce the Acts and in so doing to observe on principle which is inherent in the Acts and has been long recognised, the principle that parties cannot contract out of the Acts. . . .

LORD OLIVER OF AYLMERTON: . . .
Antoniades v *Villiers and another*   The appellants in this appeal are a young couple who at all material times were living together as man and wife. In about November 1984 they learned from a letting agency that a flat was available in a house at 6, Whiteley Road, London SE19, owned by the respondent, Mr. Antoniades. They inspected the flat together and were told that the rent would be £174 per month. They were given the choice of having the bedroom furnished with a double bed or two single beds and they chose a double bed. So, right from the inception, there was never any question but that the appellants were seeking to establish a joint home and they have, at all material times, been the sole occupants of the flat.

There is equally no question but that the premises are not suitable for occupation by more than one couple, save on a very temporary basis. The small living-room contains a sofa capable of being converted into a double bed and also a bed-table capable of being opened out to form a narrow single bed. The appellants did in fact have a friend to stay with them for a time in what the trial judge found to be cramped conditions, but the size of the accommodation and the facilities available clearly do not make the flat suitable for multiple occupation. When it came to drawing up the contractual arrangements under which the appellants were to be let into possession, each was asked to and did sign a separate licence agreement in the terms set out in the speech of my noble and learned friend, Lord Templeman, under which each assumed an individual, but not a joint, responsibility for payment of one half of the sum of £174 previously quoted as the rent.

There is an air of total unreality about these documents read as separate and individual licences in the light of the circumstance that the appellants were together seeking a flat as a quasi-matrimonial home. A separate licensee does not realistically assume responsibility for all repairs and all outgoings. Nor in the circumstances can any realistic significance be given to clauses 16 and 17 of the document. It cannot realistically have been contemplated that the respondent would either himself use or occupy any part of the flat or put some other person in to share accommodation specifically adapted for the occupation by a couple living together. These clauses cannot be considered as seriously intended to have any practical operation or to serve any purpose apart from the purely technical one of seeking to avoid the ordinary legal consequences attendant upon letting the appellants into possession at a monthly rent. The unreality is enhanced by the reservation of the right of eviction without court order, which cannot seriously have been thought to be effective, and by the accompanying agreement not to get married, which can only have been designed to prevent a situation arising in which it would be quite impossible to argue that the 'licensees' were enjoying separate rights of occupation.

The conclusion seems to me irresistible that these two so-called licences, executed contemporaneously and entered into in the circumstances already outlined, have to be read together as constituting in reality one single transaction under which the appellants became joint occupiers. That of course does not conclude the case because the question still remains, what is the effect?. . .

If the documents fall to be taken seriously at their face value and to be construed according to their terms, I see, for my part, no escape from the conclusion at which the Court of Appeal arrived. If it is once accepted that the respondent enjoyed the right—whether he exercised it or not—to share the accommodation with the appellants, either himself or by introducing one or more other persons to use the flat with them, it is, as it seems to me, incontestable that the appellants cannot claim to have had exclusive possession. . . .

If the real transaction was, as the judge found, one under which the appellants became joint tenants with exclusive possession, on the footing that the two agreements are to be construed together, then it would follow that they were together jointly and severally responsible for the whole rent. It would equally follow that they could effectively exclude the respondent and his nominees.

Although the facts are not precisely on all fours with *Somma* v *Hazelhurst* [1978] 1 WLR 1014, they are strikingly similar and the judge was, in my judgment, entitled to conclude that the appellants had exclusive possession of the premises. I read his finding that, 'the licences are artificial transactions designed to evade the Rent Acts' as a finding that they were sham documents designed to conceal the true nature of the transaction. There was, in my judgment, material on which he could properly reach this conclusion and I, too, would allow the appeal.

AG Securities v *Vaughan and others*

The facts in this appeal are startlingly different from those in the case of *Antoniades*. To begin with the appeal concerns a substantial flat in a mansion block consisting of four bedrooms, a lounge, a sitting-room and usual offices. The trial judge found, as a fact, that the premises could without difficulty provide residential accommodation for four persons. There is no question but that the agreements with which the appeal is concerned reflect the true bargain between the parties. It is the purpose and intention of both parties to each agreement that it should confer an individual right on the licensee named, that he should be liable only for the payment which he had undertaken, and that his agreement should be capable of termination without reference to the agreements with other persons occupying the flat. . . .

I pause to note that it has never been contended that any individual occupier has a tenancy of a particular room in the flat with a right to use the remainder of the flat in common with the tenants of other rooms. I can envisage that as a possibility in cases of arrangements of this kind if the facts support the marking out with the landlord's concurrence of a particular room as the exclusive domain of a particular individual. But to support that there would, I think, have to be proved the grant of an identifiable part of the flat and that simply does not fit with the system described in the evidence of the instant case.

The real question—and it is this upon which the respondents rely—is what is the position when the flat is occupied concurrently by all four licensees? What is said then is that since the licensor has now exhausted, for the time being, his right of nomination, the four occupants collectively have exclusive possession of the premises because they can collectively exclude the licensor himself. Because, it is argued, (1) they have thus exclusive possession and, (2) there is an ascertainable term during which all have the right to use and occupy, and (3) they are occupying in consideration of the payment of periodic sums of money, *Street* v *Mountford* [1985] AC 809 shows that they are collectively tenants of the premises. They are not lodgers. Therefore they must be tenants. And because each is not individually a tenant, they must together be joint tenants.

My Lords, there appear to me to be a number of fallacies here. In the first place, the assertion of an exclusive possession rests, as it seems to me, upon assuming what it is sought to prove. If, of course, each licence agreement creates a tenancy, each tenant will be sharing with other persons whose rights to be there rest upon their own estates which, once they have been granted, they enjoy in their own right independently of the landlord.

Collectively they have the right to exclude everyone other than those who have concurrent estates. But if the licence agreement is what it purports to be, that is to say, merely an agreement for permissive enjoyment as the invitee of the landlord, then each shares the use of the premises with other invitees of the same landlord. The landlord is not excluded for he continues to enjoy the premises through his invitees, even though he may for the time being have precluded himself by contract with each from withdrawing the invitation. Secondly, the fact that under each agreement an individual has the privilege of user and occupation for a term which overlaps the term of user and occupation of other persons in the premises, does not create a single indivisible term of occupation for all four consisting of an amalgam of the individual overlapping periods. Thirdly, there is no single sum of money payable in respect of use and occupation. Each person is individually liable for the amount which he has agreed, which may differ in practice from the amounts paid by all or some of the others.

The respondents are compelled to support their claims by a strange and unnatural theory that, as each occupant terminates his agreement, there is an implied surrender by the other three and an implied grant of a new joint tenancy to them together with the new incumbent when he enters under his individual agreement. With great respect to the majority in the Court of Appeal, this appears to me to be entirely unreal. For my part, I agree with the dissenting judgment of Sir George Waller in finding no unity of interest, no unity of title, certainly no unity of time and, as I think, no unity of possession. I find it impossible to say that the agreements entered into with the respondents created either individually or collectively a single tenancy either of the entire flat or of any part of it. I agree that the appeal should be allowed.

Hill, J., Shared Accommodation and Exclusive Possession (1989) 52 MLR 408

III Sham transactions

In the context of shared residential accommodation, the fact that each occupier entered a separate 'licence agreement' with the owner does not preclude the possibility that the occupiers are tenants. However, for this to be the case it must be established that the agreements are in some sense sham. While the fundamental characteristic of a sham transaction is that the form disguises the substance, it is important to be aware that not all shams are of the same type. In the present context three different types of sham should be distinguished (although it is quite possible for all three types of sham to arise in a single case). First, and least problematical, is the situation where the terminology employed in an agreement misrepresents the legal category into which the arrangement falls. Secondly, documents may include clauses by which neither party intends to be bound and which are obviously a smokescreen to cover the real intentions of both contracting parties, Thirdly, where there are a number of transactions creating a composite whole the court may look at the overall result of what is achieved rather than considering the individual transactions in isolation. For example, where a number of occupiers enter separate licence agreements the courts may treat the occupiers as joint tenants. In cases involving composite transactions the substance of the relationship between the occupiers and the owner may be determined either by reading the interdependent written agreements together (ignoring smokescreen clauses) or by reference to a parallel oral or implied agreement. . . .

IV Implications

A disappointing feature of the speeches in *AG Securities* v *Vaughan* and *Antoniades* v *Villiers* is the House of Lords' failure to address the problems which result from the fact that the exploitation of the lease/licence distinction is merely one of a number of devices employed by landlords to avoid the Rent Act 1977 (and now the Housing Act 1988). Any individual decision which appears to extend the ambit of statutory protection (such as *Antoniades* v *Villiers*) will have no more than a marginal impact in terms of its practical effects if landlords' legal advisers can continue to circumvent the legislation simply by redrafting their standard-form agreements or by employing alternative avoidance mechanisms. The absence of a broader perspective runs the risk of the rights of residential occupiers depending on arbitrary distinctions, and the courts 'awarding marks for drafting.'

Although in *Antoniades* v *Villiers* and *AG Securities* v *Vaughan* the House of Lords declined to address the issue of avoidance of statutory schemes of protection on a broader level, the principles which have been formulated in the context of the lease/licence distinction are applicable to analogous situations. It is suggested that the tripartite structure employed in the previous section offers an appropriate framework through which the courts can work out solutions to the various avoidance devices employed by private sector landlords.

In a number of cases the courts have considered the authenticity of holiday lettings (which are not within the scope of statutory schemes of protection). Although on occasion the courts have declined to question the label employed by the landlord more recently in *R v Rent Officer for London Borough of Camden, ex parte Plant* (1980) 257 EG 713 it was held that a purported 'holiday let' for six months was not genuine since the landlord knew that the occupiers were student nurses and therefore were not occupying the premises for the purpose of a holiday. This decision is consistent with the lease/licence cases in the sense that the court accepted that it was not bound by the label employed by the parties to the agreement. Similarly, although smokescreen clauses are used primarily with a view to exploiting the lease/licence distinction, the approach taken by the House of Lords in *Antoniades v Villiers* [see **17.2.5**] may be applicable in other contexts. For example, a contrived attempt to bring a tenancy agreement within the exception contained in section 7 of the Rent Act 1977 by providing 'board' might be regarded as a sham.

In relation to the lease/licence cases the third category of sham—interdependent transactions—presents the most problems. The same is true in the context of other avoidance devices, as can be seen from two cases decided by the Court of Appeal shortly before the House of Lords heard *Antoniades v Villiers* and *AG Securities v Vaughan* [see **17.2.5**]. In *Gisborne v Burton* [1988] 3 WLR 921 a landowner granted an agricultural tenancy to his wife, who immediately granted a sub-tenancy of the land to the defendant. The purpose of this arrangement was to prevent the defendant from acquiring the rights which are available to tenants under the Agricultural Holdings Act 1948. In the Court of Appeal Dillon LJ, having examined the principles employed by the courts in tax avoidance cases took the view that:

> a similar principle must be applicable wherever there is a pre-ordained series of transactions which is intended to avoid some mandatory statutory provision, even if not of a fiscal nature. You must look at the effect of the scheme as a whole, instead of concentrating on each pre-ordained step individually, and you do not, as it were, blow the whistle at half time.

Russell LJ, having noted that he had 'not derived a lot of assistance from the tax avoidance cases,' nevertheless decided that the series of transactions was a sham. Accordingly, notwithstanding the formal position the real substance of the two transactions was held to be the grant of a tenancy to the defendant.

Although one commentator expressed the view that '*Gisborne* may prove useful to residential tenants' advisers who try to argue that tenants have security of tenure, particularly in the case of 'artificial' company let agreements' in *Hilton v Plustitle Ltd* [1989] 1 WLR 149 the Court of Appeal held that a tenancy granted to an off-the-shelf company purchased by the sole occupier of residential premises was not a sham. As a result the occupier was denied the benefits of the Rent Act 1977.

The recent decisions of the House of Lords suggest that the approach taken by the Court of Appeal in *Gisborne v Burton* is the correct one. In *Antoniades v Villiers* it was held that the form of a predetermined series of transactions (two licence agreements) cannot be allowed to disguise the true substance of the arrangement (the grant of a joint tenancy). In a case such as *Hilton v Plustitle Ltd* which involves the purchase of an off-the-shelf company the artificial nature of the series of transactions is transparent. Accordingly, the true substance of the arrangement is the grant of tenancy to the occupier, rather than the company. On the other hand, where a tenancy of residential premises is granted to a company with an independent existence there is no sham since there is no pre-ordained or interdependent series of transactions.

Conclusion

Street v Mountford [1985] 1 AC 809 presented a very straightforward issue: there was a single agreement between Mrs Mountford and the landlord, and it was conceded by the landlord that Mrs Mountford had exclusive possession. From the foregoing discussion it has been seen that Lord Templeman's speech in *Street v Mountford* provides rather limited assistance when considering the questions posed by the use of licence agreements in the context of shared accommodation. The statement that 'exclusive possession for a term at a rent' results in a tenancy does not help in determining whether or not exclusive possession has been granted.

In 1987 the Law Commission said that *Street v Mountford* was 'not likely to have ended the battle; rather it settled a series of skirmishes and moved the front line.' This assessment is vindicated by the cases discussed in this note. Although in *Antoniades v Villiers* and *AG Securities v Vaughan* the House of Lords has gone some way towards clarifying the dividing line between leases and licences, some questions have not been given an unequivocal answer. More significantly, the House of Lords has still to consider expressly the viability of other avoidance devices (in particular the company let). The war is not over yet.

17.2.6   'PRETENCE' CLAUSES DESIGNED TO NEGATE EXCLUSIVE POSSESSION

ASLAN v *MURPHY* and *DUKE* v *WYNN* [1990] 1 WLR 766

FACTS: In the first case, A granted to M the use of a tiny basement room. The licence included a term that A could introduce another occupant. It also included another provision that M had no right to use the room between 1030 and 1200 hours.
HELD: Both these clauses were found to be 'pretences', and M was held to be a tenant.

FACTS: In the second case D granted to Mr and Mrs W (who had two children living with them) a three-bedroom house for two years. D again reserved the right to introduce other occupiers to the property. This clause was found to be a 'pretence'. D had no genuine intention of introducing other person(s) to the house.
HELD: Mr and Mrs W were found to have a lease.

17.3   Formalities for Leases

17.3.1   LEGAL LEASES BY EXPRESS GRANT

LAW OF PROPERTY ACT 1925

54.   Creation of interests in land by parol
   (1)   All interests in land created by parol and not put in writing and signed by the persons so creating the same, or by their agents thereunto lawfully authorised in writing, have, notwithstanding any consideration having been given for the same, the force and effect of interests at will only.
   (2)   Nothing in the foregoing provisions of this Part of this Act shall affect the creation by parol of leases taking effect in possession for a term not exceeding three years (whether or not the lessee is given power to extend the term) at the best rent which can be reasonably obtained without taking a fine.

17.3.2   LEGAL LEASES BY OPERATION OF LAW

JAVAD v *MOHAMMED AQIL* [1991] 1 WLR 1007, Court of Appeal

FACTS: The plaintiff landlord allowed the defendant to take possession of the premises upon payment of a lump sum equivalent to advance rent for the first quarter of the year. The arrangement was made in anticipation of the agreement of terms for a fixed-term lease. In the event, the parties could not agree the terms of the lease, but during the period of the negotiations the defendant remained in possession of the premises amd made two further payments in respect of quarterly rent. When the plaintiff ultimately brought proceedings for possession, the defendant claimed that he had a periodic tenancy and was therefore entitled to three months' notice before eviction.

HELD: In the circumstances the defendant was to be treated as a tenant at will. There were too many unresolved differences between the parties to infer a period tenancy.

NICHOLLS LJ: . . . A tenancy, or lease, is an interest in land. With exceptions immaterial for present purposes, a tenancy springs from a consensual arrangement between two parties: one person grants to another the right to possession of land for a lesser term than he, the grantor, has in the land. The extent of the right thus granted and accepted depends primarily upon the intention of the parties.

As with other consensually-based arrangements, parties frequently proceed with an arrangement whereby one person takes possession of another's land for payment without having agreed or directed their minds to one or more fundamental aspects of their transaction. In such cases the law, where appropriate, has to step in and fill the gaps in a way which is sensible and reasonable. The law will imply, from what was agreed and all the surrounding circumstances, the terms the parties are to be taken to have intended to apply. Thus if one party permits another to go into possession of his land on payment of a rent of so much per week or month, failing more the inference sensibly and reasonably to be drawn is that the parties intended that there should be a weekly or monthly tenancy. Likewise, if one party permits another to remain in possession after the expiration of his tenancy. But I emphasise the qualification 'failing more.' Frequently there will be more: Indeed, nowadays there normally will be other material surrounding circumstances. The simple situation is unlikely to arise often, not least because of the extent to which statute has intervened in landlord-tenant relationships. Where there is more than the simple situation, the inference sensibly and reasonably to be drawn will depend upon a fair consideration of all the circumstances, of which the payment of rent on a periodical basis is only one, albeit a very important one. This is so, however large or small may be the amount of the payment.

To this I add one observation, having in mind the facts of the present case. Where parties are negotiating the terms of a proposed lease, and the prospective tenant is let into possession or permitted to remain in possession in advance of, and in anticipation of, terms being agreed, the fact that the parties have not yet agreed terms will be a factor to be taken into account in ascertaining their intention. It will often be a weighty factor. Frequently in such cases a sum called 'rent' is paid at once in accordance with the terms of the proposed lease: for example, quarterly in advance. But, depending on all the circumstances, parties are not to be supposed thereby to have agreed that the prospective tenant shall be a quarterly tenant. They cannot sensibly be taken to have agreed that he shall have a periodic tenancy, with all the consequences flowing from that, at a time when they are still not agreed about the terms on which the prospective tenant shall have possession under the proposed lease, and when he has been permitted to go into possession or remain in possession merely as an interim measure in the expectation that all will be regulated and regularised in due course when terms are agreed and a formal lease granted.

Of course, when one party permits another to enter or remain upon his land on payment of a sum of money, and that other has no statutory entitlement to be there, almost inevitably there will be some consensual relationship between them. It may be no more than a licence determinable at any time, or a tenancy at will. But when and so long as such parties are in the throes of negotiating larger terms, caution must be exercised before inferring or imputing to the parties an intention to give to the occupant more than a very limited interest, be it licence or tenancy. Otherwise the court would be in danger of inferring or imputing from conduct, such as payment of rent and the carrying out of repairs, whose explanation lies in the parties' expectation that they will be able to reach agreement on the larger terms, an intention to grant a lesser interest, such as a periodic tenancy, which the parties never had in contemplation at all. . . .

I would dismiss this appeal. Entry into possession while negotiations proceed is one of the classic circumstances in which a tenancy at will may exist . . .

17.4   End of Chapter Assessment Question

Whether a transaction under which someone acquires the right to use another's property is a lease or a license depends largely, but not exclusively, on whether the transaction grants 'exclusive possession'.

Discuss.

17.5   End of Chapter Assessment Outline Answer

The Basic Test of Exclusive Possession

The first major case to discuss the *way* in which a lease should be distinguished from a licence was *Wells* v *Hull Corporation*. The facts of this 1875 case are very far removed from twentieth century cases, which usually involve residential properties.

Hull Corporation owned a dry dock which it 'let' for short periods (usually a week) to shipowners for the purposes of carrying out repairs. The court held that whether the transaction constituted a lease or a licence turned on whether the grantee shipowner had been given 'exclusive possession' of the dock. The grantee would have 'exclusive possession' if he had been granted the *overall general control* of the dock.

On the facts the shipowners were held only to have licences as they lacked the necessary control of the dock. Under the terms of the standard form used by the Corporation, the Corporation continued to operate the dock gates, the pumps, and also supervised the cleaning out of the dock at the end of each day's repair work. These clauses meant that the shipowners did not have exclusive possession.

Moving forward more than a hundred years it can be said that nowadays the most obvious type of licensee in modern conditions is the traditional lodger. His 'landlady' (in the colloquial sense) retains control of his room, cleaning out, tidying up and changing bed linen. In *Marchant* v *Charters* [see **17.2.2**], a case in 1977 which presumably survives *Street* v *Mountford*, the grantee was not a lodger in the time-honoured sense but the occupant of a service flat. The grantor provided daily cleaning and regular changes of bed linen; the grantee was held to have only a licence.

Service Occupancies

Reading *Wells* v *Hull Corporation* one might get the impression that there was a hard and fast rule, 'If a grant gives exclusive possession it must amount to a lease.' Even in the nineteenth century this was not the case, for the law has long recognised the concept of the 'Service Occupancy' under which an employee has a licence to occupy his employer's house/flat.

The employee usually has exclusive possession, but he in law will only have a licence if the house/flat is provided so that he can be 'ready on the job'. Normally the employee is required by his contract of employment to live in the accommodation, but in *Crane Morris* (1965) the employee was permitted but not obliged to live in a house which the employer had provided very close to the place of work. The employee was held to be a service occupier licencee.

An interesting recent case is *Norris* v *Checksfield* (1991). An employee, who was already working as a coach fitter, was granted by his employer exclusive possession of a bungalow very near the depot. It was envisaged by the employer that in the near future the employee would take a PSV driver's test and would then be 'on call' to cover for emergencies such as a regular driver going sick. The employee never took the test; it was held that he was only a service occupier licencee.

Possessory Licences from 1945 to 1985

After the second world war there were a number of cases which seemed to indicate that if a transaction (which was not a service occupancy) granted exclusive possession, a licence not a lease would arise if it could be proved that 'the intent of the parties' was that there should only be a licence.

This problematic line of cases possibly started with *Marcroft Wagons* v *Smith* in 1951. There the existing tenancy of a house had terminated, but the grantors allowed the daughter of the ex-tenants to continue to live there for six months while she sought alternative accommodation. They charged her the same rent as before, but refused to give her a rent book or any other documentation. The daughter was held to be only a licencee. The Court of Appeal held that a lease had not been 'intended'.

As a result of this and other cases grantors thought, 'If we draft our grants so that they are *called* possessory licences we are on to a winner. We will escape all the restrictions of the Rent Acts.

Things come to a head in Street v Mountford

In this case Street granted Mountford the exclusive possession of a flat. The document they both signed included the kind of provisions you would expect in a residential lease, but it also explicitly stated that the transaction was not a lease, only a licence. The Court of Appeal held that the subjective 'intent of the parties' was decisive, and that Mountford only had a licence.

Celebrations by grantors of residential properties were however very short-lived. When *Street* reached the House of Lords, the House overruled the Court of Appeal. In particular the House held that the test for whether a transaction was a lease or a licence was NOT the subjective 'intent of the parties'.

The House of Lords held (in effect reverting to the nineteenth century position) that it was the objective test of exclusive possession which determined whether a transaction was a lease or a licence. A transaction which granted exclusive possession created a lease unless it fell within certain exceptions.

The exceptions recognised by the Lords were four in number. Service occupancies and occupation by virtue of an office (e.g. a vicar in his vicarage) were two. The other two exceptions are where a purchaser of premises is allowed into possession ahead of completion and where somebody allows friend(s) to occupy his premises as an act of generosity.

The 1974 case of *Heslop* v *Burns* is a clear illustration of this last exception. There an impoverished couple lived rent free in the house of a wealthy benefactor. They were held only to be licensees. Whether *Marcroft* v *Smith* comes within this exception is more debatable. The grantors had some understandable sympathy for the daughter, but they did charge her rent!

Non-exclusive Licenses

Another trick adopted by residential grantors even prior to *Street* was examined by the House of Lords in *Antoniades* v *Villiers*. There the two partners to a cohabitation had each signed a separate 'non-exclusive' license over a very small flat. One of the clauses of each agreement read 'The licensor shall be entitled at any time to use the rooms together with the licensee and permit other persons to use all of the rooms together with the licensee.'

The House of Lords held that the documents had to be read together as creating one lease, and that the clause just quoted had to be rejected as a 'pretence'.

A case decided at the same time as *Antoniades, AG Securities* v *Vaughan* has however shown a way forward for grantors still determined to give only licences over their property. The grantors had granted four non-exclusive-licences over a four bedroom flat, each licence commencing on a different day, for a different duration and at a different rent. The House of Lords held that there were four licences, overruling a Court of Appeal decision that the four documents should be read as creating one lease.

Grantors retaining Rights over the Premises

It is quite clear that if a grantor retains keys to premises the use of which he has granted to other(s), that does not prevent the transaction from giving exclusive possession and therefore being a lease. But what if the grantor inserts into a grant a clause deliberately designed to negate exclusive possession? In *Aslan* v *Murphy* Aslan granted to Murphy the use of a tiny basement flat, but with a strange looking clause inserted that Murphy had no right to use the premises between 1030 and 1200 every day. The licensor also had 'the right' to introduce into the flat another occupant.

In practice these clauses were never enforced and the Court of Appeal in effect held that they were 'pretences' (cf. *Antoniades* v *Villiers*). Murphy was held to have a lease.

This robust approach of in effect deleting from transactions clauses inserted by grantors which *on paper but not in reality* negate the granting of exclusive possession calls into question the 1971 decision of the Court of Appeal in *Shell-Mex* v *Manchester Garages*.

Shell granted the use of a filling station to the defendants for one year. The grant included a strange clause under which Shell could alter the layout of the premises. The clause even entitled Shell to move the very extensive underground storage tanks. The Court of Appeal held that the defendants only had a licence.

It is submitted that if this case were to recur the courts would apply (in the commercial field) the same approach as has been applied to dwellings. The artificial clauses about layout would be ignored as 'pretences'; the garage would have exclusive possession and therefore a one year lease protected by the Landlord and Tenant Act 1954, Part II.

CHAPTER EIGHTEEN

OBLIGATIONS IN LEASES

18.1   Rent — Certain Basic Points

18.1.1   RENT REVIEWS

UNITED SCIENTIFIC HOLDINGS LTD v BURNLEY BOROUGH COUNCIL
[1977] 2 All ER 62, House of Lords

FACTS: A rent-review clause in a lease provided for the upwards-only variation of the rent at 10 year intervals. On the date for the first increase in rent the level of the reviewed rent had not been agreed between the parties. The tenant sought a declaration that, since time was of the essence, the landlord had lost its right to raise the rent for the second period of ten years.

HELD: Time was not of the essence. The new rent could still be determined in accordance with the formula set-out in the lease.

LORD DIPLOCK: My Lords, during the last two decades since inflation, particularly in the property market, has been rife, it has been usual to include in leases for a term of years, except when the term is very short, a clause providing for the annual rent to be reviewed at fixed intervals during the term and for the market rent current at reach review date if it be higher, to be substituted for the rent previously payable. The wording of such clauses varies; there are several different ones now included in the books of precedents; but a feature common to nearly all of them is that not only do they specify a procedure for the determination of the revised rent by agreement between the parties or, failing that, by an independent valuer or arbitrator, but they also set out a time-table for taking some or all of the steps in that procedure which, if followed, would enable the revised rent to be settled not later than the review date.

The question in both of these appeals, which have been heard together, is whether a failure to keep strictly to the time-table laid down in the review clause deprives the landlord of his right to have the rent reviewed and consequently of his right to receive an increased rent during the period that will elapse until the next review date. . . .

It is not disputed that the parties to a lease may provide expressly that time is or time is not of the essence of the contract in respect of all or any of the steps required to be taken by the landlord to obtain the determination of an increased rent, and that if they do so the court will give effect to their expressed intention. But many rent review cases that are now maturing do not contain express provision in these terms. . . .

The rent review clauses that have given rise to the two instant appeals, as well as nearly all those which have been considered in the reported cases, if they result in any alteration of the rent previously payable can only have the effect of providing for the payment of a higher rent than would be payable by the tenant if the review clause had not been brought into operation. So the only party who can benefit from a review of rent under these clauses is the landlord. It is accordingly unlikely that the tenant would take the initiative in obtaining a review of the rent, even where the clause contains provision for his doing so—as it does in the second of the instant appeals.

It was this concentration of initiative and benefit in the landlord that led the Court of Appeal in the second appeal to regard the rent review clause as conferring upon the landlord a unilateral right to bring into existence a new contractual relationship between the parties. This they regarded as sufficiently analogous to an option, to make time of the essence of the occurrence of each one of the events in the time-table laid down in a review clause for the determination of the new rent. For my part, I consider the analogy to be misleading. The determination of the new rent under the procedure stipulated in the rent review clause neither brings into existence a fresh contract between the landlord and the tenant nor does it put an end to one that had existed previously. It is an event upon the occurrence of which the tenant has in his existing contract already accepted an obligation to pay to the landlord the rent so determined for the period to which the rent review relates. The tenant's acceptance of that obligation was an inseverable part of the whole consideration of the landlord's grant of a term of years of the length agreed. Without it, in a period during which inflation was anticipated, the landlord would either have been unwilling to grant a lease for a longer period than up to the first review date or would have demanded a higher rent to be paid throughout the term than that payable before the first review date. By the time of each review of rent the tenant will have already received a substantial part of the whole benefit which it was intended that he should obtain in return for his acceptance of the obligation to pay the higher rent for the succeeding period.

My Lords, I see no relevant difference between the obligation undertaken by a tenant under a rent review clause in a lease and any other obligation in a synallagmatic contract that is expressed to arise upon the occurrence of a described event, where a postponement of that event beyond the time stipulated in the contract is not so prolonged as to deprive the obligor of substantially the whole benefit that it was intended he should obtain by accepting the obligation.

So upon the question of principle which these two appeals were brought to settle, I would hold that in the absence of any contra-indications in the express words of the lease or in the interrelation of the rent review clause itself and other clauses or in the surrounding circumstances the presumption is that the time-table specified in a rent review clause for completion of the various steps for determining the rent payable in respect of the period following the review date is not of the essence of the contract. . . .

AMHERST v JAMES WALKER GOLDSMITH & SILVERSMITH LTD
[1983] 1 Ch 305, Court of Appeal

FACTS: Amherst was the landlord of a shop and James Walker Ltd, the well-known 'high street chain', was the tenant. Amherst claimed a rent review four years late.
HELD: Amherst succeeded in his claim. The crucial point was that the rent on one shop was a relatively insignificant consideration for a big firm like James Walker.

OLIVER LJ: Essentially, as it seems to me, the question is one of construction not of remedies and what one has to ask is whether, as a matter of construction of the contract, compliance with the time stipulation is so essential to the contract that any failure to comply with it entitles the other party, without more, to treat the contract as repudiated. Of course, that does not mean either that the contract is to be treated for all purposes as if the time had never been mentioned or that, when it comes to exerting any remedies for breach of contract, the ordinary rules of specific performance are suspended or abrogated. Thus, albeit the contract is not to be construed as if time were essential, damages may still be obtained for failure to comply with the fixed date for completion if damage can be shown: see *Raineri v Miles* [1981] AC 1050.

Equally where, as a matter of construction, time is not of the essence, it does not follow that the party in default may not, by extensive delay or other conduct, disentitle himself from having it specifically performed: see, e.g., *Cornwall v Henson* [1900] 2 Ch 298 and *MEPC Ltd v Christian-Edwards* [1978] Ch 281.

But the question of how the contract should be construed and the question of whether a party in default may have deprived himself of a right to rely on the contract must now, in my judgment, be treated as logically distinct and separate questions, whatever may be the historical origin of the rule of construction.

Mr. Rich's submission treats the service of a renewal notice after the time stipulated as a submission to the court of the issue whether or not the contract should be performed. But the landlord, in serving notice, is not invoking the aid of the court to perform the contract. He is exercising the right which the contract, as properly construed, confers upon him. If it is to be construed in the sense that time is of the essence, he has no right to serve the notice. If it is not, then the right subsists, unless the tenant can show either that the contract, or that part of the contract, has been abrogated or that the landlord has precluded himself from exercising it. He may do that by showing that the contract has been repudiated—for instance, where he has served a notice calling upon the landlord to exercise his right within a reasonable time or not at all and such notice is ignored—or that some event has happened which estops the landlord from relying on his right. But I know of no ground for saying that mere delay, however lengthy, destroys the contractual right. It may put the other party in a position where, by taking the proper steps, he may become entitled to treat himself as discharged from his obligation; but that does not occur automatically and from the mere passage of time. I know of no authority for the proposition that the effect of construing a time stipulation as not being of the essence is to substitute a fresh implied term that the contract shall be performed within a reasonable time and even if such a term is to be substituted the passage of a reasonable time would not automatically abrogate the contract. It is, I think, important to distinguish between that which entitles a party to treat the contract as at an end and that which entitles the party not in default to enforce it. No one contests that, once the stipulated date is passed, proceedings may be instituted to enforce the agreement (see, e.g. *Woods* v *Mackenzie Hill Ltd* [1975] 1 WLR 613), but that is quite a different question. . . .

In my judgment, therefore, the deputy judge was right in the conclusion at which he arrived, although I would in fact go further and suggest that, despite what Lord Salmon said in *United Scientific Holdings Ltd* v *Burnley Borough Council* [1978] AC 904, even delay plus hardship to the tenants would not disentitle the landlord to exercise the right which he has on the true construction of the contract unless the combination amounted to an estoppel. In my judgment, the contractual right continues to exist unless and until it is abrogated by mutual agreement or the contract is discharged by breach or, to adopt the example of Lord Diplock in the *United Scientific* case, by the obligor being substantially deprived of the whole benefit that it was intended that he should have (which I take to be a reference, in effect, to frustration or failure of consideration and which I cannot envisage as arising in this sort of case). Apart from these circumstances, the only way in which I can envisage the landlord as being precluded from relying upon the clause is by an estoppel . . .

Finally, I should add that I am not, for my part, persuaded that in fact the instant case is one where 'unreasonable' delay has occurred. The expression 'unreasonable delay' does, I think, require some definition. It must, I think, mean something more than 'prolonged delay' and it may, I suppose, be used to express the notion either of delay for which no acceptable reason can be advanced or delay which no reasonable man would incur acting in his own interest. But if this is its meaning then the absence of reason has no necessary relation to duration. If on the other hand, as I suspect, the phrase is used to describe such delay as it would not in the circumstances be reasonable to expect the other party to put up with, then it seems to me that it contains within it, by necessary implication, the notion of hardship or prejudice, for how otherwise is the other party harmed by it?

In the instant case certainly no prejudice is shown nor does it seem to me that there has been any substantial delay which is not perfectly rationally accounted for. The landlord's solicitors tried to rectify their omission within a month of the contract date and they can hardly be blamed, in the state of the law as it then stood, for not pursuing the matter further prior to 1978. If, thereafter, they had appreciated that their original letter did not, in fact, comply with the lease not only as to date but in point of form also, they could, no doubt, have issued a fresh notice before issuing the first originating summons, so that all matters could be dealt with in one set of proceedings. That they did not do so may be unfortunate, but it has been extremely beneficial to the tenants who got a further uncovenanted reprieve; but I cannot, speaking for myself, regard their failure to do so as 'unreasonable.'. . .

18.2   Repairs

18.2.1   LIABILITY TO REPAIR – GENERAL

BARRETT v *LOUNOVA (1982) LTD* [1990] 1 QB 348, Court of Appeal

FACTS: In a lease of a dwelling house the tenant had covenanted to carry out all the internal repairs on the premises. The question was, 'who should be responsible for carrying out the external repairs?'
HELD: In order to 'give business efficacy to the agreement', there was an implied obligation on the landlord to do the external repairs.

KERR LJ: . . . I turn to the issue whether or not there is to be implied a term to the effect that the landlord was bound to keep the outside in reasonable repair, as the recorder decided.
In that regard it is common ground that he directed himself correctly when he said:

Clearly on the authorities the law does not permit the court to imply terms merely on the basis that implication would seem to be reasonable or fair. In essence, what is required before such implication is made is either a situation where the parties to the agreement, if asked about the suggested implied term would have said words such as 'Oh yes, of course we both agree. Is there any need to mention it?;' or where it is not merely desirable but necessary to imply such a term to give business efficacy or in other words necessary to make the contract workable, which amounts to the same thing.

Those two ways of putting the test as to whether or not a term should be implied, sometimes referred to as 'the officious bystander test' and the 'business efficacy test,' are of course correct.
But whether or not, on applying those tests, the implication falls to be made is not easy, and the authorities are of no direct assistance . . . on the basis that an obligation to keep the outside in a proper state of repair must be imposed on someone, three answers are possible.
First, that the tenant is obliged to keep the outside in repair as well as the inside, at any rate to such extent as may be necessary to enable him to perform his covenant. I would reject that as being unbusinesslike and unrealistic. In the case of a tenancy of this nature, which was to become a monthly tenancy after one year, the rent being paid weekly, it is clearly unrealistic to conclude that this could have been the common intention. In that context it is to be noted that in *Warren* v *Keen* [1954] 1 QB 15, this court held that a weekly tenant was under no implied obligation to do any repairs to the structure of the premises due to wear and tear or lapse of time or otherwise, and that it was doubtful whether he was even obliged to ensure that the premises remained wind and watertight. Any construction which casts upon the tenant the obligation to keep the outside in proper repair must in my view be rejected for these reasons; and also because there is an express tenant's covenant relating to the inside, so that it would be wrong, as a matter of elementary construction, to imply a covenant relating to the outside as well.
The second solution would be the implication of a joint obligation on both parties to keep the outside in good repair. I reject that as being obviously unworkable and I do not think that Mr. Pryor really suggested the contrary.
That leaves one with the third solution, an implied obligation on the landlord. In my view this is the only solution which makes business sense. The recorder reached the same conclusion by following much the same route, and I agree with him.
Accordingly I would dismiss this appeal.

18.2.2   THE LANDLORD AND TENANT ACT 1985

LANDLORD AND TENANT ACT 1985

8.   Implied terms as to fitness for human habitation
   (1)   In a contract to which this section applies for the letting of a house for human habitation there is implied, notwithstanding any stipulation to the contrary—

(a)   a condition that the house is fit for human habitation at the commencement of the tenancy, and

(b)   an undertaking that the house will be kept by the landlord fit for human habitation during the tenancy.

(2)   The landlord or person authorised by him in writing, may at reasonable times of the day, on giving 24 hours' notice in writing to the tenant or occupier, enter premises to which this section applies for the purpose of viewing their state and condition.

(3)   This section applies to a contract if—

(a)   the rent does not exceed the figure applicable in accordance with subsection (4), and

(b)   the letting is not on such terms as to the tenant's responsibility as are mentioned in subsection (5).

(4)   . . .

(5)   This section does not apply where a house is let for a term of three years or more (the lease not being determinable at the option of either party before the expiration of three years) upon terms that the tenant puts the premises into a condition reasonably fit for human habitation.

(6)   In this section 'house' includes—

(a)   a part of a house, and

(b)   any yard, garden, outhouses and appurtenances belonging to the house or usually enjoyed with it.

10.   Fitness for human habitation

In determining for the purposes of this Act whether a house is unfit for human habitation, regard shall be had to its condition in respect of the following matters—

repair,
stability,
freedom from damp,
internal arrangement,
natural lighting,
ventilation,
drainage and sanitary conveniences,
facilities for preparation and cooking of food and for the disposal of waste water;

and the house shall be regarded as unfit for human habitation if, and only if, it is so far defective in one or more of those matters that it is not reasonably suitable for occupation in that condition.

11.   Repairing obligations in short leases

(1)   In a lease to which this section applies (as to which, see sections 13 and 14) there is implied a covenant by the lessor—

(a)   to keep in repair the structure and exterior of the dwelling-house (including drains, gutters and external pipes),

(b)   to keep in repair and proper working order the installations in the dwelling-house for the supply of water, gas and electricity and for sanitation (including basins, sinks, baths and sanitary conveniences, but not other fixtures, fittings and appliances for making use of the supply of water, gas or electricity), and

(c)   to keep in repair and proper working order the installations in the dwelling-house for space heating and heating water.

(1A)   If a lease to which this section applies is a lease of a dwelling-house which forms part only of a building, then, subject to subsection (1B), the covenant implied by subsection (1) shall have effect as if—

(a)   the reference in paragraph (a) of that subsection to the dwelling-house included a reference to any part of the building in which the lessor has an estate or interest; and

(b)   any reference in paragraphs (b) and (c) of that subsection to an installation in the dwelling-house included a reference to an installation which, directly or indirectly, serves the dwelling-house and which either—

(i)   forms part of any part of a building in which the lessor has an estate or interest; or

(ii)   is owned by the lessor or under his control.

(1B)   Nothing in subsection (1A) shall be construed as requiring the lessor to carry out any works or repairs unless the disrepair (or failure to maintain in working order) is such as to affect the lessee's enjoyment of the dwelling-house or of any common parts, as defined in section 60(1) of the Landlord and Tenant Act 1987, which the lessee, as such, is entitled to use.

(2)   The covenant implied by subsection (1) ('the lessor's repairing covenant') shall not be construed as requiring the lessor—

(a)   to carry out works or repairs for which the lessee is liable by virtue of his duty to use the premises in a tenant-like manner, or would be so liable but for an express covenant on his part,

(b)   to rebuild or reinstate the premises in the case of destruction or damage by fire, or by tempest, flood or other inevitable accident, or

(c)   to keep in repair or maintain anything which the lessee is entitled to remove from the dwelling-house.

(3)   In determining the standard of repair required by the lessor's repairing covenant, regard shall be had to the age, character and prospective life of the dwelling-house and the locality in which it is situated.

(3A)   In any case where—

(a)   the lessor's repairing covenant has effect as mentioned in subsection (1A), and

(b)   in order to comply with the covenant the lessor needs to carry out works or repairs otherwise than in, or to an installation in, the dwelling-house, and

(c)   the lessor does not have a sufficient right in the part of the building or the installation concerned to enable him to carry out the required works or repairs,

then, in any proceedings relating to a failure to comply with the lessor's repairing covenant, so far as it requires the lessor to carry out the works or repairs in question, it shall be a defence for the lessor to prove that he used all reasonable endeavours to obtain, but was unable to obtain, such rights as would be adequate to enable him to carry out the works or repairs.

(4)   A covenant by the lessee for the repair of the premises is of no effect so far as it relates to the matters mentioned in subsection (1)(a) to (c), except so far as it imposes on the lessee any of the requirements mentioned in subsection (2)(a) or (c).

(5)   The reference in subsection (4) to a covenant by the lessee for the repair of the premises includes a covenant—

(a)   to put in repair or deliver up in repair,

(b)   to paint, point or render,

(c)   to pay money in lieu of repairs by the lessee, or

(d)   to pay money on account of repairs by the lessor.

(6)   In a lease in which the lessor's repairing covenant is implied there is also implied a covenant by the lessee that the lessor, or any person authorised by him in writing, may at reasonable times of the day and on giving 24 hours' notice in writing to the occupier, enter the premises comprised in the lease for the purpose of viewing their condition and state of repair.

12.   Restriction on contracting out of s. 11

(1)   A covenant or agreement, whether contained in a lease to which section 11 applies or in an agreement collateral to such a lease, is void in so far as it purports—

(a)   to exclude or limit the obligations of the lessor or the immunities of the lessee under that section, or

(b)   to authorise any forfeiture or impose on the lessee any penalty, disability or obligation in the event of his enforcing or relying upon those obligations or immunities, unless the inclusion of the provision was authorised by the county court.

(2)   The county court may, by order made with the consent of the parties, authorise the inclusion in a lease, or in an agreement collateral to a lease, of provisions excluding or modifying in relation to the lease, the provisions of section 11 with respect to the repairing obligations of the parties if it appears to the court that it is reasonable to do so, having regard to all the circumstances of the case, including the other terms and conditions of the lease.

13.   Leases to which s. 11 applies: general rule

(1)   Section 11 (repairing obligations) applies to a lease of a dwelling-house granted on or after 24th October 1961 for a term of less than seven years.

(2)   In determining whether a lease is one to which section 11 applies—

(a)   any part of the term which falls before the grant shall be left out of account and the lease shall be treated as a lease for a term commencing with the grant,

(b)   a lease which is determinable at the option of the lessor before the expiration of seven years from the commencement of the term shall be treated as a lease for a term of less than seven years, and

(c)   a lease (other than a lease to which paragraph (b) applies) shall not be treated as a lease for a term of less than seven years if it confers on the lessee an option for renewal for a term which, together with the original term, amounts to seven years or more.

(3)   This section has effect subject to—

section 14 (leases to which section 11 applies: exceptions), and

section 32(2) (provisions not applying to tenancies within Part II of the Landlord and Tenant Act 1954).

14.   Leases to which s. 11 applies: exceptions

(1)   Section 11 (repairing obligations) does not apply to a new lease granted to an existing tenant, or to a former tenant still in possession, if the previous lease was not a lease to which section 11 applied (and, in the case of a lease granted before 24th October 1961, would not have been if it had been granted on or after that date).

(2)   In subsection (1)—

'existing tenant' means a person who is when, or immediately before, the new lease is granted, the lessee under another lease of the dwelling-house;

'former tenant still in possession' means a person who—

(a)   was the lessee under another lease of the dwelling-house which terminated at some time before the new lease was granted, and

(b)   between the termination of that other lease and the grant of the new lease was continuously in possession of the dwelling-house or of the rents and profits of the dwelling-house; and

'the previous lease' means the other lease referred to in the above definitions.

(3)   Section 11 does not apply to a lease of a dwelling-house which is a tenancy of an agricultural holding within the meaning of the Agricultural Holdings Act 1986.

(4)   Section 11 does not apply to a lease granted on or after 3rd October 1980 to—

a local authority,

a new town corporation,

an urban development corporation,

the Development Board for Rural Wales,

a registered housing association,

a co-operative housing association, or

an educational institution or other body specified, or of a class specified, by regulations under section 8 of the Rent Act 1977 (bodies making student lettings)

a housing action trust established under Part III of the Housing Act 1988.

(5)   Section 11 does not apply to a lease granted on or after 3rd October 1980 to—

(a)   Her Majesty in right of the Crown (unless the lease is under the management of the Crown Estate Commissioners), or

(b)   a government department or a person holding in trust for Her Majesty for the purposes of a government department.

QUICK v TAFF ELY BOROUGH COUNCIL [1986] 1 QB 809, Court of Appeal

FACTS: The plaintiff was tenant of a council house. Condensation, created by the type of windows in the house, caused woodwork, furniture and clothes to rot. The tenant brought proceedings for an order of specific performance of the landlord's obligation to repair the 'structure and exterior' of the premises.

HELD: The council was not liable. Evidence of lack of amenity was not evidence of a need for repair.

DILLON LJ: . . . In my judgment, the key factor in the present case is that disrepair is related to the physical condition of whatever has to be repaired, and not to questions of lack of amenity or inefficiency. I find helpful the observation of Atkin LJ in *Anstruther-Gough-*

Calthorpe v *McOscar* [1924] 1 KB 716, 734 that repair 'connotes the idea of making good damage so as to leave the subject so far as possible as though it had not been damaged.' Where decorative repair is in question one must look for damage to the decorations but where, as here, the obligation is merely to keep the structure and exterior of the house in repair, the covenant will only come into operation where there has been damage to the structure and exterior which requires to be made good.

If there is such damage caused by an unsuspected inherent defect, then it may be necessary to cure the defect, and thus to some extent improve without wholly renewing the property as the only practicable way of making good the damage to the subject matter of the repairing covenant. That, as I read the case, was the basis of the decision in *Ravenseft* [1980] QB 12. There there was an inherent defect when the building, a relatively new one, was built in that no expansion joints had been included because it had not been realised that the different coefficients of expansion of the stone of the cladding and the concrete of the structure made it necessary to include such joints. There was, however, also physical damage to the subject matter of the covenant in that, because of the differing coefficients of expansion, the stones of the cladding had become bowed, detached from the structure, loose and in danger of falling. Forbes J in a very valuable judgment rejected the argument that no liability arose under a repairing covenant if it could be shown that the disrepair was due to an inherent defect in the building. He allowed in the damages under the repairing covenant the cost of putting in expansion joints, and in that respect improving the building, because, as he put it, at p. 22, on the evidence 'In no realistic sense . . . could it be said that there was any other possible way of reinstating this cladding than by providing the expansion joints which were, in fact, provided.'. . .

In the present case the liability of the council was to keep the structure and exterior of the house in repair—not the decorations. Though there is ample evidence of damage to the decorations and to bedding, clothing and other fabrics, evidence of damage to the subject matter of the covenant, the structure and exterior of the house, is far to seek. Though the condensation comes about from the effect of the warm atmosphere in the rooms on the cold surfaces of the walls and windows, there is no evidence at all of physical damage to the walls—as opposed to the decorations—or the windows. . . .

LAWTON LJ: It is with regret that I have decided that this appeal on the points taken in this court by the defendant council must be allowed. The case will have to be remitted to the county court for Judge Francis to reassess the damages, if they cannot be agreed, as I hope they will be.

When I read the papers in this case I was surprised to find that the plaintiff had not based his claim on an allegation that at all material times the house let to him by the council had not been fit for human habitation. The uncontradicted evidence, accepted by the trial judge, showed that furniture, furnishings and clothes had rotted because of damp and the sitting room could not be used because of the smell of damp.

18.2.3 THE CRUCIAL PRINCIPLE IN *O'BRIEN* v *ROBINSON*

O'BRIEN AND ANOTHER v *ROBINSON* [1973] AC 912, House of Lords

FACTS: A tenant and his wife were injured when the ceiling of their flat suddenly and unexpectedly caved in upon them. Some years ago the tenants of the flat above had caused violent vibrations of the ceiling by prolonged 'dancing' and 'banging on the floors'. The tenant sued the landlord for damages for personal injuries.
HELD: The landlord's liability to repair did not arise until latent defects had become apparent and their existence made known to him. On that basis the landlord in the present case was not liable.

LORD MORRIS OF BORTH-Y-GEST: . . . In the case of *Morgan* v *Liverpool Corporation* [1927] 2 KB 131 one basis of claim was that there had been a failure to perform the statutory undertaking that the house would be 'kept in all respects reasonably fit for human habitation.' As I have shown, there was at that date a statutory right in a landlord to enter for the purposes of inspection. The accident which gave rise to the claim was that when the upper portion of a window was being opened one of the cords of the window sash broke with the result that the top part of the window slipped down and caught and injured the plaintiff's hand. In the argument on behalf of the plaintiff in the Court of Appeal it was admitted that the defect was a latent one (of which the plaintiff did not know and about which accordingly he could not give any notice) but it was contended that there was a statutory obligation on the landlord which was different from that contained in an ordinary covenant and that in the Act (Housing Act 1925), there were no words requiring that any notice should be given to the landlord. Furthermore, reliance was placed on the statutory right of the landlord to enter and inspect. Apart from any such statutory right the facts of the case showed that there was a notice posted up in the house containing certain conditions which included a reservation by the landlord of the right of entering the house at any time without previous notice in order to view the state of repair. The Court of Appeal held that the landlord was not liable and that any liability was conditional upon his having been given notice of any defects even though they were latent ones and that this result was not affected by the fact that the landlord had a right to enter in order to inspect. There were divisions of opinion on certain points which arose: in particular on the point whether by reason of the breaking of the sash cord the particular dwelling (which was most limited in size) was rendered unfit for human habitation. But all three Lords Justices were of the opinion that the claim failed because the landlord did not have notice and because in such a case as that under consideration notice was required before the liability of the landlord to repair existed. Lord Hanworth MR said (at p. 141) that it had 'long been established law that where there is a covenant on the part of a landlord to keep the premises in repair, the tenant must give notice to the landlord of what is out of repair . . .' He held that notice was required whether or not the landlord had means of access: he said that the fact that the origin of a covenant was statutory did not give the covenant any higher authority than one inserted in a contract by the parties. Atkin LJ said that in ordinary circumstances the obligation of a landlord to do repairs does not come into existence until he has had notice of the defect which his contract to repair requires him to make good. He said, at p. 151:

> I think the power of access that is given, extensive though it may be, does not take the case away from the principle from which the courts have inferred the condition that the liability is not to arise except on notice. The position is quite a satisfactory one, because as soon as the tenant is aware of the defect he must then give notice, and if the landlord does not repair it, the landlord will be liable. If in fact the tenant is not able to ascertain the defect, there seems to be no reason why the landlord should be exposed to what remains still the same injustice of being required to repair a defect of which he does not know, which seems to me to be the real reason for the rule. This was a case in which notice was not given to the landlord. As I have said, it appears to me that, as soon as the defect became so known by the fall of the sash, the tenant was able to give notice to the landlord and did give notice. In my view the landlord then became under a liability to repair in the circumstances of this case, because if he did not, the house would be in a state not in all respects fit for human habitation; but as no notice was given, I think the landlord was not liable. . . .

LORD DIPLOCK: . . . this appeal must fail unless the tenant can show that before the ceiling fell the landlord had information about the existence of a defect in the ceiling such as would put him on inquiry as to whether works of repair to it were needed. . . .

HEATH v DROWN [1973] AC 498, House of Lords

FACTS: It became necessary to execute extensive repairs to business premises occupied by a tenant. Accordingly, the landlord sought re-possession of the premises in order to carry out the repairs.
HELD: Temporary re-possession by the landlord was consistent with the continuing existence of the tenant's lease, but extensive repairs, necessitating long-term re-possession was not. Accordingly, although the tenant might ordinarily be entitled to a statutory renewal of the lease at the end of the term, such renewal would not be granted in the present case. The landlord was granted absolute possession.

LORD REID: In my view, the crucial findings are that the work would take at least four months, that during that time it would not be reasonably possible for the appellant to carry on her business—an employment agency—in the premises, that whatever terms might be put in the new lease there were likely to be disputes which would frustrate the respondent's operations and that therefore he needs exclusive possession. The clear meaning is, I think, that the only reasonable course is that the tenant shall have no right to enter the premises while the work is in progress: it is not enough that the respondent shall have access, he must also be enabled to exclude the appellant. . . .

I do not profess to be an expert in the English law of real property and this matter was not fully argued. But I understand that the granting of a new lease would necessarily imply that the tenant is given legal possession from its commencement and throughout its duration. But it is found as a fact that the landlord needs exclusive physical possession for a period of at least four months. So far as I know it would be a novelty to provide in a lease that during so long a period the tenant, although liable for the full rent, shall have no right even to enter the demised premises. I do not see in what sense the tenant could during that period be said to have legal possession. . . .

I would therefore dismiss this appeal.

18.2.4 MEANING OF EXPRESS COVENANTS TO REPAIR

ANSTRUTHER-GOUGH-CALTHORPE v *McOSCAR AND ANOTHER*
[1924] 1 KB 716, Court of Appeal

FACTS: A 95 year lease was granted in 1825 of three houses. They were built in 1825, in a very pleasant position on the then edge of the built-up area of London. By the time the lease expired in 1920 the area (in the vicinity of King's Cross station) had become very 'run down'. The landlord brought an action against the tenant for breaking the covenant to repair.
HELD: The tenant should have maintained the property to the 1825 standard.

SCRUTTON LJ: . . . The question in dispute seems to be whether, as the purposes for which such a subject matter is ordinarily used may vary from time to time, the standard of repair is to vary from time to time, or remains as it was when the subject matter was demised. For instance, where a fashionable mansion let for a long term of years has fallen to the position of a tenement house for the poorer classes, is the standard of repair to become less onerous than when the house is let? To take an illustration of Bankes LJ, if the sub-tenants of a tenement house do not want a front door, is the tenant to be excused from keeping a properly repaired front door on the premises?

In my view this question has been decided, as far as this Court is concerned, by the decision in *Morgan* v *Hardy* (1886) 17 QBD 770. In that case the referee had to decide between the claim that the premises must be properly repaired and the contention that, as the premises and the neighbourhood had deteriorated, and in consequence of such deterioration a great portion of the repairs required 'were not suited to the said premises and were unnecessary for their use and enjoyment', they need not be considered in awarding damages. This Court, affirming Denman J, said very summarily that it was a wholly untenable proposition to say that the depreciation of the neighbourhood ought to lower the amount of damages for breach of a covenant to repair. This can only mean that the fact that the class of persons who would use the house at the end of the term had deteriorated, so that their requirements in the way of repairs were less, was immaterial in ascertaining the repairs that the tenant was bound to execute. *Morgan* v *Hardy* was the case of a fifty years' lease.

In *Proudfoot* v *Hart* (1890) 25 QBD 42 the lease was for three years only, and the covenant was to keep in good tenantable repair. There was no suggestion of any change in character of the house or its probable tenants between the beginning and the end of the term. Lopes LJ framed a definition which Lord Esher adopted as follows: 'Such repair, as having regard to the age, character, and locality of the house, would make it reasonably fit for the occupation of a reasonably minded tenant of the class who would be likely to take it.' I do not think there was any intention of suggesting that a deterioration in the class of tenants would lower the standard of repairs; the point was not before the Court, and had been decided the other way by the Court four years previously. Therefore in my view we are bound to look to the character of the house and its ordinary uses at the time of the demise. It must then be put in repair and kept in repair. An improvement of its tenants or its neighbourhood will not increase the standard of repair, nor will their deterioration lower that standard. . . .

18.2.5   THE REPAIR/RECONSTRUCTION DISTINCTION

RAVENSEFT PROPERTIES LTD v DAVSTONE (HOLDINGS) LTD
[1979] 2 WLR 897, Queen's Bench Division

FACTS: Stone-cladding on a concrete block of flats began to bow away from the wall. In order to address the risk of stones falling, the landlord made full repairs. The tenant, a property development company, had covenanted to be liable for repairs and so the landlord company brought the present action to recover the cost of the works it had carried out.

HELD: It was a question of degree whether the works carried out by the landlord were properly to be described as 'repairs' or 'improvements'. On these facts the works were to be regarded as repairs, because at the end of the lease the tenant would return to the landlord substantially the same building that the landlord had originally leased out. Accordingly, the tenant would be liable to re-imburse the landlord's costs of repair.

FORBES J: . . . it is always a question of degree whether that which the tenant is being asked to do can properly be described as repair, or whether on the contrary it would involve giving back to the landlord a wholly different thing from that which he demised.

In deciding this question, the proportion which the cost of the disputed work bears to the value or cost of the whole premises, may sometimes be helpful as a guide. In this case the figures have not been finally worked out in complete detail. I have, however, the evidence of Mr. Clark, the contracts manager for the Stone Firms Ltd, the contractors who actually carried out the work. He was not himself responsible for any of the work as he joined that company after the work was completed. He is, however, familiar with that company's methods of charging and so on, and he has studied the drawings and the analysed quotations produced by the company. From these he has been able to give me, not a detailed and accurate costing, but a reliable, broad, estimate of the cost of that part of the remedial work relating solely to the insertion of expansion joints. It is, as he said, an indication of the order of magnitude of the cost. Although cross-examined by Mr. Colyer, no rebutting evidence was called and I accept Mr. Clark's estimate that the cost would have been in the region of £5,000. The total cost of the remedial works was around £55,000, the balance of £50,000 being for re-fixing the stones and other ancillary works which was not, as I find, necessary to cure any defect of design, but to remedy what was originally defective workmanship. For comparison, the cost of building a structure of this kind in 1973 would have been in the region of £3 million, or rather more. I find myself wholly unable to accept that the cost of inserting these joints could possibly be regarded as a substantial part of the cost of the repairs, much less a substantial part of the value or cost of the building. Mr. Colyer urges me not to consider cost and that may, perhaps, in some circumstances, be right. He argues that the result of carrying out this improvement is to give back to the landlord a safe building instead of a dangerous one and this means the premises now are of a wholly different character. Further, he argues that because they are of a wholly different character, the work on expansion joints, the work necessary to cure the inherent defect, is an improvement of a character which transforms the nature of the premises demised, and, therefore, cannot fall within the ambit of the covenant to repair. I cannot accept this. The expansion joints form but a trivial part of this whole building and looking at it as a question of degree, I do not consider that they amount to such a change in the character of the building as to take them out of the ambit of the covenant to repair.

I pass to Mr. Colyer's second point, namely, that the tenant is not liable under the repair covenant for that part of any work of repair necessary to remedy an inherent defect. Again it seems to me that this must be a question of degree. . . .

LURCOTT v *WAKELY & WHEELER* [1911] 1 KB 905, Court of Appeal

FACTS: The tenant had covenanted to keep the premises in thorough repair and good condition. Shortly before the end of the term the local council condemned one wall of the house as dangerous and served notice on the landlord to demolish and replace it. Having done so, the landlord sought to recover the costs from the tenant.

HELD: The tenant was liable under the covenant to repair to reimburse the landlord.

COZENS-HARDY MR: . . . It was [in *Lister* v *Lane* [1893]] held by the Court of Appeal, and I see no reason to quarrel with their decision, that the change of circumstances which had arisen could not have been in the contemplation of the parties and that it would not be reasonable to construe the covenant to repair as applicable to that change of circumstances. But then when I come to what I should have thought was everyday experience in cases of this kind, when I come to consider what is to happen when by reason of the elements acting on an old building, say, a chimney stack is blown down, is it possible for the tenant to say he is not liable to put that up because the collapse was due merely to age and the elements? I am astonished to hear that such a contention can be raised. So, if a tenant under a repairing lease finds that a floor has become so rotten that it cannot be patched up, that it is in such a condition that it cannot bear the weight of human beings or of furniture upon it, can it be said that the tenant is exempt from the liability of replacing that floor, and repairing it in the only way in which it can be repaired in order to make the house habitable, merely because the state of the floor is due to time and the elements? I am entirely unable to follow that argument. *Proudfoot* v *Hart* (1890) 25 QBD 42 seems to lay down a perfectly sound and intelligible proposition on this point, namely, that in such a case it is the duty of the tenant, if he cannot patch up the floor so as to make it a floor, to replace that which is no longer a floor by something which is a floor. . .

18.2.6   REMEDIES FOR BREACH OF LANDLORD'S EXPRESS COVENANTS TO REPAIR

18.2.6.1   No rent-strikes, *but* . . .

LEE-PARKER AND ANOTHER v *IZZET AND OTHERS* [1971] 1 WLR 1688, Chancery Division

FACTS: Tenants, having executed certain repairs on their own account, sought to withhold rent to cover the cost they had incurred. The landlord should have carried out the repairs himself.

HELD: The tenants could withhold rent to cover the repairs. This was not by way of lien or set-off, but was an ancient common law right. The tenants would not have been able to withhold rent had they not executed the repairs themselves at their own cost.

GOFF J: . . . the third and fourth defendants further claim a lien for the cost of the repairs or alternatively for the value of any permanent improvement effected thereby, and they also claim a set off against rent in their capacity as tenants.

   First, they say that in so far as the first defendant was, as landlord, liable to do the repairs by the express or implied terms of the tenancy agreement, including the covenants imported by section 32(1) of the Housing Act 1961, they, having done them themselves, are entitled to treat the expenditure as a payment of rent, for which reliance is placed on *Taylor* v *Beal* (1591) Cro Eliz 222. That is dicta only and the actual decision must have been the other way, because one of the majority in opinion thought the point was not open on the pleadings. However, *Woodfall's Landlord and Tenant* says the case—that is, the *dicta*—would still seem to be the law: see 27th edn. (1968), vol. 1, p. 655 para. 1490. The case is dealt with in *Foa's General Law of Landlord & Tenant*, 8th edn. (1957), on the question of distress only, at p. 559, citing also *Davies* v *Stacey* (1840) 12 Ad & El 506, where the point was left open. *Foa* states, at p. 559:

   Where the lessor covenants to repair and neglects to do so, and the repairs are thereupon executed by the lessee, a payment made by the lessee for the cost of such repairs is not (it is submitted) equivalent to payment of rent so as to reduce the amount for which the landlord may distrain.

. . . I do not think this is bound up with technical rules of set off. It is an ancient common law right. I therefore declare that so far as the repairs are within the express or implied covenants of the landlord, the third and fourth defendants are entitled to recoup themselves out of future rents and defend any action for payment thereof. It does not follow however that the full amount expended by the third and fourth defendants on such repairs can properly be treated as payment of rent. It is a question of fact in every case whether and to what extent the expenditure was proper. . . .

18.2.6.2 Specific performance for breach of a repairing obligation

JEUNE v QUEENS CROSS PROPERTIES LTD [1973] 3 All ER 97, Chancery Division

FACTS: The plaintiff tenants sought an order that the defendant landlord should reinstate a York Stone balcony which had partially collapsed at the front of their house in Westbourne Terrace, London, W2.
HELD: The Court made an order for specific performance of the landlord's repairing covenant because the landlord was plainly in breach of the covenant and there was no doubt as to what precisely was required to be done to remedy the breach.

PENNYCUICK V-C: . . . the principle that a landlord cannot obtain against his tenant an order for specific performance of a covenant to repair . . . does not . . . apply to a landlord's covenant to repair, although it is said there may be some other explanation for the words, 'The difficulty upon this doctrine of a Court of Equity is, that there is no mutuality in it.'

Counsel for the plaintiff has looked through various textbooks on the law of landlord and tenant and assures me that, although *Hill* v *Barclay* (1810) 16 Ves 402 is repeatedly cited, there is no other authority in point. It is worthwhile to refer to two passages in Halsbury's Laws of England. In the landlord and tenant volume it is stated:

Unless the lease contains a proviso empowering the landlord to re-enter for forfeiture on breach of the covenant to repair, the landlord's remedy is an action for damages; for specific performance of such a covenant will not ordinarily be granted.

Reference is made there to *Hill* v *Barclay*. In the specific performance volume there is this passage: 'In particular, the court does not, as a rule, order the specific performance of a contract to build or repair.' It then goes on to refer to the circumstances in which specific performance of a contract to build will be granted.

There is nothing at all there inconsistent with a power in the court to make an order on a landlord to do specific work under a covenant to repair. I cannot myself see any reason in principle why, in an appropriate case, an order should not be made against a landlord to do some specific work pursuant to his covenant to repair. Obviously, it is a jurisdiction which should be carefully exercised. But in a case such as the present where there has been a plain breach of a covenant to repair and there is no doubt at all what is required to be done to remedy the breach, I cannot see why an order for specific performance should not be made. . . .

18.2.6.3 Appointing a receiver

SUPREME COURT ACT 1981

37. Powers of High Court with respect to injunctions and receivers
    (1) The High Court may by order (whether interlocutory or final) grant an injunction or appoint a receiver in all cases in which it appears to the court to be just and convenient to do so.
    (2) Any such order may be made either unconditionally or on such terms and conditions as the court thinks just.
    (3) The power of the High Court under subsection (1) to grant an interlocutory injunction restraining a party to any proceedings from removing from the jurisdiction of

the High Court, or otherwise dealing with, assets located within that jurisdiction shall be exercisable in cases where that party is, as well as in cases where he is not, domiciled resident or present within that jurisdiction.

(4)   The power of the High Court to appoint a receiver by way of equitable execution shall operate in relation to all legal estates and interests in land; and that power—

(a)   may be exercised in relation to an estate or interest in land whether or not a charge has been imposed on that land under section 1 of the Charging Orders Act 1979 for the purpose of enforcing the judgment, order or award in question; and

(b)   shall be in addition to, and not in derogation of, any power of any court to appoint a receiver in proceedings for enforcing such a charge.

(5)   Where an order under the said section 1 imposing a charge for the purpose of enforcing a judgment, order or award has been, or has effect as if, registered under section 6 of the Land Charges Act 1972, subsection (4) of the said section 6 (effect of non-registration of writs and orders registrable under that section) shall not apply to an order appointing a receiver made either—

(a)   in proceedings for enforcing the charge; or

(b)   by way of equitable execution of the judgment, order or award or, as the case may be, of so much of it as requires payment of moneys secured by the charge.

HART v EMELKIRK [1983] 1 WLR 1289, Chancery Division

FACTS: The landlord of two blocks of flats in London had failed to comply with a covenant to repair. The tenants therefore brought an action to force the landlord to carry out the repairs. Pending the hearing of that action, the tenants applied for the appointment of a receiver to 'stand in the landlord's shoes' and collect their rents and meet the landlord's obligations. HELD: The court appointed a receiver as requested.

GOULDING J: . . . The action is brought to obtain a mandatory injunction against the defendant company to comply with the landlord's covenants and also for damages, and counsel for the defendant company tells me that third party proceedings are likely. But what I am asked to do today by the plaintiffs in each of the two actions dealing with adjoining blocks of flats, is to appoint a named surveyor to receive the rents and profits of each property and all other moneys payable under any lease of any part thereof and to manage the property in accordance with the rights and obligations of the reversioner until trial or further order. I am asked to say that the person so appointed may give a good receipt for certain sums of money which one of the plaintiffs in each case has received as representing (or apparently representing) what remains of a reserve fund, intended under the leases to be built up by tenants' contributions, and that the receiver may have to resort to those funds in course of management.

Now, I know of no precedent for such relief but I also know of no authority that forbids it under the provisions of the Judicature Acts now represented by Supreme Court Act 1981. Section 37(1) provides:

The High Court may by order (whether interlocutory or final) . . . appoint a receiver in all cases in which it appears to the court to be just and convenient to do so.

It clearly appears to me to be just to appoint a receiver in this case because it is done to support the enforcement by the court of covenants affecting property: compare *Riches* v *Owen* (1868) LR 3 Ch App 820. It is also convenient because, as I said, the properties are in a condition that demands urgent action. . .

EVANS v CLAYHOPE PROPERTIES LTD [1987] 1 WLR 225, Chancery Division

FACTS: Tenants of a block of flats brought an action against a landlord, seeking to enforce compliance with the landlord's covenant of repair. Pending the full hearing of the action, the court appointed a receiver to receive the rent and meet the landlord's continuing obligations in respect to the premises. Unfortunately the rents received by the receiver were not sufficient to meet his own remuneration, and the landlord's obligations. The receiver brought the present action to recover his expenses from the landlord.

HELD: The receiver's application was refused. The receiver was an officer appointed by the court and could only be indemnified out of assets under the control of the court. He could not be remunerated out of the landlord's general funds.

VINELOTT J: . . . The question raised in this application is whether, where a receiver has been appointed by the court in circumstances such as those which arose in *Hart v Emelkirk Ltd* [1983] 1 WLR 1289 and the receiver incurs expenditure or becomes entitled to remuneration in excess of moneys which he was appointed to receive the court has jurisdiction on an interlocutory application while the litigation is still proceeding to order that the balance of that expenditure or remuneration over the sums available to the receiver should be paid by one of the parties to the action.

. . . The use of the court's power to appoint a receiver to enforce a landlord's obligation to repair property, is a new development which poses many novel questions. They will have to be answered in time. I think that it is undesirable that I should attempt to do more than answer the precise question raised by the application now before me. Mr. Heath also submitted that the court could and should extend the receiver's powers so as to authorise him to charge Dover Mansions to raise money for the purpose of meeting his remuneration. That application is made at a late stage. On the basis of the evidence before me, the prospect that moneys could be raised by way of charge is simply chimerical. The income derived from Dover Mansions is very small and as matters stand there is no real prospect that it could be enhanced by letting the unlet flats, whether at rack rents or at a premium, while the block remains in the present state of disrepair. There is, therefore, effectively no security which could be offered to a lender. Whether the court could authorise a receiver appointed in these circumstances to create a charge and meet his own remuneration, so indirectly throwing the burden on the landlord, is again a question which I do not think I should attempt to answer.

The position is a most unfortunate one. It may serve as a reminder of the limitations inherent in the power of the court to appoint a receiver. A receiver should not take office unless he is satisfied that the assets of which he is appointed a receiver will be adequate to meet his remuneration, or that he has an enforceable indemnity by a party to the litigation capable of meeting his remuneration. Moreover, although the appointment of a receiver in order, indirectly, to ensure that property is kept in repair in accordance with covenants to repair entered into by a landlord, is a valuable extension of the power of the court to appoint a receiver for the preservation of property in cases where urgent repairs are necessary, where the landlord is plainly in breach of a covenant to repair and where the income of the property will enable the receiver to remedy the want of repair (in particular where, as in *Hart v Emelkirk Ltd* [1983] 1 WLR 1289, a service charge capable of being recovered by the landlord, and capable of being vested in the receiver can be imposed in advance of the carrying out of works of repair to meet their eventual cost) the appointment of a receiver in a case where the income including any service charge, or any other property or money which can be put under the control of the receiver, is patently inadequate to meet the cost of repair, is likely to prove ineffective and may even frustrate the carrying out of repairs that the landlord is willing to carry out. . . .

18.2.6.4 Appointing a receiver manager

The tenants of a privately owned block of residential flats have a right to apply to court for the appointment of a receiver-manager.

LANDLORD AND TENANT ACT 1987

24. Appointment of manager by the court

(1) The court may, on an application for an order under this section, by order (whether interlocutory or final) appoint a manager to carry out in relation to any premises to which this Part applies—

(a) such functions in connection with the management of the premises, or

(b) such functions of a receiver,

or both, as the court thinks fit.

(2) The court may only make an order under this section in the following circum-stances, namely—

(a)   where the court is satisfied—

(i)   that the landlord either is in breach of any obligation owed by him to the tenant under his tenancy and relating to the management of the premises in question or any part of them or (in the case of an obligation dependent on notice) would be in breach of any such obligation but for the fact that it has not been reasonably practicable for the tenant to give him the appropriate notice, and

(ii)   that the circumstances by virtue of which he is (or would be) in breach of any such obligation are likely to continue, and

(iii)   that it is just and convenient to make the order in all the circumstances of the case; or

(b)   where the court is satisfied that other circumstances exist which make it just and convenient for the order to be made.

. . .

(4)   An order under this section may make provision with respect to—

(a)   such matters relating to the exercise by the manager of his functions under the order, and

(b)   such incidental or ancillary matters,

as the court thinks fit; and, on any subsequent application made for the purpose by the manager, the court may give him directions with respect to any such matters.

(5)   Without prejudice to the generality of subsection (4), an order under this section may provide—

(a)   for rights and liabilities arising under contracts to which the manager is not a party to become rights and liabilities of the manager;

(b)   for the manager to be entitled to prosecute claims in respect of causes of action (whether contractual or tortious) accruing before or after the date of his appointment;

(c)   for remuneration to be paid to the manager by the landlord, or by the tenants of the premises in respect of which the order is made or by all or any of those persons;

(d)   for the manager's functions to be exercisable by him (subject to subsection (9)) either during a specified period or without limit of time.

(6)   Any such order may be granted subject to such conditions as the court thinks fit, and in particular its operation may be suspended on terms fixed by the court.

(7)   . . .

(8)   The Land Charges Act 1972 and the Land Registration Act 1925 shall apply in relation to an order made under this section as they apply in relation to an order appointing a receiver or sequestrator of land. . . .

18.2.6.5   Local authorities taking action against private landlords

Where a house, flat, or block of flats is in disrepair, the local district council can serve a notice on the landlord requiring specified repairs. If the landlord fails to comply, the council can enter the property, carry out the repairs, and charge them to the landlord. (See the Housing Acts 1957–88.)

18.2.6.6   Measure of damages against landlords

CALABAR PROPERTIES LTD v STITCHER [1984] 1 WLR 287, Court of Appeal

FACTS: Defects in the external parts of certain rented premises had resulted in the interior becoming damp. Consequently, the tenants withheld payment of ground rent and were sued by the landlords. The tenants counter-claimed for damages for breach of the landlord's covenant to keep external parts in good repair. After some time the dampness, which had resulted in ill health, forced the tenants to vacate the premises. The judge at first instance found for the tenants and awarded damages for the cost of repairing the flat and for disappointment, discomfort, loss of enjoyment and ill health. However, the judge refused to award damages for loss of use and wasted rent etc. during the period for which the house was uninhabitable. The defendant appealed against the award of damages.

HELD: The appeal was dismissed. The judge had been correct to limit the award of damages to the difference in value between the flat as it was and the flat as it would have been had the repair obligations been met. No damages could be awarded in respect of the defendant's cost of renting alternative accommodation, no counterclaim had been made for those costs, and it was now too late to claim them.

GRIFFITHS LJ: . . . The object of awarding damages against a landlord for breach of his covenant to repair is not to punish the landlord but, so far as money can, to restore the tenant to the position he would have been in had there been no breach. This object will not be achieved by applying one set of rules to all cases regardless of the particular circumstances of the case. The facts of each case must be looked at carefully to see what damage the tenant has suffered and how he may be fairly compensated by a monetary award.

In this case on the findings of the judge the plaintiff landlords, after notice of the defect, neglected their obligation to repair for such a length of time that the flat eventually became uninhabitable. It was also clear that unless ordered to do so by an order of the court, the plaintiffs had no intention of carrying out the repairs. In these circumstances the defendant had two options that were reasonably open to her: either of selling the flat and moving elsewhere, or alternatively of moving into temporary accommodation and bringing an action against the plaintiffs to force them to carry out the repairs, and then returning to the flat after the repairs were done. If the defendant had chosen the first option then the measure of damages would indeed have been the difference in the price she received for the flat in its damaged condition and that which it would have fetched in the open market if the plaintiffs had observed their repairing covenant. If however the defendant did not wish to sell the flat but to continue to live in it after the plaintiffs had carried out the necessary structural repairs it was wholly artificial to award her damages on the basis of loss in market value, because once the plaintiffs had carried out the repairs and any consequential redecoration of the interior was completed there would be no loss in market value. The defendant should be awarded the cost to which she was put in taking alternative accommodation, the cost of redecorating, and some award for all the unpleasantness of living in the flat as it deteriorated until it became uninhabitable. These three heads of damage will, so far as money can, compensate the defendant for the plaintiffs' breach.

18.2.7 DAMAGES AGAINST A TENANT IN BREACH OF REPAIRING OBLIGATIONS

LEASEHOLD PROPERTY (REPAIRS) ACT 1938

1.   Restriction on enforcement of repairing covenants in long leases of small houses
   (1)   Where a lessor serves on a lessee under subsection (1) of section one hundred and forty-six of the Law of Property Act 1925, a notice that relates to a breach of a covenant or agreement to keep or put in repair during the currency of the lease [all or any of the property comprised in the lease], and at the date of the service of the notice [three] years or more of the term of the lease remain unexpired, the lessee may within twenty-eight days from that date serve on the lessor a counter-notice to the effect that he claims the benefit of this Act.
   (2)   A right to damages for a breach of such a covenant as aforesaid shall not be enforceable by action commenced at any time at which [three] years or more of the term of the lease remain unexpired unless the lessor has served on the lessee not less than one month before the commencement of the action such a notice as is specified in subsection (1) of section one hundred and forty-six of the Law of Property Act 1925, and where a notice is served under this subsection, the lessee may, within twenty-eight days from the date of the service thereof, serve on the lessor a counter-notice to the effect that he claims the benefit of this Act.
   (3)   Where a counter-notice is served by a lessee under this section, then, notwithstanding anything in any enactment or rule of law, no proceedings, by action or otherwise, shall be taken by the lessor for the enforcement of any right of re-entry or forfeiture under any proviso or stipulation in the lease for breach of the covenant or agreement in question, or for damages for breach thereof, otherwise than with the leave of the court.
   (4)   A notice served under subsection (1) of section one hundred and forty-six of the Law of Property Act 1925, in the circumstances specified in subsection (1) of this section,

and a notice served under subsection (2) of this section shall not be valid unless it contains a statement, in characters not less conspicuous than those used in any other part of the notice, to the effect that the lessee is entitled under this Act to serve on the lessor a counter-notice claiming the benefit of this Act, and a statement in the like characters specifying the time within which, and the manner in which, under this Act a counter-notice may be served and specifying the name and address for service of the lessor.

(5)   Leave for the purposes of this section shall not be given unless the lessor proves—

(a)   that the immediate remedying of the breach in question is requisite for preventing substantial diminution in the value of his reversion, or that the value thereof has been substantially diminished by the breach;

(b)   that the immediate remedying of the breach is required for giving effect in relation to the [premises] to the purposes of any enactment, or of any byelaw or other provision having effect under an enactment, [or for giving effect to any order of a court or requirement of any authority under any enactment or any such byelaw or other provision as aforesaid];

(c)   in a case in which the lessee is not in occupation of the whole of the [premises as respects which the covenant or agreement is proposed to be enforced], that the immediate remedying of the breach is required in the interests of the occupier of [those premises] or of part thereof;

(d)   that the breach can be immediately remedied at an expense that is relatively small in comparison with the much greater expense that would probably be occasioned by postponement of the necessary work; or

(e)   special circumstances which in the opinion of the court, render it just and equitable that leave should be given.

(6)   The court may, in granting or in refusing leave for the purposes of this section, impose such terms and conditions on the lessor or on the lessee as it may think fit.

2.   Restriction on right to recover expenses of survey, etc

A lessor on whom a counter-notice is served under the preceding section shall not be entitled to the benefit of subsection (3) of section one hundred and forty-six of the Law of Property Act 1925, (which relates to costs and expenses incurred by a lessor in reference to breaches of covenant), so far as regards any costs or expenses incurred in reference to the breach in question, unless he makes an application for leave for the purposes of the preceding section, and on such an application the court shall have power to direct whether and to what extent the lessor is to be entitled to the benefit thereof.

18.3   Covenants Against Assigning, Sub-letting and Parting with Possession

18.3.1   QUALIFIED COVENANTS

LANDLORD AND TENANT ACT 1927

19.   Provisions as to covenants not to assign, etc, without licence or consent

(1)   In all leases whether made before or after the commencement of this Act containing a covenant condition or agreement against assigning, underletting, charging or parting with the possession of demised premises or any part thereof without licence or consent, such covenant condition or agreement shall, notwithstanding any express provision to the contrary, be deemed to be subject—

(a)   to a proviso to the effect that such licence or consent is not to be unreasonably withheld, but this proviso does not preclude the right of the landlord to require payment of a reasonable sum in respect of any legal or other expenses incurred in connection with such licence or consent; . . .

LANDLORD AND TENANT (COVENANTS) ACT 1995

22.   Imposition of conditions regulating giving of landlord's consent to assignments

After subsection (1) of section 19 of the Landlord and Tenant Act 1927 (provisions as to covenants not to assign etc. without licence or consent) there shall be inserted—

(1A)   Where the landlord and the tenant under a qualifying lease have entered into an agreement specifying for the purposes of this subsection—

(a)   any circumstances in which the landlord may withhold his licence or consent to an assignment of the demised premises or any part of them, or

(b)   any conditions subject to which any such licence or consent may be granted,

then the landlord—

(i)   shall not be regarded as unreasonably withholding his licence or consent to any such assignment if he withholds it on the ground (and it is the case) that any such circumstances exist, and

(ii)   if he gives any such licence or consent subject to any such conditions, shall not be regarded as giving it subject to unreasonable conditions;

and section 1 of the Landlord and Tenant Act 1988 (qualified duty to consent to assignment etc.) shall have effect subject to the provisions of this subsection. . . .

LAW OF PROPERTY ACT 1925

144.   No fine to be exacted for licence to assign

In all leases containing a covenant, condition, or agreement against assigning, underletting, or parting with the possession, or disposing of the land or property leased without licence or consent, such covenant, condition, or agreement shall, unless the lease contains an express provision to the contrary, be deemed to be subject to a proviso to the effect that no fine or sum of money in the nature of a fine shall be payable for or in respect of such licence or consent; but this proviso does not preclude the right to require the payment of a reasonable sum in respect of any legal or other expense incurred in relation to such licence or consent.

18.3.2   WHEN IS A CONSENT UNREASONABLY WITHELD?

INTERNATIONAL DRILLING FLUIDS LTD v LOUISVILLE INVESTMENTS (UXBRIDGE) LTD [1986] 1 Ch 513, Court of Appeal

FACTS: A lease was granted for thirty years and provided that the demised premises should not be used 'for any purpose other than as offices'. The lease could not be assigned without the landlord's permission (known, somewhat confusingly, as the landlord's 'licence'), but such licence was not to be unreasonably witheld. The tenant requested the landlord's consent to an assignment. The landlord refused, on the ground, *inter alia*, that the proposed use of the premises as offices would reduce the value of the landlord's reversion and create parking problems. The judge held that the landlord's refusal to give consent to the assignment had been unreasonable. The landlord appealed.
HELD: The appeal was dismissed.

BALCOMBE LJ: From the authorities I deduce the following propositions of law.

(1)   The purpose of a covenant against assignment without the consent of the landlord, such consent not to be unreasonably withheld, is to protect the lessor from having his premises used or occupied in an undesirable way, or by an undesirable tenant or assignee: *per* A L Smith LJ in *Bates v Donaldson* [1896] 2 QB 241, 247, approved by all the members of the Court of Appeal in *Houlder Brothers & Co. Ltd v Gibbs* [1925] Ch 575.

(2)   As a corollary to the first proposition, a landlord is not entitled to refuse his consent to an assignment on grounds which have nothing whatever to do with the relationship of landlord and tenant in regard to the subject matter of the lease: see *Houlder Brothers & Co. Ltd v Gibbs*, a decision which (despite some criticism) is binding on this court: *Bickel v Duke of Westminster* [1977] QB 517. A recent example of a case where the landlord's consent was unreasonably withheld because the refusal was designed to achieve a collateral purpose unconnected with the terms of the lease is *Bromley Park Garden Estates Ltd v Moss* [1982] 1 WLR 1019.

(3)   The onus of proving that consent has been unreasonably withheld is on the tenant: see *Shanly v Ward* (1913) 29 TLR 714 and *Pimms Ltd v Tallow Chandlers Company* [1964] 2 QB 547, 564. [Now see Landlord and Tenant Act 1988.]

(4)   It is not necessary for the landlord to prove that the conclusions which led him to refuse consent were justified, if they were conclusions which might be reached by a reasonable man in the circumstances: *Pimms Ltd* v *Tallow Chandlers Company* [1964] 2 QB 547, 564.

(5)   It may be reasonable for the landlord to refuse his consent to an assignment on the ground of the purpose for which the proposed assignee intends to use the premises, even though that purpose is not forbidden by the lease: see *Bates* v *Donaldson* [1896] 2 QB 241, 244.

(6)   There is a divergence of authority on the question, in considering whether the landlord's refusal of consent is reasonable, whether it is permissible to have regard to the consequences to the tenant if consent to the proposed assignment is withheld. In an early case at first instance, *Sheppard* v *Hong Kong and Shanghae Banking Corporation* (1872) 20 WR 459, 460, Malins V-C said that by withholding their consent the lessors threw a very heavy burden on the lessees and they therefore ought to show good grounds for refusing it. In *Houlder Brothers & Co Ltd* v *Gibbs* [1925] Ch 575, 584, Warrington LJ said:

> An act must be regarded as reasonable or unreasonable in reference to the circumstances under which it is committed, and when the question arises on the construction of a contract the outstanding circumstances to be considered are the nature of the contract to be construed, and the relations between the parties resulting from it.

In a recent decision of this court, *Leeward Securities Ltd* v *Lilyheath Properties Ltd* (1983) 271 EG 279 concerning a sub-letting which would attract the protection of the Rent Act, both Oliver LJ and O'Connor LJ made it clear in their judgments that they could envisage circumstances in which it might be unreasonable to refuse consent to an underletting, if the result would be that there was no way in which the tenant (the sub-landlord) could reasonably exploit the premises except by creating a tenancy to which the Rent Act protection would apply, and which inevitably would affect the value of the landlord's reversion. O'Connor LJ said, at p. 283:

> It must not be thought that, because the introduction of a Rent Act tenant inevitably has an adverse effect upon the value of the reversion, that that is a sufficient ground for the landlords to say that they can withhold consent and that the court will hold that that is reasonable.

To the opposite effect are the *dicta*, *obiter* but nevertheless weighty, of Viscount Dunedin and Lord Phillimore in *Viscount Tredegar* v *Harwood* [1929] AC 72, 78, 82. There are numerous other dicta to the effect that a landlord need consider only his own interest: see, e.g., *West Layton Ltd* v *Ford* [1979] QB 593, 605, and *Bromley Park Garden Estates Ltd* v *Moss* [1982] 1 WLR 1019, 1027. Those *dicta* must be qualified, since a landlord's interests, collateral to the purposes of the lease, are in any event ineligible for consideration: see proposition (2) above. But in my judgment a proper reconciliation of those two streams of authority can be achieved by saying that while a landlord need usually only consider his own relevant interests, there may be cases where there is such a disproportion between the benefit to the landlord and the detriment to the tenant if the landlord withholds his consent to an assignment that it is unreasonable for the landlord to refuse consent.

(7)   Subject to the propositions set out above, it is in each case a question of fact, depending upon all the circumstances, whether the landlord's consent to an assignment is being unreasonably withheld: see *Bickel* v *Duke of Westminster* [1977] QB 517, 524, and *West Layton Ltd* v *Ford* [1979] QB 593, 604, 606–607.

In the present case, the judge, having made the findings of specific fact set out above, carefully considered the relevant authorities. He then reached the conclusion that the views of the landlords' expert witnesses about the effect of the proposed assignment on the value of the reversion, although views which could be held by reasonable professional men, did not in the circumstances of this case, where there was no prospect of the landlords wishing to realise the reversion, constitute a ground for reasonable apprehension of damage to their interests. That was a decision on the facts to which the judge was entitled to come. He made no error of law in reaching his decision; he took into account nothing which he ought not to have considered, and he omitted nothing which he ought to have considered. In my judgment, this court ought not to interfere.

But in any event, in my judgment, the judge reached the right decision. Although he did not expressly mention the disproportionate harm to the tenants if the landlords were entitled to refuse consent to the assignment, compared with the minimum disadvantage which he clearly considered the landlords would suffer by a diminution in the paper value of the reversion—'paper value' because he was satisfied there was no prospect of the landlords wishing to realise the reversion—he clearly recognised the curious results to which the landlords' arguments, based solely upon a consideration of their own interests, could lead. As he said in his judgment:

It seems to me that, if Mr. Lewison is right, the more substantial the lessee, the more easily the landlord would be able to justify a refusal of consent to an assignment, since unless the proposed assignee's covenant was as strong as the assignor's, a reasonable man might form the view that the market would consider the reversion less attractive if the lease were vested in the assignor. To take the matter to extremes, if a lease was made in favour of a government department it would be unassignable except to another government department; for as Mr. Matthews [one of the expert witnesses] accepted in cross-examination, the market would prefer to have the government as the lessee, whether the premises were being used as serviced offices or not, even if they were standing empty, rather than a company, however strong its covenant.

In my judgment, the gross unfairness to the tenants of the example postulated by the judge strengthens the arguments in favour, in an appropriate case of which the instant case is one, of it being unreasonable for the landlord not to consider the detriment to the tenant if consent is refused, where the detriment is extreme and disproportionate to the benefit to the landlord.

NORFOLK CAPITAL GROUP LTD v KITWAY LTD [1976] 3 All ER 787, Court of Appeal

FACTS: A long lease of a house was vested in a limited company. It was proposed to assign the lease to a human tenant who would be able to take advantage of certain sections of protective legislation not available to 'artificial persons' (as companies are often referred to). This fact would have the effect of reducing the value of the landlord's reversion.
HELD: The landlords were reasonable in vetoing the assignments.

MEGAW LJ: . . . In so far as there is any authority which can be said to bear on this question, Mr. Barnes has rightly called our attention to a decision at first instance of Lawson J in *Welch v Birrane*, in 1974, reported only in (1974) 29 P & CR 102. In that case Lawson J had to deal with the question of a refusal by a landlord to give consent to an assignment the effect of which would have been to enable the proposed assignee, in course of time, had the proposed assignee so desired, to claim the advantages of the Leasehold Reform Act 1967. There were further complications in that case which ultimately led to the decision in favour of the tenant. The judge held that the landlord in that case had waived his right to challenge the assignment that had been made without his consent. But the judge did decide, as the first question, whether the landlord in those circumstances could be said unreasonably to have refused his consent; and the judge decided that question before going on to the other question, whether there had been a waiver. Lawson J as I understand his judgment, decided that issue on two separate grounds, each of which stood apart from the other. The first of those grounds, as I understand it, was that the very fact that there is this potential disadvantage to a landlord under the Leasehold Reform Act 1967 if the proposed assignment were to go through is in itself sufficient to prevent that refusal from being unreasonable. . . .

In my judgment, the case ends where it began. Looking at it as a matter of ordinary common sense and the ordinary use of words, from which I do not think that the law ought to be regarded as departing unless there is clear authority that requires one so to hold, the refusal of the landlord, in the circumstances of this case, to give his consent to an assignment which has the potential effect that this assignment would have is something that cannot be fairly described as being 'unreasonable.' Accordingly, I would dismiss the appeal. . . .

LANDLORD AND TENANT ACT 1988

1.   Qualified duty to consent to assigning, underletting etc of premises

(1)   This section applies in any case where—

(a)   a tenancy includes a covenant on the part of the tenant not to enter into one or more of the following transactions, that is—

(i)   assigning,

(ii)   underletting

(iii)   charging, or

(iv)   parting with the possession of,

the premises comprised in the tenancy or any part of the premises without the consent of the landlord or some other person, but

(b)   the covenant is subject to the qualification that the consent is not to be unreasonably withheld (whether or not it is also subject to any other qualification).

(2)   In this section and section 2 of this Act—

(a)   references to a proposed transaction are to any assignment, underletting, charging or parting with possession to which the covenant relates, and

(b)   references to the person who may consent to such a transaction are to the person who under the covenant may consent to the tenant entering into the proposed transaction.

(3)   Where there is served on the person who may consent to a proposed transaction a written application by the tenant for consent to the transaction, he owes a duty to the tenant within a reasonable time—

(a)   to give consent, except in a case where it is reasonable not to give consent,

(b)   to serve on the tenant written notice of his decision whether or not to give consent specifying in addition—

(i)   if the consent is given subject to conditions, the conditions,

(ii)   if the consent is withheld, the reasons for withholding it.

(4)   Giving consent subject to any condition that is not a reasonable condition does not satisfy the duty under subsection (3)(a) above.

(5)   For the purposes of this Act it is reasonable for a person not to give consent to a proposed transaction only in a case where, if he withheld consent and the tenant completed the transaction, the tenant would be in breach of a covenant.

(6)   It is for the person who owed any duty under subsection (3) above—

(a)   if he gave consent and the question arises whether he gave it within a reasonable time, to show that he did,

(b)   if he gave consent subject to any condition and the question arises whether the condition was a reasonable condition, to show that it was,

(c)   if he did not give consent and the question arises whether it was reasonable for him not to do so, to show that it was reasonable,

and, if the question arises whether he served notice under that subsection within a reasonable time, to show that he did.

18.4   Surrender Clauses

BOCARDO SA v S & M HOTELS LTD AND ANOTHER [1980] 1 WLR 17, Court of Appeal

FACTS: A clause of a long commercial lease required the tenant to offer to surrender its lease to the landlord before asking for consent to assign. The tenant pleaded that such an arrangement fell foul of section 19(1) of the Landlord and Tenant Act 1927, and was void. HELD: The provision as to surrender was valid.

MEGAW LJ: . . . if one is to assume, as for the reasons which I have given it seems to me right for us to assume, that section 19(1) does not prevent or limit freedom of contract to ban assignments altogether by agreement in the lease, why should the subsection be treated as having the effect of preventing or limiting freedom of contract to ban assignments during a part of the lease? Counsel for the landlords, I think rightly, submitted that the courts could not treat section 19(1) as invalidating a contractual proviso that no assignment should be made—that no question of assignment by consent should arise—during, say, the first, or the last, seven years of a 14-year lease. Why, then, as a matter of policy or practical sense or logic should the courts hold that section 19(1) invalidates a proviso that, before the tenant's right of assignment with consent shall arise, a condition precedent shall be fulfilled: namely, the tenant's obligation first to offer a surrender? If by agreement an assignment by consent can be precluded altogether, what logical reason or policy can be invoked to preclude a limited right of the tenant to assign with consent; the limitation being that the landlord, if he wishes, can insist on a surrender?.

GREENE v CHURCH COMMISSIONERS FOR ENGLAND
[1974] 1 Ch 467, Court of Appeal

FACTS: The plaintiff had taken a lease by assignment. The original tenant had agreed to offer to surrender his lease before making any request to assign the premises. The plaintiff claimed not to be bound by the agreement to surrender. He argued that the landlord's right to require a surrender was an estate contract, registrable as a class C(iv) Land Charge, and as it had not been registered it would be void against a purchaser from the original tenant. HELD: The plaintiff's argument succeeded.

LORD DENNING MR: This case raises a point of widespread application. It concerns a clause, now common in leases, by which the landlord can insist on a surrender. The question is whether it ought to be registered as a land charge. . . .

The question is, therefore: Was this proviso a 'contract' to surrender?

. . . help is to be found by the word 'including' in Class C(iv). That word is very appropriate to show the wide meaning which the legislature attributes to 'contract' in the opening words. It uses the word 'contract' in a sense which *includes* a valid option to purchase or a right of pre-emption. So it does *include* contracts which are binding on one side only. The word 'including' is used so as to remove any doubt as to the width of the word 'contract' in the opening words. It makes it clear that it is used in the wide sense, which includes an offer binding on one side, which the other can accept or reject as he pleases. . . .

In my opinion, therefore, the word 'contract' in the opening words of Class C(iv) includes a contract which is binding on one side only. It includes a contract by which one party binds himself, in a particular event, to convey or create a legal estate, even though the other is not bound to accept it: and only becomes bound by some further act of acceptance. Such is the case where the owner of a legal estate gives another an option to purchase, or gives him a right of pre-emption, or where a lessee gives to a tenant an option to renew a lease (as in *Beesly v Hallwood Estates Ltd* itself), or where a lessee gives to a lessor a right to accept or reject a surrender (as in this case). . . .

CHAPTER NINETEEN

THE RUNNING OF COVENANTS IN A LEASE

19.1 Which Covenants Touch and Concern the Land?

KUMAR v DUNNING [1987] 2 All ER 801, Court of Appeal

FACTS: The landlord gave consent to an assignment of the lease, but made his consent conditional upon the provision by a third party of a guarantee that the new tenant would pay the rent. Such a third party is called a 'surety'. If the assignee fails to make rental payments, the surely will be required to make them instead. The question in the present case was whether a puchaser of the leasehold reversion would be entitled to enforce the guarantee. HELD: The guarantee was enforceable by the new landlord because it 'touched and concerned' the land. The guarantee was of benefit to nobody but the present owner of the freehold, it would therefore be artificial to treat the benefit of the guarantee as something personal to the original freeholder only.

SIR NICOLAS BROWNE-WILKINSON V-C: The test whether a covenant touches and concerns land is that formulated by Bayley J in *Mayor of Congleton* v *Pattison* (1808) 10 East 130 at 138, 103 ER 725 at 728 and adopted by Farwell J in *Rogers* v *Hosegood* [1900] 2 Ch 388 at 395: '. . . the covenant must either affect the land as regards mode of occupation, or it must be such as per se, and not merely from collateral circumstances, affects the value of the land'. But although the test is certain, its exact meaning when applied to different sets of circumstances is very obscure. In *Grant* v *Edmondson* [1931] 1 Ch 1 at 28, [1930] All ER Rep 48 at 59 Romer LJ said:

> In connection with the subject of covenants running with the land, it is impossible to reason by analogy. The established rules concerning it are purely arbitrary, and the distinctions, for the most part, quite illogical.

> Before seeking to analyse the authorities, I will first state how the matter strikes me as a matter of impression. The surety covenant is given as a support or buttress to covenants given by a tenant to a landlord. The covenants by the tenant relate not only to the payment of rent, but also to repair, insurance and user of the premises. All such covenants by a tenant in favour of the landlord touch and concern the land, i.e. the reversion of the landlord. The performance of some covenants by tenants relate to things done on the land itself (e.g. repair and user covenants). Other tenants' covenants (e.g. payment of rent and insurance) require nothing to be done on the land itself. They are mere covenants for the payment of money. The covenant to pay rent is the major cause of the landlord's reversion having any value during the continuance of the term. Where there is privity of estate, the tenants' covenant to pay rent touches and concerns the land: see *Parker* v *Webb* (1693) 3 Salk 5, 91 ER 656. As it seems to me, in principle a covenant by a third party guaranteeing the performance by the tenant of his obligations should touch and concern the reversion as much as do the tenants' covenants themselves.

This view accords with what, to my mind, is the commercial common sense and justice of the case. When, as in the present case, the lease has been assigned on the terms that the sureties will guarantee performance by the assignee of the lease, justice and common sense ought to require the sureties, not the original tenant, to be primarily liable in the event of default by the assignee. So long as the reversion is not assigned, that will be the position. Why should the position between the original tenant and the sureties be rendered completely different just because the reversion has been assigned, a transaction wholly outside the control of the original tenant and the sureties?

Yet in all save one of the cases decided at first instance, the court has held that the surety covenant does not touch and concern the land. The exception is *Pinemain Ltd v Tuck* (4 March 1986, unreported) where the question was left open. In *Pinemain Ltd v Welbeck International Ltd* (1984) 272 EG 1166 Edward Nugee QC sitting as a deputy High Court judge held that the surety covenant to run at law (as opposed to a negative covenant running with the land in equity) it was necessary that the covenant should require something to be done which afffected the land itself, not merely its value. I find this view difficult to reconcile with those cases which establish that a tenant's covenant to pay rent and to insure touch and concern the land. Moreover, Mr Nugee's view is, to my mind, inconsistent with the decision in *Dyson v Forster* [1909] AC 98, [1908–10] All ER Rep 212 which I will mention later. . . .

Reverting to the test laid down in the *Congleton* case, it is clear that the surety covenant in the present case does not 'affect the land as to the mode of occupation'. The question is whether it affects the value of the reversion 'per se and not merely from collateral circumstances'. The meaning of those latter words has been expounded in a number of cases which have not often been cited subsequently. In *Vernon v Smith* (1821) 5 B & Ald 1, [1814–23] All ER Rep 677 the question was whether a covenant by the tenant to insure the demised premises was enforceable by the assignee of the reversion. Although the case was one of privity of estate, the enforceability of the covenant depended on whether the covenant touched and concerned the land. It was argued that the covenant was merely to pay money to a third party. The majority of the court decided that the covenant was enforceable on the narrow point that the assignee of the reversion would have an interest in the insurance moneys.

. . . The benefit of the covenant to repay could not touch and concern the land because someone other than the owner for the time being of the term could take the benefit of it.

19.2   Liability of Original Parties after Assignment

LAW OF PROPERTY ACT 1925

141.   Rent and benefit of lessee's covenants to run with the reversion

(1)   Rent reserved by a lease, and the benefit of every covenant or provision therein contained, having reference to the subject-matter thereof, and on the lessee's part to be observed or performed, and every condition of re-entry and other condition therein contained, shall be annexed and incident to and shall go with the reversionary estate in the land, or in any part thereof, immediately expectant on the term granted by the lease, notwithstanding severance of that reversionary estates, and without prejudice to any liability affecting a covenantor or his estate.

(2)   Any such rent, covenant or provision shall be capable of being recovered, received, enforced, and taken advantage of, by the person from time to time entitled, subject to the term, to the income of the whole or any part, as the case may require, of the land leased.

ARLESFORD TRADING CO. LTD v SERVANSINGH [1971] 3 All ER 113, Court of Appeal

FACTS: The original tenant covenanted on behalf of himself and his succesors in title, for the benefit of the landlord and its successors in title, to pay, half yearly, a ground rent and cetain service charges. The tenant assigned the remainder of the term of the 99 year lease to a new tenant. The new tenant failed to make the payments of ground rent and service charges. Later, the reversion also changed hands. It was assigned by the original landlord to the plaintiff. The plaintiff brought the present action against the original tenant for recovery of the sums due.

HELD: The new landlord was successful. An original tenant generally remained liable, throughout the full term of the lease, for any breaches of covenants touching and concerning the land. This was in accordance with s. 141 of the Law of Property Act 1925.

RESSELL LJ: . . . Now it has been established in this court that an assignee of the reversion can claim, against the lessee, arrears of rent accrued prior to the assignment, and to re-enter on the ground of the failure to have paid such arrears; this is by force of s. 141 of the Law of Property Act 1925: see *London and County (A & D) Ltd* v *Wilfred Sportsman Ltd (Greenwoods (Hosiers and Outfitters) Ltd, third party)* [1917] Ch 764. In that case, however, the claim to re-enter and forfeit the lease was against the original lessee (and his chargee). It is pointed out that in the present case the defendant assigned his lease before the reversion was asigned to the plaintiffs and that there has never been privity of estate between the plaintiffs and the defendant, contrary to what appears from the note of the judgment to have been the judge's view. But it is argued for the plaintiffs that an original lessee remains at all times liable under the lessee's covenants throughout the lease, and that assignment of the reversion does not automatically release him from that liability. This agreement is in our judgment correct; so that if there is no special feature in this case the plaintiffs undoubtedly have a right as assignee of the reversion, and with it of the benefit of the lessee's covenants for rent etc to sue for arrears of rent.

Was there a special feature which denies the plaintiffs the right to sue the defendant? It is plain that Drayville Properties Ltd could not have asserted against the assignee of the lease (or his mortgagee) that there was any subsisting breach of the covenant for rent. This is because of the production of the receipt for the June 1969 instalment. It was manifestly the intention that the lease should be assigned 'clean', so to speak, of any liability for those three unpaid instalments. Equally, the plaintiffs could not have asserted against the assignee of the term (or his mortgagee) the failure in the payment of those three instalments. But does it follow from that that the postponed obligation of the defendant to pay those three instalments no longer had sufficiently the quality of an obligation to pay rent etc under the lease to enable the assignee of the reversion to assert against the defendant that the benefit of that obligation was assigned together with the reversion? In our judgment the answer is in the negative. The obligation on the defendant remained on him in his capacity as lessee under the lease, and the ability to enforce against him passed with the reversion to the plaintiffs.

In our judgment accordingly the appeal fails.

19.2.1   INDEMNITIES BETWEEN ASSIGNEES OF A LEASE

LAW OF PROPERTY ACT 1925

77.   Implied covenants in conveyance subject to rents

(1)   In addition to the covenants implied under the last preceding section, there shall in the several cases in this section mentioned, be deemed to be included and implied, a covenant to the effect in this section stated, by and with such persons as are hereinafter mentioned, that is to say:—

. . .

(C)   In a conveyance for valuable consideration, other than a mortgage, of the entirety of the land comprised in a lease, for the residue of the term or interest created by the lease, a covenant by the assignee or joint and several covenants by the assignees (if more than one) with the conveying parties and with each of them (if more than one) in the terms set out in Part IX of the Second Schedule to this Act. . . .

SECOND SCHEDULE

PART IX   COVENANT IN A CONVEYANCE FOR VALUABLE CONSIDERATION, OTHER THAN A MORTGAGE, OF THE ENTIRETY OF THE LAND COMPRISED IN A LEASE FOR THE RESIDUE OF THE TERM OR INTEREST CREATED BY THE LEASE

That the assignees, or the persons denying title under them, will at all times, from the date of the conveyance or other date therein stated, duly pay all rent becoming due under the lease creating the term or interest for which the land is conveyed, and observe and perform all the covenants, agreements and conditions therein contained and thenceforth on the part of the lessees to be observed and performed:

And also will at all times, from the date aforesaid, save harmless and keep indemnified the conveying parties and their estates and effects, from and against all proceedings, costs, claims and expenses on account of any omission to pay the said rent or any breach of any of the said covenants, agreements and conditions.

19.3   Position of Covenants Which Do Not Touch and Concern

19.3.1   POSITION OF OPTIONS TO RENEW THE LEASE

REGENT OIL CO. LTD v *J A GREGORY (HATCH END) LTD*
[1965] 3 All ER 673, Court of Appeal

FACTS: C Ltd, the tenant of a petrol filling station, borrowed £4,000 from the plaintiff and undertook to repay the sum, without interest, over ten years. Simultaneous with the mortgage, the tenant also covenated to purchase all its petrol, oil etc. from the plaintiff company, and from none other. Later, C Ltd, assigned the lease to a new tenant. The question was whether the covenants as to the purchase of petrol, oil etc touched and concerned the land, so as to run with the assignment and bind the new tenant.
HELD: The covenant touched and concerned the land and was not merely personal. The new tenant was bound.

(Note that extracts from this case are not essential here.)

19.4   Position of Equitable Leases

PURCHASE v *LICHFIELD BREWERY COMPANY*
[1915] 1 KB 184, King's Bench Division

FACTS: The tenant of an equitable lease agreed to assign a lease to new tenants, but the deed to that effect was never executed by the proposed assignees, nor did they take up possession of the demised land. The plaintiff landlord brought this action to recover rent from the proposed assignees. They refused to pay rent, on grounds that they had never taken up possession.
HELD: There could not be privity of estate between the landlord and the new tenants, because the original tenant had never possessed a legal estate capable of being assigned. Accordingly, the proposed assignees were not liable to pay rent on the premises.

HORRIDGE J: . . . Assuming that Lunnis was in a position to have enforced specific performance against the plaintiff and had the right to treat himself as being a lessee under the lease which would have been granted under a decree for specific performance, still it does not follow that his assignee is in the same position. The only case cited to establish such a right in an assignee is *Dowell* v *Dew* 12 LJ (Ch) 158; but in that case the assignee of the agreement had entered and paid rent and had been recognized as tenant by the owner of the property. Knight Bruce V-C said that the agreement was assignable 'and especially with the assent of the landlord for the time being.' In that case there was privity of contract. Even then the landlord was entitled if he thought fit to insist on the personal liability of his lessee on the covenants in the lease as if it had been granted to him. Such a case as the present one seems remote from the case which Jessel MR was considering when he said, in *Walsh* v *Lonsdale* 21 ChD 9,'There is an agreement for a lease under which possession has been given. Now since the Judicature Act the possession is held under the agreement . . .

The tenant holds under an agreement for a lease. He holds, therefore, under the same terms in equity as if a lease had been granted, it being a case in which both parties admit that relief is capable of being given by specific performance.' In my opinion as assignee of a mere agreement for a lease who never took possession and never attorned tenant could not before the Judicature Acts and cannot now in his own right enforce specific performance against the landlord. He could not establish such a direct relation between himself and the landlord as would induce a Court of Equity, regarding that as done which ought to be done, to treat him as a person in whom a lease had been vested. I do not think that the case of *Williams* v *Bosanquet* 1 Brod & B 238 applies because in that case the lease was under seal and it was validly assigned by deed to the mortgagees.

LUSH J: . . . I do not think it is necessary to say how the case might have stood if the defendants had ever taken possession. They are liable, if at all, on the principle of *Walsh* v *Lonsdale* 21 ChD 9. In that case the tenant was in possession under the agreement. In the present case the defendants never did take possession. The agreement contained a provision against assigning. The defendants were only mortgagees. It does not follow from *Walsh* v *Lonsdale* that a Court of Equity would decree specific performance against mere mortgagees who only took an assignment by way of security. In my opinion it would leave the parties to their position at law. Accordingly the matter stands thus: A tenant under an agreement, whose only title to call himself a lessee depends on his right to specific performance of the agreement, assigns his right to assignees. The assignees never had a term vested in them because no term was ever created; therefore there was never privity of estate. They never went into possession or were recognized by the landlord; therefore there was never privity of contract. It is impossible that specific performance of a contract can be decreed against a person with whom there is neither privity of contract nor privity of estate. Therefore these assignees are not liable to perform the terms of the agreement and this appeal must be allowed.

BOYER v *WARBEY* [1953] 1 QB 234, Court of Appeal

This case is included because of the following dictum of Denning LJ. The facts of the case are not essential here.

DENNING LJ: . . . I know that before the Judicature Act 1873, it was said that the doctrine of covenants running with the land only applied to covenants under seal and not to agreements under hand: see *Elliott* v *Johnson* (1868) LR 2 QB 120. But since the fusion of law and equity, the position is different. The distinction between agreements under hand and covenants under seal has been largely obliterated. There is no valid reason nowadays why the doctrine of covenants running with the land—or with the reversion—should not apply equally to agreements under hand as to covenants under seal, and I think we should so hold, not only in the case of agreements for more than three years which need the intervention of equity to perfect them, but also in the case of agreements for three years or less which do not. . . .

19.5   Position of Sub-Tenants and Head Landlords

19.5.1   RESTRICTIVE COVENANTS IN THE HEAD LEASE

A head landlord can enforce restrictive covenants in the lease against a sub-tenant, despite the absence of privity of estate, where:

(a) the lease is unregistered title and the sub-tenant has notice of the restrictive covenants (usually the sub-tenant will have notice of the restrictive covenants in the head lease as the head tenant will, for his own protection, at least tell the sub-tenant about them); or

(b) the lease is registered title. Restrictive covenants in registered leases are automatically binding on sub-tenants by virtue of the Land Registration Act 1925, s. 23(1)(a) and (2).

LAND REGISTRATION ACT 1925

23. Effect of registration of dispositions of leaseholds

(1)   In the case of a leasehold estate registered with an absolute title, a disposition (including a subdemise thereof) for valuable consideration shall, when registered, be deemed to vest in the transferee or underlessee the estate transferred or created to the extent of the registered estate, or for the term created by the subdemise, as the case may require, with all implied or expressed rights, privileges, and appurtenances attached to the estate transferred or created, including (subject to any entry to the contrary on the register) the appropriate rights and interests which would under the Law of Property Act 1925, have been transferred if the land had not been registered, but subject as follows:—

(a)   To all implied and express covenants, obligations, and liabilities incident to the estate transferred or created; and

(b)   To the incumbrances and other entries (if any) appearing in the register [and any charge for [inheritance tax] subject to which the disposition takes effect under section 73 of this Act]; and

(c)   Unless the contrary is expressed on the register, to the overriding interests, if any, effecting the estate transferred or created,

but free from all other estates and interests whatsoever, including estates and interests of His Majesty; and the transfer or subdemise shall operate in like manner as if the registered transferor or sublessor were (subject to any entry to the contrary on the register) absolutely entitled to the registered lease for his own benefit.

(2)   In the case of a leasehold estate registered with a good leasehold title, a disposition (including a subdemise thereof) for valuable consideration shall, when registered, have the same effect as it would have had if the land had been registered with an absolute title, save that it shall not effect or prejudice the enforcement of any right or interest affecting or in derogation of the title of the lessor to grant the lease.

19.6   End of Chapter Assessment Question

In 1980 Lisa leased (by deed) a house to Tommy for 40 years. The lease includes the following covenants:

   (a) the tenant should pay £2,000 per year rent;

   (b) the tenant should not use the house for any purpose other than as a private dwelling;

   (c) the tenant should not assign, sub-let or part with possession except with the landlord's consent.

The lease does not contain a forfeiture clause.

Lisa believes that Tommy intends to assign or sub-let to Percy. She is alarmed at that prospect, as Percy uses a number of houses in the area as branches of his very extensive accountacy practice.

Advise Lisa:

   (i) as to the possible legal consequences if she withheld her consent to an assignment or sub-letting to Percy;

   (ii) as to her position if she gave her consent to an assignment or sub-letting, but subsequently wishes to enforce covenants (a) or (b).

19.7   End of Chapter Assessment Outline Answer

The lease omits a forfeiture clause, thus limiting the remedies Lisa can seek for breach of covenant. She can sue for damages, and also an injunction to restrain non-residential user, but she will be unable to reclaim possession, even if the breach is extremely serious.

   A second preliminary point is that if Tommy assigned or sublet to Percy without even asking for Lisa's consent, that would be a breach of covenant. Lisa could claim damages, but the transaction would be valid (*Peabody* v *Higgins*). If Percy was a man of excellent character to whom no reasonable objection could have been taken the damages might be nominal.

   Assuming that Tommy asks (in writing) for consent to assign or sub-let to Percy, then the Landlord and Tenant Acts 1927 and 1988 apply to covenant (iii), a 'qualified covenant' against assignment etc. The 1927 Act (section 19) implies into covenant (iii) a proviso that Lisa must not unreasonably withhold her consent.

   The 1988 Act is even more significant, placing on Landlords (like Lisa) a series of duties if they receive from a tenant with respect to a qualified covenant a written request for consent to an assignment or sub-letting. Firstly, Lisa must give an answer within a 'reasonable time'. Secondly she must give consent, unless there are reasonable grounds for refusing. Thirdly, if she says 'no' then she must give written reasons. Moreover, if she breaches any of these duties, Tommy can sue for damages.

   The 1988 Act also establishes that in any dispute over a landlord's actions where there is a qualified covenant, the onus of proof will be on the landlord to show that (s)he is being reasonable.

   Thus Lisa is advised to say 'yes' to any written request from Tommy, unless she has good grounds for objecting which she can prove to the satisfaction of the court. Caselaw (particularly the *Louisville Investments* case) indicates that purely personal objections (e.g. 'I cannot stand accountants') will not suffice. The landlord's objections must relate to the character of the assignee/sub-tenant or his proposed use for the premises. If Percy were of proven bad character, e.g. a convicted criminal or male prostitute, that would be good grounds for objection.

More importantly, if Lisa could prove that Percy intended to use the premises for inappropriate purposes, e.g. that he was definitely going to use the house as an office, that would be good grounds for saying 'no'.

It follows from this discussion that the answer to part (a) largely depends on whether Lisa is confident that she has reasonable grounds of objection provable in court. If this is so, then she will win any litigation commenced by Tommy. She might even consider herself seeking an injunction to restrain the proposed sub-letting/assignment.

If, in response to Tommy, she advances inadequate reasons, she may be lucky. Tommy may not want to risk litigation, and abandon his proposed transaction. Lisa will have bluffed her way out. But Tommy may well call Lisa's bluff, and when told 'no' go ahead and assign or sub-let without consent. Proceedings then commenced by Lisa would fail.

Tommy might alternatively claim a declaration that Lisa witholding her consent unreasonably and/or a claim damages under the 1988 Act. Tommy would win. Moreover, if because of delay caused by litigation Percy lost interest in the premises, the damages could be substantial.

With respect to part (b) of the question, if Lisa wishes to enforce covenants (i) or (ii) against Tommy, then the position is the same, whether Tommy has sub-let or assigned. Tommy, being the original tenant, is liable for the duration of the lease. He contracted for forty years, so he (or his personal representatives after his death) remain liable for that period. This will be so, whether the breach about which Lisa is complaining is actually committed by Tommy, Percy or an assignee from Percy.

With respect to enforcement against Percy, it matters whether the transaction is an assignment or sub-lease. If an assignment, then Lisa and Percy will come into a relationship known as 'Privity of Estate'. Such privity exists where two parties are in a direct landlord and tenant relationship. Where parties are in Privity of Estate, then covenants which 'touch and concern the land' are enforceable between them.

Covenants to pay rent and relating to user of the premises touch and concern the land. Thus if rent arrears build up, Lisa will have the choice of suing Tommy (contract) or Percy (privity of estate). She can only recover one lot of damages. She should sue whoever has the most money.

If the house is used for other than a private dwelling, she can again sue either Tommy or Percy, though if she wants an injunction preventing the user she should sue Percy.

If the transaction is a subletting, then there is no Privity of Estate between Lisa and Percy, a there is no direct relationship of landlord and tenant. (Tommy, as it were, stands between them.) Thus the covenant to pay rent would only be enforceable against Tommy.

Covenant (iii) is special. It is a restrictive covenant, which can be enforced by a landlord (Lisa) against a subtenant (Percy), not by invoking landlord and tenant law, but by invoking restrictive covenants law. If the lease is registered title, then the covenant automatically binds a sub-tenant. (Land Registration Act section 23). If the lease is unregistered, then Percy is only bound if he has notice of the covenant. Lisa can ensure this by consenting to the sub-letting on condition that Tommy tells Percy about the covenant. (Case law and the 1988 Act allow consent on conditions, providing they are reasonable. Clearly this condition is reasonable.)

CHAPTER TWENTY

TERMINATION OF LEASES

20.1 Ways in Which Leases May Terminate

20.1.1 NATURAL EXPIRY

This occurs where the term of a fixed-term lease runs out. Also known as termination by 'Effluxion of Time'.

20.1.2 GIVING OF NOTICE

See **17.1**.

20.1.3 MERGER

This occurs where the tenant buys the landlord's reversion.

20.1.4 SURRENDER

A lease is surrendered where it is terminated by mutual agreement between landlord and tenant.

20.1.5 FRUSTRATION

NATIONAL CARRIERS LTD v *PANALPINA (NORTHERN) LTD*
[1981] 1 All ER 161, House of Lords

FACTS: In January 1974 the defendants took a ten-year lease of a warehouse. In May 1979 the local authority closed the only access road to the warehouse. The closure was likely to last 20 months. The tenants refused to pay any further rent, arguing that the lease was frustrated by the lack of any road access.
HELD: The doctrine of frustration did apply to leases, but a twenty months interruption in the enjoyment of a ten year lease was not such a drastic change in the rights of the parties as to amount to a frustration terminating the lease.

LORD HAILSHAM OF ST MARYLEBONE LC: . . . Is there anything in principle which ought to prevent a lease from ever being frustrated? I think there is not. In favour of the opposite opinion, the difference in principle between real and chattel property was strongly urged. But I find it difficult to accept this, once it has been decided, as has long been the case, that time and demise charters even of the largest ships and of considerable duration can in principle be frustrated. . . . I accept of course that systems of developed land draw a vital distinction between land, which is relatively permanent, and other types of property, which are relatively perishable. But one can overdo the contrast. Coastal erosion as well as the 'vast convulsion of nature' postulated by Viscount Simon LC in the *Cricklewood case* [1945] 1 All ER 252 at 255–256, [1945] AC 221 at 229 can, even in this island, cause houses, gardens, even villages and their churches to fall into the North Sea, and, although the law of property in Scotland is different, as may be seen from *Tay Salmon Fisheries Co. Ltd* v *Speedie* 1929 SC 593, whole estates can there, as Lord President Clyde points out (at 600), be overblown with sand for centuries and so fall subject to the *rei interitus* doctrine of the civil law. In *Taylor* v *Caldwell* (1863) 3 B & S 826 at 834, [1861–73] All ER Rep 24 at 27 itself Blackburn J, after referring to the Digest (lib XLV, title 1) on the subject of '*obligatio de certo corpore*' on which in part he founds his new doctrine, expressly says:

> ... no doubt the propriety, one might almost say the necessity, of the implied condition is more obvious when the contract relates to a living animal, whether man or brute, than when it relates to some inanimate thing (*such as in the present case a theatre*) [emphasis mine] the existence of which is not so obviously precarious as that of the live animal, but the principle is adopted in the Civil law as applicable to every obligation of which the subject is a certain thing.

He then refers to Pothier, Traité des Obligations (partie 3, ch 6, art 3, § 668) in support of his contention.

No doubt a long lease, say for example one for 999 years, is almost exactly identical with the freehold for this purpose, and therefore subject to the ordinary law regarding the incidence of risk (recognised as regards chattels in s. 7 of the former Sale of Goods Act 1893). But there is no difference between chattels in this respect and real property except in degree. Long term speculations and investments are in general less easily frustrated than short term adventures and a lease for 999 years must be in the longer class. I find myself persuaded by the argument presented by Atkin LJ in his dissenting judgment in *Matthey* v *Curling* [1922] 2 AC 180 at 199–200 and quoted with approval by Viscount Simon LC in the *Cricklewood case* [1945] 1 All ER 252 at 256, [1945] AC 221 at 230. In that passage Atkin LJ said:

> ... it does not appear to me conclusive against the application to a lease of the doctrine of frustration that the lease, in addition to containing contractual terms, grants a term of years. Seeing that the instrument as a rule expressly provides for the lease being determined at the option of the lessor upon the happening of certain specified events, I see no logical absurdity in implying a term that it shall be determined absolutely on the happening of other events—namely, those which in an ordinary contract work a frustration. . . .

... No doubt the circumstances in which the doctrine can apply to leases are, to quote Viscount Simon LC in the *Cricklewood case* [1945] 1 All ER 252 at 257, [1945] AC 221 at 231, 'exceedingly rare'. Lord Wright appears to have thought the same, whilst adhering to the view that there are cases in which frustration can apply (see [1945] 1 All ER 252 at 263, [1945] AC 221 at 241). But, as he said in the same passage: 'The doctrine of frustration is modern and flexible and is not subject to being constricted by an arbitrary formula.' To this school of thought I respectfully adhere. Like Lord Wright, I am struck by the fact that there appears to be no reported English case where a lease has ever been held to have been frustrated. I hope this fact will act as a suitable deterrent to the litigious, eager to make legal history by being first in this field. But I am comforted by the reflexion of the authority referred to in the Compleat Angler (pt i, ch 5) on the subject of strawberries: 'Doubtless God could have made a better berry, but doubtless God never did.' I only append to this observation of nature the comment that it does not follow from these premises that He never will, and, if it does not follow, an assumption that He never will becomes exceedingly rash.

In the event my opinion is that the appeal should be dismissed with costs.

20.1.6 FORFEITURE

See below.

20.2   Forfeiture of Leases

20.2.1   MODES OF FORFEITURE

CRIMINAL LAW ACT 1977

6.   Violence for securing entry

(1)   Subject to the following provisions of this section, any person who, without lawful authority, uses or threatens violence for the purpose of securing entry into any premises for himself or for any other person is guilty of an offence, provided that—

(a)   there is someone present on those premises at the time who is opposed to the entry which the violence is intended to secure; and

(b)   the person using or threatening the violence knows that that is the case.

(2)   The fact that a person has any interest in or right to possession or occupation of any premises shall not for the purposes of subsection (1) above constitute lawful authority for the use or threat of violence by him or anyone else for the purpose of securing his entry into those premises.

(3)   In any proceedings for an offence under this section it shall be a defence for the accused to prove—

(a)   that at the time of the alleged offence he or any other person on whose behalf he was acting was a displaced residential occupier of the premises in question; or

(b)   that part of the premises in question constitutes premises of which he or any other person on whose behalf he was acting was a displaced residential occupier and that the part of the premises to which he was seeking to secure entry constitutes an access of which he or, as the case may be, that other person is also a displaced residential occupier.

(4)   It is immaterial for the purposes of this section—

(a)   whether the violence in question is directed against the person or against property; and

(b)   whether the entry which the violence is intended to secure is for the purpose of acquiring possession of the premises in question or for any other purpose.

(5)   A person guilty of an offence under this section shall be liable on summary conviction to imprisonment for a term not exceeding six months or to a fine not exceeding [level 5 on the standard scale] or to both.

(6)   A constable in uniform may arrest without warrant anyone who is, or whom he, with reasonable cause, suspects to be, guilty of an offence under this section.

(7)   . . .

BILLSON v RESIDENTIAL APARTMENTS LTD [1992] 2 WCR 15, House of Lords

FACTS: A tenant undertook major reconstruction works without their landlord's consent and in express breach of covenant. The landlord served a Law of Property Act 1925, s. 146 (1) notice forfeiting the lease. Having failed to remedy the breach the landlords peaceably re-entered the vacant premises and changed the locks. Only later did the tenant apply for relief from forfeiture.

HELD: The tenants were too late to apply for relief.

LORD TEMPLEMAN: . . . When a tenant receives a section 146 notice he will not know whether the landlord can be persuaded that there is no breach or persuaded to accept in due course that any breach has been remedied and that he has been offered adequate and satisfactory compensation or whether the landlord will seek to determine the lease by issuing and serving a writ or will seek to determine the lease by re-entering the premises. The tenant will not wish to institute proceedings seeking relief from forfeiture if those proceedings will be aggressive and hostile and may be premature and unnecessary. Parliament cannot have intended that if the landlord employs the civilised method of determining the lease by issuing and serving a writ, then the tenant will be entitled to apply for relief, but if the landlord employs the dubious and dangerous method of determining the lease by re-entering the premises, then the tenant will be debarred from applying for relief. . . .

My Lords, I accept the conclusion that a landlord who serves a notice under section 146(1) can be said, for the purposes of section 146(2) to be proceeding to enforce his rights under the lease. A tenant authorised by section 146(2) to apply to the court for relief against forfeiture if he fails to comply with a section 146 notice may make that application after service of the notice for the purpose of elucidating the issues raised by the notice, ascertaining the intentions of the landlord, and setting in train the machinery by which the dispute between the landlord and the tenant can be determined by negotiation or by the court. But the fact that the tenant may apply to the court for relief after service of the section 146 notice does not mean that if he does not do so he loses the right conferred on him by section 146(2) to apply for relief if and when the landlord proceeds, not by action but 'otherwise' by exercising a right of re-entry. No absurdity follows from a construction which allows the tenant to apply for relief before and after a landlord re-enters without first obtaining a court order. . . .

The results of section 146 and the authorities are as follows. A tenant may apply for appropriate declarations and for relief from forfeiture under section 146(2) after the issue of a section 146 notice but he is not prejudiced if he does not do so. A tenant cannot apply for relief after a landlord has forfeited a lease by issuing and serving a writ, has recovered judgment and has entered into possession pursuant to that judgment. If the judgment is set aside or successfully appealed the tenant will be able to apply for relief in the landlord's action but the court in deciding whether to grant relief will take into account any consequences of the original order and repossession and the delay of the tenant. A tenant may apply for relief after a landlord has forfeited by re-entry without first obtaining a court order for that purpose but the court in deciding whether to grant relief will take into account all the circumstances, including delay, on the part of the tenant. Any past judicial observations which might suggest that a tenant is debarred from applying for relief after the landlord has re-entered without first obtaining a court order for that purpose are not to be so construed.

I would therefore allow the appeal and set aside the orders of the trial judge and the Court of Appeal.

20.2.2 FORFEITURE OF A LEASE OF A DWELLING HOUSE

PROTECTION FROM EVICTION ACT 1977

1.   Unlawful eviction and harassment of occupier
   (1)   In this section 'residential occupier', in relation to any premises, means a person occupying the premises as a residence, whether under a contract or by virtue of any enactment or rule of law giving him the right to remain in occupation or restricting the right of any other person to recover possession of the premises.
   (2)   If any person unlawfully deprives the residential occupier of any premises of his occupation of the premises or any part thereof, or attempts to do so, he shall be guilty of an offence unless he proves that he believed, and had reasonable cause to believe, that the residential occupier had ceased to reside in the premises.
   (3)   If any person with intent to cause the residential occupier of any premises—
      (a)   to give up the occupation of the premises or any part thereof; or
      (b)   to refrain from exercising any right or pursuing any remedy in respect of the premises or part thereof;
does acts [likely] to interfere with the peace or comfort of the residential occupier or members of his household, or persistently withdraws or withholds services reasonably required for the occupation of the premises as a residence, he shall be guilty of an offence.
   (3A)   Subject to subsection (3B) below, the landlord of a residential occupier or an agent of the landlord shall be guilty of an offence if—
      (a)   he does acts likely to interfere with the peace or comfort of the residential occupier or members of his household, or
      (b)   he persistently withdraws or withholds services reasonably required for the occupation of the premises in question as a residence,
and (in either case) he knows, or has reasonable cause to believe, that that conduct is likely to cause the residential occupier to give up the occupation of the whole or part of the

premises or to refrain from exercising any right or pursuing any remedy in respect of the whole or part of the premises.

(3B)   A person shall not be guilty of an offence under subsection (3A) above if he proves that he had reasonable grounds for doing the acts or withdrawing or withholding the services in question. . . .

2.   Restriction on re-entry without due process of law

Where any premises are let as a dwelling on a lease which is subject to a right of re-entry or forfeiture it shall not be lawful to enforce that right otherwise than by proceedings in the court while any person is lawfully residing in the premises or part of them.

HOUSING ACT 1988

27.   Damages for unlawful eviction

(1)   This section applies if, at any time after 9th June 1988, a landlord (in this section referred to as 'the landlord in default') or any person acting on behalf of the landlord in default unlawfully deprives the residential occupier of any premises of his occupation of the whole or part of the premises.

(2)   This section also applies if, at any time after 9th June 1988, a landlord (in this section referred to as 'the landlord in default') or any person acting on behalf of the landlord in default—

(a)   attempts unlawfully to deprive the residential occupier of any premises of his occupation of the whole or part of the premises, or

(b)   knowing or having reasonable cause to believe that the conduct is likely to cause the residential occupier of any premises—

(i)   to give up his occupation of the premises or any part thereof, or

(ii)   to refrain from exercising any right or pursuing any remedy in respect of the premises or any part thereof,

does acts likely to interfere with the peace or comfort of the residential occupier or members of his household, or persistently withdraws or withholds services reasonably required for the occupation of the premises as a residence, and, as a result, the residential occupier gives up his occupation of the premises as a residence.

(3)   Subject to the following provisions of this section, where this section applies, the landlord in default shall, by virtue of this section, be liable to pay to the former residential occupier, in respect of his loss of the right to occupy the premises in question as his residence, damages . . .

20.3   Waiver of Forfeiture

CENTRAL ESTATES (BELGRAVIA) LTD v WOOLGAR (No. 2)
[1972] 3 All ER 610, Court of Appeal

FACTS: Woolgar, an OAP and a First World War veteran, was tenant of a long lease (due to expire in 1993) of a sizeable house in central London. He had a fall from grace, and was convicted of using the premises as a (homosexual) brothel. In view of his past exemplary record he was granted a conditional discharge by the magistrates. The landlords, however, decided to forfeit the lease for breach of the covenant in the lease prohibiting illegal user, and served on Woolgar the warning notice required by section 146 of the Law of Property Act 1925. The landlords were anxious to forfeit the lease as the property would be much more valuable to them with 'vacant possession'. A minor official of the landlords then made a crucial mistake. He sent to Woolgar a rent demand for a future instalment of rent. HELD: The rent demand waived the breach, even though it had been sent out in error and Woolgar had not been in any way misled by the demand (even after the demand was sent he still personally believed that he was going to be evicted from the premises). The test of an 'unequivocal act' of waiver was what the 'reasonable onlooker' would think.

LORD DENNING MR: . . . The material question is whether the demand and acceptance of rent in September 1970 was a waiver of the forfeiture. If it was, the landlords were not entitled to issue this plaint for possession as they did in December 1970. The judge held there was not a waiver because, as he found, the tenant when he paid the rent knew full well that the landlords' intention to forfeit the lease remained unchanged.

The cases on waiver are collected in the notes to *Dumpor's Case* (1603) 4 Co Rep 119b in Smith's Leading Cases. Those notes show that the demand and acceptance of rent has a very different effect according to how the question arises. If it is sought to say there is *a new tenancy* by acceptance of rent; for instance, after a notice to quit has expired, the question always is, as Lord Mansfield said, '*quo animo* the rent was received, and what the real intention of both parties was': see *Doe d Cheny v Batten* (1775) 1 Cowp 243 and *Clarke v Grant* [1949] 1 All ER 768. But, if it is sought to say that an existing lease *continues in existence* by waiver of forfeiture, then the intention of the parties does not matter. It is sufficient if there is an unequivocal act done by the landlord which recognises the existence of the lease after having knowledge of the ground of forfeiture. The law was well stated by Parker J in *Matthews v Smallwood* [1910] 1 Ch 777, which was accepted by this court in *Oak Property Co. Ltd v Chapman* [1947] 2 All ER 1:

> It is also, I think, reasonably clear upon the cases that whether the act, coupled with the knowledge, constitutes a waiver is a question which the law decides, and therefore, it is not open to a lessor who has knowledge of the breach to say 'I will treat the tenancy as existing, and I will receive the rent, or I will take advantage of my power as landlord to distrain; but I tell you that all I shall do will be without prejudice to my right to re-enter, which I intend to reserve'. That is a position which he is not entitled to take up. If, knowing of the breach, he does distrain, or does receive the rent, then by law he waives the breach, and nothing which he can say by way of protest against the law will avail him anything.

. . . So we have simply to ask: was this rent demanded and accepted by the landlords' agents with knowledge of the breach? It does not matter that they did not intend to waive. The very fact that they accepted the rent with the knowledge constitutes the waiver. The position here is quite plain. The agents, who had full authority to manage these properties on behalf of the landlords, did demand and accept the rent with full knowledge. It may be that the instructions did not get down the chain of command from the partner to the subordinate clerk who issued the demands and gave the receipts for rent. That cannot affect, to my mind, the legal position. It comes within the general rule that the knowledge of the agent—and of his clerks—is the knowledge of the principal. A principal cannot escape the doctrine of waiver by saying that one clerk had the knowledge and the other received the rent. They must be regarded as one for this purpose. The landlords' agents knew the position and they accepted the rent with knowledge. That is a waiver. . . .

BLACKSTONES LTD v *BURNETTS* [1973] 3 All ER 782, Queen's Bench Division

FACTS: Burnetts had a lease from Blackstones of premises in central London. There was a qualified covenant against sub-letting. Burnetts got Blackstones' consent to sub-let to two people, A and D, trading in partnership. However, Burnetts actually sub-let to a different person, Flat Finders Ltd. (A and D were the directors of that company). The landlord's solicitors got to hear of what had happened. The solicitors seem to have been ignorant of the very basic principle of company law that a company is a separate person from its shareholders and directors. They sought counsel's opinion as to whether there had been a breach of the qualified covenant against sub-letting (clearly there had been such a breach). While this 'opinion' was awaited a clerk in the landlord's office sent out a rent demand for the next quarter's rent.
HELD: The rent demand had waived the breach of the qualified covenant against sub-letting.

SWANWICK J: . . . in forfeiture cases the consequences of an action relied on as a waiver are a matter of law and not of actual intention and that it is irrelevant *quo animo* such an act was done. It is also clear from the last mentioned case that a principal is affected by the knowledge of his agent and that he cannot escape the consequences of an act done by one agent by saying that it was not that agent but another that had the actual knowledge. . . .

The basic questions on this issue therefore are: (a) is a demand for future rent, if made with knowledge of a breach which entitles the landlord to forfeit, sufficient by itself to constitute an election to continue the lease and therefore a waiver? (b) If so, what knowledge is necessary and did Mr Fraser have it at the relevant time?

... My view, both on principle and on such persuasive authority as has been cited to me, is that an unambiguous demand for future rent in advance—such as was made here—does in law amount to an election and does constitute a waiver if, at the time it is made, the landlord has sufficient knowledge of the facts to put him to his election. To my perhaps simple mind there is a fundamental inconsistency between contending that a lease has been determined and demanding rent on the basis of its future continuance. ...

In my judgment, again without the guidance of any direct authority, the knowledge required to put a landlord to his election is knowledge of the basic facts that in law constitute a breach of covenant entitling him to forfeit the lease. Once he or his agent knows these facts, an appropriate act by himself or any agent will in law effect a waiver or a forfeiture. His knowledge or ignorance of the law is, in my judgment, irrelevant. If it were not so, a vast gap would be opened in the administration of the law of landlord and tenant, and a facile escape route for landlords would be provided. Indeed, if this were the position, unscrupulous landlords could hardly have failed in the past to take advantage of it long before now. ...

20.4   Relief from Forfeiture

LAW OF PROPERTY ACT 1925

146.   Restrictions on and relief against forfeiture of leases and underleases

(1)   A right of re-entry or forfeiture under any proviso or stipulation in a lease for a breach of any covenant or condition in the lease shall not be enforceable, by action or otherwise, unless and until the lessor serves on the lessee a notice—

(a)   specifying the particular breach complained of; and

(b)   if the breach is capable of remedy, requiring the lessee to remedy the breach; and

(c)   in any case, requiring the lessee to make compensation in money for the breach; and the lesee fails, within a reasonable time thereafter, to remedy the breach, if it is capable of remedy, and to make reasonable compensation in money, to the satisfaction of the lessor, for the breach.

(2)   Where a lessor is proceeding, by action or otherwise, to enforce such a right of re-entry or forfeiture, the lessee may, in the lessor's action, if any, or in any action brought by himself, apply to the court for relief; and the court may grant or refuse relief, as the court, having regard to the proceedings and conduct of the parties under the foregoing provisions of this section, and to all the other circumstances, thinks fit; and in case of relief may grant it on such terms; if any, as to costs, expenses, damages, compensation, penalty, or otherwise, including the granting of an injunction to restrain any like breach in the future, as the court, in the circumstances of each case, thinks fit.

(3)   A lessor shall be entitled to recover as a debt due to him from a lessee, and in addition to damages (if any), all reasonable costs and expenses properly incurred by the lessor in the employment of a solicitor and surveyor or valuer, or otherwise, in reference to any breach giving rise to a right of re-entry or forfeiture which, at the request of the lessee, is waived by the lessor, or from which the lessee is relieved, under the provisions of this Act.

(4)   Where a lessor is proceeding by action or otherwise to enforce a right of re-entry or forfeiture under any covenant, proviso, or stipulation in a lease, or for non-payment of rent, the court may, on application by any person claiming as under-lessee any estate or interest in the property comprised in the lease or any part thereof, either in the lessor's action (if any) or in any action brought by such person for that purpose, make an order vesting, for the whole term of the lease or any less term, the property comprised in the lease or any part thereof in any person entitled as under-lessee to any estate or interest in such property upon such conditions as to execution of any deed or other document, payment of rent, costs, expenses, damages, compensation, giving security, or otherwise, as the court in

the circumstances of each case may think fit, but in no case shall any such under-lessee be entitled to require a lease to be granted to him for any longer term than he had under his original sub-lease.

20.4.1   RELIEF FROM FORFEITURE FOR NON-PAYMENT OF RENT

BELGRAVIA INSURANCE CO. LTD v MEAH [1964] 1 QB 436, Court of Appeal

FACTS: The tenant in this case had fallen into arrears with rental payments, and did not resist an order forfeiting the lease and granting possession to the landlord. However, a mortgagee who had a mortgage of the tenant's interest applied to the court for relief from forfeiture of the lease. The mortgagee undertook to carry out outstanding repairs, and to pay arrears of rent.
HELD: Relief was granted.

LORD DENNING MR: . . . During the nineteenth century it was held (following Lord Eldon LC's views in *Hill* v *Barclay* (1810) 16 Ves 402), that the Court of Chancery had no jurisdiction to grant a lessee relief from forfeiture for any breaches except non-payment of rent. This was remedied in 1881 by section 14 of the Conveyancing Act 1881 (which did not apply to non-payment of rent). But that section did not apply to under-lessees. So Parliament enacted section 4 of the Conveyancing Act 1892, so as to include them. But this section was held to apply, not only to other breaches, but also to non-payment of rent: see *Gray* v *Bonsall* [1904] 1 KB 601. In 1925 the whole law, as so evolved, was consolidated in section 146 of the Law of Property Act 1925. Section 146(4) enabled the court to grant relief to an under-lessee, not only in case of other breaches but also non-payment of rent, on such conditions 'as the court in the circumstances of each case may think fit.' It seems to me that, in exercising this discretion, the court will, in the ordinary way, grant relief to an under-lessee on the terms of paying the rent in arrear, performing the covenants, and paying all the costs: see *Gray* v *Bonsall*, *per* Romer LJ. In short, on the same terms as the old Court of Chancery would have done. The only difference is that it is not necessary to make the lessee a party.

. . . In any case, whether under the old Chancery jurisdiction or under section 146(4) of the Law of Property Act 1925, it is clear that the court may always refuse relief, if the conduct of the applicant is such as to make it inequitable that relief should be given to him: see *Bowser* v *Colby* [1956] 2 QB 1, *per* Wigram V.-C., and *Gill* v *Lewis* (1841) 1 Hare 109, *per* Hodson LJ.

The master and the judge seem to have thought that this was such a case. The judge said that the applicant had a history which disentitled him to relief. I cannot share this view. The episode of the drains and of the proposed assignment was over four years ago and should no longer be held against him. The recent difficulties with the defendant, and the proposal about Noor, do not reflect adversely on the applicant, or at any rate not so adversely as to disentitle him to relief. It seems to me that if he is prepared to pay all the rent in arrear and all proper costs and to put the premises in repair to the satisfaction of a surveyor, he should be granted relief. . . .

SUPREME COURT ACT 1981

38.   Relief against forfeiture for non-payment of rent
   (1)   In any action in the High Court for the forfeiture of a lease for non-payment of rent, the court shall have power to grant relief against forfeiture in a summary manner, and may do so subject to the same terms and conditions as to the payment of rent, costs or otherwise as could have been imposed by it in such an action immediately before the commencement of this Act.
   (2)   Where the lessee or a person deriving title under him is granted relief under this section, he shall hold the demised premises in accordance with the terms of the lease without the necessity for a new lease.

20.4.2   FORFEITURE FOR BREACH OF COVENANT OTHER THAN RENT

20.4.2.1   Remediable or irremediable breaches?

EXPERT CLOTHING SERVICE AND SALES LTD v *HILLGATE HOUSE LTD AND ANOTHER* [1985] 2 All ER 998, Court of Appeal

FACTS: The tenant had breached a covenant to reconstruct the premises by an agreed date. The landlords served a notice under s. 146 Law of Property Act 1925 that the lease was forfeit due to an irremediable breach of covenant. The tenants claimed relief from forfeiture on the basis that the notice had been defective. They claimed that the breach was capable of remedy, and the notice had not given them an opportunity to effect that remedy.
HELD: The tenant was granted relief. The breach was 'remediable' by the tenant belatedly carrying out the works of reconstruction.

SLADE LJ: I would, for my part, accept the submission of counsel for the defendants that the breach of a positive covenant (whether it be a continuing breach or a once and for all breach) will ordinarily be capable of remedy. As Bristow J pointed out in the course of argument, the concept of capability of remedy for the purpose of s. 146 must surely be directed to the question whether the harm that has been done to the landlord by the relevant breach is for practical purposes capable of being retrieved. In the ordinary case, the breach of a promise to do something by a certain time can for practical purposes be remedied by the thing being done, even out of time. For these reasons I reject the plaintiffs' argument that the breach of the covenant to reconstruct by 28 September 1982 was not capable of remedy *merely* because it was not a continuing breach.

I would add this point. If this breach was, on these grounds alone, not capable of remedy, the very same grounds would appear to render the breach of the lessees' covenant to give notice of the charge in favour of Lloyds Bank likewise incapable of remedy. But counsel for the plaintiffs has not attempted to maintain the latter proposition, which would have been very difficult to sustain having regard to what one may suppose was the intention of the legislature in enacting s. 146(1).

As his second main line of argument in this context, he submitted that the breach of the covenant to reconstruct was not capable of remedy because of the operation of the new rent review provisions incorporated in the lease by the schedule to the order of 29 June 1981. He pointed out that under these provisions the landlords, on a rent review, would have an option which they would clearly wish to exercise, to review the rent on the basis of the premises as reconstructed. He submitted that there was no ready way in which the plaintiffs could be effectively restored to the same position under the rent review clause as that in which they would have found themselves if the premises had been reconstructed by the due date.

Respectfully differing from the judge on this point, I do not think that this submission is well founded. When the rent review clause comes to be applied, the defendants cannot rely on their own wrong (consisting of the failure to reconstruct) to reduce the rent which would otherwise have been payable as from the review date. The proper approach must be to asume for the purpose of the assessment that the required reconstruction has taken place. As counsel for the defendants pointed out, surveyors are quite accustomed to this kind of artificial assumption in rent review valuations. With the appropriate expert advice there would be little difficulty in ascertaining the rent to which the plaintiffs would have been entitled on the first rent review, and indeed on any subsequent rent review, if the defendants had complied with their building obligations in due time. While counsel for the plaintiffs pointed out that, if this had been done, the premises might have been sublet by the rent review date and this would itself have facilitated the ascertainment of a fair rack market annual rental value, there is no certainty whatever that any such subletting would have taken place. In the context of the rent review clause, any damage resulting from the relevant breach of covenant was, in my opinion, capable of being remedied simply by the payment by the defendants of an appropriate sum of money.

SCALA HOUSE AND DISTRICT PROPERTY CO. LTD v FORBES
[1973] 3 All ER 308, Court of Appeal

FACTS: A tenant broke a covenant against sub-letting and the landlord gave notice forfeiting the lease. The tenant applied for relief from forfeiture.
HELD: The breach was a once-and-for-all breach, it was incapable of remedy. Relief was refused.

RUSSELL LJ: . . . So the first question is whether a breach of covenant such as is involved in the present case is capable of remedy. If it is capable of remedy, and is remedied in reasonable time, the lessor is unable to prove that a condition precedent to his ability to seek to forfeit by action or otherwise has been fulfilled. Here at once is a problem. An unlawful subletting is a breach once and for all. The subterm has been created.
. . . breach by an unlawful subletting is not capable of remedy at all. In my judgment the introduction of such breaches into the relevant section for the first time by s. 146 of the 1925 Act operates only to confer a statutory ability to relieve the lessee from forfeiture on that ground. The subterm has been effectively created subject only to risks of forfeiture; it is a complete breach once for all; it is not in any sense a continuing breach. If the law were otherwise a lessee, when a subtenancy is current at the time of the s. 146 notice, would have a chance of remedying the situation without having to apply for relief. But if the unlawful subletting had determined before the notice, the lessee could only seek relief from forfeiture. The only escape from that wholly unsatisfactory difference would be to hold that in the second example by some analogy the lessor was disabled from issuing a writ for possession. But I can find nothing in the section to justify that limitation on the common law right of re-entry, bearing especially in mind that a lessor might discover a whole series of past expired unlawful subletting which might well justify a refusal to grant relief in forfeiture proceedings.
I stress again that where there has been an unlawful subletting which has determined (and which has not been waived) there has been a breach which at common law entitles the lessor to re-enter; nothing can be done to remedy that breach; the expiry of the subterm has not annulled or remedied the breach; in such case the lessor plainly need not, in his s. 146 notice, call on the lessee to remedy the breach which is not capable of remedy, and is free to issue his writ for possession, the possibility of relief remaining. . . .

GLASS v KENCAKES LTD AND OTHERS [1964] 3 All ER 807, Queen's Bench Division

FACTS: The tenant of a lease containing a covenant against illegal/immoral user sub-let to a sub-tenant who used the premises for the purpose of prostitution. The original tenant was not aware of the breach. When the landlord became aware of the immoral user he served a notice under s. 146 of the Law of Property Act alleging that the lease was forfeit because of an irremediable breach of covenant. The tenant, in turn, served a notice to the same effect on the sub-tenant.
HELD: The tenant was granted relief from forfeiture, but the sub-lease was declared forfeit. The judge held that the tenant had remedied his (arguably technical) breach of the head lease by evicting the sub-tenant before the property became tainted with a stigma.

PAULL J: As I see it, the result of the agreement between counsel is that cl. (2) must be taken to read:

> The above-mentioned covenants have been broken and the particular breach complained of is that the first and third floors of the said premises have been used [as] other than residential flats in that they have been used for a business purpose, that is for the purpose of prostitution, an immoral business.

It is this breach which is said to be incapable of remedy. On the strict wording of the notice clearly the plaintiff fails. That is agreed by counsel for the plaintiff. What follows in this judgment therefore must be read as based on a notice stating the words which I have set out. . . .

The question before me therefore resolves itself into a question which can be simply stated, but which I have found very difficult to decide. I would state it in these words: Where the covenant, the breach of which is complained of, is a covenant that premises shall only be used in a certain manner and that covenant is broken by a sub-tenant of the lessee, is it capable of remedy by the lessee where the user which constitutes the breach is in fact an immoral user but where the lessee does not know that there is any such or any breach and the circumstances are such that the lessee has no reason to suppose that any, and in particular any such, breach has been or is being committed by the sub-tenant? If the position is that in some circumstances such a breach is capable of remedy and in some circumstances not, is the breach in this case capable of remedy?

. . . I think that the following propositions may be stated: (i) The mere fact that the breach complained of is a breach of user by a sub-tenant contrary to a covenant in the lease does not render the breach incapable of remedy. If one of the tenants of these flats in Queensway had, unknown to the defendants, carried on a small business of dressmaking in the flats, I would hold without hesitation that the breach was capable of remedy so far as the defendants are concerned, but it may be that the remedy would have to consist not only of stopping the tenants from carrying on that business but of bringing an action for forfeiture—it being then left to the court to decide whether the particular tenants should be granted relief. (ii) The fact that the business user involves immorality does not in itself render the breach incapable of remedy provided that the lessees neither knew nor had any reason to know of the fact that the flat was being so used. The remedy in such a case, however, must involve not only that immediate steps are taken to stop such a user so soon as the user is known, but that an action for a claim for forfeiture of the sub-tenant's lease must be started within a reasonable time. If therefore the lessee has known of such a breach for a reasonable time before the notice is served, the breach is incapable of remedy unless such steps have been taken. (iii) It does not follow that such a breach is always capable of remedy. All the circumstances must be taken into consideration. For example, if the notice is not the first notice which has had to be served, or if there are particularly revolting circumstances attaching to the user, or great publicity, then it might well be that the slate could not be wiped clean, or, to use another phrase, the damage to the property might be so great as to render the breach incapable of remedy.

At first sight propositions (ii) and (iii) would seem to put the landlord in great difficulties as to the form of his notice, since a mistake would be fatal. However, Harman J, in *Hoffman's case* [*Hoffman* v *Fineberg* [1948] 1 All ER 592] said that a form calling on the tenants to remedy the breach and adding the words 'if it is capable of remedy' probably is a good notice, and I would go further and say that I can see no reason why it should not be a good notice. If such a notice is served then the landlord, having allowed a reasonable time to elapse, can bring his action claiming (a) that the breach is incapable of remedy, or (b) if it is capable of remedy that it has not been remedied, and (c) in any event asking that the court should not permit the lease to continue.

After some hesitation, in my judgment the breach in this case is capable of remedy, and indeed was remedied within a reasonable time. . . .

20.4.3   RELIEF TO SUB-TENANTS

CHATHAM EMPIRE THEATRE (1955) LTD v ULTRANS LTD AND OTHERS
[1961] 2 All ER 381, Queen's Bench Division

FACTS: A head lease had been granted by the plaintiff to the first defendant's predecessor in title. The premises subject to the head lease included a theatre, a cinema, a car park and a restaurant. The first defendant sub-let the cinema, car park and restaurant to other parties but retained possession of the theatre. The defendant company failed to pay the rent due under the head-lease and ultimately went insolvent. The plaintiff served a forfeiture notice on the first defendant company. The sub-tenants of the cinema applied for relief from forfeiture. Against the sub-tenant's application the plaintiff argued that relief should not be granted unless the sub-tenants were prepared to pay the full arrears of rent due under the head-lease.

HELD: The sub-tenants were entitled to relief from forfeiture.

SALMON J: . . . It seems to me quite plain that s. 146(4) LPA 1925 confers on the court the widest discretion as to the terms on which relief should be granted. Counsel for the defendants contends that the defendants should be required to pay only £195 per quarter for the three relevant quarters, that is to say, £585. The defendants had, of course, paid this sum to Ultrans, Ltd., who have not paid it to the plaintiffs. Counsel says that the defendants ought only to pay that part of the arrears attributable to their property, the property which was sub-let to them. Counsel for the plaintiffs says that the whole of the arrears in respect of the whole property in the head lease ought to be paid by the defendants. That really is the chief issue between the parties.

In my judgment it is clearly equitable that the landlord should be put in the same position as he was in before the forfeiture *qua* that part of the property, namely, the cinema, let to the defendants. In my judgment the defendants ought to be required as a condition of obtaining relief, to pay £585 plus an element for the premium and not the whole of the £2,730. One can envisage a case in which a block of property comprising a large number of shops and other premises is let to one corporation for £30,000 a year. The corporation then sub-lets the separate shops to various small shopkeepers at perhaps £300 a year each. After some time the corporation goes into liquidation owing perhaps half a year's rent. It is quite plain that the legislature gives the right to the small shopkeeper to come and ask for relief. If counsel for the plaintiffs' contention is correct, the apparently wide discretion conferred by s. 146(4) is so limited that the court could not give relief to the small shopkeeper unless he paid the £15,000 rent in arrear in respect of the whole block. It is suggested that that would not work any hardship because he could recoup himself from the corporation. That does not really commend itself to me as a practical argument because, in the first place, he will not be able to find the £15,000, and in any event the insolvent corporation could not pay. I cannot believe that in circumstances such as those the court's discretion is fettered as contended on behalf of the plaintiffs. I should have thought that if the shopkeeper paid his proportion of the arrears, namely, £150, and it was otherwise just and equitable that there should be relief, he should obtain relief on that basis. I can certainly conceive of cases where it would be quite wrong to give a sub-lessee relief on this basis; great hardship could be caused to the head lessor if granting relief to one or two of many sub-tenants would make it impossible for him to deal with the premises as a whole. Every case must be considered on its own facts. . . .

20.5   Leasehold Property (Repairs) Act 1938

LEASEHOLD PROPERTY (REPAIRS) ACT 1938

1.   Restriction on enforcement of repairing covenants in long leases of small houses

(1)   Where a lessor serves on a lessee under subsection (1) of section one hundred and forty-six of the Law of Property Act 1925, a notice that relates to a breach of a covenant or agreement to keep or put in repair during the currency of the lease all or any of the property comprised in the lease, and at the date of the service of the notice three years or more of the term of the lease remain unexpired, the lessee may within twenty-eight days from that date serve on the lessor a counter-notice to the effect that he claims the benefit of this Act.

(2)   A right to damages for a breach of such a covenant as aforesaid shall not be enforceable by action commenced at any time at which three years or more of the term of the lease remain unexpired unless the lessor has served on the lessee not less than one month before the commencement of the action such a notice as is specified in subsection (1) of section one hundred and forty-six of the Law of Property Act 1925, and where a notice is served under this subsection, the lessee may, within twenty-eight days from the date of the service thereof, serve on the lessor a counter-notice to the effect that he claims the benefit of this Act.

(3)   Where a counter-notice is served by a lessee under this section, then, notwithstanding anything in any enactment or rule of law, no proceedings, by action or otherwise, shall be taken by the lessor for the enforcement of any right of re-entry or forfeiture under any proviso or stipulation in the lease for breach of the covenant or agreement in question, or for damages for breach thereof, otherwise than with the leave of the court.

(4)   A notice served under subsection (1) of section one hundred and forty-six of the Law of Property Act 1925, in the circumstances specified in subsection (1) of this section, and a notice served under subsection (2) of this section shall not be valid unless it contains a statement, in characters not less conspicuous than those used in any other part of the notice, to the effect that the lessee is entitled under this Act to serve on the lessor a counter-notice claiming the benefit of this Act, and a statement in the like characters specifying the time within which, and the manner in which, under this Act a counter-notice may be served and specifying the name and address for service of the lessor.

(5)   Leave for the purposes of this section shall not be given unless the lessor proves—

(a)   that the immediate remedying of the breach in question is requisite for preventing substantial diminution in the value of his reversion, or that the value thereof has been substantially diminished by the breach;

(b)   that the immediate remedying of the breach is required for giving effect in relation to the premises to the purposes of any enactment, or of any byelaw or other provision having effect under an enactment, or for giving effect to any order of a court or requirement of any authority under any enactment or any such byelaw or other provision as aforesaid;

(c)   in a case in which the lessee is not in occupation of the whole of the premises as respects which the covenant or agreement is proposed to be enforced, that the immediate remedying of the breach is required in the interests of the occupier of those premises or of part thereof;

(d)   that the breach can be immediately remedied at an expense that is relatively small in comparison with the much greater expense that would probably be occasioned by postponement of the necessary work; or

(e)   special circumstances which in the opinion of the court, render it just and equitable that leave should be given.

(6)   The court may, in granting or in refusing leave for the purposes of this section, impose such terms and conditions on the lessor or on the lessee as it may think fit.

ASSOCIATED BRITISH PORTS v *CH BAILEY PLC* [1990] 1 All ER 929, House of Lords

FACTS: Landlords of a dry-dock which had fallen into disuse served a forfeiture notice (under s. 146 of the Law of Property Act 1925) on the tenant, alleging breaches of their repairing covenant which would cost £600,000 to remedy. The tenants served a counter notice under the Leasehold Property (Repairs) Act 1938. The landlords brought proceedings for forfeiture, claiming that the continued disrepair of the premises would cause a substantial diminution of the value of the reversion. A master, a judge and then the Court of Appeal all confirmed that the landlord should succeed. The tenant appealed to the House of Lords.

HELD: The tenant's appeal was allowed. The landlord had to prove on the balance of probabilities that forfeiture was necessary to prevent a diminution of the value of the reversion. The landlord in this case had merely shown an arguable case.

LORD TEMPLEMAN: . . . save in special circumstances, the landlord must prove that the immediate remedying of a breach of the repairing covenant is required in order to save the landlord of the LP(R)A 1938 from substantial loss or damage which the landlord would otherwise sustain. By s. 1(6) the court can specify action to be taken by the tenant or impose other conditions in granting or withholding leave for the landlord to sue for forfeiture or damages.

In *National Real Estate and Finance Co. Ltd* v *Hassan* [1939] 2 KB 61 at 78, cf [1939] 2 All ER 154 at 161 Goddard LJ said that the mischief that the 1938 Act was designed to remedy—

was speculators buying up small property in an indifferent state of repair, and then serving a schedule of dilapidations upon the tenants, which the tenants cannot comply with . . . this is the general mischief, that the speculator buys at a very low price, turns out the tenants, and gets the reversion which he has never paid for, which is a great hardship to the tenants.

Parliament must have concluded that similar mischief was caused to tenants of all properties because, by s. 51(3) of the Landlord and Tenant Act 1954, leases of all properties, except agricultural property, become subject to the 1938 Act. In the present case the landlords are not speculators or purchasers but have served a notice of dilapidation which can only be complied with by expenditure exceeding £600,000 which, according to the tenants, will be useless expenditure to the tenants and of minimal value to the landlords. If the landlords are allowed to pursue their remedies, the landlords may be able to recover the demised premises in the year 1990 instead of the year 2049.

Section 1 of the 1938 Act prevents the landlord from bringing proceedings for forfeiture and damages 'otherwise than with the leave of the court'. The immunity from suit thus conferred on the tenants is absolute unless the landlords prove that at least one of the requirements imposed by paras (a) to (e) of s. 1(5) is satisfied. The landlords have only established a prima facie or arguable case. The landlords have not proved in accordance with the balance of probabilities in the light of the evidence adduced by both the landlords and the tenants that the immediate remedying of the tenants' breach of their repairing covenant is requisite for preventing substantial diminution in the value of the landlords' reversion or that the breach has substantially diminished that value. The landlords submit that they need only establish a prima facie or arguable case and must then, on the true construction of the 1938 Act, be granted leave to institute proceedings for forfeiture and damages. In the course of those proceedings the tenants may seek to satisfy the court that they should be granted relief from forfeiture for their admitted breaches of covenant on the ground that the immediate remedying of the tenants' breaches of covenant is not required for the protection of the landlords. It is said, on behalf of the landlords, that the authorities and the practice of the courts support the view that in an application under s. 1 of the 1938 Act, the landlords are entitled to leave to pursue their remedies if they adduce evidence which consists of material on which, if it were accepted as accurate, an arguable case can be put forward. The justification for this course is said to be the avoidance of duplication and the saving of time and expense. If the landlords and the tenants produce their best evidence and the landlords prove the need for immediate remedying of breaches of covenant as required by the 1938 Act, the same or better evidence must be rehearsed in the ensuing action for forfeiture if the tenants resist forfeiture or seek relief from forfeiture. . .

SEDAC INVESTMENTS LTD v TANNER AND OTHERS [1982] 3 All ER 646, Chancery Division

FACTS: A local Conservative Club had convenanted to carry out repairs of the premises of which they were tenant, but had allowed the building to fall into a dangerous state of disrepair. The landlords (under pressure from the local authority) carried out the repairs themselves. The landlords then served a forfeiture notice under s. 146 of the Law of Property Act 1925 on the tenant. The tenant argued that the notice had been invalid for the purposes of s. 1 of the Leasehold Property (Repairs) Act 1938.
HELD: The tenant was granted relief from forfeiture. The s. 146 notice had not been validly served. It should have been served before the repairs were remedied.

MICHAEL WHEELER QC: . . . I am forced to the conclusion that in a case such as the present, where the lessor remedied the breach before attempting to serve a notice under s. 146(1), he has thereby put it out of his power to serve a valid s. 146 notice at all, with the result that he has deprived the lessee of his right to serve a counter-notice, and the consequence of this seems inevitably to be that the court has no jurisdiction to give the lessor leave to commence proceedings for damages because that jurisdiction arises, as I have already indicated, only where (and because) the lessee has served a valid counter-notice.

It is also true, as was pointed out in argument, that in the present case the lessors might have protected their position in other ways. For example, (1) they might have invoked cl. 2(4) of the lease and called on the lessees to remedy the breach; and they could have reinforced this by seeking, or threatening to seek, a mandatory injunction on the lessees to undertake the necessary remedial work; alternatively, (2) they might have served a notice under s. 146(1) (however general and imprecise the terms of that notice might, in the circumstances, have had to be) and might have also stated that in view of the urgency they regarded it as essential (and, ex hypothesi, as reasonable) that the lessees should at least commence to remedy the breach within, say, 48 hours.

As to these alternatives, they must, if they are valid, apply to any similar situation whether more or less urgent than in the present case. Suffice it to say that I do not consider either of them to be of any practical value in a case of real emergency.

In the present case, the basic trouble has arisen partly from the urgency of the repairs which were undoubtedly required (Mr. Laker's evidence on this score is uncontroverted and is accepted as correct by counsel for the lessees) and partly from the fact that at the time when the damage to the wall was first noticed neither side (and I state this as a fact rather than as a criticism) was apparently aware of their respective legal rights and obligations. The lessees were unaware of the nature and extent of their liabilities under the repairing covenant in the lease; and the lessors were unaware of their rights under cl. 2(4) of the lease.

So it was that when the emergency arose (an emergency which the lessees themselves first brought to the attention of the lessors) it was the latter who (rightly as the factual position was to prove) took immediate emergency action. True it is that they did so really on their own initiative and without, as their counsel accepted, first giving the lessees the opportunity to take remedial action themselves. But the fact remains that the emergency basically arose as a result of the lessees' failure to comply with their obligations under the repairing covenant in the lease.

Nevertheless, for the reasons which I have given, I feel bound to conclude that in the present case the lessees are correct in arguing that the purported s. 146 notice given by the lessors did not (and on the facts could not) comply with the requirements of s. 1(2) of the 1938 Act and accordingly that I have no jurisdiction to give leave to the lessors as contemplated by that section to take proceedings to enforce their claim for damages for breach of the repairing covenant. But, in case this matter should go further, I wish to make it clear that, if I felt that as a matter of law I had such jurisdiction, I would, on the facts of this case, unhesitatingly exercise my judicial discretion in favour of the plaintiff lessors. . . .

20.6   Reform of Forfeiture of Leases

Clarke, A., Property Law (1992) 45 *Current Legal Problems* 81 at 104

. . . Forfeiture displays the best and worst features of a self-help remedy. When exercised extra-judicially it is fast and effective remedy for breach, and it is sufficiently drastic in effect to deter breaches. In fact it has been so successful in this jurisdiction that it has developed at the expense of doctrines of repudiatory breach and frustration. On the other hand, its bad features are, first, that it affects the interests of third parties, who may have had no knowledge of the breach and no means of preventing it, and secondly that its effect between the parties bears no relation to the effect of the breach: it can inflict loss on the tenant quite disproportionate to the blameworthiness of the breach, and it can produce a windfall profit for the landlord. *Cardigan Properties Ltd* v *Consolidated Property Investments Ltd* [1991] 7 EG 132 provides a good illustration. The freeholder had granted a 999-year lease of a residential block at a peppercorn rent for a premium of £770,000. Twelve years later the lease was assigned to the present tenant for £6,829,000, who bought it with the aid of a loan secured by a mortgage of the lease. In circumstances which were only marginally the fault of the tenant and created no real risk to the freeholder, the freeholder sought to forfeit by actual re-entry on the grounds of breach of the tenant's covenant to insure. In fact the court found that the re-entry was premature (insufficient time had been given for the remedy of the breach): had the court not done so it would, in the present state of the law, have been powerless to prevent the freeholder obtaining a windfall worth over £6,000,000 at the expense of the tenant and its wholly blameless mortgagee.

Unsurprisingly, given its potential for producing such dramatic results, both equity and statute have from an early stage intervened to regulate the exercise of the right to forfeit. Equity intervened as part of its general jurisdiction to grant relief against penalties, forfeiture of property, and unconscionable insistence on legal rights. The first statutory intervention was in fact made to regulate the equitable jurisdiction to grant relief against forfeiture for non-payment of rent: the Landlord and Tenant Act 1730, passed to relieve landlords who had been adversely affected by the courts of equity granting relief from forfeiture for non-payment of rent long after the lease had been forfeited at law, effectively barred a tenant from relief unless application was made within six months after the landlord obtained judgment. Later statutes introduced more positive but piecemeal regulation of forfeiture, which developed parallel to, or more accurately, entwined with, developments in the equitable jurisdiction.

The present interplay between equity and the complicated network of statute in this area is difficult to follow, and a matter of current controversy. In particular, there are two complicating factors. The first is that forfeiture for non-payment of rent has developed separately from forfeiture for breach of other covenants. The second is that most of the statutory provisions deal with forfeiture and relief as procedural rather than substantive matters: as a consequence, some (whether deliberately or accidentally) deal only with court proceedings for forfeiture, making no provision for forfeiture by actual re-entry, and others deal only with county court, or only with High Court, proceedings.

For present purposes, the essential problem is this. Both equity and statute—sometimes pulling together and at other times working against each other—have sought to ensure that forfeiture is used only as security for the performance of the obligations under the lease, by allowing the tenant, and any subtenant or mortgagee of the tenant's interest, relief against the forfeiture in all appropriate cases. But given the piecemeal development of the equitable and statutory jurisdictions, it is not surprising that there are gaps in the protection. The gap currently being exploited by landlords is that in the case of a breach of covenant other than to pay rent, the court appears to have no jurisdiction to grant relief against forfeiture to a tenant, subtenant, or mortgagee once the forfeiture is completed: since forfeiture by actual re-entry is completed as soon as the landlord enters, and no notice of re-entry is required, the opportunity to apply for relief can be removed by stealth. . . .

The Law Commission (Law Com. No. 142) Codification of the Law of Landlord and Tenant: Forfeiture of Tenancies, London: HMSO, 21 March 1985

SUMMARY OF RECOMMENDATIONS

(1)   The law of forfeiture has become unnecessarily complicated, is no longer coherent and gives rise to injustices. The report recommends its replacement by a new system. In cases where the fault is that of the landlord, the tenant now has no means of terminating the tenancy. The report recommends that he should have a right to do so which is broadly analogous to that of the landlord under the new system. . . .

THE DETAILS OF THE TERMINATION ORDER SCHEMES PROPOSED

(6)   The scheme is based upon a system under which there would be no distinction between termination for non-payment of rent and termination for other reasons and under which the tenancy would continue in full force until the court made an order—a 'termination order'—determining the date on which it should end. . . .

GROUNDS FOR A TERMINATION ORDER: 'TERMINATION ORDER EVENTS'

(10)   Grounds on which the landlord may base an application for a termination order may conveniently be called 'termination order events'. They should be of three kinds. . . .

(a)   **Breaches of covenant**

(11)   All breaches of covenant by the tenant should be termination order events. We use the word 'covenant' in the wide sense, to include all the obligations owed by tenant to landlord, whether they are expressly undertaken or implied at common law or by statute. . . .

(12)   Although under the present law breaches of covenant are grounds for forfeiture only if they are expressly made so by the inclusion in the tenancy of a 'forfeiture clause', no such special provision should be necessary to make them termination order events. But:

(a)   This should not apply to tenancies granted before the date on which the implementing legislation comes into force: in such tenancies a breach of covenant should be a termination order event only if covered by a forfeiture clause.

(b)   If a tenancy, though granted after that date, is granted in pursuance of a binding obligation in existence before that date, and the obligation was such that a forfeiture clause was not to be included (or was not to be included in relation to some of the tenant's covenants) then the obligation should be interpreted as requiring the inclusion of an express term excluding the termination order scheme in relation to the tenant's covenants (or some of them as the case may be). . . .

(13)   Where an obligation entered into before the date on which the implementing legislation comes into force was such that a forfeiture clause *was* to be included in a tenancy granted after that date, that requirement should be treated as fulfilled if the tenancy maintains silence on the point, so allowing breaches of covenant to be termination order events. . . .

(b)   **Disguised breaches of covenant**

(14)   Termination order events should also include all events on the happening of which the tenancy (whether through the inclusion of a condition or limitation or for any other reason) is to cease (whether immediately or after a period) or the landlord is to have the right (whether or not on notice) to apply for a termination order, to forfeit the tenancy or to bring it to an end in any other way or to require its surrender or its assignment to a person nominated or to be nominated by him—being events against which a landlord would be expected to protect himself (if he protected himself at all) through the imposition of a covenant upon the tenant. . . .

(c)   **Insolvency events**

(15)   Termination order events should also include all events on the happening of which the tenancy (whether through the inclusion of a condition, limitation or for any other reason) is to cease (whether immediately or after a period) or the landlord is to have the right (whether or not on notice) to apply for a termination order, to forfeit the tenancy or bring it to an end in any other way, or to require its surrender or its assignment to a person nominated or to be nominated by him—being events having to do with the actual or threatened bankruptcy or insolvency of the tenant or any surety and including (but without prejudice to the generality of the foregoing words):

bankruptcy of, or the commission of any act of bankruptcy by, or the making of a receiving order against, a tenant or surety who is an individual;

entering into liquidation, compulsory or voluntary, by any tenant or surety which is a company, or having a receiver appointed in respect of any of its assets;

a tenant or surety entering into any arrangement or composition for the benefit of creditors; or

a tenant suffering the tenancy to be taken in execution; or a tenant or surety suffering any distress or execution to be levied on goods. . . .

PART VI WAIVER

(21)   The law which now governs the circumstances in which a landlord is debarred by waiver from forfeiting a tenancy on a particular ground is unsatisfactory. A termination order event should be regarded as waived if, and only if, the landlord's conduct, after he has knowledge of the event, is such that it would lead a reasonable tenant to believe, and does in fact lead the actual tenant to believe, that he will not seek a termination order on the ground of that event. . . .

(22)   And if the event is a continuing breach of covenant, it should be a question of fact whether and how far the landlord has led the tenant reasonably to believe that he has waived it for the future as well as for the past. . . .

(23)   It should be possible, according to analogous rules, for the landlord to grant a waiver which is conditional upon some action on the part of the tenant. . . .

(24)   A termination order event should generally remain available as a ground for a termination order despite the fact that its consequences may have been remedied. . . .

Wilkinson, H. W., The Rush to Simplification (1994) Conv 177

Termination of Tenancies Bill

The Law Commission seems to have taken an objection to all that beautiful and involved learning which has for so long been a delight to the industrious student. Once more it has produced proposals for 'simplifying' the law, heedless of the wise maxim derived from our transatlantic cousins, 'if it ain't real broke, don't fix it.'. . .

Outline of the Scheme

The Law Commission outlines its proposed new scheme as follows. A landlord will no longer be able to forfeit a lease for breach of covenant or insolvency, or for failure to fulfill a condition. He will instead have the right to bring termination order proceedings to end the lease. A proviso for re-entry or other such provision would not be needed in the lease, but the right to bring termination proceedings could be excluded (or presumably restricted) by an express term. The tenancy will continue until a court orders that it should end. The court order could be of two types, the first that it will end on a stated day, the other that it will end if the tenant has not taken specified remedial action within a stated period. Any derivative interests will come to an end unless the landlord or the owner of the derivative interest makes an appropriate application to the court and an order in his favour is made. A Termination of Tenancies Bill is included in the report.

The Bill and Notes
By clause 1 and 2, the landlord's power to determine a tenancy by re-entry or forfeiture is abolished and the only way in which termination may be procured is by a termination order event taking place and a court then making a termination order. Exceptions would be where the landlord believes and has reasonable cause to believe that the tenant has abandoned the whole of the property and one or more termination order events has taken place. The landlord must serve a notice on the tenant and if no counter-notice is received the tenancy will end six months later. In the meantime the landlord will be able to enter and 'take such steps as are immediately necessary for securing the property and preserving it from damage.' The explanatory note says that entering the property to secure it would not terminate the tenancy but would absolve the landlord from any liability for trespass. By clause 40(2) guidance is given as to the meaning of 'abandonment'; it has both a physical and a mental element ('is not occupying it' and 'has no intention of occupying it'). Conviction for knowingly using premises as a brothel, under the Sexual Offences Act 1956, is a ground for the landlord to require assignment of the lease to someone else, or termination in a case of non-compliance.

By clause 5, a breach of any of the tenant's obligations (meaning by clause 47(1) created by covenant and owed by the tenant to the landlord in his capacity as landlord) is a termination order event, whether an act or an omission, repudiatory or not. Now, here is the earth-shaking change. By clause 5(3) a breach of the tenant's obligation to pay rent becomes a termination order event 'without a formal demand having been made,' but there is to be a period of 21 days' grace (or such other period as is stipulated) after the date the rent is overdue for payment to be made. Some leases are so framed that they may be terminated by the landlord where an event occurs which does not arise from the act or omission of the tenant 'neutral events.' Examples are given of the grant of planning permission or the bankruptcy of a surety. By clause 39, in such cases, the landlord may determine the tenancy by giving not less than one month's notice from the date of the notice. He must give the notice not later than six months after the event came to his knowledge and he must not have waived compliance.

By clause 4 the court could make a termination order or a remedial order. Under the latter, by clauses 8 and 9 it could order a payment to the landlord, the discontinuance of a breach and the obtaining of a surety.

The Law Commission considered that the present law on waiver of breaches was too technical and that waiver was too easy to make inadvertently, such as by demanding rent through an employee of an estate agent when instructions had been given not to do so. By clause 11(1) the rule is proposed to be that a landlord may choose to waive but is only to be held to do so against his will if,

> (a) his conduct, after it came to the knowledge of the tenant, would have led a reasonable tenant to believe and in fact led the tenant to believe, that the landlord would not seek to rely on it, or;
> (b) in the case of non-compliance with a condition, that the landlord's conduct, after it came to the tenant's knowledge, would have led a reasonable tenant to believe, and did in fact lead the tenant to believe, that the landlord would not seek to rely on the breach if the condition were fulfilled and the condition was in fact fulfilled. Thus this particular breach of obligation would not remain a ground for termination after it had been remedied.

By clause 13 and 14 there are three cases in which the court will have a duty to make an absolute termination order. The first is where it is satisfied that a termination event of a serious character has occurred whilst the tenant has held the tenancy or that terminating events have been frequent during that time (even if not acted on by the landlord) and in addition it appears to the court that the tenant is therefore such an unsatisfactory tenant that he ought not to remain tenant. The purpose of this is to deal with the 'stigma' cases but to decide each on its merits. The second case is where the tenancy has been assigned to forestall the risk of an absolute order under the first provision and where in addition it appears to the court that there is a substantial risk of the continuance of the termination events (this is to prevent profitable continued misuse of the property). The third case is where there has been an assignment in breach of the tenant's obligations or an insolvency event (defined in clause 47(2)) has occurred and the court is satisfied that a remedial order will not provide an adequate remedy. . . .

The new proposals affect all types of lease, residential, agricultural and business but they do not override any special protection given by statute to various classes of tenant, such as under the Landlord and Tenant Act 1954 for business tenants.

Ah well, those who think that the law of forfeiture produces 'needless complication' may yet have their way. Next they will wish to simplify the rules of chess.

20.7 End of Chapter Assessment Question

In 1982 Letitia leased (by deed) a shop to Tamsin for 40 years. The lease includes a covenant under which the tenant undertakes to ensure that the shop is not used for illegal purposes. Rent is payable quarterly and in advance to Letitia's agent Rocky. The lease also includes a forfeiture clause which can be invoked if the tenant breaks any of the covenants.

In 1994 Tamsin lawfully assigned the lease to Ann. In early 1995 Dandy, one of Ann's shop assistants, took advantage of the fact that Ann did not normally arrive at the shop until 9.30 a.m. He started an early morning 'side-line' selling Cocaine. After only a month Ann found out about the illegal trade. She immediately dismissed Dandy and reported his activities to the police. Last week Dandy was convicted of drug-trafficking.

Letitia has just read of Dandy's conviction in the local newspaper. She has decided to endeavour to forfeit the lease. She tells you, 'The rent under the existing lease is ridiculously low; if I can get Ann out a new tenant would be willing to pay three times as much'.

Advise Letitia.

20.8 End of Chapter Assessment Outline Answer

There is one point of which Letitia should be warned almost the moment she has sat down in the office. As she wishes to forfeit the lease she should be careful not to do anything which might be construed by a court as 'Waiver'. In particular she should inform Rocky that he should neither demand nor accept any further instalments of rent.

Demanding/accepting rent is always a waiver of forfeiture even if done by an agent of the landlord who is ignorant of the landlord's intent to forfeit. (See *Belgravia* v *Woolgar*.) Letitia should immediately insist that Rocky marks his file relating to the shop 'No rent to be collected'. If Rocky uses a computer system to send out rent demands/reminders, the computer must be reprogrammed immediately.

The forfeiture process instituted by Letitia should proceed in two stages.

(1) Serve a notice under section 146 of the LPA and then (after waiting a reasonable time).
(2) Issue a writ claiming forfeiture of the lease and possession of the property.

(It is still theoretically possible to forfeit a lease without court proceedings, using 'peaceable re-entry'. Letitia might be tempted to do what the landlords did in *Billson* v *Residential Apartments*; sneak in very early one morning when no-one is at the shop.

However the House of Lords decision in *Billson* makes peaceable re-entry an undesirable course. Under the Lords' decision a tenant can claim relief from forfeiture after the landlord has peaceably re-entered, perhaps quite a long time after. Thus after the peaceable re-entry no new tenant would be keen to take a lease of the property for fear that Ann would reappear claiming relief.)

The section 146 notice should be served on Ann (the current tenant, see *Old Grovebury*). Extreme care should be taken in drafting the notice. If the notice is not correctly drafted, any court proceedings for forfeiture commenced after the notice will be abortive, and Letitia will have to start all over again.

The notice should give full details of the breach of covenant, and if Letitia wants monetary compensation the notice should contain a demand for such compensation.

If Ann's breach is 'capable of remedy' the notice should include a demand that the breach be remedied. This 'capable of remedy' point is notoriously tricky.

Normally a breach by a tenant of a covenant against illegal user is irremediable. The damage has been done; the property has been besmirched; everyone knows that the house is a brothel or the shop a drug den. . . . However Letitia's case looks slightly like the problematic case of *Glass* v *Kencakes* where Paull J (not a specialist land lawyer) held that illegal user by a sub-tenant in breach of the head lease had been remedied by evicting the sub-tenant before the property became tainted.

Letitia is therefore advised to play safe. She should include in the section 146 notice a clause, 'Remedy this breach if capable of remedy'. Moreover she should wait at least three months between serving the notice and issuing her writ. (A fortnight wait would be sufficient if the breach were irremediable.)

Having got to court (and getting there is clearly going to take at minimum a few months) Letitia should be warned that Ann will probably apply (by way of counterclaim) for relief from forfeiture. Although relief from forfeiture is in the discretion of the court, Ann's case for relief is strong. (The breach may be technically incapable of remedy, but the Court of Appeal in *Woolgar* and now the Lords in *Billson* have made it clear that relief can be granted with respect to an irremediable breach.)

Ann has a strong case for relief as the breach was not committed by her personally but by her employee. She sacked Dandy the moment she found out. To grant forfeiture would be to deprive Ann of a very valuable asset—a lease with 29 years to run at (seemingly) a cheap rent. When Ann acquired the lease in 1994 she presumably had to pay quite a substantial price to Tamsin.

Probably Letitia's only hope is to come to court in a state of righteous indignation, fuming, 'I will not have my shop used as an emporium for HARD drugs such as Cocaine. Ann should have been careful whom she employed, and should have been at the shop every day when it opened.'

It would be fatal to her chances of forfeiture for Letitia to let on that she only wanted Ann out in order to get in a tenant who was willing to pay a much higher rent (*cf. Woolgar*). Moreover, if Ann proves that Letitia already has a new tenant lined up, that would destroy any claim that the property had been tainted.

It would thus appear that Letitia is likely to spend a lot of money, time and energy pursuing forfeiture proceedings which will probably end with relief from forfeiture being granted. It is probably not worth all the effort, particularly when it is remembered that Letitia will not be able to collect any rent while the forfeiture proceedings are pending.

Letitia may feel confident that she can relet the property at a much higher rent. In the current economic climate her confidence may be misplaced. We see a lot of empty shops, even in the (relatively) prosperous South-East. If the shop was left unlet for any length of time Letitia might even have a problem with 'shop squatters'.

Letitia might, as an alternative to forfeiture, consider suing for damages. She has the choice of suing Tamsin (privity of contract) or Ann (privity of estate). However, as Letitia's reversion is not due to come into possession until 2022, it is difficult to see her recovering anything more than nominal damages.

CHAPTER TWENTY-ONE

ADVERSE POSSESSION AND THE LIMITATION ACTS

21.1 Introduction

Lawson, F. H., and Rudden, B., The Law of Property, 2nd edn,
Oxford: Clarendon Press, 1982, p. 51

LIMITATION OF ACTIONS AND RIGHTS

. . . Persons acquiring movables seldom trouble themselves with questions of title. But with land the barring of title by twelve years' adverse possession is important.

It operates as follows. Let us suppose that A has the best title to a piece of land which we shall call Blackacre—that is to say, a title which has no known title superior to it—and whilst he is away B takes possession of it. B now, by the very fact that he possesses Blackacre, has to title to it, but one that can be defeated by A. If, however, A does not take steps to recover possession for twelve years, by ousting B or bringing an action against him, he loses his title, and B's title, which was formerly the best but one, becomes the best. But his title does not then become a new one; it is still the same one that he obtained by dispossessing A; and this may have important consequences which are too technical to detain us here.

It might be thought that a purchaser of land would feel safe in limiting his researches into his vendor's title to a period of twelve years in the past. This is unfortunately not the case. For there may be persons who have rights in the land which will entitle them to possession at some future date. Until that time they will have no right to recover possession from an intruder, and the Limitation Act gives them some years from that time and not from the original intrusion in which to recover possession. No limit can be set to the period during which the purchaser should push back his investigations in order to be absolutely safe. However, as a practical matter some period must be fixed and the law has chosen to say that, unless a special agreement has been made to the contrary, a purchaser is entitled to trace back the vendor's title only to some good root of title at least fifteen years old. A good root of title is some document, such as a conveyance on sale, which transferred the interest which the purchaser seeks to acquire, which dealt completely with the title to it in law and equity, and contained nothing to cast doubts upon the title of the vendor. . . .

BUCKINGHAMSHIRE COUNTY COUNCIL v MORAN
[1989] 2 All ER 225, Court of Appeal

FACTS: In 1955, the plaintiff council had acquired a plot of land near some houses, intending at some future date to use the land for a road diversion. Before then the land was to be left vacant. In fact, the resident of a house adjoining the plot decided to maintain the plot of land and treated it as part of their own garden. The only access to the plot was through their garden. In 1971 the defendant bought the house and continued to treat the plot as if it were part of his garden, even though he was fully aware that the council owned it. Indeed, in a letter to the council he had asserted his belief that he was entitled to use the plot until the proposed road diversion was built. The council, in reply, refuted his claimed entitlement to use the land, but they took no measures to regain possession of the land at that time. Only in 1985 did they eventually issue a writ claiming possession of the plot. The defendant raised s. 15(1) of the Limitation Act 1980 in his defence, claiming that the council were time-barred from bringing an action to recover possession, on account of 12 years adverse possession.

HELD: The council's claim for possession was barred by the Limitation Act 1980. The defendant had established the necessary adverse possession.

SLADE LJ: On this appeal counsel for the council has accepted that if the plot was in adverse possession of the defendant more that 12 years before action was bought (i.e. on 28 October 1973) it has not ceased to be in adverse possession since that time. Ultimately, therefore, the crucial question will be: was the defendant in adverse possession of the plot on 28 October 1973?

Possession is never 'adverse' within the meaning of the 1980 Act if it is enjoyed under a lawful title. If, therefore a person occupies or uses land by licence of the owner with the paper title and his licence has not been duly determined, he cannot be treated as having been in 'adverse possession' as against the owner with the paper title.

Before the passing of the 1980 Act certain decisions of this court, in particular *Wallis's Cayton Bay Holiday Camp* v *Shell-Mex and BP Ltd* [1974] 3 All ER 575, [1975] QB 94 and *Gray* v *Wykeham-Martin* [1977] CA Transcript 10A, were thought to have established a general doctrine that in one special type of case there would be implied in favour of the would-be adverse possessor, *without any specific factual basis for such implication*, a licence permitting him to commit the acts of possession on which he sought to rely; the effect of implying such a licence would, of course, be to prevent the squatter's possession from being 'adverse'. That special type of case was broadly one where the acts of an intruder, however continuous and far-reaching, did not substantially interfere with any plans which the owners might have for the future use of undeveloped land.

. . . The doctrine of the implied licence has now been abrogated by para. 8(4) of Sch. 1 to the 1980 Act, which provides:

> For the purpose of determining whether a person occupying any land is in adverse possession of the land it shall not be assumed by implication of law that his occupation is by permission of the person entitled to the land merely by virtue of the fact that his occupation is not inconsistent with the latter's present or future enjoyment of the land. This provision shall not be taken as prejudicing a finding to the effect that a person's occupation of any land is by implied permission of the person entitled to the land in any case where such a finding is justified on the actual facts of the case.

In the light of this provision, it would at first sight appear that there is now no reason why the words 'possess' and 'dispossess' or similar expressions should not be given their ordinary legal meaning in the context of the 1980 Act. However, counsel for the council, while accepting that the implied licence doctrine is now abrogated, nevertheless submits that para. 8(4) (I quote from his skeleton argument)—

> leaves intact the special rule formulated by Bramwell LJ in *Leigh* v *Jack* ((1879) 5 Ex D 264) and Sir John Pennycuick in *Treloar* v *Nute* ([1977] 1 All ER 230, [1976] 1 WLR 1295) that where land is acquired or retained by the owner for a specific future purpose then acts of trespass which are not inconsistent with such purpose do not amount to dispossession. . . .

. . . it must, in my judgment, be too broad a proposition to suggest that an owner who retains a piece of land with a view to its utilisation for a specific purpose in the future can never be treated as dispossessed, however firm and obvious the intention to dispossess, and however drastic the acts of dispossession of the person seeking to dispossess him may be. . . .

I turn then to consider the first of the two requisite elements of possession. First, as at 28 October 1973 did the defendant have factual possession of the plot? I venture to repeat what I said in *Powell* v *McFarlane* (1977) 38 P & CR 452 at 470–471:

> Factual possession signifies an appropriate degree of physical control. It must be a single and [exclusive] possession . . . Thus an owner of land and a person intruding on that land without his consent cannot both be in possession of the land at the same time. The question what acts constitute a sufficient degree of exclusive physical control must depend on the circumstances, in particular the nature of the land and the manner in which land of that nature is commonly used or enjoyed.

On evidence it would appear clear that by 28 October 1973 the defendant had acquired complete and exclusive physical control of the plot. He had secured a complete enclosure of the plot and its annexation to Dolphin Place. Any intruder could have gained access to the plot only by way of Dolphin Place, unless he was prepared to climb the locked gate fronting the highway or to scramble through one or other of the hedges bordering the plot. The defendant had put a new lock and chain on the gate and had fastened it. He and his mother had been dealing with the plot as any occupying owners might have been expected to deal with it. They had incorporated it into the garden of Dolphin Place. They had planted bulbs and daffodils in the grass. They had maintained it as part of that garden and had trimmed the hedges. I cannot accept counsel's submission for the council that the defendant's acts of possession were trivial. It is hard to see what more he could have done to acquire complete physical control of the plot by October 1973. In my judgment, he had plainly acquired factual possession of the plot by that time.

[margin note: factual possession]

However as the judge said, the more difficult question is whether the defendant had the necessary *animus possidendi*. As to this, counsel for the council accepted the correctness of the following statement (so far as it went) which I made in *Powell* v *McFarlane* (at 471–472):

[margin note: Animus possidendi]

> . . . the *animus possidendi* involves the intention, in one's own name and on one's own behalf, to exclude the world at large, including the owner with the paper title if he be not himself the possessor, so far as is reasonably practicable and so far as the processes of the law will allow.

At least at first sight the following observations of Lord Halsbury in *Marshall* v *Taylor* [1895] 1 Ch 641 at 645 (which were referred to by Hoffmann J in his judgment) are very pertinent to the present case:

> The true nature of this particular strip of land is that it is inclosed. It cannot be denied that the person who says he owns it could not get to it in any ordinary way. I do not deny that he could have crept through the hedge, or, if it had been a brick wall, that he could have climbed over the wall; but that was not the ordinary and usual mode of access. That is the exclusion—the dispossession—which seems to me to be so important in this case.

As a number of authorities indicate, inclosure by itself *prima facie* indicates the requisite *animus possidendi*. As Cockburn CJ said in *Seddon* v *Smith* (1987) 36 LT 168 at 169: 'Enclosure is the strongest possible evidence of adverse possession . . .' Russell LJ in *George Wimpey & Co. Ltd* v *Sohn* [1966] 1 All ER 232 at 240, [1967] Ch 487 at 511 similarly observed: 'Ordinarily, of course, enclosure is the most cogent evidence of adverse possession and of dispossession of the true owner.' While counsel for the council pointed out that the plot was always accessible from the north where no boundary demarcation existed, it was only accessible from the defendant's own property, Dolphin Place. In my judgment, therefore, he must be treated as having inclosed it.

Counsel for the council, however, submitted that, even if inclosure had occurred, the defendant's intention must be assessed in the light of the particular circumstances of this case. The defendant knew that the council had acquired and retained the plot with the specific intention of building a road across it at some future time. The council had no use for the land in the interim. It was for all practical purposes waste land. None of the defendant's acts, he submitted, were inconsistent with the council's known future intentions. . . .

If the defendant had stopped short of placing a new lock and chain on the gate, I might perhaps have felt able to accept these submissions. Counsel for the council submitted that this act did not unequivocally show an intention to exclude the council as well as other people. It is well established that it is no use for an alleged adverse possessor to rely on acts which are merely equivocal as regards the intention to exclude the true owner: see for example *Tecbild Ltd* v *Chamberlain* (1969) 20 P & CR 633 at 642 per Sachs LJ. In my judgment, however, the placing of the new lock and chain and gate did amount to a final unequivocal demonstration of the defendant's intention to possess the land. . . .

The other main point which counsel for the council has argued in support of this appeal has caused me slightly more difficulty. In his submission there can be no sufficient *animus possidendi* to constitute adverse possession for the purpose of the 1980 Act unless there exists the intention to exclude the owner with the paper title in *all* future circumstances. The defendant's oral statements to Mr Harris in the conversation of 10 November 1975, as recorded in the attendance note, do appear to have constituted an implicit acknowledgment by the defendant that he would be obliged to leave the plot if in the future the council required it for the purpose of constructing the proposed new road. The letter of 18 December 1975, which I have concluded should be admitted in evidence, contains an express acknowledgment of this nature. If the intention to exclude the owner with the paper title in *all* future circumstances is a necessary constituent of the *animus possidendi*, the attendance notice and the letter of 18 December 1975 show that this constituent was absent in the present case.

There are some dicta in the authorities which might be read as suggesting that an intention to *own* the land is required. Lindley MR, for example, in *Littledale* v *Liverpool College* [1900] 1 Ch 19 at 23, referred to the 'acts of ownership' relied on by the plaintiffs. Russell LJ in *George Wimpey & Co. Ltd* v *Sohn* [1966] 1 All ER 232 at 240, [1967] Ch 487 at 510 said:

> . . . I am not satisfied that the actions of the *predecessors* in bricking up the doorway and maintaining a lock on the gate to the roadway were necessarily referable to an intention to occupy the [land] as their own absolute property. (Russell LJ's emphasis.)

At one point in my judgment in *Powell* v *McFarlane* (1977) 38 P & CR 452 at 478 I suggested that:

> . . . any objective informed observer might probably have inferred that the plaintiff was using the land simply for the benefit of his family's cow or cows, during such periods as the absent owner took no steps to stop him, without any intention to appropriate the land as his own.

Nevertheless, I agree with the judge that 'What is required for this purpose is not an intention to own or even an intention to acquire ownership but an intention to possess', that is to say an intention *for the time being* to possess the land to the exclusion of all other persons, including the owner with the paper title. No authorities cited to us establish the contrary proposition. The conversation with Mr Harris, as recorded in the attendance note and the letter of 18 December 1975, to my mind demonstrate the intention of the defendant for the time being to continue in possession of the plot to the exclusion of the council unless and until the proposed bypass is built. The form of the conveyance to the defendant and of the contemporaneous statutory declaration which he obtained from Mr and Mrs Wall are, of course, entirely consistent with the existence of an intention on his part to take and keep adverse possession of the plot, at least unless and until that event occurred.

In the light of the line of authorities to which we have been referred, beginning with *Leigh* v *Jack*, I have already accepted that the court should be slow to make a finding of adverse possession in a case such as the present. However, as the judge pointed out, in none of those earlier cases, where the owner with the paper title successfully defended his title, was there present the significant feature of complete inclosure of the land in question by the trespasser. On the evidence in the present case he was, in my judgment, right in concluding that the defendant had acquired adverse possession of the plot by 28 October 1973 and had remained in adverse possession of it ever since. There is no evidence that any representative of the council has even set foot on the plot since that date.

This appeal, which has been well argued on both sides, should in my judgment be dismissed.

21.2 The Limitation Act 1980

THE LIMITATION ACT 1980

15. Time limit for actions to recover land

(1) No action shall be brought by any person to recover any land after the expiration of twelve years from the date on which the right of action accrued to him or, if it first accrued to some person through whom he claims, to that person.

(2) Subject to the following provisions of this section, where—

(a) the estate or interest claimed was an estate or interest in revision or remainder or any other future estate or interest and the right of action to recover the land accrued on the date on which the estate or interest fell into possession by the determination of the preceding estate or interest; and

(b) the person entitled to the preceding estate or interest (not being a term of years absolute) was not in possession of the land on that date;

no action shall be brought by the person entitled to the succeeding estate or interest after the expiration of twelve years from the date on which the right of action accrued to the person entitled to the preceding estate or interest or six years from the date on which the right of action accrued to the person entitled to the succeeding estate or interest, whichever period last expires.

(3) Subsection (2) above shall not apply to any estate or interest which falls into possession on the determination of an entailed interest and which might have been barred by the person entitled to the entailed interest.

(4) No person shall bring an action to recover any estate or interest in land under an assurance taking effect after the right of action to recover the land had accrued to the person by whom the assurance was made or some person through whom he claimed or some person entitled to a preceding estate or interest, unless the action is brought within the period during which the person by whom the assurance was made could have brought such an action.

(5) Where any person is entitled to any estate or interest in land in possession and, while so entitled, is also entitled to any future estate or interest in that land, and his right to recover the estate or interest in possession is barred under this Act, no action shall be brought by that person, or by any person claiming through him, in respect of the future estate or interest, unless in the meantime possession of the land has been recovered by a person entitled to an intermediate estate or interest.

(6) Part I of Schedule 1 to this Act contains provisions for determining the date of accrual of rights of action to recover land in the cases there mentioned.

(7) Part II of that Schedule contains provisions modifying the provisions of this section in their application to actions brought by, or by a person claiming through, the Crown or any spiritual or eleemosynary corporation sole.

SCHEDULE I

Right of action not to accrue or continue unless there is adverse possession

8.—(1) No right of action to recover land shall be treated as accruing unless the land is in the possession of some person in whose favour the period of limitation can run (referred to below in this paragraph as 'adverse possession'); and where under the preceding provisions of this Schedule any such right of action is treated as accruing on a certain date and no person is in adverse possession on that date, the right of action shall not be treated as accruing unless and until adverse possession is taken of the land.

(2) Where a right of action to recover land has accrued and after its accrual, before the right is barred, the land ceases to be in adverse possession, the right of action shall no longer be treated as having accrued and no fresh right of action shall be treated as accruing unless and until the land is again taken into adverse possession.

(3) For the purpose of this paragraph—

(a) possession of any land subject to a rentcharge by a person (other that the person entitled to the rentcharge) who does not pay the rent shall be treated as adverse possession of the rentcharge; and

(b)   receipt of rent under a lease by a person wrongfully claiming to be entitled to the land in reversion immediately expectant on the determination of the lease shall be treated as adverse possession of the land.

(4)   For the purpose of determining whether a person occupying any land is in adverse possession of the land it shall not be assumed by implication of law that his occupation is by permission of the person entitled to the land merely by virtue of the fact that his occupation is not inconsistent with the latter's present or future enjoyment of the land.

This provision shall not be taken as prejudicing a finding to the effect that a person's occupation of any land is by implied permission of the person entitled to the land in any case where such a finding is justified on the actual facts of the case.

21.2.1   COMMENCEMENT OF ADVERSE POSSESSION

TRELOAR v NUTE [1977] 1 All ER 230, Court of Appeal

FACTS: The plaintiff and the defendant were adjoining farmers. The plaintiff (an elderly lady) had about one-seventh of an acre of waste ground which she totally forgot about. The defendant and his father in effect took over the ground. They levelled it off. (There had been a gully.) They then used it for various purposes such as an informal motor-bike trials course and a rubbish dump. Eventually the defendant started to build a bungalow on the ground. At this point Mrs. Treloar issued a writ claiming to re-possess the land.
HELD: The defendant and his father were able to prove that they had been using the ground for more than twelve years and that the possession was adverse to Mrs. Treloar's title. Her title was therefore extinguished and Nute (junior) was declared to hold a new title to the land.

SIR JOHN PENNYCUICK: . . . It is not in any doubt that under the 1939 Act as under the previous law, the person claiming by possession must show either (1) discontinuance by the paper owner followed by possession or (2) dispossession or, as it is sometimes called, 'ouster' of the paper owner. Clearly, possession concurrent with the paper owner is insufficient. On the other hand, where the person claiming by possession establishes possession in the full sense of exclusive possession, that by itself connotes absence of possession on the part of the paper owner and I doubt if there is any real difference in the concept of taking possession and the concept of dispossession except in the special type of case where the owner, although not technically in possession, has some purpose to which he intends to put the land in the future. . . .

The judge found, as we read his judgment, that the defendant's father took possession of the disputed land outside the limitation period but that this possession was not adverse by reason that it caused no inconvenience to the plaintiff. In our judgment the second part of this finding is contrary to the plain terms of [the Act], which in effect defines adverse possession as possession of some person in whose favour the period of limitation can run. It is not permissible to import into this definition a requirement that the owner must be inconvenienced or otherwise affected by that possession. Apart from the cases relating to special purpose no authority has been cited to us which would support the requirement of inconvenience to the owner and we are not ourselves aware of any such authority. On the contrary, so far as our own experience goes the typical instance in which a possessory title is treated as having been acquired is that in which a squatter establishes himself on a piece of land for which the owner has no use. Indeed, if inconvenience to the owner had to be established it would be difficult ever to acquire a possessory title since the owner if inconvenienced would be likely to take proceedings. . . .

21.2.2   THE 'ADVERSE' IN ADVERSE POSSESSION

HYDE v PEARCE [1982] 1 All ER 1029, Court of Appeal

FACTS: In 1958, the plaintiff agreed, at an auction, to purchase a plot of land. He went into possession without telling the vendors and the auctioneers agreed to lend him the keys on the understanding that he would return them on demand. Shortly after the plaintiff had moved into the premises, there arose a boundary dispute with a neighbour. The vendors sided with the neighbour and demanded that the plaintiff return the keys to the premises. He refused to do so. The vendors took no further action to remove the plaintiff. However, in 1972, the vendors sold the land to the defendant. That sale overreached any estate contract the plaintiff might have had, because he had never protected it by registering a land charge. The plaintiff was imprisoned about this time and when he emerged from prison he discovered that the defendant had demolished, reconstructed and taken possession of the house. He brought an action claiming that the vendor's title had been extinguished by his adverse possession, and that, therefore, the defendant had no title in the house.

HELD: The existence of the plaintiff's estate contract, which he had owned up until the sale to the defendant, was inconsistent with his claim to have acquired title by adverse possession. The defendant was declared the true owner of the property.

TEMPLEMAN LJ: . . . We were also referred to certain cases in which it was held that time did not begin to run under the Limitation Act because of the peculiar nature of the position of the person claiming a title under that Act. For example, in *Thomas v Thomas* (1855) 2 K & J 79, 69 ER 701, a father, who entered on property, was held not to have a possessory title as against his own children because, as I understand it, he clothed himself with the capacity of a trustee and a trustee cannot assert a possessory title against beneficiaries. . . .

. . . in the peculiar circumstances of this case, it seems to me that it is not sufficient to show that a right of action had accrued. The plaintiff must show some further quality, namely adverse possession. The plaintiff was allowed in possession as a purchaser pending completion; and he was allowed to stay there because he was a purchaser. If he had been a mere trespasser no doubt the vendors would have brought proceedings. But the vendors, in all the circumstances of the case, seem to have decided by accident or design to allow matters to drift on without taking steps to evict him from the premises, relying on the fact that it would all turn out right in the end when the purchase price was ascertained and completion took place. . . .

In my judgment, the plaintiff, having in effect been able to go in and stay under the contract, cannot now repudiate the contract with hindsight. As I have said, if, at any time, he made it clear that he was no longer bound by the contract, then different considerations would apply. Equally, no doubt, if he had made that clear, then the vendors would have taken action against him. It is only the fact that he was there as a purchaser pending completion which has enabled time to run in his favour, as he says, and which enables him to claim a title by adverse possession. Accordingly, in my judgment, although the full period by the 1939 Act has elapsed, the plaintiff has not shown that he was in adverse possession. . . .

21.2.3 THE 'APPARENTLY ABANDONED PLOT' PROBLEM

(Note that the following cases must now be read subject to the case of *Bucks C.C. v Moran* and sch. 1, para. 8(4) of the Limitation Act 1980, above.)

WILLIAMS BROTHERS DIRECT SUPPLY STORES LTD v RAFTERY [1957] 3 All ER 593, Court of Appeal

FACTS: The plaintiffs purchased in 1937 a piece of waste ground at the back of their factory. They hoped to expand their premises onto this ground, but they were prevented from doing so first by the war and then by the refusal of planning consent. In 1940 the defendant came along, saw the waste ground, and started to 'dig for victory' (that is, he used the ground as a vegetable patch as part of the war effort). After the war, he kept greyhounds on the land, erecting kennels and fencing. In 1957, the plaintiffs suddenly claimed possession of the ground. The defendant claimed that he had gained a title to the ground by adverse possession. A director of the plaintiffs testified that they had always retained development plans for the piece of land in the hope that the town planners might change their minds.

HELD: There was no adverse possession, because the defendant had never done anything to render the plaintiff's plans 'impossible'.

HODSON LJ: . . . I cannot see that any act which the defendant did is capable of being treated as sufficient to dispossess the plaintiffs. The defendant never even thought he was dispossessing the plaintiffs; he never claimed to do more than work the soil, as he thought he was permitted to do. He had some vague idea in his head, derived from a source which is not clear on the evidence, that it was quite all right for him to work it, but, as far as I know, he never had nor claimed any intention of asserting any right to the possession of this piece of ground. . . .

He approved Bramwell LJ in *Leigh* v *Jack* (1879) 5 ExD 264 who had said:

in order to defeat a title by dispossessing the former owner, acts must be done which are inconsistent with his enjoyment of the soil for the purposes for which he intended to use it; . . .

WALLIS'S CAYTON BAY HOLIDAY CAMP LTD v SHELL-MEX AND BP LTD
[1974] 3 All ER 575, Court of Appeal

FACTS: The defendants acquired one-and-a-third acres in the middle of a field for the purposes of a new filling station. This one-and-a-third acres adjoined the site of a proposed new road, but neither the road nor the one-and-a-third acres were marked off by boundary markers. All a passer-by would see was an arable field no different from its neighbours. The field belonged to Wallis's, which it farmed, together with adjoining fields, through a subsidiary company. For eleven-and-a-half years Wallis's farming activities extended to the one-and-a-third acres. Then the local authority abandoned the scheme for the new road. Shell promptly wrote to Wallis's offering to sell the one-and-a-third acres. Wallis's did not reply. Instead they carried on their farming for eight more months and then claimed that they had acquired title through adverse possession.
HELD: Wallis's failed to establish title by adverse possession. The period of adverse possession had not commenced until after Shell had abandoned its plans for the land. There had therefore only been a few months of adverse possession, not the necessary twelve years.

LORD DENNING MR: . . . There is a fundamental error in that argument. Possession by itself is not enough to give a title. It must be *adverse* possession. The true owner must have discontinued possession or have been dispossessed and another must have taken it adversely to him. There must be something in the nature of an ouster of the true owner by the wrongful possessor. That is shown by a series of cases in this court which, on their very facts, show this proposition to be true.

When the true owner of land intends to use it for a particular purpose in the future, but meanwhile has no immediate use for it, and so leaves it unoccupied, he does not lose his title to it simply because some other person enters on it and uses it for some temporary purpose, like stacking materials; or for some seasonal purpose, like growing vegetables. Not even if this temporary or seasonal purpose continues year after year for 12 years, or more: see *Leigh* v *Jack* (1879) 5 ExD 264, *Williams Brothers Direct Supply Stores Ltd* v *Raftery* [1957] 3 All ER 593, *Tecbild Ltd* v *Chamberlain* (1969) 20 P & CR 633. The reason is not because the user does not amount to actual possession. The line between acts of user and acts of possession is too fine for words. The reason behind the decisions is because it does not lie in that other person's mouth to assert that he used the land of his own wrong as a trespasser. Rather his user is to be ascribed to the licence or permission of the true owner. By using the land, knowing that it does not belong to him, he impliedly assumes that the owner will permit it; and the owner, by not turning him off, impliedly gives permission. And it has been held many times in this court that acts done under licence or permitted by the owner do not give a licensee a title under the Limitation Act 1939. They do not amount to adverse possession: see *Cobb* v *Lane* [1952] 1 All ER 1199 . . . in this court.

. . . There is a broad principle of equity dating back for at least 100 years that where a person, by his words or conduct, leads another to believe that his strict rights at law will not be enforced—and the other acts on it—the person who otherwise might have enforced those rights will not be allowed to enforce them where it would be inequitable having regard to the dealings which have taken place between the parties: see *Hughes* v *Metropolitan Railway Co.* (1877) 2 App Cas 439 per Lord Cairns LC. That principle carries out the very object for which equity was first introduced—to mitigate the rigours of the law. It has been applied in recent years so as to preclude a party to a contract from enforcing his strict rights under it: see *Central London Property Trust Ltd* v *High Trees House Ltd* [1947] KB 130. I see no reason why it should not be applied so as to preclude a squatter from enforcing his strict rights under the Limitation Act 1939. By not replying to the letters, Wallis's were plainly doing wrong. They were deliberately trespassing on the land of Shell—lying low and saying nothing—so as to acquire a title for themselves. They knew full well that it was not their land. Yet they seek to take advantage of their own wrong to say it is now their land. The judge would not allow them to do this. He said it was 'contrary to equity and natural justice'. I agree with him. I would dismiss this appeal.

21.3   Adverse Possession and Tenants

21.3.1   WHAT IF AN ADVERSE POSSESSOR DISPLACES A TENANT?

See **21.6**.

21.3.2   THE PROBLEM OF A TENANT ENCROACHING ON ADJOINING LAND

SMIRK v *LYNDALE DEVELOPMENTS LTD* [1975] 1 Ch 317, Court of Appeal

FACTS: The plaintiff, a British Railways employee, had a weekly service tenancy of a house owned by his employer. During the period of his occupation he took it upon himself to cultivate adjoining land ('the blue plot') which was also owned by his employer. His employer eventually sold the title to the house and 'the blue plot' to the defendant. The plaintiff claimed to have acquired title to 'the blue plot' by adverse possession.
HELD: Where a lessee encroaches upon other land, the encroachment is presumed to be an extension of the 'locus' of the lease (the tenant is presumed to be merely expanding the area granted to him). The plaintiff failed, therefore, to show that he had acquired title to 'the blue plot' by adverse possession.

LAWTON LJ: [Approved the following *dictum* of Pennycuik V-C in the court below] . . .

Whatever accrued or accruing right the plaintiff may have had to include the blue plot in his tenancy from British Railways, this right must have determined with his tenancy under British Railways, and obviously no new right can have accrued against [the defendant] during the short time in which [the defendant has] been his landlord. There can be no ground for treating a period of two different tenancies as continuous for the present purposes. Contrast the position where a possessory title is acquired by successive squatters or against successive freeholders. The tenant, so long as the presumption applies, can do no more than acquire an addition to the subject-matter of the tenancy and his interest in that additional subject-matter must necessarily determine together with his interest in the original subject-matter.

21.4   Time Starts Running Afresh by Acknowledgment of Title

EDGINGTON v *CLARK AND ANOTHER* [1963] 3 All ER 468, Court of Appeal

FACTS: A person in adverse possession of certain freehold property wrote a letter to an agent of the owner making an offer to purchase the land. The offer was accepted and a deposit paid, but the purchase was never completed.

HELD: The letter showed that the adverse possessor acknowledged the title of the original owner. The period of adverse possession would begin afresh from the date of that acknowledgment.

UPJOHN LJ: . . . If a man makes an offer to purchase freehold property, even though it be subject to contract, he is quite clearly saying that as between himself and the person to whom he makes the offer, he realises that the offeree has a better title to the freehold land than himself, and that would seem to be the plainest possible form of acknowledgment.

Counsel for the plaintiff, however, has ingeniously argued that when an intending purchaser makes an offer to purchase, he does not thereby acknowledge that the vendor can prove or establish the title which the purchaser is entitled to have on a sale and purchase of land, and he says that the letters properly understood merely mean: 'If you can prove your title which I am bound to accept, then I will buy', and accordingly, so the argument proceeds, there is no acknowledgment of the vendor's title. We are quite unable to accept that argument. Of course an intending purchaser does not acknowledge that the vendor has a marketable title when he makes an offer to purchase. That is a matter for inspection of title and requisitions at a later stage; but what he does acknowledge is that as between the intending purchaser and the vendor, the vendor has the better title to the land and that seems to us all that is required.

. . . The question whether a particular writing amounts to an acknowledgment must depend on the true construction of the document in all the surrounding circumstances, and it is quite plain that in that case there was no acknowledgment by the writing, for it challenges the ownership of the true owner, but offers by way of compromise to accept a tenancy. Had a bargain been concluded, then no doubt that would have been an acknowledgment because by agreeing to become a tenant, the writer could not deny his landlord's title, and that, we think, is the explanation of the concluding words at the end of the judgment. Accordingly that case does not help the plaintiff. . . .

21.4.1   ACKNOWLEDGMENT OF TITLE MADE BY PERSON IN WHOSE FAVOUR TIME HAS ALREADY RUN IS OF NO EFFECT

COLCHESTER BOROUGH COUNCIL v *SMITH AND OTHERS* [1992] 2 All ER 561,
Court of Appeal

FACTS: The fourth defendant, Maurice Tillson, had been (apparently) in adverse possession of the plaintiff's land for well over twelve years. Despite that fact, the plaintiff began proceedings for possession against him. These proceedings were compromised on the terms:

(a)   that Tillson accepted the plaintiff still owned the land;
(b)   that the plaintiff granted Tillson a lease of the land.

In later proceedings for possession brought on the expiry of the lease, Tillson claimed that he had a freehold title by virtue of adverse possession.
HELD: Tillson was bound by the earlier compromise and therefore estopped from disputing the plaintiff's title to the freehold.

BUTLER-SLOSS LJ: . . . Where parties to a dispute reach a compromise which brings that dispute to an end and avoids the need for litigation or further litigation, such a compromise is a valuable part of the resolution of disputes within the machinery of the administration of justice. The compromise has to be genuine, entered into freely by all parties to it without concealment of essential information or undue advantage taken by one party of another party, and preferably with the assistance of lawyers. Consequently, an agreement to compromise an action or a dispute which may lead to litigation is binding and is enforceable against the party seeking subsequently to repudiate it. As Roskill LJ said in *Binder* v *Alachouzos* [1972] 2 All ER 189 at 194, [1972] 2 QB 151 at 160, 'any other course would cause very great difficulty in the administration of justice'.

In my view the courts have an interest in upholding agreements to compromise disputes. The terms of the agreement to compromise under review are therefore in a wholly different position from the situations caught within the scope of the Limitation Acts, such as payment of rent or acknowledgment of title. The agreement to compromise at 3 November 1983 is therefore binding upon the appellant, and I also would dismiss this appeal.

21.5 Nature of Title acquired under Limitation Acts where Title Adversely Possessed against is Unregistered

RE NISBET AND POTTS' CONTRACT [1906] 1 Ch 386, Court of Appeal

FACTS: A 'squatter' had extinguished the unregistered title of the original freeholder by adverse possession. The question was whether this had the effect of releasing the adverse possessor's new title from a restrictive covenant to which the original freehold had been subject.
HELD: The 'squatter' was bound by the restriction. The covenantee had not, as yet, had any cause to enforce the restriction, so it would be a nonsense to hold that the enforcement of the covenant in the future had been time-barred by the squatter's adverse possession. Nor could the squatter claim to be a 'purchaser' for value of the legal estate without notice of the restrictive covenant.

COLLINS MR: . . . the Statute of Limitations, as one would expect, does not purport to annul by lapse of time any rights other than those which persons might have, and ought to have, exercised during the period limited. The statute does not begin to run in any case against a person until that person has been put to what is generally called his 'right of entry.' Unless the circumstances have been such as to put the person who is to be barred by the lapse of time upon the assertion of his right, the time does not begin to run against him. All that the statute does is this. By s. 34 it says: 'At the determination of the period limited by this Act to any person for making an entry or distress, or bringing any writ of quare impedit or other action or suit, the right and title of such person to the land, rent, or advowson, for the recovery whereof such entry, distress, action, or suit respectively might have been made or brought within such period, shall be extinguished.' That is the whole right the squatter acquires, namely, the extinguishment of a title adverse to his own. But how does that affect the question here? What machinery is there in the Statute of Limitations affecting the right of a covenantee who has the benefit of a restrictive covenant? Nothing in the Act has been pointed out to us which touches that right at all. In fact, unless and until the right of the covenantee has been in some way infringed, so that it becomes necessary for him to enforce that right, there is no reason, either in principle or in fairness, why his right should be in any way affected. . . .

21.6 Adverse Possession Where the Title Possessed Against is Registered Land

LAND REGISTRATION ACT 1925

75. Acquisition of title by possession

(1) The Limitation Acts shall apply to registered land in the same manner and to the same extent as those Acts apply to land not registered, except that where, if the land were not registered, the estate of the person registered as proprietor would be extinguished, such estate shall not be extinguished but shall be deemed to be held by the proprietor for the time being in trust for the person who, by virtue of the said Acts, has acquired title against any proprietor, but without prejudice to the estates and interests of any other person interested in the land whose estate or interest is not extinguished by those Acts.

(2) Any person claiming to have acquired a title under the Limitation Acts to a registered estate in the land may apply to be registered as proprietor thereof.

(3) The registrar shall, on being satisfied as to the applicant's title, enter the applicant as proprietor either with absolute, good leasehold, qualified, or possessory title, as the case

may require, but without prejudice to any estate or interest protected by any entry on the register which may not have been extinguished under the Limitation Acts, and such registration shall, subject as aforesaid, have the same effect as the registration of a first proprietor; but the proprietor or the applicant or any other person interested may apply to the court for the determination of any question arising under this section.

(4) . . .

(5)   Rules may be made for applying (subject to any necessary modifications) the provisions of this section to cases where an easement, right or privilege has been acquired by prescription.

21.7   Adverse Possession Against the Registered Proprietor of a Lease

21.7.1   TWELVE YEARS' ADVERSE POSSESSION BUT NO RECTIFICATE OF THE REGISTER

FAIRWEATHER v ST MARYLEBONE PROPERTY CO. LTD
[1962] 2 All ER 288, House of Lords

FACTS: A squatter had established title by adverse possession against a tenant holding land under a 99 year lease of registered title. The tenant then surrendered its lease to the landlord.
HELD: (Lord Morris of Borth y Gest dissenting) the surrender was effective to extinguish the 'squatters' right to possess the land.

LORD DENNING: My Lords, I have come to the clear conclusion that a surrender operates as a determination of the term. It is not an assignment of it. I am aware that no less an authority than Lindley LJ, once said that: 'The surrender of the term only operated as an assignment of the surrenderor's interest in it', see *David* v *Sabin* [1893] 1 Ch 533. But if that be true, it is not by any rule of the common law, only by force of statute: and then only in the case of underleases, not in the case of trespasser or squatter. . . .

The question may be asked: why did the common law on a surrender protect the underlessee from eviction? The answer is to be found in Coke on Littleton II, p. 338b, where it is said that

having regard to the parties to the surrender, the estate is absolutely drowned . . . But having regard to strangers, who were not parties or privies thereunto, lest by a voluntary surrender they may receive prejudice touching any right or interest they had before the surrender, the estate surrendered hath in consideration of law a continuance.

This passage applies in favour of an underlessee so as to protect him from eviction during the term of his underlease: but it does not apply in favour of a trespasser. The reason for the difference is because the underlessee comes in under a grant from the lessee; and the lessee cannot, by a surrender, derogate from his own grant, see *Davenport's Case* (1610) 8 Co. Rep 144b, *Mellor* v *Watkins* (1874) LR 9 QB 405 by Blackburn J. But a trespasser comes in by wrong and not by grant of the lessee. If the lessee surrenders his term, the freeholder is at once entitled to evict the trespasser for the simple reason that, on the surrender, the lease is determined, and there is no bar whatever to the freeholder recovering possession, see *Ecclesiastical Comrs of England and Wales* v *Rowe* (1880) 5 App Cas 736. And I see no reason why the same reasoning should not apply even though, at the date of the surrender, the trespasser is a squatter who has been there more than twelve years for, as against the freeholder he is still a trespasser. The freeholder's right to possession does not arise until the lease is determined by the surrender. It then comes into being and time begins to run against him under s. 6(1) of the Limitation Act 1939.

The only reason, it seems to me, which can be urged against this conclusion is that it means that a squatter's title can be destroyed by the leaseholder and freeholder putting their heads together. It is said that they can by a surrender—or by a surrender and regrant—destroy the squatter's title completely and get rid of him. So be it. There is no way of preventing it. But I would point out that, if we were to deny the two of them this right, they could achieve the same result in another way. They could easily do it by the leaseholder submitting to a forfeiture. If the leaseholder chooses not to pay the rent, the freeholder can determine the lease under the proviso for re-entry. The squatter cannot stop him. He cannot pay the rent without the authority of the leaseholder. He cannot apply for relief against forfeiture. The squatter's title can thus be defeated by a forfeiture—or by a forfeiture and regrant—just as it can by a surrender—or by a surrender and regrant. So there is nothing in the point.

My Lords, so far as these questions under the Limitation Acts are concerned, I must say that I see no difference between a surrender or merger or a forfeiture. On each of those events the lease is determined and the freeholder is entitled to evict the squatter, even though the squatter has been on the land during the lease for more than twelve years: and on the determination of the lease, time then begins to run against the freeholder. . . .

One word about s. 75(1) of the Land Registration Act, 1925. That point was not raised in the county court and its availability depends on facts which were not proved. I do not think that it is open to the appellant here. But in any case I doubt if that puts registered land on a very different footing from unregistered land. It is machinery so as to apply the Limitation Acts to registered land but it does not alter the substantive position very materially. The registered leaseholder clearly remains liable on the covenants and subject to the conditions of the lease, including the proviso for re-entry: and I do not see why, on a surrender, the freeholder should not recover possession from a squatter, just as he can on a forfeiture. The freeholder has no notice of the trust in favour of the squatter and his interests are not to be prejudiced by the fact that the leasehold is registered. I say no more because the point is not available here. Suffice it to say that for the reasons I have given, I would dismiss this appeal.

21.7.2 TWELVE YEARS' ADVERSE POSSESSION AND THERE IS RECTIFICATION OF THE REGISTER

SPECTRUM INVESTMENT CO. AND ANOTHER v HOLMES
[1981] 1 All ER 6, Chancery Division

FACTS: The facts are best understood chronologically. The freehold of the premises was registered in 1901 and a 99 year lease was granted to a lessee from Christmas Day, 1902. This lease was registered early in 1903. In 1939 the lessee granted an oral weekly tenancy to Mrs. Holmes. The lessee then assigned the lease to Mrs. David, who was duly registered as proprietor thereof. Mrs. Holmes stopped paying rent in 1944. She died in 1951 and her daughter, Miss Holmes, took up possession as her successor. Miss Holmes was registered with possessory title to the lease in 1968 and Mrs. David's registered proprietorship was removed by the rectification of the register in 1968. In April 1975 the freehold reversion was transferred to the plaintiff, Spectrum Investment Co. In May 1975 Mrs. David surrendered her lease to the plaintiff. The plaintiff then brought proceedings for possession against Miss Holmes.

HELD: The purported surrender by Mrs. David had no effect. She ceased to have any interest capable of being surrendered from the moment that the register was rectified.

BROWNE-WILKINSON J: . . . I can now shortly state the contentions of Spectrum. Spectrum submits that the Land Registration Act 1925 introduces mere machinery for proving title to and transferring land and does not affect the substantive rights which parties enjoy under the general law. Accordingly it is said that the rights of Spectrum (as established by *Fairweather* v *St Marylebone Property Co. Ltd* [1962] 2 All ER 288, [1963] AC 510) must be reflected in the provisions of the Land Registration Act 1925 and are preserved by the words in s. 11 which expressly provide that registration with possessory title 'shall not affect or prejudice the enforcement of any estate, right, or interest (whether in respect of the lessor's title or otherwise) adverse to or in derogation of' the proprietor with possessory title. So, it is said, having obtained a surrender of the lease from Mrs. David, Spectrum's right to possession as against Miss Holmes is preserved.

There is in my judgment a short answer to the claim by Spectrum. Accepting for the moment the broad proposition that the Land Registration Act 1925 was not intended to alter substantive rights, it undoubtedly was intended to alter the manner in which such rights were to be established and transferred. The surrender by Mrs. David to Spectrum is the linchpin of Spectrum's claim. But in my judgment that surrender has not been affected by the only means authorised by the 1925 Act for the disposal of a registered leasehold interest by act of the parties.

. . . It is clear from the references in s. 75(3) that s. 75 apples to leasehold interest. Under s. 75(3) the registrar is under a mandatory duty to register the squatter on the application made by the squatter under sub-s. (2) if the registrar is satisfied as to the squatter's title. For what does the squatter make application? I will read s. 75(2) again: 'Any person claiming to have acquired a title under the Limitation Acts to a registered estate in the land may apply to be registered as proprietor thereof.' To my mind the words are clear and unequivocal: the squatter claims to have acquired a title to 'a registered estate in the land' (i.e. the leasehold interest) and applies to be registered as a proprietor *'thereof'* (my emphasis). Therefore, under s. 75(2), references to the squatter having acquired title to a registered estate must include the rights which under the Limitation Act 1939 the squatter acquires in relation to leasehold interests. Subsection (2) then refers to the squatter applying to be registered as proprietor 'thereof'. This word can, in my judgment, only refer back to the registered estate in the land against which the squatter has acquired title under the 1939 Act, i.e. the leasehold interest. The clear words of the Act therefore seem to require that, once the 12 years have run, the squatter is entitled to be registered as proprietor of the lease itself, and is bound to be so registered if he applies for registration. It follows that in my judgment Miss Holmes (as the squatter) is correctly registered as proprietor of the lease itself in accordance with the clear requirements of s. 75 of the 1925 Act. If that is right, Mrs. David cannot be entitled to rectification of the register as against Miss Holmes, and she can therefore never get into a position in which she is competent to surrender the lease to Spectrum.

I am conscious that in so deciding I am reaching a conclusion which produces at least a limited divergence between squatter's rights over registered and unregistered land. Once the squatter is rightly registered as proprietor under s. 75(3) the documentary lessee and the freeholder can no longer defeat the squatter's rights by a surrender. But I am not deciding anything as to the position during the period between the date when the squatter obtains his title by adverse possession and the date on which he obtains registration of it. This is the period covered by sub-s. (1) of s. 75 which is the subsection on which Lord Radcliffe ([1962] 2 All ER 288 at 296, [1963] AC 510 at 542) and Sir John Pennycuick ([1976] 3 All ER 521 at 530, [1978] QB 264 at 275) were commenting. It may well be, as their *dicta* suggest, that during the period preceding any registration of the squatter's rights, the documentary lessee (as registered proprietor of the lease) and the freeholder can deal with the legal estate with reference to a person whose rights are not recorded on the register. But once the Act provides for registration of the squatter's title, it must in my judgment follow that the squatter's rights (once registered) cannot be overridden. The difference between registered and unregistered land in this respect is an inevitable consequence of the fact that the Land Registration Act 1925 provides for registration of the squatter as proprietor and that registered proprietors have rights. . . .

Smith, P. F., Limitation and the Land Registration Act 1925 (1981) 131 NLJ 718

The interrelation of the Limitation Act 1939 and the Land Registration Act 1925 raises two problems of some difficulty which it is the object of this article to examine. The first question concerns the nature of a squatter's title acquired against registered land; the second matter is whether in any sense it is true to say that a squatter is given by the combined effects of the Limitation Act 1939 and the Land Registration Act 1925, a 'parliamentary conveyance'.

Construction of LRA, s. 75

Neither the authorities nor the leading texts offer very much guidance as to the nature of the title conferred on the squatter (one registered) by s. 75 of the 1925 Act, but two points do emerge. The first of these is that, contrary to the position with unregistered land, the squatter with a registered title has no new estate. Secondly, despite this, the general view appears to be that s. 75(1) is in effect mere machinery and does not affect the substance of the matter. Thus, not untypically, it is said in *Williams on Title* (4th edn, p. 844) when dealing with the provision:

It is arguable that s. 75 achieves a parliamentary conveyance to the squatter, a proposition which is diametrically opposed to the accepted construction of the Limitation Acts. It is thought, however, that this conclusion will be resisted by the courts. . . .

Not surprisingly, as was suggested above, the latest authority on the point, *Spectrum Investment Ltd* v *Holmes* [1981] 1 All ER 6, was non-committal on the point, the reason for this being partly the decision that the purported surrender was invalid as an unauthorised disposition, and partly, no doubt, caution.

It is thought, with respect, that the proper construction of s. 75(1) leads to the tentative conclusion that the broad denial of its effecting a parliamentary conveyance is as misleading as its complete and unqualified acceptance would be. After all, it has already been seen that the estate of the squatter, once registered under the 1925 Act, is capable of resisting disfeasance by a subsequent 'surrender' by the documentary lessee. This is not so in the case of unregistered land where the effect of the squat is purely extinctive.

Secondly, and this is of more difficulty, if the squatter's registered leasehold title is incapable of disfeasance by subsequent surrender, it is possible that the squatter steps into the position of the lessee for the residue of the term, so that in general, the freeholder's right to possession will not vest until the term date.

Thirdly, it is fairly clear that, as is the case with unregistered land, the squatter's registration will not of itself defeat prior interests and titles, and this appears to be recognised in s. 75(1) of the Land Registration Act, in these words:

. . . without prejudice to the estates and interests of any other person interested in the land whose estate or interest is not extinguished by those Acts. . . .

Nugee, E.G., Limitation and the Land Registration Act 1925 (1981) 131 NLJ 774

Dear Madam,

Your contributor Mr P. F. Smith (*NLJ* July 9, p. 718) finds difficulties in the interrelation of the Limitation Act 1939 and the Land Registration Act 1925 some of which do not really exist. The key is that, to quote Jessel MR in *Rosenberg* v *Cook* 8 QBD 162, 165, 'The title of the disseisor is in this country a freehold title'. When a squatter takes possession of land adversely to the owner, he obtains a legal estate in fee simple from the moment he does so. True it is defeasible by the owner, but it is good against the rest of the world. The best exposition is in Megarry & Wade's *Law of Real Property* 4th edn, pp. 1002–10, especially at 1007.

The fact that the owner's title is registered is neither here nor there. If S, the squatter, acquires a legal estate in fee simple from the moment he goes into adverse possession when R's title is unregistered, he does so equally clearly if R's title is registered—R's title is quite distinct, and there is nothing in the Land Registration Act 1925 to prevent S from acquiring an independent legal estate in fee simple. His estate does not require registration in order that its legal nature be recognised, for S does not acquire it by disposition from R, and it is not within the categories of estate the registration of which is compulsory under s. 123. The law has always recognised that two legal estates in fee simple can co-exist in the same land, one being defeasible by the other; and the Land Registration Act 1925 contains nothing to alter the general law in this respect.

When 12 years have elapsed, S still has his original legal estate, but it has ceased to be defeasible by R. R, however, remains on the register as the proprietor of *his* legal estate. Since the register is intended to mirror the true legal position, the Act provides that the estate which is registered in R's name is not simply extinguished as it would have been had it been unregistered; but R ceases to have any beneficial interest in it, and becomes a bare trustee of it for S. S then has two interests in the land—his own legal estate acquired by adverse possession, and the equitable title to the estate of which R is still the registered proprietor. In practice what happens is that when S applies to be registered, the Land Registry close R's title and open a new one for S, thereby recognising that the reality of the position is that R's title has been extinguished and S's has become indefeasible.

Mr Smith's statement that 'contrary to the position with unregistered land, the squatter with a registered title' (by which he presumably means the squatter on land the title to which is registered in the name of someone else) 'has no new estate' is, with respect, wrong. The Land Registry will in fact register a squatter with possessory title before he has been in adverse possession for 12 years, at any rate if no one else has a registered title (see 27 Conv 372), and in such a case they must be accepting that there are two legal estates in fee simple co-existing, since the title of the original owner cannot have been extinguished. . . .

Yours faithfully,

E. G. Nugee QC

Lincoln's Inn

London WC2

21.8   End of Chapter Assessment Question

Edwina holds an 80 year lease (granted in 1965) over Greenacre and a freehold title to Redacre. The two plots adjoin and Edwina uses most of the land for her business as a scrap merchant. However she has left vacant part of the land ('Grey Land'). Grey Land is partly within Greenacre and partly within Redacre.

In 1982 Freda, the owner of nearby Great House, started to cultivate Grey Land as an ornamental garden. Freda admits that, 'I have known all along that Grey Land belongs to Edwina'. Indeed in 1995 Freda wrote to Edwina offering to buy Grey Land. (Edwina did not reply to this letter.)

Edwina's business is now expanding, and she wishes to regain possession of Grey Land.

Advise Edwina.

21.9   End of Chapter Assessment Outline Answer

It would appear that Freda (if she is properly advised) will claim title to Grey Land by virtue of adverse possession.

In the 1989 case of *Bucks CC* v *Moran*, Moran extended his large garden on to land which he well knew was owned by the Council and was intended to be used for a projected by-pass. Moran nevertheless took control of the Council's land, and clearly had *animus possidendi*, i.e. an intent to exclude everyone else from the relevant land. As Moran's control continued for more than twelve years the Court of Appeal held that he had destroyed the Council's title by his adverse possession and acquired a new title for himself based on his own long possession.

Similarly Freda can argue that her cultivation of Grey Land for the last fourteen years was adverse possession. (One imagines that she intended to keep everyone from trampling over her beautiful garden!) Following *Moran* it will not matter that Freda knew 'all along that Grey Land belonged to Edwina'.

Edwina may well say to us something like, 'I always intended to make use of Grey Land but I just never got round to doing so.' In the past that might well have helped Edwina, as a line of cases (one as recent as 1974, *Wallis* v *Shell*) had held that if the owner of a paper title to some disused land retained plans for that land, there could be no adverse possession against that land until those plans were either abandoned or rendered impossible.

However in 1979 Parliament passed what is now Schedule 1, para. 8(4) of the Limitation Act 1980. The wording is obscure, but in *Moran* the Court of Appeal held that para. 8(4) overrules the line of cases culminating in *Wallis*.

The *Wallis'* line of cases had produced the unfortunate result that ownership of land could depend on obscure plans locked up in the minds of paper title owners, rather than on the easily observed physical fact of long possession. It is submitted that if the interpretation of para. 8(4) in Moran was challenged in the House of Lords, the House (currently very concerned to produce a sensible and workable Land Law) would rule that *Moran* was entirely correct.

The letter which Freda wrote in 1995 has come too late for our client. If it had been written in (say) 1992 it would have constituted an acknowledgement of title which would have stopped time running in Fred's favour. But by 1994 time had already run in Fred's favour; the rights of a paper title holder (Edward) once they have been 'time barred' cannot be revived by a subsequent acknowledgment.

CHAPTER TWENTY-TWO

RECTIFICATION OF THE REGISTER OF TITLE

22.1 The Statutory Framework

LAND REGISTRATION ACT 1925

82. Rectification of the register

(1) The register may be rectified pursuant to an order of the court or by the registrar, subject to an appeal to the court, in any of the following cases, but subject to the provisions of this section:—

(a) Subject to any express provisions of this Act to the contrary, where a court of competent jurisdiction has decided that any person is entitled to any estate right or interest in or to any registered land or charge, and as a consequence of such decision such court is of opinion that a rectification of the register is required, and makes an order to that effect;

(b) Subject to any express provision of this Act to the contrary, where the court, on the application in the prescribed manner of any person who is aggrieved by any entry made in, or by the omission of any entry from, the register, or by any default being made, or unnecessary delay taking place, in the making of any entry in the register, makes an order for the rectification of the register;

(c) In any case and at any time with the consent of all persons interested;

(d) Where the court or the registrar is satisfied that any entry in the register has been obtained by fraud;

(e) Where two or more persons are, by mistake, registered as proprietors of the same registered estate or of the same charge;

(f) Where a mortgagee has been registered as proprietor of the land instead of as proprietor of a charge and a right of redemption is subsisting;

(g) Where a legal estate has been registered in the name of a person who if the land had not been registered would not have been the estate owner; and

(h) In any other case where, by reason of any error or omission in the register, or by reason of any entry made under a mistake, it may be deemed just to rectify the register.

(2) The register may be rectified under this section, notwithstanding that the rectification may affect any estates, rights, charges, or interests acquired or protected by registration, or by any entry on the register, or otherwise.

(3) The register shall not be rectified, except for the purpose of giving effect to an overriding interest [or an order of the court], so as to affect the title of the proprietor who is in possession—

(a) unless the proprietor has caused or substantially contributed to the error or omission by fraud or lack of proper care; or

(b) . . .

(c) unless for any other reason, in any particular case, it is considered that it would be unjust not to rectify the register against him.

(4) Where a person is in possession of registered land in right of a minor interest, he shall, for the purposes of this section, be deemed to be in possession as agent for the proprietor.

(5) The registrar shall obey the order of any competent court in relation to any registered land on being served with the order or an official copy thereof.

(6) On every rectification of the register the land certificate and any charge certificate which may be affected shall be produced to the registrar unless an order to the contrary is made by him.

NORWICH AND PETERBOROUGH BUILDING SOCIETY v STEED
[1993] Ch 116, Court of Appeal

FACTS: The defendant had emigrated to the United States, leaving his home in the occupation of his mother, his sister and his brother in law. He executed a power of attorney in favour of his mother, in terms which permitted her, *inter alia*, to sell the property. The sister produced a transfer showing that the mother had sold the land to her and the brother in law, her husband. The mother denied ever having consented to such a sale. In any event, the sister and brother in law were duly registered as proprietors of the property. Unfortunately, they fell behind with repayments of mortgage instalments and the building society brought proceedings for possession. The defendant resisted the building society's claim to possess the premises, and counterclaimed for rectification of the register on the basis that the transfer had been forged and was, therefore, not his deed (this plea is known as '*non est factum*'). He withdrew the allegation of forgery when expert evidence was adduced to show that the mother (who had since died) probably had executed the transfer. HELD: As the defendant no longer alleged fraud, and as his claim of *non est factum* had failed, there were no grounds for rectification. Section 82(1) of the Land Registration Act 1925 did not confer on the court a general jurisdiction to achieve a just and equitable solution.

SCOTT LJ: If an order of rectification is to be made the case must be brought within at least one of paragraphs (a) to (h) of section 82(1). . . .

There is a sense in which the power to rectify under section 82 is undoubtedly discretionary. The words in subsection (1) are 'may be rectified.' Section 83(2) shows that rectification is not automatic. The power to rectify may, in a particular case, be present but, nonetheless, there is a general discretion to refuse rectification. It does not follow, however, that there is, in every case, a general discretion to grant rectification. The power to grant rectification is limited in subsection (1) to 'any of the following cases.' The power to order rectification must, therefore, be found within one or other of the subsection (1) paragraphs and cannot be spelled out of the words 'may be rectified.'. . .

In my opinion the scheme is reasonably clear. Paragraphs (a) and (b) give power to the court to make orders of rectification in order to give effect to property rights which have been established in an action or which are clear. Paragraph (c) enables orders to be made by consent. The remaining paragraphs, (d) to (h), are intended to enable errors to be corrected. Paragraph (d), paragraph (e), paragraph (f) and paragraph (g) each deals with an error of a particular character. But, since these paragraphs might not cover comprehensively all errors, paragraph (h) was added as a catch-all provision to cover any other errors. The breadth of the catch-all provision was, I imagine, the reason why it was thought appropriate to make the power exercisable 'where . . . it may be deemed just to rectify the register.' There are no comparable words in any of the other paragraphs.

Paragraph (h) is relied on by Mr. Lloyd. But in order for the paragraph to be applicable some 'error or omission in the register' or some 'entry made under a mistake' must be shown. The entry in the charges register of the building society's legal charge was not an error and was not made under a mistake. The legal charge was executed by the Hammonds, who were at the time transferees under a transfer executed by Mrs. Steed as attorney for the registered proprietor. The voidable transfer had not been set aside. The registration of the Hammonds as proprietors took place at the same time as the registration of the legal charge. Neither registration was an error. Neither entry was made under a mistake. So the case for rectification cannot be brought under paragraph (h).

As a matter of principle, if, as I think, the defendant's case for rectification as against the building society cannot be brought under any of the paragraphs of section 82(1), I would conclude that that must be an end to the rectification claim.

22.1.1   RECTIFICATION AGAINST A REGISTERED PROPRIETOR IN POSSESSION

22.1.1.1   Registered proprietor 'to blame' for the wrong registration

RE 139 HIGH STREET, DEPTFORD [1951] 1 ChD 950, Chancery Division

FACTS: Prior to 1948 number 139 was unregistered title. In 1948 V sold to P number 139. The conveyance, which had no plan attached, described the land as 'all that shop and dwelling-house situate and known as 139, High Street, Deptford in the County of London'. P applied for first registration. Apparently V, P, their respective legal advisers, and the Land Registry all thought that number 139 included a small piece of disused land at the rear of No 139, next to a railway line. P was registered as proprietor of the dwelling house/shop and the land at the rear. In fact, this land actually 'belonged to' British Railways. The registration thus deprived the railway of that piece of land. When British Railways found out, it sought rectification of the register.
HELD: Rectification was granted. The judge held that P was caught by section 82(3)(a), because P had 'contributed' to the error at the Registry.

WYNN-PARRY J: . . . The respondent, by his solicitor, merely put forward an application in the usual form, describing the property as '139 Deptford High Street,' and accompanying the application with the conveyance containing the description to which I have already referred:

> all that shop and dwelling-house situate at and known as 139 High Street, Deptford, in the county of London.

Counsel for the respondent, on the one hand, contends that, in doing that and nothing more, the respondent did something which cannot in any sense be said to have contributed to the mistake, the mistake being that of the Land Registry in including the disputed land in the registration. It is submitted by the applicants, on the other hand, that the respondent must be said to have contributed to the mistake. The question must be one of construction as to what is included in the language of the parcels. To resolve that, reference must be made to the surrounding circumstances so far as, in accordance with the well-established rules, they can be taken into consideration. When one looks at the surrounding circumstances, one finds that at the date of the contract and the conveyance the only access to the disputed land was through the immediately adjoining premises, which, quite clearly, were known as '139 High Street, Deptford,' and that, therefore, as a matter of construction, this conveyance intended to include, and did include, the disputed land in the description '139 High Street, Deptford.' On that view it is contended by counsel for the applicants that, by putting that description forward, the respondent contributed to the mistake, because the necessary consequence of putting forward the application must have been that the Land Registry officials would make the usual inquiries and, if necessary, a survey of the premises, and they would, therefore, be led to fall into the same mistake as had been made by the respondent and his vendors. It is not an easy point to resolve, but it appears to me that the determining factor is the circumstance that, so far as the physical aspect of the matter is concerned, the disputed land must have appeared to anyone looking at the properties in question to form part of 139 High Street, Deptford. It was, apparently, so obvious that the vendors to the respondent fell into the mistake, the respondent himself fell into the mistake, and the Land Registry fell into the mistake. On that view of the matter, it appears to me, notwithstanding the arguments both practical and theoretical of counsel for the respondent, to follow, necessarily, that the respondent must be held to have contributed to the mistake, within the meaning of s. 82(3)(a) of the Act of 1925. . . .

22.1.1.2   Unjust not to rectify the register

EPPS v ESSO PETROLEUM CO. LTD [1973] 2 All ER 465, Chancery Division

FACTS: C owned a site in Gillingham on which he built a house and a garage, leaving a strip of land between them. In 1955 C's personal representatives conveyed the house and the strip to Edna Jones. She covenanted to erect a wall between the strip and the garage, but failed to do so. The existing fence between strip and house remained *in situ*. The strip therefore appeared to 'belong' to the garage. In 1957 Gillingham became an area of compulsory registration. In 1959 C's personal representatives conveyed the garage and strip to Ball. Ball applied for first registration, and was registered as proprietor of both garage and strip. There was thus a 'double conveyancing' situation, but Ball had legal title to the strip due to his registration. Since 1959 the strip had been used as part of the garage. In 1964 Ball sold the garage including the strip to Esso; Esso became registered proprietor. In 1968 Edna Jones' personal representatives sold the house and purported to sell the strip to Epps, but the Land Registry refused to register him as proprietor of the strip. He applied for rectification, and relied particularly on section 82(3)(c).

HELD: Rectification was refused.

TEMPLEMAN J: . . . if an order for rectification is made the defendants will be entitled to indemnity on 1973 values, and if the claim for rectification is refused then they will keep the land, but the plaintiffs will not get compensation.

The question I have to determine is whether that is sufficient to upset the justice of the defendants' claim that there should not be rectification in the present instance. Is it sufficient—and this is the test—to make it unjust not to rectify the register against the defendants? Counsel for the plaintiffs pointed out that as far as the defendants are concerned the disputed strip formed, he calculated, four per cent of the garage premises. He said it could not make a lot of difference to the defendants' garage; on the other hand, it was of importance to 4 Darland Avenue, because it provided a private garage, an asset which is important in commuter territory.

In my judgment, however, this cannot be solved merely on the question of money. The defendants bought the land; they bought it to exploit for their commercial purposes; they did not buy it in order to sell a strip for a 1973 value, which in real terms will not, in my judgment, adequately indemnify them. Although the strip is at the back of the garage, in the same way as it could be used as a private garage for 4 Darland Avenue, so it could be used by the defendants for commercial purposes, and in fact they say now they intend to use it in connection with a car wash; if they are deprived of it they will be in considerable difficulty, and will not have all the facilities which a modern garage requires. I think that may be putting it a bit high, but the fact of the matter is that this strip is worth more to the defendants than the pounds, shillings and pence which they will receive by indemnity, even on a 1973 basis.

Accordingly, in my judgment, that argument is not sufficient to overturn all the other arguments in favour of the defendants, and I decline to order rectification of the register.

22.2 Indemnity

LAW OF PROPERTY ACT 1925

83. Right to indemnity in certain cases

(1) Subject to the provisions of this Act to the contrary, any persons suffering loss by reason of any rectification of the register under this Act shall be entitled to be indemnified.

(2) Where an error or omission has occurred in the register, but the register is not rectified, any person suffering loss by reason of such error or omission, shall, subject to the provisions of this Act, be entitled to be indemnified.

(3) Where any person suffers loss by reason of the loss or destruction of any document lodged at the registry for inspection or safe custody or by reason of an error in any official search, he shall be entitled to be indemnified under this Act.

(4) Subject as hereinafter provided, a proprietor of any registered land or charge claiming in good faith under a forged disposition shall, where the register is rectified, be deemed to have suffered loss by reason of such rectification and shall be entitled to be indemnified under this Act.

(5) . . .

(6) Where an indemnity is paid in respect of the loss of an estate or interest in or charge on land the amount so paid shall not exceed—

(a) Where the register is not rectified, the value of the estate, interest or charge at the time when the error or omission which caused the loss was made;

(b) Where the register is rectified, the value (if there had been no rectification) of the estate, interest or charge, immediately before the time of rectification.

(7) ...

(8) ...

(9) Where indemnity is paid for a loss, the registrar, on behalf of the Crown, shall be entitled to recover the amount paid from any person who has caused or substantially contributed to the loss by his fraud.

(10) The registrar shall be entitled to enforce, on behalf of the Crown, any express or implied covenant or other right which the person who is indemnified would have been entitled to enforce in relation to the matter in respect of which indemnity has been paid.

(11) A liability to pay indemnity under this Act shall be deemed a simple contract debt; and for the purposes of [the Limitation Act 1980], the cause of action shall be deemed to arise at the time when the claimant knows, or but for his own default might have known, of the existence of his claim:

Provided that, when a claim to indemnity arises in consequence of the registration of an estate in land with an absolute or good leasehold title, the claim shall be enforceable only if made within six years from the date of such registration, except in the following cases:—

(a) Where at the date of registration the person interested is an infant, the claim by him may be made within six years from the time he attains full age;

(b) In the case of settled land, or land held on trust for sale, a claim by a person interested in remainder or reversion, may be made within six years from the time when his interest falls into possession;

(c) Where a claim arises in respect of a restrictive covenant or agreement affecting freehold land which by reason of notice or the registration of a land charge or otherwise was binding on the first proprietor at the time of first registration, the claim shall only be enforceable within six years from the breach of the covenant or agreement;

(d) Where any person interested is entitled as a proprietor of a charge or as a mortgagee protected by a caution in the specially prescribed form, the claim by him may be made within six years from the last payment in respect of principal or interest.

(12) This section applies to the Crown in like manner as it applies to a private person.

22.2.1 INDEMNITY FOR A REGISTERED PROPRIETOR WHERE RECTIFICATION IS GRANTED

RE CHOWOOD'S REGISTERED LAND [1933] 1 Ch 574, Chancery Division

FACTS: An adverse possessor had gained title to part of a piece of land of which Chowood Ltd was registered proprietor. The adverse possessor sought rectification of the register.
HELD: Rectification was granted. Chowood Ltd was held not to be entitled to any indemnity. The adverse possessor had an overriding interest under section 70(1)(f) of the Land Registration Act 1925, and Chowood lost nothing as a result of the rectification.

CLAUSON J: . . . Immediately before the rectification of the register the position, as I have indicated above, was that Chowood's estate was 'subject to rights acquired or in course of being acquired under the Limitation Acts.' On the facts as they appeared in the case of *Chowood, Ltd* v *Lyall* [1930] 2 Ch 156 (and the findings of fact in that case are by agreement to be treated as binding between the present parties), Lyall was in possession of the strip when Chowood's title was registered, and, of course, also when the Land Registration Act 1925, came into force, and also immediately before and at the date of the rectification of the register. Further, that possession was, at each of those dates, protected against any claim by Chowood to enter upon it, the protection flowing from the fact, established by Lyall in the former litigation, that Lyall and her predecessors had had possession for such length of time as would be an answer under the Limitation Acts to any such claim by Chowood. It appears to me to follow that Lyall's rights were accordingly rights acquired under the Limitation Acts. It was suggested that the words 'subject to the provisions of this Act' affect the matter. I cannot see why. The reference seems to be to s. 75, which contains very special provisions which prevent rights acquired under the Limitation Acts from operating under certain cirumstances to extinguish the estate of the registered proprietor. This does not seem to have any operation upon the position in the case with which I am now dealing. It was further suggested that Lyall's title depended to some extent on what was called a paper title, and not solely on the Limitation Acts. I do not say what the position might have been if Lyall's paper title had disclosed, for example, a grant to her by Ralli's predecessor in title which could be used to defeat Chowood's claim to the strip without recourse to the Statute of Limitations. Such a case can be dealt with when it arises. In the present case Lyall's paper title was of value simply as some evidence of length of possession, and had no other operation; the paper title, save in so far as it supported a plea of possession for the statutory period, would not have helped to defeat Chowood's claim. It results from this that Chowood's title was all along subject to the rights which Lyall has succeeded in establishing; and the loss, if it may properly be so called, which Chowood has suffered is that they have not got, and since the Act of 1925 came into force (whatever may have been the position before) have never had title to the strip, except subject to an overriding right in Lyall. That loss was occasioned by Chowood failing to ascertain that, when they bought, Lyall was in possession, and in possession under such circumstances that Ralli could not make a title to the strip. The loss was occasioned by paying Ralli for a strip to which Ralli could not make title. The rectification of the register merely recognised the existing position, and put Chowood in no worse a position than they were in before.

In these circumstances I must hold that Chowood have suffered no loss by reason of the rectification of the register. . . .

22.3   End of Chapter Assessment Question

The Aberconwy District (Llandudno, Conwy, Llanrwst etc.) became an area of compulsory registration of title on the 1 December 1988.

In 1987 Geoffrey purchased a small piece of land 'Lomasacre' situated in Aberconwy. Lomasacre formed a small part of the vast 'Brooke Estate' owned by John. Geoffrey did his own conveyancing; as a result no indorsement referring to the sale off of Lomasacre was placed on the deeds to the Brooke Estate.

Geoffrey has only visited Lomasacre on one occasion since he purchased it; on that occasion he dumped some rusting railings on part of the land.

Last week John sold the whole of the Brooke Estate to Malcolm; Malcolm believes that Lomasacre is part of the land he has purchased. He has successfully applied for registration as proprietor of the whole of the Brooke Estate.

Discuss.

22.4   End of Chapter Assessment Outline Answer

The problem scenario describes a 'double conveyancing' situation. John sold Lomasacre to Geoffrey in 1987, before it became compulsory to register Lomasacre with a separate title. In these circumstances Geoffrey should have ensured that the sale of Lomasacre had been endorsed on the deeds of the Brook Estate. He failed to do so. Recently John sold the whole of the Brooke Estate to Malcolm, with the result that Lomasacre has been conveyed twice. On these facts it is clear that Geoffrey has the best title to Lomasacre. However, to the scenario must be added the fact that Malcolm has been registered successfully as proprietor of the whole of the Brook Estate, including Lomasacre. Now Geoffrey's only hope of asserting his title to Lomasacre is to obtain rectification of the register.

In the case of *Norwich and Peterborough Building Society* v *Steed* (1993) [see **22.1**], the Court of Appeal emphasised that the court's powers to order rectification of the register are strictly confined to the grounds set out in s. 82 of the Land Registration Act 1925. The basic grounds for rectifying the register are set out in s. 82(1) of the Land Registration Act 1925. If, however, as in the present case, rectification of the register is sought against a 'registered proprietor in possession', the conditions in s. 82(3) will also have to be satisfied.

Section 82(1)(b) provides that the register may be rectified 'on the application . . . of any person who is aggrieved by any entry made in, or by the ommission of an entry from, the register'. This section covers Geoffrey's claim. Section 82(1) further provides that rectification may take place if all the parties consent (not likely here); if the court is satisfied that an entry has been obtained by fraud (there is no suggestion that Malcolm has acted fraudulently); where a legal estate has been registered in the name of a person who if the land had not been registered would not have been the estate owner (this paragraph, s. 82(1)(g), is clearly the most appropriate to Geoffrey's claim); and in any other case where by reason of any error or omission in the register, or by reason of an entry made under a mistake, it may be deemed just to rectify the register.

It is clear that Geoffrey will seek rectification under s. 82(1)(g). However, he will have to satisfy the requirements of s. 82(3) which are designed to protect registered proprietors in possession, such as Malcolm in our case. Before 1977, s. 82(3)(a) provided for rectification against a registered proprietor in possession where the proprietor had caused or substantially contributed, by his act, neglect or default, to the fraud, mistake or omission. This provision was applied in *Re 139 Deptford High Street* (1951) [see **22.1.2.1**]. In that case a purchaser applied for first registration of title, just as Malcolm has done in our case. The purchaser was registered as proprietor of a large piece of land, but he was mistakenly registered as proprietor also of a small piece of land that did not belong to him (as in our case). The true owner of the small plot applied for rectification of the register and was successful. The court held that the purchaser had 'contributed' to the error at the registry by presenting documents for registration which were inaccurate. It did not matter that the purchaser had been neither fraudulent nor negligent (in that case the vendor had mistakenly believed that the disputed piece of land had been properly sold to the purchaser, and so the purchaser had not been negligent) in putting forward the innacurate documents. Accordingly, it is likely that Geoffrey would have succeeded on the facts of the present case if he had been claiming rectification before 1977.

However, in 1977 s. 82(3)(a) was amended to give even more protection to the registered proprietor in possession. Under the new provision rectification can be granted only where '. . . the proprietor has caused or substantially contributed to the error or omission by fraud or lack of proper care'. Accordingly, Geoffrey will only obtain rectification today if he can show that Malcolm knew that the documents he had presented for registration had been inaccurate (a case of fraud) or that he ought to have known that the documents were inaccurate (a case of 'lack of proper care'). There is no evidence that Malcolm had actual knowledge of Geoffrey's right. And it is doubtful that he ought to have known. The presence of 'rusty' railings on a part of the Brook Estate, suggests, if anything, that the land has not been used for some time. Malcolm may, perhaps, have asked John how the rusty railings came to be there, and if John's answer led Malcolm to suspect the presence of a third party, it may be that Malcolm 'ought to have concluded' that a third party had rights over the land. However, this is a most unlikely set of circumstances.

The most likely conclusion is that Geoffrey will be refused rectification under s. 82(3)(a). Consequently, Geoffrey will fail to obtain rectification unless he can show that 'for any other reason . . . it would be unjust not to rectify the register' (s. 82(3)(c)). It is clear from the wording of that paragraph (particularly the use of a double negative [see 22.1]) that this provision should only be used in a case where it is absolutely clear that justice demands that the register should be rectified. One question the courts will ask is whether, if Geoffrey is refused rectification, cash compensation at the market value of his lost land will be adequate compensation (*Epps* v *Esso* (1973) [see 22.1.2.2]). Considering the infrequent and uneconomic use to which Geoffrey has put his land the conclusion seems inevitable that justice will not demand a rectification, and that rectification will be refused.

The question of compensation remains. According to s. 83(2) of the Land Registration Act 1925 [see 22.2] 'where an error or omission has occurred in the register, but the register is not rectified, any person suffering loss by reason of such error or omisssion, shall, subject to the provisions of this Act, be entitled to be indemnified'. The land 'lost' is valued at the date that the error occurred (today) which is probably bad news for Malcolm because the land will have been devalued due to the presence of the rusty railings.

CHAPTER TWENTY-THREE

THE ESSENTIAL CHARACTERISTICS OF EASEMENTS

23.1 Preliminary Considerations

MILLER v EMCER PRODUCTS LTD [1956] 1 All ER 237, Court of Appeal

FACTS: A tenant claimed the right to use a lavatory on another floor of the building in which he lived. The tenants of that floor objected to his use of it. One question was whether the right to use the toilet would be capable of being an easement.
HELD: It was.

ROMER LJ: . . . The question remains, however, as to the nature of the right which the landlords purported to include in the demise, and, in particular whether it was a licence or an easement? In my judgment, the right had all the requisite characteristics of an easement. There is no doubt what were intended to be the dominant and servient tenements respectively, and the right was appurtenant to the former and calculated to enhance its beneficial use and enjoyment. It is true that during the times when the dominant owner exercised the right, the owner of the servient tenement would be excluded, but this in greater or less degree is a common feature of many easements (e.g., rights of way) and does not amount to such an ouster of the servient owner's rights as was held by Upjohn J, to be incompatible with a legal easement in *Copeland* v *Greenhalf* [1952] 1 All ER 809. No case precisely in point on this issue was brought to our attention, but the right to use a lavatory is not dissimilar, I think, to the right to use a neighbour's kitchen for washing, the validity of which as an easement was assumed without question in *Heywood* v *Mallalieu* (1883) 25 ChD 357. No objection can fairly be made based on uncertainty, and it follows, in my judgment, that the right may properly be regarded as an easement which the landlords were professing to grant for a term of years; and such an easement would rank as an interest in or over land capable of being created at law by virtue of the Law of Property Act 1925, s. 1(2)(a).

. . . the easement which the landlords purported to grant to the tenant in relation to the lavatories is within the covenant for quiet enjoyment.

RE ELLENBOROUGH PARK [1955] 3 All ER 667, Court of Appeal

FACTS: The owners of houses situated around a 'private square' in Weston-super-Mare claimed the right to use a private garden in the middle of the square for the purpose of exercise and relaxation.
HELD: The neighbouring owners had easements over the garden.

SIR RAYMOND EVERSHED MR: For the purposes of the argument before us counsel were content to adopt, as correct, the four characteristics formulated in Dr. Cheshire's Modern Real Property (7th edn.), p. 456 et seq. They are (i) There must be a dominant and a servient tenement: (ii) an easement must accommodate the dominant tenement: (iii) dominant and servient owners must be different persons: and (iv) a right over land cannot amount to an easement unless it is capable of forming the subject-matter of a grant.

The four characteristics stated by Dr. Cheshire correspond with the qualities discussed by Gale in his second chapter, sections 2, 5, 3, and 6 and 8 respectively. Two of the four may be disregarded for present purposes, *viz*, the first and the third. If the garden or park is, as it is alleged to be, the servient tenement in the present case, then it is undoubtedly distinct from the alleged dominant tenements, *viz*, the freeholds of the several houses whose owners claim to exercise the rights. It is equally clear that if these lands respectively constitute the servient and dominant tenements, then they are owned by different persons. The argument in the case is found accordingly to turn on the meaning and application to the circumstances of the present case of the second and fourth conditions; i.e., first, whether the alleged easement can be said in truth to 'accommodate' the dominant tenement, in other words, whether there exists the required 'connection' between the one and the other; and, second, whether the right alleged is 'capable of forming the subject-matter of a grant'. The exact significance of this fourth and last condition is, at first sight perhaps, not entirely clear. As between the original parties to the 'grant' it is not in doubt that rights of this kind would be capable of taking effect by way of contract or licence. But for the purposes of the present case, as the arguments made clear, the cognate questions involved under this condition are: whether the rights purported to be given are expressed in terms of too wide and vague a character; whether, if and so far as effective, such rights would amount to rights of joint occupation or would substantially deprive the owners of the park of proprietorship or legal possession; whether, if and so far as effective, such rights constitute mere rights of recreation, possessing no quality of utility or benefit; and on such grounds cannot qualify as easements. . . .

Can it be said, then, of the right of full enjoyment of the park in question, which was granted by the conveyance of December 23, 1864, and which, for reasons already given, was, in our view, intended to be annexed to the property conveyed to Mr. Porter, that it accommodated and served that property? It is clear that the right did, in some degree enhance the value of the property and this consideration cannot be dismissed as wholly irrelevant. It is, of course, a point to be noted; but we agree with the submission of counsel for the owners of the park that it is in no way decisive of the problem; it is not sufficient to show that the right increased the value of the property conveyed unless it is also shown that it was connected with the normal enjoyment of that property. It appears to us that the question whether or not this connection exists, is primarily one of fact, and depends largely on the nature of the alleged dominant tenement and the nature of the right granted.

. . . The park became a communal garden for the benefit and enjoyment of those whose houses adjoined it or were in its close proximity. Its flower beds, lawns and walks were calculated to afford all the amenities which it is the purpose of the garden of a house to provide; and apart from the fact that these amenities extended to a number of householders instead of being confined to one (which on this aspect of the case is immaterial) we can see no difference in principle between Ellenborough Park and a garden in the ordinary signification of that word. It is the collective garden of the neighbouring houses to whose use it was dedicated by the owners of the estate and as such amply satisfied, in our judgment, the requirement of connection with the dominant tenements to which it is appurtenant. The result is not affected by the circumstance that the right to the park is in this case enjoyed by some few houses which are not immediately fronting on the park. The test for present purposes, no doubt, is that the park should constitute in a real and intelligible sense the garden (albeit the communal garden) of the houses to which the enjoyment is annexed. But we think that the test is satisfied as regards these few neighbouring, though not adjacent, houses. We think that the extension of the right of enjoyment to these few houses does not negative the presence of the necessary 'nexus' between the subject-matter enjoyed and the premises to which the enjoyment is expressed to belong. . . .

We turn next to Dr. Cheshire's fourth condition for an easement—that the right must be capable of forming the subject-matter of a grant. As we have earlier stated, satisfaction of the condition in the present case depends on a consideration of the questions, whether the right conferred is too wide and vague, whether it is inconsistent with the proprietorship or possession of the alleged servient owners, and whether it is a mere right of recreation without utility or benefit.

To the first of these questions the interpretation which we have given to the typical deed provides, in our judgment, the answer; for we have construed the right conferred as being both well defined and commonly understood. In these essential respects the right may be said to be distinct from the indefinite and unregulated privilege which, we think, would ordinarily be understood by the Latin term *'jus spatiandi'*, a privilege of wandering at will over all and every part of another's field or park, and which, though easily intelligible as the subject-matter of a personal licence, is something substantially different from the subject-matter of the grant in question, *viz*, the provision for a limited number of houses in a uniform crescent of one single large but private garden. Our interpretation of the deed also provides, we think, the answer to the second question; for the right conferred no more amounts to a joint occupation of the park with its owners, no more excludes the proprietorship or possession of the latter, than a right of way granted through a passage or than the use by the public of the gardens of Lincoln's Inn Fields (to take one of our former examples) amount to joint occupation of that garden with the London County Council, or involve an inconsistency with the possession or proprietorship of the council as lessees. It is conceded that in any event the owners of the park are entitled to cut the timber growing on the park and to retain its proceeds. We have said that in our judgment, under the deed, the flowers and shrubs grown in the garden are equally the property of the owners of the park. We see nothing repugnant to a man's proprietorship or possession of a piece of land that he should decide to make of it and maintain it as an ornamental garden, and should grant rights to a limited number of other persons to come into it for the enjoyment of its amenities.

. . . If the proposition be well-founded, we do not think that the right to use a garden of the character with which we are concerned in this case can be called one of mere recreation and amusement. . . .

The third of the questions embraced in Dr. Cheshire's fourth condition rests primarily on a proposition stated in Theobald's The Law of Land (1929), at p. 263, where it is said that an easement 'must be a right of utility and benefit and not one of mere recreation and amusement.'

PHIPPS v *PEAR* [1964] 2 All ER 35, Court of Appeal

FACTS: A house was demolished, leaving a wall of a neighbouring house exposed which had not been built to withstand the weather. When frost began to cause cracks to appear in the wall the owner of the exposed house brought an action against his neighbour, claiming an easement of protection from the weather.

HELD: There was no such right known to the law, and none should be recognised.

LORD DENNING MR: . . . There are two kinds of easement known to the law: positive easements, such as a right of way, which give the owner of land *a right himself to do something* on or to his neighbour's land: and negative easements, such as a right of light, which gives him *a right to stop his neighbour doing something* on his (the neighbour's) own land. The right of support does not fall neatly into either category. It seems in some way to partake of the nature of a positive easement rather than a negative easement. The one building, by its weight, exerts a thrust, not only downwards, but also sideways on to the adjoining building or the adjoining land, and is thus doing something to the neighbour's land, exerting a thrust on it; see *Dalton* v *Angus* (1881) 6 App Cas 740 per Lord Selborne, LC. But a right to protection from the weather (if it exists) is entirely negative. It is a right to stop your neighbour pulling down his own house. Seeing that it is a negative easement, it must be looked at with caution, because the law has been very chary of creating any new negative easements.

Take this simple instance: Suppose you have a fine view from your house. You have enjoyed the view for many years. It adds greatly to the value of your house. But if your neighbour chooses to despoil it, by building up and blocking it, you have no redress. There is no such right known to the law as a right to a prospect or view: see *Bland* v *Moseley* (1587) 9 Co. Rep 58a. The only way in which you can keep the view from your house is to get your neighbour to make a covenant with you that he will not build so as to block your view. Such a covenant is binding on him by virtue of the contract. It is also binding in equity on anyone who buys the land from him with notice of the covenant: but it is not binding on a purchaser who has no notice of it . . . if such an easement were to be permitted, it would unduly restrict your neighbour in his enjoyment of his own land. It would hamper legitimate development, see *Dalton* v *Angus* per Lord Blackburn. Likewise here, if we were to stop a man pulling down his house, we would put a brake on desirable improvement. Every man is entitled to pull down his house if he likes. If it exposes your house to the weather, that is your misfortune. It is no wrong on his part. Likewise every man is entitled to cut down his trees if he likes, even if it leaves you without shelter from the wind or shade from the sun, see the decision of the Master of the Rolls in Ireland. There is no such easement known to the law as an easement to be protected from the weather. The only way for an owner to protect himself is by getting a covenant from his neighbour that he will not pull down his house or cut down his trees. Such a covenant would be binding on him in contract; and it would be enforceable on any successor who took with notice of it, but it would not be binding on one who took without notice. . .

23.2　There Must be a Dominant and a Servient Tenement

An easement can exist only if it is attached to ('appurtenant to') a piece of dominant land. Suppose Gillian owns Wideviews Farm, situated in rural Derbyshire. She executes a deed in favour of Wendy (a keen walker) granting Wendy the right to use a path which crosses the farm. Wendy owns no land whatsoever. Though the right granted by the deed will give Wendy a lot of pleasure, it is certainly not an easement.

23.3　The Easement Must Accommodate the Dominant Tenement

PUGH v *SAVAGE* [1970] 2 All ER 353, Court of Appeal

FACTS: The question which arose in this case was whether a 'right of way' existing over one field to get to another field, where a third field lay between the dominant and servient tenements, could exist as a valid easement.
HELD: The right of way was a valid easement.

CROSS LJ: . . . *Todrick* v *Western National Omnibus Co. Ltd* [1934] Ch 561 shows that a right of way may exist for the benefit of a dominant tenement although between the dominant tenement and the servient tenement there is some intervening land. In the *Todrick* case itself, that intervening land was in fact owned by the owner of the dominant tenement, but all three members of the court expressed the view that, providing that the dominant owner was able to get across the intervening land, though only by the consent of a third party, the way claimed might still be a good right of way if it was sufficiently close to the dominant land to be sensibly described as appurtenant to and for the benefit of the dominant land. . . .

HILL v *TUPPER* (1863) 159 English Reports 51, Court of Exchequer

FACTS: The Basingstoke Canal Company owned the canal and some land on the banks of the canal. They leased the land on the banks of the canal to Hill for the purposes of a boatyard. The lease included a clause granting Hill the exclusive right to put pleasure boats on the canal. Tupper nevertheless started placing his pleasure boats on the canal. Hill sued Tupper, claiming that his 'pleasure boat monopoly' (as I like to call it) was an easement. If the court had accepted that claim, it would have meant that the pleasure boat monopoly was a property right which could be protected by suing anybody who interfered with it.
HELD: The pleasure boat monopoly was not an easement. The monopoly did not 'accommodate' the land leased to Hill. Rather it was for the benefit of Hill's business. Therefore, Hill's only remedy was to sue the canal company for breach of contract.

POLLOCK CB: . . . It is an old and well-established principle of our law that new estates cannot be created. Counsel says he sees no reason, if a man may grant a right to cut turves, or to fish, or to hunt etc, why such a right as that here claimed, or why an exclusive right to cut cabbages in a garden, or to collect the manure and droppings from cattle, which no doubt is of some value, may not also be granted. The answer is, that the law will not allow it. So the law will not permit a man to leave land alternately to a male heir and a female heir. Now rights or incidents of property cannot be created, nor can a new species of burden be imposed upon land at the pleasure of the owners. There are no instances of such new creations. It would be a new species of incorporeal hereditament. It has been contended that this is a sort of estate, but the owner of an estate must be content to take it with the rights and incidents known to and allowed by the law. A grantor may bind himself by covenant to allow what rights he pleases over his property, but the law will not permit him to carve out his property so as to enable the grantee of such a limited right to sue a stranger in the way here contended for. For these reasons, therefore, our judgment will be for the defendant.

MARTIN B: I am entirely of the same opinion. This grant is no doubt a valid grant between the canal company and their tenant, the plaintiff in this action; but in order to enable the plaintiff to maintain his action against the defendant he must establish that, by the grant, an estate vested in him so as to enable him to maintain an action on the case against a stranger for an infringement of his alleged rights, which he has failed to do. No case has been cited to show that such a right as this can be created, or that an owner can carve out his property into an indefinite number of hitherto unknown estates. To admit the right here claimed would be to open a door to the creation of such a variety of pieces and parcels of interests in land, and to such an indefinite increase of possible estates, that we ought not to do it. The plaintiff is entitled to the benefit of his covenant as against his lessors, the canal company; but if strangers infringe or molest him in the enjoyment of his rights, he must use the company's name to bring an action against such wrongdoers, and in this there is no hardship. . . .

23.4 'An Easement Must be Capable of Forming the Subject Matter of a Grant'

23.4.1 AN EASEMENT MUST BE CAPABLE OF REASONABLY EXACT DEFINITION

HARRIS v DE PINNA (1886) 33 ChD 238, Court of Appeal

FACTS: The owner of a timber-drying shed claimed the right to have an uninterrupted flow of air to his shed. He sought to enforce this right against a neighbour who had built two warehouses on nearby land.
HELD: There could be no easement for a general flow of air.

COTTON LJ: . . . Then, coming to what is said also to be a very important matter—air—have the plaintiffs made out any right in respect of air? It must be claimed either under the common law, or by a presumed grant, or under the statute.
. . . As regards light that is an entirely different matter from air. Light, the principal light which we enjoy, comes to us in a direct line, in direct pencils, and the light which is thrown over a neighbour's land goes over a very short space indeed. But here it is not a claim to air as coming in a defined channel over a neighbour's land, but it is a claim which is made in respect of a building not in any way closed up but made with openings,—merely a skeleton of a building if I may say so—with timbers supporting the floor and roof, and cross-beams to keep them in their position and make them steady; to prevent the plaintiffs' neighbour from doing anything which will prevent the current of air over his open yard from coming to the whole face of the plaintiffs' buildings as freely as it originally came when he did not choose, and it was not necessary for him, to apply the land for the purpose for which he is now intending to apply it. That, in my opinion, would be a most serious interference with the right which every one has to use his property, so long as he does not interfere with

those rights of his neighbour in respect of which the law gives such neighbour a right of complaint if they should be interfered with. In my opinion, therefore, there is no case made out here for holding that the plaintiffs are entitled to that right of air which they claim as against the defendant. . . .

COLLS v HOME AND COLONIAL STORES LTD [1904] AC 179, House of Lords

FACTS: Home and Colonial Stores Ltd held premises from which they carried on their trade. They sought an injunction to restrain Colls from building on the opposite side of the road. They based their claim on the need to protect their right to light.
HELD: The injunction was refused. It was not sufficient to show that the erection of buildings would result in there being less light than before. A substantial deprivation must be shown.

EARL OF HALSBURY LC: The question may be very simply stated thus: after an enjoyment of light for twenty years, or if the question arose before the Act for such a period as would justify the presumption of a lost grant, would the owner of the tenement in respect of which such enjoyment had been possessed be entitled to *all* the light without any diminution whatsoever at the end of such a period?

My Lords, if that were the law it would be very far-reaching in its consequences, and the application of it to its strict logical conclusion would render it almost impossible for towns to grow, and would formidably restrict the rights of people to utilise their own land. Strictly applied, it would undoubtedly prevent many buildings which have hitherto been admitted to be too far removed from others to be actionable, but if the broad proposition which underlies the judgment of the Court of Appeal be true, it is not a question of 45 degrees, but any appreciable diminution of light which has been enjoyed (that is to say, has existed uninterruptedly for twenty years) constitutes a right of action, and gives a right to the proprietor of a tenement that has had this enjoyment to prevent his neighbour building on his own land.

My Lords, I do not think this is the law. The argument seems to me to rest upon a false analogy, as though the access to and enjoyment of light constituted a sort of proprietary right in the light itself. Light, like air, is the common property of all, or, to speak more accurately, it is the common right of all to enjoy it, but it is the exclusive property of none. If the same proposition against which I am protesting could be maintained in respect of air the progressive building of any town would be impossible. The access of air is undoubtedly interfered with by the buildings which are being built every day round London. The difference between the town and country is very appreciable to the dweller in cities when he goes to the open country, or to the top of a mountain, or even a small hill in the country; but would the possessor for twenty years of a house on the edge of a town be at liberty to restrain his neighbour from building near him because he had enjoyed the free access of air without buildings near him for twenty years? No doubt this is an extreme case, but it is one of the extreme cases which tries the principle.

ALLEN v GREENWOOD [1979] 1 All ER 819, Court of Appeal

FACTS: The defendants erected a fence which reduced the light coming into the plaintiff's greenhouse. The question on appeal was how much light the plaintiff was entitled to receive.
HELD: Where a right to light is acquired by prescription under s. 3 of the Prescription Act 1832 the owner of the land benefitting from the right is entitled to receive such amounts of light as are required for the normal purposes for which the land is used. In the case of a greenhouse, as here, the owner of the right could claim an extraordinary amount of light.

GOFF LJ: . . . The starting point for the resolution of these contending arguments must be in *Colls v Home and Colonial Stores Ltd* [1904] AC 179, which does, as it seems to me, establish the basic principle that the measure of the lights to which right is acquired, of which it has to be seen whether there is such diminution as to cause a nuisance, is the light required for the beneficial use of the building for any ordinary purpose for which it is adapted. . . .

The problem, therefore, is whether a right to a specially high degree of light can be acquired by known enjoyment of that specially high degree for the full period of 20 years. . . .

It is clear that a right to a greater degree of light than such as is normally obtained by prescription could be the subject of a valid grant, and in my judgment, therefore, it is capable of being acquired by prescription. That being so, provided it is enjoyed for the full period of 20 years to the knowledge of the servient owners, I fail to see any ground on which it should be held not to have been acquired by prescription.

Of course, where the operation which needs special light is carried on indoors it may be very difficult in fact to prove sufficiently precise knowledge, but here the user was completely obvious. Blackett-Ord V-C decided this point against the plaintiffs, as I have already observed, on the ground that there was no evidence that the owners of the servient tenement knew the precise use which was being made of the greenhouse, but, with all respect to him, in my judgment the evidence was amply sufficient to prove knowledge, and sufficient knowledge. . . .

23.4.2 AN EASEMENT MUST NOT BE SO EXTENSIVE AS TO AMOUNT TO A CLAIM TO JOINT POSSESSION OF THE SERVIENT LAND

COPELAND v GREENHALF [1952] 1 All ER 809, Chancery Division

FACTS: The case involved a claim for an easement. The alleged servient land was a strip of land about 150 feet long and 20 feet wide. The servient owners used the strip to gain access to their orchard. The alleged dominant owners were 'wheelwrights' (i.e. vehicle repairers). For many years they parked vehicles awaiting repair on the strip. These vehicles often occupied a large part of the strip, but the 'wheelwrights' were always careful to leave a gap through which the 'servient owners' could pass to get to their orchard. The wheelrights eventually claimed that they had a prescriptive easement to park their vehicles on the strip.
HELD: The wheelwrights were, in effect, claiming joint possession of the land. Such a claim was too extensive to qualify as an easement.

UPJOHN J: . . . in my judgment the right claimed here goes wholly outside any normal idea of an easement, that is, a right of the occupier of a dominant tenement over a servient tenement. This claim really amounts to a claim to a joint user of the land by the defendant. Practically he is claiming the whole beneficial user of the strip of land on the south-east side of the track so that he can leave there as many or as few lorries as he likes for any time that he likes and enter on it by himself, his servants and agents, to do repair work. In my judgment, that is not a claim which can be established as an easement. It is virtually a claim to possession, if necessary to the exclusion of the owner, or, at any rate, to a joint user, and no authority has been cited to me which would justify me in coming to the conclusion that a right of this wide and undefined nature can be the proper subject-matter of an easement. It seems to me that for this claim to succeed it must really amount to a right of possession by long adverse possession. I say nothing, of course, as to the creation of such rights by grant or by covenant. I am dealing solely with the question of a claim arising by prescription. . . .

GRIGSBY v MELVILLE AND ANOTHER [1973] 1 All ER 385, Chancery Division

FACTS: A butcher had used the cellar of his cottage, which adjoined his shop, to store brine. The shop was eventually sold, and the purchaser began to store various articles in the cellar. The then owner of the cottage sought an injunction to prevent the storage of the articles. The defendant claimed an easement of storage.
HELD: The defendant's claim to possess an easement failed. A right of unlimited storage in a confined space could not amount to an easement.

BRIGHTMAN J: . . . I am left with the defendants' claim to an easement of storage. This claim is again based on the words of exception and reservation in the conveyance. There was evidence that, when the two properties had been one, the occupier, who was a butcher had used the cellar to store brine. Therefore, it was submitted, a general right of storage was enjoyed in connection with Church Hill and that right was reserved to the vendor as an easement over no 3.

There are, I think, two issues here: first, whether an easement of unlimited storage within a confined or defined space is capable of existing as a matter of law. Secondly, if so, whether such an easement was reserved in the present case. Counsel for the plaintiff referred me to *Copeland* v *Greenhalf* [see above]. Counsel for the defendants countered by observing that *Copeland* v *Greenhalf* was inconsistent with *Wright* v *Macadam* [see **22.2.4.1**], an earlier decision of the Court of Appeal in which it was held that the right of a tenant to store domestic coal in a shed on the landlord's land could exist as an easement for the benefit of the demised premises. I am not convinced that there is any real inconsistency between the two cases. The point of the decision in *Copeland* v *Greenhalf* was that the right asserted amounted in effect to a claim to the whole beneficial user of the servient tenement and for that reason could not exist as a mere easement. The precise facts in *Wright* v *Macadam* in this respect are not wholly clear from the report and it is a little difficult to know whether the tenant had exclusive use of the coal shed or of any defined portion of it. To some extent a problem of this sort may be one of degree.

In the case before me, it is, I think, clear that the defendants claim to an easement would give, to all practical intents and purposes, an exclusive right of user over the whole of the confined space representing the servient tenement. I think I would be at liberty if necessary to follow *Copeland* v *Greenhalf*. . .

LONDON AND BLENHEIM ESTATES LTD v LADBROKE RETAIL PARKS LTD
[1993] 1 All ER 307, Chancery Division

This case is referred to because it contains an interesting *obiter dictum* on whether a right to park cars on land is capable of being an easement. It was held that the right is capable of being an easement.

JUDGE PAUL BAKER QC: . . . *Wright* v *Macadam* [see **22.2.4.1**] was not cited in *Copeland* v *Greenhalf* [1952] 1 All ER 809, [1952] Ch 488, which directly concerned the parking of vehicles. The alleged servient tenement was a strip of land about 150 feet long running from the road with a width varying between 15 feet and 35 feet. It was wholly occupied with vehicles and agricultural implements save for a gangway allowing access from the road to the land beyond. The defendant was a wheelwright whose premises were on the other side of the road. The vehicles were his or his customers awaiting repair or collection. The plaintiff owned the strip and the land beyond. Upjohn J said ([1952] 1 All ER 809 at 812, [1952] Ch 488 at 498):

> . . . in my judgment the right claimed here goes wholly outside any normal idea of an easement, that is, a right of the occupier of a dominant tenement over a servient tenement. This claim really amounts to a claim to a joint user of the land by the defendant. Practically he is claiming the whole beneficial user of the strip of land on the south-east side of the track so that he can leave there as many or as few lorries as he likes for any time that he likes and enter on it by himself, his servants and agents, to do repair work. In my judgment, that is not a claim which can be established as an easement.

It is unfortunate that *Wright* v *Macadam* was not cited, but it probably would not have made any difference. The matter must be one of degree. A small coal shed in a large property is one thing. The exclusive use of a large part of the alleged servient tenement is another. Hence I do not accept the submission that *Copeland* v *Greenhalf* was wrongly decided.

. . . the grantee of a right of way cannot complain of obstructions in some part of the way so long as his right is not substantially interfered with. In the present case the right on its true construction is dependent upon the continued existence of car parking facilities for other persons. That leaves the main point under this head, whether the right to park cars can exist at all as an easement. I would not regard it as a valid objection that charges are made, whether for the parking itself or the general upkeep of the park. The essential question is one of degree. If the right granted in relation to the area over which it is to be exercisable is such that it would leave the servient owner without any reasonable use of his land whether for parking or anything else, it could not be an easement, though it might be some larger or different grant. The rights sought in the present case do not appear to approach anywhere near that degree of invasion of the servient land. If that is so—and I emphasise that I have not gone into the facts—I would regard the right claimed as a valid easement.

23.5   Access to Neighbouring Land Act 1992

The Law Commission, Working Paper No. 78, Rights of Access to Neighbouring Land, London: HMSO, 1980, p. 4

THE EXISTING LAW

...

No general right of access

2.2   There is in English law no general right of entry upon neighbouring land in order to do work on one's own property, even if the work consists of essential repairs. Unless a specific right has been created or has arisen in one of the ways mentioned below, a person who enters neighbouring land for this purpose and without consent is simply a trespasser.

2.3   This proposition, though already clear, has been strikingly illustrated in a case decided since the date of the Lord Chancellor's reference to us, *John Trenberth Ltd* v *National Westminster Bank Ltd*.

> In that case, the Bank owned premises which had become dangerous. They abutted on a highway and the Bank had a statutory duty to maintain them in a safe condition. The Bank sought access to the neighbouring property in order to erect scaffolding and carry out the necessary repairs. They offered appropriate assurances and indemnities, but the neighbouring owner did not consent and ceased after a time to answer letters. The Bank's builders then entered without consent and began to do the work. The neighbouring owner sought, by way of interlocutory relief, a court order for the removal of the scaffolding and injunctions restraining future entry.

The neighbouring owner was successful. Walton J held that although the actual damage caused to the neighbouring owner was 'so slight that if an action were brought for it, it would hardly command the smallest coin of the realm', the Bank and their builders were nonetheless trespassers against whom an immediately effective injunction should and would be granted, because people 'are not to infringe the property rights of others and then say, "And I am entitled to go on doing it because I am really doing you no tangible harm, and fivepence will amply compensate you for that harm."

Particular cases where rights of access may exist

2.4   Although there is no general right of access there are, as we have indicated above, several ways in which rights of access might come into being in particular cases. They might be created expressly, or they might arise in other ways.

(a) *Rights created expressly*

2.5   If such rights are created expressly under the present law, they exist most commonly as easements; rights of this kind are therefore considered first.

(i) Easements

2.6   Easements are perpetual rights which are attached to and exist for the benefits of one piece of land (known as the dominant land) and are exercisable by the owner for the time being of that land over some other piece of land (the servient land). A dominant landowner may thus have an easement entitling him to enter adjoining servient land in order to do work upon his own land. . . .

(ii) Other rights

2.8   A right of access which exists as a legal easement may be said to enjoy the highest legal status, since it will enure through different ownerships of the servient and dominant lands and will usually be perpetual; but rights of access may be created in other ways. Thus one landowner may covenant with another that he will permit the other to enter his land. Equally, he may grant him a licence to do so. Indeed any valid agreement may operate to confer such a right. But rights created in these ways may not always have the durability and unassailability of easements.

(b) *Rights not created expressly*

. . .

(i) Implied easements

[See **24.2**.]

(ii) Easements acquired by long usage

[see **Chapter 25**.]

(iii) Estoppel rights

2.16   Recent cases have shown that the doctrine of equitable estoppel may have a part to play in relation to rights over land. Broadly, the doctrine comes into operation in this context when one landowner has acted (for example, by spending money on his property which he would not otherwise have spent) on a belief, engendered or encouraged by the other, that the other will allow him (or will continue to allow him) some particular facility of this kind. In such circumstances the doctrine may operate to prevent the withdrawal of an existing facility which could otherwise be freely withdrawn, or to make enforceable a new facility which could not otherwise be enforced. Again, however, it is clear that such rights are rare and provide no general solution to the problem. . . .

[A general solution was eventually provided in he form of the following statute.]

ACCESS TO NEIGHBOURING LAND ACT 1992

1.   Access orders

   (1)   A person—

      (a)   who, for the purpose of carrying out works to any land (the 'dominant land'), desires to enter upon any adjoining or adjacent land (the 'servient land'), and

      (b)   who needs, but does not have, the consent of some other person to that entry,

may make an application to the court for an order under this section ('an access order') against that other person.

   (2)   On an application under this section, the court shall make an access order if, and only if, it is satisfied—

      (a)   that the works are reasonably necessary for the preservation of the whole or any part of the dominant land; and

      (b)   that they cannot be carried out, or would be substantially more difficult to carry out, without entry upon the servient land;

but this subsection is subject to subsection (3) below.

   (3)   The court shall not make an access order in any case where it is satisfied that, were it to make such an order—

      (a)   the respondent or any other person would suffer interference with, or disturbance of, his use or enjoyment of the servient land, or

      (b)   the respondent, or any other person (whether of full age or capacity or not) in occupation of the whole or any part of the servient land, would suffer hardship,

to such a degree by reason of the entry (notwithstanding any requirement of this Act or any term or condition that may be imposed under it) that it would be unreasonable to make the order.

   (4)   Where the court is satisfied on an application under this section that it is reasonably necessary to carry out any basic preservation works to the dominant land, those works shall be taken for the purposes of this Act to be reasonably necessary for the preservation

of the land; and in this subsection 'basic preservation works' means any of the following, that is to say—

(a)   the maintenance, repair or renewal of any part of a building or other structure comprised in, or situate on, the dominant land;

(b)   the clearance, repair or renewal of any drain, sewer, pipe or cable so comprised or situate;

(c)   the treatment, cutting back, felling, removal or replacement of any hedge, tree, shrub or other growing thing which is so comprised and which is, or is in danger of becoming, damaged, diseased, dangerous, insecurely rooted or dead;

(d)   the filling in, or clearance, of any ditch so comprised;

but this subsection is without prejudice to the generality of the works which may, apart from it, be regarded by the court as reasonably necessary for the preservation of any land. . . .

3.   Effect of access order

(1)   An access order requires the respondent, so far as he has power to do so, to permit the applicant or any of his associates to do anything which the applicant or associate is authorised or required to do under or by virtue of the order of this section.

(2)   Except as otherwise provided by or under this Act, an access order authorises the applicant or any of his associates, without the consent of the respondent,—

(a)   to enter upon the servient land for the purpose of carrying out the specified works;

(b)   to bring on to that land, leave there during the period permitted by the order and, before the end of that period, remove, such materials, plant and equipment as are reasonably necessary for the carrying out of those works; and

(c)   to bring on to that land any waste arising from the carrying out of those works, if it is reasonably necessary to do so in the course of removing it from the dominant land;

but nothing in this Act or in any access order shall authorise the applicant or any of his associates to leave anything in, on or over the servient land (otherwise than in discharge of their duty to make good that land) after their entry for the purpose of carrying out works to the dominant land ceases to be authorised under or by virtue of the order. . . .

CHAPTER TWENTY-FOUR

EXPRESS AND IMPLIED GRANT OF EASEMENTS

24.1 Express Grant and Reservation of Easements (and Profits)

*ST EDMUNDSBURY AND IPSWICH DIOCESAN BOARD OF FINANCE AND
ANOTHER v CLARK (No. 2)* [1975] 1 All ER 722, Court of Appeal

FACTS: The Church of England originally owned a chuchyard and the adjoining rectory grounds. In 1945 the Church of England sold the rectory and its grounds to Clark. The only access to the church building was across the rectory grounds. So the conveyance to Clark included an express reservation of an easement of way along an existing track across the rectory grounds to and from the church. Unfortunately this reservation did not make it clear whether this right of way was 'on foot only' or whether vehicles could use the track. Clark, to the inconvenience of weddings, funerals etc, insisted that the right of way was 'on foot only'. Evidence had been adduced to show that in 1945 there had been at the churchyard end of the track two solid gateposts only about four feet apart.

HELD: The physical circumstances of the pieces of land at the time of the grant/reservation had to be taken into account; if, but only if, the doubts were not resolved by looking at the physical circumstances, the court should give the benefit of the doubt to the dominant owner and construe the grant in his favour. In the present case the finding of fact as to the size of the gap between the gateposts proved fatal to the Church's claim. The Court concluded that the narrow gap through the gateposts meant that in 1945 the right of way must have been 'on foot only'. In view of that finding of fact there was no room for doubt such as would warrant an exercise of discretion in favour of the dominant owner.

SIR JOHN PENNYCUICK: . . . Counsel for the parochial church council relied, above all, on the undoubted facts that the disputed strip is wide enough—nine feet from tree root to tree root—for cars, including lorries, to drive along it without difficulty and that its surface in 1945 was sufficiently firm and even for them to do so. This is an important factor, but far from conclusive. One may well have a strip of land capable of being used by cars but not adapted or appropriate for the passage of cars.

Counsel for the parochial church council relied on another factor which seemed to us of importance, namely, that from time to time building materials would have to be taken to the church and there was no other route available. One would certainly expect the parties to have had this consideration in mind in 1945, when the church was in rather a dilapidated condition. They could not, of course, have foreseen the 1968 fire.

We mention at this point, in order to avoid misunderstanding, that if there is no right of way for vehicles over the disputed strip, the Church authorities may have a vehicular right of way of necessity to the church for the purpose of taking up building materials and the like. This possibility does not arise on the pleadings; but if there be such, it is open to Mr. Clark to select any reasonably convenient line, and he has in fact offered a longer vehicular way round to the north of the church for the repairs.

There was some evidence as to the use of a small part of the disputed strip by hearses. But this did not, we think, turn out to be a factor of much importance. No serious difficulty arises in carrying a coffin over this short stretch and it would in any event be met at the entrance to the churchyard and carried into the church. Nor did any point arise as to weddings. In a parish of this size, neither weddings nor funerals are of frequent occurrence. The ordinary churchgoer, arrived by car or on foot, would be negligibly inconvenienced by a few yards extra walk.

Counsel for the parochial church council sought to discount the gate at the churchyard end by pointing out its poor condition in 1945. This is a valid point so far as it goes. Obviously a broken-down wooden gate is of less significance than, for instance, a solid iron barrier. But the gate remains, to our mind, a factor of the first importance. . . .

24.2   Implied Grant of Easements (and Profits)

24.2.1   WAYS OF NECESSITY

CORPORATION OF LONDON v RIGGS (1880) 13 ChD 798, Master of the Rolls

FACTS: Riggs acquired a 'land-locked' piece of farm-land in the middle of Epping Forest. Epping Forest was (and still is) the property of the City of London. Riggs started building 'tea rooms' on his land. It was not disputed that Riggs had a 'way of necessity' to and from his land, but the Corporation of London objected to his building activities.
HELD: The way of necessity could only be used for those purposes for which the dominant and was being used at the time the necessity arose (i.e. at the time the land became isolated). In the present case the land had been used for farming purposes at that time, therefore neither contractors building the tea-rooms, nor his future clientele, could use the way.

JESSEL MR: . . . What does the necessity of the case require? The object of implying the re-grant, as stated by the older Judges, was that if you did not give the owner of the reserved close some right of way or other, he could neither use nor occupy the reserved close, nor derive any benefit from it. But what is the extent of the benefit he is to have? Is he entitled to say, I have reserved to myself more than that which enables me to enjoy it as it is at the time of the grant? And if that is the true rule, that he is not to have more than necessity requires, as distinguished from what convenience may require, it appears to me that the right of way must be limited to that which is necessary at the time of the grant; that is, he is supposed to take a re-grant to himself of such a right of way as will enable him to enjoy the reserved thing as it is.

That appears to me to be the meaning of a right of way of necessity. If you imply more, you reserve to him not only that which enables him to enjoy the thing he has reserved as it is, but that which enables him to enjoy it in the same way and to the same extent as if he reserved a general right of way for all purposes: that is—as in the case I have before me—a man who reserves two acres of arable land in the middle of a large piece of land is to be entitled to cover the reserved land with houses, and call on his grantee to allow him to make a wide metalled road up to it. I do not think that is a fair meaning of a way of necessity: I think it must be limited by the necessity at the time of the grant; and that the man who does not take the pains to secure an actual grant of a right of way for all purposes is not entitled to be put in a better position than to be able to enjoy that which he had at the time the grant was made. . . .

24.2.2   INTENDED EASEMENTS

CORY v DAVIES [1923] 2 Ch 95, Chancery Division

FACTS: A property developer had built three houses serviced by a private road which had openings at each end where it joined the public highway. The tenant of one of the houses locked the gates of the private road nearest to his house, so as to prevent traffic using that route. The tenants of the other houses sought an injunction preventing the defendant from locking the gate in the future. They also sought a declaration that they were entitled to use the right of way.

HELD: The circumstances showed that it had been the common intention of the tenants that the private drive should be open for their mutual benefit. Accordingly the grant of an easement to that effect would be implied into the lease of each plot.

PO LAWRENCE J: . . . the circumstances in the present case are such that, in order to give effect to the common intention of the parties, the law will imply the appropriate grants and reservations in the three contemporaneous leases of May 8 1857. This common intention would be given complete effect to, if there were implied in the lease of each plot a grant to the lessee of the right, during the term, to use the drive and entrance gates and a reservation to the lessor and to his lessees, as owner and occupiers of the houses erected on the other two plots, of the right to use the drive and entrance gates, so far as such drive and gates were constructed on the demised plot. The present case, in my opinion, falls within the second of the two classes of cases in which, according to Lord Parker's speech in *Pwllbach Colliery Co.* v *Woodman* [1915] AC 634 easements may impliedly be created. Lord Parker there states that this class of cases does not depend upon the terms of the grant itself, but upon the circumstances under which the grant was made, and that the Court will readily imply the grant or reservation of such easements as may be necessary to give effect to the common intention of the parties to the grant with reference to the manner or purpose in and for which the land granted or some land retained by the grantor is to be used, pointing out, however, that it is an essential condition of the implied creation of such easements that the parties should intend that the subject of the grant or the land retained by the grantor should be used in some definite and particular manner and that it is not enough that the user intended by the parties might or might not involve that definite and particular use. The defendants, however, contend that the Court ought not to act on this principle, because in the circumstances of this case its application would involve the implication of a reservation in favour of the lessor, and that such an implication is contrary to the principle laid down in *Wheeldon* v *Burrows* [see **24.2.3**]. That case, no doubt, lays down the general rule that, if a grantor intends to reserve any right over the tenement granted, it is his duty to reserve it expressly in the grant, and I think that there is great force in the argument that this general rule applies a fortiori where the grant, as in the present case, contains certain express reservations in favour of the grantor. It is evident, however, from the judgment in *Wheeldon* v *Burrows*, that there are exceptions to this general rule, and I am of opinion that the present case forms one of these exceptions. The three leases of May 8 1857, were really parts of one transaction, by which the lessor was at the same moment disposing of the sites of all the three plots, that is to say, of the whole of the land over which the easements were to extend, and the easements were only required for the beneficial enjoyment by the lessees of the three plots. In fact the lessor in granting the three leases containing covenants to lay out the three plots in the form of a terrace was only giving effect to the arrangement made between the three lessees, and, therefore, this is not a case where the lessor or anybody deriving title under him by virtue of a subsequent grant is claiming the benefit of an implied reservation in favour of the lessor for his own benefit. In these circumstances the Court ought not, in my opinion, to let the general rule stand in the way of holding that the appropriate grants and reservations, in order to carry out the common intention of the parties, ought to be implied. . . .

WONG v BEAUMONT PROPERTY TRUST LTD [1964] 2 All ER 119, Court of Appeal

FACTS: A landlord had granted a lease of the basement of premises to Blackaby. He covenanted—

(a) to run the premises as a 'popular restaurant';
(b) to comply with Public Health Regulations;
(c) to eliminate 'all noxious smells'.

Blackaby's attempt to run the premises as an English Restaurant were a miserable failure. He assigned the lease to Wong, who converted the restaurant to Chinese food, with resounding success. However, the tenant upstairs complained about the dreadful 'noxious smells' coming from the basement. Public Health Officers were called in. They told Wong that unless a ventilation shaft was run from the basement up the back of the above-ground floors of the building, Wong would have to close down. The landlords refused to let Wong put up the ventilating shaft, so Wong commenced proceedings claiming that he had an easement entitling him to put up the shaft. The county court judge found as a fact that, at the time the lease was granted to Blackaby, a ventilating shaft was necessary for the restaurant to function successfully and eliminate smells.

HELD: The fact that neither of the original parties realised that a ventilation shaft was necessary was not fatal to establishing an easement on the basis of an implied grant based on the intentions of the parties. The inference of an easement had been necessary to accord with their general intentions.

LORD DENNING MR: The whole question in the case now is: Is the tenant entitled to put up this duct outside the building without the landlords' consent? The Midland Bank readily consent because they dislike very much the odours and smells which come up. The public health inspector says it is absolutely essential, if the business is to be carried on at all, that this ventilation duct should be put in. But the landlords object. It is difficult to see any good reason for the landlords' refusal. The judge has found that the duct would hardly make any appreciable difference to the landlords at all. Of course, it would be unsightly for a big duct to be put up on the back wall; but the back of these premises is unsightly anyway. It faces a back street and is hardly seen by anyone.

. . . The question is: Has the tenant a right to put up this duct without the landlords' consent? If he is to have any right at all, it must be by way of easement and not merely by way of implied contract. He is not the original lessee, nor are the defendants the original lessors. Each is a successor in title. As between them, a right of this kind, if it exists at all, must be by way of an easement. In particular, an easement of necessity. The law on the matter was stated by Lord Parker of Waddington in *Pwllbach Colliery Co. Ltd v Woodman* [1915] AC 634, where he said, omitting immaterial words:

> The law will readily imply the grant or reservation of such easements as may be necessary to give effect to the common intention of the parties to a grant of real property, with reference to the manner or purposes in and for which the land granted . . . is to be used . . . But it is essential for this purpose that the parties should intend that the subject of the grant . . . should be used in some definite and particular manner. It is not enough that the subject of the grant . . . should be intended to be used in a manner which may or may not involve this definite and particular use.

That is the principle which underlies all easements of necessity. . . .

. . . Here was the grant of a lease to the lessee for the very purpose of carrying on a restaurant business. It was to be a popular restaurant, and it was to be developed and extended. There was a covenant not to cause any nuisance; and to control and eliminate all smells; and to comply with the food hygiene regulations. That was 'a definite and particular manner' in which the business had to be conducted. It could not be carried on in that manner at all unless a ventilation system was installed by a duct of this kind. In these circumstances it seems to me that, if the business is to be carried on at all—if, in the words of Rolle's Abridgment, the lessee is to 'have any benefit by the grant' at all—he must of necessity be able to put a ventilation duct up the wall. It may be that in Mr. Blackaby's time it would not have needed such a large duct as is now needed in the tenant's time; but nevertheless a duct of some kind would have had to be put up the wall. The tenant may need a bigger one. That does not matter. A man who has a right to an easement can use it in any proper way, so long as he does not substantially increase the burden on the servient tenement. In this case a bigger duct will not substantially increase the burden.

There is one point in which this case goes further than the earlier cases which have been cited. It is this. It was not realised by the parties, at the time of the lease, that this duct would be necessary. But it was in fact necessary from the very beginning. That seems to me sufficient to bring the principle into play. In order to use this place as a restaurant, there must be implied an easement, by the necessity of the case, to carry a duct up this wall. . . .

24.2.3 THE RULE IN *WHEELDON* v *BURROWS*

WHEELDON v *BURROWS* (1879) 12 ChD 31, Court of Appeal

FACTS: A workshop and an adjacent piece of land belonging to the same owner were put up for sale by auction. The piece of land was sold first, and the workshop was sold later. Both properties were sold to different purchasers. The workshop had the benefit of light coming in from the area of the piece of land.

HELD: There was no implied reservation in the sale of the workshop of the right to receive light coming from the area of the piece of land.

THESIGER LJ: . . . on the grant by the owner of a tenement or part of that tenement as it is then used and enjoyed, there will pass to the grantee all those continuous and apparent easements (by which, of course, I mean *quasi* easements), or, in other words, all those easements which are necessary to the reasonable enjoyment of the property granted, and which have been and are at the time of the grant used by the owners of the entirety for the benefit of the part granted. . . .

. . . in the case of a grant you may imply a grant of such continuous and apparent easements or such easements as are necessary to the reasonable enjoyment of the property conveyed, and have in fact been enjoyed during the unity of ownership, but that, with the exception which I have referred to of easements of necessity, you cannot imply a similar reservation in favour of the grantor of land. . . .

24.2.3.1 The almost magical conversion of 'nebulous rights' into easements

BORMAN v *GRIFFITH* [1930] 1 Ch 49, Chancery Division

FACTS: James owned a sizeable country estate. The estate included a mansion leased to Griffith for the purposes of a school. Running across the estate from the mansion to the main road was a properly made up private driveway. On that private driveway was a smaller house known as 'The Gardens'.

In 1923, James agreed to lease 'The Gardens' to Borman, a poultry farmer. This agreement said nothing about access to 'The Gardens'. However, at the time of the agreement James was constructing an alternative access route to 'The Gardens'. In wet weather this alternative route proved impassable for the lorries which served Borman's business. The lorries therefore used the main driveway, despite opposition from Griffith.

HELD: (Applying *Wheeldon* v *Burrows*, see above) An easement to use the driveway was to be implied into the 1923 agreement. The three elements of the rule were satisfied.

MAUGHAM J: . . . The plaintiff relies on s. 62, sub-ss. 1 and 2, of the Law of Property Act, 1925, under which certain general words are deemed to be included in a conveyance . . . 'conveyance' is defined in s. 205, sub-s. 1 (ii), to include 'a lease . . . and every other assurance of property or of an interest therein by any instrument, except a will.'

If the contract of October 10, 1923 is an 'assurance of property or of an interest therein,' a very curious result follows, for the definition of 'conveyance' in the Conveyancing Act, 1881, is limited to documents made by deed, and the contract in the present case is not by deed. . . .

On the whole, I think that it is not a 'conveyance,' because it is not an 'assurance of property or of an interest therein.'. . . In my view, the principles laid down in . . . *Wheeldon* v *Burrows* (1879) 12 ChD 31 . . . are applicable. Without going through all those cases in detail, I may state the principle as follows—namely, that where, as in the present case, two properties belonging to a single owner and about to be granted are separated by a common road, or where a plainly visible road exists over the one for the apparent use of the other, and that road is necessary for the reasonable enjoyment of the property, a right to use the road will pass with the quasi-dominant tenement, unless by the terms of the contract that right is excluded: and in my opinion, if the present position were that the plaintiff was claiming against the lessor specific performance of the agreement of October 10 1923, he would be entitled to be given a right of way for all reasonable purposes along the drive, including the part that passes the farm on the way to the orchard.

It is true that the easement, or, rather, quasi-easement, is not continuous. But the authorities are sufficient to show that a grantor of property, in circumstances where an obvious, i.e., visible and made road is necessary for the reasonable enjoyment of the property by the grantee, must be taken *prima facie* to have intended to grant a right to use it. . . .

West, J., *Wheeldon v Burrows* Revisited (1995) 59 Conv 346

Millman v *Ellis*, 19 March 1995

One hundred & fifteen is no age in the law. The rule in *Wheeldon v Burrows* continues to flourish like the proverbial green bay tree. Conveyancers ignore it at their peril. . . .

In the recent and as yet unreported case of *Millman v Ellis*, decided by the Court of Appeal (Bingham MR, Hirst and Aldous LJJ) on March 19, 1995, E was the vendor of a country house with a driveway which terminated in a very wide tarmacced access to the highway rather like a private lay-by. Bends on the road made it necessary for vehicles entering and leaving the property to use the whole width of the 'lay-by', as E himself had always done. The property included a coach-house which, together with part of the land, was excluded from the sale and retained by E. His intention was to convert the coach-house into a residence and at the date when contracts were exchanged his contractors were engaged in forming a second driveway leading out of the 'lay-by' which would provide the coach-house with its own means of access to the highway.

E decided that he would divide the 'lay-by', notionally though not physically, into two parts: the part adjacent to the original driveway became known as the green land, and that furthest from it the pink. He retained ownership of the whole of the 'lay-by', but the contract provided for the express grant to the purchaser of the country house, M, of an unlimited right of way across the green land. The conveyance duly included such a grant. No right of way was expressly granted to M over any part of the pink land. Following completion M regularly used the entire width of the 'lay-by'. E contended that he was only entitled to cross the green part and sought to impose limits on his use of the pink.

The Court of Appeal upheld the trial judge's finding that at the date of the grant a continuous and apparent easement was used by E over the whole 'lay-by' for the benefit of the property sold. The Court was unimpressed by the argument that the 'lay-by' was plainly and obviously, by virtue of the excavation of the coach-house driveway, going in future to serve a dual purpose instead of continuing to serve merely as an extended exit from the original drive. However the Court reversed the judge's finding that the quasi-easement so used by E up until the sale was not necessary to the reasonable enjoyment of the property sold. The judge had made that finding on the basis that in rural Herefordshire, where the property was situated, winding roads and concealed entrances calling for the utmost caution were commonplace, and that although it would be highly inconvenient for M to be confined to crossing the green land such confinement would not make his house inaccessible: albeit he would be able to turn safely only in one direction, and would be obliged before proceeding in the other to make a detour along the highway and turn round. The judge considered that the willingness of M to accept the grant of a right of way only over the green land was cogent evidence of what was considered by the parties themselves at the date of the grant to be necessary to the reasonable enjoyment of the property he bought: although he did not consider that the inclusion of the express grant in the conveyance would have precluded the creation of an easement over the pink land by implication if such an easement had in his view been necessary for the reasonable enjoyment of M's property.

The Court of Appeal's reversal of that crucial finding by the judge owed much to E's admission in evidence that he had always used both the green and pink parts of the 'lay-by' and that it would have been dangerous not to have done so. It was submitted on behalf of E as a matter of law that whether or not an easement over the pink land was necessary, no such easement could be implied since its implication was excluded by the express grant. The argument was that since the basis of the rule in *Wheeldon v Burrows* was that a grantor could not derogate from his grant there could be no room for its application where the grant in terms divided the 'lay-by' into two parts and allowed the grantee the use only of part. It was also submitted that in view of Lord Wilberforce's description of the rule, in *Sovmots Ltd* v *Environment Secretary of State for the Environment*, as 'a rule of intention', the court should apply the same test for deciding whether an easement ought to be implied into the conveyance as the courts invariably apply in deciding whether to imply terms into contracts generally — that is whether the implication needs to be made in order for the contract to be given business efficacy. It was submitted that the 'officious bystander' would have been far from satisfied at the date of contract that both parties intended there to be an easement over the pink land.

It is the Court of Appeal's rejection of these arguments, rather than the findings of fact peculiar to the case, which may be of interest to some conveyancers and concern to others. The case makes it plain that the express grant of a limited easement to a purchaser of part of a property on a sale-off will not necessarily prevent him from claiming to have acquired greater rights over the vendor's retained land by implied grant. Any conveyancer who believed that *Wheeldon* v *Burrows* could only be invoked in cases where the conveyance said nothing about, for example, rights of way, should think again. The Court of Appeal held that a vendor could indeed be guilty of derogating from his grant in circumstances such as these, and rejected the argument that the rule in *Wheeldon* v *Burrows* needed to be assimilated into ordinary contract law. . . .

The conveyancer will thus be obliged to include in the contract for the sale of part of a property some condition designed to protect the vendor from the implication in the purchaser's favour under *Wheeldon* v *Burrows* of an easement over his retained property which he does not wish to grant. As Professor Barnsley has shown (Conveyancing Law and Practice 3rd Edition pp. 165–167), that is no simple task.

24.2.4   SECTION 62 OF THE LAW OF PROPERTY ACT 1925

LAW OF PROPERTY ACT 1925

62.   General words implied in conveyances

(1)   A conveyance of land shall be deemed to include and shall by virtue of this Act operate to convey, with the land, all buildings, erections, fixtures, commons, hedges, ditches, fences, ways, waters, watercourses, liberties, privileges, easements, rights, and advantages whatsoever, appertaining or reputed to appertain to the land, or any part thereof, or, at the time of conveyance, demised, occupied, or enjoyed with or reputed or known as part or parcel of or appurtenant to the land or any part thereof. . . .

(4)   This section applies only if and as far as a contrary intention is not expressed in the conveyance, and has effect subject to the terms of the conveyance and to the provisions therein contained.

(5)   This section shall not be construed as giving to any person a better title to any property, right, or thing in this section mentioned than the title which the conveyance gives to him to the land or manor expressed to be conveyed, or as conveying to him any property, right, or thing in this section mentioned, further or otherwise than as the same could have been conveyed to him by the conveying parties. . . .

65.   Reservation of legal estates

(1)   A reservation of a legal estate shall operate at law without any execution of the conveyance by the grantee of the legal estate out of which the reservation is made, or any regrant by him, so as to create the legal estate reserved, and so as to vest the same in possession in the person (whether being the grantor or not) for whose benefit the reservation is made.

(2)   A conveyance of a legal estate expressed to be made subject to another legal estate not in existence immediately before the date of the conveyance, shall operate as a reservation unless a contrary intention appears.

(3)   This section applies only to reservations made after the commencement of this Act.

24.2.4.1   The breadth of the s. 62 principle

WRIGHT v *MACADAM* [1949] 2 All ER 565, Court of Appeal

FACTS: The defendant leased a top-floor flat to Mrs. Wright. While this first lease was still running Macadam gave Mrs. Wright permission to store her coal in a coal-shed situated in the garden to the small block of flats. When Wright's first lease ran out, it was renewed for a further period. At the time of renewal nothing was said about the coal shed. Later, during the running of the second lease, Macadam demanded that Wright pay one shilling and sixpence (seven-and-a-half new pence) per week for the use of the coal-shed. She refused. HELD: On the renewal of the lease to Wright, there was implied into the renewed lease an easement to store coal in the coal-shed. The crucial point was the existence of the privilege at the time the lease was renewed. The statutory 'magic' of the Law of Property Act 1925, s. 62 therefore converted Wright's privilege into a full easement.

JENKINS LJ: . . . The question in the present case, therefore, is whether the right to use the coal shed at the date of the letting of August 28 1943, was a liberty, privilege, easement, right or advantage appertaining, or reputed to appertain, to the land, or any part thereof, or, at the time of the conveyance, demised, occupied or enjoyed with the land—i.e., the flat—or any part thereof. It is enough for the tenants' purposes if they can bring the right claimed within the widest part of s. 62(1), i.e., if they can show that the right was at the time of the material letting demised, occupied or enjoyed with the flat or any part thereof. The predecessor of s. 62 of the Act of 1925, in the shape of s. 6 of the Act of 1881, has been the subject of a good deal of judicial discussion, and I think the effect of the cases can be thus summarised. First, the section is not confined to rights which, as a matter of law, were so annexed or appurtenant to the property conveyed at the time of the conveyance as to make them actual legally enforceable rights. Thus, on the severance of a piece of land in common ownership, the *quasi* easements *de facto* enjoyed in respect of it by one part of the land over another will pass although, of course, as a matter of law, no man can have a right appendant or appurtenant to one part of his property exercisable by him over the other part of his property. Secondly, the right, in order to pass, need not be one to which the owner or occupier for the time being of the land has had what may be described as a permanent title. A right enjoyed merely by permission is enough.

. . . I am of opinion that the learned judge came to a wrong conclusion when he held that s. 62 of the Law of Property Act 1925, had no application. He said that the right to use the coal-shed was merely a temporary right. That, as I have said, is no sufficient ground for excluding the operation of s. 62, having regard to the principle laid down in the *International Tea Stores case* [1903] 2 Ch 165. Further, he said that this was never a right or advantage appurtenant to the flat, but it is not only rights or advantages that are appurtenant to given premises that pass under s. 62. It is enough, as I have already said, that the right or advantage should, in fact, be enjoyed with the premises. Accordingly, it seems to me that the learned judge was wrong in excluding the operation of s. 62. . . .

GOLDBERG v *EDWARDS* [1950] 1 Ch 247, Court of Appeal

FACTS: Edwards owned a main building, together with an annex at the back of the main building. He leased the annex to Goldberg. That lease included an express grant of an easement of way permitting all visitors to the annex to gain access using an open yard at the side of the building. While this first lease was still in force Edwards gave permission for visitors to the annex to pass through the hallway of the main building. (That way they did not get wet!)
The first lease expired, but Goldberg was granted a new lease, with the same express clause regarding use of the open yard at the side. The new lease made no express mention of the hallway, but Goldberg claimed that the new lease impliedly granted him an easement to use the hallway.
HELD: Goldberg's claim under *Wheeldon* v *Burrows* failed, because a right to use the hallway, while it had its advantages, was not 'necessary for the reasonable or convenient enjoyment' of the annex. Despite losing on the *Wheeldon* v *Burrows* issue, Goldberg won the case; he was held to have acquired (on the renewal of his lease) an implied easement to use the hallway under the Law of Property Act 1925, s. 62.

EVERSHED MR : . . . in my judgment it does not follow that a way through the front door of another's premises and through the ground floor and passages is even *prima facie* necessary for the reasonable or convenient enjoyment of premises behind. It would take strong evidence to show that it was so, for the right to pass through another's premises, particularly when they are business premises, is, I think, a considerable burden upon the quasi-servient tenement in any case. But the evidence is that these premises at the back before the plaintiff's tenancy were wholly or partly in the occupation of another person who carried on another type of business there, and who apparently enjoyed them both reasonably and conveniently without any necessity for passing through the front part of the premises. I therefore reject the argument based on implied grant, and turn to s. 62.

. . . the privilege granted here was not temporary, like, for instance, a temporary right of light when it is obvious that buildings shortly to be erected will obscure it. The present privilege is in some ways indeed not dissimilar to that which in *Wright v Macadam* [1949] 2 KB 744 was held to be covered by s. 62, namely, a privilege for the tenant to use a shed for storing her coal. I therefore think that, if the right which I have defined was one which was being enjoyed at the time of the conveyance, it is covered by s. 62.

That therefore leaves the final point: what is the 'time of conveyance' within the meaning of s. 62, sub-ss. 1 and 2? The arrangement about this use of the passage appears to have been made at various dates, the last of which was January 13 1947. The plaintiffs went into occupation of the annexe on January 18 1947. The fitting of the bell and signboard took place after that. Several months passed (why, I know not, and it is quite immaterial) before the lease was executed on July 10 1947, though the term was expressed to run from January 18. It is plain that before July 10 there was no written instrument whatever. Possession may no doubt have been attributable to an oral agreement of which, having regard to the position, specific performance might have been granted; but I fail to find any instrument in writing within the meaning of s. 62 before the lease of July 10. It seems to me, therefore, that the phrase 'at the time of conveyance' must mean in this case July 10. I am unable to accept the view that one should construe that as meaning at the time when the term granted by the lease is stated to have begun. On July 10 1947, under the privilege granted, this right of ingress and egress was being enjoyed in fact. As I have held, though it is limited to the lessees themselves and does not extend to other persons, it would be capable of formulation and incorporation as a term of the lease, and it is, in my judgment, covered by s. 62. To that extent, therefore, but to that limited extent only, the plaintiffs are entitled to succeed. . . .

24.2.4.2 The limits on s. 62

SOVMOTS INVESTMENTS LTD v *SECRETARY OF STATE FOR THE ENVIRONMENT AND OTHERS* [1977] 2 All ER 385, House of Lords

FACTS: A London Borough Council made a compulsory purchase order of a number of maisonettes. The council argued that certain additional rights must be taken to have passed with the maisonettes, for without those rights the maisonettes could not be used for residential purposes. The rights claimed included such things as ways for water, electricity and sewage.

HELD: (Lord Russell of Killowen dissenting) The additional rights did not automatically pass with the maisonettes. Accordingly, the maisonettes could not be used for their intended residential purposes. Consequently, the Borough Council had been acting *ultra vires* in making the compulsory purchase order with a view to providing housing.

LORD WILBERFORCE: The main argument before the inspector and in the courts below was that in this case and under the compulsory purchase order as made no specific power to require the creation of ancillary rights was necessary because these would pass to the acquiring authority under either, or both, of the first rule in *Wheeldon v Burrows* (1879) 12 ChD 31 ('the rule') or of s. 62 of the Law of Property Act 1925. . . . Under s. 62 a conveyance of land operates to convey with the land all ways, watercourses, liberties, privileges, easements, rights and advantages whatsoever, appertaining or reputed to appertain to the land, or any part thereof, or, at the time of conveyance, demised, occupied or enjoyed with, or reputed or known as part or parcel or appurtenant to the land or any part thereof.

My Lords, there are very comprehensive expressions here, but it does not take much analysis to see that they have no relevance to the situation under consideration.

The rule is a rule of intention, based on the proposition that a man may not derogate from his grant. He cannot grant or agree to grant land and at the same time deny to his grantee what is at the time of the grant obviously necessary for its reasonable enjoyment. To apply this to a case where a public authority is taking from an owner his land without his will is to stand the rule on its head: it means substituting for the intention of a reasonable voluntary grantor the unilateral, opposed, intentions of the acquirer.

Moreover, and this point is relevant to a later argument, the words I have emphasised show that for the rule to apply there must be actual, and apparent, use and enjoyment at the time of the grant. But no such use or enjoyment had, at Centre Point, taken place at all.

Equally, s. 62 does not fit this case. The reason is that when land is under one ownership one cannot speak in any intelligible sense of rights, or privileges, or easements being exercised over one part for the benefit of another. Whatever the owner does, he does as owner and, until a separation occurs, of ownership or at least of occupation, the condition for the existence of rights, etc, does not exist: see *Bolton* v *Bolton* (1879) 11 ChD 968, per Fry J, and *Long* v *Gowlett* [1923] 2 Ch 177, in my opinion a correct decision.

A separation of ownership, in a case like the present, will arise on conveyance of one of the parts (e.g. the maisonettes), but this separation cannot be projected back to the stage of the compulsory purchase order so as, by anticipation, to bring into existence rights not existing in fact. . . .

LONG v *GOWLETT* [1923] 2 Ch 177, Chancery Division

FACTS: The owner of two plots of land adjoining each other sold them to separate purchasers. One of the new owners claimed a right of access to the other plot in order to effect certain repairs and maintenance works on a river which served both plots of land. Only by tending the river banks in this way could the flow of the river be assured. The claimant adduced evidence that the previous owner of both plots had occasionally made such repairs himself. The claimant sought to establish that an easement must be implied into the conveyance to him under s. 62 of the Law of Property Act 1925.
HELD: There must have been diversity of ownership or occupation before the conveyance to the claimant in order to imply an easement by the operation of s. 62. In the present case the acts of repair carried out by the original owner could not be said to have been wholly independent of his ownership of the 'servient' plot, therefore the claimant's argument must fail.

SARGANT J: . . . in order that there may be a 'privilege, easement or advantage' enjoyed with Whiteacre over Blackacre so as to pass under the statute, there must be something done on Blackacre not due to or comprehended within the general rights of an occupying owner of Blackacre, but of such a nature that it is attributable to a privilege, easement, right or advantage, however precarious, which arises out of the ownership or occupation of Whiteacre, altogether apart from the ownership or occupation of Blackacre. And it is difficult to see how, when there is a common ownership of both Whiteacre and Blackacre, there can be any such relationship between the two closes as (apart from the case of continuous and apparent easements or that of a way of necessity) would be necessary to create a 'privilege, easement, right or advantage' within the words of s. 6, sub-s. 2, of the statute. For this purpose it would seem that there must be some diversity of ownership or occupation of the two closes sufficient to refer the act or acts relied on not to mere occupying ownership, but to some advantage or privilege (however far short of a legal right) attaching to the owner or occupier of Whiteacre as such and *de facto* exercised over Blackacre. . . .

24.2.4.3   *Graham* v *Philcox*

GRAHAM v *PHILCOX* [1984] 2 All ER 643, Court of Appeal

FACTS: L owned a large garden with a house at one end of that garden. In 1960 L leased the house to T. This lease included an express grant to T of an easement of way over the garden for the duration of the lease. In 1975 (while T's lease was still running) L sold the fee simple reversion in the house to G. The 1975 conveyance made no mention of a right of way.
HELD: Section 62 implied into the 1975 conveyance the grant to G of a fee simple easement of way over the garden.

PURCHAS LJ: . . . With great respect to the judge, I think that he was wrong in deciding that the easement and right created in the first instance in the lease was coterminous with it or even with any further occupation by the grantee under statutory protection. The right of way having been created by direct grant and its use continuing even though under statutory protection at the time of the conveyance, the use and enjoyment of that easement fell within the terms of s. 62 of the 1925 Act and the judge was in error in holding that it did not. Nor, for the reasons I have already given, can I accept the submissions made by counsel for the defendants that by enlarging the physical dimensions or indeed altering the nature of the dominant tenement from two individual flats to one dwelling house has the easement, right or advantage been destroyed. The occupier of the dominant tenement, however, will be and will remain subject to the rules requiring that the character and extent of the burden imposed on the servient tenement must not be enlarged. For want of a better definition, this burden must be said to be commensurate with the reasonable user of the means of access by the occupier, his servants, agents, invitees or licensees occupying a single dwelling unit. If by any change in the nature of his enjoyment of the dominant tenement the occupier thereof increases the burden on the servient tenement beyond this, then he will be liable to the consequences of excessive user which may be imposed on any person enjoying an easement, right or benefit of this kind. . .

24.3 Implied Reservation of Easements

RE WEBB'S LEASE [1951] Ch 808, Court of Appeal

FACTS: The landlord, the head-lessee of business premises where he carried on his business of a butcher and merchant, leased the floors above his shop to Webb. The tenancy covered the outer walls of the upper floors where the landlord had for some time prior to the tenancy displayed an advertisement in respect of his trade. The landlord had neglected to reserve the right to continue to display the advertisement and claimed that the reservation of an easement to that end ought to be implied into the grant of the tenancy. HELD: The landlord's claim to an easement by reservation failed.

JENKINS LJ: . . . The landlord did not include in the provisions of the lease, as executed, any reservation of advertising rights over any part of the outer walls. At the date of the lease the advertisements now in dispute were in their present positions on the walls and plainly to be seen. Moreover, they had existed in their present positions continuously since before the commencement of the tenant's original tenancy in 1939, and the tenant never objected to their presence at any time during his original tenancy or at the time of the granting of the lease of August 11 1949, or thereafter until January 1950. There is no evidence that either party ever even mentioned the subject of the advertisements to the other during the whole of this period of more than ten years. This being in substance the whole of the available facts, the question is whether on those bare facts, without more, the court can and ought as a matter of law to imply in favour of the landlord a reservation during the term of twenty-one years granted by the lease of August 11 1949, of advertising rights over the outer walls demised, at all events, to the extent required to enable him to maintain the existing advertisements and to retain for his own benefit any periodical payments receivable from the Borough Billposting Co. in respect of the site of the Brymay poster. . . .

In *Wheeldon* v *Burrows* (12 ChD 49), Thesiger LJ, states two propositions as 'the general rules governing cases of this kind.' The first concerns easements passing to the grantee and is not relevant here. The second he states *(ibid)* as being

> . . . that, if the grantor intends to reserve any right over the tenement granted, it is his duty to reserve it expressly in the grant. Those are the general rules governing cases of this kind, but the second of those rules is subject to certain exceptions. One of those exceptions is the well-known exception which attaches to cases of what are called ways of necessity; and I do not dispute for a moment that there may be, and probably are, certain other exceptions, to which I shall refer before I close my observations upon this case. Both of the general rules which I have mentioned are founded upon a maxim which

is as well established by authority as it is consonant to reason and common sense, *viz,* that a grantor shall not derogate from his grant.

The learned lord justice deals further with the question of exceptions (*ibid,* 59), but, apart from the case of easements of necessity, he does not appear to have been disposed to admit any further exceptions other than cases of mutual easements and cases in which the same vendor sells by auction different lots to different persons at the same time, where the purchaser of one lot may be entitled to an easement over another lot even though the latter was in fact actually conveyed before the former: see *Swansborough* v *Coventry* (1832) 9 Bing 305. . . . (i) If the landlord intended to reserve any such rights over the demised premises it was his duty to reserve them expressly in the lease of August 11 1949: *Wheeldon* v *Burrows.* (ii) The landlord having failed in this duty, the onus was on him to establish the facts to prove, and prove clearly, that his case was an exception to the rule: *Aldridge* v *Wright* [1929] 2 KB 117. (iii) The mere fact that the tenant knew at the date of the lease of August 11 1949, that the landlord was using the outer walls of the demised premises for the display of the advertisements in question did not suffice to absolve the landlord from his duty of expressly reserving any rights in respect of them he intended to claim, or to take the case out of the general rule: see *Suffield* v *Brown* 4 De GJ & Sm 199, *Crossley & Sons Ltd* v *Lightowler* LR 2 Ch 478. . . .

CHAPTER TWENTY-FIVE

PRESCRIPTION FOR EASEMENTS (AND PROFITS)

25.1   The Complexities of Prescription Law

Unfortunately there are no less than three forms of prescription for easements and profits:

(a)   common law prescription;

(b)   lost modern grant;

(c)   the Prescription Act 1832.

25.2   Rules Common to All Three Forms of Prescription

User, to be prescriptive, must be 'as of right'. User is only 'as of right' if it is *nec vi, nec clam, nec precario*, i.e., 'without force, without secrecy and without permission'.

25.2.1   WITHOUT FORCE

In this context, 'force' has been given a very wide meaning, and the courts have ruled that user, to be prescriptive, must not be contentious in any way. Thus, fisticuffs man-to-man, the breaking down of barriers and the climbing over of fences are all 'forcible' user and therefore not prescriptive.

The courts have also held that user in face of express oral or written protests from the alleged servient owner should be deemed to be 'forcible', even though there is no actual violence.

25.2.2   WITHOUT SECRECY

LLOYDS BANK LIMITED AND ANOTHER v DALTON
[1942] 1 Ch 466, Chancery Division

FACTS: Dalton owned the servient building, which was a large dye-works. The dominant building was a small outhouse which claimed a prescriptive easement of support against the dye-works. The outhouse had for well over twenty years leant against the wall of the dye-works. That wall was a blank wall without any windows. The outhouse could therefore not be seen from the works, nor could it be seen from the public road.

HELD: The court rejected Dalton's contention that there was a 'secret' user, not capable of giving rise to an easement by prescription. A reasonable owner would surely go around his premises from time to time. A reasonable owner would therefore at some stage have discovered the outhouse.

BENNETT J: . . . It was not suggested that the plaintiffs' predecessors in title, in executing their works, had acted secretly. The defendant rested his case exclusively on the fact proved that in March 1939, the yard and the outbuilding were not visible from the dye-works or from a highway or other public place.

It is clear law, I think, that an easement of support cannot be acquired unless the owner of the servient tenement has knowledge that his land or his building is in fact supporting the dominant tenement. . . .

. . . in *Union Lighterage Co.* v *London Graving Dock Co.* [1902] 2 Ch 557 Romer LJ stated the principle in these terms: '. . . on principle, it appears to me that a prescriptive right to an easement over a man's land should only be acquired when the enjoyment has been open—that is to say, of such a character that an ordinary owner of the land, diligent in the protection of his interests, would have, or must be taken to have, a reasonable opportunity of becoming aware of that enjoyment.'

In the present case the dominant tenement had in fact been supported by the servient tenement for more than forty years before March 1939. The two tenements were on the slope of this hill. They were contiguous, and the defendant's tenement was below the plaintiffs' tenement. The buildings on the slope were close to one another. There was an open passage leading from Castle Terrace on to the plaintiffs' yard. Once in the plaintiffs' yard, it must have been obvious that the north-east end of that yard and of the outbuilding were supported by the dye-works, and the south-west wall of the dye-works. Lastly, the defendant was not called to give evidence at the trial. It is notorious that the owners of land and buildings are interested in their boundaries, and, in my judgment, the facts proved at the trial of this case lead irresistibly to the conclusion that the successive owners of the dye-works, assuming them to have been reasonable persons, diligent in the protection of their interests, either must have known or must be taken to have had reasonable opportunity of becoming aware of the fact that the dye-works were supporting the north-east part of the plaintiffs' yard and of the outbuilding standing thereon. For these reasons, the plea of claim, in my judgment, fails. . . .

LIVERPOOL CORPORATION v H COGHILL & SON [1918] 1 Ch 307, Chancery Division

FACTS: Coghill ran a chemical factory which operated 24 hours a day. For many years Coghill poured borax effluent into the corporation's sewers. Coghill always did so very early in the morning. This was not out of any deliberate attempt to conceal what he was doing. Discharging effluent at night suited its 'production cycle'.
HELD: Coghill could not claim a prescriptive right. Its user was in law 'secret', even though there had been no deliberate attempt at concealment.

EVE J: . . . how can this intermittent use, or rather misuse, of surface and rain water gullies and drains wholly upon and within the limits of the defendants' premises be made the foundation of a legal right to pour a poisonous waste liquor (for such *ex hypothesi* it must be, or no necessity for asserting the easement would exist) into the plaintiffs' sewers, unless notice is brought home to the plaintiffs of what the defendants were doing? There has been no assertion by conduct or otherwise on the part of the defendants that they claimed to do these things as of right, nor have they produced any evidence to prove any notice of their acts to the corporation or their predecessors, or established the existence of any state of things from which such notice could legitimately be inferred. On the contrary, I am quite satisfied on the evidence of Mr. Everett, who covers the period between 1879 and 1895, fortified by the resolution of July 30 1873, that the plaintiffs' predecessors had no knowledge of the facts. No attempt has been made to fix the corporation with notice since 1895, and when the matter of injury to the farm was taken up by their responsible officials in 1908 their whole course of conduct was quite inconsistent with their having any notice of what was going on inside the defendants' works. If, then, the methods adopted by the defendants could in any circumstances have been made the foundation of a prescriptive right, a point upon which I express no opinion, I am satisfied that in the circumstances here disclosed the enjoyment has not been of such a character as to establish any such right. It has throughout been secret, not surreptitious or actively concealed from, but unknown to and unsuspected by the plaintiffs and their predecessors, and incapable, therefore, of being relied upon as the foundation of rights to their prejudice. As Thesiger LJ says in the course of the judgment of the Court of Appeal in *Sturges* v *Bridgman* (1879) 11 ChD 852, 'Consent or acquiescence of the owner of the servient tenement lies at the root of prescription, and of the fiction of a lost grant, and hence the acts or user, which go to the proof of either the one or the other, must be in the language of the civil law, nec vi, nec clam, nec precario; for a man cannot, as a general rule, be said to consent or acquiesce in the acquisition by his neighbour of an easement through an enjoyment of which he has no knowledge, actual or constructive.' . . .

25.2.3 WITHOUT PERMISSION

MILLS v *SILVER* [1991] 1 All ER 449, Court of Appeal

FACTS: In 1986 the defendant purchased a derelict farm set some distance from a public road. The defendant relied upon an old statutory declaration which indicated that the previous owner of the farm had for many years regularly and openly used a particular track to gain access to the farm. The defendant proceeded to use the track for passage on foot and by motor vehicle. The plaintiff objected to the use of vehicles, particularly when the defendant laid down 700 tons of stone along the track, to make a solid road. They sought an injunction and damages for trespass against the defendant.
HELD: The previous owner of the 'servient' land had not given permission for the previous owner of the 'dominant' land to use the track, nor had he objected to the use of it. He had merely 'tolerated' or acquiesced in the use of the track. Nevertheless, this did not defeat the defendant's claim that an easement had been acquired by prescriptive user 'as of right'. The defendants would be able to pass and repass, with or without vehicles, over the track. However, the laying of 700 tons of stone was an excessive exercise of the right to a right of way. Damages were awarded for the trespass.

DILLON LJ: . . . I turn now to the judge's point of tolerance. The question is whether the judge has correctly directed himself in law. To put it another way, did the tolerance of the successive servient owners, James Price until 1970 and in his case tolerance out of good neighbourliness and because the use was too insignificant to matter to him or cause him any inconvenience, of such vehicular use of the disputed track as there was in Joe Phillips's time preclude a prescriptive right being acquired, even though no express permission was ever granted to Joe Phillips and no reservations as to his use of the disputed track with vehicles were ever communicated to him by anyone?

The topic of tolerance has bulked fairly large in recent decisions of this court dealing with claims to prescriptive rights, since the decision in *Alfred F Beckett Ltd* v *Lyons* [1967] 1 All ER 833, [1967] Ch 449. If passages in successive judgments are taken on their own out of context and added together, it would be easy to say, as, with all respect, it seems to me that the judge did in the present case, that there is an established principle of law that no prescriptive right can be acquired if the user by the dominant owner of the servient tenement in the particular manner for the appropriate number of years has been tolerated without objection by the servient owner.

But there cannot be any such principle of law because it is, with rights of way, fundamentally inconsistent with the whole notion of acquisition of rights by prescription. It is difficult to see how, if there is such a principle, there could ever be a prescriptive right of way. It follows that the various passages in the judgments in question cannot be taken on their own out of context. If each case is looked at on its own and regarded as a whole, none lays down any such far-reaching principle. In my judgment, the judge in the present case has misapplied the authorities, by taking passages out of context, and misdirected himself in arriving at the supposed principle of law which he has sought to apply. . . .

25.2.4 USER MUST BE CONTINUOUS

HOLLINS v *VERNEY* (1884) 13 QB 304, Court of Appeal

FACTS: The case concerned a claim to an easement of way. The alleged dominant owner had only used the right of way three times in the last twenty years.

HELD: The claim for a prescriptive easement failed. User must be regular enough for it to be reasonable to expect that the servient owner would be aware that some right was being asserted.

LINDLEY LJ: . . . as the enjoyment which is pointed out by the Prescription Act 1832 is an enjoyment which is open as well as of right, it seems to follow that no actual user can be sufficient to satisfy the statute, unless during the whole of the statutory term (whether acts of user be proved in each year or not) the user is enough at any rate to carry to the mind of a reasonable person who is in possession of the servient tenement, the fact that a continuous right to enjoyment is being asserted, and ought to be resisted if such right is not recognised, and if resistance to it is intended. Can a user which is confined to the rare occasions on which the alleged right is supposed in this instance to have been exercised, satisfy even this test? It seems to us that it cannot: that it is not, and could not reasonably be treated as the assertion of a continuous right to enjoy; and when there is no assertion by conduct of a continuous right to enjoy, it appears to us that there cannot be an actual enjoyment within the meaning of the statute. Without therefore professing to be able to draw the line sharply between long and short periods of non-user, without holding that non-user for a year or even more is necessarily fatal in all cases, without attempting to define that which the statute has left indefinite, we are of opinion that no jury can properly find that the right claimed by the defendant in this case has been established by evidence of such limited user as was mainly relied upon, and as was contended by the defendant to be sufficient in the present case.

25.2.5   USER MUST BE BY OR ON BEHALF OF A FEE SIMPLE AGAINST A FEE SIMPLE

SIMMONS v DOBSON [1991] 4 All ER 25, Court of Appeal

FACTS: The plaintiff was the tenant of one property and the defendant was tenant of an adjoining property. Freehold title to both properties was held by the same freeholder. The plaintiff sought to show that, according to the doctrine of lost modern grant, they had the right to use a passageway over the defendant's premises.
HELD: A tenant could not claim an easement by the doctrine of lost modern grant. The doctrine gave rise to a form of common law prescription, it could therefore only apply between freeholders.

FOX LJ: I come then to the contention that the plaintiff succeeds on the basis of lost modern grant.

That doctrine arises from the inadequacies of common law prescription. At common law, acquisition of a prescriptive right depended upon the claimant establishing (amongst other things) the requisite period of user. Thus, common law prescription was based upon a presumed grant. The grant would be presumed only where the appropriate user had continued from time immemorial. That was fixed as the year 1189; that date originated in a medieval statute. It was usually impossible to satisfy that test. Accordingly, the courts held that if user 'as of right' for 20 years or more was established, continued user since 1189 would be presumed. That was satisfactory as far as it went, but there were gaps. In particular the presumption of immemorial user could be rebutted by showing that, at some time since 1189, the right did not exist. For example, an easement of light could not be claimed in respect of a house built after 1189.

It was because of the unsatisfactory nature of common law prescription that the doctrine of lost modern grant was introduced. It was judge made. The doctrine presumed from long usage that an easement had, in fact, been granted since 1189 but the grant had got lost.

The form which the doctrine took was, initially, that juries were told that from user during living memory, or even during 20 years, they could presume a lost grant. After a time the jury were recommended to make that finding and finally they were directed to do so. Nobody believed that there ever was a grant. But it was a convenient and workable fiction. The doctrine was ultimately approved by the House of Lords in *Dalton* v *Henry Angus & Co.* (1881) 6 App Cas 740, [1881–5] All ER Rep 1.

Now, in relation to common law prescription generally, user had to be by or on behalf of a fee simple owner against a fee simple owner. An easement can be granted expressly by a tenant for life or tenant for years so as to bind their respective limited interests, but such rights cannot be acquired by prescription. . . .

While, therefore, there appears to be no case which directly decides that there can be no lost modern grant by or to a person who owns a lesser estate than the fee, the *dicta* are to the contrary and are very strong and of long standing. I take them to represent settled law. I should mention for completeness that the law in Ireland has gone the other way: see *Flynn v Harte* [1913] 2 IR 322 and *Tallon v Ennis* [1937] IR 549.

As to any departure from that state of the law, there are, I think, difficulties of principle. It is clear that common law prescription and prescription under the 1832 Act are, as a matter of decision, not available by or to owners of less estates than the fee. Lost modern grant is merely a form of common law prescription. It is based upon a fiction which was designed to meet, and did meet, a particular problem. It would, I think, be anomalous to extend the fiction further by departure, in relation to lost modern grant, from the fundamental principle of common law prescription referred to by Lindley LJ.

I would allow the appeal.

PALK v *SHINNER* (1852) 118 English Reports 215

FACTS: Palk leased his land to various tenants. From 1820 onwards the tenants crossed Shinner's land 'as of right' to get to the land leased to them. From 1821 onwards Shinner's land was leased to X. User as of right by the tenants continued until the dispute broke out in about 1850.

HELD: Judgment was given for Palk. His tenants were to be regarded as acting on his behalf. Palk thus acquired a fee simple easement.

LORD CAMPBELL CJ: I am of opinion that the plaintiff is entitled to our judgment. I think that there was evidence from which the jury might find that he was entitled to claim a right of way under s. 2 of stat. 2 & 3 W. 4, c. 71. I do not say that the evidence was conclusive; but it was sufficient to justify their finding; and that finding ought not to be disturbed unless the plaintiff's claim is defeated by s. 8. I am of opinion that it is not. The period during which the land over which the right of way is claimed has been leased for a term exceeding three years is not, under that section, to be excluded from the computation of a twenty years' enjoyment, though it is, no doubt, to be excluded from the computation of an enjoyment for forty years. Sect. 7 excludes certain times, including that of a tenancy for life, but not that of a tenancy for years, from the computation of the 'periods' thereinbefore 'mentioned'; and a twenty years' enjoyment is one of those periods. But s. 8 provides for the exclusion of certain other times, among which is a tenancy of more than three years, not from the periods thereinbefore mentioned, but from one particular period only, expressly mentioned, namely, that of an enjoyment for forty years. It is clear, therefore, that it was not intended to exclude from the computation of an enjoyment for twenty years. Great reliance was placed upon *Bright v Walker* (1 CM & R 211, 4 Tyr 502); but, on examination into that case, it appears that there was no necessity for the Court to give any opinion as to the effect of s. 8; for the right of way there claimed was clearly destroyed, under s. 7, by reason of a tenancy for life. But, even supposing s. 8 to apply to a twenty years' enjoyment as well as to an enjoyment for forty years, the right by enjoyment in the present case is not destroyed, inasmuch as the condition, that the claim shall be resisted by the reversioner within three years after the determination of the tenancy for years, has not been complied with.

25.3   Prescription at Common Law

(For a general discussion see the dictum of Fox LJ in *Simmons v Dobson* (25.2.5, above).)

A claim for an easement or a profit by 'prescription at common law' is very rarely successful. The theory of this form of prescription is that once upon a time a deed was executed by the then servient owner in favour of the then dominant owner granting the relevant easement or profit. However, this deed was granted so long ago that its execution is 'outside the scope of legal memory'.

Unfortunately legal memory is elephantine, and stretches back to 1189 (the year of the accession of Richard I). In effect, if you claim a prescriptive easement (or profit) at common law, you have bodly to assert that you and your predecessors have been exercising the right ever since 1189.

Fortunately you do not have to produce evidence of user covering the whole of the last 800 or so years. If 20 years' user is proved, user right back to 1189 will be presumed. But the presumption can be rebutted by showing any of the following facts:

(a)   at some time since 1189 the right was not exercised; or
(b)   at some time since 1189 the right could not have been exercised; or
(c)   at some time since 1189 dominant and servient plots were in common ownership.

25.4   Prescription by Lost Modern Grant

(For a general discussion see the dictum of Fox LJ in *Simmons v Dobson* (**25.2.5** above).)

CHARLES DALTON v HENRY ANGUS & Co. (1881) 6 App Cas 740, House of Lords

This case is included here because it contains an important statement in the House of Lords affirming the validity of the doctrine of lost modern grant.

THE LORD CHANCELLOR (LORD SELBORNE): . . . 'My Brother Hayes said, presumed grants of windows and of support were idle fictions which ought never to have been invented; perhaps so, but the fact that they were shews that the inventors and everybody else supposed that *real grants of such a nature would be* good.' The rule as to prescription is thus stated in Sir Francis North's argument in *Potter v North* 1 Vent 387: 'The law allows prescriptions but in supply of the loss of a grant. Ancient grants happen to be lost many times, and it would be hard that no title could be made to things that lie in grant but by shewing of a grant; therefore, upon usage *temps dont*, &c., the law presumes a grant and a lawful beginning, and allows such usage for a good title; but still it is but in supply of the loss of a grant; and, therefore, for such things *as can have no lawful beginning*, nor be created at this day *by any manner of grant, or reservation, or deed that can be supposed*, no prescription is good.' Ashhurst J, in *Lord Pelham v Pickersgill* 1 TR 667, laid it down as the general rule, that 'every prescription is good, if by any possibility it can be supposed to have had a legal commencement.'. . .

TEHIDY MINERALS LTD AND ANOTHER v NORMAN AND OTHERS
[1971] 2 All ER 475, Court of Appeal

FACTS: In January 1920 a group of farmers started grazing their sheep on the servient land. They continued to do so 'as of right' until October 1941, when the land was requisitioned by the war office for military training. The farmers continued to graze their sheep on the land, but it was conceded that the post 1941 grazing was by permission. (Permission came first from the war office and then, after the land had been derequisitioned, the servient owners.) The farmers claimed a prescriptive profit of pasture.

HELD: The farmers succeeded under the doctrine of 'lost modern grant'. The 'presumption' of lost modern grant arose because the claimant had produced strong evidence of twenty years user 'as of right'. It would not rebut the 'presumption' for the servient owner to show that the grant never in fact took place. The servient owner could only rebut the 'presumption' by showing that during the relevant period (in this case January 1920 to October 1921) the grant was impossible at law.

BUCKLEY LJ: No defendant has sought to prove any actual grant of common rights; at the trial the defendants relied on common law prescription, on the Prescription Act 1832, and on the doctrine of lost modern grant.

. . . The co-existence of three separate methods of prescribing is, in our view, anomalous and undesirable, for it results in much unnecessary complication and confusion. We hope that it may be possible for the legislature to effect a long overdue simplification in this branch of the law.

. . . In our judgment *Angus & Co v Dalton* decides that, where there has been upwards of 20 years' uninterrupted enjoyment of an easement, such enjoyment having the necessary qualities to fulfil the requirements of prescription, then unless, for some reason such as incapacity on the part of the person or persons who might at some time before the commencement of the 20-year period have made a grant, the existence of such a grant is impossible, the law will adopt a legal fiction that such a grant was made, in spite of any direct evidence that no such grant was in fact made. If this legal fiction is not to be displaced by direct evidence that no grant was made, it would be strange if it could be displaced by circumstantial evidence leading to the same conclusion, and in our judgment it must follow that circumstantial evidence tending to negative the existence of a grant (other than evidence establishing impossibility) should not be permitted to displace the fiction. Precisely the same reasoning must, we think, apply to a presumed lost grant of a profit à prendre as to an easement.

In the present case, if we are to presume lost grants, we must do so in respect of each of the four farms, Higher and Lower Hill, Cabilla and Pinsla Park. Each of the presumed grants must be supposed to have been made between 20 January 1920 and 28 November 1921, and to have been since lost in circumstances of which no one now has any recollection. This combination of circumstances seems to us to be exceedingly improbable, and we feel sympathy for the view expressed by Farwell J in *A-G v Simpson*, where that learned judge said:

> It cannot be the duty of a judge to presume a grant of the non-existence of which he is convinced, nor can he be constrained to hold that such a grant is reasonably possible within the meaning of the authorities.

In view, however, of the decision in *Angus & Co. v Dalton* we consider that it is not open to us in the present case to follow this line. . . .

For these reasons we think that grants of common rights of grazing over Tawna Down must be presumed to have been made since 19 January 1920 and before 6 October 1921, in respect of each of the four farms at present under consideration. We are therefore of opinion that prescriptive rights to grazing on the down must be regarded as having been in force at the date of the requisition in respect of all seven farms under discussion. What ensued thereafter can only have had the effect of suspending these rights unless it can be said that any of the claimants or any predecessor in title of his has abandoned his grazing rights. For the plaintiffs it is contended that the arrangements of October 1960 amounted to abandonment by the commoners of their rights over Tawna Down. We do not agree. For reasons which we have already indicated we think that that arrangement was of a temporary and terminable character. Abandonment of an easement or of a profit à prendre can only, we think, be treated as having taken place where the person entitled to it has demonstrated a fixed intention never at any time thereafter to assert the right himself or to attempt to transmit it to anyone else. The fact that the commoners are content for the time being to subject the management of the grazing on the down to the control of the association is not, in our view, a circumstance which gives rise to any such conclusion. The commoners may well find it more advantageous for the time being to subject themselves to the control of the association in order to obtain the benefits of the fencing and maintenance by the association of the grazing on the down than to exercise their common rights. It does not at all follow from this that if at some time in the future the arrangement should come to an end, the commoners might not wish to reassert their common rights. We do not think that any abandonment has been shown to have taken place. . . .

OAKLEY v *BOSTON* [1975] 3 All ER 405, Court of Appeal

FACTS: Land surrounding a Church of England rectory was 'glebe land' vested in the rector of the parish in his capacity as a 'corporation sole'. The owner of adjoining land had continually used, 'as of right', a pathway of the rectory land from 1914 to 1962. In 1962 the adjoining land was sold to a new owner who used the pathway only occasionally. In 1965 the rectory was sold to the plaintiffs. They sought an injunction to restrain the adjoining owner from 'trespassing' on their land.

HELD: There could be no presumption of a lost modern grant made sometime between 1914 and 1942 (the relevant period in order to establish user as of right for twenty years up to 1962). This was because a vicar who owns land in his official capacity as an 'ecclesiastical corporation sole' has no power to grant easements. The claim for prescription by lost modern grant failed because the grant was a legal impossibility.

25.5   Prescription Under the Prescription Act 1832

PRESCRIPTION ACT 1832

1.   Claims to right of common and other profits à prendre, not to be defeated after thirty years enjoyment by merely showing the commencement; after sixty years enjoyment the right to be absolute, unless had by consent or agreement

... No claim which may be lawfully made at the common law, by custom, prescription, or grant, to any right of common or other profit or benefit to be taken and enjoyed from or upon any land of our sovereign lord the King ... or any land being parcel of the duchy of Lancaster or the duchy of Cornwall, or of any ecclesiastical or lay person, or body corporate, except such matters and things as are herein specially provided for, and except tithes, rent, and services, shall, where such right, profit, or benefit have been actually taken and enjoyed by any person claiming right thereto without interruption for the full period of thirty years, be defeated or destroyed by showing only that such right, profit, or benefit was first taken or enjoyed at any time prior to such period of thirty years, but nevertheless such claim may be defeated in any other way by which the same is now liable to be defeated; and when such right, profit, or benefit shall have been so taken and enjoyed as aforesaid for the full period of sixty years, the right thereto shall be deemed absolute and indefeasible, unless it shall appear that the same was taken and enjoyed by some consent or agreement expressly made or given for that purpose by deed or writing.

2.   In claims of rights of way or other easement the periods to be twenty years and forty years

... No claim which may be lawfully made at the common law, by custom, prescription, or grant, to any way or other easement, or to any watercourse, or the use of any water, to be enjoyed or derived upon, over, or from any land or water of our said lord the King ... or being parcel of the duchy of Lancaster or of the duchy of Cornwall, or being the property of any ecclesiastical or lay person, or body corporate, when such way or other matter as herein last before mentioned shall have been actually enjoyed by any person claiming right thereto without interruption for the full period of twenty years, shall be defeated or destroyed by showing only that such way or other matter was first enjoyed at any time prior to such period of twenty years, but nevertheless such claim may be defeated in any other way by which the same is now liable to be defeated; and where such way or other matter as herein last before mentioned shall have been so enjoyed as aforesaid for the full period of forty years, the right thereto shall be deemed absolute and indefeasible, unless it shall appear that the same was enjoyed by some consent or agreement expressly given or made for that purpose by deed or writing.

3.   Right to the use of light enjoyed for twenty years indefeasible, unless shewn to have been by consent

... When the access and use of light to and for any dwelling house, workshop, or other building shall have been actually enjoyed therewith for the full period of twenty years without interruption, the right thereto shall be deemed absolute and indefeasible, any local usage or custom to the contrary notwithstanding, unless it shall appear that the same was enjoyed by some consent or agreement expressly made or given for that purpose by deed or writing.

5.   In actions on the case the claimant may allege his right generally, as at present. In pleas to trespass and other pleadings, etc, the period mentioned in this Act may be alleged; and exceptions, etc, to be replied to specially

... In all actions upon the case and other pleadings, wherein the party claiming may now by law allege his right generally, without averring the existence of such right from time immemorial, such general allegation shall still be deemed sufficient, and if the same shall be denied, all and every the matters in this Act mentioned and provided, which shall be applicable to the case, shall be admissible in evidence to sustain or rebut such allegation; and . . . in all pleadings to actions of trespass, and in all other pleadings wherein before the passing of this Act it would have been necessary to allege the right to have existed from time immemorial, it shall be sufficient to allege the enjoyment thereof as of right by the occupiers of the tenement in respect whereof the same is claimed for and during such of the periods mentioned in this Act as may be applicable to the case, and without claiming in the name or right of the owner of the fee, as is now usually done; and if the other party shall intend to rely on any proviso, exception, incapacity, disability, contract, agreement, or other matter herein-before mentioned, or on any cause or matter of fact or of law not consistent with the simple fact of enjoyment, the same shall be specially alleged and set forth in answer to the allegation of the party claiming, and shall not be received in evidence on any general traverse or denial of such allegation.

6. Restricting the presumption to be allowed in support of claims herein provided for
. . . In the several cases mentioned in and provided for by this Act, no presumption shall be allowed or made in favour or support of any claim, upon proof of the exercise or enjoyment of the right or matter claimed for any less period of time or number of years than for such period or number mentioned in this Act as may be applicable to the case and to the nature of the claim.

25.5.1 THE 'NEXT BEFORE ACTION' AND 'WITHOUT INTERRUPTION' RULES

PRESCRIPTION ACT 1832

4. Before mentioned periods to be deemed those next before suits for claiming to which such periods relate—What shall constitute an interruption
. . . Each of the respective periods of years herein-before mentioned shall be deemed and taken to be the period next before some suit or action wherein the claim or matter to which such period may relate shall have been or shall be brought into question; and . . . no act or other matter shall be deemed to be an interruption, within the meaning of this statute, unless the same shall have been or shall be submitted to or acquiesced in for one year after the party interrupted shall have had or shall have notice thereof, and of the person making or authorising the same to be made.

25.5.1.1 Interruption of user as of right in the twentieth year

FLIGHT v THOMAS (1841) 8 English Reports 91, House of Lords

FACTS: The dominant owner had enjoyed an easement of way as of right for 19 years and eleven months. He was then interrupted by an obstruction. He waited a few months before issuing the writ, thus twenty months had elapsed from the commencement of his user as of right.
HELD: The dominant owner was held to have a prescriptive easement.

THE LORD CHANCELLOR: . . . The argument at the bar rested principally on this, that there had not been 20 years' enjoyment. That there had not been one year's interruption acquiesced in is clear from the facts stated in the bill of exceptions; but the ground of the objection to the direction of the learned Judge was, that there had not been 20 years' enjoyment of the window. Now, in point of fact, there is no doubt that there had not been 20 years' enjoyment, according to the ordinary meaning and usage of that term; but the question is not whether there had been 20 years' enjoyment in the ordinary sense, but whether there had or had not been 20 years' enjoyment within the meaning of the Act; because, whatever term the Act uses, if it explains the meaning of that term, it is quite immaterial whether the word may or may not be used in any other sense where it is not explained what the meaning of the term is. Now, as I read these two sections, the meaning is that there must be 20 years from the commencement of the right of enjoyment to the commencement of the suit; and no interruption shall be considered as an interruption within the meaning of the Act, that is to say, for the purpose of interfering with the 20 years, unless that interruption shall have lasted one year. The Act, therefore, explains what it means by enjoyment without an interruption of one year's duration. Twenty years must elapse, but no interruption shall be considered as preventing the 20 years from running, unless that interruption has a duration of one year.

Now I think it was hardly disputed—although, when it was put to the learned counsel, an attempt was made to show a distinction—that within the terms of this Act, if an interruption of any duration had taken place, and had ceased during the running of the 20 years, so that at the expiration of the 20 years there was no obstruction, that would prevent the action being brought at the expiration of the 20 years: it must be so within the terms of the Act; because the objection is, not that there is not 20 years' enjoyment, but that there is not 20 years' enjoyment without interruption; and whether that interruption be in the middle or be at the end of the term, cannot, within the meaning of this clause, create any difference in the result.

That would be the construction which I should think the obvious construction of these two clauses, if there had been no decision on the subject. It does, however, so happen that in all the Courts at Westminster this question has arisen more or less directly. In the case of *Jones* v *Price* (3 Bing NC 52), the real point decided was that the 20 years must be pleaded as being next before the commencement of the suit. The right was there laid, not as next before the obstruction created, but next before the commencement of the suit. Now if the right mode of pleading be 'next before the commencement of the suit,' that of course implies that the plea would have been bad if it had been 'next before the injury complained of.' In *Richards* v *Fry* (7 Ad and E 698), it was held that the laying the term of enjoyment before the act complained of was bad, and that it ought to have been next before the commencement of the suit. There is also the case of *Wright* v *Williams* (1 Mees and W. 77), and the case of *Lawson* v *Langley* (4 Ad and El 890); which cases prove this, not only that it is good to lay the right 20 years before the commencement of the suit, but that it is bad if it is not so laid: it is bad if it is laid next before the injury complained of. Those cases decide that, according to the true construction of the Act, the 20 years are to be reckoned from the date of the commencement of the right claimed until the commencement of the suit.

Then we have only to put a construction on the words of the Act relating to the interruption. The words of the fourth section of the Act are positive that no interruption for less than one year shall be deemed an interruption within the meaning of this Act—the meaning and purpose of the Act being to give 20 years' enjoyment the effect of absolute right—that no interruption of the enjoyment of that right for less than one year shall have effect for the purposes of the Act.

Under these circumstances, I think there cannot be a doubt that the construction put upon this Act by the Court below was a correct construction; and I shall move your Lordships to affirm the judgment with costs.

25.5.2 DIFFERENCES BETWEEN LONGER AND SHORTER PERIODS UNDER THE PRESCRIPTION ACT 1832

GARDNER v *HODGSON'S KINGSTON BREWERY COMPANY LTD*
[1903] AC 229, House of Lords

FACTS: The owner of a house used a track from his stables through the yard of an adjoining inn in order to access a public road. Evidence showed that he paid fifteen shillings a year to the owners of the yard. There was no agreement in writing and no evidence to show conclusively that the payment of the fifteen shillings was in consideration of the use of the track.
HELD: The payment of fifteen shillings was presumed to have been made in consideration of the right to use the track. Therefore the use of the track had been 'by permission', not 'as of right'. Accordingly, there could be no prescription under the Prescription Act 1832.

EARL OF HALSBURY LC: In a certain sense a man has a right to enjoy what he has paid for, and, therefore, if the appellant here at any time during the year when she had paid for the right to use this way had been hindered, she would have had a right to complain that what I will call her contract had been broken, and that during the year she had a right to use the way. I do not think that this would have established a right in the proper sense, because, being but a parol licence, it might be withdrawn, and her action would be for damages, but she would have no *right* to the way. And in no sense could the right be the right contemplated by the Act. That right means a right to exercise the right claimed against the will of the person over whose property it is sought to be exercised. It does not and cannot mean a user enjoyed from time to time at the will and pleasure of the owner of the property over which the user is sought. At any time after the first year the owner of the Red Lion might refuse to renew the permission to use this way. I think, therefore, that there is no evidence whatever of a user 'as of right'.

25.5.3　PRESCRIPTION FOR EASEMENTS OF LIGHT

25.5.3.1　Rights of Light Act 1959

RIGHTS OF LIGHT ACT 1959

2.　Registration of notice in lieu of obstruction of access of light

(1)　For the purpose of preventing the access and use of light from being taken to be enjoyed without interruption, any person who is an owner of land (in this and the next following section referred to as the 'servient land') over which light passes to a dwelling-house, workshop or other building (in this and the next following section referred to as 'the dominant building') may apply to the local authority in whose area the dominant building is situated for the registration of a notice under this section. . . .

3.　Effect of registered notice and proceedings relating thereto

(1)　Where, in pursuance of an application made in accordance with the last preceding section, a notice is registered thereunder, then, for the purpose of determining whether any person is entitled (by virtue of the Prescription Act 1832, or otherwise) to a right to the access of light to the dominant building across the servient land, the access of light to that building across that land shall be treated as obstructed to the same extent, and with the like consequences, as if an opaque structure, of the dimensions specified in the application,—

(a)　had, on the date of registration of the notice, been erected in the position on the servient land specified in the application, and had been so erected by the person who made the application, and

(b)　had remained in that position during the period for which the notice has effect and had been removed at the end of that period.

(2)　For the purposes of this section a notice registered under the last preceding section shall be taken to have effect until either—

(a)　the registration is cancelled, or

(b)　the period of one year beginning with the date of registration of the notice expires, or

(c)　in the case of a notice registered in pursuance of an application accompanied by a certificate issued under paragraph (b) of subsection (3) of the last preceding section, the period specified in the certificate expires without such a further certificate as is mentioned in paragraph (c) of subsection (5) of that section having before the end of that period been lodged with the local authority,

and shall cease to have effect on the occurrence of any one of those events.

(3)　Subject to the following provisions of this section, any person who, if such a structure as is mentioned in subsection (1) of this section had been erected as therein mentioned, would have had a right of action in any court in respect of that structure, on the grounds that he was entitled to a right to the access of light to the dominant building across the servient land, and that the said right was infringed by that structure, shall have the like right of action in that court in respect of the registration of a notice under the last preceding section:

Provided that an action shall not be begun by virtue of this subsection after the notice in question has ceased to have effect.

(4)   Where, at any time during the period for which a notice registered under the last preceding section has effect, the circumstances are such that, if the access of light to the dominant building had been enjoyed continuously from a date one year earlier than the date on which the enjoyment thereof in fact began, a person would have had a right of action in any court by virtue of the last preceding subsection in respect of the registration of the notice, that person shall have the like right of action in that court by virtue of this subsection in respect of the registration of the notice.

(5)   The remedies available to the plaintiff in an action brought by virtue of subsection (3) or subsection (4) of this section (apart from any order as to costs) shall be such declaration as the court may consider appropriate in the circumstances, and an order directing the registration of the notice to be cancelled or varied, as the court may determine.

(6)   For the purposes of section four of the Prescription Act 1832 (under which a period of enjoyment of any of the rights to which that Act applies is not to be treated as interrupted except by a matter submitted to or acquiesced in for one year after notice thereof)—

(a)   as from the date of registration of a notice under the last preceding section, all persons interested in the dominant building or any part thereof shall be deemed to have notice of the registration thereof and of the person on whose application it was registered;

(b)   until such time as an action is brought by virtue of subsection (3) or subsection (4) of this section in respect of the registration of a notice under the last preceding section, all persons interested in the dominant building or any part thereof shall be deemed to acquiesce in the obstruction which, in accordance with subsection (1) of this section, is to be treated as resulting from the registration of the notice;

(c)   as from the date on which such an action is brought, no person shall be treated as submitting to or acquiescing in that obstruction:

Provided that, if in any such action, the court decides against the claim of the plaintiff, the court may direct that the preceding provisions of this subsection shall apply in relation to the notice as if that action had not been brought.

25.6   End of Chapter Assessment Questions

1.   Last month Finnegan, owner of Blackacre and Whiteacre, two neighbouring farms, sold and conveyed Blackacre to Milligan. The conveyance contained no provision relating to easements and profits.

Advise Milligan regarding the following:

(a)   The only direct access to Blackacre is a narrow footpath insufficiently wide to accommodate motor traffic. Milligan wishes to make use of the private driveway which runs from Blackacre through Whiteacre and leads into the adjoining public highway.

(b)   Some drains run from Blackacre under Whiteacre. Milligan wishes to make use of those drains.

(c)   Cyrus, the owner of Redacre, an adjoining farm, claims that he can continue to graze his sheep on a hill-side forming part of Blackacre where sheep from Redacre have been grazed 'as long as anyone can remember'.

2.   In 1973 Louise acquired the freehold to Grand House. Grand House adjoins West Field, the freehold to which was then owned by Nellie. Over the years Nellie has leased West Field to Olive for short periods.

On acquiring Grand House, Louise immediately leased it to Terry for 70 years. Soon after taking the lease, Terry started to pasture the five sheep he owned in West Field, and to take a short cut across West Field to get to the nearest station. He continued both of these activities until September 1995, without any objection from Nellie or Olive.

In September 1995 Patel acquired the freehold to West Field from Nellie, and immediately ordered Terry not to make any further use of West Field. Initially Terry complied with this demand, but now both he and Louise are threatening legal action.

It is now January 1996. Advise Patel.

25.7   End of Chapter Assessment Outline Answers

QUESTION 1

Regarding (a) and (b) Milligan will have to try and rely on the (rather complex) rules for implied grant of easements. There are no less than four separate rules in which an easement can arise by implied grant.
   The first rule is 'way of necessity'. This rule is relevant only to (a). It only applies if land is sold which is completely 'land-locked', i.e. there is absolutely no way in and out except over the vendor's land. This does not appear to be the case with Blackacre, as there is the 'narrow footpath'. This path may not be adequate for farming purposes, but its existence is sufficient to prevent there being a way of necessity.
   The second rule is the rule of 'intended easements'. If land is granted by a vendor or lessor to be used for a particular purpose *known to the vendor/lessor*, then there is implied into the conveyance/lease any easement over land retained by the vendor/lessor which is ABSOLUTELY ESSENTIAL in order to carry out that 'particular purpose'. (See the ventilation shaft case of *Wong v Beaumont*.)
   With respect to (a) Milligan must argue:

(i)   that Finnegan knew that Milligan intended to use Blackacre as a farm; AND

(ii)   that a right to use the private driveway was absolutely essential to carry on a farm business.

Milligan should have no difficulty proving point (i), but point (ii) is very problematic. Finnegan would probably sucsessfully contend that there were possible alternatives (e.g. widening and surfacing the narrow footpath to take motor traffic) and that therefore using the driveway was not *absolutely essential*.

With respect to (b) Milligan will have to argue that it is absolutely essential that he use the existing drains under Whiteacre. But Finnegan is likely to respond that alternative drains could be always laid not passing under Whiteacre. If that is the case, then Milligan has no chance under the intended easements rule.

Milligan's best chance would appear to be with the third rule of implied grant, the rule in *Wheeldon* v *Burrows*. Under this rule pre-existing nebulous rights known as 'privileges' and 'quasi-easements' can be magically converted into easements on the conveyance of the dominant land.

A 'privilege' would arise if the owner of two plots had leased one of them and then later granted the tenant some licence over the land he retained. There appears no evidence of Finnegan having done this. A quasi-easement would exist where the owner of two plots makes use of one plot for the benefit of the other in circumstances where had the plots been in separate ownership the 'use' could have been granted as an easement. It seems very likely that prior to the sale of Blackacre Finnegan made use of quasi-easements over the driveway and the drains.

If the following three conditions were satisfied one or both of these quasi-easements would be converted into full easements in favour of Blackacre the moment Blackacre was conveyed to Milligan.

(1)   The quasi-easement was 'continuous and apparent', i.e. regularly used, and detectable by inspection of the plots of land.

(2)   The quasi-easement was used for the benefit of the dominant land immediately prior to its being conveyed.

(3)   The quasi-easement was necessary for the reasonable or convenient enjoyment of the dominant land.

Element (2) is presumably satisfied with respect to both (a) and (b). (1) is clearly satisfied with respect to the driveway, but whether the drains are 'apparent' will depend upon whether there was evidence *on the surface* (man-hole covers, gratings, etc) of their existence.

It is submitted that element (3) is satisfied with respect to both (a) and (b). While the driveway and drains are probably not 'absolutely essential', they probably do satisfy the lesser test of necessity laid down for *Wheeldon* v *Burrows*.

The fourth rule for implied grant, section 62, can apply only to 'privileges'; and is therefore seemingly of no help to Milligan's claims.

With respect to (c) Cyrus is going to claim a profit of pasture by prescription. The basic idea underlying prescription for easements and profits is that if the dominant owner has been exercising his claim *'as of right'* for the past twenty years he thereby acquires an easement/profit to exercise his claim permanently.

For user to be 'as of right' it must be open ('without secrecy'), without force and without permission. Cyrus' user has clearly been open, but if his user depended upon a permission (even an oral one) granted by Finnegan or one of his predecessors, there could be no prescription. (Exceptionally, if there was a purely oral permission given more than sixty years ago and never repeated a claim under section one of the Prescription Act 1832 would apparently succeed.)

If Cyrus' user was in the face of active opposition from Finnegan (protests or more obstructive behaviour), then user would be forceable and not prescriptive. Assuming Cyrus' user was as of right he would not *ipso facto* acquire a prescriptive profit. He must also satisfy one of the three alternative prescription periods, common law, or the Prescription Act 1832 or lost modern grant.

Cyrus probably will not succeed under the common law rule, as he has to assert that he and his predecessors have been grazing sheep on the hillside since 1189. But the

Prescription Act section one will almost certainly be available, which requires thirty (not twenty) years user as of right 'next before action'.

If Cyrus can only show between twenty and thirty years user as of right he will probably be able to rely on the presumption of lost modern grant. This presumption could only be rebutted by showing that throughout the relevant period the grant of a profit was a legal impossibility.

QUESTION 2

For reasons which will emerge, there is no need to treat the claims of Louise and Terry separately. Louise will claim that a prescriptive easement of way and a prescriptive profit of pasture have been acquired over West Field, and that those rights are 'appurtenant' to the freehold in Grand House. Terry will claim that, as current Tenant of Grand House, he is automatically entitled to the benefit of those rights appurtenant to Grand House.

There are two stages to the establishing of a claim for a prescriptive easement or profit. Firstly, the dominant owner must show that certain general rules common to all three forms of Prescription are satisfied. Secondly, he/she must show that the 'User as of Right' satisfies the rules specific to one of the three forms of prescription.

The General Rules

Louise and Terry will firstly have to show that there has been continuous user as of right, i.e. open user without permission from the servient owner and without force or dispute in any form.

For user to be 'open' it must be such as would indicate to a reasonable servient owner that a right was being exercised (*Lloyds Bank v Dalton*). The grazing was obviously 'open', as presumably was the crossing the field to get to the station, unless Terry only used the short cut at night-time, which is highly unlikely.

We are told that user was 'without any objection', so there is no question of 'forcible user'. Patel's only hope under the 'user as of right' heading would be to prove that Nellie gave express permission to Terry for his activities. An oral permission would be sufficient, but it must be stressed that mere acquiescence in the prescriber's activities, which seems to be the case here, does not equal permission.

Louise and Terry must also satisfy the general rule that user be 'by or on behalf of a fee simple against a fee simple'. A prescriptive easement is always in fee simple, and is (theoretically) a grant from the servient freeholder to the dominant freeholder.

The application of this rule has two aspects. Firstly any prescriptive user by a lessee such as Terry is deemed to be as agent for his landlord. Thus Terry could not have prescribed against land owned by Louise, but any prescriptive right which he establishes against a third party such as Nellie is appurtenant to her freehold, though he gets the benefit for the seventy years of his lease.

Secondly, user as of right to be prescriptive must commence against a freeholder in physical possession. Thus if the commencement of the grazing and the 'short cutting' was during one of the 'short periods' when Nellie had let the field to Olive, Patel will be able to defeat the claims for prescriptive rights.

The Forms of Prescription

Assuming that Patel is unable to defeat the prescriptive rights under the general rules just discussed, Terry and Louise will invoke the Prescription Act 1832 for the (alleged) right of way, and lost modern grant for the profit of grazing. (Any claim under the third form of prescription, common law, is bound to fail as user clearly commenced in about 1974, long after 1189.)

Under the Prescription Act 1832 Louise and Terry will have to show user as of right for twenty years 'next before action'. Their claim will succeed (they can show user 1974–95) despite the fact that for about seven months Terry complied with the demand not to exercise his 'rights'. Provided Louise and Terry issue their writ before the break in user has lasted one year, they should win.

Section four of the 1832 Act requires the user to be 'next before action', i.e. (normally) immediately preceding the issue of the writ in the case in which the easement is disputed. But it then provides that an 'interruption' of user for less than twelve months shall not count as an interruption to defeat the claim.

Louise and Terry will not be able to rely on the 1832 Act for their claim to a prescriptive profit. This is simply because section one of the Act lays down a minimum period of 30 years user for profits. Louise and Terry (like the farmers in *Tehidy Minerals* v *Norman*) will thus have to fall back on the 'last resort' form of prescription, 'lost modern grant'.

To succeed under this heading they will have to show strong evidence of at least twenty years user as of right. If they can do so (and it seems they can) the court will, by way of legal fiction, presume that a deed was executed 'in modern times' but that deed has been mislaid. . . .

In lost modern grant cases nobody really believes that a deed existed. Yet recent cases rule that the presumption of lost grant cannot be rebutted by factual proof (however convincing) that there was no deed. The presumption can only be rebutted by showing that the grant was throughout 'the relevant time' impossible as a matter of law.

The 'relevant time' begins when user as of right commenced, and ends twenty years before user as of right ceased. In our case the relevant time would be (circa) 1974 to September 1975. If throughout those months the granting of a valid profit would have been legally impossible because (say) the land was requisitioned or because Nellie was under some special legal disability like the vicar in *Oakley* v *Boston*, then Patel would defeat the claim to a Profit. But it should be stressed that cases where the alleged servient owner can show legal impossibility are rare.

CHAPTER TWENTY-SIX

RESTRICTIVE COVENANTS — THE BASIC PRINCIPLES

26.1   Restrictive and Positive Covenants Distinguished

AUSTERBERRY v *CORPORATION OF OLDHAM* (1885) 24 ChD 750, Court of Appeal

FACTS: Mr. Elliot conveyed freehold land to trustees of a joint stock company which company wished to use the land to build a road. The trustees covenanted in the deed, for themselves, their heirs and assigns, that they would make the road and keep it in repair. The trustees duly made the road, creating an access to Mr. Elliot's land. Later Mr. Elliot sold his land to Austerberry and the trustees sold their land to the defendant. The main question in the case was whether Austerberry could enforce the repairing covenant against the defendant.

HELD: The covenant was unenforceable. This was because the covenant was a 'positive covenant', that is, one which imposed a positive burden on the owner of the servient land.

COTTON LJ: . . . where there is a restrictive covenant, the burden and benefit of which do not run at law, Courts of Equity restrain anyone who takes the property with notice of that covenant from using it in a way inconsistent with the covenant. But here the covenant which is attempted to be insisted upon on this appeal is a covenant to lay out money in doing certain work upon this land; and, that being so, in my opinion—and the Court of Appeal has already expressed a similar opinion in a case which was before it—that is not a covenant which a Court of Equity will enforce: it will not enforce a covenant not running at law when it is sought to enforce that covenant in such a way as to require the successors in title of the covenantor, to spend money, and in that way to undertake a burden upon themselves. The covenantor must not use the property for a purpose inconsistent with the use for which it was originally granted: but in my opinion a Court of Equity does not and ought not to enforce a covenant binding only in equity in such a way as to require the successors of the covenantor himself, they having entered into no covenant, to expend sums of money in accordance with what the original covenantor bound himself to do.

SMITH AND SNIPES HALL FARM LTD v *RIVER DOUGLAS CATCHMENT BOARD*
[1949] 2 All ER 179, Court of Appeal

FACTS: The defendants promised a farmer, for the benefit of his farm, that they would maintain the banks of a river. The first plaintiff took a conveyance of the farm and brought an action against the defendants when the river burst, flooding the plaintiff's land.

HELD: The plaintiff farmer was entitled to enforce the promise. On the proper construction of the covenant to repair and maintain the river banks, it was clear that the benefit of the promise had been intended by all parties to run to purchasers of the dominant land. Although the covenant had not expressly identified the land intended to benefit from the covenant, the court applied the maxim 'that is certain which can be made certain'. Accordingly, extrinsic evidence was admitted to prove the area of the land held by the original contracting parties.

TUCKER LJ: . . . It remains to consider whether, in these circumstances, the plaintiffs, or either of them, can sue in respect of this breach. It is said for the board that the benefit of the covenant does not run with the land so as to bind a stranger who has not and never had an interest in the land to be benefited and there being no servient tenement to bear the burden. Further it is contended that such a covenant must by the terms of the deed in which it is contained relate to some specific parcel of land, the precise extent and situation of which can be identified by reference to the deed alone. It is first necessary to ascertain from the deed that the covenant is one which 'touches or concerns' the land, that is, it must either affect the land as regards mode of occupation or it must be such as *per se*, and not merely from collateral circumstances, affects the value of the land, and it must then be shown that it was the intention of the parties that the benefit thereof should run with the land. The deed shows that its object was to improve the drainage of land liable to flooding and prevent future flooding. The location of the land is described as situate between the Leeds and Liverpool Canal and the River Douglas and adjoining the Eller Brook. In return for lump sum payments the board covenants to do certain work to the banks of the Eller Brook, one of such banks being, in fact, situate upon and forming part of the plaintiffs' lands, and to maintain for all time the work when completed. In my view, the language of the deed satisfies both tests. It affects the value of the land *per se* and converts it from flooded meadows to land suitable for agriculture, and shows an intention that the benefit of the obligation to maintain shall attach thereto into whosesoever hands the lands shall come.

With regard to the covenantor being a stranger, *The Prior's Case* (1368) YB 42 is referred to in *Spencer's Case* (1583) 5 Co Rep 16a in these words, as set out in Smith's Leading Cases (13th edn, vol. 1, p. 55):

[In the case of a] grandfather, father and two sons: The grandfather being seised of the manor of D, whereof a chapel was parcel: a prior, with the assent of his convent, by deed covenanted for him and his successors, with the grandfather and his heirs, that he and his convent would sing all the week in his chapel, parcel of the said manor, for the lords of the said manor and his servants, etc.; the grandfather did enfeoff one of the manor in fee, who gave it to the younger son and his wife in tail; and it was adjudged that the tenants in tail, as terre-tenants (for the elder brother was heir), should have an action of covenant against the prior, for the covenant is to do a thing which is annexed to the chapel, which is within the manor, and so annexed to the manor, as it is there said.

The notes to *Spencer's* case, in Smith's Leading Cases, at p. 73, state:

When such a covenant [namely, covenants running with the land made with the owner of the land to which they relate] is made, it seems to be of no consequence whether the covenantor be the person who conveyed the land to the covenantee, or be a mere stranger.

. . . In this state of the authorities it seems clear, despite some dicta coming to the contrary view, that such a covenant, if it runs with the land, is binding on the covenantor though a mere stranger, and that this point will not avail the board.

As to the requirement that the deed containing the covenant must expressly identify the particular land to be benefited, no authority was cited to us and in the absence of such authority I can see no valid reason why the maxim '*Id certum est quod certum reddi potest*' should not apply so as to make admissible extrinsic evidence to prove the extent and situation of the lands of the respective landowners adjoining the Eller Brook situate between the Leeds and Liverpool Canal and the River Douglas.

. . . I do not find anything in the judgments in *Austerberry* v *Oldham Corpn.* (1885) 24 ChD 750 which conflicts with the law as I have endeavoured to set it out above, and I have, accordingly, arrived at the conclusion that the covenant by the board in the agreement of April 25 1938, is one which runs with the land referred to therein, which land is capable of identification, and that it is binding on the board; and, further, that by virtue of s. 78(1) of the Law of Property Act 1925, it can be enforced at the suit of the covenantee and her successors in title and the persons deriving title under her or them so that both the plaintiff Smith and the plaintiff company can sue in respect of the damage resulting to their respective interests therein by reason of the board's breach of covenant. For these reasons, I would allow this appeal, and remit the assessment of damages to an official referee.

RHONE v STEPHENS [1994] 2 All ER 65, House of Lords

FACTS: The owners of a house and cottage under the same roof sold the cottage and covenanted in the conveyance that they would maintain the roof above the cottage. Since then both properties had been sold on to new owners. Later, the roof of the cottage began to leak. The plaintiffs, the new owners of the cottage, sought to enforce the repairing covenant against the new owners of the house.
HELD: The positive covenant was not enforceable at common law. To permit it to be so enforced would destroy the notion of privity of contract between the original parties. Nor could the burden of the covenant run in equity to bind the new owner of the house.

LORD TEMPLEMAN: . . . Equity can . . . prevent or punish the breach of a negative covenant which restricts the user of land or the exercise of other rights in connection with land. Restrictive covenants deprive an owner of a right which he could otherwise exercise. Equity cannot compel an owner to comply with a positive covenant entered into by his predecessors in title without flatly contradicting the common law rule that a person cannot be made liable upon a contract unless he was a party to it. Enforcement of a positive covenant lies in contract; a positive covenant compels an owner to exercise his rights. Enforcement of a negative covenant lies in property; a negative covenant deprives the owner of a right over property. As Lord Cottenham LC said in *Tulk v Moxhay* 2 Ph 774 at 778, [1843–60] All ER Rep 9 at 11:

. . . if an equity is attached to the property by the owner, no one purchasing with notice of that equity can stand in a different situation from the party from whom he purchased. . . .

For over 100 years it has been clear and accepted law that equity will enforce negative covenants against freehold land but has no power to enforce positive covenants against successors in title of the land. To enforce a positive covenant would be to enforce a personal obligation against a person who has not covenanted. To enforce negative covenants is only to treat the land as subject to a restriction.

Mr Munby, who argued the appeal persuasively on behalf of the plaintiffs, referred to an article by Professor Sir William Wade, 'Covenants—"a broad and reasonable view" (1972) 31 CLJ 157, and other articles in which the present state of the law is subjected to severe criticism. In 1965 the *Report of the Committee on Positive Covenants Affecting Land* (Cmnd 2719), which was a report by a committee appointed by the Lord Chancellor and under the chairmanship of Lord Wilberforce, referred to difficulties caused by the decision in the *Austerberry* case and recommended legislation to provide that positive covenants which relate to the use of land and are intended to benefit specified other land should run with the land. In *Transfer of Land: Appurtenant Rights* (Law Commission working paper no 36, published on 5 July 1971) the present law on positive rights was described as being illogical, uncertain, incomplete and inflexible. The Law Commission Report *Transfer of Land: The Law of Positive and Restrictive Covenants* (Law Com No 127) laid before Parliament in 1984 made recommendations for the reform of the law relating to positive and restrictive obligations and submitted a draft Bill for that purpose. Nothing has been done.

In these circumstances your Lordships were invited to overrule the decision of the Court of Appeal in the *Austerberry* case [(1885) 24 ChD 750]. To do so would destroy the distinction between law and equity and to convert the rule of equity into a rule of notice. It is plain from the articles, reports and papers to which we were referred that judicial legislation to overrule the *Austerberry* case would create a number of difficulties, anomalies and uncertainties and affect the rights and liabilities of people who have for over 100 years bought and sold land in the knowledge, imparted at an elementary stage to every student of the law of real property, that positive covenants affecting freehold land are not directly enforceable except against the original covenantor. Parliamentary legislation to deal with the decision in the *Austerberry* case would require careful consideration of the consequences. . . .

Snape, J., The Burden of Positive Covenants (1994) 58 Conv 477

Rhone v *Stephens (Executrix)* [1994] 2 All ER 65

In *Rhone* v *Stephens*, the House of Lords has definitively ruled that, in freehold land, the burden of a *positive* covenant (e.g. to repair) will not *in equity* run with the land. In other words, the burden of a positive covenant cannot in equity be enforced against successors in title of the original covenantor by the original covenantee/successors in title of the original covenantee. This is unsurprising although, until *Rhone* v *Stephens*, the rule had not been tested in a higher court for over a century. At common law, irrespective of whether a covenant is positive or restrictive, the burden does not generally run. The crucial difference between the equitable and common law positions, reinforced in *Rhone* v *Stephens*, is that the burden of a restrictive covenant *may* be enforced against successors in title of the original covenantor under the rule in *Tulk* v *Moxhay* [see **26.2.1**].

There are a number of ways of circumventing these rules so as to make, in effect, the *burden* of a positive covenant 'run.' Property lawyers have known about them for years. Perhaps three stand out from the others. One makes use of the rule that the original covenantor remains liable on his covenant. On selling the relevant property, the covenantor (i.e. the vendor) takes an indemnity from the purchaser in the conveyance, to cover his continuing liability for breaches of covenant by the purchaser/successors in title of the purchaser. This obviously creates a strong incentive for the purchaser to observe the covenant. Another involves the reservation of a rentcharge on the sale of the relevant property, to which is annexed a right of entry allowing the rentcharge owner (the covenantor/vendor) to enter, make good the breach and charge the cost to the purchaser in possession. A third possibility is, with extreme care, to make use of the so-called 'conditional benefit principle'. Whilst ensuring that the condition is relevant to the exercise of the right, it is necessary to make taking a benefit under the deed conditional on the assumption of the burden of the positive covenant. However, it is apparent from *Rhone* v *Stephens* itself that there are certain cases where this third possibility cannot be applied, because the person intended to be subject to the burden is not free to choose whether to take the benefit and may have no continuing interest in claiming it. . . .

26.2 Passing the Burden of a Restrictive Covenant

26.2.1 THE COVENANT MUST BE NEGATIVE IN SUBSTANCE

TULK v MOXHAY (1848) [1843–60] All ER Rep 9, Lord Chancellor's Court

FACTS: The fee simple owner of land in Leicester Square, London sold the land to Mr. Elms. Elms covenanted in the conveyance, for himself, his heirs and assigns, that he would 'keep and maintain the said piece of ground . . . uncovered with any buildings, in neat and ornamental order'. The land was later sold by Elms to the defendant. That conveyance did not recite the covenant, but the defendant admitted that he had actual notice of it in any event. The defendant intended to build on the land.

HELD: An injunction was granted against the defendant to restrain a breach of the covenant.

LORD COTTENHAM LC: That this court has jurisdiction to enforce a contract between the owner of land and his neighbour purchasing a part of it that the purchaser shall either use or abstain from using the land purchased in a particular way is what I never knew disputed. Here there is no question about the contract. The owner of certain houses in the square sells the land adjoining, with a covenant from the purchaser not to use it for any other purpose than as a square garden. It is now contended, not that the vendee could violate that contract, but that he might sell the piece of land, and that the purchaser from him may violate it without this court having any power to interfere. If that were so, it would be impossible for an owner of land to sell part of it without incurring the risk of rendering what he retains worthless. It is said that, the covenant being one which does not run with the land, this court cannot enforce it, but the question is not whether the covenant runs with the land, but whether a party shall be permitted to use the land in a manner inconsistent with the contract entered into by his vendor, with notice of which he purchased. Of course, the price would be affected by the covenant, and nothing could be more inequitable than that the original purchaser should be able to sell the property the next day for a greater price, in consideration of the assignee being allowed to escape from the liability which he had himself undertaken. . . .

Note that in *Haywood* v *Brunswick Permanent Benefit Building Society* (1881) 8 QBD 403 Cotton LJ suggested a simple test for determining whether a covenant is restrictive (i.e. negative in substance). He held that a covenant will not be restrictive if the covenantor is required 'to put his hand into his pocket' in order to fulfil his covenant.

26.2.2 THE COVENANT MUST BE MADE WITH AN INTENT TO BURDEN THE SERVIENT LAND

LAW OF PROPERTY ACT 1925

79. Burden of covenants relating to land

(1)   A covenant relating to any land of a covenantor or capable of being bound by him, shall, unless a contrary intention is expressed, be deemed to be made by the covenantor on behalf of himself his successors in title and the persons deriving title under him or them, and, subject as aforesaid, shall have effect as if such successors and other persons were expressed.

This subsection extends to a covenant to do some act relating to the land, notwithstanding that the subject-matter may not be in existence when the covenant is made.

(2)   For the purposes of this section in connexion with covenants restrictive of the user of land 'successors in title' shall be deemed to include the owners and occupiers for the time being of such land.

(3)   This section applies only to covenants made after the commencement of this Act.

26.2.3 THE COVENANT MUST BE MADE TO PROTECT DOMINANT LAND RETAINED BY THE COVENANTEE

LONDON COUNTY COUNCIL v *ALLEN* [1914] 3 KB 642, Court of Appeal

FACTS: The LCC sold a large amount of land to Mr. Allen, a builder. With respect to one small part of the land, Mr. Allen covenanted not to build upon it. This small parcel was intended as an open space for the local residents. The LCC retained no other land in the vicinity. Mr. Allen sold the small parcel to his wife, who commenced building work. The LCC sought an injunction.
HELD: The injunction was refused. The LCC had no dominant land, so it could not claim the benefit of the restrictive covenant.

BUCKLEY LJ: . . . The reasoning of Lord Cottenham's judgment in *Tulk* v *Moxhay* [1843–60] All ER Rep 9 is that if an owner of land sells part of it reserving the rest, and takes from his purchaser a covenant that the purchaser shall use or abstain from using the land purchased in a particular way, that covenant (being one for the protection of the land reserved) is enforceable against a sub-purchaser with notice. The reason given is that, if that were not so, it would be impossible for an owner of land to sell part of it without incurring the risk of rendering what he retains worthless. If the vendor has retained no land which can be protected by the restrictive covenant, the basis of the reasoning of the judgment is swept away. In *Haywood* v *Brunswick Permanent Benefit Building Society* (1881) 8 QBD 403 the Court of Appeal declined to extend the doctrine of *Tulk* v *Moxhay* [1843–60] All ER Rep 9 to covenants other than restrictive covenants. They rejected the doctrine that, inasmuch as the defendants took the land with notice of the covenants, they were bound in equity to perform them. That therefore is not the principle upon which the equitable doctrine rests. In the present case we are asked to extend the doctrine of *Tulk* v *Moxhay* so as to affirm that a restrictive covenant can be enforced against a derivative owner taking with notice by a person who never has had or who does not retain any land to be protected by the restrictive covenant in question. In my opinion the doctrine does not extend to that case. The doctrine is that a covenant not running with the land, but being a negative covenant entered into by an owner of land with an adjoining owner, binds the land in equity and is enforceable against a derivative owner taking with notice. The doctrine ceases to be applicable when the person seeking to enforce the covenant against the derivative owner has no land to be protected by the negative covenant. The fact of notice is in that case irrelevant. . . .

NEWTON ABBOT CO-OP v WILLIAMS AND TREADGOLD [1952] 1 All ER 279, Chancery Division

FACTS: Mrs. Mardon owned two shops in the small central Devon town of Bovey Tracey. The shops were about fifty yards apart on opposite sides of the street. In 1923 Mrs. Mardon sold one of the shops. In the conveyance of that shop there was imposed a restrictive covenant which said that no ironmongery was to be sold from the shop. The restrictive covenant did not identify the dominant land. However, the shop across the road retained by Mrs. Mardon was an ironmongers.

HELD: There was a valid restrictive covenant which bound a subsequent purchaser of the shop sold by Mrs. Mardon in 1923. Although the dominant land was not expressly identified in the conveyance which contained the restrictive covenant, it could be identified by examining the geography of the locality. That, in the view of the judge, was sufficient.

UPJOHN J: . . . the sole issue before me is whether the plaintiffs are entitled to the benefit of the restrictive covenant, and, if so, whether they are entitled to enforce it against the defendants. I will deal with the first point first. Counsel for the plaintiffs submitted, first, that the benefit of the restrictive covenant was annexed to Devonia so as to pass with the assignment of Devonia in equity without any express mention in such subsequent assignment—in other words, that the covenant runs with the land. Alternatively, he said that the plaintiffs are the express assigns of the benefit of the covenant, and as such are entitled to enforce it. In this difficult branch of the law one thing, in my judgment, is clear, *viz*, that in order to annex the benefit of a restrictive covenant to land so that it runs with the land without express assignment on a subsequent assignment of the land, the land for the benefit of which it is taken must be clearly identified in the conveyance containing the covenant. That has been established in a number of cases of high authority.

. . . Looking at the 1923 conveyance, I can find nothing whatever which identifies the land for the benefit of which the covenant is alleged to be taken. Counsel for the plaintiffs relies on the fact that Mrs. Mardon is described as of Devonia, Fore Street, but that, in my judgment, is quite insufficient to annex the benefit of the covenant to those premises. There is no other mention whatever of Devonia in the conveyance. In my judgment, therefore, the plaintiffs fail on this point.

I turn, then, to his second submission, *viz*, that the plaintiffs are express assigns of the benefit of the restrictive covenant. Counsel for the defendants contends that, even if his submissions (with which I shall deal later) are wrong and the covenant was taken by Mrs. Mardon for the benefit of Devonia to enable her to dispose of it to better advantage, yet there is here no complete chain of assignments vesting the benefit in the plaintiffs. He says that there was never any assignment of the benefit of the covenant by the executors of Mrs. Mardon to Leonard Soper Mardon, and, therefore, he was not in a position to assign the benefit of the covenant to the plaintiffs' predecessors in title. He relied on *Ives v Brown* [1919] 2 Ch 314 and *Lord Northbourne v Johnston & Son* [1922] 2 Ch 309. In my judgment, those authorities do not support his contention. The position as I see it was this. On the footing that the restrictive covenant was not annexed to the land so as to run with it, the benefit of the covenant is capable of passing by operation of law as well as by express assignment and formed part of Mrs. Mardon's personal estate on her death: see *Ives v Brown*. It follows, therefore, that when her estate was duly wound up and adminis- tered—and this case has been argued before me on the footing that that happened many years ago—the benefit of the covenant was held by the executors as bare trustees for the residuary legatee, Leonard Soper Mardon, who was himself one of the executors. He, therefore, became entitled to the benefit of this restrictive covenant in equity, and, in my judgment, he was entitled to assign the benefit in equity on an assignment of Devonia. No doubt, had the covenant been assigned to him by the executors, he could also have assigned it at law.

> . . . Counsel's second point was that in order that the benefit of the covenant may be assignable the land for which the benefit of the covenant is taken must in some way be referred to in the conveyance creating the covenant. . . .

In my judgment, therefore, the problem which I have to consider is, first, when Mrs. Mardon took the covenant in 1923, did she retain other land capable of being benefited by the covenant? If not, *cadit quaestio*. Secondly, was such land 'ascertainable' or 'certain' in this sense, that the existence and situation of the land must be indicated in the conveyance or otherwise shown with reasonable certainty. Apart from the fact that Mrs. Mardon is described as of Devonia, there is nothing in the 1923 conveyance to define the land for the benefit of which the restrictive covenant was taken, and I do not think that carries one very far, but, for the reasons I have given, I am, in my judgment, entitled to look at the surrounding circumstances to see if the land to be benefited is shown 'otherwise' with reasonable certainty. That is a question of fact, and, on the admitted facts, bearing in mind the close juxtaposition of Devonia and the defendants' premises, in my judgment, the only reasonable inference to draw from the circumstances at the time of the 1923 conveyance was that Mrs. Mardon took the covenant restrictive of the user of the defendants' premises for the benefit of her own business of ironmonger and of her property Devonia where at all material times she was carrying on that business, which last-mentioned fact must have been apparent to the purchasers in 1923. I should, perhaps, mention that at the date of her death, Mrs. Mardon owned other property in Fore Street, but counsel on neither side founded any argument on that circumstance. It follows, therefore, in my judgment, that Mrs. Mardon could on any subsequent sale of her land Devonia, if she so chose, as part of the transaction of sale, assign the benefit of the covenant so as to enable the purchaser from her and his assignees of the land and covenant to enforce it against an owner of the defendants' premises taking with notice and her legatee, Leonard Soper Mardon, was in no worse position. I do not regard the fact that he assigned the covenant in the deed containing the assignment of the business as affecting the matter. I say nothing as to the position when the plaintiffs' lease expires so that their estate in Devonia comes to an end, nor whether Leonard Soper Mardon, having apparently assigned away the entire benefit of the covenant, will then be in any position further to enforce it. . . .

26.3   Remedies to Enforce a Restrictive Covenant

WROTHAM PARK ESTATE COMPANY v PARKSIDE HOMES LTD AND OTHERS
[1974] 2 All ER 321, Chancery Division

FACTS: In 1935, the Wrotham Park Estate, then owned by the Earl of Strafford, extended to about 4,000 acres. In that year the Earl sold 47 acres out of the Estate. This land was subject to a restrictive covenant 'not to develop the . . . land for building purposes except in strict accordance with plans [approved by the owners of Wrotham Park Estate].' The covenant was expressed to be for the benefit of 'Wrotham Park Estate'. The plaintiff company later acquired Wrotham Park Estate. The defendant, Parkside Homes Ltd, acquired a small part of the servient land. The defendant obtained planning permission from the local authority to build 13 'middle class' houses on the land. It did not, however, submit its plans to the plaintiff for approval. It believed that the plaintiff was not entitled to enforce the covenant. In January 1972, the defendant started to lay the foundations. On 14 February the plaintiff issued a writ claiming an injunction to restrain building. The plaintiff failed, however, to seek an 'interlocutory' (temporary) injunction to restrain development pending the full trial of the dispute. Parkside, accordingly, completed the building operations and the first residents moved into their new homes.
HELD: The judge refused to order that the houses should be demolished. Instead, he awarded the plaintiff damages equivalent to the 'price' it could reasonably have asked for releasing the covenant.

BRIGHTMAN J: . . . There can be obvious cases where a restrictive covenant clearly is, or clearly is not, of benefit to an estate. Between these two extremes there is inevitably an area where the benefit to the estate is a matter of personal opinion, where responsible and reasonable persons can have divergent views sincerely and reasonably held. In my judgment, in such cases, it is not for the court to pronounce which is the correct view. I think that the court can only decide whether a particular view is one which can reasonably be held. If a restriction is bargained for at the time of sale with the intention of giving the vendor a protection which he desires for the land he retains, and the restriction is expressed to be imposed for the benefit of the estate so that both sides are apparently accepting that the restriction is of value to the retained land, I think that the validity of the restriction should be upheld so long as an estate owner may reasonably take the view that the restriction remains of value to his estate, and that the restriction should not be discarded merely because others may reasonably argue that the restriction is spent. I think that this accords with the judgment of Sargant J in the *Northbourne* case [1922] 2 Ch 309 and of Wilberforce J in the *Marten* case [see **27.2.1.3**]. The view expressed by Mr Byng and by Mr Parker is, in my judgment, a reasonable one, although it may be a matter of opinion whether it is correct or not. My own opinion is that it is correct, and I would so hold. For it seems to me that an estate owner, living on a residential and agricultural estate sandwiched between two developing towns, is properly interested in the standard of development of those towns. To take an extreme case, which is not this case, a Wrotham Park estate lying between two overcrowded slum districts would be a less desirable and less marketable property than a Wrotham Park estate lying between two carefully developed and uncrowded districts. If the rest of areas 14, 10 and 12 were subjected to the same kind of exploitation that the allotment site has suffered, it seems to me that a reasonable owner of the Wrotham Park estate might well fear that the quality of the development on the periphery of his estate was deteriorating to his disadvantage. I therefore conclude that the layout covenant imposed on area 14 is still capable of benefiting the Wrotham Park estate, or, at any rate, that the contrary has not been proved. . . .

I must now consider the relief to which the plaintiffs are entitled, that is to say a mandatory injunction or damages (both are not sought): if damages, whether substantial or nominal; or a declaration of the plaintiffs' rights as the sole relief. The plaintiffs made it abundantly clear at the outset of the case that the relief they primarily sought was a mandatory injunction. This did not spring from outraged feelings or from indifference to the welfare of those who have made the offending houses their homes. It sprang from the belief, sincerely held, that there was no other effective way of preserving the integrity of the planning restrictions imposed by the terms of the Blake conveyance. Quite apart from the benefit to the Wrotham Park estate, the plaintiffs, as I have already said, take the view that they have a moral obligation towards the residents of the building estates to enforce the restrictive covenants so far as they are lawfully entitled to do so. I agree. The plaintiffs do not seek to bulldoze the occupiers out of their homes but are content that they shall have a period of two years in which to acquire other homes with the help of the £20,000 or so that will come to each of them under the indemnity assurance that has been arranged. . . .

Counsel for the plaintiffs submitted, and I accept, that it is no answer to a claim for a mandatory injunction that the plaintiffs, having issued proceedings, deliberately held their hand and did not seek the assistance of the court for the purpose of preserving the status quo. On the other hand, it is, in my view, equally true that a plaintiff is not entitled 'as of course' to have everything pulled down that was built after the issue of the writ. The erection of the houses, whether one likes it or not, is a fait accompli and the houses are now the homes of people. I accept that this particular fait accompli is reversible and could be undone. But I cannot close my eyes to the fact that the houses now exist. It would, in my opinion, be an unpardonable waste of much needed houses to direct that they now be pulled down and I have never had a moment's doubt during the hearing of this case that such an order ought to be refused. No damage of a financial nature has been done to the plaintiffs by the breach of the layout stipulation. The plaintiffs' use of the Wrotham Park estate has not been and will not be impeded. It is totally unnecessary to demolish the houses in order to preserve the integrity of the restrictive covenants imposed on the rest of area 14. Without hesitation I decline to grant a mandatory injunction. But the fact that these houses will remain does not spell out a charter entitling others to despoil adjacent areas of land in breach of valid restrictions imposed by the conveyances. A developer who tries that course may be in for a rude awakening.

... In my judgment a just substitute for a mandatory injunction would be such a sum of money as might reasonably have been demanded by the plaintiffs from Parkside as a quid pro quo for relaxing the covenant. The plaintiffs submitted that that sum should be a substantial proportion of the development value of the land. This is currently put at no less than £10,000 per plot, i.e. £140,000 on the assumption that the plots are undeveloped. Mr Parker gave evidence that a half or a third of the development value was commonly demanded by a landowner whose property stood in the way of a development. I do not agree with that approach to damages in this type of case. I bear in mind the following factors: (1) The layout covenant is not an asset which the estate owner ever contemplated he would have either the opportunity or the desire to turn to account. It has no commercial or even nuisance value. For it cannot be turned to account except to the detriment of the existing residents who are people the estate owner professes to protect. (2) The breach of covenant which has actually taken place is over a very small area and the impact of this particular breach on the Wrotham Park estate is insignificant. The validity of the covenant over the rest of area 14 is unaffected.

... I think that damages must be assessed in such a case on a basis which is fair and, in all the circumstances, in my judgment a sum equal to 5 per cent of Parkside's anticipated profit is the most that is fair. I accordingly award the sum of £2,500 in substitution for mandatory injunctions. ...

CHAPTER TWENTY-SEVEN

THE PASSING OF THE BENEFIT OF RESTRICTIVE COVENANTS

27.1 Introduction

LAW OF PROPERTY ACT 1925

78. Benefit of covenants relating to land

(1) A covenant relating to any land of the covenantee shall be deemed to be made with the covenantee and his successors in title and the persons deriving title under him or them, and shall have effect as if such successors and other persons were expressed.

For the purposes of this subsection in connexion with covenants restrictive of the user of land 'successors in title' shall be deemed to include the owners and occupiers for the time being of the land of the covenantee intended to be benefited.

(2) This section applies to covenants made after the commencement of this Act, but the repeal of section fifty-eight of the Conveyancing Act 1881 does not affect the operation of covenants to which that section applied.

FEDERATED HOMES LTD v *MILL LODGE PROPERTIES LTD* [1980] 1 All ER 371, Court of Appeal

FACTS: A firm called Mackenzie Hill Ltd owned a large amount of development land in Newport Pagnell (just north of Milton Keynes). It had outline planning permission to develop the land with 1,250 houses. It sold part of that land to Mill Lodge. The conveyance included a restrictive covenant:—

> In carrying out the development of the . . . land the purchaser shall not build at a greater density than a total of 300 dwellings so as not to reduce the number of units which the vendor might eventually erect on the retained land under the existing planning consent.

Mackenzie Hill later sold the land they retained in the area to Federated Homes. The Court of Appeal had (*inter alia*) to decide whether the above clause effected an annexation so that on the sale of the 'retained land' the right to enforce the covenant passed automatically to Federated Homes.
HELD: The clause effected a valid annexation of the benefit of the covenant to the land owned by Federated Homes Ltd.

BRIGHTMAN LJ: In my judgment the benefit of this covenant was annexed to the retained land, and I think that this is a consequence of s. 78 of the Law of Property Act 1925, which reads:

> (1) A covenant relating to any land of the covenantee shall be deemed to be made with the covenantee and his successors in title and the persons deriving title under him or them, and shall have effect as if such successors and other persons were expressed. For the purposes of this subsection in connexion with covenants restrictive of the user of

land 'successors in title' shall be deemed to include the owners and occupiers for the time being of the land of the covenantee intended to be benefited.

(2)   This section applies to covenants made after the commencement of this Act, but the repeal of section fifty-eight of the Conveyancing Act 1881, does not affect the operation of covenants to which that section applied.

Counsel for the defendants submitted that there were three possible views about s. 78. One view, which he described as 'the orthodox view' hitherto held, is that it is merely a statutory shorthand for reducing the length of legal documents. A second view, which was the one that counsel for the defendants was inclined to place in the forefront of his argument, is that the section only applies, or at any rate only achieves annexation, when the land intended to be benefited is signified in the document by express words or necessary implication as the intended beneficiary of the covenant. A third view is that the section applies if the covenant in fact touches and concerns the land of the covenantee, whether that be gleaned from the document itself or from evidence outside the document.

For myself, I reject the narrowest interpretation of s. 78, the supposed orthodox view, which seems to me to fly in the face of the wording of the section. Before I express my reasons I will say that I do not find it necessary to choose between the second and third views because, in my opinion, this covenant relates to land of the covenantee on either interpretation of s. 78. Clause 5(iv) shows quite clearly that the covenant is for the protection of the retained land and that land is described in cl. 2 as 'any adjoining or adjacent property retained by the Vendor'. This formulation is sufficient for annexation purposes: see *Rogers* v *Hosegood* [1900] 2 Ch 388.

There is in my judgment no doubt that this covenant 'related to the land of the covenantee', or, to use the old-fashioned expression, that it touched and concerned the land, even if counsel for the defendants is correct in his submission that the document must show an intention to benefit identified land. The result of such application is that one must read cl. 5(iv) as if it were written: 'The purchaser hereby covenants with the vendor and its successors in title and the persons deriving title under it or them, including the owners and occupiers for the time being of the retained land, that in carrying out the development of the blue land the purchaser shall not build at a greater density than a total of 300 dwellings so as not to reduce the number of units which the vendor might eventually erect on the retained land under the existing planning consent.' I leave out of consideration s. 79 as unnecessary to be considered in this context, since Mill Lodge is the original covenantor.

The first point to notice about s. 78(1) is that the wording is significantly different from the wording of its predecessor, s. 58(1) of the Conveyancing and Law of Property Act 1881. The distinction is underlined by sub-s. (2) of s. 78, which applies sub-s. (1) only to covenants made after the commencement of the Act. Section 58(1) of the earlier Act did not include the covenantee's successors in title or persons deriving title under him or them, nor the owners or occupiers for the time being of the land of the covenantee intended to be benefited. The section was confined, in relation to realty, to the covenantee, his heirs and assigns, words which suggest a more limited scope of operation than is found in s. 78.

If, as the language of s. 78 implies, a covenant relating to land which is restrictive of the user thereof is enforceable at the suit of (1) a successor in title of the covenantee, (2) a person deriving title under the covenantee or under his successors in title, and (3) the owner or occupier of the land intended to be benefited by the covenant, it must, in my view, follow that the covenant runs with the land, because ex hypothesi every successor in title to the land, every derivative proprietor of the land and every other owner and occupier has a right by statute to the covenant. In other words, if the condition precedent of s. 78 is satisfied, that is to say, there exists a covenant which touches and concerns the land of the covenantee, that covenant runs with the land for the benefit of his successors in title, persons deriving title under him or them and other owners and occupiers.

This approach to s. 78 has been advocated by distinguished textbook writers: see Dr Radcliffe in the Law Quarterly Review, Professor Wade in the Cambridge Law Journal under the apt cross-heading 'What is wrong with section 78?', and Megarry and Wade on the Law of Real Property. Counsel pointed out to us that the fourth edition of Megarry and Wade's textbook indicates a change of mind on this topic since the third edition was published in 1966.

Although the section does not seem to have been extensively used in the course of argument in this type of case, the construction of s. 78 which appeals to me appears to be consistent with at least two cases decided in this court. The first is *Smith v River Douglas Catchment Board* [1949] 2 All ER 179. In that case an agreement was made in April 1938 between certain landowners and the catchment board under which the catchment board undertook to make good the banks of a certain brook and to maintain the same, and the landowners undertook to contribute towards the cost. In 1940 the first plaintiff took a conveyance from one of the landowners of a part of the land together with an express assignment of the benefit of the agreement. In 1944 the second plaintiff took a tenancy of that land without any express assignment of the benefit of the agreement. In 1946 the brook burst its banks and the land owned by the first plaintiff and tenanted by the second plaintiff was inundated. The two important points are that the agreement was not expressed to be for the benefit of the landowner's successors in title; and there was no assignment of the benefit of the agreement in favour of the second plaintiff, the tenant. In reliance, as I understand the case, on s. 78 of the Law of Property Act 1925, it was held that the second plaintiff was entitled to sue the catchment board for damages for breach of the agreement. It seems to me that that conclusion can only have been reached on the basis that s. 78 had the effect of causing the benefit of the agreement to run with the land so as to be capable of being sued on by the tenant. . . .

I find the idea of the annexation of a covenant to the whole of the land but not to a part of it a difficult conception fully to grasp. I can understand that a covenantee may expressly or by necessary implication retain the benefit of a covenant wholly under his own control, so that the benefit will not pass unless the covenantee chooses to assign; but I would have thought, if the benefit of a covenant is, on a proper construction of a document, annexed to the land, *prima facie* it is annexed to every part thereof, unless the contrary clearly appears. . . .

In the end, I come to the conclusion that s. 78 of the Law of Property Act 1925 caused the benefit of the restrictive covenant in question to run with the red land and therefore to be annexed to it, with the result that the plaintiff company is able to enforce the covenant against Mill Lodge, not only in its capacity as owner of the green land, but also in its capacity as owner of the red land. . . .

27.2   Annexation

Todd, P. N., Annexation After Federated Homes (1985) 49 Conv 177

. . . the view of the operation of section 78 taken by Brightman LJ in *Federated Homes* is very radical. It seems to be that at least for any post-1926 covenant, once the covenant 'relates to' the benefited land, annexation is a matter of law:

> If the condition precedent of section 78 is satisfied—that is to say, there exists a covenant which touches and concerns the land of the covenantee—that covenant runs with the land for the benefit of his successors in title, persons deriving title under them and other owners and occupiers.

On the widest interpretation of this statement, restrictive covenants run with land automatically. The question does not seem to depend on words expressing or implying annexation, or on surrounding circumstances, and may even be independent of the intention of the parties. Thus, Mr. Newsom, commenting on the above statement of Brightman LJ states:

> This can only mean that the benefit of the covenant is automatically annexed to 'the land of the covenantee' which it 'touches and concerns.' This is a new doctrine and it is at least a little surprising that Parliament should have forced annexation upon the parties even if they clearly did *not* intend it; but that is what the Lord Justice implied.

Indeed, the case is ostensibly even more radical than this, as the automatic annexation doctrine applies not merely for the benefit of the land as a whole, but for the benefit of each and every part of the land.

Given that this interpretation of the case is widely held, it is perhaps not surprising that *Federated Homes* has attracted such extensive comment and criticism. If the decision is correct, the wide view of it suggests that the law on the passing of benefit of all restrictive covenants has been revolutionised, and is much simpler than had previously been thought. . . .

Though it is no doubt possible to argue this very wide interpretation of *Federated Homes*, however, I would suggest that a much narrower view is probably more appropriate. The case may not be an authority for automatic annexation at all, and may not, I suggest, apply to all post-1926 covenants.

A NARROWER VIEW

. . . There are other reasons also for inferring that Brightman LJ did not intend annexation to be independent of intention. He relies heavily on the academic authority of Professor H W R Wade, as expressed in an article in the *Cambridge Law Journal* in 1972, where he asked 'What is wrong with Section 78.' In this article, Professor Wade argued that the rules for the transmission of restrictive covenants both should be and have been recently relaxed. He believed that there had been a relaxation of the law by the Chancery judges in the 20 years prior to 1972, such that the precise words of the conveyance became less important, and evidence of intention to annex gleaned from the surrounding circumstances more important. One result of this, he suggested, was that the words implied into a conveyance by section 78 should be sufficient to annex any covenant to land, if they can be taken along with surrounding circumstances indicating intention to so annex. It is important to note that he does not seem to assume that the words of the section are sufficient to automatically annex any covenant to land:

> If the covenant in fact relates to any land of the covenantee, his successors in title, widely defined for the purposes of restrictive covenants, are presumed to be intended to benefit,

but

> Whether, if so capable [of 'touching and concerning' or 'relating to' land], it [a covenant] actually does so relate to any given land is a matter of intention, to be collected from the deed and the surrounding circumstances; there are no rules of formality.

This suggests that far from arguing for automatic annexation, Professor Wade would gather intention from surrounding circumstances, both as to whether the covenant actually relates to the land, and also if it does, (possibly) as to whether the presumption of intention to benefit is rebutted. In relation to section 78 in particular, therefore, what seems to be argued is that if from the surrounding circumstances an intention to annex is apparent, no further words of annexation are required apart from those implied anyway by section 78. . . .

My conclusion, therefore, is that *Federated Homes* does not, in fact, stand for such an automatic annexation theory, but that Brightman LJ's views are similar to Professor Wade's, namely that the wording of section 78 is sufficient without more to annex a covenant to land so long as enough evidence can be found from surrounding circumstances that it is intended to 'relate to' the land in question. . . .

27.2.1   THE TRADITIONAL VIEWPOINT ON ANNEXATION

JAMAICA MUTUAL LIFE ASSURANCE SOCIETY v *HILLSBOROUGH AND OTHERS*
[1989] 1 WLR 1101, Privy Council

FACTS: The owners of land sold plots to various parties, subject to a covenant against sub-division of the plots and prohibiting the use of the plots for the carrying on of any trade or business. The instruments of transfer of the plots did not expressly identify the land which the covenants were intended to benefit. One of the owners of the plots applied to the Supreme Court of Jamaica for a declaration as to the extent to which they were bound by the restrictive covenants contained in the instrument of transfer.

HELD: In the absence of express assignment of the benefit of the covenant to the vendors' successors in title, and in the absence of any possible inference that the vendors intended to annex the benefit of the covenants to the land retained by them, the benefit of the covenant had not passed and could not be enforced against the owner of the plot.

LORD JAUNCEY of Tullichettle: . . . There were in the instrument of transfer to Maurice William Facey no words stating that the restrictions therein were intended for the benefit of any land retained by Dunn and others. . . .
   In *Renals v Cowlishaw* (1878) 9 ChD 125, 130, Hall V-C said:

> that in order to enable a purchaser as an assign (such purchaser not being an assign of all that the vendor retained when he executed the conveyance containing the covenants, and that conveyance not shewing that the benefit of the covenant was intended to enure for the time being of each portion of the estate so retained or of the portion of the estate of which the plaintiff is assign) to claim the benefit of a restrictive covenant, this, at least, must appear, that the assign acquired his property with the benefit of the covenant, that is, it must appear that the benefit of the covenant was part of the subject-matter of the purchase.

In *Rogers v Hosegood* [1900] 2 Ch 388, 407–408, Collins LJ said:

> When, as in *Renals v Cowlishaw*, there is no indication in the original conveyance, or in the circumstances attending it, that the burden of the restrictive covenant is imposed for the benefit of the land reserved, or any particular part of it, then it becomes necessary to examine the circumstances under which any part of the land reserved is sold, in order to see whether a benefit, not originally annexed to it, has become annexed to it on the sale, so that the purchaser is deemed to have bought it with the land . . .

Both *Renals v Cowlishaw* and *Rogers v Hosegood* were referred to with approval in *Reid v Bickerstaff* [1909] 2 Ch 305 where Cozens-Hardy MR in the context of a submission that the benefit of a covenant was annexed to adjoining lands of the vendors said, at p. 321:

> As to the second proposition the plaintiffs have a more plausible case, but I think they fail in establishing it. It is plain that they are not assignees of the covenant, of the existence of which they were not aware. It is equally plain that there is nothing in the deed of 1840, or in any document prior or subsequent thereto, to indicate that the covenant was entered into for the benefit of the particular parcels of which the plaintiffs are now owners. I cannot hold that the mere fact that the plaintiffs' land is adjacent and would be more valuable if the covenant were annexed to the land suffices to justify the court in holding that it was so annexed as to pass without mention by a simple conveyance of the adjacent land.

Applying the principles to be derived from these three cases to the matters to which their Lordships have just referred their Lordships consider that Carey JA was mistaken in concluding that the covenant in the applicant's title was annexed to any land. . . .

27.2.1.1 Annexation to the whole or each and every part?
On the traditional view of the law, a restrictive covenant which is annexed to 'Blackacre' is presumptively annexed only to the whole of Blackacre. This presumption can be rebutted if the conveyance includes some phrase such as 'this covenant is annexed to Blackacre and each and every part thereof'.
   When drafting a restrictive covenant for the benefit of a large piece of land, the solicitor acting for the dominant owner needs to decide whether:

(a)   to annex the covenant only to the whole of the dominant land; or
(b)   to annex the covenant to 'each and every part of the dominant land'.

Each alternative has its advantages and disadvantages.

27.2.1.2 The disadvantages of annexation only to the whole of the dominant land—the 'small plot–big plot' situation

RE BALLARD'S CONVEYANCE [1937] 2 All ER 691, Chancery Division

FACTS: The owners of the 'Childwickbury Estate' sold sixteen acres on the edge of their 1,700 acre estate, subject to a restrictive covenant that the land sold should be used for agricultural purposes only. The covenant was expressed to be for the benefit of 'the whole of the Childwickbury Estate'.

HELD: There was no valid annexation. For a valid annexation the current owners of Childwickbury would have to have proved that all 1,700 acres were benefited by the 'agriculture only' covenant. In the judge's view, those parts of the estate close to the sixteen acres were capable of benefiting from the covenant, but those further away were not. The covenant was therefore unenforceable.

CLAUSON J: I . . . hold that the land for the benefit of which the covenant was taken was the land (about 1,700 acres) now vested in Childwickbury Stud, Ltd, by conveyance from Mr. Joel, and that the fact that it claims by virtue of a purchase from Mrs. Ballard would not affect its title to sue.

That brings me to the remaining question, namely: Is the covenant one which, in the circumstances of the case, comes within the category of a covenant the benefit of which is capable of running with the land for the benefit of which it was taken? A necessary qualification, in order that the covenant may come within that category, is that it concerns or touches the land with which it is to run : see *per* Farwell J, in *Rogers* v *Hosegood* [1900] 2 Ch 388, at p. 395. That land is an area of some 1,700 acres. It appears to me quite obvious that, while a breach of the stipulations might possibly affect a portion of that area in the vicinity of Mr. Wright's land, far the largest part of this area of 1,700 acres could not possibly be affected by any breach of any of the stipulations.

Counsel for the respondent company asked for an adjournment in order to consider whether it would call evidence (as I was prepared to allow it to do) to prove that a breach of the stipulations, or of some of them, might affect the whole of this large area. However, ultimately no such evidence was called.

The result seems to me to be that I am bound to hold that, while the covenant may concern or touch some comparatively small portion of the land to which it has been sought to annex it, it fails to concern or touch far the largest part of the land. I asked in vain for any authority which would justify me in severing the covenant, and treating it as annexed to or running with such part of the land as is touched by or concerned with it, though, as regards the remainder of the land, namely, such part as is not touched by or concerned with the covenant, the covenant is not, and cannot be, annexed to it, and accordingly does not, and cannot, run with it. . . .

27.2.1.3 The modern trend in 'small plot' 'big plot' cases

MARTEN v FLIGHT REFUELLING LTD [1961] 2 All ER 696, Chancery Division

FACTS: Mrs. Marten had a beneficial interest under a strict settlement in the 7,500 acre Crichel Estate, Dorset. When she was still an infant, the trustees of the settlement sold a farm comprising part of the estate (562 acres, in fact) to Mr. Harding. He covenanted that he would use the land for agricultural purposes only. In course of time the defendant company came to own the 'farm', and began to use the land for industrial purposes. When Mrs. Marten attained majority, the trustees executed an assent vesting the estate in her, but the assent made no express mention of the covenant. Mrs. Marten brought the present action for an injunction restraining the defendant's industrial use of the 'farm' land.

HELD: She was entitled to the benefit of the restrictive covenant. Accordingly, the injunction was granted.

WILBERFORCE J: . . . an intention to benefit may be found from surrounding or attending circumstances. . .

. . . it was said that a mere examination of the figures showed that the covenant could not benefit the estate: the Crichel Estate extends to some seven thousand five hundred acres, and it was asked how such covenant could benefit the estate as a whole. In my view, there is no such manifest impossibility about this. I have already referred to the character of the estate, and I can well imagine that for the owner of it, whether he wished to retain it in his family or to sell it as a whole, it might be of very real benefit to be able to preserve a former outlying portion from development. This seems to me to be a question of fact to be determined on the evidence: and I note that, when a similar argument was placed before the court in *Re Ballard's Conveyance* [see **27.2.1.2**], Clauson J, while accepting it in the absence of evidence, showed it to be his opinion that evidence could have been called. . . .

27.2.1.4   Annexation destroyed on sub-division of the dominant land

RUSSEL v *ARCHDALE* [1962] 3 All ER 305, Chancery Division

FACTS: A company owned certain land which it conveyed to the defendant, the company retaining other land in the neighbourhood. The defendant purchaser entered into various restrictive covenants 'so as to . . . benefit and protect the vendor's adjoining and neighbouring land'. Some years later the plaintiffs bought *part* of the company's retained land. The conveyance was expressed to include the benefit of the covenants entered into by the defendants. On the question whether the plaintiffs could enforce the restrictive covenants:
HELD: The annexation of the covenants to 'the vendor's adjoining and neighbouring land' was an annexation to the *whole* of the vendor's adjoining and neighbouring land and not to *each and every part* of it. Accordingly, as the plaintiffs had acquired a part only of the land, they could not enforce the benefit of the covenant.

BUCKLEY J: No doubt every case of this kind, being one of construction, must be determined on the facts and the actual language used, but . . . I cannot see that the mere fact that the land intended to be benefited is described by such an expression as 'the land retained by the vendor', is sufficient to enable the court to come to the conclusion that the covenant is intended to benefit each and every part of that land. . . . That being so, it must follow that the plaintiffs cannot enforce the covenant merely by reason of its annexation to the 'adjoining and neighbouring land' of the vendors under the conveyance of July 6 1938, since they (the plaintiffs) have acquired part only of that land.

27.2.1.5   The disadvantage of annexation to each and every part

When the dominant land is sub-divided, the number of owners entitled to enforce the covenant is bound to increase; with a large dominant area the number of dominant owners could initially be one, but later be enormous.

27.2.2   THE POTENTIAL EFFECTS OF THE *FEDERATED HOMES* CASE— A HIGHLY QUESTIONABLE NEW FORM OF ANNEXATION

27.2.2.1   Drafting of restrictive covenants in the light of *Federated Homes*

ROAKE v *CHADHA AND ANOTHER* [1983] 3 All ER 503, Chancery Division

FACTS: A clause in a 1934 conveyance expressly stated that the benefit of a number of restrictive convenants was not to pass by annexation.
HELD: The judge rejected an argument that the benefit of the covenants had nevertheless been annexed by virtue of section 78 of the Law of Property Act 1925. Careful drafting had excluded the effect of section 78.

HIS HONOUR JUDGE PAUL BAKER QC: . . . Counsel for the plaintiffs' method of applying it is simplicity itself. The *Federated Homes* case shows that s. 78 brings about annexation, and that the operation of the section cannot be excluded by a contrary intention. As I have indicated, he supports this last point by reference to s. 79, which is expressed to operate 'unless a contrary intention is expressed', a qualification which, as we have already noticed, is absent from s. 78. Counsel for the plaintiffs could not suggest any reason of policy why s. 78 should be mandatory, unlike, for example, s. 146 of the 1925 Act, which deals with restrictions on the right to forfeiture of leases and which, by an express provision, 'has effect notwithstanding any stipulation to the contrary'.

I am thus far from satisfied that s. 78 has the mandatory operation which counsel for the plaintiffs claimed for it. But, even if one accepts that it is not subject to a contrary intention, I do not consider that it has the effect of annexing the benefit of the covenant in each and every case irrespective of the other express terms of the covenant. I notice that Brightman LJ did not go so far as that, for he said in the *Federated Homes* case [1980] 1 All ER 371 at 381, [1980] 1 WLR 594 at 606:

> I find the idea of the annexation of a covenant to the whole of the land but not to a part of it a difficult conception fully to grasp. I can understand that a covenantee may expressly or by necessary implication retain the benefit of a covenant wholly under his own control, so that the benefit will not pass unless the covenantee chooses to assign; but I would have thought, if the benefit of a covenant is, on a proper construction of a document, annexed to the land, *prima facie* it is annexed to every part thereof, unless the contrary clearly appears.

So at least in some circumstances Brightman LJ is considering that despite s. 78 the benefit may be retained and not pass or be annexed to and run with land. In this connection, I was also referred by counsel for the defendants to Sir Lancelot Elphinstone's *Covenants Affecting Land* (1946) p. 17, where the author says, with reference to this point (and I quote from a footnote on that page):

> ... but it is thought that, as a covenant must be construed as a whole, the court would give due effect to words excluding or modifying the operation of the section.

The true position as I see it is that, even where a covenant is deemed to be made with successors in title as s. 78 requires, one still has to construe the covenant as a whole to see whether the benefit of the covenant is annexed. Where one finds, as in the *Federated Homes* case, the covenant is not qualified in any way, annexation may be readily inferred; but, where, as in the present case, it is expressly provided that 'this covenant shall not enure for the benefit of any owner or subsequent purchaser of any part of the Vendor's Sudbury Court Estate at Wembley unless the benefit of this covenant shall be expressly assigned', one cannot just ignore these words. . . .

27.3 Assignment of the Benefit of Restrictive Covenants

27.3.1 THE RULES FOR A VALID ASSIGNMENT

MILES v *EASTER* [1933] Ch 611, Court of Appeal

FACTS: A 1908 conveyance contained a covenant made by the purchasers that they would not do anything which might cause a nuisance to the vendor's land. The conveyance showed that the vendors retained land in the vicinity, referring as it did to a 'foreshore belonging to the vendors', but the deed did not go further in defining the land.
HELD: Due to uncertainty as to the land intended to benefit, the plaintiff had failed to show that the benefit of the restrictive covenant made in the 1908 deed had vested in them.

ROMER LJ: . . . It is plain, however, from these and other cases, and notably that of *Renals v Cowlishaw* (1878) 9 ChD 125, that if the restrictive covenant be taken not merely for some personal purpose or object of the vendor, but for the benefit of some other land of his in the sense that it would enable him to dispose of that land to greater advantage, the covenant, though not annexed to such land so as to run with any part of it, may be enforced against an assignee of the covenantor taking with notice, both by the covenantee and by persons to whom the benefit of such covenant has been assigned, subject however to certain conditions. In the first place, the 'other land' must be land that is capable of being benefited by the covenant—otherwise it would be impossible to infer that the object of the covenant was to enable the vendor to dispose of his land to greater advantage. In the next place, this land must be 'ascertainable' or 'certain,' to use the words of Romer and Scrutton LJJ respectively. For, although the Court will readily infer the intention to benefit the other land of the vendor where the existence and situation of such land are indicated in the conveyance or have been otherwise shown with reasonable certainty, it is impossible to do so from vague references in the conveyance or in other documents laid before the Court as to the existence of other lands of the vendor, the extent and situation of which are undefined. In the third place, the covenant cannot be enforced by the covenantee against an assign of the purchaser after the covenantee has parted with the whole of his land.

This last point was decided, and in our opinion rightly decided, by Sargant J in *Chambers* v *Randall* [1923] 1 Ch 149. As pointed out by that learned judge, the covenant having been entered into to enable the covenantee to dispose of his property to advantage, that result will in fact have been obtained when all that property has been disposed of. There is therefore no longer any reason why the Court should extend to him the benefit of the equitable doctrine of *Tulk* v *Moxhay* [1843–60] All ER Rep 9. That is only done when it is sought to enforce the covenant in connection with the enjoyment of land that the covenant was intended to protect. But it was also held by Sargant J in the same case, and in our opinion rightly held, that although on a sale of the whole or part of the property intended to be protected by the covenant the right to enforce the covenant may be expressly assigned to the purchaser, such an assignment will be ineffective if made at a later date when the covenantee has parted with the whole of his land. The covenantee must, indeed, be at liberty to include in any sale of the retained property the right to enforce the covenants. He might not otherwise be able to dispose of such property to the best advantage, and the intention with which he obtained the covenant would be defeated. But if he has been able to sell any particular part of his property without assigning to the purchaser the benefit of the covenant, there seems no reason why he should at a later date and as an independent transaction be at liberty to confer upon the purchaser such benefit. To hold that he could do so would be to treat the covenant as having been obtained, not only for the purpose of enabling the covenantee to dispose of his land to the best advantage, but also for the purpose of enabling him to dispose of the benefit of the covenant to the best advantage. Where, at the date of the assignment of the benefit of the covenant, the covenantee has disposed of the whole of his land, there is an additional reason why the assignee should be unable to enforce it. For at the date of the assignment the covenant had ceased to be enforceable at the instance of the covenantee himself, and he cannot confer any greater rights upon the assignee than he possessed himself.

. . . it is impossible to ascertain with any certainty what lands retained by the covenantees when the conveyance of October 23 1908, was executed were intended to be protected by the covenant so that the covenantees might thereafter dispose of them to greater advantage. That conveyance shows that the vendors were possessed of other land in the vicinity, reference being made in the deed to 'foreshore belonging to the vendors west of the harbour entrance,' without further defining it, and to land coloured yellow on the plan attached to the deed in terms that clearly indicate their ownership of such land. But our attention is also called to certain transactions between the covenantees and a company called The Service Land Company Ltd, in the month of January 1912, that show that in October 1908, the covenantees were possessed of still other lands at Lancing and Shoreham of considerable, though, so far as the Court is concerned, of undefined extent. Referring to these other lands, Bennett J said: 'There was no evidence before me as to where such other lands were situate or as to the area thereof. There was no evidence before me as to the purposes for which the Shoreham Company acquired these lands, whether for the purpose of resale or for development as a building estate. . . . I am really left to guess at the reasons, if any, which led to the introduction in the conveyance of October 23 1908, of the purchaser's covenant.' In these circumstances, the learned judge declined to draw the conclusion that the covenant was inserted in the conveyance for the protection of all the other lands of the Shoreham Company so as to enable them to dispose of such lands to the best advantage. And he was justified in so doing. It is impossible to ascertain whether all or some, and if so which, part of such lands were capable of being protected by the reservation of the covenant. When, therefore, by indentures of October 19 1920, and

October 15 1921, the Shoreham Company and the Seaside Company (to whom the Shoreham Company had previously sold the whole of their still unsold lands) purported to assign to the defendant Easter the benefit of the restrictive covenant, there can be no sure ground for thinking that any of such still unsold lands were lands for the protection of which the covenant had been obtained. It is plain that at that time all the lands coloured green had been disposed of. The defendants have accordingly failed to show that there is now vested in them, or either of them, the right to enforce the restrictive covenant contained in the deed of October 23, 1908. . . .

27.4   Building Schemes or Schemes of Development

27.4.1   THE CONDITIONS REQUIRED FOR A VALID BUILDING SCHEME

ELLISTON v REACHER [1908] 2 Ch 374, Chancery Division

FACTS: A building scheme was created in 1861. The plots were sold from an office in Ipswich, but the scheme itself was on 10 acres of land at Felixstowe. Anybody entering the office at Ipswich would have seen on the wall a large plan of the scheme, with the restrictive covenants endorsed prominently on the plan. Potential purchasers could buy a copy of this plan for 1s 6d. The covenants were of a kind to preserve the 'exclusive' nature of the area.
HELD: It was a natural inference from the advertising that the creator of the scheme intended the covenants to be mutually enforceable.

PARKER J: I pass, therefore, to the consideration of the question whether the plaintiffs can enforce these restrictive covenants. In my judgment, in order to bring the principles of *Renals* v *Cowlishaw* (1878) 9 ChD 125 and *Spicer* v *Martin* (1888) 14 App Cas 12 into operation it must be proved that both the plaintiffs and defendants derive title under a common vendor; that previously to selling the lands to which the plaintiffs and defendants are respectively entitled the vendor laid out his estate, or a defined portion thereof (including the lands purchased by the plaintiffs and defendants respectively), for sale in lots subject to restrictions intended to be imposed on all the lots, and which, though varying in details as to particular lots, are consistent and consistent only with some general scheme of development; that these restrictions were intended by the common vendor to be and were for the benefit of all the lots intended to be sold, whether or not they were also intended to be and were for the benefit of other land retained by the vendor; and that both the plaintiffs and the defendants, or their predecessors in title, purchased their lots from the common vendor upon the footing that the restrictions subject to which the purchases were made were to enure for the benefit of the other lots included in the general scheme whether or not they were also to enure for the benefit of other lands retained by the vendors. If these four points be established, I think that the plaintiffs would in equity be entitled to enforce the restrictive covenants entered into by the defendants or their predecessors with the common vendor irrespective of the dates of the respective purchases. I may observe, with reference to the third point, that the vendor's object in imposing the restrictions must in general be gathered from all the circumstances of the case, including in particular the nature of the restrictions. If a general observance of the restrictions is in fact calculated to enhance the values of the several lots offered for sale, it is an easy inference that the vendor intended the restrictions to be for the benefit of all the lots, even though he might retain other land the value of which might be similarly enhanced, for a vendor may naturally be expected to aim at obtaining the highest possible price for his land. Further, if the first three points be established, the fourth point may readily be inferred, provided the purchasers have notice of the facts involved in the three first points; but if the purchaser purchases in ignorance of any material part of those facts, it would be difficult, if not impossible, to establish the fourth point. It is also observable that the equity arising out of the establishment of the four points I have mentioned has been sometimes explained by the implication of mutual contracts between the various purchasers, and sometimes by the implication of a contract between each purchaser and the common vendor, that each purchaser is to have the benefit of all the covenants by the other purchasers, so that each purchase is in equity an assign of the benefit of these covenants. In my opinion the implication of mutual contract is not always a perfectly satisfactory explanation. It may be satisfactory where all the lots are sold by auction at the same time, but when, as in cases such as *Spicer* v *Martin*, there is no sale by auction, but all the various sales are by private treaty and at various intervals of time, the circumstances may, at the date of one or more of the sales, be such as to preclude the possibility of any actual contract. For example, a prior purchaser may be dead or incapable of contracting at the time of a subsequent purchase, and in any event it is unlikely that the prior and subsequent purchasers are ever brought into personal relationship, and yet the equity may exist between them. It is, I think, enough to say, using Lord Macnaghten's words in *Spicer* v *Martin*, that where the four points I have mentioned are established, the community of interest imports in equity the reciprocity of obligation which is in fact contemplated by each at the time of his own purchase. . . .

Proceeding with the facts as we know them, it appears that, though the lots were according to the sale plan to be offered to the members of the society in August 1860, the society did not complete its title to the property until early in January 1861. The unexecuted engrossment bears date a few days after such completion. It appears also that the society prepared and procured to be printed a form of conveyance for use on the sale of every lot, and that such printed form was in fact used on the sales of the lots purchased by the predecessors in title of the plaintiffs and defendants respectively. Further, a copy of the sale plan was pasted on canvas and hung up in the offices of the society, and as and when plots were sold such plots were marked off on the plan in Indian ink. Most if not all of the plots were so marked off as sold before the end of the year 1865. . . .

Under all the circumstances of the case it is in my opinion sufficiently established not only that the predecessors of the plaintiffs and the defendants respectively had notice of the intention of their common vendors that the restrictions in question should enure for the benefit of all the lots offered for sale, but that they made their respective purchases on that footing. . . .

27.4.2 PROVING THAT THE CREATOR OF THE SCHEME INTENDED MUTUAL ENFORCEABILITY

BAXTER v *FOUR OAKS PROPERTIES LTD* [1965] 1 All ER 906, Chancery Division

FACTS: The 288 acre 'Four Oaks Estate' was sold in plots of various sizes over a period of ten years, each purchaser entering a mutual deed of covenants for the benefit of the owners of the other plots.
HELD: Where there was a mutual deed of covenant, the fact that the vendor had not laid out his land in plots before sale did not preclude a finding that a building scheme was in existence.

CROSS J: . . . In 1891 Lord Clanrikarde owned an estate of some 288 acres at Sutton Coldfield known as the 'Four Oaks Estate', the eastern boundary of which was formed by a public road called at the south end the Lichfield Road, and further north the Four Oaks Road. By various conveyances executed over a period of some ten years he sold the whole of the estate for building development in plots of various sizes. It was his intention that the whole estate should be residential but that the cost of the houses to be erected should not be uniform throughout. To effect the purpose which he had in mind, the whole estate was divided into several parts, the part with which this action is concerned being that abutting on the Lichfield and Four Oaks Road.

The first purchaser of a plot on this part was one Samuel Hope. On April 27 1891, an indenture (which I will call the 'Lichfield Road deed of covenant') was expressed to be made between Lord Clanrikarde of the one part and Samuel Hope and all other persons whose names are or might thereafter be entered in the second column of Sch. 2 thereto, being purchasers of lands forming parts of the Four Oaks Estate as delineated on the plan thereto annexed of the other part. The recital and operative part of this Indenture were as follows:

WHEREAS by an Indenture of Conveyance bearing even date with these presents and made between the said Marquess of Clanrikarde of the one part and the said Samuel Hope of the other part for the consideration therein mentioned the said Marquess of Clanrikarde hath conveyed to the said Samuel Hope his heirs and assigns a certain piece or parcel of land being part of the Four Oaks Estate and fronting on a road shown on the said plan and leading from Sutton Coldfield to Lichfield and Little Aston being the piece or parcel of land coloured blue on the said plan and identified by the name 'Hope' written upon it TO HOLD the same unto and to the use of the said Samuel Hope his heirs and assigns AND in the said Indenture of Conveyance is contained a covenant by the said Samuel Hope with the said Marquess of Clanrikarde that he the said Samuel Hope his heirs and assigns and all persons claiming under him will at all times hereafter perform and observe certain covenants and conditions as to building on the said piece or parcel of land and as to the user of the said piece or parcel of land therein specified AND WHEREAS it is intended that all other persons who may be or become purchasers of any lands forming part of the said Four Oaks Estate and fronting on the said road shall enter into covenants as to building on such lands as to the user thereof similar to the covenant in that behalf contained in the hereinbefore recited Indenture of Conveyance to the said Samuel Hope NOW THIS INDENTURE WITNESSETH that for giving effect to such covenants respectively IT IS HEREBY AGREED AND DECLARED that the said Samuel Hope and every other person who shall be or become a purchaser of any land forming part of the said Four Oaks Estate and fronting on the said road and their respective heirs and assigns and all persons claiming under them respectively shall whether they shall or shall not have respectively executed these presents perform and observe the covenants and conditions contained in Sch. 1 hereunder written so far as such covenants and conditions respectively may relate to the lands purchased by them respectively AND IT IS HEREBY FURTHER AGREED AND DECLARED that in the event of any breach by the said Samuel Hope or any such other person as aforesaid or by their respective heirs or assigns or by any person or persons claiming under them respectively of the said covenants and conditions respectively or any of them it shall be lawful for any other person for the time being entitled to any land being part of the said Four Oaks Estate and fronting on the said road or having any estate or interest in such land without any further consent or concurrence of the said Marquess of Clanrikarde his heirs or assigns to bring such action or take such steps as may be necessary or proper or restrain such breach PROVIDED ALWAYS that the covenant and conditions contained in Sch. 1 hereunder written shall not apply to or affect any lands forming part of the Four Oaks Estate other than such lands as front on the said road.

The covenants and conditions in Sch. 1 were as follows:

1. No dwellinghouse or other building (other than the existing cottage adjoining Doe Bank House or other than a building used for the purposes of and as appurtenant to a dwellinghouse) of a less cost for materials and labour of construction than £750 or in the case of a pair of semi-detached houses than £1,200 shall be erected or built or suffered to remain upon any part of the lands above mentioned between Hartopp Road and Bracebridge Road or of a less cost than £1,000 in the case of a single house or £1,500 in the case of a pair of semi-detached houses upon any part of the lands above mentioned between Bracebridge Road and Blackroot Road. 2. No dwellinghouse or other building other than a porch or oriel or bow window or balcony shall be erected or built or suffered to remain upon any part of the lands above mentioned so as to project beyond the building line shown on the plan hereto annexed. 3. No dwellinghouse or other building on any part of the lands above mentioned shall be used for the sale or supply of wine beers or spirits or for the sale or supply of victuals or as an hotel or inn or for any trade or business whatever or otherwise than as a private residence or for any purpose which may be or grow to the annoyance damage or disturbance of any person who may be or become the owner or occupier of any other part of the lands above mentioned. . . .

It is, of course, clear that a vendor who sells a piece of land to 'A' and subsequently sells another piece of land to 'B' cannot, as part of the later transaction, annex to 'A's' land the benefit of a restrictive covenant entered into by 'B' if it was not part of his bargain with 'A' at the time of the sale to him that 'A' should have the benefit of it. On the other hand, for well over one hundred years past where the owner of land deals with it on the footing of imposing restrictive obligations on the use of various parts of it as and when he sells them off for the common benefit of himself (in so far as he retains any land) and of the various purchasers *inter se* a court of equity has been prepared to give effect to this common intention notwithstanding any technical difficulties involved. In the early days it was not unusual for the common vendor to have prepared a deed of mutual covenant to be executed by each purchaser. If the various sales all took place at the same time—as they would, for instance, if all the land in question was put up for sale by auction in lots—then the various purchasers would, no doubt, be brought into direct contractual relations with one another on signing the deed; but if the common vendor sold off different lots of land at intervals, it might well happen that by the time a later purchaser executed the deed, one of the earlier purchasers was dead. In such a case it would be difficult to found the right of the successors in title of the deceased earlier purchaser to enforce the covenants against the later purchaser or his successors in title on any contract between the two original purchasers, even though each signed the deed.

The view taken by the courts has been rather that the common vendor imposed a common law on a defined area of land and that whenever he sold a piece of it to a purchaser who knew of the common law, that piece of land automatically became entitled to the benefit of, and subject to the burden of, the common law. With the passage in time it became apparent that there was no particular virtue in the execution of a deed of mutual covenant—save as evidence of the intention of the parties—and what came to be called 'building schemes' were enforced by the courts if satisfied that it was the intention of the parties that the various purchasers should have rights *inter se*, even though no attempt was made to bring them into direct contractual relations. . . .

LAW OF PROPERTY ACT 1925

56.   Persons taking who are not parties and as to indentures

(1)   A person may take an immediate or other interest in land or other property, or the benefit of any condition, right of entry, covenant or agreement over or respecting land or other property, although he may not be named as a party to the conveyance or other instrument.

(2)   A deed between parties, to effect its objects, has the effect of an indenture though not intended or expressed to be an indenture.

27.4.3   MODERN CASES EXPANDING THE BUILDING SCHEME PRINCIPLES

BAXTER v FOUR OAKS [1965] 1 All ER 906

FACTS: There was a Victorian building scheme with one special feature. The common vendor had fixed the area of his scheme but had not divided his land into plots before commencing selling. Rather, he had sold each purchaser as much land as he (the purchaser) desired.
HELD: Cross J found that the special feature of the case did not prevent there being a building scheme. In *Baxter* there was an organised scheme of covenants for a defined area, and those covenants had been incorporated into a mutual deed of covenant.

RE DOLPHIN'S CONVEYANCE [1970] 2 All ER 664

FACTS: In 1871, two sisters were tenants in common of the 30-acre 'Selly Hill Estate' on the (then) south-west edge of Birmingham. They started selling off sizeable parts of this estate. They then gave the remaining parts of Selly Hill to their nephew. He sold off further chunks of Selly Hill, until it had all gone by 1891.

As each chunk of Selly Hill was sold, restrictive covenants were imposed on the land. The purchasers (usually builders) promised to build only high class housing; each house was to have a minimum of a quarter of an acre of grounds.

On each sale the vendors (the sisters or the nephew) covenanted that if they sold further parts of Selly Hill, the same restrictive covenants would be imposed. The judge inferred from this promise by the vendors an intention that the covenants restricting the area to high-class housing were to be mutually enforceable.

HELD: The judge went on to hold that although:

    (a)   there had been no scheme of restrictive covenants for the whole area decided upon before sale commenced; and

    (b)   the selling of the estate had been spread over 20 years;

there was nevertheless in his view a situation within the building scheme principle. Thus current owners of large houses on Selly Hill could enforce the covenants against Birmingham Corporation, who had bought other parts of Selly Hill for high-density council housing.

27.5   The Chaotic State of the Law on the Running of Benefits of Covenants

The Law Commission (Law Com. No. 127) Transfer of Land: The Law of Positive and Restrictive Covenants, London: HMSO, 26 January 1984

4.10   A traveller in this area of the law, old though it is, walks on ground which is still shifting. Particularly striking examples come from the same two topics: the *Federated Homes* case has made radical and controversial changes in what was thought to be the law about annexation, and successive court decisions in recent years have altered the conditions thought to be essential for the establishment of a binding scheme.

4.11   Shifts in the law as interpreted by the courts may be wholly beneficial so far as future covenants are concerned, but they must of course apply equally to existing covenants and here their effects are much more mixed. If a land-owner sought legal advice periodically about the enforceability of a particular covenant, he would have to be told different things at different times; and his lot would not be a happy one if he had acted in good faith on advice given one year only to find it invalidated the next. . . .

[The Law Commission proposed that a new 'land obligation' should be created to replace existing and future restrictive covenants.]

4.22 . . . the new interest will, like an easement, normally subsist as a legal interest in land, and be enforceable by legal remedies, including an action for common law damages. The highly technical rules determining whether the benefit and the burden of restrictive covenants may pass to new owners of the land affected will also disappear; and any doubt which might otherwise arise as to whether an obligation was intended to run with the land or operate only between the parties will be removed by requiring parties who intend to create an obligation running with the land to label it by express words as a 'land obligation'. . . . It will not be enforceable between the original parties after they have parted with the land.

CHAPTER TWENTY-EIGHT

ESCAPING FROM RESTRICTIVE COVENANTS

28.1 Carry on Regardless

Some developers may boldly say, 'Let's ignore those restrictive covenants,' and start work hoping that no 'dominant owner' will come along and object. In some types of situation there is little risk in doing this.

28.2 'Doing a Parkside Homes'

In the Wrotham Park case—see **26.3** the defendants, Parkside Homes, commenced their building work, but took out an insurance policy to protect themselves (and the purchasers of their houses) should anyone succeed in a claim that the covenant could still be enforced. As we know, a claim to enforce the covenant did (unexpectedly) succeed. The £2,500 damages awarded by Brightman J was paid (as his Lordship well knew) by the insurers.

28.3 Attempt to Buy Out the Dominant Owners

You must first realise that if there are (say) 10 dominant owners, then all 10 must be persuaded to give up their rights to enforce the covenant. You must also appreciate that as a result of the chaos caused by modern cases such as *Federated Homes* and *Wrotham Park* (see **27.1** and **26.3**), it is often impossible to be certain that you have 'persuaded' every dominant owner.

28.4 Take Proceedings Under the Law of Property Act 1925, Section 84(2)

LAW OF PROPERTY ACT 1925

84. Power to discharge or modify restrictive covenants affecting land

(1)   [the Lands Tribunal] shall (without prejudice to any concurrent jurisdiction of the court) have power from time to time, on the application of any person interested in any freehold land affected by any restriction arising under covenant or otherwise as to the user thereof or the building thereon, by order wholly or partially to discharge or modify any such restriction . . . on being satisfied—

(a)   that by reason of changes in the character of the property or the neighbourhood or other circumstances of the case which [the Lands Tribunal] may deem material, the restriction ought to be deemed obsolete, or

(aa)   that in a case falling within subsection (1A) below the continued existence thereof would impede some reasonable user of the land for public or private purposes . . . or, as the case may be, would unless modified so impede such user; or

(b)   that the persons of full age and capacity for the time being or from time to time entitled to the benefit of the restriction, whether in respect of estates in fee simple or any lesser estates or interests in the property to which the benefit of the restriction is annexed, have agreed, either expressly or by implication, by their acts or omissions, to the same being discharged or modified; or

(c)   that the proposed discharge or modification will not injure the persons entitled to the benefit of the restriction:

and an order discharging or modifying a restriction under this subsection may direct the applicant to pay to any person entitled to the benefit of the restriction such sum by way of consideration as the Tribunal may think it just to award under one, but not both, of the following heads, that is to say, either—

(i)   a sum to make up for any loss or disadvantage suffered by that person in consequence of the discharge or modification; or

(ii)   a sum to make up for any effect which the restriction had, at the time when it was imposed, in reducing the consideration then received for the land affected by it.

(1A)   Subsection (1)(aa) above authorises the discharge or modification of a restriction by reference to its impeding some reasonable user of land in any case in which the Lands Tribunal is satisfied that the restriction, in impeding that user, either—

(a)   does not secure to persons entitled to the benefit of it any practical benefits of substantial value or advantage to them; or

(b)   is contrary to the public interest;

and that money will be an adequate compensation for the loss or disadvantage (if any) which any such person will suffer from the discharge or modification.

(1B)   In determining whether a case is one falling within subsection (1A) above, and in determining whether (in any such case or otherwise) a restriction ought to be discharged or modified, the Lands Tribunal shall take into account the development plan and any declared or ascertainable pattern for the grant or refusal of planning permissions in the relevant areas, as well as the period at which and context in which the restriction was created or imposed and any other material circumstances.

(1C)   It is hereby declared that the power conferred by this section to modify a restriction includes power to add such further provisions restricting the user of or the building on the land affected as appear to the Lands Tribunal to be reasonable in view of the relaxation of the existing provisions, and as may be accepted by the applicant; and the Lands Tribunal may accordingly refuse to modify a restriction without some such addition.

(2)   The court shall have power on the application of any person interested—

(a)   To declare whether or not in any particular case any freehold land is or would in any given event be affected by a restriction imposed by any instrument; or

(b)   To declare what, upon the true construction of any instrument purporting to impose a restriction, is the nature and extent of the restriction thereby imposed and whether the same is [or would in any given event be] enforceable and if so by whom. Neither subsections (7) and (11) of this section nor, unless the contrary is expressed, any later enactment providing for this section not to apply to any restrictions shall affect the operation of this subsection or the operation for purposes of this subsection of any other provisions of this section.

(3)   The Lands Tribunal shall, before making any order under this section, direct such enquiries, if any, to be made of any government department or local authority, and such notices, if any, whether by way of advertisement or otherwise, to be given to such of the persons who appear to be entitled to the benefit of the restriction intended to be discharged, modified, or dealt with as, having regard to any enquiries notices or other proceedings previously made, given or taken, the Lands Tribunal may think fit.

(3A)   On an application to the Lands Tribunal under this section the Lands Tribunal shall give any necessary directions as to the persons who are or are not to be admitted (as appearing to be entitled to the benefit of the restriction) to oppose the application, and no appeal shall lie against any such direction; but rules under the Lands Tribunal Act 1949 shall make provision whereby, in cases in which there arises on such an application (whether or not in connection with the admission of persons to oppose) any such question as is referred to in subsection (2)(a) or (b) of this section, the proceedings on the application can and, if the rules so provide, shall be suspended to enable the decision of the court to be obtained on that question by an application under that subsection, or by means of a case stated by the Lands Tribunal, or otherwise, as may be provided by those rules or by rules of court.

(4) . . .

(5) Any order made under this section shall be binding on all persons, whether ascertained or of full age or capacity or not, then entitled or thereafter capable of becoming entitled to the benefit of any restriction, which is thereby discharged, modified, or dealt with, and whether such persons are parties to the proceedings or have been served with notice or not. . . .

(6) An order may be made under this section notwithstanding that any instrument which is alleged to impose the restriction intended to be discharged, modified, or dealt with, may not have been produced to the court or the Lands Tribunal, and the court or [the Lands Tribunal] may act on such evidence of that instrument as it may think sufficient.

(7) . . .

(8) This section applies whether the land affected by the restrictions is registered or not, but, in the case of registered land, the Land Registrar shall give effect on the register to any order under this section in accordance with the Land Registration Act 1925.

(9) . . .

(10) . . .

(11) . . .

(12) Where a term of more than forty years is created in land (whether before or after the commencement of this Act) this section shall, after the expiration of twenty-five years of the term, apply to restrictions affecting such leasehold land in like manner as it would have applied had the land been freehold:

Providing that this subsection shall not apply to mining leases.

RE 6, 8, 10 AND 12 ELM AVENUE, NEW MILTON, EX PARTE NEW FOREST DISTRICT COUNCIL [1984] 3 All ER 632, Chancery Division

In this case the judge gave a clear exposition of the special procedure to be adopted when seeking, under s. 84(2) of the Law of Property Act 1925, a High Court declaration of a complete list of dominant owners entitled to claim the benefit of a restrictive covenant.

SCOTT J: . . . [This] brings me to consider the approach which ought to be adopted on an application for a declaration under s. 84(2) of the Law of Property Act 1925, as amended. The subsection provides a means by which the owners of land, which may appear to be subject to restrictive covenants, can come to the court and ask for a declaration that it is not so subject. If the court makes that declaration it has an *in rem* effect and the property is not then so subject. The negative is established by the declaration sought. The position seems to me to be not in the least comparable to the situation which pertains where there is a lis between somebody claiming to be entitled to the benefit of restrictions on the one hand and the owner of the property said to be subject to the restrictions and denying the entitlement of the plaintiff on the other hand. In such a case it is plain that the onus of establishing, on a balance of probabilities, that there is a scheme, and that the property for the benefit of which it is claimed is so entitled, lies on the person asserting those matters. But when an owner of land comes to the court for a declaration under s. 84(2) it does not seem to me that he can claim to be entitled to the declaration simply on the basis that if there had been an opponent who had been arguing for the benefit of the restrictions that opponent would, on the evidence before the court, have failed on a balance of probabilities. That seems to me to be an erroneous approach. If there had been such a person, what inquiries and what case would have been made by such person is not able to be identified. It is the practice that as a preliminary to bringing before the court a claim for a declaration under s. 84(2) notice should be given to all persons in the area who might conceivably be interested in claiming the benefit of the restrictions. That has been done in this case. But it has been done in this case in the context of the wish of the local authority to construct its car park and it is entirely possible that the overwhelming consents to the construction of the car park that have been received from persons living in the neighbourhood may be simply a reflection of the need for a car park in the area. I think I would be wrong in assuming that by giving those consents the persons giving them were acknowledging that they were not entitled to the benefit of the restrictions.

However that may be, in my judgment if a declaration is to be made under s. 84(2), the court ought to be clear that the property is not burdened by the relevant restrictions. On the evidence before me I am not so clear. It seems to me likely that there was a building scheme created by Mr Merefield in the 1920s. It seems to be at least possible that, subject to the local authority's position as having acquired for statutory purposes, that building scheme may still be enforceable. In those circumstances I do not feel prepared to make a declaration the effect of which would be not simply that the local authority can proceed to construct the car park without fear of interference by way of claims for injunction, but would also have the effect of precluding anyone from coming and claiming compensation for injurious affection. Any person so claiming must of course establish, and would have the onus of proving on the balance of probabilities, that he is entitled to the benefit of the restrictions. It may very well be that nobody can do that but I do not think it would be right for me to make a declaration which would prevent any person who desired to do that from attempting to do so. . . .

28.5 Commence Proceedings in the Lands Tribunal Under Section 84(1)

RE FORGACS' APPLICATION (1976) 32 P & CR 464, Lands Tribunal

FACTS: A plot of land had two buildings on it, but was subject to a restriction that not more than one dwelling-house be built on that land. One of the buildings was already being used as a dwelling. The applicant sought a modification of the restriction so as to allow the second building to be used as an independent dwelling house.
HELD: Application granted.

J. H. EMLYN JONES FRICS: . . . I should say first of all that I accept Lord Colville's submissions founded on the evidence of the objectors that the restrictions which it is now sought to set aside in so far as they protect the concept of 'one plot, one house,' are of continuing value to the objectors. Notwithstanding the minor changes which have taken place, for example, by the conversion of houses into flats I accept Mr. Bradley's evidence and agree that the Wimbledon House Estate in general and Parkside Gardens in particular is an attractive, quiet locality with pleasant houses in peaceful surroundings. I cannot accept that the restriction which it is now sought to modify ought to be deemed obsolete. It seems to me that such an allegation is of general application and I agree with Mr. Rose that the modification asked for might well have serious consequences elsewhere on the estate if it were to be granted on the grounds contained in paragraph (a) of section 84(1).

I leave for the moment paragraph (aa) and turn to consideration of the grounds contained in paragraph (c) 'that the proposed modification will not injure the persons entitled to the benefit of the restriction.' The evidence of both expert witnesses really came to the same thing, namely, that the proposed modification looked at in isolation would not injure the persons entitled to the benefit of the restriction. Having inspected the property I must say that I do not see how they could have come to any other conclusion. The coach-house is there modification it will continue to house small families in the future. As a building it remains virtually the same (if anything rather improved) and I am not persuaded that there would be any material difference in the flow of traffic in and out through the gateway giving access on to Parkside Gardens. The only difference would be that the occupiers of the coach-house would no longer be servants of the occupiers of 'Snettisham.' I observe that there are two other coach-houses in Parkside Gardens which are similarly severed from their main houses, and I cannot see that any harmful effect has resulted from these changes. At first sight this conclusion suggests that the application succeeds under paragraph (c). It remains to consider how far the modification if granted would in Mr. Rose's words cause injury in the long-term. In my judgment the argument of the 'thin end of the wedge' can have no bearing on the facts of the present case. It seems to me that the circumstances of the present application are almost unique and looking at the merits of the application I am quite unable to see how the proposed modification can cause any injury. Lord Colville suggested that it was not so much the thin end of the wedge but rather as he put it damage to the system of covenants. But the system of covenants has been breached in minor ways in circumstances where little or no injury has been caused. Any future application it seems to me, must similarly be looked at on its merits. . . . I come to the conclusion therefore that this application succeeds under paragraph (c) of section 84(1) on the ground that it will cause no injury to the persons entitled to the benefit of the restriction. It is not necessary therefore for me to consider paragraph (aa) except to observe that prima facie an application which succeeds under paragraph (c) should succeed *a fortiori* under paragraph (aa).

RE BASS LTD'S APPLICATION (1973) 26 P & CR 156, Lands Tribunal

FACTS: The applicants had bought some land in 'inner-city' Birmingham which was 'zoned' for industrial use. They obtained planning permission to establish a large depot for long distance beer-transporting lorries. It was estimated that some 250 lorries a day would come in and out of the depot. The land was, however, subject to a 'residential purposes only' restrictive covenant. Local residents, claiming to be the dominant owners of the covenant resisted Bass's application to have the restriction removed.
HELD: Bass's application failed, despite the finding that Bass performed 'so useful and agreeable a function.'

J STUART DANIEL QC: . . . The issue, which I think is a difficult one, is then whether the application should succeed under section 84(1)(aa). I accept Mr. Eyre's distillation of the questions which therefore arise and I proceed to them. *Question* 1. *Is the proposed user a reasonable user of the land for private purposes?* In order to answer this question it is right, I think, to consider the question on the assumption that the covenants do not exist, otherwise the question is begged. The planning permissions are very persuasive in this connexion . . . I would not like it to be thought that the first question arising, that of reasonable user, could always be concluded in the affirmative by the production of a planning permission, but on balance and after some doubt, and assuming that the covenants were not there, I have decided that in the present case the proposal does in all the difficulties of the situation constitute a reasonable user of the land for private purposes.
Question 2. *Do the covenants impede the proposed user?*
   There is no question but that the covenants do impede the proposed user.
Question 5. *Is impeding the proposed user contrary to the public interest?*
   I am following Mr. Eyre in taking his question 5 before giving my answers to his Questions 3 and 4. In doing so I recognise that it is right and sensible to juxtapose question 5 with question 2 because this enables the question of reasonable user and of public interest to be considered consecutively. But that does not of course mean that the questions are the same, they are simply related and sometimes overlapping; the proposition that a user is reasonable may be assisted by a planning permission; the proposition that impeding that user is contrary to public interest may also be assisted by a planning permission but in rather a different way. As I have just said a planning permission is immediately persuasive on the general question whether a user is reasonable. Mr. Eyre submitted that prima facie a planning permission also meant that the proposal was in the public interest. But that is not the question. The question is whether impeding the proposal is contrary to the public interest. There is here more than a narrow nuance of difference; a planning permission only says, in effect, that a proposal will be allowed; it implies perhaps that such a proposal will not be a bad thing but it does not necessarily imply that it will be positively a good thing and in the public interest, and that failure of the proposal to materialise would be positively bad. Many planning permissions have got through by the skin of their teeth, and I think that the assistance derived from a planning permission at this stage of things is little more than the negative assistance of enabling it to be said that at any rate there was not a refusal. Thus the proving that impeding the present proposal is contrary to public interest raises a different onus from the onus of proving the user to be a reasonable one. This is really obvious from the drafting of the section but I have spelled it out in the present case because I think it is necessary. I am by no means satisfied that to stop this proposal would be contrary to public interest. There is private interest, of course, and to serve the private interest of so large a concern as Bass Limited which performs so useful and agreeable a function does to some extent serve the public interest, but that is really as far as it goes and

I do not think it goes far enough. . . . I do not think the planning documents prove anything on this issue. . . . I am not satisfied that impeding this proposal is contrary to the public interest, and that conclusion is made after having full regard to what I am now about to say on Question 3, to which I now turn.

Question 3. Does impeding the proposed user secure to the objectors practical benefits?

This opens up the general merits on the amenity front and in particular the question of noise.

The Tribunal then considered the evidence in some further detail and concluded: The residents of City Road are already subjected to noise which is not only undesirable but is beyond the limit of what is acceptable. And this application proposes to increase it.

In that situation I feel quite unable to be satisfied that impeding this proposal does not secure to the objectors benefits of substantial value or advantage. The objectors' evidence made it very clear how they feared and disliked this proposal. It does not seem to me that any authority is needed for the proposition that prevention of such a proposal and therefore the assuaging of the fear and dislike it engenders is indeed a benefit of substantial advantage.

It is not only the noise. That perhaps is the factor most amenable to measurement, difficult though that is. Fumes, vibration, dirt, the appearance of things and the risk of accidents all add to the aggregate of debts and cumulatively strengthen my opinion that in impeding this proposal the objectors do secure practical benefits of substantial value and advantage. . . .

Questions 6 and 7 do not arise, because I have given an affirmative answer to Question 4 and a negative answer to Question 5. . . .

[Question 6 was—'If the answer to Question 4 is negative, would money be an adequate compensation?

Question 7 was—'If the answer to Question 5 is affirmative, would money be an adequate compensation?']

GILBERT v *SPOOR* [1982] 2 All ER 576, Court of Appeal

FACTS: This case involved an application to the Lands Tribunal for an order under section 84(1) for the discharge or modification of a restrictive covenant against building. The applicant had obtained planning permission to build houses on the servient land.
HELD: The restrictive covenant would not be modified or discharged. The grant of planning permission was not a conclusive consideration.

EVELEIGH LJ: . . . We are only concerned with one restriction and the ground for the application based on s. 84(1)(aa) although the original application covered a wider field.

The resriction is contained in the first schedule to a conveyance dated 3 November 1954. So far as is material it reads:

Not to erect on the piece of land hereby conveyed any building whatsoever other than one private dwellinghouse with proper offices and outbuildings (including at the Purchaser's option a private garage). . .

The application was for an order that the restriction be discharged wholly or modified by—

Permitting the erection and maintenance on the said land of three dwelling houses with proper offices, outbuildings and garages, of design and specification approved by the Castle Morpeth Borough Council by and or pursuant to the said Council's grant of planning permission to the Applicant dated the 11th day of October one thousand nine hundred and seventy six. . .

It is clear from the introductory sentence of sub-s. (1) of s. 84 of the 1925 Act that its provisions apply as between the original parties and to restrictions of any kind: see the observations in *Ridley* v *Taylor* [1965] 2 All ER 51, [1965] 1 WLR 611. I therefore do not think that it is permissible to construe sub-s. (1A) only in the context of restrictive covenants which run with the land. The first task is to construe the section in isolation and then to relate it to the facts of the present case.

The words of the subsection, in my opinion, are used quite generally. The phrase 'any practical benefits of substantial value or advantage to them' is wide. The subsection does not speak of a restriction for the benefit or protection of land, which is a reasonably common phrase, but rather to a restriction which secures any practical benefits. The expression 'any practical benefits' is so wide that I would require very compelling considerations before I felt able to limit them in the manner contended for. When one remembers that Parliament is authorising the Lands Tribunal to take away from a person a vested right either in law or in equity, it is not surprising that the tribunal is required to consider the adverse effects on a broad basis.

Had this application been one where all the original parties were concerned, I do not understand counsel for the applicant to argue that the preservation of the view could not be said to be a practical benefit secured by the restriction. If this is correct, and I think that it is, I see no reason to give the words a different meaning because successors in title are involved. The successor in title may well have to establish certain conditions before the covenant is enforceable by him, but that fact will not alter the nature of the benefits or advantage in fact secured to him by the existence of the restriction.

In my judgment the tribunal was entitled to hold that the view was a benefit whether or not that benefit could be said to touch and concern the land. However, I am also of the view that the land of the objectors is, in each case, touched and concerned by the covenant. The covenant is intended to preserve the amenity or standard of the neighbourhood generally. The covenant is specifically aimed at density of housing. Extensive building can effect the amenity of a district in many ways. An estate can easily lose its character when buildings obstruct the views. It seems to me to be perfectly reasonable to say that the loss of a view 'at a point just a short distance from the land' may have an adverse effect on the land itself for the loss of the view could prove detrimental to the estate as a whole. In my opinion therefore the tribunal was entitled to find as it did. . . .

28.6 End of Chapter Assessment Question

In 1870 Mark bought the fee simple in Broadacre. Broadacre was then 10 acres of poor quality farm land, so Mark decided to sell the land for high class housing.

From 1871 to 1875 he sold off the whole of Broadacre in 40 plots of approximately a quarter of an acre each. In each conveyance he imposed restrictive covenants which (inter alia) prohibited the building of more than one house on each plot.

Luke has just purchased 'Redgables', a house built in 1873 on one of the plots sold by Mark. He has obtained planning permission to build a second house in the garden of 'Redgables'.

Luke's plans have caused alarm amongst some of his neighbours, and they are threatening proceedings for an injunction, claiming that they are entitled to enforce the 'one house per plot' restrictive covenant.

Other neighbours have indicated to Luke that they support him, and that they are also considering applying for planning permission to build a second house in their gardens.

Advise Luke.

28.7 End of Chapter Assessment Outline Answer

Prima facie there would appear to be a building scheme here, in which the restrictive covenants are mutually enforceable between the current owners of the plots. Compare, for instance, *Re Dolphin's Conveyance* (1970) [see **27.4.3**]. In that case the judge held that there was a valid building scheme of restrictive covenants for the whole estate, notwithstanding the fact that (as in the present case) the estate had not been divided into separate plots prior to the first plots being sold.

Assuming that each plot on Broadacre is subject to the scheme of restrictive covenants the question arises whether Luke can escape from the covenant restricting him to building one house on his plot.

A number of possible avenues of escape may be available to him.

First, he might carry on regardless and build a second house on his plot. Although, with neighbours threatening to seek an injunction against further building on his land this would appear to be inadvisable. Normally it will not be difficult for Luke's neighbours to obtain an interlocutory injunction, all they need to show is an 'arguable case' against Luke's plans. However, an injunction is an equitable remedy granted in the discretion of the court and it will not be awarded if the applicant has 'unclean hands'. Thus, if the neighbours who oppose Luke can be shown to have breached (substantially) any of the scheme covenants, they will be unlikely to obtain an injunction against him.

Secondly, he might carry on regardless, but take out insurance against the possibility that he might be subjected to an injunction. However, in the light of the threats he has received it is likely that insurance cover will be prohibitively expensive, or even refused altogether.

Thirdly, Luke might seek to identify all the 'dominant' owners (neighbours who are able to enforce the restrictive covenant) and attempt to persuade them to support him, perhaps by 'buying them out', although he is unlikely to be able to buy them all out without the financial support of those neighbours who support his plans. But how will Luke know that he has pursuaded all the dominant owners? The answer is that under s. 84(2) of the Law of Property Act 1925 the High Court can declare a definitive list of the dominant owners. Once such a declaration has been made Luke need not fear the claims of any dominant owner not appearing on the list. The High Court will only make a declaration under s. 84(2) if Luke has first circularised all his neighbours informing them that proceedings are pending, that they can be joined as parties and that they will be bound by the result (*Re Sunnyfield* [1932] 1 Ch 79).

If Luke is unable to pursuade all the dominant owners to release him from the restrictive covenant he may commence proceedings in the Lands Tribunal under s. 84(1) of the Law of Property Act 1925. The Lands Tribunal has the power, on such an application, to modify or discharge out of date restrictive covenants.

Under s. 84(1) there are a number of grounds on which a restrictive covenant may be discharged or modified [see **28.4**]. Luke is most likely to succeed under ground s. 84(1)(aa), which was introduced in 1969. The ground is that: 'the continued existence [of the restrictive covenant undischarged/modified] would impede some reasonable user of the land for public or private purposes'.

Section 84(1A) provides that two elements must be satisfied in order to succeed under s. 84(1)(aa). First, the restrictive covenant must (a) 'not secure to [the dominant owner(s)] any practical benefits of substantial value or advantage ...' **or** (b) must be 'contrary to the public interest'. Secondly, money must be 'an adequate compensation for the loss or disadvantage (if any) which any [dominant owner] will suffer from the discharge or modification'. In determining these issues '. . . the Lands Tribunal shall take into account the development plan and any declared or ascertainable pattern for the grant or refusal of planning permissions in the relevant area . . .' (s. 84(1B)). Thus Luke will rely on the development plan for his area if it suggests that there is a shortage of local housing. But it will not satisfy s. 84(1B) for Luke to point, merely, to the individual planning permission that has been granted to him.

In *Re Bass' Application* (1973) the tribunal analysed a ground (aa) application in terms of a series of questions [see **28.5**]. Applying those questions to the present case it is fairly clear that, (1) Luke's proposed user is reasonable (the grant of planning permission is usually conclusive evidence of this); (2) the covenants clearly impede that reasonable user; (3) impeding the user secures a practical benefit to the objectors (it preserves the appearance of his plot in keeping with the rest of Broadacre, and may prevent the obstruction of light from neighbouring premises); (4) the practical benefit (in 3) is substantial (but see below); (5) it is not against the public interest to impede the development (a grant of planning permission shows only that the development is not against the public interest); and consequently the tribunal is unlikely to discharge or modify the restrictive covenant.

If, on the other hand, the geography of Broadacre is such that Luke could build a second house without depriving his neighbours of a 'substantial' practical benefit (perhaps his plot is on the edge of the estate and obscured by trees) he might succeed under ground (aa) (*Re Banks' Application* (1976) P & CR 138). If such is the case the restrictive covenant will be modified or discharged, but only if money would be an adequate compensation to the dominant owners for the loss of the restriction. If compensation is awarded it will be calculated as 'a sum to make up for any loss' or, alternatively, 'as a sum to make up for the effect which the restriction had, at the time it was imposed, in reducing the consideration then received for the land affected by it'. One problem with the latter measure of compensation is that it is not inflation proof, another problem is that historic valuations are difficult to carry out. Accordingly, the first, less complicated, measure is the one normally used.

CHAPTER TWENTY-NINE

THE CREATION OF MORTGAGES

29.1 Introduction

Lawson, F. H. and Rudden, B., The Law of Property, 2nd edn,
Oxford: Clarendon Press, 1982, p. 198

. . .

The function of land mortgages
Since the days when the law of land mortgages was worked out two important changes have taken place. Firstly, ordinary people and not just the wealthy or the business community enter into mortgages to acquire their homes. Secondly, in this field, the private lender has almost disappeared along with the form of the mortgage that expected periodic payment only of *interest* with the capital advanced being repaid in a lump sum.

Nowadays the great mortgagees are the Building Societies who lend money to enable citizens to acquire a home and stipulate for repayment of both capital and income by instalments, so that after twenty or so years the debt and the mortgage are both extinguished. Their business is to earn money in the form of interest on loans made to purchasers of houses and mortgages are merely security for those loans. But they are *trustees* of their funds for their depositors. In one sense, therefore, the great lenders are merely conduit pipes. Ordinary people hand over their savings to them and receive interest on the money; and the funds thus amassed are lent to other ordinary people at interest.

Thus a mortgage looks two ways. The lender benefits the borrower by financing him, usually in the purchase of something like a home; the borrower benefits the lender by offering him a sound and safe investment. Any problems that might arise over a lender who suddenly needs his money back are solved by the interposition of Building Societies so that both lender and borrower are relieved from the anxieties of a one-to-one transaction.

29.2 Legal Mortgages of Fees Simple after 1925

29.2.1 MORTGAGE BY LONG LEASE ('MORTGAGE BY DEMISE')

The mortgagor grants to the mortgagee a lease for a very long period (usually 3,000 years) subject to a proviso for cesser on redemption, i.e. a provision that on the debt being repaid on a named date the lease should automatically terminate. This named date is the legal redemption date and is still usually fixed at a nominal six months from the date of the creation of the mortgage. The equitable right to redeem remains all important.

Any attempt after 1925 to create a mortgage by conveyance of the fee simple is converted by the Law of Property Act 1925, s. 85(2) to a mortgage by demise for 3,000 years, with a proviso for cesser on redemption.

Any legal mortgage existing on 1 January 1926 which had been created by conveyance of the fee simple was automatically converted into a mortgage by demise for 3,000 years. The fee simple was automatically revested in the mortgagor.

29.2.2 CHARGE BY WAY OF LEGAL MORTGAGE

LAW OF PROPERTY ACT 1925

Section 117   FOURTH SCHEDULE

FORMS RELATING TO STATUTORY CHARGES OR MORTGAGES OF FREEHOLD OR
LEASEHOLD LAND

FORM NO 1

STATUTORY CHARGE BY WAY OF LEGAL MORTGAGE

This Legal Charge made by way of Statutory Mortgage the .... day of ....
19 .. , between *A.* of [etc.] of the one part and *M.* of [etc.] of the other part Witnesseth that
in consideration of the sum of £............. now paid to *A.* by *M.* of which sum *A.* hereby
acknowledges the receipt *A.* As Mortgagor and As Beneficial Owner hereby charges by
way of legal mortgage All That [etc.] with the payment to *M.* on the .... day of ....
19 .. , of the principal sum of £............. as the mortgage money with interest thereon at the
rate of .... per centum per annum.
    In witness etc.

29.3   Equitable Mortgages of Legal Estates

29.3.1   EQUITABLE MORTGAGES AFTER 26 SEPTEMBER 1989

UNITED BANK OF KUWAIT PLC v SAHIB AND OTHERS [1995] 2 WLR 94,
Chancery Division

FACTS: The plaintiff obtained judgment against the first defendant. The first defendant
then confirmed in writing to another bank, the second defendant, that the land certificate
to his land (he held the freehold jointly with his wife) was being held for the defendant
bank as security for a loan made by the defendant bank to him. The plaintiff claimed to be
entitled to an equitable charge on the freehold by deposit of the land certificate.
HELD: Section 2 of the Law of Property (Miscellaneous Provisions) Act 1989 precluded the
valid creation of an equitable mortgage in favour of the defendant bank. There was no
document in writing signed by both parties which amounted to a specifically enforceable
contract. The informal deposit of the land certificate could not be effective to create an
equitable mortgage because it failed the formality requirements laid down in s. 53(1)(c) of
the Law of Property Act 1925, which required any disposition of a subsisting equitable
interest to be made by signed writing. The subsisting equitable interest here was the first
defendant's interest under the trust for sale on which the land was held. There was no
room to avoid the formality requirements by finding a resulting, implied or constructive
trust under s. 53(2) of the Law of Property Act 1925.

CHADWICK J: . . . Mr. Boggis on behalf of the plaintiff bank—without accepting that
Sogenal has any interest at all as a mortgagee or chargee—sought to persuade me that
priority between Sogenal and the plaintiff bank would be governed by the rule in *Dearle* v
Hall (1828) 3 Russ 1. Where the rule applies priority depends upon the order in which
notice of the mortgage or charge is received by the trustees for sale: see section 137(2)(ii) of
the Law of Property Act 1925. . . .
    . . . the plaintiff bank can gain no assistance from the rule in *Dearle* v *Hall*, 3 Russ 1. If
Sogenal became entitled to a charge over Mr. Sahib's beneficial interest in 37c before the
charging order nisi was made on 12 October 1992, then Sogenal's charge has priority over
the charge created in favour of the plaintiff bank by the charging order. It is necessary,
therefore, to decide whether Sogenal did, indeed, become entitled to the charge which it
claims.

For the reasons which I have already set out, the only interest in 37c over or in respect of which Mr. Sahib, acting alone, was capable of creating a mortgage or charge was his equitable interest under the trust for sale. The only interest which Sogenal could have acquired from Mr. Sahib was as an equitable mortgagee or chargee of Mr. Sahib's equal undivided share in the proceeds of sale. An equitable mortgage or charge over or in respect of an existing equitable interest may arise in a number of ways. First, it may be created expressly by a disposition in writing made for that purpose. In the case of an equitable mortgage the disposition would take the form of an assignment of the interest by way of security with a proviso (express or implied) for reassignment upon satisfaction of the obligation. An equitable charge not made by way of mortgage may be made, without assignment, by charging the equitable interest with the payment of the debt. Writing, signed by the person creating the mortgage or charge or by his agent, is essential if the requirements of section 53(1)(c) of the Law of Property Act 1925 are to be satisfied. There is nothing in the present case which could amount to a disposition in writing sufficient, in itself, to create an equitable mortgage or charge over or in respect of Mr. Sahib's equal undivided share in the proceeds of sale of 37c. . . .

An equitable mortgage or charge may also arise out of a specifically enforceable contract to create a security. The principle was explained by Buckley LJ in *Swiss Bank Corporation* v *Lloyds Bank Ltd* [1982] AC 584, 595:

A contract to mortgage property, real or personal, will, normally at least, be specifically enforceable, for a mere claim to damages or repayment is obviously less valuable than a security in the event of the debtor's insolvency. If it is specifically enforceable, the obligation to confer the proprietary interest will give rise to an equitable charge upon the subject matter by way of mortgage.

Similar reasoning supports the conclusion that a contract to create a charge will, normally and without more, take effect as an equitable charge. Equity looks on that as done which ought to be done. . . .

The effect of section 2(1) of the Law of Property (Miscellaneous Provisions) Act 1989 is that a contract to mortgage or charge land (including a contract to charge an interest in the proceeds of sale of land) will be void if it is not made in a written document (or documents) incorporating all the terms which the parties have agreed and signed by or on behalf of each party.

In the present case, there being no exchange of contracts incorporating the same terms, the whole contract must be found in a document signed by both parties. There is no document signed by both parties; indeed, there was no document signed by or on behalf of either party, at the time when the contract was said to have been made, which identifies the obligation which is now said to be secured, namely the new advance of £130,000 or, more strictly, the amount due from Mr. Sahib in respect of the time deposit current for the time being and the balance on account 320/260.834.

It must follow that there is no contract, recognisable at law or in equity, between Mr. Sahib and Sogenal in relation to the giving of security over 37c. . . .

Mr. Pymont sought to escape the rigour of section 2(1) of the Act of 1989 by disclaiming reliance on any contract between Mr. Sahib and Sogenal. He submitted that the confirmation given by Wilde Sapte on behalf of Mr. Sahib in their letter of 10 September 1990—that they would hold the land certificate in respect of 37c to the order to Sogenal—was to be treated as a notional deposit of the certificate, so that Sogenal was in the same position as it would have been in if there had been actual delivery of the land certificate by Mr. Sahib to Sogenal. He relied on the rule that a deposit of title deeds as security for a loan was, without more, sufficient to create an equitable charge in the land to which those deeds relate. This, he submitted, was a third way in which an equitable charge could arise: it was outside the provisions of section 2(1) of the Act of 1989 and (notwithstanding that the interest charged was an existing equitable interest) it was also outside the provisions of section 53(1)(c) of the Law of Property Act 1925.

A convenient statement of the rule is to be found in *Coote on Mortgages*, 9th edn. (1927), vol. 1, p. 86, in a passage cited by the Court of Appeal in *Thames Guaranty Ltd* v *Campbell* [1985] QB 210, 232–233:

A deposit of title deeds by the owner of freeholds or leaseholds with his creditor for the purpose of securing either a debt antecedently due, or a sum of money advanced at the time of the deposit, operates as an equitable mortgage or charge, by virtue of which the depositee acquires, not merely the right of holding the deeds until the debt is paid, but also an equitable interest in the land itself. A mere delivery of the deeds will have this operation without any express agreement, whether in writing or oral, as to the conditions or purpose of the delivery, as the court would infer the intent and agreement to create a security from the relation of debtor and creditor subsisting between the parties, unless the contrary were shown; and the delivery would be sufficient part performance of such agreement to take the case out of [section 40 of the Law of Property Act 1925].

It is, I think, important to keep in mind that (as is made clear in the passage just cited) it was not the mere deposit of title deeds which gave rise to an equitable mortgage or charge; it was necessary to establish that the deeds were deposited for the purpose of securing an obligation. In most cases there would be evidence of something said, written or done from which that purpose could be established and the obligation identified. But in some cases there would be no evidence other than that the depositor and the depositee were, or were about to become, debtor and creditor. In those cases the court could infer the purpose and identify the obligation from that fact alone. But the basis of the rule, as explained in *Coote on Mortgages*, was that the equitable charge arose because the court was satisfied from whatever evidence there was that the parties had made an agreement (expressly or by implication) that the debtor should grant security for an obligation which the court could identify, that the agreement was (or, but for the provision of section 40 of the Law of Property Act 1925, would have been) specifically enforceable, and that the deposit of the title deeds was treated as an act of part performance sufficient to take the case out of section 40 and so enable the agreement to be enforced notwithstanding the absence of any memorandum in writing capable of satisfying subsection (1) of that section. In other words, the equitable charge which arose upon the deposit of title deeds was contract-based.

If this is a correct analysis of the basis of the rule that a deposit of title deeds for the purpose of securing a debt operated, without more, as an equitable mortgage or charge, then it is difficult to see how the rule can have survived section 2 of the Act of 1989. . . .

. . . I find no support in the decided cases for the view . . . that a charge created by deposit of title deeds is properly to be regarded as something distinct from an equitable charge arising from agreement. . . .

I should, perhaps, add (without seeking to decide the point) that I am far from persuaded that section 53(2) of the Law of Property Act 1925 can have any application in a case where it is sought to avoid the effect of section 53(1)(c) by relying on an oral contract to make the disposition which section 53(1)(c) requires to be in writing. The point arose in *Oughtred* v *Inland Revenue Commissioners* [1960] AC 206. It was put, succinctly, by counsel for the Inland Revenue (Mr. Wilberforce QC) in argument, at p 221: 'It cannot be right that an oral contract can transfer property when an oral disposition cannot.'. . .

29.4 Equitable Mortgages of Equitable Interests

LAW OF PROPERTY ACT 1925

53. Instruments required to be in writing

(1) Subject to the provisions hereinafter contained with respect to the creation of interests in land by parol—

(a) no interest in land can be created or disposed of except by writing signed by the person creating or conveying the same, or by his agent thereunto lawfully authorised in writing, or by will, or by operation of law;

(b) a declaration of trust respecting any land or any interest therein must be manifested and proved by some writing signed by some person who is able to declare such trust or by his will;

(c) a disposition of an equitable interest or trust subsisting at the time of the disposition, must be in writing signed by the person disposing of the same, or by his agent thereunto lawfully authorised in writing or by will.

(2) This section does not affect the creation or operation of resulting, implied or constructive trusts.

CHAPTER THIRTY

THE REMEDIES OF MORTGAGEES

30.1 Introduction

Radcliffe, G. R. Y. and Cross, G., The English Legal System, 3rd edn, London: Butterworth & Co., 1954, p. 137

... A mortgage in the seventeenth century took the form of a conveyance of the property intended as security by the borrower to the lender, with a stipulation that if the money lent was repaid with interest on a given day the lender would reconvey the property to the borrower. If the money was not repaid the property would, according to the tenor of the bond, become the lender's. Cases, however, might arise in which it would be inequitable to hold that the property was forfeited for non-payment on the fixed day. For instance, the lender might intentionally evade payment by hiding or some unexpected accident might prevent the borrower from having the money ready. In such cases, since the common law adhered to the letter of the bond, equity gave relief, provided the money with interest and any costs which the lender had incurred were paid within a reasonable time. Gradually it came to be felt that the true object of the conveyance at law was to give the lender security for repayment of his loan and not to give him the chance of making a profit by forfeiting the estate, and that the lender ought not to be able in any case to claim to retain the security if his money was forthcoming from the borrower within a reasonable time of his demanding it. Thus there grew up the doctrine that although the time fixed at law for redemption was passed the borrower still had in equity a right to redeem which could only be extinguished by the lender's applying to the Chancery to destroy it. The Chancery would then calculate what was due, give the borrower six months to pay, and on his default declare the estate forfeited in equity as well as law to the lender.

The right to redeem a mortgaged estate by application to the Chancery was known as an 'equity of redemption' and was viewed by the seventeenth-century Chancellors as an equitable estate in the property remaining in the borrower. This estate could be dealt with by its owner with the same freedom with which a beneficiary could deal with an equitable interest in land held on trust for him by a trustee. Since a very large proportion of the land in the country was either held by trustees or incumbered with mortgages a great amount of the litigation regarding real property found its way into the Court of Chancery. This foothold which the Chancery gained in the sphere of the land law in the eighteenth century by reason of its jurisdiction in cases of equitable interests under settlements and over mortgages enabled the court in the nineteenth century, after the Court of Chancery Procedure Act 1852, gave it power to decide for itself the true construction of legal as opposed to equitable limitations of land without having to submit these questions to the common law courts, gradually to draw nearly the whole land law into its orbit. Thus to-day the branch of the law which was once the special province of the common lawyers in the Temple is now the recognised sphere of the equity lawyer in Lincoln's Inn. . . .

30.2   Foreclosure

30.2.1   FORECLOSURE AND DWELLING HOUSES

(See s. 8(3) of the Administration of Justice Act 1973 at **30.4.1.2.**)

30.3   The Mortgagee's Statutory Power of Sale

LAW OF PROPERTY ACT 1925

101.   Powers incident to estate or interest of mortgage

(1)   A mortgagee, where the mortgage is made by deed, shall, by virtue of this Act, have the following powers, to the like extent as if they had been in terms conferred by the mortgage deed, but not further (namely):—

(i)   A power, when the mortgage money has become due, to sell, or to concur with any other person in selling, the mortgaged property, or any part thereof, either subject to prior charges or not, and either together or in lots, by public auction or by private contract, subject to such conditions respecting title, or evidence of title, or other matter, as the mortgagee thinks fit, with power to vary any contract for sale, and to buy in at an auction, or to rescind any contract for sale, and to re-sell, without being answerable for any loss occasioned thereby; and

(ii)   A power, at any time after the date of the mortgage deed, to insure and keep insured against loss or damage by fire any building, or any effects or property of an insurable nature, whether affixed to the freehold or not, being or forming part of the property which or an estate or interest wherein is mortgaged, and the premiums paid for any such insurance shall be a charge on the mortgaged property or estate or interest, in addition to the mortgage money, and with the same priority, and with interest at the same rate, as the mortgage money; and

(iii)   A power, when the mortgage money has become due, to appoint a receiver of the income of the mortgaged property, or any part thereof; or, if the mortgaged property consists of an interest in income, or of a rentcharge or an annual or other periodical sum, a receiver of that property or any part thereof; and

(iv)   A power, while the mortgagee is in possession, to cut and sell timber and other trees ripe for cutting, and not planted or left standing for shelter or ornament, or to contract for any such cutting and sale, to be completed within any time not exceeding twelve months from the making of the contract.

(2)   Where the mortgage deed is executed after the thirty-first day of December, nineteen hundred and eleven, the power of sale aforesaid includes the following powers as incident thereto (namely):—

(i)   A power to impose or reserve or make binding, as far as the law permits, by covenant, condition, or otherwise, on the unsold part of the mortgaged property or any part thereof, or on the purchaser and any property sold, any restriction or reservation with respect to building on or other user of land, or with respect to mines and minerals, or for the purpose of the more beneficial working thereof, or with respect to any other thing:

(ii)   A power to sell the mortgaged property, or any part thereof, or all or any mines and minerals apart from the surface:—

(a)   With or without a grant or reservation of rights of way, rights of water, easements, rights, and privileges for or connected with building or other purposes in relation to the property remaining in mortgage or any part thereof, or to any property sold: and

(b)   With or without an exception or reservation of all or any of the mines and minerals in or under the mortgaged property, and with or without a grant or reservation of powers of working, wayleaves, or rights of way, rights of water and drainage and other powers, easements, rights, and privileges for or connected with mining purposes in relation to the property remaining unsold or any part thereof, or to any property sold: and

(c) With or without covenants by the purchaser to expend money on the land sold.

(3) The provisions of this Act relating to the foregoing powers, comprised either in this section, or in any other section regulating the exercise of those powers, may be varied or extended by the mortgage deed, and, as so varied or extended, shall, as far as may be, operate in the like manner and with all the like incidents, effects, and consequences, as if such variations or extensions were contained in this Act.

(4) This section applies only if and as far as a contrary intention is not expressed in the mortgage deed, and has effect subject to the terms of the mortgage deed and to the provisions therein contained. . . .

102. Provision as to mortgages of undivided shares in land

(1) A person who was before the commencement of this Act a mortgagee of an undivided share in land shall have the same power to sell his share in the proceeds of sale of the land and in the rents and profits thereof until sale, as, independently of this Act, he would have had in regard to the share in the land; and shall also have a right to require the trustees for sale in whom the land is vested to account to him for the income attributable to that share or to appoint a receiver to receive the same from such trustees corresponding to the right which, independently of this Act, he would have had to take possession or to appoint a receiver of the rents and profits attributable to the same share.

(2) The powers conferred by this section are exercisable by the persons deriving title under such mortgagee.

103. Regulation of exercise of power of sale

A mortgagee shall not exercise the power of sale conferred by this Act unless and until—

(i) Notice requiring payment of the mortgage money has been served on the mortgagor or one of two or more mortgagors, and default has been made in payment of the mortgage money, or of part thereof, for three months after such service; or

(ii) Some interest under the mortgage is in arrear and unpaid for two months after becoming due; or

(iii) There has been a breach of some provision contained in the mortgage deed or in this Act, or in an enactment replaced by this Act, and on the part of the mortgagor, or of some person concurring in making the mortgage, to be observed or performed, other than and besides a covenant for payment of the mortgage money or interest thereon.

30.3.1 MORTGAGEE'S DUTIES ON SELLING THE PROPERTY

CUCKMERE BRICK CO. LTD v MUTUAL FINANCE LTD [1971] 2 All ER 633,
Court of Appeal

FACTS: A property company owned a sizeable vacant site on the edge of Maidstone. The company had planning permission to develop the site for houses or flats. The mortgagees exercised their power of sale. They sold by auction. The adverts for the auction mentioned that there was planning permission for houses, but not the permission for flats. Because of this omission the site did not fetch as high a price as it should have.
HELD: The mortgagee had to account for the difference in price between what should have been obtained and what was actually obtained.

SALMON LJ: . . . It is well settled that a mortgagee is not a trustee of the power of sale for the mortgagor. Once the power has accrued, the mortgagee is entitled to exercise it for his own purposes whenever he chooses to do so. It matters not that the moment may be unpropitious and that by waiting a higher price could be obtained. He has the right to realise his security by turning it into money when he likes. Nor, in my view, is there anything to prevent a mortgagee from accepting the best bid he can get at an auction, even though the auction is badly attended and the bidding exceptionally low. Providing none of those adverse factors is due to any fault of the mortgagee, he can do as he likes. If the mortgagee's interests, as he sees them, conflict with those of the mortgagor, the mortgagee can give preference to his own interests, which of course he could not do were he a trustee of the power of sale for the mortgagor.

Counsel for the defendants contends that the mortgagee's sole obligation to the mortgagor in relation to a sale is to act in good faith; there is no duty of care, and accordingly no question of negligence by the mortgagee in the conduct of the sale can arise. If this contention is correct it follows that, even on the facts found by the learned judge, the defendants should have succeeded. It is impossible to pretend that the state of the authorities on this branch of the law is entirely satisfactory. There are some dicta which suggest that unless a mortgagee acts in bad faith he is safe. His only obligation to the mortgagor is not to cheat him. There are other *dicta* which suggest that, in addition to the duty of acting in good faith, the mortgagee is under a duty to take reasonable care to obtain whatever is the true market value of the mortgaged property at the moment he chooses to sell it: compare, for example, *Kennedy v de Trafford* [1896] 1 Ch 762 with *Tomlin v Luce* (1889) 43 ChD 191. The proposition that the mortgagee owes both duties, in my judgment, represents the true view of the law. Approaching the matter first of all on principle, it is to be observed that if the sale yields a surplus over the amount owed under the mortgage, the mortgagee holds this surplus in trust for the mortgagor. If the sale shows a deficiency, the mortgagor has to make it good out of his own pocket. The mortgagor is vitally affected by the result of the sale but its preparation and conduct is left entirely in the hands of the mortgagee. The proximity between them could scarcely be closer. Surely they are 'neighbours'. Given that the power of sale is for the benefit of the mortgagee and that he is entitled to choose the moment to sell which suits him, it would be strange indeed if he were under no legal obligation to take reasonable care to obtain what I call the true market value at the date of the sale. Some of the textbooks refer to the 'proper price', others to the 'best price'. Vaisey J in *Reliance Permanent Building Society v Harwood-Stamper* [1944] 2 All ER 75, seems to have attached great importance to the difference between these two descriptions of 'price'. My difficulty is that I cannot see any real difference between them. 'Proper price' is perhaps a little nebulous, and 'the best price' may suggest an exceptionally high price. That is why I prefer to call it 'the true market value'.

. . . I accordingly conclude, both on principle and authority, that a mortgagee in exercising his power of sale does owe a duty to take reasonable precaution to obtain the true market value of the mortgaged property at the date on which he decides to sell it. No doubt in deciding whether he has fallen short of that duty, the facts must be looked at broadly and he will not be adjudged to be in default unless he is plainly on the wrong side of the line.

CHINA AND SOUTH SEA BANK LTD v *TAN* [1989] 3 All ER 839, Privy Council

FACTS: A surety had guaranteed the repayment of a loan which the plaintiff bank had made to a company. The company defaulted on the loan at a time when the shares in the company were adequate security for the loan. However, the bank did not enforce its security (by selling the shares) until the shares were virtually worthless. The bank sought repayment of the loan under the guarantee given by the surety. The surety, in his defence, argued that the bank owed him a duty to have sold the shares at the time when the proceeds would have been sufficient to pay off the loan.
HELD: The surety was obliged to pay-off the company's debt to the bank.

LORD TEMPLEMAN: . . . If the creditor does nothing and the debtor declines into bankruptcy the mortgaged securities become valueless and if the surety decamps abroad the creditor loses his money. If disaster strikes the debtor and the mortgaged securities but the surety remains capable of repaying the debt then the creditor loses nothing. The surety contracts to pay if the debtor does not pay and the surety is bound by his contract. If the surety, perhaps less indolent or less well protected than the creditor, is worried that the mortgaged securities may decline in value then the surety may request the creditor to sell and if the creditor remains idle then the surety may bustle about, pay off the debt, take over the benefit of the securities and sell them. No creditor could carry on the business of lending if he could become liable to a mortgagee and to a surety or to either of them for a decline in value of mortgaged property, unless the creditor remas personally responsible for the decline. Applying the rule as specified by Pollock CB in *Watts v Shuttleworth* (1860) 5 H & N 235 at 247–248, 157 ER 1171 at 1176, it appears to their Lordships that in the present case the creditor did no act injurious to the surety, did no act inconsistent with the rights of the surety and the creditor did not omit any act which his duty enjoined him to do. The creditor was not under a duty to exercise his power of sale over the mortgaged securities at any particular time or at all. . . .

PARKER-TWEEDALE v *DUNBAR BANK PLC AND OTHERS (No. 1)* [1990] 2 All ER 577, Court of Appeal

FACTS: A matrimonial home was held by the wife on trust for sale for herself and her husband. Having defaulted in repaying a loan to the defendant bank, which it had secured by way of mortgage on the matrimonial home, the bank took possession and sold the house. The house was sold to a development company for £575,000 and one week later it was sold on to another company for £700,000. The husband brought this present action against the bank, claiming that the bank had owed him a duty of care to obtain a proper price upon sale of the property.

HELD: The duty of care owed by the bank to the mortgagor (the wife) did not extend to the husband, whose only interest in the house was a beneficial interest under a trust for sale.

NOURSE LJ: . . . It was settled by the decision of this court in *Cuckmere Brick Co. Ltd* v *Mutual Finance Ltd* [1972] 2 All ER 633, [1971] Ch 949 that a mortgagee, although he may exercise his power of sale at any time of his own choice, owes the mortgagor a duty to take reasonable care to obtain a proper price for the mortgaged property at that time. But there is no support, either in the authorities or on principle, for the proposition that where the mortgagor is a trustee, even a bare trustee, of the mortgaged property a like duty is owed to a beneficiary under the trust of whose interest the mortgagee has notice.

In seeking to support that proposition the plaintiff relied on the decision of this court in *Jarrett* v *Barclays Bank Ltd* [1946] 2 All ER 266, [1947] Ch 187. For reasons which were stated by Peter Gibson J and need not be repeated here, that case does not assist him. He also relied on the following passage in the judgment of Salmon LJ in *Cuckmere Brick Co. Ltd* v *Mutual Finance Ltd* [1971] 2 All ER 633 at 643–644, [1971] Ch 949 at 966:

> Approaching the matter first of all on principle, it is to be observed that if the sale yields a surplus over the amount owed under the mortgage, the mortgagee holds this surplus in trust for the mortgagor. If the sale shows a deficiency, the mortgagor has to make it good out of his own pocket. The mortgagor is vitally affected by the result of the sale but its preparation and conduct is left entirely in the hands of the mortgagee. The proximity between them could scarcely be closer. Surely they are 'neighbours'. Given that the power of sale is for the benefit of the mortgagee and that he is entitled to choose the moment to sell which suits him, it would be strange indeed if he were under no legal obligation to take reasonable care to obtain what I call the true market value at the date of the sale.

This reference to 'neighbours' has enabled the plaintiff to argue that the duty is owed to all those who are within the neighbourhood principle, i.e. to adapt the words of Lord Atkin in *Donoghue (or M'Alister)* v *Stevenson* [1932] AC 562 at 580–581, [1932] All ER Rep 1 at 11–12, to all persons who are so closely and directly affected by the sale that the mortgagee ought reasonably to have them in contemplation as being so affected when he is directing his mind to the sale. Further support for the application of the neighbourhood principle in this context can be gained from the judgment of Lord Denning MR in *Standard Chartered Bank Ltd* v *Walker* [1982] 3 All ER 938 at 942, [1982] 1 WLR 1410 at 1415, where it was held that the duty to take reasonable care to obtain a proper price was owed to a surety for the mortgage debt as well as to the mortgagor himself.

In my respectful opinion it is both unnecessary and confusing for the duties owed by a mortgagee to the mortgagor and the surety, if there is one, to be expressed in terms of the tort of negligence. The authorities which were considered in the careful judgments of this court in *Cuckmere Brick Co. Ltd* v *Mutual Finance Ltd* demonstrate that the duty owed by the mortgagee to the mortgagor was recognised by equity as arising out of the particular relationship between them. Thus Salmon LJ himself said ([1971] 2 All ER 633 at 644, [1971] Ch 949 at 967):

It would seem, therefore, that many years before the modern development of the law of negligence, the courts of equity had laid down a doctrine in relation to mortgages which is entirely consonant with the general principles later evolved by the common law.

The duty owed to the surety arises in the same way. In *China and South Sea Bank Ltd* v *Tan* [1989] 3 All ER 839 at 841, [1990] 2 WLR 56 at 58 Lord Templeman, in delivering the judgment of the Privy Council, having pointed out that the surety in that case admitted that the moneys secured by the guarantee were due, continued:

> But the surety claims that the creditor owed the surety a duty to exercise the power of sale conferred by the mortgage and in that case the liability of the surety under the guarantee would either have been eliminated or very much reduced. The Court of Appeal [in Hong Kong] sought to find such a duty in the tort of negligence but the tort of negligence has not yet submitted all torts and does not supplant the principles of equity or contradict contractual promises . . . Equity intervenes to protect a surety.

Once it is recognised that the duty owed by the mortgagee to the mortgagor arises out of the particular relationship between them, it is readily apparent that there is no warrant for extending its scope so as to include a beneficiary or beneficiaries under a trust of which the mortgagor is the trustee. The correctness of that view was fully established in the clear and compelling argument of counsel for Dunbar, who drew particular attention to the rights and duties of the trustee to protect the trust property against dissipation or depreciation in value and the impracticabilities and potential rights of double recovery inherent in giving the beneficiary an additional right to sue the mortgagee, a right which is in any event unnecessary.

The only exception for which counsel for Dunbar allowed was the special case where the trustee has unreasonably refused to sue on behalf of the trust or has committed some other breach of its duties to the beneficiaries, e.g. by consenting to an improvident sale, which disables or disqualifies him from acting on behalf of the trust. In such a case the beneficiary is permitted to sue on behalf of the trust. This exception is established by a series of authorities, some of which were recently considered by the Privy Council in *Hayim* v *Citibank NA* [1987] AC 730. In delivering the judgment of their Lordships, Lord Templeman said (at 748):

> These authorities demonstrate that a beneficiary has no cause of action against a third party save in special circumstances which embrace a failure, excusable or inexcusable, by the trustees in the performance of the duty owed by the trustees to the beneficiary to protect the trust estate or to protect the interests of the beneficiary in the trust estate.

It is important to emphasise that when a beneficiary sues under the exception he does so in right of the trust and in the room of the trustee. . . .

30.4   Mortgagees Taking Possession

ASHLEY GUARANTEE PLC v *ZACARIA AND ANOTHER* [1993] 1 All ER 254, Court of Appeal

FACTS: The plaintiff mortgagee lent money to a company which was secured by mortgage on the defendant's family home. The company defaulted in re-payment of the loan and the plaintiff brought an action to recover the sum of £151,000, or in default possession of the family home. The defendants contended that the company had counter-claims for unliquidated damages against the plaintiff, which if successful would yield funds sufficient to re-pay the loan. Accordingly, the defendants resisted the plaintiff's action for possession. HELD: The mortgagee was entitled to enter into possession at any time, subject only to the usual limitations on the re-possession of residential property. The existence of counter-claims was no ground for postponing possession and sale of the family home. The fact that the defendants were guarantors of the loan and not the principal debtors was no ground for allowing them to resist the order for possession.

NOURSE LJ: . . . Contract and statute apart, a legal mortgagee's right to possession of the mortgaged property cannot be defeated by a cross-claim on the part of the mortgagor, even if it is both liquidated and admitted and even if it exceeds the amount of the mortgage arrears.

. . . In my judgment that question must be answered in the negative. I can see no distinction in principle between a case where the mortgagor is the principal debtor of the mortgagee and one where he is only a guarantor. In each case the mortgagee has, as an incident of his estate in the land, a right to possession of the mortgaged property. In each case the cross-claims cannot be unilaterally appropriated in discharge of the mortgage debt. The fact that in the latter case the mortgagor is not primarily liable for payment of the debt is immaterial. When he comes to be made liable his position vis-à-vis the appropriation of the cross-claims is at best no different from, and certainly cannot be better than, that of a mortgagor who is the primary debtor. . . .

30.4.1   MORTGAGEE TAKING POSSESSION OF A DWELLING-HOUSE

30.4.1.1   The 1970 'Reform'

ADMINISTRATION OF JUSTICE ACT 1970

36.   Additional powers of court in action by mortgagee for possession of dwelling-house

(1)   Where the mortgagee under a mortgage of land which consists of or includes a dwelling-house brings an action in which he claims possession of the mortgaged property, not being an action for foreclosure in which a claim for possession of the mortgaged property is also made, the court may exercise any of the powers conferred on it by subsection (2) below if it appears to the court that in the event of its exercising the power the mortgagor is likely to be able within a reasonable period to pay any sums due under the mortgage or to remedy a default consisting of a breach of any other obligation arising under or by virtue of the mortgage.

(2)   The court—
   (a)   may adjourn the proceedings, or
   (b)   on giving judgment, or making an order, for delivery of possession of the mortgaged property, or at any time before the execution of such judgment or order, may—
      (i)   stay or suspend execution of the judgment or order, or
      (ii)   postpone the date for delivery of possession,
for such period or periods as the court thinks reasonable.

(3)   Any such adjournment, stay, suspension or postponement as is referred to in subsection (2) above may be made subject to such conditions with regard to payment by the mortgagor of any sum secured by the mortgage or the remedying of any default as the court thinks fit.

(4)   The court may from time to time vary or revoke any condition imposed by virtue of this section. . . .

30.4.1.2   A further 'reform' in 1973

ADMINISTRATION OF JUSTICE ACT 1973

8.   Extension of powers of court in action by mortgagee of dwelling-house

(1)   Where by a mortgage of land which consists of or includes a dwelling-house, or by any agreement between the mortgagee under such a mortgage and the mortgagor, the mortgagor is entitled or is to be permitted to pay the principal sum secured by instalments or otherwise to defer payment of it in whole or in part, but provision is also made for earlier payment in the event of any default by the mortgagor or of a demand by the mortgagee or otherwise, then for purposes of section 36 of the Administration of Justice Act 1970 (under which a court has power to delay giving a mortgagee possession of the mortgaged property so as to allow the mortgagor a reasonable time to pay any sums due under the mortgage) a court may treat as due under the mortgage on account of the principal sum

secured and of interest on it only such amounts as the mortgagor would have expected to be required to pay if there had been no such provision for earlier payment.

(2)   A court shall not exercise by virtue of subsection (1) above the powers conferred by section 36 of the Administration of Justice Act 1970 unless it appears to the court not only that the mortgagor is likely to be able within a reasonable period to pay any amounts regarded (in accordance with subsection (1) above) as due on account of the principal sum secured, together with the interest on those amounts, but also that he is likely to be able by the end of that period to pay any further amounts that he would have expected to be required to pay by then on account of that sum and of interest on it if there had been no such provision as is referred to in subsection (1) above for earlier payment.

(3)   Where subsection (1) above would apply to an action in which a mortgagee only claimed possession of the mortgaged property, and the mortgagee brings an action for foreclosure (with or without also claiming possession of the property), then section 36 of the Administration of Justice Act 1970 together with subsections (1) and (2) above shall apply as they would apply if it were an action in which the mortgagee only claimed possession of the mortgaged property, except that—

(a)   section 36(2)(b) shall apply only in relation to any claim for possession; and

(b)   section 36(5) shall not apply. . . .

CHELTENHAM AND GLOUCESTER BUILDING SOCIETY v NORGAN, *The Times,* 8 December 1995, Court of Appeal

FACTS: Mrs Norgan had lived with her husband and five sons in a period farmhouse in Wiltshire with eight acres of land, total value £225,000. They had borrowed £90,000 from the building society in 1986, on an instalment mortgage. The Cheltenham society was a member of the Council of Mortgage Lenders whose statement of current practice provided means of helping some borrowers in difficulty. Those included lengthening the term of a repayment loan, deferring interest payments for a period and capitalising interest.

HELD: The logic and spirit of the legislation required, especially where the lender was acting within the statement of current practice, that the court should take as its starting point the full term of the mortgage and pose at the outset the question: would it be possible for the borrower to maintain payment-off of the arrears by instalments over that period?

WAITE LJ: . . . at common law the court had only a very limited jurisdiction to grant relief to a borrower in default under a mortgage. It could only adjourn the application for a short time to give the borrower the chance to pay up in full: *Birmingham Citizens Permanent Building Society* v *Caunt* [1962] Ch 883, 912.

The Administration of Justice Acts of 1970 and 1973 had mitigated the rigour of that position allowing the court at its discretion to treat the sum due under the mortgage as being only the arrears of instalments or interest and allow a reasonable period for the borrower to pay off the arrears if it appeared he was likely to be able to do so.

The question was what exactly constituted a 'reasonable period' for bringing payments up to date. . . . It seemed to his Lordship that the logic and spirit of the legislation required, especially in cases where the parties were proceeding the type of arrangement provided in the statement of current practice, that the court should take as its starting point the full term of the mortgage and pose at the outset the question: would it be possible for the borrower to maintain payment-off of the arrears by instalments over that period?

That approach would be liable to demand a more detailed analysis of present figures and future projections than had hitherto been customary. Borrowers might need to provide a detailed budget.

The court would also have to resolve disputes over how much of the outstanding debt should be attributed to interest and how much to principal. And expert evidence might be needed to determine if and when the lenders security might be put at risk as a result of imposing postponement of payments in arrear. But such problems should not be allowed to stand in the way of giving effect to the clearly intended scheme of the legislation.

Another factor strongly favouring the adoption of the full term of the mortgage as the starting point for calculating the 'reasonable period' was the cost of multiple applications under section 36 of the 1970 Act.

One advantage of taking the period most favourable to the borrower at the outset was that if his or her hopes of repayment proved to be ill-founded and the new instalments initially ordered as a condition of suspension were not maintained but themselves fell into arrear, the lender could be heard with justice to say that the borrower had had his chance and that the section 36 powers should not be used repeatedly to compel a lending institution to accept assurances of future payment from a borrower in whom it had lost confidence. . . .

EVANS LJ: . . . The statement issued by the Council of Mortgage Lenders said that members sought to take possession only as a last resort.

Given its stated policy, his Lordship did not see how the building society could properly say that it was not appropriate to take account of the whole of the remaining part of the original term when assessing a reasonable period for the payment of arrears.

Considerations which were likely to be relevant in establishing a reasonable period were:

(a) How much could the borrower reasonably afford to pay, both now and in the future?

(b) If the borrower had a temporary difficulty in meeting his obligations, how long was the difficulty likely to last?

(c) What was the reason for the arrears which had accumulated?

(d) How much remained of the original term?

(e) What were the relevant contractual terms and what type of mortgage was it, that is, when was the principal due to be repaid?

(f) Was it a case where the court should exercise its power to disregard accelerated payment provisions (section 8 of the 1973 Act)?

(g) Was it reasonable to expect the lender, in the circumstances of the particular case, to recoup the arrears of interest (i) over the whole of the original term, or (ii) within a shorter period, or even (iii) within a longer period, that is, by extending the repayment period? Was it reasonable to expect the lender to capitalise the interest or not?

(h) Were there any reasons affecting the security which should influence the length of the period for payment?

In the light of the answers to those questions, the court could proceed to exercise its overall discretion, taking account also of any further factors which might arise in the particular case. . . .

30.4.2 DUTY OF MORTGAGEE IN POSSESSION TO ACCOUNT STRICTLY

WHITE v CITY OF LONDON BREWERY COMPANY (1889) 42 ChD 237, Court of Appeal

FACTS: A pub, originally a 'free house', was mortgaged to a brewery, the mortgage (surprisingly) not containing a tie clause. The brewery took possession and leased the pub as a 'tied house'. The fact that the pub was tied to one brewery meant, in those days, that the pub attracted a lower rent than it would have, had it been a 'free house'.
HELD: In determining the amount owed by White to the brewery, under the mortgage, the brewery had to account on the basis of the higher rent which a 'free house' would have commanded.

COTTON LJ: . . . A mortgagee in possession must account for the rents which, but for his wilful default, he would have received. The plaintiff says that if he fails as to the brewers' profits yet he ought to have a larger sum in respect of the rents which the mortgagees would, but for their wilful default, have received. I think the learned Judge was a little indulgent to the plaintiff, but in these days if there is a question to be decided on the evidence before the Court, we are not inclined to restrict the suitor very closely to the pleadings. The learned Judge has allowed an addition of £20 a year from 19 August, 1874, down to the date of the sale, in addition to the rent obtained by the mortgagees. Before 1873, there had been a period during which the brewers were in occupation by their servant, then a period during which they let nominally at £30, but really at £15 a year, since half the £30 was paid by the tenant for the furniture and fixtures which belonged to the brewers; and then a period of letting at £60 a year. I was rather struck at first at there being no occupation rent charged against the brewers while they were in possession by their servant; it does not appear to have been asked for, but if it had been, is any case made for giving it? I think the evidence is the other way. At the time the brewers took possession, the trade in the neighbourhood was in a bad state. We know that when trade is in a bad state workmen have not money to spend in beer, so the custom would fall off, and when a public-house has got into a low state there is a difficulty in re-establishing its business. This house at the time when the brewers took possession could not be let, because nobody could carry it on without a loss, as the brewers found by experience. As soon after as they could let it at all, they let it to Moulton, who found a rent of £40 too high, and was allowed to remain at a rent of £30. On the evidence before us, there is nothing which satisfies my mind that they could by any possibility have obtained a larger rent than that, during the tenancy of Mr. Moulton. Then I think the learned Judge was right in saying, when there was a change in the tenancy, that there was no ground for charging the brewers with more than the £60 rent which they received from Hake during the first year of his occupation; but after that time, when he had established himself, the learned Judge thought that something more ought to be allowed. The evidence on that question is of a somewhat doubtful character, but I think the Plaintiff has not established that more should be given him than what the learned Judge has allowed, viz. £20 a year, which comes altogether, as the Master of the Rolls has said, to £100. . . .

30.5   Power to Appoint a Receiver

DOWNSVIEW NOMINEES LTD AND ANOTHER v FIRST CITY CORP LTD AND ANOTHER [1993] 3 All ER 626, Privy Council

FACTS: A mortgagor brought this action against a mortgagee and a receiver appointed by it, claiming that the receiver had acted fraudulently, recklessly and in breach of his duties. HELD: A mortgagee must exercise its power to appoint receivers in good faith and for the sole purpose of enforcing its security, however the mortgagee owes the mortgagor no duty to be careful in selecting the receiver appointed.

LORD TEMPLEMAN: . . . Several centuries ago equity evolved principles for the enforcement of mortgages and the protection of borrowers. The most basic principles were, first, that a mortgage is security for the repayment of a debt and, secondly, that a security for repayment of a debt is only a mortgage. From these principles flowed two rules, first, that powers conferred on a mortgagee must be exercised in good faith for the purpose of obtaining repayment and secondly that, subject to the first rule, powers conferred on a mortgagee may be exercised although the consequences may be disadvantageous to the borrower. These principles and rules apply also to a receiver and manager appointed by the mortgagee.

It does not follow that a receiver and manager must immediately upon appointment seize all the cash in the coffers of the company and sell all the company's assets or so much of the assets as he chooses and considers sufficient to complete the redemption of the mortgage. He is entitled, but not bound, to allow the company's business to be continued by himself or by the existing or other executives. The decisions of the receiver and manager whether to continue the business or close down the business and sell assets chosen by him cannot be impeached if those decisions are taken in good faith while protecting the interests of the debenture holder in recovering the moneys due under the debenture, even though the decisions of the receiver and manager may be disadvantageous for the company.

The nature of the duties owed by a receiver and manager appointed by a debenture holder were authoritatively defined by Jenkins LJ in a characteristically learned and comprehensive judgment in Re B Johnson & Co. (Builders) Ltd [1955] 2 All ER 775 at 790–791, [1955] Ch 634 at 661–663:

. . . the phrase 'manager of the company', *prima facie*, according to the ordinary meaning of the words, connotes a person holding, whether *de jure* or *de facto*, a post in or with the company of a nature charging him with the duty of managing the affairs of the company for the company's benefit; whereas a receiver and manager for debenture-holders is a person appointed by the debenture-holders to whom the company has given powers of management pursuant to the contract of loan constituted by the debenture and as a condition of obtaining the loan, to enable him to preserve and realise the assets comprised in the security for the benefit of the debenture-holders. The company gets the loan on terms that the lenders shall be entitled, for the purpose of making their security effective, to appoint a receiver with powers of sale and of management pending sale, and with full discretion as to the exercise and mode of exercising those powers. The primary duty of the receiver is to the debenture-holders and not to the company. He is receiver and manager of the property of the company for the debenture-holders, not manager of the company. The company is entitled to any surplus of assets remaining after the debenture debt has been discharged, and is entitled to proper accounts. The whole purpose of the receiver and manager's appointment would obviously be stultified if the company could claim that a receiver and manager owes it any duty comparable to the duty owed to a company by its own directors or managers. In determining whether a receiver and manager for the debenture-holders of a company has broken any duty owed by him to the company, regard must be had to the fact that he is a receiver and manager—i.e., a receiver, with ancillary powers of management—for the debenture-holders, and not simply a person appointed to manage the company's affairs for the benefit of the company . . . The duties of a receiver and manager for debenture-holders are widely different from those of a manager of the company. He is under no obligation to carry on the company's business at the expense of the debenture-holders. Therefore he commits no breach of duty to the company by refusing to do so, even though his discontinuance of the business may be detrimental from the company's point of view. Again, his power of sale is, in effect, that of a mortgagee, and he therefore commits no breach of duty to the company by a *bona fide* sale, even though he might have obtained a higher price and even though, from the point of view of the company, as distinct from the debenture-holders, the terms might be regarded as disadvantageous. In a word, in the absence of fraud or mala fides . . . the company cannot complain of any act or omission of the receiver and manager, provided that he does nothing that he is not empowered to do, and omits nothing that he is enjoined to do by the terms of his appointment. If the company conceives that it has any claim against the receiver and manager for breach of some duty owed by him to the company, the issue is not whether the receiver and manager has done or omitted to do anything which it would be wrongful in a manager of a company to do or omit, but whether he has exceeded or abused or wrongfully omitted to use the special powers and discretions vested in him pursuant to the contract of loan constituted by the debenture for the special purpose of enabling the assets comprised in the debenture-holders' security to be preserved and realised.

The duties owed by a receiver and manager do not compel him to adopt any particular course of action, by selling the whole or part of the mortgaged property or by carrying on the business of the company or by exercising any other powers and discretions vested in him. But since a mortgage is only security for a debt, a receiver and manager commits a breach of his duty if he abuses his powers by exercising them otherwise than 'for the special purpose of enabling the assets comprised in the debenture holders' security to be preserved and realised' for the benefit of the debenture holder. . . .

. . . The general duty of care said to be owed by a mortgagee to subsequent incumbrancers and the mortgagor in negligence is inconsistent with the right of the mortgagee and the duties which the courts applying equitable principles have imposed on the mortgagee. If a mortgagee enters into possession he is liable to account for rent on the basis of wilful default; he must keep mortgage premises in repair; he is liable for waste. Those duties were imposed to ensure that a mortgagee is diligent in discharging his mortgage and returning the property to the mortgagor. If a mortgagee exercises his power of sale in good faith for the purpose of protecting his security, he is not liable to the mortgagor even though he might have obtained a higher price and even though the terms might be regarded as disadvantageous to the mortgagor. *Cuckmere Brick Co. Ltd v Mutual Finance Ltd* [1971] 2 All ER 633, [1971] Ch 949 is Court of Appeal authority for the proposition that, if the mortgagee decides to sell, he must take reasonable care to obtain a proper price but is no authority for any wider proposition. A receiver exercising his power of sale also owes the same specific duties as the mortgagee. But that apart, the general duty of a receiver and manager appointed by a debenture holder, as defined by Jenkins LJ in *Re B Johnson & Co. (Builders) Ltd* [1955] 2 All ER 775 at 790–791, [1955] Ch 634 at 661–663, leaves no room for the imposition of a general duty to use reasonable care in dealing with the assets of the company. The duties imposed by equity on a mortgagee and on a receiver and manager would be quite unnecessary if there existed a general duty in negligence to take reasonable care in the exercise of powers and to take reasonable care in dealing with the assets of the mortgagor company....

Similar considerations apply to Downsview. A mortgagee owes a general duty to subsequent incumbrancers and to the mortgagor to use his powers for the sole purpose of securing repayment of the moneys owing under his mortgage and a duty to act in good faith. He also owes the specific duties which equity has imposed on him in the exercise of his powers to go into possession and his powers of sale. It may well be that a mortgagee who appoints a receiver and manager, knowing that the receiver and manager intends to exercise his powers for the purpose of frustrating the activities of the second mortgagee or for some other improper purpose or who fails to revoke the appointment of a receiver and manager when the mortgagee knows that the receiver and manager is abusing his powers, may himself be guilty of bad faith but in the present case this possibility need not be explored.

The liability of Mr Russell in the present case is firmly based not on negligence but on the breach of duty....

30.6 A Lifeline to Mortgagors with Negative Equity

PALK AND ANOTHER v MORTGAGE SERVICES FUNDING PLC [1993] 2 All ER 481,
Court of Appeal

FACTS: The Palks owned a house encumbered with a debt amounting to £358,000. They had found a prospective purchaser willing to pay just £283,000, and they wanted to sell the property and make up the difference out of their personal resources. The mortgagee refused to agree to this, and took proceedings for possession. It was the mortgagee's intention not to sell the house until 'the market improved', and in the meantime to let the house to a tenant. It was clear that the rent obtainable would be substantially less than the interest continuing to accrue. Thus the amount owed by the Palks would steadily increase, as would the amount of the 'negative equity'. The Palks therefore applied for an order of sale under section 91(2) of the Law of Property Act 1925, a provision granting the court a discretion to order a sale of mortgaged property.

HELD: The order for sale was granted. The mortgagee must not exercise its various powers in a manner wholly unfair to the mortgagor.

SIR DONALD NICHOLLS V-C: Anthony Palk is a victim of the recession.

In January 1990 he obtained an advance of £300,000 from Mortgage Services Funding plc (Mortgage Services). The loan was secured by a mortgage over the house owned by him and his wife Margaret: The Thatch, Warren Lane, Cross-in-Hand, Heathfield, East Sussex....

Mr. Palk is now bankrupt. His wife has appealed against the judge's decision. The amount, including interest, now owing under the mortgage is approximately £409,000.

The statute

The jurisdiction being invoked by Mrs. Palk is statutory. Section 91(2) of the Law of Property Act 1925 provides:

In any action, whether for foreclosure, or for redemption, or for sale, or for the raising and payment in any manner of mortgage money, the court, on the request of the mortgagee, or of any person interested either in the mortgage money or in the right of redemption, and, notwithstanding that—(a) any other person dissents; or (b) the mortgagee or any person so interested does not appear in the action; and without allowing any time for redemption or for payment of any mortgage money, may direct a sale of the mortgaged property, on such terms as it thinks fit, including the deposit in court of a reasonable sum fixed by the court to meet the expenses of sale and to secure performance of the terms.

. . . a mortgagee can sit back and do nothing. He is not obliged to take steps to realise his security. But if he does take steps to exercise his rights over his security, common law and equity alike have set bounds to the extent to which he can look after himself and ignore the mortgagor's interests. In the exercise of his rights over his security the mortgagee must act fairly towards the mortgagor. His interest in the property has priority over the interest of the mortgagor, and he is entitled to proceed on that footing. He can protect his own interest, but he is not entitled to conduct himself in a way which unfairly prejudices the mortgagor. If he takes possession he might prefer to do nothing and bide his time, waiting indefinitely for an improvement in the market, with the property empty meanwhile. That he cannot do. He is accountable for his actual receipts from the property. He is also accountable to the mortgagor for what he would have received but for his default. So he must take reasonable care to maximise his return from the property. He must also take reasonable care of the property. Similarly, if he sells the property: he cannot sell hastily at a knock-down price sufficient to pay off his debt. The mortgagor also has an interest in the property and is under a personal liability for the shortfall. The mortgagee must keep that in mind. He must exercise reasonable care to sell only at the proper market value. . . .

I have given two examples where the law imposes a duty on a mortgagee when he is exercising his powers: if he lets the property he must obtain a proper market rent, and if he sells he must obtain a proper price. . . .

However, and this is my second observation on the mortgagee's argument, whether in these circumstances Mortgage Services is in breach of any duty it owes to Mrs. Palk is not a crucial question on this appeal, for this reason: an exercise by the court of its statutory power to direct a sale even against the wishes of Mortgage Services is not dependent on there first having been a breach of duty by the company. The discretion given to the court by s. 91(2) of the 1925 Act is not hedged about with preconditions. The question on this appeal is how ought the court to exercise its discretion under the statute in the particular circumstances and against the background that a mortgagee owes at least some duties in law to a mortgagor when exercising his rights over the mortgaged property. That Mortgage Services is not, or may not be, in breach of any duty it owes Mrs. Palk is only one of the circumstances to be taken into account. . . .

In my view this is a case in which a sale should be directed even though there will be a deficiency. It is just and equitable to order a sale because otherwise unfairness and injustice will follow. I can summarise the four factors which combine to produce this result. First, there is a substantial income shortfall: the rental under the proposed letting would fall significantly short of the interest Mrs. Palk would save if the house were sold. Second, the only prospect of recoupment of the shortfall lies in the hope that there will be a substantial rise in house prices generally. This is not a case where a sale is being postponed for a reason specific to this property: for example, pending the outcome of an application for planning permission for development. Following on from this, third, on the scanty evidence before the court the likelihood of Mrs. Palk suffering increased loss if the company's plan proceeds is so high as to make the plan oppressive to her. Her liability is open-ended and will increase indefinitely. This risk of increased loss to her under her repayment obligation far outweighs the prospect of any gain the company may make from its proposed realisation scheme for the house. The one is unacceptably disproportionate to the other. Fourth, directing a sale will not preclude the mortgagee from having the opportunity to wait and see what happens to house prices. The mortgagee can buy the property. A mortgagee cannot buy property from itself, but here the sale is directed by the court; it is not a sale by a mortgagee in exercise of its own power of sale. . . .

30.7   Reform

The Law Commission (Law Com. No. 204) Transfer of Land—Land Mortgages, London: HMSO, 13 November 1991

7.27   Foreclosure is not . . . an inevitable feature of a mortgage system . . . we recommend that foreclosure be abolished, and that a mortgagee under a formal land mortgage should be entitled to sell to himself in exercise of the statutory power of sale, subject to the following:

(a)   the mortgagee must first obtain leave of the court; and

(b)   the court should not grant leave unless satisfied by the mortgagee that this is the most advantageous method of realising the security, from the point of view of the mortgagor, any guarantors of the mortgagor, and any subsequent encumbrancers.

Standard Terms

5.5   The question of standardising the *content* of mortgages by producing standard terms or conditions raises rather different issues. In this context, statutory mortgage conditions can fulfil three different functions. The first is that, by setting out the *prima facie* rights and duties of the parties, they define the nature of the relationship created by the new mortgage. To the extent that standard terms are fulfilling this function they should be largely overriding (that is, not variable by the parties), to ensure that the essential nature of the transaction is preserved. While the parties would not be able to vary overriding provisions, either in the mortgage document or by any other oral or written agreement at that time or later, it will be seen that they are not all inflexible. For example, the mortgagee's duty to repair the property while in possession would be the equivalent of whatever obligation was imposed on the mortgagor during his period of possession of the property, and the mortgagor's statutory repairing duty would be capable of variation or total exclusion in accordance with the parties' wishes. Again, the freedom which the mortgagor would have to grant leases while he was in possession would be modified by the fact that no lease would bind the mortgagee or a receiver unless the mortgagee had given his written consent to it; the mortgagee would therefore have a complete discretion in deciding whether to be bound by leases created by the mortgagor.

5.6   The second function of standard terms is to provide minimum rights and protection for protected mortgagors. To the extent that standard terms have this mortgagor protection function, they should be overriding in protected mortgages but largely variable in non-protected mortgages. The third function is to produce simple, uniform, and modern formulations of provisions commonly found in all mortgages. The objective in drafting such conditions is to produce a formulation acceptable to most mortgagors and mortgagees in most circumstances, so that the parties would not usually choose to vary the standard conditions (whilst they remain free to do so). Some conditions may of course fulfil more than one of these functions. . . .

Redemption

6.42   Although we recommend below the abolition of the equitable jurisdiction to set aside any provision of a mortgage which constitutes a clog or fetter on the equity of redemption, we do not intend to interfere with the equitable right to redeem. In other words, under a formal or informal land mortgage (as in any other mortgage or charge over any other kind of property) the mortgagor will remain entitled to redeem the property freed from the mortgage by paying and discharging all obligations under it, even after the contractual date for payment and discharge has passed, up until the time when the mortgagor's interest is destroyed by a sale by the mortgagee. In the case of protected mortgages, we consider that further steps should be taken to ensure that redemption and discharge are not discouraged or penalised. In our view this is particularly important because of the lack of control protected mortgagors have over the identity of the mortgagee and over the rate of interest from time to time charged. . . . Nevertheless, mortgagees must inevitably retain a significant degree of discretion in both areas, and ultimately the only recourse of mortgagors dissatisfied with their mortgagees, or with the rate of interest charged, is to redeem the mortgage and borrow elsewhere. Whilst a shortage of mortgage funds may often make the right to redeem illusory in practice, we take the view that, in the case of protected mortgages, no restriction on the right to redeem at any any time ought to be permitted. Although most lenders would prefer to retain the flexibility of being able to impose whatever terms they consider appropriate in relation to redemption, they made no very strong objections to the provisions which we proposed in the Working Paper and recommend here, and which were strongly supported by consumers' organisations. Also, it should be noted that mortgagors whose mortgages secure regulated agreements under the Consumer Credit Act 1974 are already entitled to discharge the mortgage at any time.

6.43   Accordingly we recommend that in the case of protected mortgages:

(a)   any term of the mortgage which postpones the mortgagor's right to redeem should be void, unless the property includes non-residential premises (in which case the postponement of the right to redeem should be dealt with in the same way as in non-protected mortgages, that is subject to challenge under the court's general jurisdiction: see Part VIII below);

(b)   any term of the mortgage which requires the mortgagor to give notice of intention to redeem, or requires payment of interest in lieu of notice, should be void: such provisions, which were once very common in residential mortgage deeds although now not in regular use by institutional lenders, impose a financial penalty on mortgagors who want to repay early;

(c)   mortgagors whose repayments are calculated on the basis of the loan remaining outstanding for a specified period should be entitled to the appropriate rebate on earlier repayment; this should be dealt with by regulations similar to those currently achieving the same objective in relation to mortgages securing a regulated agreement under the Consumer Credit Act 1974.

30.8   End of Chapter Assessment Question

In 1990 Bertha borrowed £40,000 from the Doorway Building Society. The loan is secured by a first legal mortgage of Bertha's freehold house 'Arkwrite Towers'.

In 1992 Bertha borrowed a further £20,000 from Princewest Finance Ltd secured by a second legal mortage on Arkwrite Towers. The interest on this loan is 23%, and Bertha has fallen into arrears with her repayments to Princewest.

(a)   Explain whether it will be possible for Princewest to take possession of and sell Arkwrite Towers, and how such a sale would affect the position of the Doorway Building Society.

(b)   If Princewest sells Arkwrite Towers at less than its open market value, consider whether Bertha would have any remedy against either:

   (i)   Princewest, or

   (ii)   the purchaser from Princewest.

(c)   How must Princewest apply the proceeds of any sale of Arkwrite Towers?

30.9   End of Chapter Assessment Outline Answer

(a)   In order to take possession under the Criminal Law Act 1967, a mortgagee seeking possession in practice always seeks a court possession order. In the case of residential property repossession is always illegal unless it takes place by order of the court. Thus, assuming that 'Arkwrite Towers' is a dwelling house, Princewest will need to apply to court for a possession order under s. 36 of the Administration of Justice Act 1970.

Section 36 gives the court a wide discretion to adjourn possession proceedings, or to make a possession order but suspend its operation. The intention is to give the mortgagor time to find the money to pay off the mortgage. Possession will only be suspended or adjourned if it appears that the mortgagor will be able to repay the loan within a 'reasonable period'. Further protection is given to mortgagors of instalment mortgages by s. 8 of the Administration of Justice Act 1973 (most mortgages of dwelling houses are paid off by instalments). Section 8 authorises the court to suspend or adjourn possession in cases where it appears likely that the mortgagor will, within a reasonable period, be able to pay off instalments that are in arrears and catch-up with current instalment payments. A reasonable period will normally be around two years (depending upon the economic climate) although in the recent case of *Cheltenham and Gloucester Building Society* v *Norgan, The Times*, 8 December 1995, the Court of Appeal held that the court should take the full term of the mortgage (usually 25 years) as its starting point in determining the 'reasonable period' for repayment. Waite LJ stated that courts should ask at the outset the question: would it be possible for the borrower to maintain payment-off of the arrears by instalments over that period? It remains to be seen whether this radical decision will survive an appeal to the House of Lords.

Assuming that the building society has gained possession of the house it will now be able to sell, provided that the power of sale has arisen and has become exercisable. It will **arise** if the mortgage is by deed and if the legal redemption date has passed (the mortgage is four years old, and so the power of sale will almost certainly have arisen). The power to sell is **exercisable** if interest repayments are at least two months in arrears, as appears to be the case in the present scenario. Accordingly, it appears from the facts that sale will be possible if possession is secured.

The effect of a sale on the first mortgagee, Doorway, depends upon whether Doorway had allowed the sale to take place from its rights. If it did, Doorway will be entitled only to recover its share of the sale proceeds. If Doorway refused to allow the sale to continue free from its rights, the sale could still go ahead, but the house would yield greatly reduced sale proceeds, as any purchaser would be bound by the first mortgage.

(b)(i)   The Court of Appeal in *Cuckmere Brick Co.* v *Mutual Finance Co.* [1971] 2 All ER 633 held that in deciding **when** to sell the mortgagee is entitled to consult its own interests to the total exclusion of the mortgagor's interests. However, having decided to sell at a particular time, in conducting the sale a mortgagee owes a duty of care to the mortgagor to obtain the best price reasonably obtainable at that time. If the mortgagee fails to obtain the best price he will have to account for the difference. The onus of proving that the mortgagee is in breach of this duty is on the mortgagor, unless the purchaser from the mortgagee has a personal connection with the mortgagee, in which case the onus is on the mortgagee to show that reasonable efforts were made to obtain the best price (*Tse Kwong Lam* v *Wong Chit Sen* [1983] 1 WLR 1349).

(ii)   If a mortgagee attempts to convey the property before the power of sale has arisen, any conveyance will be completely invalid. Once the power of sale has arisen, a mortgagee can convey a good title to a purchaser free of the mortgagor's rights, whether or not the power of sale has become exercisable. A purchaser in good faith from a mortgagee need satisfy himself only that the power of sale has arisen; he is under no duty to enquire whether the power has become exercisable.

A purchaser from the mortgagee is under no duty to pay the best price. Provided he acts in good faith he will get a good title, even if the mortgagee should have obtained a higher price by taking greater care. It would be acting in bad faith if the purchaser conspired with the mortgagee to purchase at an undervalue.

(c)   Princewest is treated as 'trustee of the proceeds of sale'. Proceeds from the sale must be applied in the following order: First, in paying off the total debt owed to the prior mortgagee, Doorway Building Society, if Doorway had permitted the sale to proceed free from its mortgage. Secondly, in discharging any costs of sale and any attempted sale. Thirdly, in discharging the total debt (capital and interest) owed to Princewest. Finally, the balance (if any) must be paid to Bertha. If Princewest departs from this strict order it may be liable for breach of its trust.

CHAPTER THIRTY-ONE

SPECIAL LEGAL RULES GOVERNING MORTGAGES

31.1   Fire Insurance of the Mortgaged Property

See Law of Property Act 1925, s. 101(1)(ii) at **30.3**.

31.2   Leasing of the Mortgaged Property

CHATSWORTH PROPERTIES LTD v EFFIOM [1971] 1 All ER 604, Court of Appeal

FACTS: A mortgagee who had appointed a receiver of rented property gave the tenants the impression that the mortgagee was the new landlord of the premises. It had written to the tenants saying, 'Do not pay your rent to your former landlord, but to the receiver we have appointed'.

HELD: The mortgagee was held to have created a tenancy by estoppel in favour of the tenants.

SALMON LJ: . . . The vital letter in this case is a letter of 23 December 1968, written to the defendant by the plaintiffs' solicitors acting on their behalf. The letter is in these terms:

> We act for [the plaintiffs], who have to-day appointed a Receiver of the income, rents and profits of the above property. The Receiver is Mr. R C Richardson of Messrs. C H & J W Willmott, 65 Goldhawk Road, W12. Please take notice that henceforth you should not pay any sums to your former landlords, Mr. and Mrs. Lamptey, but to Mr. Richardson or to whom he shall direct. Further take notice that no credit will be given for monies paid from now on to Mr. and Mrs. Lamptey. Yours faithfully.

Then it is signed by the solicitors. Now what does this letter mean? Counsel for the plaintiffs says, quite rightly, that the test (sometimes described as 'objective') is not, what did the defendant understand by it? but, what would this letter mean to the ordinary reasonable man? Counsel for the plaintiffs says that a receiver appointed under a mortgage deed is the agent of the mortgagor and not of the mortgagee. I entirely agree. He says that the true view of this letter is that it is giving notice to the defendant that the plaintiffs have appointed a receiver under a mortgage into which Mr. and Mrs. Lamptey had entered, that it gave the defendant notice that Mr. Richardson was Mr. and Mrs. Lamptey's agent to receive the rents, and that in future the rent should be paid to Mr. Richardson as agent for Mr. and Mrs. Lamptey and not to them.

I am afraid that, persuasively as counsel for the plaintiffs has put the argument, I am quite unable to accept it. I do not think that the letter means anything of the kind. To begin with, it is to be noticed that it does not say a word about any 'mortgage deed' or 'legal charge'. There is not a spark of evidence that the defendant had any idea that the Lampteys had mortgaged their leasehold interest in the premises. The natural meaning to the ordinary person would be that Mr. Richardson was appointed as the agent of the plaintiffs, on behalf of whom the letter was written, to receive the rent due to them in respect of the premises. It is said: well, that cannot be right; surely the fact that the word 'Receiver' is used in the letter—particularly with a large 'R'—ought to put the ordinary man on some sort of enquiry, even if he is not a lawyer. But even if one were to accede to that argument, and I am afraid I do not, the rest of the letter seems to me to make it abundantly plain that the one thing that would not be communicated to the mind of the ordinary man by this letter is that the plaintiffs had appointed Mr. Richardson a receiver to collect rents on behalf of Mr. and Mrs. Lamptey as landlords. The passage to which I draw particular attention is the passage in which the letter says 'henceforth you should not pay any sums to your *former* landlords, Mr. and Mrs. Lamptey'. I think that that can only mean, to the ordinary person, that Mr. and Mrs. Lamptey were no longer his landlords: the rent must be paid to Mr. Richardson, presumably as agents for the landlord. If any reasonable man received a letter such as that written on behalf of the plaintiffs, I think that he would come to the conclusion, a very sensible conclusion, that the letter was telling him not only that Mr. and Mrs. Lamptey had ceased to be his landlords but that the plaintiffs, on behalf of whom the letter was written, were his landlords and that they had appointed Mr. Richardson to collect the rents from him on their behalf. Thereafter, without more ado, Mr. Richardson collected the rent from the defendant in accordance with the terms of that letter. A new rent book was issued to the defendant describing the landlord as 'R C Richardson Receiver'. This in the circumstances would convey to the defendant only that Mr. Richardson was the landlord's agent. In my view a fresh tenancy had indeed been created between the plaintiffs and the defendant; at any rate the plaintiffs are precluded from denying that they did become the defendant's landlords. . . .

31.3   The Rules of Equity Protecting the Equitable Right to Redeem

31.3.1   NO IRREDEEMABLE MORTGAGES

One consequence of this is that it is impossible to include, as a term of the mortgage, a provision giving the mortgage an option to purchase the mortgaged property. But if, after the land has been mortgaged, the mortgagor as a completely separate transaction grants an option to the mortgagee, the option is valid.

31.3.2   POSTPONEMENT OF REDEMPTION

JAMES FAIRCLOUGH v *SWAN BREWERY COMPANY LIMITED* [1912] AC 565, Privy Council

FACTS: A lease of a hotel with seventeen-and-a-half years to run was mortgaged to a brewery, redemption being postponed until there were just six weeks to run on the lease. HELD: The postponement of redemption was invalid.

LORD MACNAGHTEN: . . . It will be observed that the lease is made to expire on June 12 1925, and that the instrument of mortgage provides that without the consent in writing of the company the mortgage debt of £500 is not to be wholly paid off until May 1 1925, that is just six weeks before the actual expiration of the lease.

In December 1909, the company were prevented by accidental circumstances from supplying the appellant with beer in accordance with a covenant on their part contained in the mortgage deed. The appellant thereupon assumed to treat the tie as at an end, and obtained beer from other quarters. The company brought an action for damages and for an injunction. The appellant, who apparently had already offered to redeem, counterclaimed for redemption. McMillan J gave judgment for the company in the action, and assessed the damages at £8. On the counter-claim he gave judgment for the appellant, holding that by law he was entitled to redeem. On appeal to the Full Court an order was made in the action in favour of the company with a reference as to damages. The counter-claim was dismissed with costs. Hence the present appeal.

The arguments of counsel ranged over a very wide field. But the real point is a narrow one. It depends upon a doctrine of equity, which is not open to question.

'There is,' as Kindersley V-C said in *Gossip v Wright* (1863) 32 LJ Ch 648, 'no doubt that the broad rule is this: that the Court will not allow the right of redemption in any way to be hampered or crippled in that which the parties intended to be a security either by any contemporaneous instrument with the deed in question, or by anything which this Court would regard as a simultaneous arrangement or part of the same transaction.' The rule in comparatively recent times was unsettled by certain decisions in the Court of Chancery in England which seem to have misled the learned judges in the Full Court. But it is now firmly established by the House of Lords that the old rule still prevails and that equity will not permit any device or contrivance being part of the mortgage transaction or contemporaneous with it to prevent or impede redemption. The learned counsel on behalf of the respondents admitted, as he was bound to admit, that a mortgage cannot be made irredeemable. That is plainly forbidden. Is there any difference between forbidding redemption and permitting it, if the permission be a mere pretence? Here the provision for redemption is nugatory. The incumbrance on the lease the subject of the mortgage according to the letter of the bargain falls to be discharged before the lease terminates, but at a time when it is on the very point of expiring, when redemption can be of no advantage to the mortgagor even if he should be so fortunate as to get his deeds back before the actual termination of the lease. For all practical purposes this mortgage is irredeemable. It was obviously meant to be irredeemable. It was made irredeemable in and by the mortgage itself.

Their Lordships are therefore of opinion that the order of the Full Court should be discharged with costs, and the decision of McMillan J restored. Their Lordships will humbly advise His Majesty accordingly. . . .

ESSO PETROLEUM CO. LTD v HARPER'S GARAGE (STOURPORT) LTD
[1966] 1 All ER 725, Court of Appeal

FACTS: A mortgage of a petrol filling station included a term postponing redemption for 21 years, and another term requiring the mortgagor to buy the mortgagee's petrol.
HELD: The postponement was invalid. The mortgagor was able to repay the mortgage and thereby free themselves from the 'tie' to Esso.

LORD DENNING MR: . . . In my opinion if a covenant in a mortgage is bad as being in unreasonable restraint of trade, then a court of equity should refuse to enforce it just as much as a court of law. Equity should follow the law. It is true of course that in applying the doctrine of restraint of trade to a mortgage, it is very relevant that the mortgagee has lent money. In many cases it may be quite reasonable for the mortgagee to stipulate for a tie so long as the loan is outstanding. But in that case he must not preclude the mortgagor from paying off the loan. At any rate he must not insert a clause making the loan irredeemable for an unduly long period. If he does so, then the tie is bad as being in unreasonable restraint of trade and the proviso forbidding redemption is bad as being unconscionable or oppressive. It is the coupling of the two together—the tie for the long period and the proviso forbidding redemption for the same period—which makes both bad if the period is so long as to be in unreasonable restraint of trade.

I find nothing in the cases contrary to this view. The cases on mortgages to brewers do not help because the doctrine of restraint of trade was not considered in them. The actual decisions are quite consistent with what I have said. In *Biggs v Hoddinott* [1895–99] All ER Rep 625, the restraint was *reasonable* and a proviso forbidding redemption for five years was held valid. In *Morgan v Jeffreys* [1910] Ch 620, the restraint was unreasonable and a proviso against redemption for twenty-eight years was held invalid.

I hold, therefore, that the doctrine of restraint of trade does apply to mortgages. Applied to this case I think that the tie for twenty-one years—coupled with a proviso forbidding redemption for twenty-one years—was unreasonable and invalid. It might have been reasonable, when they were making a loan of £7,000, to provide for a tie for five years and no right to redeem for that period. But twenty-one years is far too long.

I would, therefore, dismiss Esso's claim for an injunction; because the tie clause was in unreasonable restraint of trade. I would allow Harpers' counter-claim for redemption; because the proviso prohibiting redemption for twenty-one years (seeing that it was coupled with the tie) was unconscionable or oppressive. I would allow the appeal accordingly.

KNIGHTSBRIDGE ESTATES TRUST LTD v *BYRNE* [1938] 4 All ER 618, Court of Appeal

FACTS: A London property company mortgaged land to an insurance company. The mortgage contained a term postponing redemption for forty years.
HELD: The postponement was valid.

SIR WILFRID GREENE MR: . . . The first argument was that the postponement of the contractual right to redeem for 40 years was void in itself. In other words, the making of such an agreement between mortgagor and mortgagee was prohibited by a rule of equity. It was not contended that a provision in a mortgage deed making the mortgage irredeemable for a period of years is necessarily void. The argument was that such a period must be a 'reasonable' one, and it was said that the period in the present case was an unreasonable one, by reason merely of its length. This argument was not the one accepted by the judge.

An argument such as this requires the closest scrutiny, for, if it is correct, it means that an agreement made between two competent parties, acting under expert advice and presumably knowing their own business best, is one which the law forbids them to make upon the ground that it is not 'reasonable'. If we were satisfied that the rule of equity was what it is said to be, we should be bound to give effect to it. However, in the absence of compelling authority, we are not prepared to say that such an agreement cannot lawfully be made. A decision to that effect would, in our view, involve an unjustified interference with the freedom of business men to enter into agreements best suited to their interests, and would impose upon them a test of 'reasonableness' laid down by the courts without reference to the business realities of the case. It is important to remember what those realities were. The appellants are a private company, and do not enjoy the facilities for raising money by a public issue possessed by public companies. They were the owners of a large and valuable block of property, and, so far as we know, they had no other assets. The property was subject to a mortgage at a high rate of interest, and this mortgage was liable to be called in at any time. In these circumstances, the respondents were, when the negotiations began, desirous of obtaining for themselves two advantages, (i) a reduction in the rate of interest, and (ii) the right to repay the mortgage moneys by instalments spread over a long period of years. The desirability of obtaining these terms from a business point of view is manifest, and it is not to be assumed that these respondents were actuated by anything but pure considerations of business in seeking to obtain them. The sum involved was a very large one, and the length of the period over which the instalments were spread is to be considered with reference to this fact. In the circumstances, it was the most natural thing in the world that the respondents should address themselves to a body desirous of obtaining a long-term investment for its money. The resulting agreement was a commercial agreement between two important corporations experienced in such matters, and has none of the features of an oppressive bargain where the borrower is at the mercy of an unscrupulous lender. In transactions of this kind, it is notorious that there is competition among the large insurance companies and other bodies having large funds to invest, and we are not prepared to view the agreement made as anything but a proper business transaction. It is said, however, not only that the period of postponement must be a reasonable one, but also that, in judging the 'reasonableness' of the period, the considerations which we have mentioned cannot be regarded, and that the court is bound to judge 'reasonableness' by a consideration of the terms of the mortgage deed itself, without regard to extraneous matters. In the absence of clear authority, we emphatically decline to consider a question of 'reasonableness' from a standpoint so unreal. To hold that the law is to tell business men what is reasonable in such circumstances, and to refuse to take into account the business considerations involved, would bring the law into disrepute. Fortunately, we do not find ourselves forced to come to any such conclusion. . . .

31.4   Collateral Advantages

31.4.1   VALIDITY WHILE THE MORTGAGE SUBSISTS

MULTISERVICE BOOKBINDING LTD v *MARDEN* [1978] 2 All ER 489,
Chancery Division

FACTS: A clause in a mortgage deed provided for the capital repayments to increase proportionate to the decrease in value of the pound sterling against the Swiss franc ('the Swiss franc uplift'). The question was whether such a clause was an invalid collateral advantage.
HELD: The clause was valid as being neither oppressive or unconscionable.

BROWNE-WILKINSON J: I turn then to the question whether the mortgage is unconscionable or unreasonable. The plaintiffs' starting point on this aspect of the case is a submission that a lender on mortgage is only entitled to repayment of principal, interest and costs. If the lender additionally stipulates for a premium or other collateral advantage the court will not enforce such additional stipulation unless it is reasonable. Then it is submitted that cl 6 (providing for the payment of the Swiss franc uplift in addition to the nominal amount of capital and interest) is a premium which in all the circumstances is unreasonable. Alternatively it is said that the terms of the mortgage taken together are unreasonable. In my judgment the argument so advanced is based on a false premise. Since the repeal of the usury laws there has been no general principle that collateral advantages in mortgages have to be 'reasonable'. . . .

I therefore approach the second point on the basis that, in order to be freed from the necessity to comply with all the terms of the mortgage, the plaintiffs must show that the bargain, or some of its terms, was unfair and unconscionable; it is not enough to show that, in the eyes of the court, it was unreasonable.

In my judgment a bargain cannot be unfair and unconscionable unless one of the parties to it has imposed the objectionable terms in a morally reprehensible manner, that is to say, in a way which affects his conscience.

The classic example of an unconscionable bargain is where advantage has been taken of a young, inexperienced or ignorant person to introduce a term which no sensible well-advised person or party would have accepted. But I do not think the categories of unconscionable bargains are limited; the court can and should intervene where a bargain has been procured by unfair means.

. . . The defendant made a hard bargain. But the test is not reasonableness. The parties made a bargain which the plaintiffs, who are businessmen, went into with their eyes open, with the benefit of independent advice, without any compelling necessity to accept a loan on these terms and without any sharp practice by the defendant. I cannot see that there was anything unfair or oppressive or morally reprehensible in such a bargain entered into in such circumstances. . . .

CONSUMER CREDIT ACT 1974

137. Extortionate credit bargains
  (1) If the court finds a credit bargain extortionate it may reopen the credit agreement so as to do justice between the parties.
  (2) In this section and sections 138 to 140—
    (a) 'credit agreement' means any agreement between an individual (the 'debtor') and any other person (the 'creditor') by which the creditor provides the debtor with credit of any amount, and
    (b) 'credit bargain'—
      (i) where no transaction other than the credit agreement is to be taken into account in computing the total charge for credit, means the credit agreement, or
      (ii) where one or more other transactions are to be so taken into account, means the credit agreement and those other transactions, taken together.

138. When bargains are extortionate

(1)   A credit bargain is extortionate if it—

(a)   requires the debtor or a relative of his to make payments (whether unconditionally, or on certain contingencies) which are grossly exorbitant,

or

(b)   otherwise grossly contravenes ordinary principles of fair dealing.

(2)   In determining whether a credit bargain is extortionate, regard shall be had to such evidence as is adduced concerning—

(a)   interest rates prevailing at the time it was made,

(b)   the factors mentioned in subsections (3) to (5), and

(c)   any other relevant considerations.

(3)   Factors applicable under subsection (2) in relation to the debtor include—

(a)   his age, experience, business capacity and state of health; and

(b)   the degree to which, at the time of making the credit bargain, he was under financial pressure, and the nature of that pressure.

(4)   Factors applicable under subsection (2) in relation to the creditor include—

(a)   the degree of risk accepted by him, having regard to the value of any security provided;

(b)   his relationship to the debtor; and

(c)   whether or not a colourable cash price was quoted for any goods or services included in the credit bargain.

(5)   Factors applicable under subsection (2) in relation to a linked transaction include the question how far the transaction was reasonably required for the protection of debtor or creditor, or was in the interest of the debtor.

DAVIES v DIRECTLOANS LTD [1986] 2 All ER 783, Chancery Division

FACTS: The terms of a loan granted to a co-habiting couple to enable them to buy a house included an interest rate of 21.6% at a time when the market rate was approximately 17%. The couple's income was uncertain (they were professional artists) and they were unable to borrow from institutional lenders. When the mortgagors fell behind with repayments the mortgagee brought proceedings for possession. Before those proceedings were heard the plaintiffs managed to sell their property to an estate agent. The present action was brought to re-open the charge on the basis that it had been an 'extortionate credit bargain' within the terms of the Consumer Credit Act 1974, s. 138.

HELD: In view of the uncertain security against which the mortgagee had risked the loan, and in view of the fact that the loan had been made with the independent advice of a solicitor, the high rate of interest could not be described as 'extortionate' under s. 138 of the Consumer Credit Act 1974.

EDWARD NUGEE QC: On these facts the question posed by s. 138(1)(a) of the 1974 Act is whether the defendant has proved that the legal charge required the plaintiffs to make payments which were not grossly exorbitant. These words are not defined by the Act and must be given their ordinary meaning. 'Exorbitant' is defined by the *Shorter Oxford English Dictionary* as 'Exceeding ordinary or proper bounds; excessive; outrageously large'; 'grossly' is defined as 'excessively; flagrantly'. . . .

However that may be, whether the word 'grossly' adds any additional weight or not, I am more than satisfied that the payments which the defendant required the plaintiffs to make in the present case fall far short of rendering the credit bargain constituted by the legal charge extortionate within the meaning of s. 138 of the 1974 Act. I take into account that the rate of interest was fixed throughout the term of the mortgage (although the plaintiffs could, of course, redeem at any time if they could obtain finance more cheaply elsewhere or they wished to sell). But this is an inevitable feature of an agreement under which a loan is repayable by equal fixed instalments over a period of years, and one that may operate in favour of either party. Rates of interest in general rose substantially between the date of the contract and the date of the legal charge, but the defendant did not increase the rate of interest which it required the plaintiffs to pay, although by the date of the legal charge it was under no legal obligation to abide by the original terms of the brokerage agreement. Rates fell again during the period between the date of the legal charge and its redemption, but the building society rate never fell as low as it was at the date of the contract.

Counsel for the plaintiffs asked that, if the bargain was reopened, it should be on the basis that the proper rate of interest to charge was 18%. Although I accept his submission that the court should be astute to protect borrowers, and indeed this is clearly the policy underlying the 1974 Act, I cannot regard the difference between the 18% which he submitted was proper and the 21.6% which the defendant actually charged as anywhere near large enough to render the latter grossly exorbitant. Similarly there is in my judgment nothing in the terms of the legal charge or in any other of the facts in this case which comes anywhere near satisfying the terms of s. 138(1)(b) and rendering the credit bargain one which grossly contravenes ordinary principles of fair dealing.

Sir John Donaldson MR said in *Wills v Wood* [1983] CCLR 7 at 15:

> It is, of course, clear that the Consumer Credit Act 1974 gives and is intended to give the court the widest possible control over credit bargains which, for a variety of reasons, might be considered 'extortionate'. But the word is 'extortionate', not 'unwise'. The jurisdiction seems to me to contemplate at least a substantial imbalance in bargaining power of which one party has taken advantage.

If the plaintiffs appear in retrospect to have been unwise, their lack of wisdom lay in contracting to buy the house at a time when their finances were not established on a sufficiently firm foundation. Given that initial decision, which was taken with the full benefit of advice from their own solicitor, I do not consider that it was unwise of them to have entered into the legal charge so as to enable them to complete the contract; and I am wholly satisfied that the defendant did not, either then or at the earlier contract stage, take advantage of such imbalance in bargaining power as existed, and that there was nothing extortionate about the terms of the legal charge. Accordingly the plaintiffs' claim fails and I dismiss this action.

31.4.2   COLLATERAL ADVANTAGES AFTER REDEMPTION

JAMES BRADLEY AND WILLIAM M BRADLEY v *CARRITT* [1902] AC 253,
House of Lords

FACTS: The mortgagor was the controlling shareholder of a tea company. The mortgagor was not the tea company itself, which of course is in law a separate person. The property mortgaged was the shares themselves. The mortgagee was a tea-broker. The mortgage included a collateral advantage under which the mortgagor promised that the mortgagee should always remain broker to the company.

HELD: The mortgagor, having paid off the mortgage, was released from the promise of permanent employment for the mortgagee.

LORD DAVEY: . . . In the present case the agreement is that the appellant W M Bradley will, 'as a shareholder,' use his best endeavours to secure the sale of the company's teas to the respondent or his firm, and in the event of the teas being sold through another broker will pay to the respondent the amount of the commission which he or his firm might have earned. In other words, he agrees to use the voting power attached to his shares in a particular way for the respondent's benefit. Now, what is a share? It is but a bundle of rights, of which the right of voting at meetings of the company is not the least valuable. My Lords, can it be said that the mortgagee does not retain a hold upon the shares which form the mortgaged property, or that the mortgagor has full redemption of it, when the latter is not free to exercise an important right in such manner as he may think most conducive to his own interests? He may think it advantageous to the company to employ another broker, or that the change would produce a better return on his shares, but if he gives effect to his opinion he incurs what is in effect a heavy penalty. Again, the appellant could not part with or otherwise deal with his shares without losing the influence in the company's counsels which might enable him to secure the performance of the first part of the agreement, or running a serious risk of liability under the second part. . . .

Prima facie a clause in a mortgage contract is limited to the duration of the mortgage relation between the contracting parties. In this clause we have the words 'always hereafter'; but I observe that in two other clauses (the third and the fifth) a similar phrase, 'at any time hereafter,' is used and is limited by the context to the duration of the mortgage. I am disposed to say that the words 'always hereafter,' having regard to the nature and purport of the agreement, in like manner mean at any time hereafter during the currency of the loan. But in the view which I take of the case it is not necessary for me to express a decided opinion on this question.

With regard to the appellant, James Bradley's, agreement, I think it was part of the same transaction and ancillary to the principal agreement, and by way of further security to the respondent and increased remuneration to him for the use of his money. And I am of opinion that it must be construed in the same way, and stand or fall with the principal agreement....

31.4.3   A COLLATERAL ADVANTAGE AS AN INDEPENDENT AGREEMENT

KREGLINGER v NEW PATAGONIA MEAT AND COLD STORAGE COMPANY LIMITED [1914] AC 25, Privy Council

FACTS: The meat company were mortgagors, while the mortgagees were a firm of woolbrokers. The mortgage contained a provision that for the next five years the company should not sell any sheepskins to any other person without first offering them to the woolbrokers at the best price obtainable elsewhere. The woolbrokers accepted a slightly reduced rate of interest in return for this guarantee. The mortgagor repaid the debt after only two years.
HELD: The 'sheepskins clause' remained valid for the full five years, even though the mortgagors had redeemed the mortgage. The sheepskins agreement was not a collateral advantage of the mortgage, but was an 'independent' collateral contract, entered into as a condition of obtaining the loan.

VISCOUNT HALDANE LC: . . . My Lords, the question in the present case is whether the right to redeem has been interfered with. And this must, for the reasons to which I have adverted in considering the history of the doctrine of equity, depend on the answer to a question which is primarily one of fact. What was the true character of the transaction? Did the appellants make a bargain such that the right to redeem was cut down, or did they simply stipulate for a collateral undertaking, outside and clear of the mortgage, which would give them an exclusive option of purchase of the sheepskins of the respondents? The question is in my opinion not whether the two contracts were made at the same moment and evidenced by the same instrument, but whether they were in substance a single and undivided contract or two distinct contracts. Putting aside for the moment considerations turning on the character of the floating charge, such an option no doubt affects the freedom of the respondents in carrying on their business even after the mortgage has been paid off. But so might other arrangements which would be plainly collateral, an agreement, for example, to take permanently into the firm a new partner as a condition of obtaining fresh capital in the form of a loan. The question is one not of form but of substance, and it can be answered in each case only by looking at all the circumstances, and not by mere reliance on some abstract principle, or upon the *dicta* which have fallen *obiter* from judges in other and different cases. Some, at least, of the authorities on the subject disclose an embarrassment which has, in my opinion, arisen from neglect to bear this in mind. In applying a principle the ambit and validity of which depend on confining it steadily to the end for which it was established, the analogies of previous instances where it has been applied are apt to be misleading. For each case forms a real precedent only in so far as it affirms a principle, the relevancy of which in other cases turns on the true character of the particular transaction, and to that extent on circumstances.

My Lords, if in the case before the House your Lordships arrive at the conclusion that the agreement for an option to purchase the respondents' sheepskins was not in substance a fetter on the exercise of their right to redeem, but was in the nature of a collateral bargain the entering into which was a preliminary and separate condition of the loan, the decided cases cease to present any great difficulty....

There is a further remark which I wish to make about *Bradley* v *Carritt* [1902] AC 253. It is impossible to read the report without seeing that there was a marked divergence of opinion among those members of your Lordships' House who took part in the decision as to the test by which the validity of contracts collateral to a mortgage is to be determined. Lord Davey observes that he cannot understand how, consistently with the doctrine of equity, a mortgagee can insist on retaining the benefit of a covenant in the mortgage contract materially affecting the enjoyment of the mortgaged property after redemption. Lord Lindley, on the other hand, doubts whether the covenant in question, a covenant that the mortgagor would use his influence as a shareholder to secure for the mortgagee in permanence the brokerage business of the company, ought to be looked on as really forming part of the terms of the security. He points out that when the usury laws were in force, and when every device for evading them had to be defeated by equity, the proposition that everything that was part of the mortgage transaction must cease with it, if it was not to infringe the doctrine that once a mortgage always a mortgage, was a convenient statement and as free from objection as most concise statements are, but that when the usury laws were abolished the language was too wide to be accurate.

My Lords, the views expressed by Lord Davey and Lord Lindley are not, so far as mere words go, contradictory. But I cannot shut my eyes to the fact that they represent divergent tendencies. Lord Davey seems to suggest that the doctrine about which, when expressed in general terms, there is little controversy had become finally crystallised in the particular expressions used in certain of the earlier authorities, and that, having become thus rigid, it is to-day fatal to the freedom of mortgagor and mortgagee to make their own bargains, even in cases where the reason for applying the doctrine has ceased to exist. The tendency of Lord Lindley's language is, on the other hand, to treat the application of such a rule as a question in which the Courts must not lose sight of the dominating principle underlying the reasons which originally influenced the terms of the rule, reasons which have, in certain cases, become modified as public policy has changed. Speaking for myself, and notwithsanding the high authority of Lord Davey, I think that the tendency of Lord Lindley's conclusion is the one which is most consonant with principle, and I see no valid reason why this House should not act in accordance with it in the case now under consideration. . . .

31.5   Redemption of Mortgages

31.5.1   MACHINERY OF REDEMPTION

LAW OF PROPERTY ACT 1925

115.   Reconveyances of mortgages by endorsed receipts

(1)   A receipt endorsed on, written at the foot of, or annexed to, a mortgage for all money thereby secured, which states the name of the person who pays the money and is executed by the chargee by way of legal mortgage or the person in whom the mortgaged property is vested and who is legally entitled to give a receipt for the mortgage money shall operate, without any reconveyance, surrender, or release—

(a)   Where a mortgage takes effect by demise or subdemise, as a surrender of the term, so as to determine the term or merge the same in the reversion immediately expectant thereon;

(b)   Where the mortgage does not take effect by demise or subdemise, as a reconveyance thereof to the extent of the interest which is the subject matter of the mortgage, to the person who immediately before the execution of the receipt was entitled to the equity of redemption;

and in either case, as a discharge of the mortgaged property from all principal money and interest secured by, and from all claims under the mortgage, but without prejudice to any term or other interest which is paramount to the estate or interest of the mortgagee or other person in whom the mortgaged property was vested.

(2)   Provided that, where by the receipt the money appears to have been paid by a person who is not entitled to the immediate equity of redemption, the receipt shall operate as if the benefit of the mortgage had by deed been transferred to him; unless—

    (a)   it is otherwise expressly provided; or

    (b)   the mortgage is paid off out of capital money, or other money in the hands of a personal representative or trustee properly applicable for the discharge of the mortgage, and it is not expressly provided that the receipt is to operate as a transfer. . . .

31.6   Consolidation of Mortgages

Consolidation of mortgages occurs where a mortgagee has two mortgages created by the same mortgagor, and insists that if one mortgage is redeemed the other mortgage is redeemed as well. This right of consolidation is of practical value where the mortgagor proposes to repay a well-secured loan, but to leave a poorly-secured loan outstanding. The following conditions must be satisfied for consolidation to be effected:

    (a)   At least one of the two mortgages must confer a right of consolidation. (Modern mortgages always include a clause entitling the mortgagee to consolidate.)

    (b)   The legal redemption date on each mortgage must be past.

    (c)   Both mortgages must have been made by the same mortgagor.

    (d)   At some point of time (however long or short) both mortgages were in common ownership, and both equities of redemption were in common ownership.

CHAPTER THIRTY-TWO

PRIORITY OF MORTGAGES OF UNREGISTERED TITLES

32.1 Priority of Mortgages Where an Unregistered Legal Estate is Mortgaged

32.1.1 MORTGAGES REGISTRABLE AS LAND CHARGES

LAND CHARGES ACT 1972

4. Effect of land charges and protection of purchasers

(5) A land charge of Class B and a land charge of Class C (other than an estate contract) created or arising on or after 1st January 1926 shall be void as against a purchaser of the land charged with it, or of any interest in such land, unless the land charge is registered in the appropriate register before the completion of the purchase.

32.1.2 SECTION 97 OF THE LAW OF PROPERTY ACT 1925

LAW OF PROPERTY ACT 1925

97. Priorities as between puisne mortgages

Every mortgage affecting a legal estate in land made after the commencement of this Act, whether legal or equitable (not being a mortgage protected by the deposit of documents relating to the legal estate affected) shall rank according to its date of registration as a land charge pursuant to the Land Charges Act 1925.

This section does not apply [to mortgages or charges to which the Land Charges Act 1972 does not apply by virtue of section 14(3) of that Act (which excludes certain land charges created by instruments necessitating registration under the Land Registration Act 1925), or] to mortgages or charges of registered land. . . .

32.2 Tacking of Further Advances

32.2.1 WHEN CAN A FURTHER ADVANCE BE TACKED?

LAW OF PROPERTY ACT 1925

94. Tacking and further advances

(1) After the commencement of this Act, a prior mortgagee shall have a right to make further advances to rank in priority to subsequent mortgages (whether legal or equitable)—

(a) if an arrangement has been made to that effect with the subsequent mortgagees; or

(b)   if he had no notice of such subsequent mortgages at the time when the further advance was made by him; or

(c)   whether or not he had such notice as aforesaid, where the mortgage imposes an obligation on him to make such further advances.

This subsection applies whether or not the prior mortgage was made expressly for securing further advances.

(2)   In relation to the making of further advances after the commencement of this Act a mortgagee shall not be deemed to have notice of a mortgage merely by reason that it was registered as a land charge if it was not so registered at the time when the original mortgage was created or when the last search (if any) by or on behalf of the mortgagee was made, whichever last happened.

This subsection only applies where the prior mortgage was made expressly for securing a current account or other further advances.

(3)   Save in regard to the making of further advances as aforesaid, the right to tack is hereby abolished:

Provided that nothing in this Act shall affect any priority acquired before the commencement of this Act by tacking, or in respect of further advances made without notice of a subsequent incumbrance or by arrangement with the subsequent incumbrancer.

(4)   This section applies to mortgages of land made before or after the commencement of this Act, but not to charges registered under the Land Registration Act 1925, or any enactment replaced by that Act.

CHAPTER THIRTY-THREE

MORTGAGES OF REGISTERED LAND

33.1 Introduction

MORTGAGE CORP LTD v NATIONWIDE CREDIT CORP LTD [1993] 4 All ER 623,
Court of Appeal

FACTS: X mortgaged a registered property to A by executing a charge. A did not register the charge or protect its rights in any other way. X then executed a charge in favour of B who (somewhat unusually) protected its interest by entering an ordinary notice on the register. The question was whether A or B had priority.

HELD: If B had actually substantively registered its charge, B would undoubtedly have gained priority. But entering an ordinary notice, while guaranteeing that the mortgage binds later purchasers/mortgagees, does not give the mortgage priority over an earlier created right, even though the earlier created right has not been protected by entry on the register. A had priority, applying the general principle of 'first in time first in right'.

DILLON LJ: One of the oddities in the present case is that it is not clear whether the plaintiffs' charge was in fact registered as a registered charge before the sale of the property to the purchasers took place. On the other hand, there is a letter from the Land Registry of 19 March 1991, which says that the plaintiffs' charge had been substantively registered under s. 26 of the 1925 Act and this is apparently echoed in a further letter from another representative of the Land Registry. On the other hand, in the only affidavit sworn in the proceedings, it is said by the plaintiffs' solicitor in relation to the plaintiffs' charge that it was lodged in the registry for registration against the title in June 1990 but the registration was still pending at the date of the affidavit, 10 June 1991, which was after completion of the sale to the purchaser. In these circumstances, we must, I apprehend, conclude that it is not shown, on the balance of probabilities, that the plaintiffs' charge was substantially registered as a registered charge. Consequently the defendants do not bring the case within s. 27(3) of the 1925 Act.

It is anyhow necessary, however, to turn to s. 52 of the 1925 [Land Registration] Act, which is concerned with the effect of notice under s. 49 of the Act. Section 52 provides as follows:

(1) A disposition by the proprietor shall take effect subject to all estates, rights, and claims which are protected by way of notice on the register at the date of the registration or entry of notice of the disposition, but only if and so far as such estates, rights, and claims may be valid and are not (independently of this Act) overridden by the disposition.

(2) Where notice of a claim is entered on the register, such entry shall operate by way of notice only, and shall not operate to render the claim valid whether made adversely to or for the benefit of the registered land or charge.

The judge construed s. 52(1) as applying only where the document which gave rise to the estate, right or claim protected by the notice on the register had been entered into at a date which was earlier than the date on which the disposition whose registration was in question had been made, that is as he put it, the effect of a notice is limited to giving priority to a person who has registered the notice only in relation to interests granted subsequently to his interest.

As I read s. 52(1), the opening part applies generally irrespective of the date of the execution of the document which gave rise to the estate, right or claim protected by the notice on the register or the date of the making of the rival disposition which is to be registered or to be the subject of the entry of a later notice. So far as the opening part is concerned, the only relevant date is the date of registration or entry of notice. But the general effect of the opening part is then cut down by the final proviso, *viz*:

... but only if and so far as such estates, rights, and claims may be valid and are not (independently of this Act) overridden by the disposition.

In the present case there is no difficulty over the first half of that proviso 'so far as such estates, rights, and claims may be valid', since the defendants' charge is unquestionably valid.

It is therefore necessary to consider the second half of the proviso: 'and are not (independently of this Act) overridden by the disposition.' As I see it, independently of the 1925 Act, the defendants' charge is necessarily overridden by the plaintiffs' charge. If, by virtue of s. 106, neither charge having been registered, both are regarded as taking effect only in equity, then the equitable rule as to the priorities that *qui prior est tempore potior est jure* applies; if they are considered independently even of s. 106 of the 1925 Act, then they are both charges by way of legal mortgage, and the later, in time, the defendants' charge can only take effect as a charge on the equity of redemption in the property subject to the plaintiffs' charge. I therefore agree with the judge's conclusion, though I am not sure that I have followed quite the same course of reasoning as he did.

In my judgment, s. 52 is enacted to prescribe the effect of a notice entered on the register. That may not necessarily be the same as the effect of a caution since the effect of a caution is prescribed by ss. 54 and 55. The effect of a notice, as determined under s. 52, will cut down any apparently wider effect that the general wording in other sections such as ss. 20 and 27(3) would otherwise have had. The particular qualifications imposed by the proviso to s. 52(1) are, first of all, that the interest protected by the notice must be valid apart from the notice and secondly that the interest protected by the notice would not independently of the 1925 Act be overridden by the rival disposition. Notice is indeed notice, but it does not give validity, if validity is not otherwise there, and it does not give priority which would not, apart from the 1925 Act, have been there. Therefore the plaintiffs' charge has priority to the defendants' charge. . . .

33.2   End of Chapter Assessment Question

'The rules governing the priority of mortgages of an unregistered title are both complex and uncertain. The rules governing the priority of mortgages of a registered title are by comparison straightforward, though the recent case of *Mortgage Corporation* v *Nationwide Credit Corporation* does create a problem for lenders who take a deposit of the land certificate.')

Discuss.

33.3   End of Chapter Assessment Outline Answer

Mortgages of Unregistered Titles

Where the mortgagee takes possession of the title deeds at the time the mortgage is created (usual in the case of a first mortgage)

A mortgage of this nature will not be registrable as a land charge. If the mortgage is legal the mortgagee can lose priority to a later mortgagee in limited circumstances only. Namely, (a) by deliberately (or in gross negligence) permitting the mortgagor to retake possession of the title deeds, thus allowing the mortgagor fraudulently to represent to a new lender that the property is not mortgaged; or (b) by prematurely endorsing a receipt on the mortgagee, thereby giving later mortgagees the impression that the first mortgage has been fully paid off. If the mortgage is equitable the same principles ((a) and (b)) apply. In addition, an equitable mortgage where the mortgagee has taken the title deeds is an example of an equitable interest not registrable as a land charge but still subject to the doctrine of notice. Therefore, such an equitable mortgagee could theoretically lose priority to a later legal mortgagee who took without notice of the earlier equitable mortgage. The risk is purely theoretical, however, because the absence of title deeds in such a case would give any later mortgagee notice of the first mortgage.

Where the mortgagee does not take possession of the title deeds at the time the mortgage is created

In such a case the mortgage will be registrable as a land charge. If it is a legal mortgage it will be a 'puisne' mortgage registrable as a class C(i) land charge. If it is an equitable mortgage it will be a general equitable charge registrable as a class C(iii) land charge. If a registrable mortgage is in fact promptly registered as a land charge then it is bound to have priority over subsequently created mortgages. The real 'complexity and uncertainty' in this area of law arises if a registrable mortgage is not registered, or is registered late (after the creation of a second mortgage of the land). In such a case s. 4(5) of the Land Charges Act 1972 and s. 97 of the Law of Property Act 1925 will apply.

Section 4(5) provides that if a registrable mortgage is not in fact registered it 'shall be void as against a purchaser of the land charged therewith, or any interest in that land'. Accordingly, in the normal course of events, if X grants a registrable mortgage to A which A omits to register, and then X grants a mortgage to B, it is B's mortgage which will have priority.

The picture becomes more confused if we now imagine that B's mortgage is also registrable, but has not been registered. According to s. 4(5) of the Land Charges Act 1972 nothing turns on whether B's mortgage has been registered, but s. 97 of the Law of Property Act 1925 could change the situation entirely. Section 97 provides that 'every mortgage affecting a legal estate in land . . . shall rank according to its date of registration as a land charge pursuant to the Land Charges Act'. If s. 97 is read literally, A, in the example given above, could regain priority over B by registering his mortgage after B has obtained her mortgage, but before B has registered her mortgage as a land charge. In short, there is a conflict in the results which flow from a literal application of ss. 4(5) and 97.

Which section should be followed? The conflict has existed for about 70 years and has not yet been resolved by any decided case, so the question is clearly not an easy one to answer. A literal reading of s. 4(5) suggests that an unregistered mortgage is rendered 'void' against the holder of a subsequent mortgage, and the usual rule is that once an interest in land is void against a purchaser (or mortgagee) subsequent registration cannot make it valid again. In further support of s. 4(5) it could be argued that a literal reading of s. 97 makes it clear that s. 97 is 'pursuant to the Land Charges Act' [see **32.1.1**] and that, accordingly, s. 4(5) of the 1972 Act should be followed.

Nevertheless, another literal reading of s. 97 leads to the clear conclusion that priority between registrable mortgages is to be determined, and to be determined only, according to the date of registration. Perhaps s. 97 will ultimately be favoured, but it would make mortgages distinct from other land charges (which would not be ideal), but it would at least be simple to apply. It would also make the rule for unregistered title similar to that for registered title.

Mortgages of Registered Titles

In contrast to the above, the rule for determining priority of mortgages of a registered title is very straightforward. If there is a series of registered charges, they rank in priority in the order they are entered on the register, not in the order of their creation. The rule is not dissimilar to the rule in s. 97 as applied to land charges in unregistered land, and lends further support to a literal application of s. 97.

Having stated that the rule is relatively straightforward it is true that the recent case of *Mortgage Corporation Ltd* v *Nationwide Credit Corporation Ltd* (1993) [see **33.1** for the facts] does create a problem for lenders who take a deposit of the land certificate instead of substantively registering their mortgage as a 'registered charge' (it is cheaper simply to take a deposit of the land certificate!). In the *Mortgage Corporation* case it was held that mortgagees will only gain priority over earlier unregistered mortgages if they 'substantively register' their mortgage charge. It will not suffice to merely register an 'ordinary notice' of the existence of the mortgage. Lenders who take a deposit of the land certificate do not 'substantively' register their mortgage and their only protection is usually to enter a 'notice' of their mortgage on the registered title at the land registry. Consequently, such lenders may find themselves bound by earlier mortgages even if those earlier mortgages have not been protected in any way. The reason given for this result in the *Mortgage Corporation* case was that if neither mortgage has been registered both mortgages will be deemed (by s. 106 of the Land Registration Act 1925) to take effect only in equity. Then the equitable rule as to priorities will apply, which is *qui prior est tempore potior est jure*, which roughly translates as 'the first in time has priority'. In the future, institutional lenders will no doubt be advised to incur the expense of substantive registration. While registration of a 'notice' is good protection against future mortgagees and purchasers, it is no protection against earlier mortgages affecting the registered title.